12
Plays
A Portable Anthology

12

Plays

A Portable Anthology

Edited by

JANET E. GARDNER

University of Massachusetts at Dartmouth

Bedford/St. Martin's   BOSTON   ◆   NEW YORK

For Bedford/St. Martin's

Executive Editor: Steve Scipione
Development Editor: Emily Goodall
Production Editor: Arthur Johnson
Production Supervisor: Tina Cameron
Marketing Manager: Jenna Bookin Barry
Copyeditor: Rosemary Winfield
Text Design: Sandra Rigney
Cover Design: Mark McKie
Cover Art: Franz Mertz's design for a 1952 production of *Oedipus Rex* directed by
    G. R. Sellner at Darmstadt, Landestheater. Museum für Gestaltung Zurich.
Composition: Stratford Publishing Services, Inc.
Printing and Binding: Haddon Craftsmen, Inc., an RR Donnelley & Sons
    Company

President: Joan E. Feinberg
Editorial Director: Denise B. Wydra
Editor in Chief: Karen S. Henry
Director of Marketing: Karen Melton
Director of Editing, Design, and Production: Marcia Cohen
Managing Editor: Elizabeth M. Schaaf

Library of Congress Control Number: 2002109608

For information, write: Bedford/St. Martin's, 75 Arlington Street, Boston, MA 02116 (617-399-4000)

ISBN-10: 0-312-40209-0
ISBN-13: 978-0-312-40209-9

Preface

There are, of course, many fine large drama anthologies for instructors to choose from, but I have long felt the need for a small anthology, affordable to students and comfortable both to carry and to read. I was, therefore, pleased to be invited to edit *12 Plays: A Portable Anthology.* It took very little time to realize what a daunting task it is, particularly for a lover of theater, to choose just twelve representative plays from among so many exciting and important works of world drama. The plays selected for this volume are all central to the dramatic tradition in Western culture. While the world of theater offers much more—from Japanese noh plays to contemporary performance art— the plays included here offer students a chance to become familiar with some of the most powerful theatrical voices of all time. They thus provide a foundation that, I hope, will lead to a lifetime of enjoyment reading plays and attending theater.

Some of the playwrights included here have long been regarded as the backbone of the tradition, perennial hot tickets like Sophocles and Shakespeare. Several—for instance Ibsen, Beckett, and Miller—belong to the realm of modern classics. Still others are newer voices, like Churchill and Wilson, who have recently emerged in the tradition and have in a short time established their importance as creators of powerful theater and sophisticated literature. In addition to their literary quality, though, all of the plays here have been widely classroom tested and are known to teach well: both students and instructors enjoy the richness they offer and the challenges they provide. My research on drama pedagogy confirms that the plays and playwrights included in this *Portable Anthology* are among those most frequently taught by instructors of introductory drama classes in American colleges and universities. This volume, therefore, can serve as the principal text in an introductory course, either on its own or supplemented with any number of inexpensive and readily available play texts.

Unlike most fiction or poetry, plays are written primarily as performance blueprints, meant to be seen and heard in the communal setting of the theater. Because of this, play reading calls on our intellectual and imaginative abilities to envision the work in performance. One of the principal purposes of this book is to help students acquire and develop those abilities by reading and studying a variety of well-written plays. The focus, therefore, is on the literary texts themselves, and editorial apparatus has been kept to a minimum, as it has for the other books in this series—*250 Poems*, a portable anthology of poetry, and *40 Short Stories*, a portable anthology of short fiction. Following the plays is a brief history of Western theater, providing context for the plays by describing the evolution of dramatic traditions from classical Greece to contemporary Europe and America. Biographical and textual notes offer brief explanations of the cultural importance of each playwright and work in the book, while a glossary familiarizes students with key terms used in discussions of drama and theater. Finally, a list of selected video resources offers students and instructors opportunities to see stage and film interpretations of each of the works here anthologized. The *12 Plays* companion Web site at www.bedfordstmartins.com/12Plays provides additional resources, including *LitLinks*, which presents concise annotations and links to several Web sites about the playwrights included in this anthology.

I owe a huge debt of thanks to the many people whose support has been invaluable in the creation of this book, beginning with my students and colleagues at the University of Massachusetts at Dartmouth. Among the many fine teachers who made a difference to me, I must single out Stephanie Tucker, whose infectious love of drama helped guide me as a student and whose friendship remains an inspiration. Parmita Kapadia's understanding and friendship have helped me more than she can know. Patrick McCorkle has been my biggest supporter and toughest critic for years, and he surely deserves a special award. Among the many good people at Bedford/ St. Martin's, I owe particular thanks to Chuck Christensen, Joan Feinberg, and Elizabeth Schaaf. Karen Henry and Maura Shea both offered insightful suggestions at several points in the process and helped to shape this volume. Steve Scipione, as usual, supported me when he could, pushed me when he had to, and never let our friendship interfere with work (or vice versa). I thank production editor (and permissions editor) Arthur Johnson for keeping that end of the project on track. My most profound thanks, though, must be reserved for my editor, Emily Goodall, whose professionalism, enthusiasm, hard work, and unflagging good spirits made working on this book a real pleasure for me.

Contents

Oedipus Rex

SOPHOCLES [c. 496–c. 406 b.c.]

TRANSLATED BY DUDLEY FITTS AND ROBERT FITZGERALD

Characters

OEDIPUS, *King of Thebes, supposed son of Polybos and Merope, King and Queen of Corinth*

IOKASTE,° *wife of Oedipus and widow of the late King Laios*

KREON,° *brother of Iokaste, a prince of Thebes*

TEIRESIAS, *a blind seer who serves Apollo*

PRIEST

MESSENGER, *from Corinth*

SHEPHERD, *former servant of Laios*

SECOND MESSENGER, *from the palace*

CHORUS OF THEBAN ELDERS

CHORAGOS, *leader of the Chorus*

ANTIGONE *and* ISMENE, *young daughters of Oedipus and Iokaste. They appear in the Exodos but do not speak.*

SUPPLIANTS, GUARDS, SERVANTS

Scene: *Before the palace of Oedipus, King of Thebes. A central door and two lateral doors open onto a platform which runs the length of the facade. On the platform, right and left, are altars; and three steps lead down into the orchestra, or chorus-ground. At the beginning of the action these steps are crowded by suppliants who have brought branches and chaplets of olive leaves and who sit in various attitudes of despair. Oedipus enters.*

PROLOGUE°

OEDIPUS: My children, generations of the living
In the line of Kadmos,° nursed at his ancient hearth:

Iokaste: Traditional Western spelling is *Jocasta*.   **Kreon:** Traditional Western spelling is *Creon*.   **Prologue:** First part of the play explaining the background and introducing the scene.   **2. Kadmos:** Founder of Thebes.

1

Why have you strewn yourselves before these altars
In supplication, with your boughs and garlands?
The breath of incense rises from the city   5
With a sound of prayer and lamentation.
                                        Children,
I would not have you speak through messengers,
And therefore I have come myself to hear you—
I, Oedipus, who bear the famous name.
(*To a Priest.*) You, there, since you are eldest in the company,   10
Speak for them all, tell me what preys upon you,
Whether you come in dread, or crave some blessing:
Tell me, and never doubt that I will help you
In every way I can; I should be heartless
Were I not moved to find you suppliant here.   15
PRIEST: Great Oedipus, O powerful king of Thebes!
You see how all the ages of our people
Cling to your altar steps: here are boys
Who can barely stand alone, and here are priests
By weight of age, as I am a priest of God,   20
And young men chosen from those yet unmarried;
As for the others, all that multitude,
They wait with olive chaplets in the squares,
At the two shrines of Pallas,° and where Apollo°
Speaks in the glowing embers.
                                  Your own eyes   25
Must tell you: Thebes is tossed on a murdering sea
And can not lift her head from the death surge.
A rust consumes the buds and fruits of the earth;
The herds are sick; children die unborn,
And labor is vain. The god of plague and pyre   30
Raids like detestable lightning through the city,
And all the house of Kadmos is laid waste,
All emptied, and all darkened: Death alone
Battens upon the misery of Thebes.

You are not one of the immortal gods, we know;   35
Yet we have come to you to make our prayer
As to the man surest in mortal ways
And wisest in the ways of God. You saved us

---

24. Pallas: Daughter of Zeus, goddess of wisdom, and protectress of Athens.
Apollo: Son of Zeus and god of the sun, of light, and of healing.

From the Sphinx,° that flinty singer, and the tribute
We paid to her so long; yet you were never   40
Better informed than we, nor could we teach you:
A god's touch, it seems, enabled you to help us.

Therefore, O mighty power, we turn to you:
Find us our safety, find us a remedy,
Whether by counsel of the gods or of men.   45
A king of wisdom tested in the past
Can act in a time of troubles, and act well.
Noblest of men, restore
Life to your city! Think how all men call you
Liberator for your boldness long ago;   50
Ah, when your years of kingship are remembered,
Let them not say *We rose, but later fell* —
Keep the State from going down in the storm!
Once, years ago, with happy augury,
You brought us fortune; be the same again!   55
No man questions your power to rule the land:
But rule over men, not over a dead city!
Ships are only hulls, high walls are nothing,
When no life moves in the empty passageways.
OEDIPUS: Poor children! You may be sure I know   60
All that you longed for in your coming here.
I know that you are deathly sick; and yet,
Sick as you are, not one is as sick as I.
Each of you suffers in himself alone
His anguish, not another's; but my spirit   65
Groans for the city, for myself, for you.

I was not sleeping, you are not waking me.
No, I have been in tears for a long while
And in my restless thought walked many ways.
In all my search I found one remedy,   70
And I have adopted it: I have sent Kreon,
Son of Menoikeus, brother of the queen,

---

39. Sphinx: A winged monster with the body of a lion and the face of a woman. The Sphinx tormented Thebes with a riddle—"What goes on four legs in the morning, two at noon, and three in the evening?"—and killed those who could not answer correctly. When Oedipus solved the riddle, the Sphinx killed herself.

To Delphi,° Apollo's place of revelation,
To learn there, if he can,
What act or pledge of mine may save the city.   75
I have counted the days, and now, this very day,
I am troubled, for he has overstayed his time.
What is he doing? He has been gone too long.
Yet whenever he comes back, I should do ill
Not to take any action the god orders.   80
PRIEST: It is a timely promise. At this instant
   They tell me Kreon is here.
OEDIPUS: O Lord Apollo!
   May his news be fair as his face is radiant!
PRIEST: Good news, I gather! he is crowned with bay,
   The chaplet is thick with berries.
OEDIPUS: We shall soon know;   85
   He is near enough to hear us now. (*Enter Kreon.*) O prince:
   Brother: son of Menoikeus:
   What answer do you bring us from the god?
KREON: A strong one. I can tell you, great afflictions
   Will turn out well, if they are taken well.   90
OEDIPUS: What was the oracle? These vague words
   Leave me still hanging between hope and fear.
KREON: Is it your pleasure to hear me with all these
   Gathered around us? I am prepared to speak,
   But should we not go in?
OEDIPUS: Speak to them all,   95
   It is for them I suffer, more than for myself.
KREON: Then I will tell you what I heard at Delphi.
   In plain words
   The god commands us to expel from the land of Thebes
   An old defilement we are sheltering.   100
   It is a deathly thing, beyond cure;
   We must not let it feed upon us longer.
OEDIPUS: What defilement? How shall we rid ourselves of it?
KREON: By exile or death, blood for blood. It was
   Murder that brought the plague-wind on the city.   105
OEDIPUS: Murder of whom? Surely the god has named him?
KREON: My Lord: Laios once ruled this land,
   Before you came to govern us.
OEDIPUS: I know;
   I learned of him from others; I never saw him.

73. **Delphi:** Site of the oracle, the preeminent shrine of Apollo.

KREON: He was murdered; and Apollo commands us now   110
   To take revenge upon whoever killed him.
OEDIPUS: Upon whom? Where are they? Where shall we find a clue
   To solve that crime, after so many years?
KREON: Here in this land, he said. Search reveals
   Things that escape an inattentive man.   115
OEDIPUS: Tell me: Was Laios murdered in his house,
   Or in the fields, or in some foreign country?
KREON: He said he planned to make a pilgrimage.
   He did not come home again.
OEDIPUS: And was there no one,
   No witness, no companion, to tell what happened?   120
KREON: They were all killed but one, and he got away
   So frightened that he could remember one thing only.
OEDIPUS: What was that one thing? One may be the key
   To everything, if we resolve to use it.
KREON: He said that a band of highwaymen attacked them,   125
   Outnumbered them, and overwhelmed the king.
OEDIPUS: Strange, that a highwayman should be so daring—
   Unless some faction here bribed him to do it.
KREON: We thought of that. But after Laios' death
   New troubles arose and we had no avenger.   130
OEDIPUS: What troubles could prevent your hunting down the killers?
KREON: The riddling Sphinx's song
   Made us deaf to all mysteries but her own.
OEDIPUS: Then once more I must bring what is dark to light.
   It is most fitting that Apollo shows,   135
   As you do, this compunction for the dead.
   You shall see how I stand by you, as I should,
   Avenging this country and the god as well,
   And not as though it were for some distant friend,
   But for my own sake, to be rid of evil.   140
   Whoever killed King Laios might—who knows?—
   Lay violent hands even on me—and soon.
   I act for the murdered king in my own interest.

   Come, then, my children: leave the altar steps,
   Lift up your olive boughs!
                         One of you go   145
   And summon the people of Kadmos to gather here.
   I will do all that I can; you may tell them that.   (*Exit a Page.*)
   So, with the help of God,
   We shall be saved—or else indeed we are lost.

PRIEST: Let us rise, children. It was for this we came,   150
 And now the king has promised it.
 Phoibos° has sent us an oracle; may he descend
 Himself to save us and drive out the plague.

(*Exeunt° Oedipus and Kreon into the palace by the central door. The Priest and
the Suppliants disperse right and left. After a short pause the Chorus enters the
orchestra.*)

PARODOS°   *Strophe° 1*

CHORUS: What is God singing in his profound
 Delphi of gold and shadow?
 What oracle for Thebes, the Sunwhipped city?
 Fear unjoints me, the roots of my heart tremble.
 Now I remember, O Healer, your power, and wonder: 5
 Will you send doom like a sudden cloud, or weave it
 Like nightfall of the past?
 Speak to me, tell me, O
 Child of golden Hope, immortal Voice.

Antistrophe° 1

Let me pray to Athene, the immortal daughter of Zeus,   10
 And to Artemis° her sister
 Who keeps her famous throne in the market ring,
 And to Apollo, archer from distant heaven—
 O gods, descend! Like three streams leap against
 The fires of our grief, the fires of darkness;   15
 Be swift to bring us rest!
 As in the old time from the brilliant house
 Of air you stepped to save us, come again!

Strophe 2

Now our afflictions have no end,
 Now all our stricken host lies down   20

---

152. **Phoibos:** Apollo. [S.D.] *Exeunt:* Latin for "they go out."   **Parodos:** The
song chanted by the Chorus on their entry.   **Strophe:** Song sung by the Chorus
as they danced from stage right to stage left.   **Antistrophe:** Song sung by the
Chorus as they danced back from stage left to stage right.   **11. Artemis:**
Daughter of Zeus, twin sister of Apollo, goddess of the hunt and female chastity.

And no man fights off death with his mind;
The noble plowland bears no grain,
And groaning mothers can not bear—
See, how our lives like birds take wing,
Like sparks that fly when a fire soars,   25
To the shore of the god of evening.

Antistrophe 2

The plague burns on, it is pitiless,
Though pallid children laden with death
Lie unwept in the stony ways,
And old gray women by every path   30
Flock to the strand about the altars
There to strike their breasts and cry
Worship of Phoibos in wailing prayers:
Be kind, God's golden child!

Strophe 3

There are no swords in this attack by fire,   35
No shields, but we are ringed with cries.
Send the besieger plunging from our homes
Into the vast sea-room of the Atlantic
Or into the waves that foam eastward of Thrace—
For the day ravages what the night spares—   40
Destroy our enemy, lord of the thunder!
Let him be riven by lightning from heaven!

Antistrophe 3

Phoibos Apollo, stretch the sun's bowstring,
That golden cord, until it sing for us,
Flashing arrows in heaven!
                              Artemis, Huntress,   45
Race with flaring lights upon our mountains!
O scarlet god,° O golden-banded brow,
O Theban Bacchos in a storm of Maenads,°

(*Enter Oedipus, center.*)

---

47. scarlet god: Bacchus, god of wine (also called Dionysus).   **48. Maenads:**
Bacchus's female devotees.

Whirl upon Death, that all the Undying hate!
Come with blinding torches, come in joy!   50

SCENE 1

OEDIPUS: Is this your prayer? It may be answered. Come,
Listen to me, act as the crisis demands,
And you shall have relief from all these evils.

Until now I was a stranger to this tale,
As I had been a stranger to the crime.   5
Could I track down the murderer without a clue?
But now, friends,
As one who became a citizen after the murder,
I make this proclamation to all Thebans:
If any man knows by whose hand Laios, son of Labdakos,   10
Met his death, I direct that man to tell me everything,
No matter what he fears for having so long withheld it.
Let it stand as promised that no further trouble
Will come to him, but he may leave the land in safety.
Moreover: If anyone knows the murderer to be foreign,   15
Let him not keep silent: he shall have his reward from me.
However, if he does conceal it; if any man
Fearing for his friend or for himself disobeys this edict,
Hear what I propose to do:

I solemnly forbid the people of this country,   20
Where power and throne are mine, ever to receive that man
Or speak to him, no matter who he is, or let him
Join in sacrifice, lustration, or in prayer.
I decree that he be driven from every house,
Being, as he is, corruption itself to us: the Delphic   25
Voice of Apollo has pronounced this revelation.
Thus I associate myself with the oracle
And take the side of the murdered king.

As for the criminal, I pray to God —
Whether it be a lurking thief, or one of a number —   30
I pray that that man's life be consumed in evil and wretchedness.
And as for me, this curse applies no less
If it should turn out that the culprit is my guest here,

Sharing my hearth.
               You have heard the penalty.
I lay it on you now to attend to this   35
For my sake, for Apollo's, for the sick
Sterile city that heaven has abandoned.
Suppose the oracle had given you no command:
Should this defilement go uncleansed for ever?
You should have found the murderer: your king,   40
A noble king, had been destroyed!
                Now I,
Having the power that he held before me,
Having his bed, begetting children there
Upon his wife, as he would have, had he lived—
Their son would have been my children's brother,   45
If Laios had had luck in fatherhood!
(And now his bad fortune has struck him down)—
I say I take the son's part, just as though
I were his son, to press the fight for him
And see it won! I'll find the hand that brought   50
Death to Labdakos' and Polydoros' child,
Heir of Kadmos' and Agenor's line.°
And as for those who fail me,
May the gods deny them the fruit of the earth,
Fruit of the womb, and may they rot utterly!   55
Let them be wretched as we are wretched, and worse!

For you, for loyal Thebans, and for all
Who find my actions right, I pray the favor
Of justice, and of all the immortal gods.
CHORAGOS:° Since I am under oath, my lord, I swear   60
   I did not do the murder, I can not name
   The murderer. Phoibos ordained the search;
   Why did he not say who the culprit was?
OEDIPUS: An honest question. But no man in the world
   Can make the gods do more than the gods will.   65
CHORAGOS: There is an alternative, I think—
OEDIPUS: Tell me.
   Any or all, you must not fail to tell me.
CHORAGOS: A lord clairvoyant to the lord Apollo,

51–52. Labdakos, Polydoros, Kadmos, and Agenor: Father, grandfather, great-grandfather, and great-great-grandfather of Laios.   **60. Choragos:** Chorus leader.

As we all know, is the skilled Teiresias.
One might learn much about this from him, Oedipus.   70
OEDIPUS: I am not wasting time:
   Kreon spoke of this, and I have sent for him—
   Twice, in fact; it is strange that he is not here.
CHORAGOS: The other matter—that old report—seems useless.
OEDIPUS: What was that? I am interested in all reports.   75
CHORAGOS: The king was said to have been killed by highwaymen.
OEDIPUS: I know. But we have no witnesses to that.
CHORAGOS: If the killer can feel a particle of dread,
   Your curse will bring him out of hiding!
OEDIPUS: No.
   The man who dared that act will fear no curse.   80

(*Enter the blind seer Teiresias, led by a Page.*)

CHORAGOS: But there is one man who may detect the criminal.
   This is Teiresias, this is the holy prophet
   In whom, alone of all men, truth was born.
OEDIPUS: Teiresias: seer: student of mysteries,
   Of all that's taught and all that no man tells,   85
   Secrets of Heaven and secrets of the earth:
   Blind though you are, you know the city lies
   Sick with plague; and from this plague, my lord,
   We find that you alone can guard or save us.

   Possibly you did not hear the messengers?   90
   Apollo, when we sent to him,
   Sent us back word that this great pestilence
   Would lift, but only if we established clearly
   The identity of those who murdered Laios.
   They must be killed or exiled.
                              Can you use   95
   Birdflight° or any art of divination
   To purify yourself, and Thebes, and me
   From this contagion? We are in your hands.
   There is no fairer duty
   Than that of helping others in distress.   100
TEIRESIAS: How dreadful knowledge of the truth can be
   When there's no help in truth! I knew this well,
   But did not act on it; else I should not have come.

96. Birdflight: Prophets believed they could predict the future based on the flight
of birds.

OEDIPUS: What is troubling you? Why are your eyes so cold?
TEIRESIAS: Let me go home. Bear your own fate, and I'll   105
  Bear mine. It is better so: trust what I say.
OEDIPUS: What you say is ungracious and unhelpful
  To your native country. Do not refuse to speak.
TEIRESIAS: When it comes to speech, your own is neither temperate
  Nor opportune. I wish to be more prudent.   110
OEDIPUS: In God's name, we all beg you—
TEIRESIAS: You are all ignorant.
  No; I will never tell you what I know.
  Now it is my misery; then, it would be yours.
OEDIPUS: What! You do know something, and will not tell us?
  You would betray us all and wreck the State?   115
TEIRESIAS: I do not intend to torture myself, or you.
  Why persist in asking? You will not persuade me.
OEDIPUS: What a wicked old man you are! You'd try a stone's
  Patience! Out with it! Have you no feeling at all?
TEIRESIAS: You call me unfeeling. If you could only see   120
  The nature of your own feelings . . .
OEDIPUS: Why,
  Who would not feel as I do? Who could endure
  Your arrogance toward the city?
TEIRESIAS: What does it matter?
  Whether I speak or not, it is bound to come.
OEDIPUS: Then, if "it" is bound to come, you are bound to tell me.   125
TEIRESIAS: No, I will not go on. Rage as you please.
OEDIPUS: Rage? Why not!
               And I'll tell you what I think:
  You planned it, you had it done, you all but
  Killed him with your own hands: if you had eyes,
  I'd say the crime was yours, and yours alone.   130
TEIRESIAS: So? I charge you, then,
  Abide by the proclamation you have made:
  From this day forth
  Never speak again to these men or to me;
  You yourself are the pollution of this country.   135
OEDIPUS: You dare say that! Can you possibly think you have
  Some way of going free, after such insolence?
TEIRESIAS: I have gone free. It is the truth sustains me.
OEDIPUS: Who taught you shamelessness? It was not your craft.
TEIRESIAS: You did. You made me speak. I did not want to.   140
OEDIPUS: Speak what? Let me hear it again more clearly.
TEIRESIAS: Was it not clear before? Are you tempting me?

•

OEDIPUS: I did not understand it. Say it again.
TEIRESIAS: I say that you are the murderer whom you seek.
OEDIPUS: Now twice you have spat out infamy. You'll pay for it!   145
TEIRESIAS: Would you care for more? Do you wish to be really angry?
OEDIPUS: Say what you will. Whatever you say is worthless.
TEIRESIAS: I say you live in hideous shame with those
    Most dear to you. You can not see the evil.
OEDIPUS: Can you go on babbling like this for ever?   150
TEIRESIAS: I can, if there is power in truth.
OEDIPUS: There is:
    But not for you, not for you,
    You sightless, witless, senseless, mad old man!
TEIRESIAS: You are the madman. There is no one here
    Who will not curse you soon, as you curse me.   155
OEDIPUS: You child of total night! I would not touch you;
    Neither would any man who sees the sun.
TEIRESIAS: True: it is not from you my fate will come.
    That lies within Apollo's competence,
    As it is his concern.
OEDIPUS: Tell me, who made   160
    These fine discoveries? Kreon? or someone else?
TEIRESIAS: Kreon is no threat. You weave your own doom.
OEDIPUS: Wealth, power, craft of statemanship!
    Kingly position, everywhere admired!
    What savage envy is stored up against these,   165
    If Kreon, whom I trusted, Kreon my friend,
    For this great office which the city once
    Put in my hands unsought — if for this power
    Kreon desires in secret to destroy me!

    He has bought this decrepit fortune-teller, this   170
    Collector of dirty pennies, this prophet fraud —
    Why, he is no more clairvoyant than I am!
                                Tell us:
    Has your mystic mummery ever approached the truth?
    When that hellcat the Sphinx was performing here,
    What help were you to these people?   175
    Her magic was not for the first man who came along:
    It demanded a real exorcist. Your birds —
    What good were they? or the gods, for the matter of that?
    But I came by,
    Oedipus, the simple man, who knows nothing —   180
    I thought it out for myself, no birds helped me!
    And this is the man you think you can destroy,

That you may be close to Kreon when he's king!
Well, you and your friend Kreon, it seems to me,
Will suffer most. If you were not an old man,   185
You would have paid already for your plot.
CHORAGOS: We can not see that his words or yours
    Have been spoken except in anger, Oedipus,
    And of anger we have no need. How to accomplish
    The god's will best: that is what most concerns us.   190
TEIRESIAS: You are a king. But where argument's concerned
    I am your man, as much a king as you.
    I am not your servant, but Apollo's.
    I have no need of Kreon or Kreon's name.

    Listen to me. You mock my blindness, do you?   195
    But I say that you, with both your eyes, are blind:
    You can not see the wretchedness of your life,
    Nor in whose house you live, no, nor with whom.
    Who are your father and mother? Can you tell me?
    You do not even know the blind wrongs   200
    That you have done them, on earth and in the world below.
    But the double lash of your parents' curse will whip you
    Out of this land some day, with only night
    Upon your precious eyes.
    Your cries then—where will they not be heard?   205
    What fastness of Kithairon° will not echo them?
    And that bridal-descant of yours—you'll know it then,
    The song they sang when you came here to Thebes
    And found your misguided berthing.
    All this, and more, that you can not guess at now,   210
    Will bring you to yourself among your children.

    Be angry, then. Curse Kreon. Curse my words.
    I tell you, no man that walks upon the earth
    Shall be rooted out more horribly than you.
OEDIPUS: Am I to bear this from him?—Damnation   215
    Take you! Out of this place! Out of my sight!
TEIRESIAS: I would not have come at all if you had not asked me.
OEDIPUS: Could I have told that you'd talk nonsense, that
    You'd come here to make a fool of yourself, and of me?
TEIRESIAS: A fool? Your parents thought me sane enough.   220

---

206. Kithairon: The mountain near Thebes where Oedipus was abandoned as an infant.

OEDIPUS: My parents again!—Wait: who were my parents?
TEIRESIAS: This day will give you a father, and break your heart.
OEDIPUS: Your infantile riddles! Your damned abracadabra!
TEIRESIAS: You were a great man once at solving riddles.
OEDIPUS: Mock me with that if you like; you will find it true.   225
TEIRESIAS: It was true enough. It brought about your ruin.
OEDIPUS: But if it saved this town?
TEIRESIAS (*to the Page*):   Boy, give me your hand.
OEDIPUS: Yes, boy; lead him away.
                                        —While you are here
    We can do nothing. Go; leave us in peace.
TEIRESIAS: I will go when I have said what I have to say.   230
    How can you hurt me? And I tell you again:
    The man you have been looking for all this time,
    The damned man, the murderer of Laios,
    That man is in Thebes. To your mind he is foreign-born,
    But it will soon be shown that he is a Theban,   235
    A revelation that will fail to please.
                                A blind man,
    Who has his eyes now; a penniless man, who is rich now;
    And he will go tapping the strange earth with his staff.
    To the children with whom he lives now he will be
    Brother and father—the very same; to her   240
    Who bore him, son and husband—the very same
    Who came to his father's bed, wet with his father's blood.
    Enough. Go think that over.
    If later you find error in what I have said,
    You may say that I have no skill in prophecy.   245

                (*Exit Teiresias, led by his Page. Oedipus goes into the palace.*)

                        ODE° 1   *Strophe 1*

CHORUS: The Delphic stone of prophecies
    Remembers ancient regicide
    And a still bloody hand.
    That killer's hour of flight has come.
    He must be stronger than riderless   5
    Coursers of untiring wind,
    For the son of Zeus° armed with his father's thunder

Ode: Song sung by the Chorus.   **7. son of Zeus:** Apollo.

Leaps in lightning after him;
And the Furies° hold his track, the sad Furies.

Antistrophe 1

Holy Parnassos'° peak of snow   10
Flashes and blinds that secret man,
That all shall hunt him down:
Though he may roam the forest shade
Like a bull gone wild from pasture
To rage through glooms of stone.   15
Doom comes down on him; flight will not avail him;
For the world's heart calls him desolate,
And the immortal voices follow, for ever follow.

Strophe 2

But now a wilder thing is heard
From the old man skilled at hearing Fate in the wing-beat of a bird.   20
Bewildered as a blown bird, my soul hovers and can not find
Foothold in this debate, or any reason or rest of mind.
But no man ever brought — none can bring
Proof of strife between Thebes' royal house,
Labdakos' line,° and the son of Polybos;°   25
And never until now has any man brought word
Of Laios' dark death staining Oedipus the King.

Antistrophe 2

Divine Zeus and Apollo hold
Perfect intelligence alone of all tales ever told;
And well though this diviner works, he works in his own night;   30
No man can judge that rough unknown or trust in second sight,
For wisdom changes hands among the wise.
Shall I believe my great lord criminal
At a raging word that a blind old man let fall?
I saw him, when the carrion woman° faced him of old,   35
Prove his heroic mind. These evil words are lies.

---

9. Furies: Powerful avenging divinities. **10. Parnassos:** Mountain sacred to
Apollo. **25. Labdakos' line:** Laios's family. **Polybos:** King of Corinth who
adopted Oedipus. **35. woman:** The Sphinx.

SCENE 2

KREON: Men of Thebes:
I am told that heavy accusations
Have been brought against me by King Oedipus.

I am not the kind of man to bear this tamely.

If in these present difficulties   5
He holds me accountable for any harm to him
Through anything I have said or done—why, then,
I do not value life in this dishonor.
It is not as though this rumor touched upon
Some private indiscretion. The matter is grave.   10
The fact is that I am being called disloyal
To the State, to my fellow citizens, to my friends.
CHORAGOS: He may have spoken in anger, not from his mind.
KREON: But did you not hear him say I was the one
Who seduced the old prophet into lying?   15
CHORAGOS: The thing was said; I do not know how seriously.
KREON: But you were watching him! Were his eyes steady?
Did he look like a man in his right mind?
CHORAGOS: I do not know.
I can not judge the behavior of great men.
But here is the king himself.

(*Enter Oedipus.*)

OEDIPUS: So you dared come back.   20
Why? How brazen of you to come to my house,
You murderer!
                        Do you think I do not know
That you plotted to kill me, plotted to steal my throne?
Tell me, in God's name: am I coward, a fool,
That you should dream you could accomplish this?   25
A fool who could not see your slippery game?
A coward, not to fight back when I saw it?
You are the fool, Kreon, are you not? hoping
Without support or friends to get a throne?
Thrones may be won or bought: you could do neither.   30
KREON: Now listen to me. You have talked; let me talk, too.
You can not judge unless you know the facts.
OEDIPUS: You speak well: there is one fact; but I find it hard
To learn from the deadliest enemy I have.

KREON: That above all I must dispute with you.   35
OEDIPUS: That above all I will not hear you deny.
KREON: If you think there is anything good in being stubborn
    Against all reason, then I say you are wrong.
OEDIPUS: If you think a man can sin against his own kind
    And not be punished for it, I say you are mad.   40
KREON: I agree. But tell me: what have I done to you?
OEDIPUS: You advised me to send for that wizard, did you not?
KREON: I did. I should do it again.
OEDIPUS: Very well. Now tell me:
    How long has it been since Laios—
KREON: What of Laios?
OEDIPUS: Since he vanished in that onset by the road?   45
KREON: It was long ago, a long time.
OEDIPUS: And this prophet,
    Was he practicing here then?
KREON: He was; and with honor, as now.
OEDIPUS: Did he speak of me at that time?
KREON: He never did,
    At least, not when I was present.
OEDIPUS: But . . . the enquiry?
    I suppose you held one?
KREON: We did, but we learned nothing.   50
OEDIPUS: Why did the prophet not speak against me then?
KREON: I do not know; and I am the kind of man
    Who holds his tongue when he has no facts to go on.
OEDIPUS: There's one fact that you know, and you could tell it.
KREON: What fact is that? If I know it, you shall have it.   55
OEDIPUS: If he were not involved with you, he could not say
    That it was I who murdered Laios.
KREON: If he says that, you are the one that knows it!—
    But now it is my turn to question you.
OEDIPUS: Put your questions. I am no murderer.   60
KREON: First, then: You married my sister?
OEDIPUS: I married your sister.
KREON: And you rule the kingdom equally with her?
OEDIPUS: Everything that she wants she has from me.
KREON: And I am the third, equal to both of you?
OEDIPUS: That is why I call you a bad friend.   65
KREON: No. Reason it out, as I have done.
    Think of this first: would any sane man prefer
    Power, with all a king's anxieties,
    To that same power and the grace of sleep?

Certainly not I.   70
I have never longed for the king's power—only his rights.
Would any wise man differ from me in this?
As matters stand, I have my way in everything
With your consent, and no responsibilities.
If I were king, I should be a slave to policy.   75
How could I desire a scepter more
Than what is now mine—untroubled influence?
No, I have not gone mad; I need no honors,
Except those with the perquisites I have now.
I am welcome everywhere; every man salutes me,   80
And those who want your favor seek my ear,
Since I know how to manage what they ask.
Should I exchange this ease for that anxiety?
Besides, no sober mind is treasonable.
I hate anarchy   85
And never would deal with any man who likes it.
Test what I have said. Go to the priestess
At Delphi, ask if I quoted her correctly.
And as for this other thing: if I am found
Guilty of treason with Teiresias,   90
Then sentence me to death. You have my word
It is a sentence I should cast my vote for—
But not without evidence!
                           You do wrong
When you take good men for bad, bad men for good.
A true friend thrown aside—why, life itself   95
Is not more precious!
                       In time you will know this well:
For time, and time alone, will show the just man,
Though scoundrels are discovered in a day.
CHORAGOS: This is well said, and a prudent man would ponder it.
   Judgments too quickly formed are dangerous.   100
OEDIPUS: But is he not quick in his duplicity?
   And shall I not be quick to parry him?
   Would you have me stand still, hold my peace, and let
   This man win everything, through my inaction?
KREON: And you want—what is it, then? To banish me?   105
OEDIPUS: No, not exile. It is your death I want,
   So that all the world may see what treason means.
KREON: You will persist, then? You will not believe me?
OEDIPUS: How can I believe you?
KREON: Then you are a fool.

OEDIPUS: To save myself?
KREON: In justice, think of me.   110
OEDIPUS: You are evil incarnate.
KREON: But suppose that you are wrong?
OEDIPUS: Still I must rule.
KREON: But not if you rule badly.
OEDIPUS: O city, city!
KREON: It is my city, too!
CHORAGOS: Now, my lords, be still. I see the queen,
   Iokaste, coming from her palace chambers;   115
   And it is time she came, for the sake of you both.
   This dreadful quarrel can be resolved through her.

(*Enter Iokaste.*)

IOKASTE: Poor foolish men, what wicked din is this?
   With Thebes sick to death, is it not shameful
   That you should take some private quarrel up?   120
   (*To Oedipus.*) Come into the house.
                              —And you, Kreon, go now:
   Let us have no more of this tumult over nothing.
KREON: Nothing? No, sister: what your husband plans for me
   Is one of two great evils: exile or death.
OEDIPUS: He is right.
                     Why, woman I have caught him squarely   125
   Plotting against my life.
KREON: No! Let me die
   Accurst if ever I have wished you harm!
IOKASTE: Ah, believe it, Oedipus!
   In the name of the gods, respect this oath of his
   For my sake, for the sake of these people here!   130

Strophe 1

CHORAGOS: Open your mind to her, my lord. Be ruled by her, I beg you!
OEDIPUS: What would you have me do?
CHORAGOS: Respect Kreon's word. He has never spoken like a fool,
   And now he has sworn an oath.
OEDIPUS: You know what you ask?
CHORAGOS: I do.
OEDIPUS: Speak on, then.
CHORAGOS: A friend so sworn should not be baited so,   135
   In blind malice, and without final proof.

OEDIPUS: You are aware, I hope, that what you say
   Means death for me, or exile at the least.

Strophe 2

CHORAGOS: No, I swear by Helios, first in heaven!
   May I die friendless and accurst,   140
   The worst of deaths, if ever I meant that!
   It is the withering fields
      That hurt my sick heart:
   Must we bear all these ills,
   And now your bad blood as well?   145
OEDIPUS: Then let him go. And let me die, if I must,
   Or be driven by him in shame from the land of Thebes.
   It is your unhappiness, and not his talk,
   That touches me.
                  As for him —
   Wherever he goes, hatred will follow him.   150
KREON: Ugly in yielding, as you were ugly in rage!
   Natures like yours chiefly torment themselves.
OEDIPUS: Can you not go? Can you not leave me?
KREON: I can.
   You do not know me; but the city knows me,
   And in its eyes I am just, if not in yours.   (*Exit Kreon.*) 155

Antistrophe 1

CHORAGOS: Lady Iokaste, did you not ask the King to go to his
   chambers?
IOKASTE: First tell me what has happened.
CHORAGOS: There was suspicion without evidence; yet it rankled
   As even false charges will.
IOKASTE: On both sides?
CHORAGOS: On both.
IOKASTE: But what was said?   160
CHORAGOS: Oh let it rest, let it be done with!
   Have we not suffered enough?
OEDIPUS: You see to what your decency has brought you:
   You have made difficulties where my heart saw none.

Antistrophe 2

CHORAGOS: Oedipus, it is not once only I have told you —   165
    You must know I should count myself unwise
    To the point of madness, should I now forsake you —
        You, under whose hand,
          In the storm of another time,
        Our dear land sailed out free.   170
        But now stand fast at the helm!
IOKASTE: In God's name, Oedipus, inform your wife as well:
    Why are you so set in this hard anger?
OEDIPUS: I will tell you, for none of these men deserves
    My confidence as you do. It is Kreon's work,   175
    His treachery, his plotting against me.
IOKASTE: Go on, if you can make this clear to me.
OEDIPUS: He charges me with the murder of Laios.
IOKASTE: Has he some knowledge? Or does he speak from
    hearsay?
OEDIPUS: He would not commit himself to such a charge,   180
    But he has brought in that damnable soothsayer
    To tell his story.
IOKASTE: Set your mind at rest.
    If it is a question of soothsayers, I tell you
    That you will find no man whose craft gives knowledge
    Of the unknowable.
              Here is my proof: 185
    An oracle was reported to Laios once
    (I will not say from Phoibos himself, but from
    His appointed ministers, at any rate)
    That his doom would be death at the hands of his own son —
    His son, born of his flesh and of mine!   190

    Now, you remember the story: Laios was killed
    By marauding strangers where three highways meet;
    But his child had not been three days in this world
    Before the king had pierced the baby's ankles
    And left him to die on a lonely mountainside.   195

    Thus, Apollo never caused that child
    To kill his father, and it was not Laios' fate
    To die at the hands of his son, as he had feared.
    This is what prophets and prophecies are worth!

Have no dread of them.
                         It is God himself   200
Who can show us what he wills, in his own way.
OEDIPUS: How strange a shadowy memory crossed my mind,
   Just now while you were speaking; it chilled my heart.
IOKASTE: What do you mean? What memory do you speak of?
OEDIPUS: If I understand you, Laios was killed   205
   At a place where three roads meet.
IOKASTE: So it was said;
   We have no later story.
OEDIPUS: Where did it happen?
IOKASTE: Phokis, it is called: at a place where the Theban Way
   Divides into the roads toward Delphi and Daulia.
OEDIPUS: When?
IOKASTE: We had the news not long before you came   210
   And proved the right to your succession here.
OEDIPUS: Ah, what net has God been weaving for me?
IOKASTE: Oedipus! Why does this trouble you?
OEDIPUS: Do not ask me yet.
   First, tell me how Laios looked, and tell me
   How old he was.
IOKASTE: He was tall, his hair just touched   215
   With white; his form was not unlike your own.
OEDIPUS: I think that I myself may be accurst
   By my own ignorant edict.
IOKASTE: You speak strangely.
   It makes me tremble to look at you, my king.
OEDIPUS: I am not sure that the blind man can not see.   220
   But I should know better if you were to tell me—
IOKASTE: Anything—though I dread to hear you ask it.
OEDIPUS: Was the king lightly escorted, or did he ride
   With a large company, as a ruler should?
IOKASTE: There were five men with him in all: one was a herald;   225
   And a single chariot, which he was driving.
OEDIPUS: Alas, that makes it plain enough!
                                But who—
Who told you how it happened?
IOKASTE: A household servant,
   The only one to escape.
OEDIPUS: And is he still
   A servant of ours?
IOKASTE: No; for when he came back at last   230

And found you enthroned in the place of the dead king,
He came to me, touched my hand with his, and begged
That I would send him away to the frontier district
Where only the shepherds go—
As far away from the city as I could send him.   235
I granted his prayer; for although the man was a slave,
He had earned more than this favor at my hands.
OEDIPUS: Can he be called back quickly?
IOKASTE: Easily.
    But why?
OEDIPUS: I have taken too much upon myself   240
    Without enquiry; therefore I wish to consult him.
IOKASTE: Then he shall come.
                            But am I not one also
    To whom you might confide these fears of yours?
OEDIPUS: That is your right; it will not be denied you,
    Now least of all; for I have reached a pitch   245
    Of wild foreboding. Is there anyone
    To whom I should sooner speak?

Polybos of Corinth is my father.
My mother is a Dorian: Merope.
I grew up chief among the men of Corinth   250
Until a strange thing happened—
Not worth my passion, it may be, but strange.
At a feast, a drunken man maundering in his cups
Cries out that I am not my father's son!
I contained myself that night, though I felt anger   255
And a sinking heart. The next day I visited
My father and mother, and questioned them. They stormed,
Calling it all the slanderous rant of a fool;
And this relieved me. Yet the suspicion
Remained always aching in my mind;   260
I knew there was talk; I could not rest;
And finally, saying nothing to my parents,
I went to the shrine at Delphi.

The god dismissed my question without reply;
He spoke of other things.
                        Some were clear,   265
Full of wretchedness, dreadful, unbearable:
As, that I should lie with my own mother, breed

Children from whom all men would turn their eyes;
And that I should be my father's murderer.

I heard all this, and fled. And from that day   270
Corinth to me was only in the stars
Descending in that quarter of the sky,
As I wandered farther and farther on my way
To a land where I should never see the evil
Sung by the oracle. And I came to this country   275
Where, so you say, King Laios was killed.

I will tell you all that happened there, my lady.
There were three highways
Coming together at a place I passed;
And there a herald came towards me, and a chariot   280
Drawn by horses, with a man such as you describe
Seated in it. The groom leading the horses
Forced me off the road at his lord's command;
But as this charioteer lurched over towards me
I struck him in my rage. The old man saw me   285
And brought his double goad down upon my head
As I came abreast.

                 He was paid back, and more!
Swinging my club in this right hand I knocked him
Out of his car, and he rolled on the ground.

                           I killed him.

I killed them all.   290
Now if that stranger and Laios were—kin,
Where is a man more miserable than I?
More hated by the gods? Citizen and alien alike
Must never shelter me or speak to me—
I must be shunned by all.

                 And I myself   295
Pronounced this malediction upon myself!

Think of it: I have touched you with these hands,
These hands that killed your husband. What defilement!

Am I all evil, then? It must be so,
Since I must flee from Thebes, yet never again   300
See my own countrymen, my own country,
For fear of joining my mother in marriage

And killing Polybos, my father.
                                                Ah,
If I was created so, born to this fate,
Who could deny the savagery of God?   305

O holy majesty of heavenly powers!
May I never see that day! Never!
Rather let me vanish from the race of men
Than know the abomination destined me!
CHORAGOS: We too, my lord, have felt dismay at this.   310
    But there is hope: you have yet to hear the shepherd.
OEDIPUS: Indeed, I fear no other hope is left me.
IOKASTE: What do you hope from him when he comes?
OEDIPUS: This much:
    If his account of the murder tallies with yours,
    Then I am cleared.
IOKASTE: What was it that I said   315
    Of such importance?
OEDIPUS: Why, "marauders," you said,
    Killed the king, according to this man's story.
    If he maintains that still, if there were several,
    Clearly the guilt is not mine: I was alone.
    But if he says one man, singlehanded, did it,   320
    Then the evidence all points to me.
IOKASTE: You may be sure that he said there were several;
    And can he call back that story now? He can not.
    The whole city heard it as plainly as I.
    But suppose he alters some detail of it: 325
    He can not ever show that Laios' death
    Fulfilled the oracle: for Apollo said
    My child was doomed to kill him; and my child—
    Poor baby!—it was my child that died first.

No. From now on, where oracles are concerned,   330
    I would not waste a second thought on any.
OEDIPUS: You may be right.
                        But come: let someone go
    For the shepherd at once. This matter must be settled.
IOKASTE: I will send for him.
    I would not wish to cross you in anything,   335
    And surely not in this.—Let us go in.

                                (*Exeunt into the palace.*)

ODE 2   *Strophe 1*

CHORUS: Let me be reverent in the ways of right,
  Lowly the paths I journey on;
  Let all my words and actions keep
  The laws of the pure universe
  From highest Heaven handed down.   5
  For Heaven is their bright nurse,
  Those generations of the realms of light;
  Ah, never of mortal kind were they begot,
  Nor are they slaves of memory, lost in sleep:
  Their Father is greater than Time, and ages not.   10

Antistrophe 1

  The tyrant is a child of Pride
  Who drinks from his great sickening cup
  Recklessness and vanity,
  Until from his high crest headlong
  He plummets to the dust of hope.   15
  That strong man is not strong.
  But let no fair ambition be denied;
  May God protect the wrestler for the State
  In government, in comely policy,
  Who will fear God, and on his ordinance wait.   20

Strophe 2

  Haughtiness and the high hand of disdain
  Tempt and outrage God's holy law;
  And any mortal who dares hold
  No immortal Power in awe
  Will be caught up in a net of pain: 25
  The price for which his levity is sold.
  Let each man take due earnings, then,
  And keep his hands from holy things,
  And from blasphemy stand apart—
  Else the crackling blast of heaven   30
  Blows on his head, and on his desperate heart.
  Though fools will honor impious men,
  In their cities no tragic poet sings.

Antistrophe 2

Shall we lose faith in Delphi's obscurities,
We who have heard the world's core   35
Discredited, and the sacred wood
Of Zeus at Elis praised no more?
The deeds and the strange prophecies
Must make a pattern yet to be understood.
Zeus, if indeed you are lord of all,   40
Throned in light over night and day,
Mirror this in your endless mind:
Our masters call the oracle
Words on the wind, and the Delphic vision blind!
Their hearts no longer know Apollo,   45
And reverence for the gods has died away.

SCENE 3

(*Enter Iokaste.*)

IOKASTE: Princes of Thebes, it has occurred to me
    To visit the altars of the gods, bearing
    These branches as a suppliant, and this incense.
    Our king is not himself: his noble soul
    Is overwrought with fantasies of dread,   5
    Else he would consider
    The new prophecies in the light of the old.
    He will listen to any voice that speaks disaster,
    And my advice goes for nothing. (*She approaches the
        altar, right.*)
                        To you, then, Apollo,
    Lycean lord, since you are nearest, I turn in prayer   10
    Receive these offerings, and grant us deliverance
    From defilement. Our hearts are heavy with fear
    When we see our leader distracted, as helpless sailors
    Are terrified by the confusion of their helmsman.

(*Enter Messenger.*)

MESSENGER: Friends, no doubt you can direct me: 15
    Where shall I find the house of Oedipus,
    Or, better still, where is the king himself?

CHORAGOS: It is this very place, stranger; he is inside.
  This is his wife and mother of his children.
MESSENGER: I wish her happiness in a happy house,   20
  Blest in all the fulfillment of her marriage.
IOKASTE: I wish as much for you: your courtesy
  Deserves a like good fortune. But now, tell me:
  Why have you come? What have you to say to us?
MESSENGER: Good news, my lady, for your house and your husband.   25
IOKASTE: What news? Who sent you here?
MESSENGER: I am from Corinth.
  The news I bring ought to mean joy for you,
  Though it may be you will find some grief in it.
IOKASTE: What is it? How can it touch us in both ways?
MESSENGER: The word is that the people of the Isthmus   30
  Intend to call Oedipus to be their king.
IOKASTE: But old King Polybos—is he not reigning still?
MESSENGER: No. Death holds him in his sepulchre.
IOKASTE: What are you saying? Polybos is dead?
MESSENGER: If I am not telling the truth, may I die myself.   35
IOKASTE (to a Maidservant): Go in, go quickly; tell this to your master.
  O riddlers of God's will, where are you now!
  This was the man whom Oedipus, long ago,
  Feared so, fled so, in dread of destroying him—
  But it was another fate by which he died.   40

(Enter Oedipus, center.)

OEDIPUS: Dearest Iokaste, why have you sent for me?
IOKASTE: Listen to what this man says, and then tell me
  What has become of the solemn prophecies.
OEDIPUS: Who is this man? What is his news for me?
IOKASTE: He has come from Corinth to announce your father's death!   45
OEDIPUS: Is it true, stranger? Tell me in your own words.
MESSENGER: I can not say it more clearly: the king is dead.
OEDIPUS: Was it by treason? Or by an attack of illness?
MESSENGER: A little thing brings old men to their rest.
OEDIPUS: It was sickness, then?
MESSENGER: Yes, and his many years.   50
OEDIPUS: Ah!
  Why should a man respect the Pythian hearth,° or
  Give heed to the birds that jangle above his head?

52. Pythian hearth: A site in Delphi where ritualistic offerings were made.

They prophesied that I should kill Polybos,
Kill my own father; but he is dead and buried,   55
And I am here—I never touched him, never,
Unless he died of grief for my departure,
And thus, in a sense, through me. No. Polybos
Has packed the oracles off with him underground.
They are empty words.
IOKASTE: Had I not told you so?   60
OEDIPUS: You had; it was my faint heart that betrayed me.
IOKASTE: From now on never think of those things again.
OEDIPUS: And yet—must I not fear my mother's bed?
IOKASTE: Why should anyone in this world be afraid
     Since Fate rules us and nothing can be foreseen?   65
     A man should live only for the present day.

     Have no more fear of sleeping with your mother:
     How many men, in dreams, have lain with their mothers!
     No reasonable man is troubled by such things.
OEDIPUS: That is true, only—   70
     If only my mother were not still alive!
     But she is alive. I can not help my dread.
IOKASTE: Yet this news of your father's death is wonderful.
OEDIPUS: Wonderful. But I fear the living woman.
MESSENGER: Tell me, who is this woman that you fear?   75
OEDIPUS: It is Merope, man; the wife of King Polybos.
MESSENGER: Merope? Why should you be afraid of her?
OEDIPUS: An oracle of the gods, a dreadful saying.
MESSENGER: Can you tell me about it or are you sworn to silence?
OEDIPUS: I can tell you, and I will.   80
     Apollo said through his prophet that I was the man
     Who should marry his own mother, shed his father's blood
     With his own hands. And so, for all these years
     I have kept clear of Corinth, and no harm has come—
     Though it would have been sweet to see my parents again.   85
MESSENGER: And is this the fear that drove you out of Corinth?
OEDIPUS: Would you have me kill my father?
MESSENGER: As for that
     You must be reassured by the news I gave you.
OEDIPUS: If you could reassure me, I would reward you.
MESSENGER: I had that in mind, I will confess: I thought   90
     I could count on you when you returned to Corinth.
OEDIPUS: No: I will never go near my parents again.

MESSENGER: Ah, son, you still do not know what you are doing—
OEDIPUS: What do you mean? In the name of God tell me!
MESSENGER: —If these are your reasons for not going home.   95
OEDIPUS: I tell you, I fear the oracle may come true.
MESSENGER: And guilt may come upon you through your parents?
OEDIPUS: That is the dread that is always in my heart.
MESSENGER: Can you not see that all your fears are groundless?
OEDIPUS: Groundless? Am I not my parents' son?   100
MESSENGER: Polybos was not your father.
OEDIPUS: Not my father?
MESSENGER: No more your father than the man speaking to you.
OEDIPUS: But you are nothing to me!
MESSENGER: Neither was he.
OEDIPUS: Then why did he call me son?
MESSENGER: I will tell you:
    Long ago he had you from my hands, as a gift.   105
OEDIPUS: Then how could he love me so, if I was not his?
MESSENGER: He had no children, and his heart turned to you.
OEDIPUS: What of you? Did you buy me? Did you find me by chance?
MESSENGER: I came upon you in the woody vales of Kithairon.
OEDIPUS: And what were you doing there?
MESSENGER: Tending my flocks.   110
OEDIPUS: A wandering shepherd?
MESSENGER: But your savior, son, that day.
OEDIPUS: From what did you save me?
MESSENGER: Your ankles should tell you that.
OEDIPUS: Ah, stranger, why do you speak of that childhood pain?
MESSENGER: I pulled the skewer that pinned your feet together.
OEDIPUS: I have had the mark as long as I can remember.   115
MESSENGER: That was why you were given the name you bear.°
OEDIPUS: God! Was it my father or my mother who did it?
    Tell me!
MESSENGER: I do not know. The man who gave you to me
    Can tell you better than I.
OEDIPUS: It was not you that found me, but another?   120
MESSENGER: It was another shepherd gave you to me.
OEDIPUS: Who was he? Can you tell me who he was?
MESSENGER: I think he was said to be one of Laios' people.
OEDIPUS: You mean the Laios who was king here years ago?
MESSENGER: Yes; King Laios; and the man was one of his herdsmen.   125
OEDIPUS: Is he still alive? Can I see him?

116. name you bear: "Oedipus" literally means swollen foot.

MESSENGER: These men here
  Know best about such things.
OEDIPUS: Does anyone here
  Know this shepherd that he is talking about?
  Have you seen him in the fields, or in the town?
  If you have, tell me. It is time things were made plain.   130
CHORAGOS: I think the man he means is that same shepherd
  You have already asked to see. Iokaste perhaps
  Could tell you something.
OEDIPUS: Do you know anything
  About him, Lady? Is he the man we have summoned?
  Is that the man this shepherd means?
IOKASTE: Why think of him?   135
  Forget this herdsman. Forget it all.
  This talk is a waste of time.
OEDIPUS: How can you say that,
  When the clues to my true birth are in my hands?
IOKASTE: For God's love, let us have no more questioning!
  Is your life nothing to you?   140
  My own is pain enough for me to bear.
OEDIPUS: You need not worry. Suppose my mother a slave,
  And born of slaves: no baseness can touch you.
IOKASTE: Listen to me, I beg you: do not do this thing!
OEDIPUS: I will not listen; the truth must be made known.   145
IOKASTE: Everything that I say is for your own good!
OEDIPUS: My own good
  Snaps my patience, then; I want none of it.
IOKASTE: You are fatally wrong! May you never learn who you are!
OEDIPUS: Go, one of you, and bring the shepherd here.
  Let us leave this woman to brag of her royal name.   150
IOKASTE: Ah, miserable!
  That is the only word I have for you now.
  That is the only word I can ever have.   (*Exit into the palace.*)
CHORAGOS: Why has she left us, Oedipus? Why has she gone
  In such a passion of sorrow? I fear this silence: 155
  Something dreadful may come of it.
OEDIPUS: Let it come!
  However base my birth, I must know about it.
  The Queen, like a woman, is perhaps ashamed
  To think of my low origin. But I
  Am a child of Luck, I can not be dishonored.   160
  Luck is my mother; the passing months, my brothers,
  Have seen me rich and poor.

> If this is so,
> How could I wish that I were someone else?
> How could I not be glad to know my birth?

ODE 3   *Strophe*

CHORUS: If ever the coming time were known
   To my heart's pondering,
   Kithairon, now by Heaven I see the torches
   At the festival of the next full moon
   And see the dance, and hear the choir sing   5
   A grace to your gentle shade:
   Mountain where Oedipus was found,
   O mountain guard of a noble race!
   May the god° who heals us lend his aid,
   And let that glory come to pass   10
   For our king's cradling-ground.

Antistrophe

Of the nymphs that flower beyond the years,
   Who bore you, royal child,
   To Pan° of the hills or the timberline Apollo,
   Cold in delight where the upland clears,   15
   Or Hermes° for whom Kyllene's° heights are piled?
   Or flushed as evening cloud,
   Great Dionysos, roamer of mountains,
   He — was it he who found you there,
   And caught you up in his own proud   20
   Arms from the sweet god-ravisher
   Who laughed by the Muses'° fountains?

---

9. god: Apollo.   **14. Pan:** God of nature and fertility, depicted as an ugly man with the horns and legs of a goat. Pan was considered playful and amorous. **16. Hermes:** Son of Zeus, messenger of the gods.   **Kyllene:** Hermes' birthplace. **22. Muses:** Nine sister goddesses of poetry, music, art, and sciences.

SCENE 4

OEDIPUS: Sirs: though I do not know the man,
   I think I see him coming, this shepherd we want:
   He is old, like our friend here, and the men
   Bringing him seem to be servants of my house.
   But you can tell, if you have ever seen him.   5

(*Enter Shepherd escorted by Servants.*)

CHORAGOS: I know him, he was Laios' man. You can trust him.
OEDIPUS: Tell me first, you from Corinth: is this the shepherd
   We were discussing?
MESSENGER: This is the very man.
OEDIPUS (*to Shepherd*): Come here. No, look at me. You must answer
   Everything I ask. — You belonged to Laios?   10
SHEPHERD: Yes: born his slave, brought up in his house.
OEDIPUS: Tell me: what kind of work did you do for him?
SHEPHERD: I was a shepherd of his, most of my life.
OEDIPUS: Where mainly did you go for pasturage?
SHEPHERD: Sometimes Kithairon, sometimes the hills near-by.   15
OEDIPUS: Do you remember ever seeing this man out there?
SHEPHERD: What would he be doing there? This man?
OEDIPUS: This man standing here. Have you ever seen him before?
SHEPHERD: No. At least, not to my recollection.
MESSENGER: And that is not strange, my lord. But I'll refresh   20
   His memory: he must remember when we two
   Spent three whole seasons together, March to September,
   On Kithairon or thereabouts. He had two flocks;
   I had one. Each autumn I'd drive mine home
   And he would go back with his to Laios' sheepfold. —   25
   Is this not true, just as I have described it?
SHEPHERD: True, yes; but it was all so long ago.
MESSENGER: Well, then: do you remember, back in those days,
   That you gave me a baby boy to bring up as my own?
SHEPHERD: What if I did? What are you trying to say?   30
MESSENGER: King Oedipus was once that little child.
SHEPHERD: Damn you, hold your tongue!
OEDIPUS: No more of that!
   It is your tongue needs watching, not this man's.
SHEPHERD: My king, my master, what is it I have done wrong?
OEDIPUS: You have not answered his question about the boy.   35
SHEPHERD: He does not know . . . He is only making trouble . . .

OEDIPUS: Come, speak plainly, or it will go hard with you.
SHEPHERD: In God's name, do not torture an old man!
OEDIPUS: Come here, one of you; bind his arms behind him.
SHEPHERD: Unhappy king! What more do you wish to learn?   40
OEDIPUS: Did you give this man the child he speaks of?
SHEPHERD: I did.
   And I would to God I had died that very day.
OEDIPUS: You will die now unless you speak the truth.
SHEPHERD: Yet if I speak the truth, I am worse than dead.
OEDIPUS (to Attendant): He intends to draw it out, apparently—   45
SHEPHERD: No! I have told you already that I gave him the boy.
OEDIPUS: Where did you get him? From your house? From somewhere
   else?
SHEPHERD: Not from mine, no. A man gave him to me.
OEDIPUS: Is that man here? Whose house did he belong to?
SHEPHERD: For God's love, my king, do not ask me any more!   50
OEDIPUS: You are a dead man if I have to ask you again.
SHEPHERD: Then . . . Then the child was from the palace of Laios.
OEDIPUS: A slave child? or a child of his own line?
SHEPHERD: Ah, I am on the brink of dreadful speech!
OEDIPUS: And I of dreadful hearing. Yet I must hear.   55
SHEPHERD: If you must be told, then . . .
                                  They said it was Laios' child;
   But it is your wife who can tell you about that.
OEDIPUS: My wife—Did she give it to you?
SHEPHERD: My lord, she did.
OEDIPUS: Do you know why?
SHEPHERD: I was told to get rid of it.
OEDIPUS: Oh heartless mother!
SHEPHERD: But in dread of prophecies . . .   60
OEDIPUS: Tell me.
SHEPHERD: It was said that the boy would kill his own father.
OEDIPUS: Then why did you give him over to this old man?
SHEPHERD: I pitied the baby, my king,
   And I thought that this man would take him far away
   To his own country.
              He saved him—but for what a fate!   65
   For if you are what this man says you are,
   No man living is more wretched than Oedipus.
OEDIPUS: Ah God!
   It was true!
        All the prophecies!
              —Now,

O Light, may I look on you for the last time!   70
I, Oedipus,
Oedipus, damned in his birth, in his marriage damned,
Damned in the blood he shed with his own hand!

(*He rushes into the palace.*)

ODE 4   *Strophe 1*

CHORUS: Alas for the seed of men.
  What measure shall I give these generations
  That breathe on the void and are void
  And exist and do not exist?
  Who bears more weight of joy   5
  Than mass of sunlight shifting in images,
  Or who shall make his thought stay on
  That down time drifts away?
  Your splendor is all fallen.
  O naked brow of wrath and tears,   10
  O change of Oedipus!
  I who saw your days call no man blest—
  Your great days like ghosts gone.

Antistrophe 1

That mind was a strong bow.
Deep, how deep you drew it then, hard archer,   15
At a dim fearful range,
And brought dear glory down!
You overcame the stranger°—
The virgin with her hooking lion claws—
And though death sang, stood like a tower   20
To make pale Thebes take heart.
Fortress against our sorrow!
True king, giver of laws,
Majestic Oedipus!
No prince in Thebes had ever such renown,   25
No prince won such grace of power.

---

18. **stranger:** The Sphinx.

Strophe 2

And now of all men ever known
Most pitiful is this man's story:
His fortunes are most changed; his state
Fallen to a low slave's   30
Ground under bitter fate.
O Oedipus, most royal one!
The great door° that expelled you to the light
Gave at night—ah, gave night to your glory:
As to the father, to the fathering son.   35
All understood too late.
How could that queen whom Laios won,
The garden that he harrowed at his height,
Be silent when that act was done?

Antistrophe 2

But all eyes fail before time's eye,   40
All actions come to justice there.
Though never willed, though far down the deep past,
Your bed, your dread sirings,
Are brought to book at last.
Child by Laios doomed to die,   45
Then doomed to lose that fortunate little death,
Would God you never took breath in this air
That with my wailing lips I take to cry:
For I weep the world's outcast.
I was blind, and now I can tell why: 50
Asleep, for you had given ease of breath
To Thebes, while the false years went by.

EXODOS°

(*Enter, from the palace, Second Messenger.*)

SECOND MESSENGER: Elders of Thebes, most honored in this land,
    What horrors are yours to see and hear, what weight
    Of sorrow to be endured, if, true to your birth,

---

33. door: Iokaste's womb.   **Exodos:** Final scene.

You venerate the line of Labdakos!
I think neither Istros nor Phasis, those great rivers,   5
Could purify this place of all the evil
It shelters now, or soon must bring to light—
Evil not done unconsciously, but willed.

The greatest griefs are those we cause ourselves.
CHORAGOS: Surely, friend, we have grief enough already;   10
   What new sorrow do you mean?
SECOND MESSENGER: The queen is dead.
CHORAGOS: O miserable queen! But at whose hand?
SECOND MESSENGER: Her own.
   The full horror of what happened you can not know,
   For you did not see it; but I, who did, will tell you
   As clearly as I can how she met her death.   15

When she had left us,
In passionate silence, passing through the court,
She ran to her apartment in the house,
Her hair clutched by the fingers of both hands.
She closed the doors behind her; then, by that bed   20
Where long ago the fatal son was conceived—
That son who should bring about his father's death—
We heard her call upon Laios, dead so many years,
And heard her wail for the double fruit of her marriage,
A husband by her husband, children by her child.   25

Exactly how she died I do not know:
For Oedipus burst in moaning and would not let us
Keep vigil to the end: it was by him
As he stormed about the room that our eyes were caught.
From one to another of us he went, begging a sword,   30
Hunting the wife who was not his wife, the mother
Whose womb had carried his own children and himself.
I do not know: it was none of us aided him,
But surely one of the gods was in control!
For with a dreadful cry   35
He hurled his weight, as though wrenched out of himself,
At the twin doors: the bolts gave, and he rushed in.
And there we saw her hanging, her body swaying
From the cruel cord she had noosed about her neck.
A great sob broke from him, heartbreaking to hear,   40
As he loosed the rope and lowered her to the ground.

I would blot out from my mind what happened next!
For the king ripped from her gown the golden brooches
That were her ornament, and raised them, and plunged them down
Straight into his own eyeballs, crying, "No more,   45
No more shall you look on the misery about me,
The horrors of my own doing! Too long you have known
The faces of those whom I should never have seen,
Too long been blind to those for whom I was searching!
From this hour, go in darkness!" And as he spoke,   50
He struck at his eyes—not once, but many times;
And the blood spattered his beard,
Bursting from his ruined sockets like red hail.

So from the unhappiness of two this evil has sprung,
A curse on the man and woman alike. The old   55
Happiness of the house of Labdakos
Was happiness enough: where is it today?
It is all wailing and ruin, disgrace, death—all
The misery of mankind that has a name—
And it is wholly and for ever theirs.   60
CHORAGOS: Is he in agony still? Is there no rest for him?
SECOND MESSENGER: He is calling for someone to open the
        doors wide
So that all the children of Kadmos may look upon
His father's murderer, his mother's—no,
I can not say it!
                And then he will leave Thebes,   65
Self-exiled, in order that the curse
Which he himself pronounced may depart from the house.
He is weak, and there is none to lead him,
So terrible is his suffering.
                        But you will see:
Look, the doors are opening; in a moment   70
You will see a thing that would crush a heart of stone.

(*The central door is opened; Oedipus, blinded, is led in.*)

CHORAGOS: Dreadful indeed for men to see.
    Never have my own eyes
    Looked on a sight so full of fear.

    Oedipus!   75
    What madness came upon you, what demon

Leaped on your life with heavier
Punishment than a mortal man can bear?
No: I can not even
Look at you, poor ruined one.   80
And I would speak, question, ponder,
If I were able. No.
You make me shudder.
OEDIPUS: God. God.
Is there a sorrow greater?   85
Where shall I find harbor in this world?
My voice is hurled far on a dark wind.
What has God done to me?
CHORAGOS: Too terrible to think of, or to see.

Strophe 1

OEDIPUS: O cloud of night,   90
Never to be turned away: night coming on,
I can not tell how: night like a shroud!
My fair winds brought me here.
                              O God. Again
The pain of the spikes where I had sight,
The flooding pain   95
Of memory, never to be gouged out.
CHORAGOS: This is not strange.
You suffer it all twice over, remorse in pain,
Pain in remorse.

Antistrophe 1

OEDIPUS: Ah dear friend   100
Are you faithful even yet, you alone?
Are you still standing near me, will you stay here,
Patient, to care for the blind?
                              The blind man!
Yet even blind I know who it is attends me,
By the voice's tone—   105
Though my new darkness hide the comforter.
CHORAGOS: Oh fearful act!
What god was it drove you to rake black
Night across your eyes?

Strophe 2

OEDIPUS: Apollo. Apollo. Dear   110
  Children, the god was Apollo.
  He brought my sick, sick fate upon me.
  But the blinding hand was my own!
  How could I bear to see
  When all my sight was horror everywhere?   115
CHORAGOS: Everywhere; that is true.
OEDIPUS: And now what is left?
  Images? Love? A greeting even,
  Sweet to the senses? Is there anything?
  Ah, no, friends: lead me away.   120
  Lead me away from Thebes.
                         Lead the great wreck
  And hell of Oedipus, whom the gods hate.
CHORAGOS: Your misery, you are not blind to that.
  Would God you had never found it out!

Antistrophe 2

OEDIPUS: Death take the man who unbound   125
  My feet on that hillside
  And delivered me from death to life! What life?
  If only I had died,
  This weight of monstrous doom
  Could not have dragged me and my darlings down.   130
CHORAGOS: I would have wished the same.
OEDIPUS: Oh never to have come here
  With my father's blood upon me! Never
  To have been the man they call his mother's husband!
  Oh accurst! Oh child of evil,   135
  To have entered that wretched bed—
                      the selfsame one!
  More primal than sin itself, this fell to me.
CHORAGOS: I do not know what words to offer you.
  You were better dead than alive and blind.
OEDIPUS: Do not counsel me any more. This punishment   140
  That I have laid upon myself is just.
  If I had eyes,
  I do not know how I could bear the sight
  Of my father, when I came to the house of Death,
  Or my mother: for I have sinned against them both   145

So vilely that I could not make my peace
By strangling my own life.
                       Or do you think my children,
Born as they were born, would be sweet to my eyes?
Ah never, never! Nor this town with its high walls,
Nor the holy images of the gods.
                    For I,   150
Thrice miserable! — Oedipus, noblest of all the line
Of Kadmos, have condemned myself to enjoy
These things no more, by my own malediction
Expelling that man whom the gods declared
To be a defilement in the house of Laios.   155
After exposing the rankness of my own guilt,
How could I look men frankly in the eyes?
No, I swear it,
If I could have stifled my hearing at its source,
I would have done it and made all this body   160
A tight cell of misery, blank to light and sound:
So I should have been safe in my dark mind
Beyond external evil.
              Ah Kithairon!
Why did you shelter me? When I was cast upon you,
Why did I not die? Then I should never   165
Have shown the world my execrable birth.

Ah Polybos! Corinth, city that I believed
The ancient seat of my ancestors: how fair
I seemed, your child! And all the while this evil
Was cancerous within me!
                 For I am sick   170
In my own being, sick in my origin.
O three roads, dark ravine, woodland and way
Where three roads met; you, drinking my father's blood,
My own blood, spilled by my own hand: can you remember
The unspeakable things I did there, and the things   175
I went on from there to do?
               O marriage, marriage!
The act that engendered me, and again the act
Performed by the son in the same bed —
                   Ah, the net
Of incest, mingling fathers, brothers, sons,
With brides, wives, mothers: the last evil   180
That can be known by men: no tongue can say

How evil!
        No. For the love of God, conceal me
Somewhere far from Thebes; or kill me; or hurl me
Into the sea, away from men's eyes for ever.

Come, lead me. You need not fear to touch me.   185
Of all men, I alone can bear this guilt.

(*Enter Kreon.*)

CHORAGOS: Kreon is here now. As to what you ask,
  He may decide the course to take. He only
  Is left to protect the city in your place.
OEDIPUS: Alas, how can I speak to him? What right have I   190
  To beg his courtesy whom I have deeply wronged?
KREON: I have not come to mock you, Oedipus,
  Or to reproach you, either.
  (*To Attendants.*)   —You, standing there:
  If you have lost all respect for man's dignity,
  At least respect the flame of Lord Helios:°   195
  Do not allow this pollution to show itself
  Openly here, an affront to the earth
  And Heaven's rain and the light of day. No, take him
  Into the house as quickly as you can.
  For it is proper   200
  That only the close kindred see his grief.
OEDIPUS: I pray you in God's name, since your courtesy
  Ignores my dark expectation, visiting
  With mercy this man of all men most execrable:
  Give me what I ask—for your good, not for mine.   205
KREON: And what is it that you turn to me begging for?
OEDIPUS: Drive me out of this country as quickly as may be
  To a place where no human voice can ever greet me.
KREON: I should have done that before now—only,
  God's will had not been wholly revealed to me.   210
OEDIPUS: But his command is plain: the parricide
  Must be destroyed. I am that evil man.
KREON: That is the sense of it, yes; but as things are,
  We had best discover clearly what is to be done.
OEDIPUS: You would learn more about a man like me?   215
KREON: You are ready now to listen to the god.

195. Lord Helios: The sun god.

OEDIPUS: I will listen. But it is to you
    That I must turn for help. I beg you, hear me.

    The woman is there—
    Give her whatever funeral you think proper: 220
    She is your sister.
                —But let me go, Kreon!
    Let me purge my father's Thebes of the pollution
    Of my living here, and go out to the wild hills,
    To Kithairon, that has won such fame with me,
    The tomb my mother and father appointed for me,   225
    And let me die there, as they willed I should.
    And yet I know
    Death will not ever come to me through sickness
    Or in any natural way: I have been preserved
    For some unthinkable fate. But let that be.   230

    As for my sons, you need not care for them.
    They are men, they will find some way to live.
    But my poor daughters, who have shared my table,
    Who never before have been parted from their father—
    Take care of them, Kreon; do this for me.   235

    And will you let me touch them with my hands
    A last time, and let us weep together?
    Be kind, my lord,
    Great prince, be kind!
                Could I but touch them,
    They would be mine again, as when I had my eyes.   240

(*Enter Antigone and Ismene, attended.*)

    Ah, God!
    Is it my dearest children I hear weeping?
    Has Kreon pitied me and sent my daughters?
KREON: Yes, Oedipus: I knew that they were dear to you
    In the old days, and know you must love them still.   245
OEDIPUS: May God bless you for this—and be a friendlier
    Guardian to you than he has been to me!

    Children, where are you?
    Come quickly to my hands: they are your brother's—
    Hands that have brought your father's once clear eyes   250

To this way of seeing—
                              Ah dearest ones,
I had neither sight nor knowledge then, your father
By the woman who was the source of his own life!
And I weep for you—having no strength to see you—,
I weep for you when I think of the bitterness   255
That men will visit upon you all your lives.
What homes, what festivals can you attend
Without being forced to depart again in tears?
And when you come to marriageable age,
Where is the man, my daughters, who would dare   260
Risk the bane that lies on all my children?
Is there any evil wanting? Your father killed
His father; sowed the womb of her who bore him;
Engendered you at the fount of his own existence!
That is what they will say of you.

                              Then, whom   265
Can you ever marry? There are no bridegrooms for you,
And your lives must wither away in sterile dreaming.

O Kreon, son of Menoikeus!
You are the only father my daughters have,
Since we, their parents, are both of us gone for ever.   270
They are your own blood: you will not let them
Fall into beggary and loneliness;
You will keep them from the miseries that are mine!
Take pity on them; see, they are only children,
Friendless except for you. Promise me this,   275
Great prince, and give me your hand in token of it.

(*Kreon clasps his right hand.*)

Children:
I could say much, if you could understand me,
But as it is, I have only this prayer for you:
Live where you can, be as happy as you can—
Happier, please God, than God has made your father.   280
KREON: Enough. You have wept enough. Now go within.
OEDIPUS: I must, but it is hard.
KREON: Time eases all things.
OEDIPUS: You know my mind, then?
KREON: Say what you desire.
OEDIPUS: Send me from Thebes!

KREON: God grant that I may!   285
OEDIPUS: But since God hates me . . .
KREON: No, he will grant your wish.
OEDIPUS: You promise?
KREON: I can not speak beyond my knowledge.
OEDIPUS: Then lead me in.
KREON: Come now, and leave your children.   290
OEDIPUS: No! Do not take them from me!
KREON: Think no longer
   That you are in command here, but rather think
   How, when you were, you served your own destruction.

(*Exeunt into the house all but the Chorus; the Choragos chants directly to the audience.*)

CHORAGOS: Men of Thebes: look upon Oedipus.

   This is the king who solved the famous riddle   295
   And towered up, most powerful of men.
   No mortal eyes but looked on him with envy,
   Yet in the end ruin swept over him.

   Let every man in mankind's frailty
   Consider his last day; and let none   300
   Presume on his good fortune until he find
   Life, at his death, a memory without pain.

c. 430 B.C.

Lysistrata

ARISTOPHANES [c. 448–c. 385 B.C.]

TRANSLATED BY DUDLEY FITTS

Persons Represented

LYSISTRATA,
KALONIKE, } *Athenian women*
MYRRHINE,
LAMPITO, *a Spartan woman*
CHORUS
COMMISSIONER
KINESIAS, *husband of Myrrhine*
SPARTAN HERALD
SPARTAN AMBASSADOR
A SENTRY
[BABY SON OF KENESIAS
STRATYLLIS
SPARTANS
ATHENIANS]

Scene: *Athens. First, a public square; later, beneath the walls of the Akropolis;° later, a courtyard within the Akropolis.*

PROLOGUE

(Athens; a public square; early morning; Lysistrata alone.)

LYSISTRATA: If someone had invited them to a festival —
  of Bacchos,° say; or to Pan's° shrine, or to Aphrodite's°

Akropolis: (Acropolis) Fortress sacred to the goddess Athena.   **2. Bacchos:** (Bacchus) God of wine and the instigator of wild, orgiastic ritual (also called Dionysus).   **Pan:** God of nature and fertility, depicted as an ugly man with the horns and legs of a goat. Pan was considered playful and lecherous.   **Aphrodite:** Goddess of love.

over at Kolias—, you couldn't get through the streets,
what with the drums and the dancing. But now,
not a woman in sight!
                         Except—oh, yes!   5

(*Enter Kalonike.*)

Here's one of my neighbors, at last. Good
    morning, Kalonike.
KALONIKE: Good morning, Lysistrata.
                                             Darling,
    don't frown so! You'll ruin your face!
LYSISTRATA: Never mind my face.
    Kalonike,
    the way we women behave! Really, I don't blame the men   10
    for what they say about us.
KALONIKE: No; I imagine they're right.
LYSISTRATA: For example: I call a meeting
    to think out a most important matter—and what happens?
    The women all stay in bed!
KALONIKE: Oh, they'll be along.
    It's hard to get away, you know: a husband, a cook,   15
    a child . . . Home life can be *so* demanding!
LYSISTRATA: What I have in mind is even more demanding.
KALONIKE: Tell me: what is it?
LYSISTRATA: It's big.
KALONIKE: Goodness! *How* big?
LYSISTRATA: Big enough for all of us.
KALONIKE: But we're not all here!
LYSISTRATA: We would be, if *that's* what was up!
                                             No, Kalonike,   20
    this is something I've been turning over for nights,
        long sleepless nights.
KALONIKE: It must be getting worn down, then,
    if you've spent so much time on it.
LYSISTRATA: Worn down or not,
    it comes to this: Only we women can save Greece!
KALONIKE: Only we women? Poor Greece!
LYSISTRATA: Just the same,   25
    it's up to us. First, we must liquidate
    the Peloponnesians—
KALONIKE: Fun, fun!

LYSISTRATA: —and then the Boiotians.°
KALONIKE: Oh! But not those heavenly eels!
LYSISTRATA: You needn't worry.
  I'm not talking about eels. —But here's the point:
  If we can get the women from those places —   30
  all those Boiotians and Peloponnesians —
  to join us women here, why, we can save all Greece!
KALONIKE: But dearest Lysistrata!
  How can women do a thing so austere, so
  political? We belong at home. Our only armor's   35
  our perfumes, our saffron dresses and
  our pretty little shoes!
LYSISTRATA: Exactly. Those
  transparent dresses, the saffron, the perfume, those
      pretty shoes —
KALONIKE: Oh?
LYSISTRATA: Not a single man would lift
  his spear —
KALONIKE: I'll send my dress to the dyer's tomorrow!
LYSISTRATA: —or grab a shield —
KALONIKE: The sweetest little negligee —   40
LYSISTRATA: —or haul out his sword.
KALONIKE: I know where
  I can buy the dreamiest sandals!
LYSISTRATA: Well, so you see. Now, shouldn't
  the women have come?
KALONIKE: Come? They should have *flown*!
LYSISTRATA: Athenians are always late.
                                   But imagine!
  There's no one here from the South Shore, or from Salamis.   45
KALONIKE: Things are hard over in Salamis, I swear.
  They have to get going at dawn.
LYSISTRATA: And nobody from Acharnai.
  I thought they'd be here hours ago.
KALONIKE: Well, you'll get
  that awful Theagenes woman: she'll be
  a sheet or so in the wind.
                              But look!   50
  Someone at last! Can you see who they are?

(*Enter Myrrhine and other women.*)

27. **Boiotians:** Boorish inhabitants of Boiotia, a region known for its seafood.

LYSISTRATA: They're from Anagyros.
KALONIKE: They certainly are.
  You'd know them anywhere, by the scent.
MYRRHINE: Sorry to be late, Lysistrata.
                              Oh come,
  don't scowl so. Say something!
LYSISTRATA: My dear Myrrhine,   55
  what is there to say? After all,
  you've been pretty casual about the whole thing.
MYRRHINE: Couldn't find
  my girdle in the dark, that's all.
                     But what *is*
  "the whole thing"?
KALONIKE: No, we've got to wait
  for those Boiotians and Peloponnesians.   60
LYSISTRATA: That's more like it. — But, look!
  Here's Lampito!

(*Enter Lampito with women from Sparta.*)

LYSISTRATA: Darling Lampito,
  how pretty you are today! What a nice color!
  Goodness, you look as though you could strangle a bull!   65
LAMPITO: Ah think Ah could! It's the work-out
  in the gym every day; and, of co'se that dance of ahs
  where y' kick yo' own tail.
KALONIKE: What an adorable figure!
LAMPITO: Lawdy, when y' touch me lahk that,
  Ah feel lahk a heifer at the altar!
LYSISTRATA: And this young lady?   70
  Where is she from?
LAMPITO: Boiotia. Social-Register type.
LYSISTRATA: Ah. "Boiotia of the fertile plain."
KALONIKE: And if you look,
  you'll find the fertile plain has just been mowed.
LYSISTRATA: And this lady?
LAMPITO: Hagh, wahd, handsome.
  She comes from Korinth.   75
KALONIKE: High and wide's the word for it.
LAMPITO: Which one of you
  called this heah meeting, and why?
LYSISTRATA: I did.
LAMPITO: Well, then, tell us:
  What's up?
MYRRHINE: Yes, darling, what *is* on your mind, after all?

LYSISTRATA: I'll tell you. — But first, one little question.
MYRRHINE: Well?
LYSISTRATA: It's your husbands. Fathers of your children. Doesn't it
    bother you   80
    that they're always off with the Army? I'll stake my life,
    not one of you has a man in the house this minute!
KALONIKE: Mine's been in Thrace the last five months, keeping an eye
    on that General.
MYRRHINE: Mine's been in Pylos for seven.
LAMPITO: And mahn,
    whenever he gets a *dis*charge, he goes raht back   85
    with that li'l ole shield of his, and enlists again!
LYSISTRATA: And not the ghost of a lover to be found!
    From the very day the war began —
                                        those Milesians!
    I could skin them alive!
                            — I've not seen so much, even,
    as one of those leather consolation prizes. —   90
    But there! What's important is: If I've found a way
    to end the war, are you with me?
MYRRHINE: I should *say* so!
    Even if I have to pawn my best dress and
    drink up the proceeds.
KALONIKE: Me, too! Even if they split me
    right up the middle, like a flounder.
LAMPITO: Ah'm shorely with you.   95
    Ah'd crawl up Taygetos° on mah knees
    if that'd bring peace.
LYSISTRATA: All right, then; here it is:
    Women! Sisters!
    If we really want our men to make peace,
    we must be ready to give up —
MYRRHINE: Give up what?   100
    Quick, tell us!
LYSISTRATA: But *will* you?
MYRRHINE: We will, even if it kills us.
LYSISTRATA: Then we must give up going to bed with our men.

(*Long silence.*)

    Oh? So now you're sorry? Won't look at me?
    Doubtful? Pale? All teary-eyed?
                            But come: be frank with me.

---

96. Taygetos: A mountain range.

Will you do it, or not? Well? Will you do it?
MYRRHINE: I couldn't. No.   105
  Let the war go on.
KALONIKE: Nor I. Let the war go on.
LYSISTRATA: You, you little flounder,
  ready to be split up the middle?
KALONIKE: Lysistrata, no!
  I'd walk through fire for you—you *know* I would!—but don't
  ask us to give up *that*! Why, there's nothing like it!   110
LYSISTRATA: And you?
BOIOTIAN: No. I must say *I'd* rather walk through fire.
LYSISTRATA: What an utterly perverted sex we women are!
  No wonder poets write tragedies about us.
  There's only one thing we can think of.
                                    But you from Sparta:
  if you stand by me, we may win yet! Will you?   115
  It means so much!
LAMPITO: Ah sweah, it means *too* much!
  By the Two Goddesses,° it does! Asking a girl
  to sleep—Heaven knows how long!—in a great big bed
  with nobody there but herself! But Ah'll stay with you!
  Peace comes first!
LYSISTRATA: Spoken like a true Spartan!   120
KALONIKE: But if—
                oh dear!
                        —if we give up what you tell us to,
  will there *be* any peace?
LYSISTRATA: Why, mercy, of course there will!
  We'll just sit snug in our very thinnest gowns,
  perfumed and powdered from top to bottom, and those men
  simply won't stand still! And when we say No,   125
  they'll go out of their minds! And there's your peace.
  You can take my word for it.
LAMPITO: Ah seem to remember
  that Colonel Menelaos threw his sword away
  when he saw Helen's breast° all bare.
KALONIKE: But, goodness me!
  What if they just get up and leave us?

---

117. **Two Goddesses:** A woman's oath referring to Demeter, the earth goddess, and her daughter Persephone, goddess of fertility. **128–29. Colonel Menelaos . . . Helen's breast:** King Menelaos's wife, Helen, was abducted by Paris and taken to Troy, which led to the Trojan War.

LYSISTRATA: In that case   130
we'll have to fall back on ourselves, I suppose.
But they won't.
KALONIKE: I must say that's not much help. But
what if they drag us into the bedroom?
LYSISTRATA: Hang on to the door.
KALONIKE: What if they slap us?
LYSISTRATA: If they do, you'd better give in.
But be sulky about it. Do I have to teach you how?   135
You know there's no fun for men when they have to force you.
There are millions of ways of getting them to see reason.
Don't you worry: a man
doesn't like it unless the girl cooperates.
KALONIKE: I suppose so. Oh, all right. We'll go along.   140
LAMPITO: Ah imagine us Spahtans can arrange a peace. But you
Athenians! Why, you're just war-mongerers!
LYSISTRATA: Leave that to me.
I know how to make them listen.
LAMPITO: Ah don't see how.
After all, they've got their boats; and there's lots of money
piled up in the Akropolis.
LYSISTRATA: The Akropolis? Darling,   145
we're taking over the Akropolis today!
That's the older women's job. All the rest of us
are going to the Citadel to sacrifice — you understand me?
And once there, we're in for good!
LAMPITO: Whee! Up the rebels!
Ah can see you're a good strate*e*gist.
LYSISTRATA: Well, then, Lampito,   150
what we have to do now is take a solemn oath.
LAMPITO: Say it. We'll sweah.
LYSISTRATA: This is it.
— But where's our Inner Guard?
                         — Look. Guard: you see this shield?
Put it down here. Now bring me the victim's entrails.
KALONIKE: But the oath?
LYSISTRATA: You remember how in Aischylos' *Seven*°   155
they killed a sheep and swore on a shield? Well, then?
KALONIKE: But I don't see how you can swear for peace on a shield.
LYSISTRATA: What else do you suggest?

155. *Seven*: Aeschylus's *Seven against Thebes* is based on a legend in which Oedipus's
sons fought for the throne of Thebes.

KALONIKE: Why not a white horse?
  We could swear by that.
LYSISTRATA: And where will you get a white horse?
KALONIKE: I never thought of that. *What* can we do?
LYSISTRATA: I have it!   160
  Let's set this big black wine-bowl on the ground
  and pour in a gallon or so of Thasian,° and swear
  not to add one drop of water.
LAMPITO: Ah lahk *that* oath!
LYSISTRATA: Bring the bowl and the wine-jug.
KALONIKE: Oh, what a simply *huge* one!
LYSISTRATA: Set it down. Girls, place your hands on the gift-offering.   165
  O Goddess of Persuasion! And thou, O Loving-cup:
  Look upon this our sacrifice, and
  be gracious!
KALONIKE: See the blood spill out. How red and pretty it is!
LAMPITO: And Ah must say it smells good.
MYRRHINE: Let me swear first!   170
KALONIKE: No, by Aphrodite, we'll match for it!
LYSISTRATA: Lampito: all of you women: come, touch the bowl,
  and repeat after me—remember, this is an oath—:
  I WILL HAVE NOTHING TO DO WITH MY HUSBAND OR
      MY LOVER
KALONIKE: *I will have nothing to do with my husband or my lover*   175
LYSISTRATA: THOUGH HE COME TO ME IN PITIABLE CONDITION
KALONIKE: *Though he come to me in pitiable condition*
  (Oh Lysistrata! This is killing me!)
LYSISTRATA: IN MY HOUSE I WILL BE UNTOUCHABLE
KALONIKE: *In my house I will be untouchable*   180
LYSISTRATA: IN MY THINNEST SAFFRON SILK
KALONIKE: *In my thinnest saffron silk*
LYSISTRATA: AND MAKE HIM LONG FOR ME.
KALONIKE: *And make him long for me.*
LYSISTRATA: I WILL NOT GIVE MYSELF   185
KALONIKE: *I will not give myself*
LYSISTRATA: AND IF HE CONSTRAINS ME
KALONIKE: *And if he constrains me*
LYSISTRATA: I WILL BE COLD AS ICE AND NEVER MOVE
KALONIKE: *I will be cold as ice and never move*   190
LYSISTRATA: I WILL NOT LIFT MY SLIPPERS TOWARD THE CEILING
KALONIKE: *I will not lift my slippers toward the ceiling*

---

162. Thasian: Wine from Thasos.

LYSISTRATA: OR CROUCH ON ALL FOURS LIKE THE LIONESS IN
   THE CARVING
KALONIKE: *Or crouch on all fours like the lioness in the carving*
LYSISTRATA: AND IF I KEEP THIS OATH LET ME DRINK FROM
   THIS BOWL   195
KALONIKE: *And if I keep this oath let me drink from this bowl*
LYSISTRATA: IF NOT, LET MY OWN BOWL BE FILLED WITH WATER.
KALONIKE: *If not, let my own bowl be filled with water.*
LYSISTRATA: You have all sworn?
MYRRHINE: We have.
LYSISTRATA: Then thus
   I sacrifice the victim.

(*Drinks largely.*)

KALONIKE: Save some for us!   200
   Here's to you, darling, and to you, and to you!

(*Loud cries offstage.*)

LAMPITO: What's all *that* whoozy-goozy?
LYSISTRATA: Just what I told you.
   The older women have taken the Akropolis.
   Now you, Lampito,
   rush back to Sparta. We'll take care of things here. Leave   205
   these girls here for hostages.
                    The rest of you,
   up to the Citadel: and mind you push in the bolts.
KALONIKE: But the men? Won't they be after us?
LYSISTRATA: Just you leave
   the men to me. There's not fire enough in the world,
   or threats either, to make me open these doors   210
   except on my own terms.
KALONIKE: I hope not, by Aphrodite!
   After all,
   we've got a reputation for bitchiness to live up to.

                                      (*Exeunt.°*)

[S.D.] *Exeunt:* Latin, "they go out."

PARODOS:° CHORAL EPISODE

(The hillside just under the Akropolis. Enter Chorus of Old Men with burning torches and braziers; much puffing and coughing.)

KORYPHAIOS^(man):° Forward march, Drakes, old friend: never you mind
  that damn big log banging hell down on your back.

Strophe° 1

CHORUS^(men): There's this to be said for longevity:
  You see things you thought that you'd never see.
    Look, Strymodoros, who would have thought it?   5
    We've caught it—
        the New Femininity!
  The wives of our bosom, our board, our bed—
  Now, by the gods, they've gone ahead
  And taken the Citadel (Heaven knows why!),
  Profanèd the sacred statuar-y,   10
        And barred the doors,
        The subversive whores!
KORYPHAIOS^(m): Shake a leg there, Philurgos, man: the Akropolis or bust!
  Put the kindling around here. We'll build one almighty big
  bonfire for the whole bunch of bitches, every last one;   15
  and the first we fry will be old Lykon's woman.

Antistrophe° 1

CHORUS^(m): They're not going to give me the old horse-laugh!
  No, by Demeter, they won't pull this off!
    Think of Kleomenes: even he
    Didn't go free
        till he brought me his stuff.   20
  A good man he was, all stinking and shaggy,
  Bare as an eel except for the bag he
  Covered his rear with. God, what a mess!
  Never a bath in six years, I'd guess.

Parodos: The song chanted by the Chorus on their entry. **1. Koryphaios:** Leader of the Chorus (also called *Choragos*). **Strophe:** Song sung by the Chorus as they danced from stage right to stage left. **Antistrophe:** Song sung by the Chorus as they danced back from stage left to stage right.

Pure Sparta, man!   25
He also ran.
KORYPHAIOS^(m): That was a siege, friends! Seventeen ranks strong
we slept at the Gate. And shall we not do as much
against these women, whom God and Euripides hate?
If we don't, I'll turn in my medals from Marathon.   30

Strophe 2

CHORUS^(m): Onward and upward! A little push,
  And we're there.
Ouch, my shoulders! I could wish
  For a pair
Of good strong oxen. Keep your eye   35
  On the fire there, it mustn't die.
   Akh! Akh!
The smoke would make a cadaver cough!

Antistrophe 2

Holy Herakles, a hot spark
  Bit my eye!   40
Damn this hellfire, damn this work!
  So say I.
Onward and upward just the same.
(Laches, remember the Goddess: for shame!)
   Akh! Akh!   45
The smoke would make a cadaver cough!
KORYPHAIOS^(m): At last (and let us give suitable thanks to God
for his infinite mercies) I have managed to bring
my personal flame to the common goal. It breathes, it lives.
Now, gentlemen, let us consider. Shall we insert   50
the torch, say, into the brazier, and thus extract
a kindling brand? And shall we then, do you think,
push on to the gate like valiant sheep? On the whole yes.
But I would have you consider this, too: if they—
I refer to the women—should refuse to open,   55
what then? Do we set the doors afire
and smoke them out? At ease, men. Meditate.
Akh, the smoke! Woof! What we really need
is the loan of a general or two from the Samos Command.°

59. **Samos Command:** Headquarters of the Athenian military.

At least we've got this lumber off our backs.   60
That's something. And now let's look to our fire.
O Pot, brave Brazier, touch my torch with flame!
Victory, Goddess, I invoke thy name!
Strike down these paradigms of female pride
And we shall hang our trophies up inside.   65

(*Enter Chorus of Old Women on the walls of the Akropolis, carrying jars of water.*)

KORYPHAIOS[(woman)]: Smoke, girls, smoke! There's smoke all over
    the place!
Probably fire, too. Hurry, girls! Fire! Fire!

Strophe 1

CHORUS[(women)]: Nikodike, run!
  Or Kalyke's done
  To a turn, and poor Kritylla's   70
  Smoked like a ham.
          Damn
These old men! Are we too late?
I nearly died down at the place
Where we fill our jars:
    Slaves pushing and jostling—   75
  Such a hustling
I never saw in all my days.

Antistrophe 1

But here's water at last.
Haste, sisters, haste!
Slosh it on them, slosh it down,   80
The silly old wrecks!
          Sex
Almighty! What they want's
A hot bath? Good. Send one down.
Athena of Athens town,
    Trito-born!° Helm of Gold!   85
  Cripple the old
Firemen! Help us help them drown!

85. **Trito-born:** Athena was said to have been born near Lake Tritonis in Libya.

(The old men capture a woman, Stratyllis.)

STRATYLLIS: Let me go! Let me go!
KORYPHAIOS⁽ʷ⁾:   You walking corpses,
  have you no shame?
KORYPHAIOS⁽ᵐ⁾:   I wouldn't have believed it!
  An army of women in the Akropolis!   90
KORYPHAIOS⁽ʷ⁾: So we scare you, do we? Grandpa, you've seen
  only our pickets yet!
KORYPHAIOS⁽ᵐ⁾:   Hey, Phaidrias!
  Help me with the necks of these jabbering hens!
KORYPHAIOS⁽ʷ⁾: Down with your pots, girls! We'll need both hands
  if these antiques attack us!
KORYPHAIOS⁽ᵐ⁾:   Want your face kicked in?   95
KORYPHAIOS⁽ʷ⁾: Want your balls chewed off?
KORYPHAIOS⁽ᵐ⁾:   Look out! I've got a stick!
KORYPHAIOS⁽ʷ⁾: You lay a half-inch of your stick on Stratyllis,
  and you'll never stick again!
KORYPHAIOS⁽ᵐ⁾: Fall apart!
KORYPHAIOS⁽ʷ⁾:   I'll spit up your guts!
KORYPHAIOS⁽ᵐ⁾:   Euripides! Master!
  How well you knew women!
KORYPHAIOS⁽ʷ⁾:   Listen to him, Rhodippe,   100
  up with the pots!
KORYPHAIOS⁽ᵐ⁾:   Demolition of God,
  what good are your pots?
KORYPHAIOS⁽ʷ⁾:   You refugee from the tomb,
  what good is your fire?
KORYPHAIOS⁽ᵐ⁾:   Good enough to make a pyre
  to barbecue you!
KORYPHAIOS⁽ʷ⁾:   We'll squizzle your kindling!
KORYPHAIOS⁽ᵐ⁾: You think so?
KORYPHAIOS⁽ʷ⁾:   Yah! Just hang around a while!   105
KORYPHAIOS⁽ᵐ⁾: Want a touch of my torch?
KORYPHAIOS⁽ʷ⁾:   It needs a good soaping.
KORYPHAIOS⁽ᵐ⁾: How about you?
KORYPHAIOS⁽ʷ⁾:   Soap for a senile bridegroom!
KORYPHAIOS⁽ᵐ⁾: Senile? Hold your trap
KORYPHAIOS⁽ʷ⁾:   Just *you* try to hold it!
KORYPHAIOS⁽ᵐ⁾: The yammer of women!
KORYPHAIOS⁽ʷ⁾:   Oh is that so?
  You're not in the jury room now, you know.   110
KORYPHAIOS⁽ᵐ⁾: Gentlemen, I beg you, burn off that woman's hair!
KORYPHAIOS⁽ʷ⁾: Let it come down!

(They empty their pots on the men.)

KORYPHAIOS[(m)]: What a way to drown!
KORYPHAIOS[(w)]:   Hot, hey?
KORYPHAIOS[(m)]:   Say, enough!
KORYPHAIOS[(w)]: Dandruff
  needs watering. I'll make you   115
  nice and fresh.
KORYPHAIOS[(m)]:   For God's sake, you,
  hold off!

SCENE 1

(Enter a Commissioner accompanied by four constables.)

COMMISSIONER: These degenerate women! What a racket of little drums,
  what a yapping for Adonis° on every house-top!
  It's like the time in the Assembly when I was listening
  to a speech — out of order, as usual — by that fool
  Demostratos,° all about troops for Sicily,°   5
  that kind of nonsense —
                          and there was his wife
  trotting around in circles howling
  Alas for Adonis! —
                      and Demostratos insisting
  we must draft every last Zakynthian that can walk —
  and his wife up there on the roof,   10
  drunk as an owl, yowling
  Oh weep for Adonis! —
                        and that damned ox Demostratos
  mooing away through the rumpus. That's what we get
  for putting up with this wretched woman-business!
KORYPHAIOS[(m)]: Sir, you haven't heard the half of it. They laughed at us! 15
  Insulted us! They took pitchers of water
  and nearly drowned us! We're still wringing out our clothes,
  for all the world like unhousebroken brats.
COMMISSIONER: Serves you right, by Poseidon!
  Whose fault is it if these women-folk of ours   20
  get out of hand? We coddle them,

2. Adonis: Beautiful young man who was loved by Aphrodite.   **5. Demostratos:**
Athenian orator and politician.   **Sicily:** Reference to the Sicilian Expedition
(415–413 B.C.), where Athens was defeated.

we teach them to be wasteful and loose. You'll see a husband
go into a jeweler's. "Look," he'll say,
"jeweler," he'll say, "you remember that gold choker
you made for my wife? Well, she went to a dance last night   25
and broke the clasp. Now, I've got to go to Salamis,
and can't be bothered. Run over to my house tonight,
will you, and see if you can put it together for her."
Or another one
goes to a cobbler—a good strong workman, too,   30
with an awl that was never meant for child's play. "Here,"
he'll tell him, "one of my wife's shoes is pinching
her little toe. Could you come up about noon
and stretch it out for her?"
                          Well, what do you expect?
Look at me, for example, I'm a Public Officer,   35
and it's one of my duties to pay off the sailors.
And where's the money? Up there in the Akropolis!
And those blasted women slam the door in my face!
But what are we waiting for?
                          —Look here, constable,
stop sniffing around for a tavern, and get us   40
some crowbars. We'll force their gates! As a matter of fact,
I'll do a little forcing myself.

(*Enter Lysistrata, above, with Myrrhine, Kalonike, and the Boiotian.*)

LYSISTRATA: No need of forcing.
   Here I am, of my own accord. And all this talk
   about locked doors—! We don't need locked doors,
   but just the least bit of common sense.   45
COMMISSIONER: Is that so, ma'am!
                          —Where's my constable?
                                              —Constable,
   arrest that woman, and tie her hands behind her.
LYSISTRATA: If he touches me, I swear by Artemis
   there'll be one scamp dropped from the public pay-roll tomorrow!
COMMISSIONER: Well, constable? You're not afraid, I suppose? Grab her,   50
   two of you, around the middle!
KALONIKE: No, by Pandrosos!°
   Lay a hand on her, and I'll jump on you so hard
   your guts will come out the back door!
COMMISSIONER: That's what *you* think!
   Where's the sergeant?—Here, you: tie up that trollop first,

---

51. Pandrosos: A woman's oath referring to a daughter of the founder of Athens.

the one with the pretty talk!

MYRRHINE: By the Moon-Goddess,°   55
just try! They'll have to scoop you up with a spoon!

COMMISSIONER: Another one!
                                   Officer, seize that woman! I swear
I'll put an end to this riot!

BOIOTIAN: By the Taurian,°
one inch closer, you'll be one screaming bald-head!

COMMISSIONER: Lord, what a mess! And my constables seem ineffective.   60
But—women get the best of us? By God, no!
                                             —Skythians!°
Close ranks and forward march!

LYSISTRATA: "Forward," indeed!
By the Two Goddesses, what's the sense in *that*?
They're up against four companies of women
armed from top to bottom.

COMMISSIONER: Forward, my Skythians!   65

LYSISTRATA: Forward, yourselves, dear comrades!
You grainlettucebeanseedmarket girls!
You garlicandonionbreadbakery girls!
Give it to 'em! Knock 'em down! Scratch 'em!
Tell 'em what you think of 'em!

(*General melee, the Skythians yield.*)

                                   —Ah, that's enough!   70
Sound a retreat: good soldiers don't rob the dead.

COMMISSIONER: A nice day *this* has been for the police!

LYSISTRATA: Well, there you are. — Did you really think we women
would be driven like slaves? Maybe now you'll admit
that a woman knows something about spirit.

COMMISSIONER: Spirit enough,   75
especially spirits in bottles! Dear Lord Apollo!

KORYPHAIOS[m]: Your Honor, there's no use talking to them. Words
mean nothing whatever to wild animals like these.
Think of the sousing they gave us! and the water
was not, I believe, of the purest.   80

KORYPHAIOS[w]: You shouldn't have come after us. And if you try it again,
you'll be one eye short! — Although, as a matter of fact,
what I like best is just to stay at home and read,
like a sweet little bride: never hurting a soul, no,

---

55. **Moon-Goddess:** Artemis, goddess of the hunt and of fertility, daughter of
Zeus.   58. **Taurian:** Reference to Artemis, who was believed to have been wor-
shiped in a cult at Taurica Chersonesos.   61. **Skythians:** Athenian archers.

never going out. But if you *must* shake hornets' nests,   85
look out for the hornets.

Strophe 1

CHORUS^(m): Of all the beasts that God hath wrought
    What monster's worse than woman?
Who shall encompass with his thought
    Their guile unending? No man.   90

They've seized the Heights, the Rock, the Shrine —
    But to what end? I wot not.
Sure there's some clue to their design!
    Have you the key? I thought not.
KORYPHAIOS^(m): We might question them, I suppose. But I warn you, sir,   95
don't believe anything you hear! It would be un-Athenian
not to get to the bottom of this plot.
COMMISSIONER: Very well.
My first question is this: Why, so help you God,
did you bar the gates of the Akropolis?
LYSISTRATA: Why?
To keep the money, of course. No money, no war.   100
COMMISSIONER: You think that money's the cause of war?
LYSISTRATA: I do.
Money brought about that Peisandros° business
and all the other attacks on the State. Well and good!
They'll not get another cent here!
COMMISSIONER: And what will you do?   105
LYSISTRATA: What a question! From now on, we intend
to control the Treasury.
COMMISSIONER: Control the Treasury!
LYSISTRATA: Why not? Does that seem strange? After all,
we control our household budgets.
COMMISSIONER: But that's different!
LYSISTRATA: "Different"? What do you mean?
COMMISSIONER: I mean simply this: 110
it's the Treasury that pays for National Defense.
LYSISTRATA: Unnecessary. We propose to abolish war.
COMMISSIONER: Good God. — And National Security?
LYSISTRATA: Leave that to us.
COMMISSIONER: You?

103. **Peisandros:** Conspirator against the Athenian democracy.

LYSISTRATA: Us.
COMMISSIONER: We're done for, then!
LYSISTRATA: Never mind.   115
  We women will save you in spite of yourselves.
COMMISSIONER: What nonsense!
LYSISTRATA: If you like. But you must accept it, like it or not.
COMMISSIONER: Why, this is downright subversion!
LYSISTRATA: Maybe it is.
  But we're going to save you, Judge.
COMMISSIONER: I don't *want* to be saved.
LYSISTRATA: Tut. The death-wish. All the more reason.   120
COMMISSIONER: But the idea of women bothering themselves about
  peace and war!
LYSISTRATA: Will you listen to me?
COMMISSIONER: Yes. But be brief, or I'll—
LYSISTRATA: This is no time for stupid threats.
COMMISSIONER: By the gods,
  I can't stand any more!
AN OLD WOMAN: Can't stand? Well, well.
COMMISSIONER: That's enough out of you, you old buzzard!   125
  Now, Lysistrata: tell me what you're thinking.
LYSISTRATA: Glad to.
                    Ever since this war began
  We women have been watching you men, agreeing with you,
  keeping our thoughts to ourselves. That doesn't mean
  we were happy: we weren't, for we saw how things were going;   130
  but we'd listen to you at dinner
  arguing this way and that.
                        —Oh you, and your big
  Top Secrets!—
                    And then we'd grin like little patriots
  (though goodness knows we didn't feel like grinning) and ask you:
  "Dear, did the Armistice come up in Assembly today?"   135
  And you'd say, "None of your business! Pipe down!" you'd say.
  And so we would.
AN OLD WOMAN: *I* wouldn't have, by God!
COMMISSIONER: You'd have taken a beating, then!
                                    —Go on.
LYSISTRATA: Well, we'd be quiet. But then, you know, all at once
  you men would think up something worse than ever.   140
  Even *I* could see it was fatal. And, "Darling," I'd say,
  "have you gone completely mad?" And my husband would look at me
  and say, "Wife, you've got your weaving to attend to.

Mind your tongue, if you don't want a slap.
'War's a man's affair!'"°   145
COMMISSIONER: Good words, and well pronounced.
LYSISTRATA: You're a fool if you think so.
                                   It was hard enough
to put up with all this banquet-hall strategy.
But then we'd hear you out in the public square:
"Nobody left for the draft-quota here in Athens?"   150
you'd say; and, "No," someone else would say, "not a man!"
And so we women decided to rescue Greece.
You might as well listen to us now: you'll have to, later.
COMMISSIONER: *You* rescue Greece? Absurd.
LYSISTRATA: You're the absurd one.
COMMISSIONER: You expect me to take orders from a woman?
                                              I'd die first! 155
LYSISTRATA: Heavens, if that's what's bothering you, take my veil,
here, and wrap it around your poor head.
KALONIKE: Yes
and you can have my market-basket, too.
Go home, tighten your girdle, do the washing, mind
your beans! "War's   160
a woman's affair!"
KORYPHAIOS⁽ʷ⁾:   Ground pitchers! Close ranks!

Antistrophe

CHORUS⁽ʷ⁾: This is a dance that I know well,
     My knees shall never yield.
Wobble and creak I may, but still
     I'll keep the well-fought field.
Valor and grace march on before,   165
     Love prods us from behind.
Our slogan is EXCELSIOR,
     Our watchword SAVE MANKIND.
KORYPHAIOS⁽ʷ⁾: Women, remember your grandmothers! Remember   170
that little old mother of yours, what a stinger she was!
On, on, never slacken. There's a strong wind astern!
LYSISTRATA: O Eros of delight! O Aphrodite! Kyprian!°

144–45. 'War's a man's affair!': Quoted from Homer's *Iliad*, VI, 492, Hector's
farewell to his wife, Andromache.   **173. Kyprian:** Reference to Aphrodite's association with Cyprus (Kyprus), the site of her worship.

If ever desire has drenched our breasts or dreamed
in our thighs, let it work so now on the men of Hellas°   175
that they shall tail us through the land, slaves, slaves
to Woman, Breaker of Armies!
COMMISSIONER: And if we do?
LYSISTRATA: Well, for one thing, we shan't have to watch you
   going to market, a spear in one hand, and heaven knows
   what in the other.
KALONIKE: Nicely said, by Aphrodite!   180
LYSISTRATA: As things stand now, you're neither men nor women.
   Armor clanking with kitchen pans and pots—
   You sound like a pack of Korybantes!°
COMMISSIONER: A man must do what a man must do.
LYSISTRATA: So I'm told.
   But to see a General, complete with Gorgon-shield,   185
   jingling along the dock to buy a couple of herrings!
KALONIKE: *I* saw a Captain the other day—lovely fellow he was,
   nice curly hair—sitting on his horse; and— can you believe it?—
   he'd just bought some soup, and was pouring it into his helmet!
   And there was a soldier from Thrace   190
   swishing his lance like something out of Euripides,
   and the poor fruit-store woman got so scared
   that she ran away and let him have his figs free!
COMMISSIONER: All this is beside the point.
                                     Will you be so kind
   as to tell me how you mean to save Greece?
LYSISTRATA: Of course.   195
   Nothing could be simpler.
COMMISSIONER: I assure you, I'm all ears.
LYSISTRATA: Do you know anything about weaving?
   Say the yarn gets tangled: we thread it
   this way and that through the skein, up and down,
   until it's free. And it's like that with war.   200
   We'll send our envoys
   up and down, this way and that, all over Greece,
   until it's finished.
COMMISSIONER: Yarn? Thread? Skein?
   Are you out of your mind? I tell you,
   war is a serious business.

175. **Hellas:** Greece.   183. **Korybantes:** Priestesses of Cybele, a fertility goddess
who was celebrated by the ritualistic beating of cymbals.

LYSISTRATA: So serious   205
    that I'd like to go on talking about weaving.
COMMISSIONER: All right. Go ahead.
LYSISTRATA: The first thing we have to do
    is to wash our yarn, get the dirt out of it.
    You see? Isn't there too much dirt here in Athens?
    You must wash those men away.
                              Then our spoiled wool —   210
    that's like your job-hunters, out for a life
    of no work and big pay. Back to the basket,
    citizens or not, allies or not,
    or friendly immigrants.
                        And your colonies?
    Hanks of wool lost in various places. Pull them   215
    together, weave them into one great whole,
    and our voters are clothed for ever.
COMMISSIONER: It would take a woman
    to reduce state questions to a matter of carding and weaving.
LYSISTRATA: You fool! Who were the mothers whose sons sailed off
    to fight for Athens in Sicily?
COMMISSIONER: Enough!   220
    I beg you, do not call back those memories.
LYSISTRATA: And then,
    instead of the love that every woman needs,
    we have only our single beds, where we can dream
    of our husbands off with the Army.
                              Bad enough for wives!
    But what about our girls, getting older every day,   225
    and older, and no kisses?
COMMISSIONER: Men get older, too.
LYSISTRATA: Not in the same sense.
                        A soldier's discharged,
    and he may be bald and toothless, yet he'll find
    a pretty young thing to go to bed with.
                              But a woman!
    Her beauty is gone with the first gray hair.   230
    She can spend her time
    consulting the oracles and the fortune-tellers,
    but they'll never send her a husband.
COMMISSIONER: Still, if a man can rise to the occasion —
LYSISTRATA: Rise? Rise, yourself!   235

(*Furiously.*)

Go invest in a coffin!
>You've money enough.
>>I'll bake you
a cake for the Underworld.
>And here's your funeral wreath!

(*She pours water upon him.*)

MYRRHINE: And here's another!

(*More water.*)

KALONIKE: And here's
my contribution!

(*More water.*)

LYSISTRATA: What are you waiting for?
All aboard Styx Ferry!
>Charon's° calling for you!   240
It's sailing-time: don't disrupt the schedule!
COMMISSIONER: The insolence of women! And to me!
No, by God, I'll go back to town and show
the rest of the Commission what might happen to them.

>(*Exit Commissioner.*)

LYSISTRATA: Really, I suppose we should have laid out his corpse   245
on the doorstep, in the usual way.
>But never mind.
We'll give him the rites of the dead tomorrow morning.

>(*Exit Lysistrata with Myrrhine and Kalonike.*)

PARABASIS:° CHORAL EPISODE   *Ode*° 1

KORYPHAIOS$^{(m)}$: Sons of Liberty, awake! The day of glory is at hand.
CHORUS$^{(m)}$: I smell tyranny afoot, I smell it rising from the land.
I scent a trace of Hippias,° I sniff upon the breeze
A dismal Spartan hogo that suggests King Kleisthenes.°

---

240. Charon: Ferryman who brought the souls of the newly dead across the Styx
to Hades.   **Parabasis:** Part of the play in which the author reveals his own views
(through the Koryphaios) directly to the audience.   **Ode:** Song sung by the
Chorus.   **3. Hippias:** An Athenian tyrant.   **4. Kleisthenes:** A bisexual Athenian.

Strip, strip for action, brothers!   5
Our wives, aunts, sisters, mothers
Have sold us out: the streets are full of godless female rages.
Shall we stand by and let our women confiscate our wages?

                                                            [Epirrhema° 1]

KORYPHAIOS(m): Gentlemen, it's a disgrace to Athens, a disgrace
to all that Athens stands for, if we allow these grandmas   10
to jabber about spears and shields and making friends
with the Spartans. What's a Spartan? Give me a wild wolf
any day. No. They want the Tyranny back, I suppose.
Are we going to take that? No. Let us look like
the innocent serpent, but be the flower under it,   15
as the poet sings. And just to begin with,
I propose to poke a number of teeth
down the gullet of that harridan over there.

Antode° 1

KORYPHAIOS(w): Oh, is that so? When you get home, your own mamma
     won't know you!
CHORUS(w): Who do you think we are, you senile bravos? Well, I'll show
     you.   20
I bore the sacred vessels in my eighth year,° and at ten
I was pounding out the barley for Athena Goddess;° then
     They made me Little Bear
     At the Brauronian Fair;°
I'd held the Holy Basket° by the time I was of age,   25
The Blessed Dry Figs had adorned my plump decolletage.

                                                          [Antepirrhema° 1]

KORYPHAIOS(w): A "disgrace to Athens," and I, just at the moment
I'm giving Athens the best advice she ever had?
Don't I pay taxes to the State? Yes, I pay them

Epirrhema: Satiric speech made by the Koryphaios following an ode delivered
by his or her half of the Chorus.   **Antode:** Lyric song sung by half of the Chorus
in response to the Ode sung by the other half.   **21. eighth year:** Young girls
between the ages of seven and eleven served in the temple of Athena in the
Akropolis.   **22. pounding out the barley for Athena Goddess:** Young girls were
sometimes chosen to grind the sacred grain of Athena.   **24. Brauronian Fair:** A
ritual in the cult of Artemis in which young girls in bear costumes danced for
the goddess.   **25. Holy Basket:** As a ritual, young girls carried baskets of objects sacred to Athena.   **Antepirrhema:** The speech delivered by the second
Koryphaios after the second half of the Chorus had sung an ode.

in baby boys. And what do you contribute, 30
you impotent horrors? Nothing but waste: all
our Treasury,° dating back to the Persian Wars,
gone! rifled! And not a penny out of your pockets!
Well, then? Can you cough up an answer to that?
Look out for your own gullet, or you'll get a crack 35
from this old brogan that'll make your teeth see stars!

Ode 2

CHORUS(m): Oh insolence!
  Am I unmanned?
  Incontinence!
  Shall my scarred hand 40
  Strike never a blow
  To curb this flow-
  ing female curse?

  Leipsydrion!°
  Shall I betray 45
  The laurels won
  On that great day?
  Come, shake a leg,
  Shed old age, beg
  The years reverse! 50

[Epirrhema 2]

KORYPHAIOS(m): Give them an inch, and we're done for! We'll have them
  launching boats next and planning naval strategy,
  sailing down on us like so many Artemisias.
  Or maybe they have ideas about the cavalry.
  That's fair enough, women are certainly good 55
  in the saddle. Just look at Mikon's paintings,
  all those Amazons wrestling with all those men!
  On the whole, a straitjacket's their best uniform.

Antode 2

CHORUS(w): Tangle with me,
  And you'll get cramps. 60

32. Treasury: Funds collected by Athens to finance a war against Persia were raided by Athenian politicians.   **44. Leipsydrion:** A place where Athenian patriots had valiantly fought.

Ferocity
's no use now, Gramps!
By the Two,
I'll get through
To you wrecks yet!   65

I'll scramble your eggs,
I'll burn your beans,
With my two legs.
You'll see such scenes
As never yet   70
Your two eyes met.
A curse? You bet!

                                                        [Antepirrhema 2]
KORYPHAIOS[(w)]: If Lampito stands by me, and that delicious Theban girl,
    Ismenia—what good are *you*? You and your seven
    Resolutions! Resolutions? Rationing Boiotian eels   75
    and making our girls go without them at Hekate's° Feast!
    That was statesmanship! And we'll have to put up with it
    and all the rest of your decrepit legislation
    until some patriot—God give him strength!—
    grabs you by the neck and kicks you off the Rock.   80

SCENE 2

(*Reenter Lysistrata and her lieutenants.*)

KORYPHAIOS[(w)] (*tragic tone*): Great Queen, fair Architect of our emprise,
    Why lookst thou on us with foreboding eyes?
LYSISTRATA: The behavior of these idiotic women!
    There's something about the female temperament
    that I can't bear!
KORYPHAIOS[(w)]:   What in the world do you mean?   5
LYSISTRATA: Exactly what I say.
KORYPHAIOS[(w)]: What dreadful thing has happened?
    Come, tell us: we're all your friends.
LYSISTRATA: It isn't easy
    to say it; yet, God knows, we can't hush it up.
KORYPHAIOS[(w)]: Well, then? Out with it!

76. **Hekate:** Patron of successful wars, object of a Boiotian cult.

LYSISTRATA: To put it bluntly,   10
we're dying to get laid.
KORYPHAIOS[(w)]:   Almighty God!
LYSISTRATA: Why bring God into it?—No, it's just as I say.
I can't manage them any longer: they've gone man-crazy,
they're all trying to get out.
                              Why, look:
one of them was sneaking out the back door   15
over there by Pan's cave; another
was sliding down the walls with rope and tackle;
another was climbing aboard a sparrow, ready to take off
for the nearest brothel—I dragged *her* back by the hair!
They're all finding some reason to leave.
                                     Look there!   20
There goes another one.
                          —Just a minute, you!
Where are you off to so fast?
FIRST WOMAN: I've got to get home.
I've a lot of Milesian wool, and the worms are spoiling it.
LYSISTRATA: Oh bother you and your worms! Get back inside!
FIRST WOMAN: I'll be back right away, I swear I will.   25
I just want to get it stretched out on my bed.
LYSISTRATA: You'll do no such thing. You'll stay right here.
FIRST WOMAN: And my wool?
You want it ruined?
LYSISTRATA: Yes, for all I care.
SECOND WOMAN: Oh dear! My lovely new flax from Amorgos—
I left it at home, all uncarded!
LYSISTRATA: Another one!   30
And all she wants is someone to card her flax.
Get back in there!
SECOND WOMAN: But I swear by the Moon-Goddess
the minute I get it done, I'll be back!
LYSISTRATA: I say No.
If you, why not all the other women as well?
THIRD WOMAN: O Lady Eileithyia!° Radiant goddess! Thou   35
intercessor for women in childbirth! Stay, I pray thee,
oh stay this parturition. Shall I pollute
a sacred spot?°

---

35. Eileithyia: Goddess of childbirth.   **37–38. pollute a sacred spot:** As the
Akropolis was considered sacred ground, giving birth there was prohibited.

LYSISTRATA: And what's the matter with *you?*
THIRD WOMAN: I'm having a baby—any minute now.
LYSISTRATA: But you weren't pregnant yesterday.
THIRD WOMAN: Well, I am today.   40
   Let me go home for a midwife, Lysistrata:
   there's not much time.
LYSISTRATA: I never heard such nonsense.
   What's that bulging under your cloak?
THIRD WOMAN: A little baby boy.
LYSISTRATA: It certainly isn't. But it's something hollow,
   like a basin or—Why, it's the helmet of Athena!   45
   And you said you were having a baby.
THIRD WOMAN: Well, I am! So there!
LYSISTRATA: Then why the helmet?
THIRD WOMAN: I was afraid that my pains
   might begin here in the Akropolis; and I wanted
   to drop my chick into it, just as the dear doves do.
LYSISTRATA: Lies! Evasions!—But at least one thing's clear: 50
   you can't leave the place before your purification.°
THIRD WOMAN: But I can't stay here in the Akropolis! Last night
      I dreamed
   of the Snake.
FIRST WOMAN: And those horrible owls, the noise they make!
   I can't get a bit of sleep; I'm just about dead.
LYSISTRATA: You useless girls, that's enough: Let's have no more lying.   55
   Of course you want your men. But don't you imagine
   that they want you just as much? I'll give you my word,
   their nights must be pretty hard.
                          Just stick it out!
   A little patience, that's all, and our battle's won.
   I have heard an Oracle. Should you like to hear it?   60
FIRST WOMAN: An Oracle? Yes, tell us!
LYSISTRATA: Here is what it says:
   WHEN SWALLOWS SHALL THE HOOPOE SHUN
      AND SPURN HIS HOT DESIRE,
   ZEUS WILL PERFECT WHAT THEY'VE BEGUN
      AND SET THE LOWER HIGHER.   65
FIRST WOMAN: Does that mean we'll be on top?
LYSISTRATA: BUT IF THE SWALLOWS SHALL FALL OUT
      AND TAKE THE HOOPOE'S BAIT,
   A CURSE MUST MARK THEIR HOUR OF DOUBT,
      INFAMY SEAL THEIR FATE.   70

51. **purification:** Ritualistic cleansing of a woman after childbirth.

THIRD WOMAN: I swear, *that* Oracle's all too clear.
FIRST WOMAN: Oh the dear gods!
LYSISTRATA: Let's not be downhearted, girls. Back to our places!
   The god has spoken. How can we possibly fail him?

(*Exit Lysistrata with the dissident women.*)

CHORAL EPISODE   *Strophe*

CHORUS^(m): I know a little story that I learned way back in school
   Goes like this:
   Once upon a time there was a young man— and no fool—
   Named Melanion; and his
   One aversion was marriage. He loathed the very thought.   5
   So he ran off to the hills, and in a special grot
   Raised a dog, and spent his days
   Hunting rabbits. And it says
   That he never never never did come home.
   It might be called a refuge *from* the womb.   10
   All right,
             all right,
                   all right!
   We're as bright as young Melanion, and we hate the very sight
   Of you women!
A MAN: How about a kiss, old lady?
A WOMAN: Here's an onion for your eye!   15
A MAN: A kick in the guts, then?
A WOMAN: Try, old bristle-tail, just try!
A MAN: Yet they say Myronides
   On hands and knees
   Looked just as shaggy fore and aft as I!   20

Antistrophe

CHORUS^(w): Well, *I* know a little story, and it's just as good as yours.
   Goes like this:
   Once there was a man named Timon—a rough diamond, of course,
   And that whiskery face of his
   Looked like murder in the shrubbery. By God, he was a son   25
   Of the Furies, let me tell you! And what did he do but run
   From the world and all its ways,
   Cursing mankind! And it says
   That his choicest execrations as of then

Were leveled almost wholly at *old* men.   30
All right,
          all right,
                    all right!
But there's one thing about Timon: he could always stand the sight
of us women.
A WOMAN: How about a crack in the jaw, Pop?
A MAN: I can take it, Ma—no fear!   35
A WOMAN: How about a kick in the face?
A MAN: You'd reveal your old caboose?
A WOMAN: What I'd show,
    I'll have you know,
    Is an instrument you're too far gone to use.   40

SCENE 3

(*Reenter Lysistrata.*)

LYSISTRATA: Oh, quick, girls, quick! Come here!
A WOMAN: What is it?
LYSISTRATA: A man.
    A man simply bulging with love.
                              O Kyprian Queen,°
    O Paphian, O Kythereian! Hear us and aid us!
A WOMAN: Where is this enemy?
LYSISTRATA: Over there, by Demeter's shrine.
A WOMAN: Damned if he isn't. But who *is* he?
MYRRHINE: My husband.   5
    Kinesias.
LYSISTRATA: Oh then, get busy! Tease him! Undermine him!
    Wreck him! Give him everything—kissing, tickling, nudging,
    whatever you generally torture him with—: give him everything
    except what we swore on the wine we would not give.
MYRRHINE: Trust me.
LYSISTRATA: I do. But I'll help you get him started.   10
    The rest of you women, stay back.

(*Enter Kinesias.*)

KINESIAS: Oh God! Oh my God!
    I'm stiff from lack of exercise. All I can do to stand up.

2. **Kyprian Queen:** Aphrodite.

LYSISTRATA: Halt! Who are you, approaching our lines?
KINESIAS: Me? I.
LYSISTRATA: A man?
KINESIAS: You have eyes, haven't you?
LYSISTRATA: Go away.   15
KINESIAS: Who says so?
LYSISTRATA: Officer of the Day.
KINESIAS: Officer, I beg you,
     by all the gods at once, bring Myrrhine out.
LYSISTRATA: Myrrhine? And who, my good sir, are you?
KINESIAS: Kinesias. Last name's Pennison. Her husband.
LYSISTRATA: Oh, of course. I beg your pardon. We're glad to see you.   20
     We've heard so much about you. Dearest Myrrhine
     is always talking about Kinesias — never nibbles an egg
     or an apple without saying
     "Here's to Kinesias!"
KINESIAS: Do you really mean it?
LYSISTRATA: I do.
     When we're discussing men, she always says   25
     "Well, after all, there's nobody like Kinesias!"
KINESIAS: Good God. — Well, then, please send her down here.
LYSISTRATA: And what do *I* get out of it?
KINESIAS: A standing promise.
LYSISTRATA: I'll take it up with her.

                                          (*Exit Lysistrata.*)

KINESIAS: But be quick about it!
     Lord, what's life without a wife? Can't eat. Can't sleep.   30
     Every time I go home, the place is so empty, so
     insufferably sad. Love's killing me, Oh,
     hurry!

(*Enter Manes, a slave, with Kinesias's baby; the voice of Myrrhine is heard offstage.*)

MYRRHINE: But of course I love him! Adore him —
                                        But no,
     he hates love. No. I won't go down.

(*Enter Myrrhine, above.*)

KINESIAS: Myrrhine!
     Darlingest Myrrhinette! Come down quick!   35
MYRRHINE: Certainly not.
KINESIAS: Not? But why, Myrrhine?

MYRRHINE: Why? You don't need me.
KINESIAS: Need you? My God, *look* at me!
MYRRHINE: So long!

(*Turns to go.*)

KINESIAS: Myrrhine, Myrrhine, Myrrhine!
  If not for my sake, for our child!

(*Pinches Baby.*)

                                          —All right, you: pipe up!
BABY: Mummie! Mummie! Mummie!
KINESIAS: You hear that?   40
  Pitiful, I call it. Six days now
  with never a bath; no food; enough to break your heart!
MYRRHINE: My darlingest child! What a father *you* acquired!
KINESIAS: At least come down for his sake.
MYRRHINE: I suppose I must.
  Oh, this mother business!   (*Exit.*)
KINESIAS: How pretty she is! And younger!   45
  The harder she treats me, the more bothered I get.

(*Myrrhine enters, below.*)

MYRRHINE: Dearest child,
  you're as sweet as your father's horrid. Give me a kiss.
KINESIAS: Now don't you see how wrong it was to get involved
  in this scheming League of women? It's bad
  for us both.
MYRRHINE: Keep your hands to yourself!
KINESIAS: But our house   50
  going to rack and ruin?
MYRRHINE: *I* don't care.
KINESIAS: And your knitting
  all torn to pieces by the chickens? Don't you care?
MYRRHINE: Not at all.
KINESIAS: And our debt to Aphrodite?
  Oh, *won't* you come back?
MYRRHINE: No. —At least, not until you men   55
  make a treaty and stop this war.
KINESIAS: Why, I suppose
  that might be arranged.
MYRRHINE: Oh? Well, I suppose
  I might come down then. But meanwhile,
  I've sworn not to.

KINESIAS: Don't worry. — Now let's have fun.
MYRRHINE: No! Stop it! I said no!
                                            — Although, of course,   60
  I *do* love you.
KINESIAS: I know you do. Darling Myrrhine: come, shall we?
MYRRHINE: Are you out of your mind? In front of the child?
KINESIAS: Take him home, Manes.

                                            (*Exit Manes with Baby.*)

                             There. He's gone.
                                            Come on!
  There's nothing to stop us now.
MYRRHINE: You devil! But where?
KINESIAS: In Pan's cave. What could be snugger than that?   65
MYRRHINE: But my purification before I go back to the Citadel?
KINESIAS: Wash in the Klepsydra.°
MYRRHINE: And my oath?
KINESIAS: Leave the oath to me.
  After all, I'm the man.
MYRRHINE: Well . . . if you say so.
                                 I'll go find a bed.
KINESIAS: Oh, bother a bed! The ground's good enough for me.
MYRRHINE: No. You're a bad man, but you deserve something better
      than dirt.   (*Exit Myrrhine.*) 70
KINESIAS: What a love she is! And how thoughtful!

(*Reenter Myrrhine.*)

MYRRHINE: Here's your bed.
  Now let me get my clothes off.
                             But, good horrors!
  We haven't a mattress.
KINESIAS: Oh, forget the mattress!
MYRRHINE: No.
  Just lying on blankets? Too sordid.
KINESIAS: Give me a kiss.
MYRRHINE: Just a second.   (*Exit Myrrhine.*)
KINESIAS: I swear, I'll explode!

(*Reenter Myrrhine.*)

MYRRHINE: Here's your mattress.   75

---

67. Klepsydra: A sacred spring beneath the walls of the Akropolis. Kinesias's suggestion borders on blasphemy.

I'll just take my dress off.
                              But look —
    where's our pillow?
KINESIAS: I don't *need* a pillow!
MYRRHINE: Well, *I* do.

                                                  (*Exit Myrrhine.*)

KINESIAS: I don't suppose even Herakles°
    would stand for this!

(*Reenter Myrrhine.*)

MYRRHINE: There we are. Ups-a-daisy!
KINESIAS: So we are. Well, come to bed.
MYRRHINE: But I wonder: 80
    is everything ready now?
KINESIAS: I can swear to that. Come, darling!
MYRRHINE: Just getting out of my girdle.
                              But remember, now,
    what you promised about the treaty.
KINESIAS: Yes, yes, yes!
MYRRHINE: But no coverlet!
KINESIAS: Damn it, I'll be your coverlet!
MYRRHINE: Be right back.   (*Exit Myrrhine.*)
KINESIAS: This girl and her coverlets   85
    will be the death of me.

(*Reenter Myrrhine.*)

MYRRHINE: Here we are. Up you go!
KINESIAS: Up? I've been up for ages.
MYRRHINE: Some perfume?
KINESIAS: No, by Apollo!
MYRRHINE: Yes, by Aphrodite!
    I don't care whether you want it or not.

                                                  (*Exit Myrrhine.*)

KINESIAS: For love's sake, hurry!   90

(*Reenter Myrrhine.*)

MYRRHINE: Here, in your hand. Rub it right in.
KINESIAS: Never cared for perfume.
    And this is particularly strong. Still, here goes.
MYRRHINE: What a nitwit I am! I brought you the Rhodian bottle.

78. Herakles: Greek hero (Hercules).

KINESIAS: Forget it.
MYRRHINE: No trouble at all. You just wait here.   95

(*Exit Myrrhine.*)

KINESIAS: God damn the man who invented perfume!

(*Reenter Myrrhine.*)

MYRRHINE: At last! The right bottle!
KINESIAS: I've got the rightest
    bottle of all, and it's right here waiting for you.
    Darling, forget everything else. Do come to bed.
MYRRHINE: Just let me get my shoes off.
                                  —And, by the way,   100
    you'll vote for the treaty?
KINESIAS: I'll think about it.

(*Myrrhine runs away.*)

    There! That's done it! The damned woman,
    she gets me all bothered, she half kills me,
    and off she runs! What'll I do? Where
    can I get laid?
                        —And you, little prodding pal,   105
    who's going to take care of *you*? No, you and I
    had better get down to old Foxdog's Nursing Clinic.
CHORUS(m): Alas for the woes of man, alas
        Specifically for you.
    She's brought you to a pretty pass: 110
        What are you going to do?
    Split, heart! Sag, flesh! Proud spirit, crack!
    Myrrhine's got you on your back.
KINESIAS: The agony, the protraction!
KORYPHAIOS(m):   Friend,
        What woman's worth a damn?   115
    They bitch us all, world without end.
KINESIAS: Yet they're so damned sweet, man!
KORYPHAIOS(m): Calamitous, that's what I say.
    You should have learned that much today.
CHORUS(m): O blessed Zeus, roll womankind   120
        Up into one great ball;
    Blast them aloft on a high wind,
        And once there, let them fall.
    Down, down they'll come, the pretty dears,
    And split themselves on our thick spears.   125

(*Exit Kinesias.*)

SCENE 4

(*Enter a Spartan Herald.*)

HERALD: Gentlemen, Ah beg you will be so kind
as to direct me to the Central Committee.
Ah have a communication.

(*Reenter Commissioner.*)

COMMISSIONER: Are you a man,
or a fertility symbol?
HERALD: Ah refuse to answer that question!
Ah'm a certified herald from Spahta, and Ah've come   5
to talk about an ahmistice.
COMMISSIONER: Then why
that spear under your cloak?
HERALD: Ah have no speah!
COMMISSIONER: You don't walk naturally, with your tunic
poked out so. You have a tumor, maybe,
or a hernia?
HERALD: You lost yo' mahnd, man?
COMMISSIONER: Well,   10
something's up, I can see that. And I don't like it.
HERALD: Colonel, Ah resent this.
COMMISSIONER: So I see. But what *is* it?
HERALD: A staff
with a message from Spahta.
COMMISSIONER: Oh, I know about those staffs.
Well, then, man, speak out: How are things in Sparta?
HERALD: Hahd, Colonel, hahd! We're at a standstill.   15
Cain't seem to think of anything but women.
COMMISSIONER: How curious! Tell me, do you Spartans think
that maybe Pan's to blame?
HERALD: Pan? No, Lampito and her little naked friends.
They won't let a man come nigh them.   20
COMMISSIONER: How are you handling it?
HERALD: Losing our mahnds,
if y' want to know, and walking around hunched over
lahk men carrying candles in a gale.
The women have swohn they'll have nothing to do with us
until we get a treaty.
COMMISSIONER: Yes. I know.   25
It's a general uprising, sir, in all parts of Greece.

But as for the answer—
                    Sir: go back to Sparta
and have them send us your Armistice Commission.
I'll arrange things in Athens.
                                And I may say
that my standing is good enough to make them listen.   30
HERALD: A man after mah own haht! Seh, Ah thank you.

                                            (*Exit Herald.*)

CHORAL EPISODE   *Strophe*

CHORUS^(m): Oh these women! Where will you find
  A slavering beast that's more unkind?
      Where's a hotter fire?
  Give me a panther, any day.
  He's not so merciless as they,   5
      And panthers don't conspire.

Antistrophe

CHORUS^(w): We may be hard, you silly old ass,
  But who brought you to this stupid pass?
      You're the ones to blame.
  Fighting with us, your oldest friends,   10
  Simply to serve your selfish ends—
      Really, you have no shame!
KORYPHAIOS^(m): No, I'm through with women for ever.
KORYPHAIOS^(w):   If you say so.
  Still, you might put some clothes on. You look too absurd
  standing around naked. Come, get into this cloak.   15
KORYPHAIOS^(m): Thank you; you're right. I merely took it off
  because I was in such a temper.
KORYPHAIOS^(w):   That's much better.
  Now you resemble a man again.
                            Why have you been so horrid?
  And look: there's some sort of insect in your eye.
  Shall I take it out?
KORYPHAIOS^(m):   An insect, is it? So that's   20
  what's been bothering me. Lord, yes: take it out!
KORYPHAIOS^(w): You might be more polite.
                            —But, heavens!
  What an enormous mosquito!

KORYPHAIOS[(m)]:   You've saved my life.
That mosquito was drilling an artesian well
in my left eye.
KORYPHAIOS[(w)]: Let me wipe   25
those tears away. — And now: one little kiss?
KORYPHAIOS[(m)]: No, no kisses.
KORYPHAIOS[(w)]: You're so difficult.
KORYPHAIOS[(m)]: You impossible women! How you do get around us!
The poet was right: Can't live with you, or without you.   30
But let's be friends.
And to celebrate, you might join us in an Ode.

Strophe 1

CHORUS[(m and w)]: Let it never be said
   That my tongue is malicious:
   Both by word and by deed   35
I would set an example that's noble and gracious.
   We've had sorrow and care
   Till we're sick of the tune.
   Is there anyone here
   Who would like a small loan?   40
     My purse is crammed,
     As you'll soon find;
And you needn't pay me back if the Peace gets signed.

Strophe 2

   I've invited to lunch
   Some Karystian° rips —   45
   An esurient bunch,
But I've ordered a menu to water their lips.
   I can still make soup
   And slaughter a pig.
   You're all coming, I hope?   50
   But a bath first, I beg!
     Walk right up
     As though you owned the place,
And you'll get the front door slammed to in your face.

45. **Karystian:** The Karystians were allies of Athens known for their crude
manners.

SCENE 5

(*Enter Spartan Ambassador, with entourage.*)

KORYPHAIOS(m): The Commission has arrived from Sparta.

                                        How oddly
they're walking!
                Gentlemen, welcome to Athens!
How is life in Lakonia?
AMBASSADOR: Need we discuss that?
Simply use your eyes.
CHORUS(m):   The poor man's right:
                        What a sight!
AMBASSADOR: Words fail me.   5
But come, gentlemen, call in your Commissioners,
and let's get down to a Peace.
CHORAGOS(m):   The state we're in! Can't bear
a stitch below the waist. It's a kind of pelvic
paralysis.
COMMISSIONER: Won't somebody call Lysistrata?
                                        — Gentlemen,
we're no better off than you.
AMBASSADOR: So I see.   10
A SPARTAN: Seh, do y'all feel a certain strain early in the morning?
AN ATHENIAN: I do, sir. It's worse than a strain.
A few more days, and there's nothing for us but Kleisthenes,
that broken blossom.
CHORAGOS(m):   But you'd better get dressed again.
You know these people going around Athens with chisels   15
looking for statues of Hermes.°
ATHENIAN: Sir, you are right.
SPARTAN: He certainly is! Ah'll put mah own clothes back on.

(*Enter Athenian Commissioners.*)

COMMISSIONER: Gentlemen from Sparta, welcome. This is a sorry
        business.
SPARTAN (*to one of his own group*): Colonel, we got dressed just in time.
        Ah sweah,
if they'd seen us the way we were, there'd have been a new wah   20
between the states.

16. **statues of Hermes:** The usual representation of Hermes was with an erect phallus. Right before the sailing of the Sicilian Expedition, vandals destroyed these statues.

COMMISSIONER: Shall we call the meeting to order?

Now, Lakonians,
  what's your proposal?
AMBASSADOR: We propose to consider peace.
COMMISSIONER: Good. That's on our minds, too.

—Summon Lysistrata.
  We'll never get anywhere without her.
AMBASSADOR: Lysistrata?   25
  Summon Lysis-*any*body! Only, summon!
KORYPHAIOS[m]:   No need to summon:
  here she is, herself.

(*Enter Lysistrata.*)

COMMISSIONER: Lysistrata! Lion of women!
  This is your hour to be
  hard and yielding, outspoken and shy, austere and
  gentle. You see here   30
  the best brains of Hellas (confused, I admit,
  by your devious charming) met as one man
  to turn the future over to you.
LYSISTRATA: That's fair enough,
  unless you men take it into your heads
  to turn to each other instead of to us. But I'd know   35
  soon enough if you did.
                    —Where is Reconciliation?
  Go, some of you: bring her here.

(*Exeunt two women.*)

And now, women,
  lead the Spartan delegates to me: not roughly
  or insultingly, as our men handle them, but gently,
  politely, as ladies should. Take them by the hand,   40
  or by anything else if they won't give you their hands.

(*The Spartans are escorted over.*)

There. —The Athenians next, by any convenient handle.

(*The Athenians are escorted.*)

Stand there, please. —Now, all of you, listen to me.

(*During the following speech the two women reenter, carrying an enormous statue of a naked girl; this is Reconciliation.*)

I'm only a woman, I know; but I've a mind,
and, I think, not a bad one: I owe it to my father   45
and to listening to the local politicians.
So much for that.
                         Now, gentlemen,
since I have you here, I intend to give you a scolding.
We are all Greeks.
Must I remind you of Thermopylai,° of Olympia,   50
of Delphoi? names deep in all our hearts?
Are they not a common heritage?
                              Yet you men
go raiding through the country from both sides,
Greek killing Greek, storming down Greek cities—
and all the time the Barbarian across the sea   55
is waiting for his chance!
                         —That's my first point.
AN ATHENIAN: Lord! I can hardly contain myself.
LYSISTRATA: As for you Spartans:
Was it so long ago that Perikleides°
came here to beg our help? I can see him still,
his gray face, his sombre gown. And what did he want?   60
An army from Athens. All Messene
was hot at your heels, and the sea-god splitting your land.
Well, Kimon and his men,
four thousand strong, marched out and saved all Sparta.
And what thanks do we get? You come back to murder us.   65
AN ATHENIAN: They're aggressors, Lysistrata!
A SPARTAN: Ah admit it.
When Ah look at those laigs, Ah sweah Ah'll aggress mahself!
LYSISTRATA: And you, Athenians: do you think you're blameless?
Remember that bad time when we were helpless,
and an army came from Sparta,   70
and that was the end of the Thessalian menace,
the end of Hippias and his allies.
                              And that was Sparta,
and only Sparta; but for Sparta, we'd be
cringing slaves today, not free Athenians.

(*From this point, the male responses are less to Lysistrata than to the statue.*)

50. **Thermopylai:** The place where, in 480 B.C., an army of three hundred
Spartans held out for three days against a superior Persian force.
58. **Perikleides:** Spartan ambassador to Athens who successfully convinced
Athenians to aid Sparta in suppressing a rebellion.

A SPARTAN: A well shaped speech.
AN ATHENIAN: Certainly it has its points.   75
LYSISTRATA: Why are we fighting each other? With all this history
   of favors given and taken, what stands in the way
   of making peace?
AMBASSADOR: Spahta is ready, ma'am,
   so long as we get that place back.
LYSISTRATA: What place, man?
AMBASSADOR: Ah refer to Pylos.
COMMISSIONER: Not a chance, by God!   80
LYSISTRATA: Give it to them, friend.
COMMISSIONER: But—what shall we have to bargain with?
LYSISTRATA: Demand something in exchange.
COMMISSIONER: Good idea. — Well, then:
   Cockeville first, and the Happy Hills, and the country
   between the Legs of Megara.
AMBASSADOR: Mah government objects.   85
LYSISTRATA: Overruled. Why fuss about a pair of legs?

(*General assent. The statue is removed.*)

AN ATHENIAN: I want to get out of these clothes and start my plowing.
A SPARTAN: Ah'll fertilize mahn first, by the Heavenly Twins!
LYSISTRATA: And so you shall,
   once you've made peace. If you are serious,   90
   go, both of you, and talk with your allies.
COMMISSIONER: Too much talk already. No, we'll stand together.
   We've only one end in view. All that we want
   is our women; and I speak for our allies.
AMBASSADOR: Mah government concurs.
AN ATHENIAN: So does Karystos.   95
LYSISTRATA: Good. — But before you come inside
   to join your wives at supper, you must perform
   the usual lustration. Then we'll open
   our baskets for you, and all that we have is yours.
   But you must promise upright good behavior   100
   from this day on. Then each man home with his woman!
AN ATHENIAN: Let's get it over with.
A SPARTAN: Lead on. Ah follow.
AN ATHENIAN: Quick as a cat can wink!

(*Exeunt all but the Choruses.*)

Antistrophe 1

CHORUS[(w)]: Embroideries and
    Twinkling ornaments and   105
    Pretty dresses—I hand
Them all over to you, and with never a qualm.
    They'll be nice for your daughters
    On festival days
    When the girls bring the Goddess   110
    The ritual prize.
    Come in, one and all:
    Take what you will.
I've nothing here so tightly corked that you can't make it spill.

Antistrophe 2

    You may search my house   115
    But you'll not find
    The least thing of use,
Unless your two eyes are keener than mine.
    Your numberless brats
    Are half starved? and your slaves?   120
    Courage, grandpa! I've lots
    Of grain left, and big loaves.
    I'll fill your guts,
    I'll go the whole hog;
But if you come too close to me, remember: 'ware the dog!   125

(Exeunt Choruses.)

EXODOS°

(A Drunken Citizen enters, approaches the gate, and is halted by a sentry.)

CITIZEN: Open. The. Door.
SENTRY: Now, friend, just shove along!
   —So you want to sit down. If it weren't such an old joke,
   I'd tickle your tail with this torch. Just the sort of gag
   this audience appreciates.
CITIZEN: I. Stay. Right. Here.

Exodos: Final scene.

SENTRY: Get away from there, or I'll scalp you!   5
  The gentlemen from Sparta
  are just coming back from dinner.

(*Exit Citizen; the general company reenters; the two Choruses now represent Spartans and Athenians.*)

A SPARTAN: Ah must say,
  Ah never tasted better grub.
AN ATHENIAN: And those Lakonians!
  They're gentlemen, by the Lord! Just goes to show,
  a drink to the wise is sufficient.
COMMISSIONER: And why not?   10
  A sober man's an ass.
  Men of Athens, mark my words: the only efficient
  Ambassador's a drunk Ambassador. Is that clear?
  Look: we go to Sparta,
  and when we get there we're dead sober. The result?   15
  Everyone cackling at everyone else. They make speeches;
  and even if we understand, we get it all wrong
  when we file our reports in Athens. But today—!
  Everybody's happy. Couldn't tell the difference
  between *Drink to Me Only* and   20
  The Star-Spangled Athens.
                         What's a few lies,
  washed down in good strong drink?

(*Reenter the Drunken Citizen.*)

SENTRY: God almighty,
  he's back again!
CITIZEN: I. Resume. My. Place.
A SPARTAN (*to an Athenian*): Ah beg yo', seh,
  take yo' instrument in yo' hand and play for us.   25
  Ah'm told
  yo' understand the intricacies of the floot?
  Ah'd lahk to execute a song and dance
  in honor of Athens,
                    and, of cohse, of Spahta.
CITIZEN: Toot. On. Your. Flute.   30

(*The following song is a solo—an aria—accompanied by the flute. The Chorus of Spartans begins a slow dance.*)

A SPARTAN: O Memory,
  Let the Muse speak once more

In my young voice. Sing glory.
Sing Artemision's shore,
Where Athens fluttered the Persians. *Alalai,*°   35
Sing glory, that great
Victory! Sing also
Our Leonidas and his men,
Those wild boars, sweat and blood
Down in a red drench. Then, then   40
The barbarians broke, though they had stood
Numberless as the sands before!

O Artemis,
Virgin Goddess, whose darts
Flash in our forests: approve   45
This pact of peace and join our hearts,
From this day on, in love.
Huntress, descend!
LYSISTRATA: All that will come in time.

                                                  But now, Lakonians,
take home your wives. Athenians, take yours.   50
Each man be kind to his woman; and you, women
be equally kind. Never again, pray God,
shall we lose our way in such madness.
KORYPHAIOS^(Athenian):   And now let's dance our joy.

(From this point the dance becomes general.)

CHORUS^(Athenian): Dance, you Graces
                       Artemis, dance
Dance, Phoibos,° Lord of dancing
                       Dance,   55
In a scurry of Maenads,° Lord Dionysos
                        Dance, Zeus Thunderer
           Dance, Lady Hera°
Queen of the sky
               Dance, dance, all you gods
Dance witness everlasting of our pact
Evohi Evohe°   60
Dance for the dearest
               the Bringer of Peace
Deathless Aphrodite!

---

35. *Alalai:* War cry. **55. Phoibos:** Apollo, god of the sun. **56. Maenads:** Bacchus's female devotees. **57. Hera:** Wife of Zeus. **60.** *Evohi Evohe:* "Come forth! Come forth!" An orgiastic exclamation often cried at rituals of Bacchus.

COMMISSIONER: Now let us have another song from Sparta.
CHORUS^(Spartan): From Taygetos, from Taygetos,
   Lakonian Muse, come down.   65
   Sing to the Lord Apollo
      Who rules Amyklai Town.

Sing Athena of the House of Brass!°
Sing Leda's Twins,° that chivalry
   Resplendent on the shore   70
Of our Eurotas; sing the girls
   That dance along before:
Sparkling in dust their gleaming feet,
   Their hair a Bacchant fire,
And Leda's daughter, thyrsos° raised,   75
   Leads their triumphant choir.
CHORUS^(S and A): *Evohe!*
           Evohai!
               Evohe!
                  We pass
          Dancing
              dancing
                   to greet
   Athena of the House of Brass.

                              411 B.C.

---

68. *House of Brass:* Temple to Athena on the Akropolis of Sparta.   **69. Leda's
Twins:** Leda, raped by Zeus, bore quadruplets, two daughters (one of whom was
Helen) and two sons.   **75. thyrsos:** An ivy-twined staff carried by Bacchus and
his followers.

Hamlet, Prince of Denmark

WILLIAM SHAKESPEARE [1564–1616]

[**Dramatis Personae**
CLAUDIUS, *King of Denmark*
HAMLET, *son to the late King Hamlet, and nephew to the present King*
POLONIUS, *Lord Chamberlain*
HORATIO, *friend to Hamlet*
LAERTES, *son to Polonius*
VOLTIMAND,
CORNELIUS,
ROSENCRANTZ,
GUILDENSTERN, *courtiers*
OSRIC,
GENTLEMAN,
PRIEST, OR DOCTOR OF DIVINITY
MARCELLUS, *officers*
BERNARDO,
FRANCISCO, *a solider*
REYNALDO, *servant to Polonius*
PLAYERS
TWO CLOWNS, *grave-diggers*
FORTINBRAS, *Prince of Norway*
CAPTAIN
ENGLISH AMBASSADORS

GERTRUDE, *Queen of Denmark, mother to Hamlet*
OPHELIA, *daughter to Polonius*

LORDS, LADIES, OFFICERS, SOLDIERS, SAILORS, MESSENGERS, AND OTHER
ATTENDANTS
GHOST *of Hamlet's father*

Scene: *Denmark.*]

Note: The text of *Hamlet* has come down to us in different versions — such as the first quarto, the second quarto, and the first Folio. The copy of the text used here is largely drawn from the second quarto. Passages enclosed in square brackets are taken from one of the other versions, in most cases the first Folio.

{ACT I   *Scene 1*}°

(*Enter Bernardo and Francisco, two sentinels, [meeting].*)

BERNARDO: Who's there?
FRANCISCO: Nay, answer me.° Stand and unfold yourself.
BERNARDO: Long live the King!
FRANCISCO: Bernardo?
BERNARDO: He.   5
FRANCISCO: You come most carefully upon your hour.
BERNARDO: 'Tis now struck twelve. Get thee to bed, Francisco.
FRANCISCO: For this relief much thanks. 'Tis bitter cold,
    And I am sick at heart.
BERNARDO: Have you had quiet guard?
FRANCISCO: Not a mouse stirring.   10
BERNARDO: Well, good night.
    If you do meet Horatio and Marcellus,
    The rivals° of my watch, bid them make haste.

(*Enter Horatio and Marcellus.*)

FRANCISCO: I think I hear them. Stand, ho! Who is there?
HORATIO: Friends to this ground.
MARCELLUS: And liegemen to the Dane.°   15
FRANCISCO: Give you° good night.
MARCELLUS: O, farewell, honest soldier.
    Who hath relieved you?
FRANCISCO: Bernardo hath my place.
    Give you good night.   (*Exit Francisco.*)
MARCELLUS: Holla, Bernardo!
BERNARDO: Say,
    What, is Horatio there?
HORATIO: A piece of him.
BERNARDO: Welcome, Horatio. Welcome, good Marcellus.   20
HORATIO: What, has this thing appear'd again tonight?
BERNARDO: I have seen nothing.
MARCELLUS: Horatio says 'tis but our fantasy,
    And will not let belief take hold of him
    Touching this dreaded sight, twice seen of us.   25
    Therefore I have entreated him along

I, I. **Location:** Elsinore castle. A guard platform.   **2. me:** Francisco emphasizes
that *he* is the sentry currently on watch.   **13. rivals:** Partners.   **15. liegemen to
the Dane:** Men sworn to serve the Danish king.   **16. Give you:** God give you.

With us to watch the minutes of this night,
That if again this apparition come
He may approve° our eyes and speak to it.
HORATIO: Tush, tush, 'twill not appear.
BERNARDO: Sit down awhile,   30
And let us once again assail your ears,
That are so fortified against our story,
What we have two nights seen.
HORATIO: Well, sit we down,
And let us hear Bernardo speak of this.
BERNARDO: Last night of all,   35
When yond same star that's westward from the pole°
Had made his° course t' illume that part of heaven
Where now it burns, Marcellus and myself,
The bell then beating one—

(*Enter Ghost.*)

MARCELLUS: Peace, break thee off! Look where it comes again!   40
BERNARDO: In the same figure, like the King that's dead.
MARCELLUS: Thou art a scholar.° Speak to it, Horatio.
BERNARDO: Looks 'a° not like the King? Mark it, Horatio.
HORATIO: Most like. It harrows me with fear and wonder.
BERNARDO: It would be spoke to.
MARCELLUS: Speak to it,° Horatio.   45
HORATIO: What art thou that usurp'st this time of night,
Together with that fair and warlike form
In which the majesty of buried Denmark°
Did sometimes° march? By heaven I charge thee speak!
MARCELLUS: It is offended.
BERNARDO: See, it stalks away.   50
HORATIO: Stay! Speak, speak. I charge thee, speak.

                                        (*Exit Ghost.*)

MARCELLUS: 'Tis gone, and will not answer.
BERNARDO: How now, Horatio? You tremble and look pale.
Is not this something more than fantasy?
What think you on 't?   55

___

29. approve: Corroborate.   36. pole: Polestar.   37. his: Its.   42. scholar: One
learned in Latin and able to address spirits.   43. 'a: He.   45. It . . . it: A ghost
could not speak until spoken to.   48. buried Denmark: The buried king of
Denmark.   49. sometimes: Formerly.

HORATIO: Before my God, I might not this believe
Without the sensible° and true avouch
Of mine own eyes.
MARCELLUS: Is it not like the King?
HORATIO: As thou art to thyself.
Such was the very armor he had on   60
When he the ambitious Norway° combated.
So frown'd he once when, in an angry parle,°
He smote the sledded° Polacks° on the ice.
'Tis strange. ·
MARCELLUS: Thus twice before, and jump° at this dead hour,   65
With martial stalk hath he gone by our watch.
HORATIO: In what particular thought to work I know not,
But, in the gross and scope° of mine opinion,
This bodes some strange eruption to our state.
MARCELLUS: Good now,° sit down, and tell me, he that knows,   70
Why this same strict and most observant watch
So nightly toils° the subject° of the land,
And why such daily cast° of brazen cannon,
And foreign mart° for implements of war,
Why such impress° of shipwrights, whose sore task   75
Does not divide the Sunday from the week.
What might be toward,° that this sweaty haste
Doth make the night joint-laborer with the day?
Who is 't that can inform me?
HORATIO: That can I,
At least, the whisper goes so. Our last king,   80
Whose image even but now appear'd to us,
Was, as you know, by Fortinbras of Norway,
Thereto prick'd on° by a most emulate° pride,
Dar'd to the combat; in which our valiant Hamlet—
For so this side of our known world esteem'd him—   85
Did slay this Fortinbras; who, by a seal'd compact,
Well ratified by law and heraldry,
Did forfeit, with his life, all those his lands
Which he stood seiz'd° of, to the conqueror;

---

57. sensible: Confirmed by the senses.   **61. Norway:** King of Norway.   **62. parle:**
Parley.   **63. sledded:** Traveling on sleds.   **Polacks:** Poles.   **65. jump:** Exactly.
68. gross and scope: General view.   **70. Good now:** An expression denoting
entreaty or expostulation.   **72. toils:** Causes to toil.   **subject:** Subjects.   **73. cast:**
Casting.   **74. mart:** Buying and selling.   **75. impress:** Impressment, conscrip-
tion.   **77. toward:** In preparation.   **83. prick'd on:** Incited.   **emulate:** Ambitious.
89. seiz'd: Possessed.

Against the° which a moi'ty competent°   90
Was gaged° by our king, which had return'd
To the inheritance of Fortinbras
Had he been vanquisher, as, by the same comart°
And carriage° of the article design'd,
His fell to Hamlet. Now, sir, young Fortinbras,   95
Of unimproved° mettle hot and full,
Hath in the skirts° of Norway here and there
Shark'd up° a list of lawless resolutes°
For food and diet° to some enterprise
That hath a stomach° in 't, which is no other—   100
As it doth well appear unto our state—
But to recover of us, by strong hand
And terms compulsatory, those foresaid lands
So by his father lost. And this, I take it,
Is the main motive of our preparations,   105
The source of this our watch, and the chief head°
Of this post-haste and romage° in the land.
BERNARDO: I think it be no other but e'en so.
Well may it sort° that this portentous figure
Comes armed through our watch so like the King   110
That was and is the question of these wars.
HORATIO: A mote° it is to trouble the mind's eye.
In the most high and palmy° state of Rome,
A little ere the mightiest Julius fell,
The graves stood tenantless and the sheeted° dead   115
Did squeak and gibber in the Roman streets;
As° stars with trains of fire and dews of blood,
Disasters° in the sun; and the moist star°
Upon whose influence Neptune's° empire stands°
Was sick almost to doomsday° with eclipse.   120

90. **Against the:** In return for.... **moi'ty competent:** Sufficient portion.
91. **gaged:** Engaged, pledged. 93. **comart:** Joint bargain (?). 94. **carriage:**
Import, bearing. 96. **unimproved:** Not turned to account (?) or untested (?).
97. **skirts:** Outlying regions, outskirts. 98. **Shark'd up:** Got together in haphazard fashion. **resolutes:** Desperadoes. 99. **food and diet:** No pay but their
keep. 100. **stomach:** Relish of danger. 106. **head:** Source. 107. **romage:**
Bustle, commotion. 109. **sort:** Suit. 112. **mote:** Speck of dust. 113. **palmy:**
Flourishing. 115. **sheeted:** Shrouded. 117. **As:** This abrupt transition suggests that matter is possibly omitted between lines 116 and 117. 118. **Disasters:** Unfavorable signs of aspects. **moist star:** Moon, governing tides.
119. **Neptune:** God of the sea. **stands:** Depends. 120. **sick ... doomsday:**
See Matt. 24:29 and Rev. 6:12.

And even the like precurse° of fear'd events,
As harbingers° preceding still° the fates
And prologue to the omen° coming on,
Have heaven and earth together demonstrated
Unto our climatures° and countrymen.   125

(*Enter Ghost.*)

But soft, behold! Lo where it comes again!
I'll cross° it, though it blast me. Stay, illusion!
If thou hast any sound, or use of voice,
Speak to me!   (*It spreads his arms.*)
If there be any good thing to be done   130
That may to thee do ease and grace to me,
Speak to me!
If thou art privy to thy country's fate,
Which, happily,° foreknowing may avoid,
O, speak!   135
Or if thou hast uphoarded in thy life
Extorted treasure in the womb of earth,
For which, they say, you spirits oft walk in death,

(*The cock crows.*)

Speak of it. Stay, and speak! Stop it, Marcellus.
MARCELLUS: Shall I strike at it with my partisan?°   140
HORATIO: Do, if it will not stand.   [*They strike at it.*]
BERNARDO: 'Tis here!
HORATIO: 'Tis here!
MARCELLUS: 'Tis gone.   [*Exit Ghost.*]
We do it wrong, being so majestical,
To offer it the show of violence;
For it is, as the air, invulnerable,   145
And our vain blows malicious mockery.
BERNARDO: It was about to speak when the cock crew.
HORATIO: And then it started like a guilty thing
Upon a fearful summons. I have heard,
The cock, that is the trumpet to the morn,   150
Doth with his lofty and shrill-sounding throat
Awake the god of day, and, at his warning,
Whether in sea or fire, in earth or air,

---

121. precurse: Heralding, foreshadowing. **122. harbingers:** Forerunners.
still: Continually. **123. omen:** Calamitous event. **125. climatures:** Regions.
127. cross: Meet, face directly. **134. happily:** Haply, perchance. **140. partisan:** Long-handled spear.

Th' extravagant and erring° spirit hies
To his confine; and of the truth herein   155
This present object made probation.°
MARCELLUS: It faded on the crowing of the cock.
  Some say that ever 'gainst° that season comes
  Wherein our Savior's birth is celebrated,
  The bird of dawning singeth all night long,   160
  And then, they say, no spirit dare stir abroad;
  The nights are wholesome, then no planets strike,°
  No fairy takes,° nor witch hath power to charm,
  So hallowed and so gracious° is that time.
HORATIO: So have I heard and do in part believe it.   165
  But, look, the morn, in russet mantle clad,
  Walks o'er the dew of yon high eastward hill.
  Break we our watch up, and by my advice
  Let us impart what we have seen tonight
  Unto young Hamlet; for, upon my life,   170
  This spirit, dumb to us, will speak to him.
  Do you consent we shall acquaint him with it,
  As needful in our loves, fitting our duty?
MARCELLUS: Let's do 't, I pray, and I this morning know
  Where we shall find him most conveniently.   175

                                              (*Exeunt.*)°

                        {*Scene II*}°

(*Flourish. Enter Claudius, King of Denmark, Gertrude the Queen, Councilors,
Polonius and his son Laertes, Hamlet, cum aliis*° [*including Voltimand and
Cornelius*].)

KING: Though yet of Hamlet our dear brother's death
  The memory be green, and that it us befitted
  To bear our hearts in grief and our whole kingdom
  To be contracted in one brow of woe,
  Yet so far hath discretion fought with nature   5
  That we with wisest sorrow think on him,
  Together with remembrance of ourselves.

---

154. extravagant and erring: Wandering. (The words have similar meaning.)
156. probation: Proof.   **158. 'gainst:** Just before.   **162. strike:** Exert evil influence.   **163. takes:** Bewitches.   **164. gracious:** Full of goodness.   [S.D.] *Exeunt:* Latin for "they go out."   I, II. **Location:** The castle.   [S.D.] *cum aliis:*
With others.

Therefore our sometime sister, now our queen,
Th' imperial jointress° to this warlike state,
Have we, as 'twere with a defeated joy—   10
With an auspicious and a dropping eye,
With mirth in funeral and with dirge in marriage,
In equal scale weighing delight and dole—
Taken to wife. Nor have we herein barr'd
Your better wisdoms, which have freely gone   15
With this affair along. For all, our thanks.
Now follows that you know° young Fortinbras,
Holding a weak supposal° of our worth,
Or thinking by our late dear brother's death
Our state to be disjoint and out of frame,   20
Colleagued with° this dream of his advantage,°
He hath not fail'd to pester us with message
Importing° the surrender of those lands
Lost by his father, with all bands° of law,
To our most valiant brother. So much for him.   25
Now for ourself and for this time of meeting.
Thus much the business is: we have here writ
To Norway, uncle of young Fortinbras—
Who, impotent and bed-rid, scarcely hears
Of this his nephew's purpose—to suppress   30
His° further gait° herein, in that the levies,
The lists, and full proportions are all made
Out of his subject;° and we here dispatch
You, good Cornelius, and you, Voltimand,
For bearers of this greeting to old Norway,   35
Giving to you no further personal power
To business with the King, more than the scope
Of these delated° articles allow.   [*Gives a paper.*]
Farewell, and let your haste commend your duty.
CORNELIUS, VOLTIMAND: In that, and all things, will we show our duty.   40
KING: We doubt it nothing. Heartily farewell.

                [*Exit Voltimand and Cornelius.*]

9. jointress: Woman possessed of a joint tenancy of an estate.   17. know: Be
informed (that).   18. weak supposal: Low estimate.   21. Colleagued with:
Joined to, allied with.   dream . . . advantage: Illusory hope of success.
23. Importing: Pertaining to.   24. bands: Contracts.   31. His: Fortinbras's.
gait: Proceeding.   31–33. in that . . . subject: Since the levying of troops and
supplies is drawn entirely from the King of Norway's own subjects.   38. delated:
Detailed. (Variant of *dilated*.)

And now, Laertes, what's the news with you?
You told us of some suit; what is 't, Laertes?
You cannot speak of reason to the Dane°
And lose your voice.° What wouldst thou beg, Laertes,   45
That shall not be my offer, not thy asking?
The head is not more native° to the heart,
The hand more instrumental° to the mouth,
Than is the throne of Denmark to thy father.
What wouldst thou have, Laertes?
LAERTES: My dread lord,   50
Your leave and favor to return to France,
From whence though willingly I came to Denmark
To show my duty in your coronation,
Yet now I must confess, that duty done,
My thoughts and wishes bend again toward France   55
And bow them to your gracious leave and pardon.°
KING: Have you your father's leave? What says Polonius?
POLONIUS: H'ath, my lord, wrung from me my slow leave
By laborsome petition, and at last
Upon his will I seal'd my hard° consent.   60
I do beseech you, give him leave to go.
KING: Take thy fair hour, Laertes. Time be thine,
And thy best graces spend it at thy will!
But now, my cousin° Hamlet, and my son—
HAMLET: A little more than kin, and less than kind.°   65
KING: How is it that the clouds still hang on you?
HAMLET: Not so, my lord. I am too much in the sun.°
QUEEN: Good Hamlet, cast thy nighted color off,
And let thine eye look like a friend on Denmark.
Do not forever with thy veiled° lids   70
Seek for thy noble father in the dust.
Thou know'st 'tis common,° all that lives must die,
Passing through nature to eternity.

---

44. the Dane: The Danish king. **45. lose your voice:** Waste your speech.
47. native: Closely connected, related. **48. instrumental:** Serviceable.
56. leave and pardon: Permission to depart. **60. hard:** Reluctant. **64. cousin:**
Any kin not of the immediate family. **65. A little . . . kind:** Closer than an ordinary nephew (since I am stepson), and yet more separated in natural feeling (with
pun on *kind*, meaning affectionate and natural, lawful). This line is often read as
an aside, but it need not be. **67. sun:** The sunshine of the King's royal favor
(with pun on *son*). **70. veiled:** Downcast. **72. common:** Of universal occurrence. (But Hamlet plays on the sense of *vulgar* in line 74.)

HAMLET: Ay, madam, it is common.
QUEEN: If it be,
  Why seems it so particular with thee?   75
HAMLET: Seems, madam! Nay, it is. I know not "seems."
  'Tis not alone my inky cloak, good mother,
  Nor customary suits of solemn black,
  Nor windy suspiration of forc'd breath,
  No, nor the fruitful° river in the eye,   80
  Nor the dejected havior of the visage,
  Together with all forms, moods, shapes of grief,
  That can denote me truly. These indeed seem,
  For they are actions that a man might play.
  But I have that within which passes show;   85
  These but the trappings and the suits of woe.
KING: 'Tis sweet and commendable in your nature, Hamlet,
  To give these mourning duties to your father.
  But you must know your father lost a father,
  That father lost, lost his, and the survivor bound   90
  In filial obligation for some term
  To do obsequious° sorrow. But to persever°
  In obstinate condolement° is a course
  Of impious stubbornness. 'Tis unmanly grief.
  It shows a will most incorrect to heaven,   95
  A heart unfortified, a mind impatient,
  An understanding simple and unschool'd.
  For what we know must be and is as common
  As any the most vulgar thing to sense,°
  Why should we in our peevish opposition   100
  Take it to heart? Fie, 'tis a fault to heaven,
  A fault against the dead, a fault to nature,
  To reason most absurd, whose common theme
  Is death of fathers, and who still hath cried,
  From the first corse° till he that died today,   105
  "This must be so." We pray you, throw to earth
  This unprevailing° woe, and think of us
  As of a father; for let the world take note,
  You are the most immediate° to our throne,
  And with no less nobility of love   110

---

80. fruitful: Abundant.   92. obsequious: Suited to obsequies or funerals.   persever: Persevere.   93. condolement: Sorrowing.   99. As . . . sense: As the most ordinary experience.   105. corse: Corpse.   107. unprevailing: Unavailing.   109. most immediate: Next in succession.

Than that which dearest father bears his son
Do I impart toward you. For your intent
In going back to school in Wittenberg,°
It is most retrograde° to our desire,
And we beseech you, bend you° to remain　　　　　　　115
Here in the cheer and comfort of our eye,
Our chiefest courtier, cousin, and our son.
QUEEN: Let not thy mother lose her prayers, Hamlet.
I pray thee stay with us, go not to Wittenberg.
HAMLET: I shall in all my best obey you, madam.　　　　　120
KING: Why, 'tis a loving and a fair reply.
Be as ourself in Denmark. Madam, come.
This gentle and unforc'd accord of Hamlet
Sits smiling to my heart, in grace whereof
No jocund° health that Denmark drinks today　　　　125
But the great cannon to the clouds shall tell,
And the King's rouse° the heaven shall bruit again,°
Respeaking earthly thunder.° Come away.

(*Flourish. Exeunt all but Hamlet.*)

HAMLET: O, that this too too sullied° flesh would melt,
Thaw, and resolve itself into a dew!　　　　　　　130
Or that the Everlasting had not fix'd
His canon° 'gainst self-slaughter! O God, God,
How weary, stale, flat, and unprofitable
Seem to me all the uses of this world!
Fie on 't, ah, fie! 'Tis an unweeded garden　　　　135
That grows to seed. Things rank and gross in nature
Possess it merely.° That it should come to this!
But two months dead—nay, not so much, not two.
So excellent a king, that was to° this
Hyperion° to a satyr; so loving to my mother　　　　140
That he might not beteem° the winds of heaven
Visit her face too roughly. Heaven and earth,
Must I remember? Why, she would hang on him
As if increase of appetite had grown

---

113. Wittenberg: Famous German university founded in 1502. **114. retrograde:** Contrary. **115. bend you:** Incline yourself. **125. jocund:** Merry. **127. rouse:** Draft of liquor. **bruit again:** Loudly echo. **128. thunder:** Of trumpet and kettledrum sounded when the King drinks, see I, IV, 8–12. **129. sullied:** Defiled. (The early quartos read *sallied*, the Folio *solid*.) **132. canon:** Law. **137. merely:** Completely. **139. to:** In comparison to. **140. Hyperion:** Titan sun-god, father of Helios. **141. beteem:** Allow.

By what it fed on, and yet, within a month—   145
Let me not think on 't. Frailty, thy name is woman!—
A little month, or ere those shoes were old
With which she followed my poor father's body,
Like Niobe,° all tears, why she, even she—
O God, a beast, that wants discourse of reason,°   150
Would have mourn'd longer—married with my uncle,
My father's brother, but no more like my father
Than I to Hercules. Within a month,
Ere yet the salt of most unrighteous tears
Had left the flushing in her galled° eyes,   155
She married. O, most wicked speed, to post
With such dexterity to incestuous° sheets!
It is not nor it cannot come to good.
But break, my heart, for I must hold my tongue.

(*Enter Horatio, Marcellus, and Bernardo.*)

HORATIO: Hail to your lordship!
HAMLET: I am glad to see you well.   160
  Horatio!—or I do forget myself.
HORATIO: The same, my lord, and your poor servant ever.
HAMLET: Sir, my good friend; I'll change° that name with you.
  And what make° you from Wittenberg, Horatio?
  Marcellus?   165
MARCELLUS: My good lord.
HAMLET: I am very glad to see you. [*To Bernardo.*] Good even, sir.—
  But what, in faith, make you from Wittenberg?
HORATIO: A truant disposition, good my lord.
HAMLET: I would not hear your enemy say so,   170
  Nor shall you do my ear that violence
  To make it truster of your own report
  Against yourself. I know you are no truant.
  But what is your affair in Elsinore?
  We'll teach you to drink deep ere you depart.   175
HORATIO: My lord, I came to see your father's funeral.

---

149. Niobe: Tantalus's daughter, Queen of Thebes, who boasted that she had
more sons and daughters than Leto; for this, Apollo and Artemis, children of
Leto, slew her fourteen children. She was turned by Zeus into a stone that continually dropped tears.   **150. wants . . . reason:** Lacks the faculty of reason.
155. galled: Irritated, inflamed.   **157. incestuous:** In Shakespeare's day, the marriage of a man like Claudius to his deceased brother's wife was considered incestuous.   **163. change:** Exchange (i.e., the name of friend).   **164. make:** Do.

HAMLET: I prithee do not mock me, fellow student;
   I think it was to see my mother's wedding.
HORATIO: Indeed, my lord, it followed hard° upon.
HAMLET: Thrift, thrift, Horatio! The funeral bak'd meats   180
   Did coldly furnish forth the marriage tables.
   Would I had met my dearest° foe in heaven
   Or° ever I had seen that day, Horatio!
   My father!—Methinks I see my father.
HORATIO: Where, my lord?
HAMLET: In my mind's eye, Horatio.   185
HORATIO: I saw him once. 'A° was a goodly king.
HAMLET: 'A was a man, take him for all in all,
   I shall not look upon his like again.
HORATIO: My lord, I think I saw him yesternight.
HAMLET: Saw? Who?   190
HORATIO: My lord, the King your father.
HAMLET: The King my father?
HORATIO: Season your admiration° for a while
   With an attent° ear, till I may deliver,
   Upon the witness of these gentlemen,
   This marvel to you.
HAMLET: For God's love, let me hear!   195
HORATIO: Two nights together had these gentlemen,
   Marcellus and Bernardo, on their watch,
   In the dead waste and middle of the night,
   Been thus encount'red. A figure like your father,
   Armed at point° exactly, cap-a-pe,°   200
   Appears before them, and with solemn march
   Goes slow and stately by them. Thrice he walk'd
   By their oppress'd and fear-surprised eyes
   Within his truncheon's° length, whilst they, distill'd
   Almost to jelly with the act° of fear,   205
   Stand dumb and speak not to him. This to me
   In dreadful secrecy impart they did,
   And I with them the third night kept the watch,
   Where, as they had delivered, both in time,
   Form of the thing, each word made true and good,   210
   The apparition comes. I knew your father;

---

179. hard: Close. 182. dearest: Direst. 183. Or: Ere, before. 186. 'A: He.
192. Season your admiration: Restrain your astonishment. 193. attent:
Attentive. 200. at point: Completely. cap-a-pe: From head to foot.
204. truncheon: Officer's staff. 205. act: Action, operation.

These hands are not more like.

HAMLET: But where was this?

MARCELLUS: My lord, upon the platform where we watch.

HAMLET: Did you not speak to it?

HORATIO: My lord, I did,
But answer made it none. Yet once methought   215
It lifted up it° head and did address
Itself to motion, like as it would speak;
But even then the morning cock crew loud,
And at the sound it shrunk in haste away,
And vanish'd from our sight.

HAMLET: 'Tis very strange.   220

HORATIO: As I do live, my honor'd lord, 'tis true,
And we did think it writ down in our duty
To let you know of it.

HAMLET: Indeed, indeed, sirs. But this troubles me.
Hold you the watch tonight?

ALL: We do, my lord.   225

HAMLET: Arm'd, say you?

ALL: Arm'd, my lord.

HAMLET: From top to toe?

ALL: My lord, from head to foot.

HAMLET: Then saw you not his face?

HORATIO: O, yes, my lord. He wore his beaver° up.   230

HAMLET: What, looked he frowningly?

HORATIO: A countenance more
In sorrow than in anger.

HAMLET: Pale or red?

HORATIO: Nay, very pale.

HAMLET: And fix'd his eyes upon you?

HORATIO: Most constantly.

HAMLET: I would I had been there.

HORATIO: It would have much amaz'd you.   235

HAMLET: Very like, very like. Stay'd it long?

HORATIO: While one with moderate haste might tell° a hundred.

MARCELLUS, BERNARDO: Longer, longer.

HORATIO: Not when I saw 't.

HAMLET: His beard was grizzl'd, — no?

HORATIO: It was, as I have seen it in his life,   240
A sable silver'd.°

---

216. it: Its.   **230. beaver:** Visor on the helmet.   **237. tell:** Count.   **241. sable silver'd:** Black mixed with white.

HAMLET: I will watch tonight.
   Perchance 'twill walk again.
HORATIO: I warr'nt it will.
HAMLET: If it assume my noble father's person,
   I'll speak to it, though hell itself should gape
   And bid me hold my peace. I pray you all,   245
   If you have hitherto conceal'd this sight,
   Let it be tenable° in your silence still,
   And whatsomever else shall hap tonight,
   Give it an understanding, but no tongue.
   I will requite your loves. So, fare you well.   250
   Upon the platform, 'twixt eleven and twelve,
   I'll visit you.
ALL: Our duty to your honor.
HAMLET: Your loves, as mine to you. Farewell.

                                   (*Exeunt [all but Hamlet]*.)

   My father's spirit in arms! All is not well.
   I doubt° some foul play. Would the night were come!   255
   Till then sit still, my soul. Foul deeds will rise,
   Though all the earth o'erwhelm them, to men's eyes.

                                              (*Exit.*)

                    {*Scene III*}°

(*Enter Laertes and Ophelia, his sister.*)

LAERTES: My necessaries are embark'd. Farewell.
   And, sister, as the winds give benefit
   And convoy is assistant,° do not sleep
   But let me hear from you.
OPHELIA: Do you doubt that?
LAERTES: For Hamlet, and the trifling of his favor,   5
   Hold it a fashion and a toy in blood,°
   A violet in the youth of primy° nature,
   Forward,° not permanent, sweet, not lasting,
   The perfume and suppliance° of a minute—
   No more.

---

247. tenable: Held tightly.   **255. doubt:** Suspect.   **I, III. Location:** Polonius's chambers.   **3. convoy is assistant:** Means of conveyance are available.   **6. toy in blood:** Passing amorous fancy.   **7. primy:** In its prime, springtime. **8. Forward:** Precocious.   **9. suppliance:** Supply, filler.

OPHELIA: No more but so?
LAERTES: Think it no more.   10
   For nature crescent° does not grow alone
   In thews° and bulk, but, as this temple° waxes,
   The inward service of the mind and soul
   Grows wide withal.° Perhaps he loves you now,
   And now no soil° nor cautel° doth besmirch   15
   The virtue of his will;° but you must fear,
   His greatness weigh'd,° his will is not his own.
   [For he himself is subject to his birth.]
   He may not, as unvalued persons do,
   Carve° for himself; for on his choice depends   20
   The safety and health of this whole state,
   And therefore must his choice be circumscrib'd
   Unto the voice and yielding° of that body
   Whereof he is the head. Then if he says he loves you,
   It fits your wisdom so far to believe it   25
   As he in his particular act and place
   May give his saying deed,° which is no further
   Than the main voice of Denmark goes withal.
   Then weigh what loss your honor may sustain
   If with too credent° ear you list° his songs,   30
   Or lose your heart, or your chaste treasure open
   To his unmaster'd importunity.
   Fear it, Ophelia, fear it, my dear sister,
   And keep you in the rear of your affection,
   Out of the shot° and danger of desire.   35
   The chariest° maid is prodigal enough
   If she unmask her beauty to the moon.
   Virtue itself scapes not calumnious strokes.
   The canker galls° the infants of the spring
   Too oft before their buttons° be disclos'd,°   40
   And in the morn and liquid dew° of youth
   Contagious blastments° are most imminent.
   Be wary then; best safety lies in fear.

11. **crescent:** Growing, waxing.   12. **thews:** Bodily strength.   **temple:** Body.
14. **Grows wide withal:** Grows along with it.   15. **soil:** Blemish.   **cautel:**
Deceit.   16. **will:** Desire.   17. **greatness weigh'd:** High position considered.
20. **Carve:** Choose pleasure.   23. **voice and yielding:** Assent, approval.
27. **deed:** Effect.   30. **credent:** Credulous.   **list:** Listen to.   35. **shot:** Range.
36. **chariest:** Most scrupulously modest.   39. **canker galls:** Cankerworm destroys.   40. **buttons:** Buds.   **disclos'd:** Opened.   41. **liquid dew:** Time when
dew is fresh.   42. **blastments:** Blights.

Youth to itself rebels, though none else near.
OPHELIA: I shall the effect of this good lesson keep   45
  As watchman to my heart. But, good my brother,
  Do not, as some ungracious pastors do,
  Show me the steep and thorny way to heaven,
  Whiles, like a puff'd° and reckless libertine,
  Himself the primrose path of dalliance treads,   50
  And recks° not his own rede.°

(*Enter Polonius.*)

LAERTES: O, fear me not.
  I stay too long. But here my father comes.
  A double blessing is a double° grace;
  Occasion° smiles upon a second leave.
POLONIUS: Yet here, Laertes? Aboard, aboard, for shame!   55
  The wind sits in the shoulder of your sail,
  And you are stay'd for. There—my blessing with thee!
  And these few precepts in thy memory
  Look thou character.° Give thy thoughts no tongue
  Nor any unproportion'd thought his° act.   60
  Be thou familiar,° but by no means vulgar.°
  Those friends thou hast, and their adoption tried,°
  Grapple them to thy soul with hoops of steel,
  But do not dull thy palm with entertainment
  Of each new-hatch'd, unfledg'd courage.° Beware   65
  Of entrance to a quarrel, but, being in,
  Bear't that° th' opposed may beware of thee.
  Give every man thy ear, but few thy voice;
  Take each man's censure,° but reserve thy judgment.
  Costly thy habit as thy purse can buy,   70
  But not express'd in fancy; rich, not gaudy,
  For the apparel oft proclaims the man,
  And they in France of the best rank and station
  Are of a most select and generous chief° in that.
  Neither a borrower nor a lender be,   75
  For loan oft loses both itself and friend,
  And borrowing dulleth edge of husbandry.°

49. **puff'd:** Bloated. 51. **recks:** Heeds. **rede:** Counsel. 53. **double:** I.e., Laertes has already bidden his father good-bye. 54. **Occasion:** Opportunity. 59. **character:** Inscribe. 60. **his:** Its. 61. **familiar:** Sociable. **vulgar:** Common. 62. **tried:** Tested. 65. **courage:** Young man of spirit. 67. **Bear't that:** Manage it so that. 69. **censure:** Opinion, judgment. 74. **generous chief:** Noble eminence (?). 77. **husbandry:** Thrift.

This above all: to thine own self be true,
And it must follow, as the night the day,
Thou canst not then be false to any man.   80
Farewell. My blessing season° this in thee!
LAERTES: Most humbly do I take my leave, my lord.
POLONIUS: The time invests° you. Go, your servants tend.°
LAERTES: Farewell, Ophelia, and remember well
   What I have said to you.   85
OPHELIA: 'Tis in my memory lock'd,
   And you yourself shall keep the key of it.
LAERTES: Farewell.   (*Exit Laertes.*)
POLONIUS: What is 't, Ophelia, he hath said to you?
OPHELIA: So please you, something touching the Lord Hamlet.   90
POLONIUS: Marry,° well bethought.
   'Tis told me he hath very oft of late
   Given private time to you, and you yourself
   Have of your audience been most free and bounteous.
   If it be so—as so 'tis put on° me,   95
   And that in way of caution—I must tell you
   You do not understand yourself so clearly
   As it behooves my daughter and your honor.
   What is between you? Give me up the truth.
OPHELIA: He hath, my lord, of late made many tenders°   100
   Of his affection to me.
POLONIUS: Affection? Pooh! You speak like a green girl,
   Unsifted° in such perilous circumstance.
   Do you believe his tenders, as you call them?
OPHELIA: I do not know, my lord, what I should think.   105
POLONIUS: Marry, I will teach you. Think yourself a baby
   That you have ta'en these tenders° for true pay,
   Which are not sterling.° Tender° yourself more dearly,
   Or—not to crack the wind° of the poor phrase,
   Running it thus—you'll tender me a fool.°   110
OPHELIA: My lord, he hath importun'd me with love
   In honorable fashion.
POLONIUS: Ay, fashion° you may call it. Go to, go to.

81. season: Mature.   **83. invests:** Besieges. . . .   **tend:** Attend, wait.   **91. Marry:**
By the Virgin Mary (a mild oath).   **95. put on:** Impressed on, told to.   **100. tenders:** Offers.   **103. Unsifted:** Untried.   **107. tenders:** With added meaning
here of *promises to pay.*   **108. sterling:** Legal currency.   **Tender:** Hold.
109. crack the wind: Run it until it is broken, winded.   **110. tender me a fool:**
(1) Show yourself to me as a fool, (2) show me up as a fool, (3) present me with a
grandchild (*fool* was a term of endearment for a child).   **113. fashion:** Mere
form, pretense.

OPHELIA: And hath given countenance° to his speech, my lord,
   With almost all the holy vows of heaven.   115
POLONIUS: Ay, springes° to catch woodcocks.° I do know,
   When the blood burns, how prodigal the soul
   Lends the tongue vows. These blazes, daughter,
   Giving more light than heat, extinct in both
   Even in their promise, as it is a-making,   120
   You must not take for fire. From this time
   Be something scanter of your maiden presence.
   Set your entreatments° at a higher rate
   Than a command to parle.° For Lord Hamlet,
   Believe so much in him° that he is young,   125
   And with a larger tether may he walk
   Than may be given you. In few,° Ophelia,
   Do not believe his vows, for they are brokers,°
   Not of that dye° which their investments° show,
   But mere implorators° of unholy suits,   130
   Breathing° like sanctified and pious bawds,
   The better to beguile. This is for all:
   I would not, in plain terms, from this time forth
   Have you so slander° any moment leisure
   As to give words or talk with the Lord Hamlet.   135
   Look to 't, I charge you. Come your ways.
OPHELIA: I shall obey, my lord.   (*Exeunt.*)

{*Scene IV*}°

(*Enter Hamlet, Horatio, and Marcellus.*)

HAMLET: The air bites shrewdly; it is very cold.
HORATIO: It is a nipping and an eager air.
HAMLET: What hour now?
HORATIO: I think it lacks of twelve.
MARCELLUS: No, it is struck.

---

114. countenance: Credit, support. **116. springes:** Snares. **woodcocks:**
Birds easily caught; here used to connote gullibility. **123. entreatments:**
Negotiations for surrender (a military term). **124. parle:** Discuss terms with the
enemy. (Polonius urges his daughter, in the metaphor of military language, not to
meet with Hamlet and consider giving in to him merely because he requests an
interview.) **125. so . . . him:** This much concerning him. **127. In few:** Briefly.
128. brokers: Go-betweens, procurers. **129. dye:** Color or sort. **investments:**
Clothes (i.e., they are not what they seem). **130. mere implorators:** Out-and-
out solicitors. **131. Breathing:** Speaking. **134. slander:** Bring disgrace or
reproach upon. **I, IV. Location:** The guard platform.

HORATIO: Indeed? I heard it not.
  It then draws near the season   5
  Wherein the spirit held his wont to walk.

(*A flourish of trumpets, and two pieces° go off* [*within*].)

  What does this mean, my lord?
HAMLET: The King doth wake° tonight and takes his rouse,°
  Keeps wassail,° and the swagg'ring up-spring° reels;
  And as he drains his draughts of Rhenish° down,   10
  The kettle-drum and trumpet thus bray out
  The triumph of his pledge.°
HORATIO: Is it a custom?
HAMLET: Ay, marry, is 't,
  But to my mind, though I am native here
  And to the manner° born, it is a custom   15
  More honor'd in the breach than the observance.°
  This heavy-headed revel east and west°
  Makes us traduc'd and tax'd of° other nations.
  They clepe° us drunkards, and with swinish phrase°
  Soil our addition;° and indeed it takes   20
  From our achievements, though perform'd at height,°
  The pith and marrow of our attribute.
  So, oft it chances in particular men,
  That for some vicious mole of nature° in them,
  As in their birth—wherein they are not guilty,   25
  Since nature cannot choose his° origin—
  By the o'ergrowth of some complexion,°
  Oft breaking down the pales° and forts of reason,
  Or by some habit that too much o'er-leavens°
  The form of plausive° manners, that these men,   30
  Carrying, I say, the stamp of one defect,

[S.D.] *pieces:* I.e., of ordnance, cannon. **8. wake:** Stay awake and hold revel. **rouse:** Carouse, drinking bout. **9. wassail:** Carousal. **up-spring:** Wild German dance. **10. Rhenish:** Rhine wine. **12. triumph . . . pledge:** His feat in draining the wine in a single draft. **15. manner:** Custom (of drinking). **16. More . . . observance:** Better neglected than followed. **17. east and west:** I.e., everywhere. **18. tax'd of:** Censured by. **19. clepe:** Call. **with swinish phrase:** By calling us swine. **20. addition:** Reputation. **21. at height:** Outstandingly. **24. mole of nature:** Natural blemish in one's constitution. **26. his:** Its. **27. complexion:** Humor (i.e., one of the four humors or fluids thought to determine temperament). **28. pales:** Palings, fences (as of a fortification). **29. o'er-leavens:** Induces a change throughout (as yeast works in dough). **30. plausive:** Pleasing.

Being nature's livery,° or fortune's star,°
Their virtues else, be they as pure as grace,
As infinite as man may undergo,
Shall in the general censure take corruption   35
From that particular fault. The dram of eale°
Doth all the noble substance of a doubt°
To his own scandal.°

(*Enter Ghost.*)

HORATIO: Look, my lord, it comes!
HAMLET: Angels and ministers of grace defend us!
  Be thou a spirit of health° or goblin damn'd,   40
  Bring with thee airs from heaven or blasts from hell,
  Be thy intents wicked or charitable,
  Thou com'st in such a questionable° shape
  That I will speak to thee. I'll call thee Hamlet,
  King, father, royal Dane. O, answer me!   45
  Let me not burst in ignorance, but tell
  Why thy canoniz'd° bones, hearsed° in death,
  Have burst their cerements;° why the sepulcher
  Wherein we saw thee quietly interr'd
  Hath op'd his ponderous and marble jaws   50
  To cast thee up again. What may this mean,
  That thou, dead corse, again in complete steel
  Revisits thus the glimpses of the moon,°
  Making night hideous, and we fools of nature°
  So horridly to shake our disposition   55
  With thoughts beyond the reaches of our souls?
  Say, why is this? Wherefore? What should we do?

                        ([*Ghost*] *beckons* [*Hamlet*].)

HORATIO: It beckons you to go away with it,
  As if it some impartment° did desire
  To you alone.

---

32. nature's livery: Endowment from nature. **fortune's star:** Mark placed by
fortune. **36. dram of eale:** Small amount of evil (?). **37. of a doubt:** A famous
crux, sometimes emended to *oft about* or *often dout,* i.e., often erase or do out, or
to *antidote,* counteract. **38. To . . . scandal:** To the disgrace of the whole enterprise. **40. of health:** Of spiritual good. **43. questionable:** Inviting question or
conversation. **47. canoniz'd:** Buried according to the canons of the church.
hearsed: Coffined. **48. cerements:** Grave-clothes. **53. glimpses of the moon:**
Earth by night. **54. fools of nature:** Mere men, limited to natural knowledge.
59. impartment: Communication.

MARCELLUS: Look with what courteous action   60
  It waves you to a more removed ground.
  But do not go with it.
HORATIO: No, by no means.
HAMLET: It will not speak. Then I will follow it.
HORATIO: Do not, my lord.
HAMLET: Why, what should be the fear?
  I do not set my life at a pin's fee,°   65
  And for my soul, what can it do to that,
  Being a thing immortal as itself?
  It waves me forth again. I'll follow it.
HORATIO: What if it tempt you toward the flood, my lord
  Or to the dreadful summit of the cliff   70
  That beetles o'er° his° base into the sea,
  And there assume some other horrible form
  Which might deprive your sovereignty of reason,°
  And draw you into madness? Think of it.
  The very place puts toys of desperation,°   75
  Without more motive, into every brain
  That looks so many fathoms to the sea
  And hears it roar beneath.
HAMLET: It waves me still.
  Go on, I'll follow thee.
MARCELLUS: You shall not go, my lord.

                                        [*They try to stop him.*]

HAMLET: Hold off your hands!   80
HORATIO: Be rul'd, you shall not go.
HAMLET: My fate cries out,
  And makes each petty artery° in this body
  As hardy as the Nemean lion's° nerve.°
  Still am I call'd. Unhand me, gentlemen.
  By heaven, I'll make a ghost of him that lets° me!   85
  I say, away! Go on. I'll follow thee.

                                        (*Exeunt Ghost and Hamlet.*)

HORATIO: He waxes desperate with imagination.
MARCELLUS: Let's follow. 'Tis not fit thus to obey him.

---

65.   fee: Value. **71.   beetles o'er:** Overhangs   threateningly. **his:** Its.
73. deprive . . . reason: Take away the rule of reason over your mind. **75. toys of
desperation:** Fancies of   desperate   acts, i.e., suicide. **82. artery:** Sinew.
83. Nemean lion: One of the monsters slain by Hercules in his twelve labors.
nerve: Sinew   **85. lets:** Hinders.

HORATIO: Have after. To what issue° will this come?
MARCELLUS: Something is rotten in the state of Denmark.   90
HORATIO: Heaven will direct it.°
MARCELLUS: Nay, let's follow him.   (*Exeunt.*)

{*Scene v*}°

(*Enter Ghost and Hamlet.*)

HAMLET: Whither wilt thou lead me? Speak. I'll go no further.
GHOST: Mark me.
HAMLET: I will.
GHOST: My hour is almost come,
    When I to sulph'rous and tormenting flames
    Must render up myself.
HAMLET: Alas, poor ghost!
GHOST: Pity me not, but lend thy serious hearing   5
    To what I shall unfold.
HAMLET: Speak. I am bound to hear.
GHOST: So art thou to revenge, when thou shalt hear.
HAMLET: What?
GHOST: I am thy father's spirit,   10
    Doom'd for a certain term to walk the night,
    And for the day confin'd to fast° in fires,
    Till the foul crimes° done in my days of nature
    Are burnt and purg'd away. But that° I am forbid
    To tell the secrets of my prison-house,   15
    I could a tale unfold whose lightest word
    Would harrow up thy soul, freeze thy young blood,
    Make thy two eyes, like stars, start from their spheres,°
    Thy knotted and combined locks° to part,
    And each particular hair to stand an end,°   20
    Like quills upon the fearful porpentine.°
    But this eternal blazon° must not be
    To ears of flesh and blood. List, list, O, list!
    If thou didst ever thy dear father love—
HAMLET: O God!   25

---

89. issue: Outcome. **91. it:** The outcome. **I, v. Location:** The battlements of
the castle. **12. fast:** Do penance. **13. crimes:** Sins. **14. But that:** Were it not
that. **18. spheres:** Eye sockets, here compared to the orbits or transparent
revolving spheres in which, according to Ptolemaic astronomy, the heavenly bodies were fixed. **19. knotted . . . locks:** Hair neatly arranged and confined.
20. an end: On end. **21. fearful porpentine:** Frightened porcupine. **22. eternal blazon:** Revelation of the secrets of eternity.

GHOST: Revenge his foul and most unnatural murder.
HAMLET: Murder?
GHOST: Murder most foul, as in the best it is,
   But this most foul, strange, and unnatural.
HAMLET: Haste me to know 't, that I, with wings as swift   30
   As meditation or the thoughts of love,
   May sweep to my revenge.
GHOST: I find thee apt;
   And duller shouldst thou be than the fat weed
   That roots itself in ease on Lethe° wharf,°
   Wouldst thou not stir in this. Now, Hamlet, hear.   35
   'Tis given out that, sleeping in my orchard,
   A serpent stung me. So the whole ear of Denmark
   Is by a forged process° of my death
   Rankly abus'd.° But know, thou noble youth,
   The serpent that did sting thy father's life   40
   Now wears his crown.
HAMLET: O my prophetic soul!
   My uncle!
GHOST: Ay, that incestuous, that adulterate° beast,
   With witchcraft of his wits, with traitorous gifts —
   O wicked wit and gifts, that have the power   45
   So to seduce! — won to his shameful lust
   The will of my most seeming-virtuous queen.
   O Hamlet, what a falling-off was there!
   From me, whose love was of that dignity
   That it went hand in hand even with the vow   50
   I made to her in marriage, and to decline
   Upon a wretch whose natural gifts were poor
   To those of mine!
   But virtue, as it never will be moved,
   Though lewdness court it in a shape of heaven,°   55
   So lust, though to a radiant angel link'd,
   Will sate itself in a celestial bed,
   And prey on garbage.
   But, soft, methinks I scent the morning air.
   Brief let me be. Sleeping within my orchard,   60
   My custom always of the afternoon,
   Upon my secure° hour thy uncle stole,

---

34. Lethe: The river of forgetfulness in Hades. **wharf:** Bank. **38. forged process:** Falsified account. **39. abus'd:** Deceived. **43. adulterate:** Adulterous. **55. shape of heaven:** Heavenly form. **62. secure:** Confident, unsuspicious.

With juice of cursed hebona° in a vial,
And in the porches of my ears did pour
The leprous° distillment, whose effect   65
Holds such an enmity with blood of man
That swift as quicksilver it courses through
The natural gates and alleys of the body,
And with a sudden vigor it doth posset°
And curd, like eager° droppings into milk,   70
The thin and wholesome blood. So did it mine,
And a most instant tetter° bark'd° about,
Most lazar-like,° with vile and loathsome crust,
All my smooth body.
Thus was I, sleeping, by a brother's hand   75
Of life, of crown, of queen, at once dispatch'd,°
Cut off even in the blossoms of my sin,
Unhous'led,° disappointed,° unanel'd,°
No reck'ning made, but sent to my account
With all my imperfections on my head.   80
O, horrible! O, horrible, most horrible!
If thou hast nature° in thee, bear it not.
Let not the royal bed of Denmark be
A couch for luxury° and damned incest.
But, howsomever thou pursues this act,   85
Taint not thy mind, nor let thy soul contrive
Against thy mother aught. Leave her to heaven
And to those thorns that in her bosom lodge,
To prick and sting her. Fare thee well at once.
The glow-worm shows the matin° to be near,   90
And 'gins to pale his uneffectual fire.°
Adieu, adieu, adieu! Remember me.   [*Exit.*]
HAMLET: O all you host of heaven! O earth! What else?
And shall I couple° hell? O fie! Hold, hold, my heart,
And you, my sinews, grow not instant old,   95

---

63. hebona: Poison. (The word seems to be a form of *ebony*, though it is thought
perhaps to be related to *henbane*, a poison, or to *ebenus*, yew.)   **65. leprous:**
Causing leprosy-like disfigurement.   **69. posset:** Coagulate, curdle.   **70. eager:**
Sour, acid.   **72. tetter:** Eruption of scabs.   **bark'd:** Covered with a rough covering, like bark on a tree.   **73. lazar-like:** Leper-like.   **76. dispatch'd:** Suddenly
deprived.   **78. Unhous'led:** Without having received the sacrament [of Holy
Communion].   **disappointed:** Unready (spiritually) for the last journey.
unanel'd: Without having received extreme unction.   **82. nature:** The promptings of a son.   **84. luxury:** Lechery.   **90. matin:** Morning.   **91. uneffectual
fire:** Cold light.   **94. couple:** Add.

But bear me stiffly up. Remember thee!
Ay, thou poor ghost, whiles memory holds a seat
In this distracted globe.° Remember thee!
Yea, from the table° of my memory
I'll wipe away all trivial fond° records,   100
All saws° of books, all forms,° all pressures° past
That youth and observation copied there,
And thy commandment all alone shall live
Within the book and volume of my brain,
Unmix'd with baser matter. Yes, by heaven!   105
O most pernicious woman!
O villain, villain, smiling, damned villain!
My tables — meet it is I set it down,
That one may smile, and smile, and be a villain.
At least I am sure it may be so in Denmark.   110

                                                          [*Writing.*]

So, uncle, there you are. Now to my word;
It is "Adieu, adieu! Remember me."
I have sworn 't.

(*Enter Horatio and Marcellus.*)

HORATIO: My lord, my lord!
MARCELLUS: Lord Hamlet!
HORATIO: Heavens secure him!
HAMLET: So be it!   115
MARCELLUS: Illo, ho, ho, my lord!
HAMLET: Hillo, ho, ho,° boy! Come, bird, come.
MARCELLUS: How is 't, my noble lord?
HORATIO: What news, my lord?
HAMLET: O, wonderful!
HORATIO: Good my lord, tell it.
HAMLET: No, you will reveal it.   120
HORATIO: Not I, my lord, by heaven.
MARCELLUS: Nor I, my lord.
HAMLET: How say you, then, would heart of man once think it?
  But you'll be secret?
HORATIO, MARCELLUS: Ay, by heaven, my lord.
HAMLET: There's never a villain dwelling in all Denmark
  But he's an arrant° knave.   125

---

98. globe: Head.   **99. table:** Writing tablet.   **100. fond:** Foolish.   **101. saws:**
Wise sayings.   **forms:** Images.   **pressures:** Impressions stamped.   **117. Hillo,
ho, ho:** A falconer's call to a hawk in air. Hamlet is playing upon Marcellus's *Illo,*
i.e., *halloo.*   **125. arrant:** Thoroughgoing.

HORATIO: There needs no ghost, my lord, come from the grave
  To tell us this.
HAMLET: Why, right, you are in the right.
  And so, without more circumstance° at all,
  I hold it fit that we shake hands and part,
  You, as your business and desire shall point you—   130
  For every man hath business and desire,
  Such as it is—and for my own poor part,
  Look you, I'll go pray.
HORATIO: These are but wild and whirling words, my lord.
HAMLET: I am sorry they offend you, heartily;   135
  Yes, faith, heartily.
HORATIO: There's no offense, my lord.
HAMLET: Yes, by Saint Patrick,° but there is, Horatio,
  And much offense too. Touching this vision here,
  It is an honest° ghost, that let me tell you.
  For your desire to know what is between us,   140
  O'ermaster 't as you may. And now, good friends
  As you are friends, scholars, and soldiers,
  Give me one poor request.
HORATIO: What is 't, my lord? We will.
HAMLET: Never make known what you have seen tonight.   145
HORATIO, MARCELLUS: My lord, we will not.
HAMLET: Nay, but swear 't.
HORATIO: In faith,
  My lord, not I.
MARCELLUS: Nor I, my lord, in faith.
HAMLET: Upon my sword.°   [*Holds out his sword.*]
MARCELLUS: We have sworn, my lord, already.
HAMLET: Indeed, upon my sword, indeed.

                         (*Ghost cries under the stage.*)

GHOST: Swear.   150
HAMLET: Ha, ha, boy, say'st thou so? Art thou there, truepenny?°
  Come on, you hear this fellow in the cellarage.
  Consent to swear.
HORATIO: Propose the oath, my lord.
HAMLET: Never to speak of this that you have seen,
  Swear by my sword.   155

---

128. circumstance: Ceremony.   **137. Saint Patrick:** The keeper of purgatory
and patron saint of all blunders and confusion.   **139. honest:** I.e., a real ghost
and not an evil spirit.   **148. sword:** The hilt in the form of a cross.
151. truepenny: Honest old fellow.

GHOST [*beneath*]: Swear.
HAMLET: Hic et ubique?° Then we'll shift our ground.

[*He moves to another spot.*]

  Come hither, gentlemen,
And lay your hands again upon my sword.
Swear by my sword   160
Never to speak of this that you have heard.
GHOST [*beneath*]: Swear by his sword.
HAMLET: Well said, old mole! Canst work i' th' earth so fast?
  A worthy pioner!° Once more remove, good friends.

[*Moves again.*]

HORATIO: O day and night, but this is wondrous strange!   165
HAMLET: And therefore as a stranger give it welcome.
  There are more things in heaven and earth, Horatio,
  Than are dreamt of in your philosophy.°
  But come;
  Here, as before, never, so help you mercy,   170
  How strange or odd soe'er I bear myself—
  As I perchance hereafter shall think meet
  To put an antic° disposition on—
  That you, at such times seeing me, never shall,
  With arms encumb'red° thus, or this headshake,   175
  Or by pronouncing of some doubtful phrase,
  As "Well, well, we know," or "We could, an if° we would,"
  Or "If we list° to speak," or "There be, an if they might,"
  Or such ambiguous giving out,° to note°
  That you know aught of me—this do swear,   180
  So grace and mercy at your most need help you.
GHOST [*beneath*]: Swear.   [*They swear.*]
HAMLET: Rest, rest, perturbed spirit! So, gentlemen,
  With all my love I do commend me to you;
  And what so poor a man as Hamlet is   185
  May do, t' express his love and friending to you,
  God willing, shall not lack. Let us go in together,
  And still° your fingers on your lips, I pray.

---

157. **Hic et ubique:** Here and everywhere (Latin).   164. **pioner:** Pioneer, digger,
miner.   168. **your philosophy:** This subject called "natural philosophy" or "science" that people talk about.   173. **antic:** Fantastic.   175. **encumb'red:** Folded
or entwined.   177. **an if:** If.   178. **list:** Were inclined.   179. **giving out:**
Profession of knowledge.   **note:** Give a sign, indicate.   188. **still:** Always.

The time is out of joint. O cursed spite,
That ever I was born to set it right!   190

> [*They wait for him to leave first.*]

Nay, come, let's go together.   (*Exeunt.*)

{ACT II   *Scene 1*}°

(*Enter old Polonius, with his man [Reynaldo].*)

POLONIUS: Give him this money and these notes, Reynaldo.
REYNALDO: I will, my lord.
POLONIUS: You shall do marvel's° wisely, good Reynaldo,
  Before you visit him, to make inquire
  Of his behavior.
REYNALDO: My lord, I did intend it.   5
POLONIUS: Marry, well said, very well said. Look you, sir,
  Inquire me first what Danskers° are in Paris,
  And how, and who, what means,° and where they keep,°
  What company, at what expense; and finding
  By this encompassment° and drift° of question   10
  That they do know my son, come you more nearer
  Than your particular demands will touch it.°
  Take° you, as 'twere, some distant knowledge of him,
  As thus, "I know his father and his friends,
  And in part him." Do you mark this, Reynaldo?   15
REYNALDO: Ay, very well, my lord.
POLONIUS: "And in part him, but," you may say, "not well.
  But, if 't be he I mean, he's very wild,
  Addicted so and so," and there put on° him
  What forgeries° you please — marry, none so rank   20
  As may dishonor him, take heed of that,
  But, sir, such wanton,° wild, and usual slips,
  As are companions noted and most known
  To youth and liberty.

II, I. **Location:** Polonius's chambers.   **3. marvel's:** Marvelous(ly).   **7. Danskers:** Danes.   **8. what means:** What wealth (they have).   **keep:** Dwell.   **10. encompassment:** Roundabout talking.   **drift:** Gradual approach or course.   **11–12. come . . . it:** You will find out more this way than by asking pointed questions (particular demands).   **13. Take:** Assume, pretend.   **19. put on:** Impute to.   **20. forgeries:** Invented tales.   **22. wanton:** Sportive, unrestrained.

REYNALDO: As gaming, my lord.
POLONIUS: Ay, or drinking, fencing, swearing,   25
  Quarreling, drabbing°—you may go so far.
REYNALDO: My lord, that would dishonor him.
POLONIUS: Faith, no, as you may season° it in the charge.
  You must not put another scandal on him
  That he is open to incontinency;°   30
  That's not my meaning. But breathe his faults so quaintly°
  That they may seem the taints of liberty,°
  The flash and outbreak of a fiery mind,
  A savageness in unreclaimed° blood,
  Of general assault.°
REYNALDO: But, my good lord—   35
POLONIUS: Wherefore should you do this?
REYNALDO: Ay, my lord,
  I would know that.
POLONIUS: Marry, sir, here's my drift,
  And, I believe, it is a fetch of wit.°
  You laying these slight sullies on my son,
  As 'twere a thing a little soil'd i' th' working,°   40
  Mark you,
  Your party in converse,° him you would sound,°
  Having ever° seen in the prenominate crimes°
  The youth you breathe° of guilty, be assur'd
  He closes with you in this consequence:°   45
  "Good sir," or so, or "friend," or "gentleman,"
  According to the phrase or the addition°
  Of man and country.
REYNALDO: Very good, my lord.
POLONIUS: And then, sir, does 'a this—'a does—what was I about to
  say?
  By the mass, I was about to say something.   50
  Where did I leave?
REYNALDO: At "closes in the consequence."

26. **drabbing:** Whoring. **28. season:** Temper, soften. **30. incontinency:** Habitual loose behavior. **31. quaintly:** Delicately, ingeniously. **32. taints of liberty:** Faults resulting from freedom. **34. unreclaimed:** Untamed. **35. general assault:** Tendency that assails all unrestrained youth. **38. fetch of wit:** Clever trick. **40. soil'd i' th' working:** Shopworn. **42. converse:** Conversation. **sound:** Sound out. **43. Having ever:** If he has ever. **prenominate crimes:** Before-mentioned offenses. **44. breathe:** Speak. **45. closes . . . consequence:** Follows your lead in some fashion as follows. **47. addition:** Title.

POLONIUS: At "closes in the consequence," ay, marry.
 He closes thus: "I know the gentleman;
 I saw him yesterday, or th' other day,
 Or then, or then, with such, or such, and, as you say,   55
 There was 'a gaming, there o'ertook in 's rouse,°
 There falling out° at tennis," or perchance,
 "I saw him enter such a house of sale,"
 Videlicet,° a brothel, or so forth. See you now,
 Your bait of falsehood takes this carp° of truth;   60
 And thus do we of wisdom and of reach,°
 With windlasses° and with assays of bias,°
 By indirections find directions° out.
 So by my former lecture and advice
 Shall you my son. You have me, have you not?   65
REYNALDO: My lord, I have.
POLONIUS: God buy ye; fare ye well.
REYNALDO: Good my lord.
POLONIUS: Observe his inclination in yourself.°
REYNALDO: I shall, my lord.
POLONIUS: And let him ply° his music.
REYNALDO: Well, my lord.   70
POLONIUS: Farewell.   (*Exit Reynaldo.*)

(*Enter Ophelia.*)

     How now, Ophelia, what's the matter?
OPHELIA: O, my lord, my lord, I have been so affrighted!
POLONIUS: With what, i' th' name of God?
OPHELIA: My lord, as I was sewing in my closet,°
 Lord Hamlet, with his doublet° all unbrac'd,°   75
 No hat upon his head, his stockings fouled,
 Ungart'red, and down-gyved to his ankle,°
 Pale as his shirt, his knees knocking each other,
 And with a look so piteous in purport

56. o'ertook in 's rouse: Overcome by drink. **57. falling out:** Quarreling.
59. Videlicet: Namely. **60. carp:** A fish. **61. reach:** Capacity, ability.
62. windlasses: Circuitous paths (literally, circuits made to head off the game in
hunting). **assays of bias:** Attempts through indirection (like the curving path of
the bowling ball, which is biased or weighted to one side). **63. directions:** The
way things really are. **68. in yourself:** In your own person (as well as by asking
questions). **70. let him ply:** See that he continues to study. **74. closet:** Private
chamber. **75. doublet:** Close-fitting jacket. **unbrac'd:** Unfastened. **77. down-
gyved to his ankle:** Fallen to the ankles (like gyves or fetters).

As if he had been loosed out of hell   80
To speak of horrors — he comes before me.
POLONIUS: Mad for thy love?
OPHELIA: My lord, I do not know,
  But truly I do fear it.
POLONIUS: What said he?
OPHELIA: He took me by the wrist and held me hard.
  Then goes he to the length of all his arm,   85
  And, with his other hand thus o'er his brow
  He falls to such perusal of my face
  As 'a would draw it. Long stay'd he so.
  At last, a little shaking of mine arm
  And thrice his head thus waving up and down,   90
  He rais'd a sigh so piteous and profound
  As it did seem to shatter all his bulk°
  And end his being. That done, he lets me go,
  And, with his head over his shoulder turn'd,
  He seem'd to find his way without his eyes,   95
  For out o' doors he went without their helps,
  And, to the last, bended their light on me.
POLONIUS: Come, go with me. I will go seek the King.
  This is the very ecstasy° of love
  Whose violent property° fordoes° itself   100
  And leads the will to desperate undertakings
  As oft as any passion under heaven
  That does afflict our natures. I am sorry.
  What, have you given him any hard words of late?
OPHELIA: No, my good lord, but, as you did command,   105
  I did repel his letters and denied
  His access to me.
POLONIUS: That hath made him mad.
  I am sorry that with better heed and judgment
  I had not quoted° him. I fear'd he did but trifle
  And meant to wrack thee; but, beshrew my jealousy!°   110
  By heaven, it is as proper to our age°
  To cast beyond° ourselves in our opinions
  As it is common for the younger sort
  To lack discretion. Come, go we to the King.

---

92. **bulk:** Body.   99. **ecstasy:** Madness.   100. **property:** Nature.   **fordoes:**
Destroys.   109. **quoted:** Observed.   110. **beshrew my jealousy:** A plague upon
my suspicious nature.   111. **proper . . . age:** Characteristic of us (old) men.
112. **cast beyond:** Overshoot, miscalculate.

This must be known, which, being kept close,° might move   115
More grief to hide than hate to utter love.°
Come.   (*Exeunt.*)

[*Scene II*]°

(*Flourish. Enter King and Queen, Rosencrantz, and Guildenstern [with others].*)

KING: Welcome, dear Rosencrantz and Guildenstern.
    Moreover that° we much did long to see you,
    The need we have to use you did provoke
    Our hasty sending. Something have you heard
    Of Hamlet's transformation—so call it,   5
    Sith° nor th' exterior nor° the inward man
    Resembles that° it was. What it should be,
    More than his father's death, that thus hath put him
    So much from th' understanding of himself,
    I cannot dream of. I entreat you both   10
    That, being of so young days° brought up with him,
    And sith so neighbor'd to his youth and havior,
    That you vouchsafe your rest° here in our court
    Some little time, so by your companies
    To draw him on to pleasures, and to gather   15
    So much as from occasion you may glean,
    Whether aught to us unknown afflicts him thus,
    That, open'd,° lies within our remedy.
QUEEN: Good gentlemen, he hath much talk'd of you
    And sure I am two men there is not living   20
    To whom he more adheres. If it will please you
    To show us so much gentry° and good will
    As to expend your time with us awhile
    For the supply and profit° of our hope,
    Your visitation shall receive such thanks   25
    As fits a king's remembrance.
ROSENCRANTZ: Both your Majesties
    Might, by the sovereign power you have of us,

115. close: Secret.   **115–16. might . . . love:** Might cause more grief (to others)
by hiding the knowledge of Hamlet's strange behavior to Ophelia than hatred by
telling it.   **II, II. Location:** The castle.   **2. Moreover that:** Besides the fact that.
6. Sith: Since.   **nor . . . nor:** Neither . . . nor.   **7. that:** What.   **11. of . . . days:**
From such early youth.   **13. vouchsafe your rest:** Please to stay.   **18. open'd:**
Revealed.   **22. gentry:** Courtesy.   **24. supply and profit:** Aid and successful
outcome.

Put your dread pleasures more into command
Than to entreaty.
GUILDENSTERN: But we both obey,
  And here give up ourselves in the full bent°   30
  To lay our service freely at your feet,
  To be commanded.
KING: Thanks, Rosencrantz and gentle Guildenstern.
QUEEN: Thanks, Guildenstern and gentle Rosencrantz.
  And I beseech you instantly to visit   35
  My too much changed son. Go, some of you,
  And bring these gentlemen where Hamlet is.
GUILDENSTERN: Heavens make our presence and our practices
  Pleasant and helpful to him!
QUEEN: Ay, amen!

      (*Exeunt Rosencrantz and Guildenstern* [*with some Attendants*].)

(*Enter Polonius.*)

POLONIUS: Th' ambassadors from Norway, my good lord,   40
  Are joyfully return'd.
KING: Thou still° hast been the father of good news.
POLONIUS: Have I, my lord? I assure my good liege
  I hold my duty, as I hold my soul,
  Both to my God and to my gracious king;   45
  And I do think, or else this brain of mine
  Hunts not the trail of policy so sure
  As it hath us'd to do, that I have found
  The very cause of Hamlet's lunacy.
KING: O, speak of that! That do I long to hear.   50
POLONIUS: Give first admittance to th' ambassadors.
  My news shall be the fruit° to that great feast.
KING: Thyself do grace to them, and bring them in.

                               (*Exit Polonius.*)

He tells me, my dear Gertrude, he hath found
The head and source of all your son's distemper.   55
QUEEN: I doubt° it is no other but the main,°
  His father's death, and our o'erhasty marriage.

(*Enter Ambassadors* [*Voltimand and Cornelius, with Polonius*].)

---

30. in . . . bent: To the utmost degree of our capacity. **42. still:** Always.
52. fruit: Dessert. **56. doubt:** Fear, suspect. **main:** Chief point, principal
concern.

KING: Well, we shall sift him. — Welcome, my good friends!
    Say, Voltimand, what from our brother Norway?
VOLTIMAND: Most fair return of greetings and desires.   60
    Upon our first,° he sent out to suppress
    His nephew's levies, which to him appear'd
    To be a preparation 'gainst the Polack,
    But, better look'd into, he truly found
    It was against your Highness. Whereat griev'd   65
    That so his sickness, age, and impotence
    Was falsely borne in hand,° sends out arrests
    On Fortinbras, which he, in brief, obeys,
    Receives rebuke from Norway, and in fine°
    Makes vow before his uncle never more   70
    To give th' assay° of arms against your Majesty.
    Whereon old Norway, overcome with joy,
    Gives him three score thousand crowns in annual fee,
    And his commission to employ those soldiers,
    So levied as before, against the Polack,   75
    With an entreaty, herein further shown,

                                [Giving a paper.]

    That it might please you to give quiet pass
    Through your dominions for this enterprise,
    On such regards of safety and allowance°
    As therein are set down.
KING: It likes° us well;   80
    And at our more consider'd° time we'll read,
    Answer, and think upon this business.
    Meantime we thank you for your well-took labor.
    Go to your rest; at night we'll feast together.
    Most welcome home!   *(Exeunt Ambassadors.)*
POLONIUS: This business is well ended.   85
    My liege, and madam, to expostulate°
    What majesty should be, what duty is,
    Why day is day, night night, and time is time,
    Were nothing but to waste night, day, and time.
    Therefore, since brevity is the soul of wit,°   90

---

61. **Upon our first:** At our first words on the business.   67. **borne in hand:** Deluded, taken advantage of.   69. **in fine:** In the end.   71. **assay:** Trial. 79. **On . . . allowance:** With such pledges of safety and provisos.   80. **likes:** Pleases.   81. **consider'd:** Suitable for deliberation.   86. **expostulate:** Expound. 90. **wit:** Sound sense or judgment.

And tediousness the limbs and outward flourishes,
I will be brief. Your noble son is mad.
Mad call I it, for, to define true madness,
What is 't but to be nothing else but mad?
But let that go.
QUEEN: More matter, with less art.   95
POLONIUS: Madam, I swear I use no art at all.
That he is mad, 'tis true; 'tis true 'tis pity,
And pity 'tis 'tis true—a foolish figure,°
But farewell it, for I will use no art.
Mad let us grant him, then, and now remains   100
That we find out the cause of this effect,
Or rather say, the cause of this defect,
For this effect defective comes by cause.°
Thus it remains, and the remainder thus.
Perpend.°   105
I have a daughter—have while she is mine—
Who, in her duty and obedience, mark,
Hath given me this. Now gather, and surmise.
[Reads the letter.] "To the celestial and my soul's idol,
the most beautified Ophelia"—   110
That's an ill phrase, a vile phrase; "beautified" is a vile
phrase. But you shall hear. Thus: [Reads.]
"In her excellent white bosom, these, etc."
QUEEN: Came this from Hamlet to her?
POLONIUS: Good madam, stay awhile; I will be faithful.   [Reads.] 115
   "Doubt° thou the stars are fire,
      Doubt that the sun doth move,
   Doubt truth to be a liar,
      But never doubt I love.
O dear Ophelia, I am ill at these numbers.° I have   120
not art to reckon° my groans. But that I love thee
best, O most best, believe it. Adieu.
            Thine evermore, most dear lady, whilst this
                  machine° is to him, Hamlet."
This in obedience hath my daughter shown me,   125
And, more above,° hath his solicitings,

---

98. figure: Figure of speech.   **103. For . . . cause:** I.e., for this defective behavior,
this madness has a cause.   **105. Perpend:** Consider.   **116. Doubt:** Suspect,
question.   **120. ill . . . numbers:** Unskilled at writing verses.   **121. reckon:**
(1) Count, (2) number metrically, scan.   **124. machine:** Body.   **126. more above:**
Moreover.

As they fell out° by time, by means, and place,
  All given to mine ear.
KING: But how hath she
  Receiv'd his love?
POLONIUS: What do you think of me?
KING: As of a man faithful and honorable.   130
POLONIUS: I would fain prove so. But what might you think,
  When I had seen this hot love on the wing—
  As I perceiv'd it, I must tell you that,
  Before my daughter told me—what might you,
  Or my dear Majesty your Queen here, think,   135
  If I had play'd the desk or table-book,°
  Or given my heart a winking,° mute and dumb,
  Or look'd upon this love with idle sight?°
  What might you think? No, I went round° to work,
  And my young mistress thus I did bespeak:°   140
  "Lord Hamlet is a prince, out of thy star;°
  This must not be." And then I prescripts gave her,
  That she should lock herself from his resort,
  Admit no messengers, receive no tokens.
  Which done, she took the fruits of my advice;   145
  And he, repelled—a short tale to make—
  Fell into a sadness, then into a fast,
  Thence to a watch,° thence into a weakness,
  Thence to a lightness,° and, by this declension,°
  Into the madness wherein now he raves,   150
  And all we mourn for.
KING: Do you think this?
QUEEN: It may be, very like.
POLONIUS: Hath there been such a time—I would fain know that—
  That I have positively said "'Tis so,"
  When it prov'd otherwise?
KING: Not that I know.   155
POLONIUS [*pointing to his head and shoulder*]: Take this from this, if this
    be otherwise.
  If circumstances lead me, I will find

---

127. **fell out:** Occurred.   136. **play'd . . . table-book:** Remained shut up, concealing the information.   137. **winking:** Closing of the eyes.   138. **with idle sight:** Complacently or uncomprehendingly.   139. **round:** Roundly, plainly.   140. **bespeak:** Address.   141. **out of thy star:** Above your sphere, position.   148. **watch:** State of sleeplessness.   149. **lightness:** Light-headedness.   **declension:** Decline, deterioration.

Where truth is hid, though it were hid indeed
Within the center.°
KING: How may we try it further?
POLONIUS: You know, sometimes he walks four hours together   160
  Here in the lobby.
QUEEN: So he does indeed.
POLONIUS: At such a time I'll loose my daughter to him.
  Be you and I behind an arras° then.
  Mark the encounter. If he love her not
  And be not from his reason fall'n thereon,°   165
  Let me be no assistant for a state,
  But keep a farm and carters.
KING: We will try it.

(*Enter Hamlet* [*reading on a book*].)

QUEEN: But look where sadly the poor wretch comes reading.
POLONIUS: Away, I do beseech you both, away.
  I'll board° him presently.

(*Exeunt King and Queen* [*with Attendants*].)

                O, give me leave.   170
How does my good Lord Hamlet?
HAMLET: Well, God-a-mercy.°
POLONIUS: Do you know me, my lord?
HAMLET: Excellent well. You are a fishmonger.°
POLONIUS: Not I, my lord.   175
HAMLET: Then I would you were so honest a man.
POLONIUS: Honest, my lord?
HAMLET: Ay, sir. To be honest, as this world goes, is to be one man pick'd
  out of ten thousand.
POLONIUS: That's very true, my lord.   180
HAMLET: For if the sun breed maggots in a dead dog, being a good kiss-
  ing carrion°—Have you a daughter?
POLONIUS: I have, my lord.
HAMLET: Let her not walk i' th' sun.° Conception° is a blessing, but as
  your daughter may conceive, friend, look to 't.   185

---

159. center: Middle point of the earth (which is also the center of the Ptolemaic universe).   **163. arras:** Hanging, tapestry.   **165. thereon:** On that account. **170. board:** Accost.   **172. God-a-mercy:** Thank you.   **174. fishmonger:** Fish merchant (with connotation of *bawd, procurer*[?]).   **181–82. good kissing carrion:** A good piece of flesh for kissing, or for the sun to kiss.   **184. i' th' sun:** With additional implication of the sunshine of princely favors.   **Conception:** (1) Understanding, (2) pregnancy.

POLONIUS [*aside*]: How say you by that? Still harping on my daughter. Yet he knew me not at first; 'a said I was a fishmonger. 'A is far gone. And truly in my youth I suff'red much extremity for love, very near this. I'll speak to him again. — What do you read, my lord?

HAMLET: Words, words, words.   190

POLONIUS: What is the matter,° my lord?

HAMLET: Between who?

POLONIUS: I mean, the matter that you read, my lord.

HAMLET: Slanders, sir, for the satirical rogue says here that old men have gray beards, that their faces are wrinkled, their eyes purging° thick 195 amber and plum-tree gum, and that they have a plentiful lack of wit, together with most weak hams. All which, sir, though I most powerfully and potently believe, yet I hold it not honesty° to have it thus set down, for you yourself, sir, shall grow old as I am, if like a crab you could go backward.   200

POLONIUS [*aside*]: Though this be madness, yet there is method in 't. — Will you walk out of the air, my lord?

HAMLET: Into my grave.

POLONIUS: Indeed, that's out of the air. [*Aside.*] How pregnant° sometimes his replies are! A happiness° that often madness hits on, which 205 reason and sanity could not so prosperously° be deliver'd of. I will leave him, [and suddenly contrive the means of meeting between him] and my daughter. — My honorable lord, I will most humbly take my leave of you.

HAMLET: You cannot, sir, take from me any thing that I will more will- 210 ingly part withal — except my life, except my life, except my life.

(*Enter Guildenstern and Rosencrantz.*)

POLONIUS: Fare you well, my lord.

HAMLET: These tedious old fools!°

POLONIUS: You go to seek the Lord Hamlet; there he is.

ROSENCRANTZ [*to Polonius*]: God save you, sir!   215

                                                      [*Exit Polonius.*]

GUILDENSTERN: My honor'd lord!

ROSENCRANTZ: My most dear lord!

HAMLET: My excellent good friends! How dost thou, Guildenstern? Ah, Rosencrantz! Good lads, how do you both?

---

191. matter: Substance (but Hamlet plays on the sense of *basis for a dispute*). **195. purging:** Discharging. **198. honesty:** Decency. **204. pregnant:** Full of meaning. **205. happiness:** Felicity of expression. **206. prosperously:** Successfully. **213. old fools:** I.e., old men like Polonius.

ROSENCRANTZ: As the indifferent° children of the earth.   220
GUILDENSTERN: Happy in that we are not over-happy. On Fortune's cap
   we are not the very button.
HAMLET: Nor the soles of her shoe?
ROSENCRANTZ: Neither, my lord.
HAMLET: Then you live about her waist, or in the middle of her favors?   225
GUILDENSTERN: Faith, her privates° we.
HAMLET: In the secret parts of Fortune? O, most true; she is a strumpet.°
   What news?
ROSENCRANTZ: None, my lord, but the world's grown honest.
HAMLET: Then is doomsday near. But your news is not true. [Let me   230
   question more in particular. What have you, my good friends, deserv'd
   at the hands of Fortune that she sends you to prison hither?
GUILDENSTERN: Prison, my lord?
HAMLET: Denmark's a prison.
ROSENCRANTZ: Then is the world one.   235
HAMLET: A goodly one, in which there are many confines,° wards,° and
   dungeons, Denmark being one o' th' worst.
ROSENCRANTZ: We think not so, my lord.
HAMLET: Why then 'tis none to you, for there is nothing either good or
   bad but thinking makes it so. To me it is a prison.   240
ROSENCRANTZ: Why then, your ambition makes it one. 'Tis too narrow
   for your mind.
HAMLET: O God, I could be bounded in a nutshell and count myself a
   king of infinite space, were it not that I have bad dreams.
GUILDENSTERN: Which dreams indeed are ambition, for the very sub-   245
   stance of the ambitious° is merely the shadow of a dream.
HAMLET: A dream itself is but a shadow.
ROSENCRANTZ: Truly, and I hold ambition of so airy and light a quality
   that it is but a shadow's shadow.
HAMLET: Then are our beggars bodies,° and our monarchs and out-   250
   stretch'd° heroes the beggars' shadows. Shall we to th' court? For, by
   my fay,° I cannot reason.
ROSENCRANTZ, GUILDENSTERN: We'll wait upon° you.

220. **indifferent:** Ordinary.   226. **privates:** Close acquaintances (with sexual
pun on *private parts*).   227. **strumpet:** Prostitute (a common epithet for indis-
criminate Fortune, see line 449 p. 137).   236. **confines:** Places of confinement.
wards: Cells.   245–46. **the very . . . ambitious:** That seemingly very substantial
thing which the ambitious pursue.   250. **bodies:** Solid substances rather than
shadows (since beggars are not ambitious).   250–51. **outstretch'd:** (1) Far-
reaching in their ambition, (2) elongated as shadows.   252. **fay:** Faith.
253. **wait upon:** Accompany, attend.

HAMLET: No such matter. I will not sort° you with the rest of my servants, for, to speak to you like an honest man, I am most dreadfully   255
attended.°] But, in the beaten way° of friendship, what make° you at
Elsinore?

ROSENCRANTZ: To visit you, my lord, no other occasion.

HAMLET: Beggar that I am, I am even poor in thanks; but I thank you,
and sure, dear friends, my thanks are too dear a halfpenny.° Were you   260
not sent for? Is it your own inclining? Is it a free visitation? Come,
come, deal justly with me. Come, come; nay, speak.

GUILDENSTERN: What should we say, my lord?

HAMLET: Why, anything, but to th' purpose. You were sent for; and there
is a kind of confession in your looks which your modesties have not   265
craft enough to color. I know the good King and Queen have sent
for you.

ROSENCRANTZ: To what end, my lord?

HAMLET: That you must teach me. But let me conjure° you, by the rights
of our fellowship, by the consonancy of our youth,° by the obligation   270
of our ever-preserv'd love, and by what more dear a better proposer°
could charge° you withal, be even° and direct with me, whether you
were sent for, or no?

ROSENCRANTZ [aside to Guildenstern]: What say you?

HAMLET [aside]: Nay then, I have an eye of° you. —If you love me, hold   275
not off.

GUILDENSTERN: My lord, we were sent for.

HAMLET: I will tell you why; so shall my anticipation prevent your discovery,° and your secrecy to the King and Queen molt no feather.° I
have of late—but wherefore I know not—lost all my mirth, forgone   280
all custom of exercises; and indeed it goes so heavily with my disposition that this goodly frame, the earth, seems to me a sterile promon-
tory; this most excellent canopy, the air, look you, this brave°
o'erhanging firmament, this majestical roof fretted° with golden fire,
why, it appeareth nothing to me but a foul and pestilent congregation   285
of vapors. What a piece of work is a man! How noble in reason, how

---

254. sort: Class, associate.   **255–56. dreadfully attended:** Waited upon in
slovenly fashion.   **256. beaten way:** Familiar path.   **make:** Do.   **260. dear a
halfpenny:** Expensive at the price of a halfpenny, i.e., of little worth.   **269. con-
jure:** Adjure, entreat.   **270. consonancy of our youth:** The fact that we are of
the same age.   **271. better proposer:** More skillful propounder.   **272. charge:**
Urge.   **even:** Straight, honest.   **275. of:** On.   **278–79. prevent your discovery:**
Forestall your disclosure.   **279. molt no feather:** Not diminish in the least.
283. brave: Splendid.   **284. fretted:** Adorned (with fret-work, as in a vaulted
ceiling).

infinite in faculties, in form and moving how express° and admirable,
in action how like an angel, in apprehension how like a god! The
beauty of the world, the paragon of animals! And yet, to me, what is
this quintessence° of dust? Man delights not me—no, nor woman nei-   290
ther, though by your smiling you seem to say so.
ROSENCRANTZ: My lord, there was no such stuff in my thoughts.
HAMLET: Why did you laugh then, when I said "man delights not me"?
ROSENCRANTZ: To think, my lord, if you delight not in man, what lenten
entertainment° the players shall receive from you. We coted° them on   295
the way, and hither are they coming, to offer you service.
HAMLET: He that plays the king shall be welcome; his Majesty shall have
tribute of me. The adventurous knight shall use his foil and target,°
the lover shall not sigh gratis, the humorous man° shall end his part in
peace, [the clown shall make those laugh whose lungs are tickle o' th'   300
sere°], and the lady shall say her mind freely, or the blank verse shall
halt° for 't. What players are they?
ROSENCRANTZ: Even those you were wont to take such delight in, the
tragedians of the city.
HAMLET: How chances it they travel? Their residence,° both in reputa-   305
tion and profit, was better both ways.
ROSENCRANTZ: I think their inhibition° comes by the means of the
innovation.°
HAMLET: Do they hold the same estimation they did when I was in the
city? Are they so follow'd?   310
ROSENCRANTZ: No, indeed, are they not.
[HAMLET: How comes it? Do they grow rusty?
ROSENCRANTZ: Nay, their endeavor keeps in the wonted° pace. But there
is, sir, an aery° of children, little eyases,° that cry out on the top of
question,° and are most tyrannically° clapp'd for 't. These are now the   315

---

287. express: Well-framed (?), exact (?).   **290. quintessence:** The fifth essence
of ancient philosophy, beyond earth, water, air, and fire, supposed to be the substance of the heavenly bodies and to be latent in all things.   **294–95. lenten
entertainment:** Meager reception (appropriate to Lent).   **295. coted:** Overtook
and passed beyond.   **298. foil and target:** Sword and shield.   **299. humorous
man:** Eccentric character, dominated by one trait or "humor."   **300–01. tickle o'
th' sere:** Easy on the trigger, ready to laugh easily. (*Sere* is part of a gunlock.)
302. halt: Limp.   **305. residence:** Remaining in one place, i.e., in the city.
307. inhibition: Formal prohibition (from acting plays in the city).   **308. innovation:** I.e., the new fashion in satirical plays performed by boy actors in the "private" theaters; or possibly a political uprising; or the strict limitations set on the
theater in London in 1600.   **313. wonted:** Usual.   **314. aery:** Nest.   **eyases:**
Young hawks.   **314–15. cry ... question:** Speak shrilly, dominating the controversy (in decrying the public theaters).   **315. tyrannically:** Outrageous.

fashion, and so berattle° the common stages°—so they call them—
that many wearing rapiers° are afraid of goose-quills° and dare scarce
come thither.

HAMLET: What, are they children? Who maintains 'em? How are they
escoted?° Will they pursue the quality° no longer than they can sing?° 320
Will they not say afterwards, if they should grow themselves to
common° players—as it is most like, if their means are no better—
their writers do them wrong, to make them exclaim against their own
succession?°

ROSENCRANTZ: Faith, there has been much to do° on both sides, and the 325
nation holds it no sin to tarre° them to controversy. There was, for a
while, no money bid for argument° unless the poet and the player
went to cuffs in the question.°

HAMLET: Is 't possible?

GUILDENSTERN: O, there has been much throwing about of brains. 330

HAMLET: Do the boys carry it away?°

ROSENCRANTZ: Ay, that they do, my lord—Hercules and his load° too.°]

HAMLET: It is not very strange, for my uncle is King of Denmark, and
those that would make mouths° at him while my father liv'd, give
twenty, forty, fifty, a hundred ducats° apiece for his picture in little.° 335
'Sblood,° there is something in this more than natural, if philosophy
could find it out.

(A flourish [of trumpets within].)

GUILDENSTERN: There are the players.

HAMLET: Gentlemen, you are welcome to Elsinore. Your hands, come
then. Th' appurtenance of welcome is fashion and ceremony. Let me 340
comply° with you in this garb,° lest my extent° to the players, which, I

---

316. berattle: Berate. common stages: Public theaters. 317. many wearing
rapiers: Many men of fashion, who were afraid to patronize the common players
for fear of being satirized by the poets who wrote for the children. goose-quills:
Pens of satirists. 320. escoted: Maintained. quality: (Acting) profession.
no longer . . . sing: Only until their voices change. 322. common: Regular,
adult. 324. succession: Future careers. 325. to do: Ado. 326. tarre: Set on
(as dogs). 327. argument: Plot for a play. 328. went . . . question: Came to
blows in the play itself. 331. carry it away: Win the day. 332. Hercules . . .
load: Thought to be an allusion to the sign of the Globe Theatre, which was
Hercules bearing the world on his shoulder. 312–32. How . . . load too: The
passage, omitted from the early quartos, alludes to the so-called War of
the Theatres, 1599–1602, the rivalry between the children companies and the
adult actors. 334. mouths: Faces. 335. ducats: Gold coins. in little: In
miniature. 336. 'Sblood: By His (God's, Christ's) blood. 341. comply: Observe the formalities of courtesy. garb: Manner. my extent: The extent of my
showing courtesy.

tell you, must show fairly outwards,° should more appear like enter-
tainment° than yours. You are welcome. But my uncle-father and
aunt-mother are deceiv'd.

GUILDENSTERN: In what, my dear lord?   345

HAMLET: I am but mad north-north-west.° When the wind is southerly I
know a hawk from a handsaw.°

(*Enter Polonius.*)

POLONIUS: Well be with you, gentlemen!

HAMLET: Hark you, Guildenstern, and you too; at each ear a hearer. That
great baby you see there is not yet out of his swaddling-clouts.°   350

ROSENCRANTZ: Happily° he is the second time come to them; for they say
an old man is twice a child.

HAMLET: I will prophesy he comes to tell me of the players; mark it.—
You say right, sir, o' Monday morning, 'twas then indeed.

POLONIUS: My lord, I have news to tell you.   355

HAMLET: My lord, I have news to tell you. When Roscius° was an actor in
Rome—

POLONIUS: The actors are come hither, my lord.

HAMLET: Buzz,° buzz!

POLONIUS: Upon my honor—   360

HAMLET: Then came each actor on his ass—

POLONIUS: The best actors in the world, either for tragedy, comedy,
history, pastoral, pastoral-comical, historical-pastoral, tragical-
historical, tragical-comical-historical-pastoral, scene individable,° or
poem unlimited.° Seneca° cannot be too heavy, nor Plautus° too light. 365
For the law of writ and the liberty,° these are the only men.

HAMLET: O Jephthah, judge of Israel,° what a treasure hadst thou!

POLONIUS: What a treasure had he, my lord?

---

342. **show fairly outwards:** Look cordial to outward appearances.   342–43. **entertainment:** A (warm) reception.   346. **north-north-west:** Only partly, at times.
347. **hawk, handsaw:** Mattock (or *hack*) and a carpenter's cutting tool respectively;
also birds, with a play on *hernshaw* or heron.   350. **swaddling-clouts:** Cloths in
which to wrap a newborn baby.   351. **Happily:** Haply, perhaps.   356. **Roscius:**
A famous Roman actor who died in 62 B.C.   359. **Buzz:** An interjection used to
denote stale news.   364. **scene individable:** A play observing the unity of place.
365. **poem unlimited:** A play disregarding the unities of time and place.
Seneca: Writer of Latin tragedies.   **Plautus:** Writer of Latin comedy.
366. **law . . . liberty:** Dramatic composition both according to rules and without
rules, i.e., "classical" and "romantic" dramas.   367. **Jephthah . . . Israel:**
Jephthah had to sacrifice his daughter; see Judges 11. Hamlet goes on to quote
from a ballad on the theme.

HAMLET: Why,
 "One fair daughter, and no more,   370
 The which he loved passing° well."
POLONIUS [*aside*]: Still on my daughter.
HAMLET: Am I not i' th' right, old Jephthah?
POLONIUS: If you call me Jephthah, my lord, I have a daughter that I love
 passing well.   375
HAMLET: Nay, that follows not.
POLONIUS: What follows, then, my lord?
HAMLET: Why,
 "As by lot, God wot,"°
 and then, you know,   380
 "It came to pass, as most like° it was."
 The first row° of the pious chanson° will show you more, for look
  where my abridgement° comes.

(*Enter the Players.*)

You are welcome, masters; welcome, all. I am glad to see thee well.
Welcome, good friends. O, old friend! Why, thy face is valanc'd° since I   385
saw thee last. Com'st thou to beard° me in Denmark? What, my young
lady° and mistress? By 'r lady, your ladyship is nearer to heaven than
when I saw you last, by the altitude of a chopine.° Pray God your
voice, like a piece of uncurrent° gold, be not crack'd within the ring.°
Masters, you are all welcome. We'll e'en to 't like French falconers, fly   390
at anything we see. We'll have a speech straight.° Come, give us a taste
of your quality; come, a passionate speech.
FIRST PLAYER: What speech, my good lord?
HAMLET: I heard thee speak me a speech once, but it was never acted, or,
if it was, not above once, for the play, I remember, pleas'd not the mil-   395
lion; 'twas caviary to the general.° But it was—as I receiv'd it, and others, whose judgments in such matters cried in the top of° mine—an

---

371. passing: Surpassingly.   **379. wot:** Knows.   **381. like:** Likely, probable.
382. row: Stanza.   **chanson:** Ballad, song.   **383. my abridgement:** Something
that cuts short my conversation; also, a diversion.   **385. valanc'd:** Fringed (with a
beard).   **386. beard:** Confront (with obvious pun).   **386–87. young lady:** Boy
playing women's parts.   **388. chopine:** Thick-soled shoe of Italian fashion.
389. uncurrent: Not passable as lawful coinage.   **crack'd . . . ring:** Changed
from adolescent to male voice, no longer suitable for women's roles. (Coins fea-
tured rings enclosing the sovereign's head; if the coin was cracked within this ring,
it was unfit for currency.)   **391. straight:** At once.   **396. caviary to the general:**
Caviar to the multitude, i.e., a choice dish too elegant for coarse tastes.
397. cried in the top of: Spoke with greater authority than.

excellent play, well digested in the scenes, set down with as much
modesty as cunning.° I remember one said there were no sallets° in
the lines to make the matter savory, nor no matter in the phrase that   400
might indict° the author of affectation, but call'd it an honest method,
as wholesome as sweet, and by very much more handsome than fine.°
One speech in 't I chiefly lov'd: 'twas Aeneas' tale to Dido, and there-
about of it especially when he speaks of Priam's slaughter.° If it live in
your memory, begin at this line: let me see, let me see —   405
"The rugged Pyrrhus,° like th' Hyrcanian beast"° —
'Tis not so. It begins with Pyrrhus:
"The rugged Pyrrhus, he whose sable° arms,
Black as his purpose, did the night resemble
When he lay couched in the ominous horse,°   410
Hath now this dread and black complexion smear'd
With heraldry more dismal.° Head to foot
Now is he total gules,° horridly trick'd°
With blood of fathers, mothers, daughters, sons,
Bak'd and impasted° with the parching streets,°   415
That lend a tyrannous and a damned light
To their lord's° murder. Roasted in wrath and fire,
And thus o'er-sized° with coagulate gore,
With eyes like carbuncles, the hellish Pyrrhus
Old grandsire Priam seeks."   420
So proceed you.
POLONIUS: 'Fore God, my lord, well spoken, with good accent and good
  discretion.
FIRST PLAYER: "Anon he finds him
  Striking too short at Greeks. His antique sword,   425
  Rebellious to his arm, lies where it falls,
  Repugnant° to command. Unequal match'd,

---

399. cunning: Skill. **sallets:** Salad, i.e., spicy improprieties. **401. indict:**
Convict. **402. fine:** Elaborately ornamented, showy. **404. Priam's slaughter:**
The slaying of the ruler of Troy, when the Greeks finally took the city.
406. Pyrrhus: A Greek hero in the Trojan War, also known as Neoptolemus, son
of Achilles. **Hyrcanian beast:** I.e., the tiger. (See Virgil, *Aeneid*, IV, 266; compare the whole speech with Marlowe's *Dido Queen of Carthage*, II, I, 214 ff.)
408. sable: Black (for reasons of camouflage during the episode of the Trojan
horse). **410. ominous horse:** Trojan horse, by which the Greeks gained access
to Troy. **412. dismal:** Ill-omened. **413. gules:** Red (a heraldic term). **trick'd:**
Adorned, decorated. **415. impasted:** Crusted, like a thick paste. **with . . .
streets:** By the parching heat of the streets (because of the fires everywhere).
417. their lord's: Priam's. **418. o'er-sized:** Covered as with size or glue.
427. Repugnant: Disobedient, resistant.

Pyrrhus at Priam drives, in rage strikes wide,
But with the whiff and wind of his fell° sword
Th' unnerved father falls. [Then senseless Ilium,°]   430
Seeming to feel this blow, with flaming top
Stoops to his° base, and with a hideous crash
Takes prisoner Pyrrhus' ear. For, lo! His sword,
Which was declining on the milky head
Of reverend Priam, seem'd i' th' air to stick.   435
So as a painted° tyrant Pyrrhus stood,
And, like a neutral to his will and matter,°
Did nothing.
But, as we often see, against° some storm,
A silence in the heavens, the rack° stand still,   440
The bold winds speechless, and the orb below
As hush as death, anon the dreadful thunder
Doth rend the region,° so, after Pyrrhus' pause,
Aroused vengeance sets him new a-work,
And never did the Cyclops'° hammers fall   445
On Mars's armor forg'd for proof eterne°
With less remorse than Pyrrhus' bleeding sword
Now falls on Priam.
Out, out, thou strumpet Fortune! All you gods,
In general synod,° take away her power!   450
Break all the spokes and fellies° from her wheel,
And bowl the round nave° down the hill of heaven,
As low as to the fiends!"
POLONIUS: This is too long.
HAMLET: It shall to the barber's with your beard.—Prithee say on. He's   455
    for a jig° or a tale of bawdry, or he sleeps. Say on, come to Hecuba.°
FIRST PLAYER: "But who, ah woe! had seen the mobled° queen"—
HAMLET: "The mobled queen?"
POLONIUS: That's good. "Mobled queen" is good.
FIRST PLAYER: "Run barefoot up and down, threat'ning the flames   460
    With bisson rheum,° a clout° upon that head

429. fell: Cruel. **430. senseless Ilium:** Insensate Troy. **432. his:** Its.
436. painted: Painted in a picture. **437. like . . . matter:** As though poised inde-
cisively between his intention and its fulfillment. **439. against:** Just before.
440. rack: Mass of clouds. **443. region:** Sky. **445. Cyclops:** Giant armor
makers in the smithy of Vulcan. **450. synod:** Assembly. **451. fellies:** Pieces of wood forming the rim
of a wheel. **452. nave:** Hub. **456. jig:** Comic song and dance often given at
the end of a play. **Hecuba:** Wife of Priam. **457. mobled:** Muffled. **461. bis-
son rheum:** Blinding tears. **clout:** Cloth.

Where late the diadem stood, and for a robe,
About her lank and all o'er-teemed° loins,
A blanket, in the alarm of fear caught up—
Who this had seen, with tongue in venom steep'd,   465
'Gainst Fortune's state° would treason have pronounc'd.°
But if the gods themselves did see her then
When she saw Pyrrhus make malicious sport
In mincing with his sword her husband's limbs,
The instant burst of clamor that she made,   470
Unless things mortal move them not at all,
Would have made milch° the burning eyes of heaven,
And passion in the gods."

POLONIUS: Look whe'er° he has not turn'd his color and has tears in 's
eyes. Prithee, no more.   475

HAMLET: 'Tis well; I'll have thee speak out the rest of this soon. Good my
lord, will you see the players well bestow'd?° Do you hear, let them be
well us'd, for they are the abstract° and brief chronicles of the time.
After your death you were better have a bad epitaph than their ill
report while you live.   480

POLONIUS: My lord, I will use them according to their desert.

HAMLET: God's bodkin,° man, much better! Use every man after his
desert, and who shall scape whipping? Use them after your own honor
and dignity. The less they deserve, the more merit is in your bounty.
Take them in.   485

POLONIUS: Come, sirs.

HAMLET: Follow him, friends. We'll hear a play tomorrow. [*As they start to
leave, Hamlet detains the First Player.*] Dost thou hear me, old friend? Can
you play the Murder of Gonzago?

FIRST PLAYER: Ay, my lord.   490

HAMLET: We'll ha 't tomorrow night. You could, for need, study a speech
of some dozen or sixteen lines, which I would set down and insert in 't,
could you not?

FIRST PLAYER: Ay, my lord.

HAMLET: Very well. Follow that lord, and look you mock him not.—My 495
good friends, I'll leave you till night. You are welcome to Elsinore.

(*Exeunt Polonius and Players.*)

---

463. o'er-teemed: Worn out with bearing children.   466. state: Rule, managing.
pronounc'd: Proclaimed.   472. milch: Milky moist with tears.   474. whe'er:
Whether.   477.   bestow'd: Lodged.   478.   abstract: Summary   account.
482. God's bodkin: By God's (Christ's) little body, *bodykin* (not to be confused
with *bodkin*, dagger).

ROSENCRANTZ: Good my lord!

(Exeunt [Rosencrantz and Guildenstern].)

HAMLET: Ay, so, God buy you.—Now I am alone.
O, what a rogue and peasant slave am I!
Is it not monstrous that this player here,   500
But in a fiction, in a dream of passion,
Could force his soul so to his own conceit°
That from her working all his visage wann'd,°
Tears in his eyes, distraction in his aspect,
A broken voice, and his whole function suiting   505
With forms to his conceit?° And all for nothing!
For Hecuba!
What's Hecuba to him, or he to Hecuba,
That he should weep for her? What would he do,
Had he the motive and the cue for passion   510
That I have? He would drown the stage with tears
And cleave the general ear with horrid speech,
Make mad the guilty and appall the free,°
Confound the ignorant, and amaze indeed
The very faculties of eyes and ears. Yet I,   515
A dull and muddy-mettled° rascal, peak,°
Like John-a-dreams,° unpregnant of° my cause,
And can say nothing—no, not for a king
Upon whose property° and most dear life
A damn'd defeat was made. Am I a coward?   520
Who calls me villain? Breaks my pate across?
Plucks off my beard, and blows it in my face?
Tweaks me by the nose? Gives me the lie° i' th' throat,
As deep as to the lungs? Who does me this?
Ha, 'swounds, I should take it; for it cannot be   525
But I am pigeon-liver'd,° and lack gall
To make oppression bitter, or ere this
I should have fatted all the region kites°
With this slave's offal. Bloody, bawdy villain!

---

502. conceit: Conception. **503. wann'd:** Grew pale. **505–06. his whole . . . conceit:** His whole being responded with actions to suit his thought. **513. free:** Innocent. **516. muddy-mettled:** Dull-spirited. **peak:** Mope, pine. **517. John-a-dreams:** Sleepy dreaming idler. **unpregnant of:** Not quickened by. **519. property:** The crown; perhaps also character, quality. **523. Gives me the lie:** Calls me a liar. **526. pigeon-liver'd:** The pigeon or dove was popularly supposed to be mild because it secreted no gall. **528. region kites:** Kites (birds of prey) of the air, from the vicinity.

Remorseless, treacherous, lecherous, kindless° villain!   530
[O, vengeance!]
Why, what an ass am I! This is most brave,
That I, the son of a dear father murder'd,
Prompted to my revenge by heaven and hell,
Must, like a whore, unpack my heart with words,   535
And fall a-cursing, like a very drab,°
A stallion!° Fie upon 't, foh! About,° my brains!
Hum, I have heard
That guilty creatures sitting at a play
Have by the very cunning of the scene   540
Been struck so to the soul that presently°
They have proclaim'd their malefactions;
For murder, though it have no tongue, will speak
With most miraculous organ. I'll have these players
Play something like the murder of my father   545
Before mine uncle. I'll observe his looks;
I'll tent° him to the quick. If 'a do blench,°
I know my course. The spirit that I have seen
May be the devil, and the devil hath power
T' assume a pleasing shape; yea, and perhaps   550
Out of my weakness and my melancholy,
As he is very potent with such spirits,°
Abuses° me to damn me. I'll have grounds
More relative° than this. The play's the thing
Wherein I'll catch the conscience of the King.   555

(*Exit.*)

{ACT III   *Scene 1*}°

(*Enter King, Queen, Polonius, Ophelia, Rosencrantz, Guildenstern, Lords.*)

KING: And can you, by no drift of conference,°
   Get from him why he puts on this confusion,

---

530. kindless: Unnatural.   **536. drab:** Prostitute.   **537. stallion:** Prostitute
(male or female). (Many editors follow the Folio reading of *scullion.*)   **About:**
About it, to work.   **541. presently:** At once.   **547. tent:** Probe.   **blench:** Quail,
flinch.   **552.   spirits:** Humors   (of   melancholy).   **553.   Abuses:** Deludes.
554. relative: Closely related, pertinent.   III, I. **Location:** The castle.   **1. drift
of conference:** Direction of conversation.

Grating so harshly all his days of quiet
With turbulent and dangerous lunacy?
ROSENCRANTZ: He does confess he feels himself distracted,   5
But from what cause 'a will by no means speak.
GUILDENSTERN: Nor do we find him forward° to be sounded,°
But with a crafty madness keeps aloof
When we would bring him on to some confession
Of his true state.
QUEEN: Did he receive you well?   10
ROSENCRANTZ: Most like a gentleman.
GUILDENSTERN: But with much forcing of his disposition.°
ROSENCRANTZ: Niggard of question,° but of our demands
Most free in his reply.
QUEEN: Did you assay° him
To any pastime?   15
ROSENCRANTZ: Madam, it so fell out that certain players
We o'er-raught° on the way. Of these we told him,
And there did seem in him a kind of joy
To hear of it. They are here about the court,
And, as I think, they have already order   20
This night to play before him.
POLONIUS: 'Tis most true,
And he beseech'd me to entreat your Majesties
To hear and see the matter.
KING: With all my heart, and it doth much content me
To hear him so inclin'd.   25
Good gentlemen, give him a further edge,°
And drive his purpose into these delights.
ROSENCRANTZ: We shall, my lord.

                    (*Exeunt Rosencrantz and Guildenstern.*)

KING: Sweet Gertrude, leave us too,
For we have closely° sent for Hamlet hither,
That he, as 'twere by accident, may here   30
Affront° Ophelia.
Her father and myself, [lawful espials,°]
Will so bestow ourselves that seeing, unseen,
We may of their encounter frankly judge,

---

7. forward: Willing. **sounded:** Tested deeply. **12. disposition:** Inclination.
13. question: Conversation. **14. assay:** Try to win. **17. o'er-raught:** Overtook
and passed. **26. edge:** Incitement. **29. closely:** Privately. **31. Affront:** Confront, meet. **32. espials:** Spies.

And gather by him, as he is behav'd,   35
    If 't be th' affliction of his love or no
    That thus he suffers for.
QUEEN: I shall obey you.
    And for your part, Ophelia, I do wish
    That your good beauties be the happy cause
    Of Hamlet's wildness. So shall I hope your virtues   40
    Will bring him to his wonted way again,
    To both your honors.
OPHELIA: Madam, I wish it may.

                                              [*Exit Queen.*]

POLONIUS: Ophelia, walk you here.—Gracious,° so please you,
    We will bestow ourselves. [*To Ophelia.*] Read on this book,
                                          [*Gives her a book.*]
    That show of such an exercise° may color°   45
    Your loneliness. We are oft to blame in this—
    'Tis too much prov'd°—that with devotion's visage
    And pious action we do sugar o'er
    The devil himself.
KING [*aside*]: O, 'tis too true!   50
    How smart a lash that speech doth give my conscience!
    The harlot's cheek, beautied with plast'ring art,
    Is not more ugly to° the thing° that helps it
    Than is my deed to my most painted word.
    O heavy burden!   55
POLONIUS: I hear him coming. Let's withdraw, my lord.
                          [*King and Polonius withdraw.°*]

(*Enter Hamlet.* [*Ophelia pretends to read a book.*])

HAMLET: To be, or not to be, that is the question:
    Whether 'tis nobler in the mind to suffer
    The slings and arrows of outrageous fortune,
    Or to take arms against a sea of troubles,   60
    And by opposing end them. To die, to sleep—
    No more—and by a sleep to say we end

43. Gracious: Your Grace (i.e., the King).   **45. exercise:** Act of devotion. (The book
she reads is one of devotion.)   **color:** Give a plausible appearance to.   **47. too
much prov'd:** Too often shown to be true, too often practiced.   **53. to:** Compared
to.   **thing:** I.e., the cosmetic.   [s.d.] *withdraw:* The King and Polonius may retire
behind an arras. The stage directions specify that they "enter" again near the end
of the scene.

The heart-ache and the thousand natural shocks
That flesh is heir to. 'Tis a consummation
Devoutly to be wish'd. To die, to sleep;   65
To sleep, perchance to dream. Ay, there's the rub,°
For in that sleep of death what dreams may come
When we have shuffled° off this mortal coil,°
Must give us pause. There's the respect°
That makes calamity of so long life.°   70
For who would bear the whips and scorns of time,
Th' oppressor's wrong, the proud man's contumely,°
The pangs of despis'd° love, the law's delay,
The insolence of office,° and the spurns°
That patient merit of th' unworthy takes,   75
When he himself might his quietus° make
With a bare bodkin?° Who would fardels° bear,
To grunt and sweat under a weary life,
But that the dread of something after death,
The undiscover'd country from whose bourn°   80
No traveler returns, puzzles the will,
And makes us rather bear those ills we have
Than fly to others that we know not of?
Thus conscience does make cowards of us all
And thus the native hue° of resolution   85
Is sicklied o'er with the pale cast° of thought,
And enterprises of great pitch° and moment°
With this regard° their currents° turn awry,
And lose the name of action. — Soft you now,
The fair Ophelia. Nymph, in thy orisons°   90
Be all my sins rememb'red.
OPHELIA: Good my lord,
How does your honor for this many a day?
HAMLET: I humbly thank you; well, well, well.
OPHELIA: My lord, I have remembrances of yours,
That I have longed long to re-deliver.   95
I pray you, now receive them.   [*Offers tokens.*]

---

66. rub: Literally, an obstacle in the game of bowls. **68. shuffled:** Sloughed, cast. **coil:** Turmoil. **69. respect:** Consideration. **70. of . . . life:** So long-lived.
72. contumely: Insolent abuse. **73. despis'd:** Rejected. **74. office:** Officialdom.
spurns: Insults. **76. quietus:** Acquittance; here, death. **77. bodkin:** Dagger.
fardels: Burdens. **80. bourn:** Boundary. **85. native hue:** Natural color, complexion. **86. cast:** Shade of color. **87. pitch:** Height (as of a falcon's flight).
moment: Importance. **88. regard:** Respect, consideration. **currents:** Courses.
90. orisons: Prayers.

HAMLET: No, not I, I never gave you aught.
OPHELIA: My honor'd lord, you know right well you did,
    And with them words of so sweet breath compos'd
    As made these things more rich. Their perfume lost,   100
    Take these again, for to the noble mind
    Rich gifts wax poor when givers prove unkind.
    There, my lord.   [*Gives tokens.*]
HAMLET: Ha, ha! Are you honest?°
OPHELIA: My lord?   105
HAMLET: Are you fair?°
OPHELIA: What means your lordship?
HAMLET: That if you be honest and fair, your honesty° should admit no
    discourse° to your beauty.
OPHELIA: Could beauty, my lord, have better commerce° than with 110
    honesty?
HAMLET: Ay, truly, for the power of beauty will sooner transform honesty
    from what it is to a bawd than the force of honesty can translate
    beauty into his likeness. This was sometime° a paradox,° but now the
    time° gives it proof. I did love you once.   115
OPHELIA: Indeed, my lord, you made me believe so.
HAMLET: You should not have believ'd me, for virtue cannot so inocu-
    late° our old stock but we shall relish of it.° I lov'd you not.
OPHELIA: I was the more deceiv'd.
HAMLET: Get thee to a nunn'ry.° Why wouldst thou be a breeder of sin- 120
    ners? I am myself indifferent honest;° but yet I could accuse me of
    such things that it were better my mother had not borne me: I am very
    proud, revengeful, ambitious, with more offenses at my beck° than I
    have thoughts to put them in, imagination to give them shape, or time
    to act them in. What should such fellows as I do crawling between 125
    earth and heaven? We are arrant knaves, all; believe none of us. Go thy
    ways to a nunn'ry. Where's your father?
OPHELIA: At home, my lord.
HAMLET: Let the doors be shut upon him, that he may play the fool
    nowhere but in 's own house.   130
    Farewell.

---

104. honest: (1) Truthful; (2) chaste.   **106. fair:** (1) Beautiful; (2) just, honorable.   **108. your honesty:** Your chastity.   **109. discourse:** Familiar dealings.
110. commerce: Dealings.   **114. sometime:** Formerly.   **paradox:** A view opposite to commonly held opinion.   **114–15. the time:** The present age.
117–18. inoculate: Graft, be engrafted to.   **118. but . . . it:** That we do not still
have about us a taste of the old stock; i.e., retain our sinfulness.   **120. nunn'ry:**
(1) Convent, (2) brothel.   **121. indifferent honest:** Reasonably virtuous.
123. beck: Command.

OPHELIA: O, help him, you sweet heavens!

HAMLET: If thou dost marry, I'll give thee this plague for thy dowry: be
thou as chaste as ice, as pure as snow, thou shalt not escape calumny.
Get thee to a nunn'ry, farewell. Or, if thou wilt needs marry, marry a   135
fool, for wise men know well enough what monsters° you° make of
them. To a nunn'ry, go, and quickly too. Farewell.

OPHELIA: Heavenly powers, restore him!

HAMLET: I have heard of your paintings too, well enough. God hath
given you one face, and you make yourselves another. You jig,° and   140
amble, and you lisp, you nickname God's creatures, and make your
wantonness your ignorance.° Go to, I'll no more on 't; it hath made me
mad. I say, we will have no moe marriage. Those that are married
already — all but one — shall live. The rest shall keep as they are. To a
nunn'ry, go.   (*Exit.*)   145

OPHELIA: O, what a noble mind is here o'erthrown!
The courtier's, soldier's, scholar's, eye, tongue, sword,
Th' expectancy and rose of the fair state,°
The glass of fashion and the mold of form,°
Th' observ'd of all observers,° quite, quite down!   150
And I, of ladies most deject and wretched,
That suck'd the honey of his music vows,
Now see that noble and most sovereign reason,
Like sweet bells jangled, out of time and harsh,
That unmatch'd form and feature of blown° youth   155
Blasted with ecstasy.° O, woe is me,
T' have seen what I have seen, see what I see!

(*Enter King and Polonius.*)

KING: Love? His affections do not that way tend;
Nor what he spake, though it lack'd form a little,
Was not like madness. There's something in his soul,   160
O'er which his melancholy sits on brood,
And I do doubt° the hatch and the disclose°
Will be some danger; which for to prevent,
I have in quick determination

136. monsters: An allusion to the horns of a cuckold. you: You women.
140. jig: Dance and sing affectedly and wantonly. 141–42. make . . . ignorance:
Excuse your affection on the grounds of your ignorance. 148. Th' expectancy . . . state: The hope and ornament of the kingdom made fair (by him).
149. The glass . . . form: The mirror of fashion and the pattern of courtly behavior. 150. observ'd . . . observers: The center of attention and honor in the
court. 155. blown: Blooming. 156. ecstasy: Madness. 162. doubt: Fear.
disclose: Disclosure.

Thus set it down: he shall with speed to England,   165
For the demand of° our neglected tribute.
Haply the seas and countries different
With variable° objects shall expel
This something-settled° matter in his heart,
Whereon his brains still beating puts him thus   170
From fashion of himself.° What think you on 't?
POLONIUS: It shall do well. But yet do I believe
The origin and commencement of his grief
Sprung from neglected love. — How now, Ophelia?
You need not tell us what Lord Hamlet said;   175
We heard it all. — My lord, do as you please,
But, if you hold it fit, after the play
Let his queen mother all alone entreat him
To show his grief. Let her be round° with him;
And I'll be plac'd, so please you, in the ear   180
Of all their conference. If she find him not,
To England send him, or confine him where
Your wisdom best shall think.
KING: It shall be so.
Madness in great ones must not unwatch'd go.

                                                        (*Exeunt.*)

                    {*Scene II*}°

(*Enter Hamlet and three of the Players.*)

HAMLET: Speak the speech, I pray you, as I pronounc'd it to you, trip-
pingly on the tongue. But if you mouth it, as many of our players° do, I
had as lief the town-crier spoke my lines. Nor do not saw the air too
much with your hand, thus, but use all gently; for in the very torrent,
tempest, and, as I may say, whirlwind of your passion, you must   5
acquire and beget a temperance that may give it smoothness. O, it
offends me to the soul to hear a robustious° periwig-pated° fellow tear
a passion to tatters, to very rags, to split the ears of the groundlings,°
who for the most part are capable of° nothing but inexplicable dumb-

---

166. For ... of: To demand.   **168. variable:** Various.   **169. something-settled:**
Somewhat settled.   **171. From ... himself:** Out of his natural manner.
179. round: Blunt.   **III, II. Location:** The castle.   **2. our players:** Indefinite
use; i.e., *players nowadays.*   **7. robustious:** Violent, boisterous.   **periwig-pated:**
Wearing a wig.   **8. groundlings:** Spectators who paid least and stood in the yard
of the theater.   **9. capable of:** Susceptible of being influenced by.

shows and noise. I would have such a fellow whipp'd for o'er-doing   10
Termagant.° It out-herods Herod.° Pray you, avoid it.

FIRST PLAYER: I warrant your honor.

HAMLET: Be not too tame neither, but let your own discretion be your
tutor. Suit the action to the word, the word to the action, with this special observance, that you o'erstep not the modesty of nature. For any-   15
thing so o'erdone is from° the purpose of playing, whose end, both at
the first and now, was and is, to hold, as 't were, the mirror up to
nature, to show virtue her feature, scorn her own image, and the very
age and body of the time his° form and pressure.° Now this overdone,
or come tardy off,° though it makes the unskillful laugh, cannot but   20
make the judicious grieve, the censure of which one° must in your
allowance o'erweigh a whole theater of others. O, there be players that
I have seen play, and heard others praise, and that highly, not to speak
it profanely, that, neither having th' accent of Christians nor the gait of
Christian, pagan, nor man, have so strutted and bellow'd that I have   25
thought some of nature's journeymen° had made men and not made
them well, they imitated humanity so abominably.

FIRST PLAYER: I hope we have reform'd that indifferently° with us, sir.

HAMLET: O, reform it altogether. And let those that play your clowns
speak no more than is set down for them; for there be of them° that   30
will themselves laugh, to set on some quantity of barren° spectators to
laugh too, though in the mean time some necessary question of the
play be then to be consider'd. That's villainous, and shows a most pitiful ambition in the fool that uses it. Go, make you ready.

                                        [*Exeunt Players.*]

(*Enter Polonius, Guildenstern, and Rosencrantz.*)

How now, my lord? Will the King hear this piece of work?   35

POLONIUS: And the Queen too, and that presently.°

HAMLET: Bid the players make haste.

                                        [*Exit Polonius.*]

Will you two help to hasten them?

11. Termagant: A god of the Saracens; a character in the St. Nicholas play, where
one of his worshipers, leaving him in charge of goods, returns to find them stolen;
whereupon he beats the god or idol, which howls vociferously.   **Herod:** Herod of
Jewry. (A character in *The Slaughter of the Innocents* and other cycle plays. The
part was played with great noise and fury.)   **16. from:** Contrary to.   **19. his:** Its.
pressure: Stamp, impressed character.   **20. come tardy off:** Inadequately done.
21. the censure . . . one: The judgment of even one of whom.   **26. journeymen:**
Laborers not yet masters in their trade.   **28. indifferently:** Tolerably.   **30. of**
them: Some among them.   **31. barren:** I.e., of wit.   **36. presently:** At once.

ROSENCRANTZ: Ay, my lord.   (*Exeunt they two.*)
HAMLET: What ho, Horatio!

(*Enter Horatio.*)

HORATIO: Here, sweet lord, at your service.   40
HAMLET: Horatio, thou art e'en as just a man
  As e'er my conversation cop'd withal.°
HORATIO: O, my dear lord—
HAMLET: Nay, do not think I flatter;
  For what advancement may I hope from thee
  That no revenue hast but thy good spirits,   45
  To feed and clothe thee? Why should the poor be flatter'd?
  No, let the candied° tongue lick absurd pomp,
  And crook the pregnant° hinges of the knee
  Where thrift° may follow fawning. Dost thou hear?
  Since my dear soul was mistress of her choice   50
  And could of men distinguish her election,
  Sh' hath seal'd thee for herself, for thou hast been
  As one, in suff'ring all, that suffers nothing,
  A man that Fortune's buffets and rewards
  Hast ta'en with equal thanks; and blest are those   55
  Whose blood° and judgment are so well commeddled°
  That they are not a pipe for Fortune's finger
  To sound what stop° she please. Give me that man
  That is not passion's slave, and I will wear him
  In my heart's core, ay, in my heart of heart,   60
  As I do thee.—Something too much of this.—
  There is a play tonight before the King.
  One scene of it comes near the circumstance
  Which I have told thee of my father's death.
  I prithee, when thou seest that act afoot,   65
  Even with the very comment of thy soul°
  Observe my uncle. If his occulted° guilt
  Do not itself unkennel in one speech,
  It is a damned° ghost that we have seen,
  And my imaginations are as foul   70
  As Vulcan's stithy.° Give him heedful note,

---

42. my . . . withal: My contact with people provided opportunity for encounter
with.   47. candied: Sugared, flattering.   48. pregnant: Compliant.   49. thrift:
Profit.   56. blood: Passion. commeddled: Commingled.   58. stop: Hole in a
wind instrument for controlling the sound.   66. very . . . soul: Inward and saga-
cious criticism.   67. occulted: Hidden.   69. damned: In league with Satan.
71. stithy: Smithy, place of stiths (anvils).

For I mine eyes will rivet to his face,
And after we will both our judgments join
In censure of his seeming.°
HORATIO: Well, my lord.
If 'a steal aught the whilst this play is playing,   75
And scape detecting, I will pay the theft.

([*Flourish.*] *Enter trumpets and kettledrums, King, Queen, Polonius, Ophelia,*
[*Rosencrantz, Guildenstern, and other Lords, with Guards carrying torches*].)

HAMLET: They are coming to the play. I must be idle. Get you a place.

[*The King, Queen, and courtiers sit.*]

KING: How fares our cousin Hamlet?
HAMLET: Excellent, i' faith, of the chameleon's dish:° I eat the air, promise-
cramm'd. You cannot feed capons so.   80
KING: I have nothing with° this answer, Hamlet. These words are not
mine.°
HAMLET: No, nor mine now. [*To Polonius.*] My lord, you played once i' th'
university, you say?
POLONIUS: That did I, my lord; and was accounted a good actor.   85
HAMLET: What did you enact?
POLONIUS: I did enact Julius Caesar. I was killed i' th' Capitol; Brutus
kill'd me.
HAMLET: It was a brute part of him to kill so capital a calf there. Be the
players ready?   90
ROSENCRANTZ: Ay, my lord; they stay upon your patience.
QUEEN: Come hither, my dear Hamlet, sit by me.
HAMLET: No, good mother, here's metal more attractive.
POLONIUS [*to the King*]: O, ho, do you mark that?
HAMLET: Lady, shall I lie in your lap?   95

[*Lying down at Ophelia's feet.*]

OPHELIA: No, my lord.
[HAMLET: I mean, my head upon your lap?
OPHELIA: Ay, my lord.]
HAMLET: Do you think I meant country° matters?
OPHELIA: I think nothing, my lord.   100

---

74. censure of his seeming: Judgment of his appearance or behavior.
79. chameleon's dish: Chameleons were supposed to feed on air. Hamlet deliberately misinterprets the King's *fares* as *feeds*. By his phrase *eat the air* he also plays
on the idea of feeding himself with the promise of succession, of being the *heir.*
81. have . . . with: Make nothing of.   **81–82. are not mine:** Do not respond to
what I asked.   **99. country:** With a bawdy pun.

HAMLET: That's a fair thought to lie between maids' legs.
OPHELIA: What is, my lord?
HAMLET: Nothing.
OPHELIA: You are merry, my lord.
HAMLET: Who, I?   105
OPHELIA: Ay, my lord.
HAMLET: O God, your only jig-maker.° What should a man do but be
    merry? For look you how cheerfully my mother looks, and my father
    died within 's° two hours.
OPHELIA: Nay, 'tis twice two months, my lord.   110
HAMLET: So long? Nay then, let the devil wear black for I'll have a suit of
    sables.° O heavens! Die two months ago, and not forgotten yet? Then
    there's hope a great man's memory may outlive his life half a year. But,
    by 'r lady, 'a must build churches, then, or else shall 'a suffer not think-
    ing on,° with the hobby-horse, whose epitaph is "For, O, for, O, the   115
    hobby-horse is forgot."°

(*The trumpets sound. Dumb show follows.*)

(*Enter a King and a Queen* [*very lovingly*]; *the Queen embracing him, and he
her.* [*She kneels and makes show of protestation unto him.*] *He takes her up,
and declines his head upon her neck. He lies him down upon a bank of flowers.
She, seeing him asleep, leaves him. Anon comes in another man, takes off his
crown, kisses it, pours poison in the sleeper's ears, and leaves him. The Queen
returns; finds the King dead, makes passionate action. The Poisoner, with some
three or four, come in again, seem to condole with her. The dead body is carried
away. The Poisoner woos the Queen with gifts; she seems harsh awhile but in
the end accepts love.*)

                                                                    [*Exeunt.*]

OPHELIA: What means this, my lord?
HAMLET: Marry, this' miching mallecho;° it means mischief.
OPHELIA: Belike° this show imports the argument° of the play.

(*Enter Prologue.*)

---

107. only jig-maker: Very best composer of jigs (song and dance).   **109. within 's:**
Within this.   **111–12. suit of sables:** Garments trimmed with the fur of the sable
and hence suited for a wealthy person, not a mourner (with a pun on *sable* black).
114–15. suffer . . . on: Undergo oblivion.   **115–16. "For . . . forgot":** Verse of a
song occurring also in *Love's Labor's Lost*, III, I, 30. The hobby-horse was a character made up to resemble a horse, appearing in the Morris dance and such May-
game sports. This song laments the disappearance of such customs under
pressure from the Puritans.   **118. this' miching mallecho:** This is sneaking mischief.   **119. Belike:** Probably.   **argument:** Plot.

HAMLET: We shall know by this fellow. The players cannot keep counsel;° 120
  they'll tell all.
OPHELIA: Will 'a tell us what this show meant?
HAMLET: Ay, or any show that you will show him. Be not you° asham'd to
  show, he'll not shame to tell you what it means.
OPHELIA: You are naught, you are naught.° I'll mark the play.   125
PROLOGUE: For us, and for our tragedy,
      Here stooping° to your clemency,
      We beg your hearing patiently.   [*Exit.*]
HAMLET: Is this a prologue, or the posy of a ring?°
OPHELIA: 'Tis brief, my lord.   130
HAMLET: As woman's love.

(*Enter* [*two Players as*] *King and Queen.*)

PLAYER KING: Full thirty times hath Phoebus' cart° gone round
      Neptune's salt wash° and Tellus'° orbed ground,
      And thirty dozen moons with borrowed° sheen
      About the world have times twelve thirties been,   135
      Since love our hearts and Hymen° did our hands
      Unite commutual° in most sacred bands.
PLAYER QUEEN: So many journeys may the sun and moon
      Make us again count o'er ere love be done!
      But, woe is me, you are so sick of late,   140
      So far from cheer and from your former state,
      That I distrust you. Yet, though I distrust,°
      Discomfort you, my lord, it nothing° must.
      For women's fear and love hold quantity;°
      In neither aught, or in extremity.   145
      Now, what my love is, proof° hath made you know,
      And as my love is siz'd, my fear is so.
      Where love is great, the littlest doubts are fear;
      Where little fears grow great, great love grows there.
PLAYER KING: Faith, I must leave thee, love, and shortly too;   150
      My operant° powers their functions leave to do.°

---

120. counsel: Secret.   **123. Be not you:** If you are not.   **125. naught:** Indecent.
127. stooping: Bowing.   **129. posy . . . ring:** Brief motto in verse inscribed in a
ring.   **132. Phoebus' cart:** The sun god's chariot.   **133. salt wash:** The sea.
Tellus: Goddess of the earth, of the *orbed ground.*   **134. borrowed:** Reflected.
136. Hymen: God of matrimony.   **137. commutual:** Mutually.   **142. distrust:**
Am anxious about.   **143. nothing:** Not at all.   **144. hold quantity:** Keep proportion with one another.   **146. proof:** Experience.   **151. operant:** Active.   **leave
to do:** Cease to perform.

And thou shalt live in this fair world behind,
Honor'd, belov'd; and haply one as kind
For husband shalt thou—
PLAYER QUEEN: O, confound the rest!
　　Such love must needs be treason in my breast.   155
　　In second husband let me be accurst!
　　None wed the second but who kill'd the first.
HAMLET: Wormwood, wormwood.
PLAYER QUEEN: The instances° that second marriage move°
　　Are base respects of thrift,° but none of love.   160
　　A second time I kill my husband dead,
　　When second husband kisses me in bed.
PLAYER KING: I do believe you think what now you speak,
　　But what we do determine oft we break.
　　Purpose is but the slave to memory,°   165
　　Of violent birth, but poor validity,°
　　Which now, like fruit unripe, sticks on the tree,
　　But fall unshaken when they mellow be.
　　Most necessary 'tis that we forget
　　To pay ourselves what to ourselves is debt.°   170
　　What to ourselves in passion we propose,
　　The passion ending, doth the purpose lose.
　　The violence of either grief or joy
　　Their own enactures° with themselves destroy.
　　Where joy most revels, grief doth most lament;   175
　　Grief joys, joy grieves, on slender accident.
　　This world is not for aye,° nor 'tis not strange
　　That even our loves should with our fortunes change;
　　For 'tis a question left us yet to prove,
　　Whether love lead fortune, or else fortune love.   180
　　The great man down, you mark his favorite flies;
　　The poor advanc'd makes friends of enemies.
　　And hitherto doth love on fortune tend;
　　For who not needs° shall never lack a friend,
　　And who in want° a hollow friend doth try,°   185

---

159. **instances:** Motives.   **move:** Motivate.   160. **base . . . thrift:** Ignoble considerations of material prosperity.   165. **Purpose . . . memory:** Our good intentions   are   subject   to   forgetfulness.   166.   **validity:** Strength,   durability.
169–70. **Most . . . debt:** It's inevitable that in time we forget the obligations we
have   imposed   on   ourselves.   174. **enactures:** Fulfillments.   177. **aye:** Ever.
184. **who not needs:** He who is not in need (of wealth).   185. **who in want:** He
who is in need.   **try:** Test (his generosity).

Directly seasons him° his enemy.
But, orderly to end where I begun,
Our wills and fates do so contrary run
That our devices still° are overthrown;
Our thoughts are ours, their ends° none of our own.   190
So think thou wilt no second husband wed,
But die thy thoughts when thy first lord is dead.

PLAYER QUEEN: Nor earth to me give food, nor heaven light,
Sport and repose lock from me day and night,
To desperation turn my trust and hope,   195
An anchor's cheer° in prison be my scope!°
Each opposite° that blanks° the face of joy
Meet what I would have well and it destroy!
Both here and hence° pursue me lasting strife,
If, once a widow, ever I be wife!   200

HAMLET: If she should break it now!

PLAYER KING: 'Tis deeply sworn. Sweet, leave me here awhile;
My spirits grow dull, and fain I would beguile
The tedious day with sleep.   [*Sleeps.*]

PLAYER QUEEN: Sleep rock thy brain,
And never come mischance between us twain!   205

                                                 [*Exit.*]

HAMLET: Madam, how like you this play?

QUEEN: The lady doth protest too much, methinks.

HAMLET: O, but she'll keep her word.

KING: Have you heard the argument?° Is there no offense in 't?

HAMLET: No, no, they do but jest, poison in jest; no offense i' th' world.   210

KING: What do you call the play?

HAMLET: "The Mouse-trap." Marry, how? Tropically.° This play is the
image of a murder done in Vienna. Gonzago is the Duke's name; his
wife, Baptista. You shall see anon. 'Tis a knavish piece of work, but
what of that? Your Majesty, and we that have free° souls, it touches us   215
not. Let the gall'd jade° winch,° our withers° are unwrung.°

---

186. **seasons him:** Ripens him into.   189. **devices still:** Intentions continually.
190. **ends:** Results.   196. **anchor's cheer:** Anchorite's or hermit's fare.   **my
scope:** The extent of my happiness.   197. **opposite:** Adverse thing.   **blanks:**
Causes to blanch or grow pale.   199. **hence:** In the life hereafter.   209. **argument:**
Plot.   212. **Tropically:** Figuratively. (The first quarto reading, *trapically*, suggests a
pun on *trap* in *Mouse-trap.*)   215. **free:** Guiltless.   216. **gall'd jade:** Horse whose
hide is rubbed by saddle or harness.   **winch:** Wince.   **withers:** The part between
the horse's shoulder blades.   **unwrung:** Not rubbed sore.

(*Enter Lucianus.*)

This is one Lucianus, nephew to the King.

OPHELIA: You are as good as a chorus,° my lord.

HAMLET: I could interpret between you and your love, if I could see the
puppets dallying.°   220

OPHELIA: You are keen, my lord, you are keen.

HAMLET: It would cost you a groaning to take off mine edge.

OPHELIA: Still better, and worse.°

HAMLET: So° you mistake° your husbands. Begin, murderer, leave thy
damnable faces, and begin. Come, the croaking raven doth bellow for   225
revenge.

LUCIANUS: Thoughts black, hands apt, drugs fit, and time agreeing,
Confederate season,° else no creature seeing,
Thou mixture rank, of midnight weeds collected,
With Hecate's ban° thrice blasted, thrice infected,   230
Thy natural magic and dire property
On wholesome life usurp immediately.

[*Pours the poison into the sleeper's ears.*]

HAMLET: 'A poisons him i' th' garden for his estate. His name's Gonzago.
The story is extant, and written in very choice Italian. You shall see
anon how the murderer gets the love of Gonzago's wife.   235

[*Claudius rises.*]

OPHELIA: The King rises.

[HAMLET: What, frighted with false fire?°]

QUEEN: How fares my lord?

POLONIUS: Give o'er the play.

KING: Give me some light. Away!   240

POLONIUS: Lights, lights, lights!

(*Exeunt all but Hamlet and Horatio.*)

---

218. chorus: In many Elizabethan plays the forthcoming action was explained by
an actor known as the "chorus"; at a puppet show the actor who spoke the dialogue
was known as an "interpreter," as indicated by the lines following.   **220. dallying:**
With sexual suggestion, continued in *keen,* i.e., sexually aroused, *groaning,* i.e.,
moaning in pregnancy, and *edge,* i.e., sexual desire or impetuosity.   **223. Still . . .
worse:** More keen-witted and less decorous.   **224. So:** Even thus (in marriage).
mistake: Mistake, take erringly, falseheartedly.   **228. Confederate season:** The
time and occasion conspiring (to assist the murderer).   **230. Hecate's ban:** The
curse of Hecate, the goddess of witchcraft.   **237. false fire:** The blank discharge of
a gun loaded with powder but not shot.

HAMLET: "Why, let the strucken deer go weep,
    The hart ungalled° play.
For some must watch,° while some must sleep;
    Thus runs the world away."°   245
Would not this,° sir, and a forest of feathers°—if the rest of my for-
tunes turn Turk with° me—with two Provincial roses° on my raz'd°
shoes, get me a fellowship in a cry of players?°
HORATIO: Half a share.
HAMLET: A whole one, I.   250
"For thou dost know, O Damon dear,
    This realm dismantled° was
Of Jove himself, and now reigns here
    A very, very—pajock."°
HORATIO: You might have rhym'd.   255
HAMLET: O good Horatio, I'll take the ghost's word for a thousand
pound. Didst perceive?
HORATIO: Very well, my lord.
HAMLET: Upon the talk of pois'ning?
HORATIO: I did very well note him.   260
HAMLET: Ah, ha! Come, some music! Come, the recorders!°
"For if the King like not the comedy,
    Why then, belike, he likes it not, perdy"°
Come, some music!

(*Enter Rosencrantz and Guildenstern.*)

GUILDENSTERN: Good my lord, vouchsafe me a word with you.   265
HAMLET: Sir, a whole history.
GUILDENSTERN: The King, sir—
HAMLET: Ay, sir, what of him?
GUILDENSTERN: Is in his retirement marvelous distemp'red.
HAMLET: With drink, sir?   270

---

243. ungalled: Unafflicted. **244. watch:** Remain awake. **242–45. Why . . .
away:** Probably from an old ballad, with allusion to the popular belief that a
wounded deer retires to weep and die; cf. *As You Like It*, II, i, 66. **246. this:** The
play. **feathers:** Allusion to the plumes that Elizabethan actors were fond of
wearing. **247. turn Turk with:** Turn renegade against, go back on. **Provincial
roses:** Rosettes of ribbon like the roses of a part of France. **raz'd:** With orna-
mental slashing. **248. fellowship . . . players:** Partnership in a theatrical company. **252. dismantled:** Stripped, divested. **254. pajock:** Peacock, a bird with
a bad reputation (here substituted for the obvious rhyme-word *ass*). **261. recorders:** Wind instruments like the flute. **263. perdy:** A corruption of
the French *par dieu*, by God.

GUILDENSTERN: No, my lord, with choler.°

HAMLET: Your wisdom should show itself more richer to signify this to the doctor, for for me to put him to his purgation would perhaps plunge him into more choler.

GUILDENSTERN: Good my lord, put your discourse into some frame° and start not so wildly from my affair.   275

HAMLET: I am tame, sir. Pronounce.

GUILDENSTERN: The Queen, your mother, in most great affliction of spirit, hath sent me to you.

HAMLET: You are welcome.   280

GUILDENSTERN: Nay, good my lord, this courtesy is not of the right breed. If it shall please you to make me a wholesome answer, I will do your mother's commandment; if not, your pardon° and my return shall be the end of my business.

HAMLET: Sir, I cannot.   285

ROSENCRANTZ: What, my lord?

HAMLET: Make you a wholesome answer; my wit's diseas'd. But, sir, such answer as I can make, you shall command, or rather, as you say, my mother. Therefore no more, but to the matter. My mother, you say—

ROSENCRANTZ: Then thus she says: your behavior hath struck her into   290 amazement and admiration.°

HAMLET: O wonderful son, that can so stonish a mother! But is there no sequel at the heels of this mother's admiration? Impart.

ROSENCRANTZ: She desires to speak with you in her closet,° ere you go to bed.   295

HAMLET: We shall obey, were she ten times our mother. Have you any further trade with us?

ROSENCRANTZ: My lord, you once did love me.

HAMLET: And do still, by these pickers and stealers.°

ROSENCRANTZ: Good my lord, what is your cause of distemper? You do   300 surely bar the door upon your own liberty, if you deny your griefs to your friend.

HAMLET: Sir, I lack advancement.

ROSENCRANTZ: How can that be, when you have the voice of the King himself for your succession in Denmark?   305

---

271. choler: Anger. (But Hamlet takes the word in its more basic humors sense of *bilious disorder*.)   **275. frame:** Order.   **283. pardon:** Permission to depart.   **291. admiration:** Wonder.   **294. closet:** Private chamber.   **299. pickers and stealers:** Hands (so called from the catechism, "to keep my hands from picking and stealing").

HAMLET: Ay, sir, but "While the grass grows"°—the proverb is some-
thing° musty.

(*Enter the Players with recorders.*)

O, the recorders! Let me see one. [*He takes a recorder.*] To withdraw°
with you: why do you go about to recover the wind° of me, as if you
would drive me into a toil?°   310

GUILDENSTERN: O, my lord, if my duty be too bold, my love is too
unmannerly.°

HAMLET: I do not well understand that. Will you play upon this pipe?

GUILDENSTERN: My lord, I cannot.

HAMLET: I pray you.   315

GUILDENSTERN: Believe me, I cannot.

HAMLET: I do beseech you.

GUILDENSTERN: I know no touch of it, my lord.

HAMLET: It is as easy as lying. Govern these ventages° with your fingers
and thumb, give it breath with your mouth, and it will discourse most   320
eloquent music. Look you, these are the stops.

GUILDENSTERN: But these cannot I command to any utt'rance of harmony; I have not the skill.

HAMLET: Why, look you now, how unworthy a thing you make of me! You
would play upon me, you would seem to know my stops, you would   325
pluck out the heart of my mystery, you would sound me from my low-
est note to the top of my compass,° and there is much music, excellent
voice, in this little organ,° yet cannot you make it speak. 'Sblood, do
you think I am easier to be play'd on than a pipe? Call me what instrument you will, though you can fret° me, you cannot play upon me.   330

(*Enter Polonius.*)

God bless you, sir!

POLONIUS: My lord, the Queen would speak with you, and presently.°

HAMLET: Do you see yonder cloud that's almost in shape of a camel?

POLONIUS: By th' mass, and 'tis like a camel, indeed.

HAMLET: Methinks it is like a weasel.   335

306. Whil . . . grows: The rest of the proverb is "the silly horse starves"; Hamlet
may not live long enough to succeed to the kingdom. **306–07. something:**
Somewhat. **308. withdraw:** Speak privately. **309. recover the wind:** Get the
windward side. **310. toil:** Snare. **311–12. if . . . unmannerly:** If I am using an
unmannerly boldness, it is my love that occasions it. **319. ventages:** Stops of the
recorder. **327. compass:** Range (of voice). **328. organ:** Musical instrument.
330. fret: Irritate (with a quibble on *fret* meaning the piece of wood, gut, or metal
that regulates the fingering on an instrument). **332. presently:** At once.

POLONIUS: It is back'd like a weasel.
HAMLET: Or like a whale?
POLONIUS: Very like a whale.
HAMLET: Then I will come to my mother by and by.° [*Aside.*] They fool
    me° to the top of my bent.° —I will come by and by.   340
POLONIUS: I will say so.   [*Exit.*]
HAMLET: "By and by" is easily said. Leave me, friends.

                                  [*Exeunt all but Hamlet.*]

'Tis now the very witching time° of night,
When churchyards yawn and hell itself breathes out
Contagion to this world. Now could I drink hot blood,   345
And do such bitter business as the day
Would quake to look on. Soft, now to my mother.
O heart, lose not thy nature! Let not ever
The soul of Nero° enter this firm bosom.
Let me be cruel, not unnatural;   350
I will speak daggers to her, but use none.
My tongue and soul in this be hypocrites:
How in my words somever° she be shent,°
To give them seals° never, my soul, consent!

                                    (*Exit.*)

                    [*Scene III*]°

(*Enter King, Rosencrantz, and Guildenstern.*)

KING: I like him not, nor stands it safe with us
    To let his madness range. Therefore prepare you.
    I your commission will forthwith dispatch,°
    And he to England shall along with you.
    The terms° of our estate° may not endure   5
    Hazard so near 's as doth hourly grow
    Out of his brows.°

---

339. by and by: Immediately.   **339–40. fool me:** Make me play the fool.
340. top of my bent: Limit of my ability or endurance (literally, the extent to which
a bow may be bent).   **343. witching time:** Time when spells are cast and evil is
abroad.   **349. Nero:** Murderer of his mother, Agrippina.   **353. How . . . somever:**
However much by my words.   **shent:** Rebuked.   **354. give them seals:** Confirm
them with deeds.   **III, III. Location:** The castle.   **3. dispatch:** Prepare, cause to
be drawn up.   **5. terms:** Condition, circumstances.   **our estate:** My royal position.   **7. brows:** Effronteries, threatening frowns (?), brain (?).

GUILDENSTERN: We will ourselves provide.
Most holy and religious fear it is
To keep those many many bodies safe
That live and feed upon your Majesty.   10
ROSENCRANTZ: The single and peculiar° life is bound
With all the strength and armor of the mind
To keep itself from noyance,° but much more
That spirit upon whose weal depends and rests
The lives of many. The cess° of majesty   15
Dies not alone, but like a gulf° doth draw
What's near it with it; or it is a messy wheel
Fix'd on the summit of the highest mount,
To whose huge spokes ten thousand lesser things
Are mortis'd and adjoin'd, which, when it falls,   20
Each small annexment, petty consequence,
Attends° the boist'rous ruin. Never alone
Did the King sigh, but with a general groan.
KING: Arm° you, I pray you, to this speedy voyage,
For we will fetters put about this fear,   25
Which now goes too free-footed.
ROSENCRANTZ: We will haste us.

          (Exeunt Gentlemen [Rosencrantz and Guildenstern].)

(Enter Polonius.)

POLONIUS: My lord, he's going to his mother's closet.
Behind the arras° I'll convey myself
To hear the process.° I'll warrant she'll tax him home,°
And, as you said, and wisely was it said,   30
'Tis meet that some more audience than a mother,
Since nature makes them partial, should o'erhear
The speech, of vantage.° Fare you well, my liege.
I'll call upon you ere you go to bed,
And tell you what I know.
KING: Thanks, dear my lord.   35

                    (Exit [Polonius].)

---

11. single and peculiar: Individual and private. **13. noyance:** Harm. **15. cess:**
Decease. **16. gulf:** Whirlpool. **22. Attends:** Participates in. **24. Arm:** Prepare.
28. arras: Screen of tapestry placed around the walls of household apartments.
(On the Elizabethan stage, the arras was presumably over a door or discovery
space in the tiring-house façade.) **29. process:** Proceedings. **tax him home:**
Reprove him severely. **33. of vantage:** From an advantageous place.

O, my offense is rank, it smells to heaven;
It hath the primal eldest curse° upon 't,
A brother's murder. Pray can I not,
Though inclination be as sharp as will.°
My stronger guilt defeats my strong intent,   40
And, like a man to double business bound,
I stand in pause where I shall first begin,
And both neglect. What if this cursed hand
Were thicker than itself with brother's blood,
Is there not rain enough in the sweet heavens   45
To wash it white as snow? Whereto serves mercy
But to confront the visage of offense?°
And what's in prayer but this twofold force,
To be forestalled° ere we come to fall,
Or pardon'd being down? Then I'll look up;   50
My fault is past. But, O, what form of prayer .
Can serve my turn? "Forgive me my foul murder"?
That cannot be, since I am still possess'd
Of those effects for which I did the murder,
My crown, mine own ambition, and my queen.   55
May one be pardon'd and retain th' offense?
In the corrupted currents° of this world
Offense's gilded hand° may shove by justice,
And oft 'tis seen the wicked prize° itself
Buys out the law. But 'tis not so above.   60
There is no shuffling,° there the action lies°
In his° true nature, and we ourselves compell'd,
Even to the teeth and forehead° of our faults,
To give in evidence. What then? What rests?°
Try what repentance can. What can it not?   65
Yet what can it, when one cannot repent?
O wretched state! O bosom black as death!
O limed° soul, that, struggling to be free,

37. **primal eldest curse:** The curse of Cain, the first murderer; he killed his brother Abel.   39. **Though . . . will:** Though my desire is as strong as my determination.   46–47. **Whereto . . . offense:** For what function does mercy serve other than to undo the effects of sin?   49. **forestalled:** Prevented (from sinning).   57. **currents:** Courses.   58. **gilded hand:** Hand offering gold as a bribe.   59. **wicked prize:** Prize won by wickedness.   61. **shuffling:** Escape by trickery. **the action lies:** The accusation is made manifest, comes up for consideration (a legal metaphor).   62. **his:** Its.   63. **teeth and forehead:** Face to face, concealing nothing.   64. **rests:** Remains.   68. **limed:** Caught as with birdlime, a sticky substance used to ensnare birds.

Art more engag'd!° Help, angels! Make assay.°
Bow, stubborn knees, and heart with strings of steel,   70
Be soft as sinews of the new-born babe!
All may be well.

                                                                      [*He kneels.*]

(*Enter Hamlet* [*with sword drawn*].)

HAMLET: Now might I do it pat,° now 'a is a-praying;
    And now I'll do 't. And so 'a goes to heaven;
    And so am I reveng'd. That would be scann'd:°   75
    A villain kills my father, and for that,
    I, his sole son, do this same villain send
    To heaven.
    Why, this is hire and salary, not revenge.
    'A took my father grossly,° full of bread,°   80
    With all his crimes broad blown,° as flush° as May;
    And how his audit° stands who knows save heaven?
    But in our circumstance and course° of thought,
    'Tis heavy with him. And am I then reveng'd,
    To take him in the purging of his soul,   85
    When he is fit and season'd for his passage?
    No!
    Up, sword, and know thou a more horrid hent.°

                                                              [*Puts up his sword.*]

    When he is drunk asleep, or in his rage,
    Or in th' incestuous pleasure of his bed,   90
    At game a-swearing, or about some act
    That has no relish of salvation in 't—
    Then trip him, that his heels may kick at heaven,
    And that his soul may be as damn'd and black
    As hell, whereto it goes. My mother stays.   95
    This physic° but prolongs thy sickly days.   (*Exit.*)
KING: My words fly up, my thoughts remain below.
    Words without thoughts never to heaven go.

                                                                      (*Exit.*)

---

69. engag'd: Embedded. **assay:** Trial. **73. pat:** Opportunely. **75. would be scann'd:** Needs to be looked into. **80. grossly:** Not spiritually prepared. **full of bread:** Enjoying his worldly pleasures. (See Ezek. 16:49.) **81. crimes broad blown:** Sins in full bloom. **flush:** Lusty. **82. audit:** Account. **83. in . . . course:** As we see it in our mortal situation. **88. know . . . hent:** Await to be grasped by me on a more horrid occasion. **96. physic:** Purging (by prayer).

{*Scene IV*}°

(*Enter* [*Queen*] *Gertrude and Polonius.*)

POLONIUS: 'A will come straight. Look you lay° home to him.
  Tell him his pranks have been too broad° to bear with,
  And that your Grace hath screen'd and stood between
  Much heat° and him. I'll sconce° me even here.
  Pray you, be round° [with him.   5
HAMLET (*within*): Mother, mother, mother!]
QUEEN: I'll warrant you, fear me not.
  Withdraw, I hear him coming.

                                              [*Polonius hides behind the arras.*]

(*Enter Hamlet.*)

HAMLET: Now, mother, what's the matter?
QUEEN: Hamlet, thou hast thy father° much offended.   10
HAMLET: Mother, you have my father much offended.
QUEEN: Come, come, you answer with an idle° tongue.
HAMLET: Go, go, you question with a wicked tongue.
QUEEN: Why, how now, Hamlet?
HAMLET: What's the matter now?
QUEEN: Have you forgot me?
HAMLET: No, by the rood,° not so: 15
  You are the Queen, your husband's brother's wife
  And—would it were not so!—you are my mother.
QUEEN: Nay, then, I'll set those to you that can speak.
HAMLET: Come, come, and sit you down; you shall not budge.
  You go not till I set you up a glass   20
  Where you may see the inmost part of you.
QUEEN: What wilt thou do? Thou wilt not murder me?
  Help, ho!
POLONIUS [*behind*]: What, ho! Help!
HAMLET [*drawing*]: How now? A rat? Dead, for a ducat, dead!   25

                                              [*Makes a pass through the arras.*]

POLONIUS [*behind*]: O, I am slain! [*Falls and dies.*]
QUEEN: O me, what hast thou done?
HAMLET: Nay, I know not. Is it the King?

III, IV. Location: The queen's private chamber.   1. lay: Thrust (i.e., reprove him
soundly).   2. broad: Unrestrained.   4. Much heat: The king's anger.   sconce:
Ensconce, hide.   5. round: Blunt.   10. thy father: Your stepfather, Claudius.
12. idle: Foolish.   15. rood: Cross.

QUEEN: O, what a rash and bloody deed is this!
HAMLET: A bloody deed—almost as bad, good mother,
  As kill a king, and marry with his brother.   30
QUEEN: As kill a king!
HAMLET: Ay, lady, it was my word.

                     [Parts the arras and discovers Polonius.]

  Thou wretched, rash, intruding fool, farewell!
  I took thee for thy better. Take thy fortune.
  Thou find'st to be too busy is some danger.—
  Leave wringing of your hands. Peace, sit you down,   35
  And let me wring your heart, for so I shall,
  If it be made of penetrable stuff,
  If damned custom° have not braz'd° it so
  That it be proof° and bulwark against sense.°
QUEEN: What have I done, that thou dar'st wag thy tongue   40
  In noise so rude against me?
HAMLET: Such an art
  That blurs the grace and blush of modesty,
  Calls virtue hypocrite, takes off the rose
  From the fair forehead of an innocent love
  And sets a blister° there, makes marriage-vows   45
  As false as dicers' oaths. O, such a deed
  As from the body of contraction° plucks
  The very soul, and sweet religion° makes
  A rhapsody° of words. Heaven's face does glow
  O'er this solidity and compound mass   50
  With heated visage, as against the doom,
  Is thought-sick at the act.°
QUEEN: Ay me, what act,
  That roars so loud and thunders in the index?°
HAMLET: Look here, upon this picture, and on this,
  The counterfeit presentment° of two brothers.   55

                     [Shows her two likenesses.]

---

38. damned custom: Habitual wickedness. **braz'd:** Brazened, hardened.
39. proof: Armor. **sense:** Feeling. **45. sets a blister:** Brands as a harlot.
47. contraction: The marriage contract. **48. religion:** Religious vows.
49. rhapsody: Senseless string. **49–52. Heaven's . . . act:** Heaven's face flushes
with anger to look down upon this solid world, this compound mass, with hot
face as though the day of doom were near, and is thought-sick at the deed (i.e.,
Gertrude's marriage). **53. index:** Table of contents, prelude, or preface.
55. counterfeit presentment: Portrayed representation.

See, what a grace was seated on this brow:
Hyperion's° curls, the front° of Jove himself,
An eye like Mars, to threaten and command,
A station° like the herald Mercury
New-lighted on a heaven-kissing hill—   60
A combination and a form indeed,
Where every god did seem to set his seal,
To give the world assurance of a man.
This was your husband. Look you now, what follows:
Here is your husband, like a mildew'd ear,°   65
Blasting his wholesome brother. Have you eyes?
Could you on this fair mountain leave to feed,
And batten° on this moor?° Ha, have you eyes?
You cannot call it love, for at your age
The heyday° in the blood is tame, it's humble,   70
And waits upon the judgment, and what judgment
Would step from this to this? Sense,° sure, you have,
Else could you not have motion, but sure that sense
Is apoplex'd,° for madness would not err,
Nor sense to ecstasy was ne'er so thrall'd   75
But it reserv'd some quantity of choice
To serve in such a difference. What devil was 't
That thus hath cozen'd° you at hoodman-blind?°
Eyes without feeling, feeling without sight,
Ears without hands or eyes, smelling sans° all,   80
Or but a sickly part of one true sense
Could not so mope.°
O shame, where is thy blush? Rebellious hell,
If thou canst mutine° in a matron's bones,
To flaming youth let virtue be as wax,   85
And melt in her own fire. Proclaim no shame
When the compulsive ardor gives the charge,
Since frost itself as actively doth burn,

57. **Hyperion:** The sun god. **front:** Brow. 59. **station:** Manner of standing.
65. **ear:** I.e., of grain. 68. **batten:** Gorge. **moor:** Barren upland. 70. **hey-
day:** State of excitement. 72. **Sense:** Perception through the five senses (the
functions of the middle or sensible soul). 74. **apoplex'd:** Paralyzed. (Hamlet
goes on to explain that without such a paralysis of will, mere madness would not
so err, nor would the five senses so enthrall themselves to *ecstasy* or lunacy; even
such deranged states of mind would be able to make the obvious choice between
Hamlet Senior and Claudius.) 78. **cozen'd:** Cheated. **hoodman-blind:**
Blindman's bluff. 80. **sans:** Without. 82. **mope:** Be dazed, act aimlessly.
84. **mutine:** Mutiny.

And reason panders will.°
QUEEN: O Hamlet, speak no more!   90
   Thou turn'st mine eyes into my very soul,
   And there I see such black and grained° spots
   As will not leave their tinct.°
HAMLET: Nay, but to live
   In the rank sweat of an enseamed° bed,
   Stew'd in corruption, honeying and making love   95
   Over the nasty sty—
QUEEN: O, speak to me no more.
   These words, like daggers, enter in my ears.
   No more, sweet Hamlet!
HAMLET: A murderer and a villain,
   A slave that is not twentieth part the tithe°   100
   Of your precedent° lord, a vice° of kings,
   A cutpurse of the empire and the rule,
   That from a shelf the precious diadem stole,
   And put it in his pocket!
QUEEN: No more!   105

(*Enter Ghost* [*in his nightgown*].)

HAMLET: A king of shreds and patches°—
   Save me, and hover o'er me with your wings,
   You heavenly guards! What would your gracious figure?
QUEEN: Alas, he's mad!
HAMLET: Do you not come your tardy son to chide,   110
   That, laps'd in time and passion,° lets go by
   Th' important° acting of your dread command?
   O, say!
GHOST: Do not forget. This visitation
   Is but to whet thy almost blunted purpose.   115
   But, look, amazement° on thy mother sits.
   O, step between her and her fighting soul!

86–89. Proclaim . . . will: Call it no shameful business when the compelling ardor of youth delivers the attack, i.e., commits lechery, since the frost of advanced age burns with as active a fire of lust and reason perverts itself by fomenting lust rather than restraining it.   **92. grained:** Dyed in grain, indelible.   **93. tinct:** Color.   **94. enseamed:** Laden with grease.   **100. tithe:** Tenth part.   **101. precedent:** Former (i.e., the elder Hamlet).   **vice:** Buffoon (a reference to the vice of the morality plays).   **106. shreds and patches:** Motley, the traditional costume of the clown or fool.   **111. laps'd . . . passion:** Having allowed time to lapse and passion to cool.   **112. important:** Importunate, urgent.   **116. amazement:** Distraction.

Conceit° in weakest bodies strongest works.
Speak to her, Hamlet.
HAMLET: How is it with you, lady?
QUEEN: Alas, how is 't with you,   120
  That you do bend your eye on vacancy,
  And with th' incorporal° air do hold discourse?
  Forth at your eyes your spirits wildly peep,
  And, as the sleeping soldiers in th' alarm,
  Your bedded° hair, like life in excrements,°   125
  Start up and stand an° end. O gentle son,
  Upon the heat and flame of thy distemper
  Sprinkle cool patience. Whereon do you look?
HAMLET: On him, on him! Look you how pale he glares!
  His form and cause conjoin'd,° preaching to stones,   130
  Would make them capable.°—Do not look upon me,
  Lest with this piteous action you convert
  My stern effects.° Then what I have to do
  Will want true color°—tears perchance for blood.
QUEEN: To whom do you speak this?   135
HAMLET: Do you see nothing there?
QUEEN: Nothing at all, yet all that is I see.
HAMLET: Nor did you nothing hear?
QUEEN: No, nothing but ourselves.
HAMLET: Why, look you there, look how it steals away!   140
  My father, in his habit° as he lived!
  Look, where he goes, even now, out at the portal!

                                                          (*Exit Ghost.*)

QUEEN: This is the very coinage of your brain.
  This bodiless creation ecstasy°
  Is very cunning in.   145
HAMLET: Ecstasy?
  My pulse, as yours, doth temperately keep time,
  And makes as healthful music. It is not madness
  That I have utter'd. Bring me to the test,
  And I the matter will reword, which madness   150

118. Conceit: Imagination.   122. incorporal: Immaterial.   125. bedded: Laid
in smooth layers.   excrements: Outgrowths.   126. an: On.   130. His . . . conjoin'd: His appearance joined to his cause for speaking.   131. capable:
Receptive.   132–33. convert . . . effects: Divert me from my stern duty.
134. want true color: Lack plausibility so that (with a play on the normal sense
of *color*) I shall shed tears instead of blood.   141. habit: Dress.   144. ecstasy:
Madness.

Would gambol° from. Mother, for love of grace,
Lay not that flattering unction° to your soul
That not your trespass but my madness speaks.
It will but skin and film the ulcerous place,
Whiles rank corruption, mining° all within,   155
Infects unseen. Confess yourself to heaven,
Repent what's past, avoid what is to come,
And do not spread the compost° on the weeds
To make them ranker. Forgive me this my virtue;°
For in the fatness° of these pursy° times   160
Virtue itself of vice must pardon beg,
Yea, curb° and woo for leave° to do him good.
QUEEN: O Hamlet, thou hast cleft my heart in twain.
HAMLET: O, throw away the worser part of it,
And live the purer with the other half.   165
Good night. But go not to my uncle's bed;
Assume a virtue, if you have it not.
That monster, custom, who all sense doth eat,°
Of habits devil,° is angel yet in this,
That to the use of actions fair and good   170
He likewise gives a frock or livery°
That aptly is put on. Refrain tonight,
And that shall lend a kind of easiness
To the next abstinence; the next more easy;
For use° almost can change the stamp of nature,   175
And either° . . . the devil, or throw him out
With wondrous potency. Once more, good night;
And when you are desirous to be bless'd,°
I'll blessing beg of you. For this same lord,

                              [*Pointing to Polonius.*]

I do repent; but heaven hath pleas'd it so   180
To punish me with this, and this with me,

---

151. gambol: Skip away. **152. unction:** Ointment. **155. mining:** Working
under the surface. **158. compost:** Manure. **159. this my virtue:** My virtuous
talk in reproving you. **160. fatness:** Grossness. **pursy:** Short-winded, corpu-
lent. **162. curb:** Bow, bend the knee. **leave:** Permission. **168. who . . . eat:**
Who consumes all proper or natural feeling. **169. Of habits devil:** Devil-like in
prompting evil habits. **171. livery:** An outer appearance, a customary garb (and
hence a predisposition easily assumed in time of stress). **175. use:** Habit.
176. And either: A defective line usually emended by inserting the word *master*
after *either*, following the fourth quarto and early editors. **178. be bless'd:**
Become blessed, i.e., repentant.

That I must be their scourge and minister.°
I will bestow° him, and will answer well
The death I gave him. So, again, good night.
I must be cruel only to be kind.   185
Thus bad begins and worse remains behind.°
One word more, good lady.
QUEEN: What shall I do?
HAMLET: Not this, by no means, that I bid you do:
    Let the bloat° king tempt you again to bed,
    Pinch wanton on your cheek, call you his mouse,   190
    And let him, for a pair of reechy° kisses,
    Or paddling in your neck with his damn'd fingers,
    Make you to ravel all this matter out,
    That I essentially am not in madness,
    But mad in craft. 'Twere good° you let him know,   195
    For who that's but a queen, fair, sober, wise,
    Would from a paddock,° from a bat, a gib,°
    Such dear concernings° hide? Who would do so?
    No, in despite of sense and secrecy,
    Unpeg the basket° on the house's top,   200
    Let the birds fly, and, like the famous ape,°
    To try conclusions,° in the basket creep
    And break your own neck down.
QUEEN: Be thou assur'd, if words be made of breath,
    And breath of life, I have no life to breathe   205
    What thou hast said to me.
HAMLET: I must to England; you know that?
QUEEN: Alack,
    I had forgot. 'Tis so concluded on.
HAMLET: There's letters seal'd, and my two school-fellows,
    Whom I will trust as I will adders fang'd,   210
    They bear the mandate; they must sweep my way,°
    And marshal me to knavery. Let it work.

---

182. their scourge and minister: Agent of heavenly retribution. (By *scourge*, Hamlet also suggests that he himself will eventually suffer punishment in the process of fulfilling heaven's will.) **183. bestow:** Stow, dispose of. **186. behind:** To come. **189. bloat:** Bloated. **191. reechy:** Dirty, filthy. **195. good:** Said ironically; also the following eight lines. **197. paddock:** Toad. **gib:** Tomcat. **198. dear concernings:** Important affairs. **200. Unpeg the basket:** Open the cage, i.e., let out the secret. **201. famous ape:** In a story now lost. **202. conclusions:** Experiments (in which the ape apparently enters a cage from which birds have been released and then tries to fly out of the cage as they have done, falling to his death). **211. sweep my way:** Go before me.

For 'tis the sport to have the enginer°
Hoist with° his own petar,° and 't shall go hard
But I will delve one yard below their mines,°   215
And blow them at the moon. O, 'tis most sweet,
When in one line two crafts° directly meet.
This man shall set me packing.°
I'll lug the guts into the neighbor room.
Mother, good night indeed. This counselor   220
Is now most still, most secret, and most grave,
Who was in life a foolish prating knave.
Come, sir, to draw toward an end° with you.
Good night, mother.

(*Exeunt [severally, Hamlet dragging in Polonius]*.)

{ACT IV   Scene I}°

(*Enter King and Queen, with Rosencrantz and Guildenstern.*)

KING: There's matter in these sighs, these profound heaves
  You must translate; 'tis fit we understand them.
  Where is your son?
QUEEN: Bestow this place on us a little while.

[*Exeunt Rosencrantz and Guildenstern.*]

  Ah, mine own lord, what have I seen tonight!   5
KING: What, Gertrude? How does Hamlet?
QUEEN: Mad as the sea and wind when both contend
  Which is the mightier. In his lawless fit,
  Behind the arras hearing something stir,
  Whips out his rapier, cries, "A rat, a rat!"   10
  And, in this brainish apprehension,° kills
  The unseen good old man.

---

213. enginer: Constructor of military contrivances. **214. Hoist with:** Blown up by. **petar:** Petard, an explosive used to blow in a door or make a breach. **215. mines:** Tunnels used in warfare to undermine the enemy's emplacements; Hamlet will countermine by going under their mines. **217. crafts:** Acts of guile, plots. **218. set me packing:** Set me to making schemes, and set me to lugging (him) and, also, send me off in a hurry. **223. draw . . . end:** Finish up (with a pun on *draw*, pull). **IV, I. Location:** The castle. **11. brainish apprehension:** Headstrong conception.

KING: O heavy deed!
  It had been so with us, had we been there.
  His liberty is full of threats to all—
  To you yourself, to us, to everyone.   15
  Alas, how shall this bloody deed be answer'd?
  It will be laid to us, whose providence°
  Should have kept short,° restrain'd, and out of haunt°
  This mad young man. But so much was our love
  We would not understand what was most fit,   20
  But, like the owner of a foul disease,
  To keep it from divulging,° let it feed
  Even on the pith of life. Where is he gone?
QUEEN: To draw apart the body he hath kill'd,
  O'er whom his very madness, like some ore°   25
  Among a mineral° of metals base,
  Shows itself pure: 'a weeps for what is done.
KING: O Gertrude, come away!
  The sun no sooner shall the mountains touch
  But we will ship him hence, and this vile deed   30
  We must, with all our majesty and skill,
  Both countenance and excuse. Ho, Guildenstern!

(*Enter Rosencrantz and Guildenstern.*)

  Friends both, go join you with some further aid.
  Hamlet in madness hath Polonius slain,
  And from his mother's closet hath he dragg'd him.   35
  Go seek him out; speak fair, and bring the body
  Into the chapel. I pray you, haste in this.

                  [*Exeunt Rosencrantz and Guildenstern.*]

  Come, Gertrude, we'll call up our wisest friends
  And let them know both what we mean to do
  And what's untimely done°   40
  Whose whisper o'er the world's diameter,°
  As level° as the cannon to his blank,°
  Transports his pois'ned shot, may miss our name,

---

17. **providence:** Foresight. 18. **short:** On a short tether. **out of haunt:**
Secluded. 22. **divulging:** Becoming evident. 25. **ore:** Vein of gold. 26. **min-
eral:** Mine. 40. **And . . . done:** A defective line; conjectures as to the missing
words include *so, haply, slander* (Capell and others); *for, haply, slander* (Theobald
and others). 41. **diameter:** Extent from side to side. 42. **As level:** With as
direct aim. **blank:** White spot in the center of a target.

And hit the woundless° air. O, come away!
My soul is full of discord and dismay.   (*Exeunt.*) 45

{*Scene II*}°

(*Enter Hamlet.*)

HAMLET: Safely stow'd.
[ROSENCRANTZ, GUILDENSTERN (*within*): Hamlet! Lord Hamlet!]
HAMLET: But soft, what noise? Who calls on Hamlet? O, here they come.

(*Enter Rosencrantz and Guildenstern.*)

ROSENCRANTZ: What have you done, my lord, with the dead body?
HAMLET: Compounded it with dust, whereto 'tis kin.   5
ROSENCRANTZ: Tell us where 'tis, that we may take it thence
  And bear it to the chapel.
HAMLET: Do not believe it.
ROSENCRANTZ: Believe what?
HAMLET: That I can keep your counsel and not mine own. Besides, to be 10
  demanded of° a sponge, what replication° should be made by the son
  of a king?
ROSENCRANTZ: Take you me for a sponge, my lord?
HAMLET: Ay, sir, that soaks up the King's countenance,° his rewards, his
  authorities. But such officers do the King best service in the end. He 15
  keeps them, like an ape an apple, in the corner of his jaw, first
  mouth'd, to be last swallow'd. When he needs what you have glean'd, it
  is but squeezing you, and, sponge, you shall be dry again.
ROSENCRANTZ: I understand you not, my lord.
HAMLET: I am glad of it. A knavish speech sleeps in° a foolish ear.   20
ROSENCRANTZ: My lord, you must tell us where the body is, and go with
  us to the King.
HAMLET: The body is with the King, but the King is not with the body.°
  The King is a thing—
GUILDENSTERN: A thing, my lord?   25
HAMLET: Of nothing.° Bring me to him. [Hide fox, and all after.°]

                                                        (*Exeunt.*)

---

44. woundless: Invulnerable. **IV, II. Location:** The castle. **11. demanded of:**
Questioned by. **replication:** Reply. **14. countenance:** Favor. **20. sleeps in:**
Has no meaning to. **23. The . . . body:** Perhaps alludes to the legal commonplace of "the king's two bodies," which drew a distinction between the sacred
office of kingship and the particular mortal who possessed it at any given time.
26. Of nothing: Of no account. **Hide . . . after:** An old signal cry in the game of
hide-and-seek, suggesting that Hamlet now runs away from them.

{*Scene III*}°

(*Enter King, and two or three.*)

KING: I have sent to seek him, and to find the body.
How dangerous is it that this man goes loose!
Yet must not we put the strong law on him.
He's lov'd of the distracted° multitude,
Who like not in their judgment, but their eyes,   5
And where 'tis so, th' offender's scourge° is weigh'd,°
But never the offense. To bear° all smooth and even,
This sudden sending him away must seem
Deliberate pause.° Diseases desperate grown
By desperate appliance are reliev'd,   10
Or not at all.

(*Enter Rosencrantz, [Guildenstern,] and all the rest.*)   }

           How now? What hath befall'n?
ROSENCRANTZ: Where the dead body is bestow'd, my lord,
  We cannot get from him.
KING: But where is he?
ROSENCRANTZ: Without, my lord; guarded, to know your pleasure.
KING: Bring him before us.
ROSENCRANTZ: Ho! Bring in the lord.   15

(*They enter [with Hamlet].*)

KING: Now, Hamlet, where's Polonius?
HAMLET: At supper.
KING: At supper? Where?
HAMLET: Not where he eats, but where 'a is eaten. A certain convocation
of politic worms° are e'en at him. Your worm is your only emperor for   20
diet.° We fat all creatures else to fat us, and we fat ourselves for maggots. Your fat king and your lean beggar is but variable service,° two
dishes, but to one table—that's the end.
KING: Alas, alas!
HAMLET: A man may fish with the worm that hath eat° of a king, and eat   25
of the fish that hath fed of that worm.

IV, III. Location: The castle.   4. distracted: Fickle, unstable.   6. scourge:
Punishment.   weigh'd: Taken into consideration.   7. bear: Manage.   9. Deliberate pause: Carefully considered action.   20. politic worms: Crafty worms
(suited to a master spy like Polonius).   21. diet: Food, eating (with perhaps a
punning reference to the Diet of Worms, a famous convocation held in 1521).
22. variable service: Different courses of a single meal.   25. eat: Eaten (pronounced "et").

KING: What dost thou mean by this?
HAMLET: Nothing but to show you how a king may go a progress°
    through the guts of a beggar.
KING: Where is Polonius? 30
HAMLET: In heaven. Send thither to see. If your messenger find him not
    there, seek him i' th' other place yourself. But if indeed you find him
    not within this month, you shall nose him as you go up the stairs into
    the lobby.
KING [*to some Attendants*]: Go seek him there. 35
HAMLET: 'A will stay till you come.

                                        [*Exit Attendants.*]

KING: Hamlet, this deed, for thine especial safety.—
    Which we do tender,° as we dearly° grieve
    For that which thou hast done—must send thee hence
    [With fiery quickness.] Therefore prepare thyself. 40
    The bark° is ready, and the wind at help,
    Th' associates tend,° and everything is bent°
    For England.
HAMLET: For England!
KING: Ay, Hamlet. 45
HAMLET: Good.
KING: So is it, if thou knew'st our purposes.
HAMLET: I see a cherub° that sees them. But, come, for England! Farewell,
    dear mother.
KING: Thy loving father, Hamlet. 50
HAMLET: My mother. Father and mother is man and wife, man and wife
    is one flesh, and so, my mother. Come, for England! (*Exit.*)
KING: Follow him at foot;° tempt him with speed aboard.
    Delay it not; I'll have him hence tonight.
    Away! For everything is seal'd and done 55
    That else leans on° th' affair. Pray you, make haste.

                                      [*Exeunt all but the King.*]

And, England,° if my love thou hold'st at aught—
    As my great power thereof may give thee sense,
    Since yet thy cicatrice° looks raw and red

---

28. progress: Royal journey of state. **38. tender:** Regard, hold dear. **dearly:**
Intensely. **41. bark:** Sailing vessel. **42. tend:** Wait. **bent:** In readiness.
48. cherub: Cherubim are angels of knowledge. **53. at foot:** Close behind, at
heel. **56. leans on:** Bears upon, is related to. **57. England:** King of England.
59. cicatrice: Scar.

After the Danish sword, and thy free awe°   60
Pays homage to us—thou mayst not coldly set°
Our sovereign process,° which imports at full,
By letters congruing° to that effect,
The present° death of Hamlet. Do it, England,
For like the hectic° in my blood he rages,   65
And thou must cure me. Till I know 'tis done,
Howe'er my haps,° my joys were ne'er begun.

                                                              (*Exit.*)

{*Scene IV*}°

(*Enter Fortinbras with his Army over the stage.*)

FORTINBRAS: Go, captain, from me greet the Danish king.
    Tell him that, by his license,° Fortinbras
    Craves the conveyance° of a promis'd march
    Over his kingdom. You know the rendezvous.
    If that his Majesty would aught with us,   5
    We shall express our duty in his eye;°
    And let him know so.
CAPTAIN: I will do 't, my lord.
FORTINBRAS: Go softly° on.   [*Exeunt all but the Captain.*]

(*Enter Hamlet, Rosencrantz, [Guildenstern,] etc.*)

HAMLET: Good sir, whose powers° are these?
CAPTAIN: They are of Norway, sir.   10
HAMLET: How purposed, sir, I pray you?
CAPTAIN: Against some part of Poland.
HAMLET: Who commands them, sir?
CAPTAIN: The nephew to old Norway, Fortinbras.
HAMLET: Goes it against the main° of Poland, sir,   15
    Or for some frontier?
CAPTAIN: Truly to speak, and with no addition,°
    We go to gain a little patch of ground
    That hath in it no profit but the name.

---

60. free awe: Voluntary show of respect. **61. set:** Esteem. **62. process:**
Command. **63. congruing:** Agreeing. **64. present:** Immediate. **65. hectic:**
Persistent fever. **67. haps:** Fortunes. **IV, IV. Location:** The coast of Denmark.
2. license: Permission. **3. conveyance:** Escort, convoy. **6. eye:** Presence.
8. softly: Slowly. **9. powers:** Forces. **15. main:** Main part. **17. addition:**
Exaggeration.

To pay° five ducats, five, I would not farm it;°   20
Nor will it yield to Norway or the Pole
A ranker° rate, should it be sold in fee.°
HAMLET: Why, then the Polack never will defend it.
CAPTAIN: Yes, it is already garrison'd.
HAMLET: Two thousand souls and twenty thousand ducats   25
   Will not debate the question of this straw.°
This is th' imposthume° of much wealth and peace,
That inward breaks, and shows no cause without
Why the man dies. I humbly thank you, sir.
CAPTAIN: God buy you, sir.   [*Exit.*]
ROSENCRANTZ: Will 't please you go, my lord?   30
HAMLET: I'll be with you straight. Go a little before.

                                    [*Exit all except Hamlet.*]

How all occasions do inform against° me,
And spur my dull revenge! What is a man,
If his chief good and market of° his time
Be but to sleep and feed? A beast, no more.   35
Sure he that made us with such large discourse,°
Looking before and after, gave us not
That capability and god-like reason
To fust° in us unus'd. Now, whether it be
Bestial oblivion,° or some craven scruple   40
Of thinking too precisely on th' event°—
A thought which, quarter'd, hath but one part wisdom
And ever three parts coward—I do not know
Why yet I live to say "This thing's to do,"
Sith° I have cause and will and strength and means   45
To do 't. Examples gross° as earth exhort me:
Witness this army of such mass and charge°
Led by a delicate and tender prince,
Whose spirit, with divine ambition puff'd
Makes mouths° at the invisible event,   50
Exposing what is mortal and unsure
To all that fortune, death, and danger dare,

20. To pay: I.e., for a yearly rental of.   **farm it:** Take a lease of it.   **22. ranker:** Higher.   **in fee:** Fee simple, outright.   **26. debate . . . straw:** Settle this trifling matter.   **27. imposthume:** Abscess.   **32. inform against:** Denounce, betray; take shape against.   **34. market of:** Profit of compensation for.   **36. discourse:** Power of reasoning.   **39. fust:** Grow moldy.   **40. oblivion:** Forgetfulness.   **41. event:** Outcome.   **45. Sith:** Since.   **46. gross:** Obvious.   **47. charge:** Expense.   **50. Makes mouths:** Makes scornful faces.

Even for an egg-shell. Rightly to be great
Is not to stir without great argument,
But greatly to find quarrel in a straw   55
When honor's at the stake. How stand I then,
That have a father kill'd, a mother stain'd,
Excitements of° my reason and my blood,
And let all sleep, while, to my shame, I see
The imminent death of twenty thousand men,   60
That, for a fantasy° and trick° of fame,
Go to their graves like beds, fight for a plot°
Whereon the numbers cannot try the cause,°
Which is not tomb enough and continent°
To hide the slain? O, from this time forth,   65
My thoughts be bloody, or be nothing worth!

                                                        (*Exit.*)

                        {*Scene v*}°

(*Enter Horatio, [Queen] Gertrude, and a Gentleman.*)

QUEEN: I will not speak with her.
GENTLEMAN: She is importunate, indeed distract.
    Her mood will needs be pitied.
QUEEN: What would she have?
GENTLEMAN: She speaks much of her father, says she hears
    There's tricks° i' th' world, and hems, and beats her heart,°   5
    Spurns enviously at straws,° speaks things in doubt°
    That carry but half sense. Her speech is nothing,
    Yet the unshaped use° of it doth move
    The hearers to collection;° they yawn° at it,
    And botch° the words up fit to their own thoughts,   10
    Which, as her winks and nods and gestures yield° them,
    Indeed would make one think there might be thought,°

---

58. **Excitements of:** Promptings by. 61. **fantasy:** Fanciful caprice. **trick:**
Trifle. 62. **plot:** I.e., of ground. 63. **Whereon . . . cause:** On which there is
insufficient room for the soldiers needed to engage in a military contest.
64. **continent:** Receptacle, container. IV, v. **Location:** The castle. 5. **tricks:**
Deceptions. **heart:** Breast. 6. **Spurns . . . straws:** Kicks spitefully, takes
offense at trifles. **in doubt:** Obscurely. 8. **unshaped use:** Distracted manner.
9. **collection:** Inference, a guess at some sort of meaning. **yawn:** Wonder,
grasp. 10. **botch:** Patch. 11. **yield:** Delivery, bring forth (her words).
12. **thought:** Conjectured.

Though nothing sure, yet much unhappily.
HORATIO: 'twere good she were spoken with, for she may strew
    Dangerous conjectures in ill-breeding° minds.   15
QUEEN: Let her come in.   [*Exit Gentlemen.*]
  [*Aside.*] To my sick soul, as sin's true nature is,
  Each toy° seems prologue to some great amiss.°
  So full of artless jealousy is guilt,
  It spills itself in fearing to be spilt.°   20

(*Enter Ophelia* [*distracted*].)

OPHELIA: Where is the beauteous majesty of Denmark?
QUEEN: How now, Ophelia?
OPHELIA (*she sings*): "How should I your true love know
    From another one?
  By his cockle hat° and staff,   25
    And his sandal shoon."°
QUEEN: Alas, sweet lady, what imports this song?
OPHELIA: Say you? Nay, pray you, mark.
  "He is dead and gone, lady,   (*Song.*)
    He is dead and gone;   30
  At his head a grass-green turf,
    At his heels a stone."
  O, ho!
QUEEN: Nay, but Ophelia—
OPHELIA: Pray you mark.   35
  [*Sings.*] "White his shroud as the mountain snow"—

(*Enter King.*)

QUEEN: Alas, look here, my lord.
OPHELIA: "Larded° all with flowers   (*Song.*)
  Which bewept to the ground did not go
    With true-love showers."   40
KING: How do you, pretty lady?
OPHELIA: Well, God 'ild° you! They say the owl° was a baker's daughter.
  Lord, we know what we are, but know not what we may be. God be at
  your table!

15. ill-breeding: Prone to suspect the worst. **18. toy:** Trifle. **amiss:** Calamity.
19–20. So . . . spilt: Guilt is so full of suspicion that it unskillfully betrays itself in
fearing betrayal. **25. cockle hat:** Hat with cockleshell stuck in it as a sign that
the wearer had been a pilgrim to the shrine of St. James of Compostella in Spain.
26. shoon: Shoes. **38. Larded:** Decorated. **42. God 'ild:** God yield or reward.
owl: Refers to a legend about a baker's daughter who was turned into an owl for
refusing Jesus bread.

KING: Conceit° upon her father.   45
OPHELIA: Pray let's have no words of this; but when they ask you what it
   means, say you this:
   "Tomorrow is Saint Valentine's° day.   (*Song.*)
      All in the morning betime,
   And I a maid at your window,   50
      To be your Valentine.
   Then up he rose, and donn'd his clo'es,
      And dupp'd° the chamber-door,
   Let in the maid, that out a maid
      Never departed more."   55
KING: Pretty Ophelia!
OPHELIA: Indeed, la, without an oath, I'll make an end on 't:
   [*Sings.*] "By Gis° and by Saint Charity,
      Alack, and fie for shame!
   Young men will do 't, if they come to 't;   60
      By Cock,° they are to blame.
   Quoth she, 'Before you tumbled me,
      You promised me to wed.'"
   He answers:
   "'So would I ha' done, by yonder sun,   65
      An thou hadst not come to my bed.'"
KING: How long hath she been thus?
OPHELIA: I hope all will be well. We must be patient, but I cannot choose
   but weep, to think they would lay him i' th' cold ground. My brother
   shall know of it; and so I thank you for your good counsel. Come, my 70
   coach! Good night, ladies; good night, sweet ladies; good night, good
   night.

                                                              [*Exit.*]

KING: Follow her close; give her good watch, I pray you.

                                                       [*Exit Horatio.*]

   O, this is the poison of deep grief; it springs
   All from her father's death—and now behold!   75
   O Gertrude, Gertrude,
   When sorrows come, they come not single spies,°
   But in battalions. First, her father slain;
   Next, your son gone, and he most violent author

---

45. Conceit: Brooding.   **48. Valentine's:** This song alludes to the belief that the
first girl seen by a man on the morning of this day was his valentine or true love.
53. dupp'd: Opened.   **58. Gis:** Jesus.   **61. Cock:** A perversion of *God* in oaths.
77. spies: Scouts sent in advance of the main force.

Of his own just remove; the people muddied,°   80
Thick and unwholesome in their thoughts and whispers,
For good Polonius' death; and we have done but greenly,°
In hugger-mugger° to inter him; poor Ophelia
Divided from herself and her fair judgment,
Without the which we are pictures, or mere beasts;   85
Last, and as much containing as all these,
Her brother is in secret come from France,
Feeds on his wonder, keeps himself in clouds,°
And wants° not buzzers° to infect his ear
With pestilent speeches of his father's death,   90
Wherein necessity, of matter beggar'd,°
Will nothing stick our person to arraign
In ear and ear.° O my dear Gertrude, this,
Like to a murd'ring-piece,° in many places
Gives me superfluous death.   (*A noise within.*) 95
[QUEEN: Alack, what noise is this?]
KING: Attend!
    Where are my Switzers?° Let them guard the door.

(*Enter a Messenger.*)

    What is the matter?
MESSENGER: Save yourself, my lord!
    The ocean, overpeering of his list,°   100
    Eats not the flats° with more impiteous° haste
    Than young Laertes, in a riotous head,°
    O'erbears your officers. The rabble call him lord,
    And, as° the world were now but to begin,
    Antiquity forgot, custom not known,   105
    The ratifiers and props° of every word,°
    They cry, "Choose we! Laertes shall be king!"
    Caps, hands, and tongues applaud it to the clouds,
    "Laertes shall be king, Laertes king!"

                        (*A noise within.*)

---

80. **muddied:** Stirred up, confused. 82. **greenly:** Imprudently, foolishly.
83. **hugger-mugger:** Secret haste. 88. **in clouds:** I.e., of suspicion and rumor.
89. **wants:** Lacks. **buzzers:** Gossipers, informers. 91. **of matter beggar'd:**
Unprovided with facts. 92–93. **Will . . . and ear:** Will not hesitate to accuse my
(royal) person in everybody's ears. 94. **murd'ring-piece:** Cannon loaded so as to
scatter its shot. 98. **Switzers:** Swiss guards, mercenaries. 100. **overpeering of
his list:** Overflowing its shore. 101. **flats:** Flatlands near shore. **impiteous:**
Pitiless. 102. **head:** Armed force. 104. **as:** As if. 106. **ratifiers and props:**
Refer to *antiquity* and *custom.* **word:** Promise.

QUEEN: How cheerfully on the false trail they cry!   110
  O, this is counter,° you false Danish dogs!

(*Enter Laertes with others.*)

KING: The doors are broke.
LAERTES: Where is this King? Sirs, stand you all without.
ALL: No, let's come in.
LAERTES: I pray you, give me leave.
ALL: We will, we will.   115

                       [*They retire without the door.*]

LAERTES: I thank you. Keep the door. O thou vile king,
  Give me my father!
QUEEN: Calmly, good Laertes.

                       [*She tries to hold him back.*]

LAERTES: That drop of blood that's calm proclaims me bastard,
  Cries cuckold to my father, brands the harlot
  Even here, between the chaste unsmirched brow   120
  Of my true mother.
KING: What is the cause, Laertes,
  That thy rebellion looks so giant-like?
  Let him go, Gertrude. Do not fear our° person.
  There's such divinity doth hedge a king
  That treason can but peep to what it would,°   125
  Acts little of his will.° Tell me, Laertes,
  Why thou art thus incens'd. Let him go, Gertrude.
  Speak, man.
LAERTES: Where is my father?
KING: Dead.
QUEEN: But not by him.
KING: Let him demand his fill.
LAERTES: How came he dead? I'll not be juggled with.   130
  To hell, allegiance! Vows, to the blackest devil!
  Conscience and grace, to the profoundest pit!
  I dare damnation. To this point I stand,
  That both the worlds I give to negligence,°

---

111. counter: A hunting term meaning to follow the trail in a direction opposite to
that which the game has taken.   **123. fear our:** Fear for my.   **125. can . . . would:**
Can only glance; as from far off or through a barrier, at what it would intend.
126. Acts . . . will: (But) performs little of what it intends.   **134. both . . . negli-**
gence: Both this world and the next are of no consequence to me.

Let come what comes, only I'll be reveng'd   135
Most throughly° for my father.
KING: Who shall stay you?
LAERTES: My will, not all the world's.°
And for my means, I'll husband them so well,
They shall go far with little.
KING: Good Laertes,
If you desire to know the certainty   140
Of your dear father, is 't writ in your revenge
That, swoopstake,° you will draw both friend and foe,
Winner and loser?
LAERTES: None but his enemies.
KING: Will you know them then?
LAERTES: To his good friends thus wide I'll ope my arms,   145
And, like the kind life-rend'ring pelican,°
Repast° them with my blood.
KING: Why, now you speak
Like a good child and a true gentleman.
That I am guiltless of your father's death,
And am most sensibly° in grief for it,   150
It shall as level° to your judgment 'pear
As day does to your eye.
                        (*A noise within:*) "Let her come in."
LAERTES: How now? What noise is that?

(*Enter Ophelia.*)

O heat, dry up my brains! Tears seven times salt
Burn out the sense and virtue° of mine eye!   155
By heaven, thy madness shall be paid with weight°
Till our scale turn the beam.° O rose of May!
Dear maid, kind sister, sweet Ophelia!
O heavens, is 't possible a young maid's wits
Should be as mortal as an old man's life?   160
[Nature is fine in° love, and where 'tis fine,
It sends some precious instance° of itself

---

136. throughly: Thoroughly.   **137. My will . . . world's:** I'll stop (*stay*) when my will is accomplished, not for anyone else's.   **142. swoopstake:** Literally, taking all stakes on the gambling table at once, i.e., indiscriminately; *draw* is also a gambling term.   **146. pelican:** Refers to the belief that the female pelican fed its young with its own blood.   **147. Repast:** Feed.   **150. sensibly:** Feelingly.   **151. level:** Plain.   **155. virtue:** Faculty, power.   **156. paid with weight:** Repaid, avenged equally or more.   **157. beam:** Crossbar of a balance.   **161. fine in:** Refined by.   **162. instance:** Token.

After the thing it loves.°]
OPHELIA: "They bore him barefac'd on the bier;

(*Song.*)

[Hey non nonny, nonny, hey nonny,]   165
And in his grave rain'd many a tear"—
Fare you well, my dove!
LAERTES: Hadst thou thy wits, and didst persuade° revenge,
It could not move thus.
OPHELIA: You must sing "A-down a-down,   170
And you call him a-down-a."
O, how the wheel° becomes it! It is the false steward° that stole his
master's daughter.
LAERTES: This nothing's more than matter.°
OPHELIA: There's rosemary,° that's for remembrance; pray you, love,   175
remember. And there is pansies,° that's for thoughts.
LAERTES: A document° in madness, thoughts and remembrance fitted.
OPHELIA: There's fennel° for you, and columbines.° There's rue° for you,
and here's some for me; we may call it herb of grace o' Sundays. You
may wear your rue with a difference.° There's a daisy.° I would give   180
you some violets,° but they wither'd all when my father died. They say
'a made a good end—
[*Sings.*] "For bonny sweet Robin is all my joy."
LAERTES: Thought° and affliction, passion, hell itself,
She turns to favor° and to prettiness.   185
OPHELIA: "And will 'a not come again? (*Song.*)
And will 'a not come again?
No, no, he is dead,
Go to thy death-bed,
He never will come again.   190

---

163. After . . . loves: Into the grave, along with Polonius.   **168. persuade:** Argue cogently for.   **172. wheel:** Spinning wheel as accompaniment to the song, or refrain.   **false steward:** The story is unknown.   **174. This . . . matter:** This seeming nonsense is more meaningful than sane utterance.   **175. rosemary:** Used as a symbol of remembrance both at weddings and at funerals.   **176. pansies:** Emblems of love and courtship; perhaps from French *pensées*, thoughts.   **177. document:** Instruction, lesson.   **178. fennel:** Emblem of flattery.   **columbines:** Emblems of unchastity (?) or ingratitude (?).   **rue:** Emblem of repentance; when mingled with holy water, it was known as *herb of grace.*   **180. with a difference:** Suggests that Ophelia and the queen have different causes of sorrow and repentance; perhaps with a play on *rue* in the sense of ruth, pity.   **daisy:** Emblem of dissembling, faithlessness.   **181. violets:** Emblems of faithfulness.   **184. Thought:** Melancholy.   **185. favor:** Grace.

"His beard was as white as snow,
All flaxen was his poll.°
    He is gone, he is gone,
    And we cast away moan.
God 'a' mercy on his soul!"   195
And of all Christians' souls, I pray God. God buy you.

                                                    [*Exit.*]

LAERTES: Do you see this, O God?
KING: Laertes, I must commune with your grief,
    Or you deny me right. Go but apart,
    Make choice of whom your wisest friends you will,   200
    And they shall hear and judge 'twixt you and me.
    If by direct or by collateral° hand
    They find us touch'd,° we will our kingdom give,
    Our crown, our life, and all that we call ours,
    To you in satisfaction; but if not,   205
    Be you content to lend your patience to us,
    And we shall jointly labor with your soul
    To give it due content.
LAERTES: Let this be so.
    His means of death, his obscure funeral—
    No trophy,° sword, nor hatchment° o'er his bones,   210
    No noble rite nor formal ostentation°—
    Cry to be heard, as 'twere from heaven to earth,
    That I must call 't in question.
KING: So you shall;
    And where th' offense is, let the great ax fall.
    I pray you go with me.   (*Exeunt.*) 215

{*Scene VI*}°

(*Enter Horatio and others.*)

HORATIO: What are they that would speak with me?
GENTLEMAN: Seafaring men, sir. They say they have letters for you.
HORATIO: Let them come in.   [*Exit Gentleman.*]
    I do not know from what part of the world
    I should be greeted, if not from lord Hamlet.   5

---

192. poll: Head. **202. collateral:** Indirect. **203. us touch'd:** Me implicated.
210. trophy: Memorial. **hatchment:** Tablet displaying the armorial bearings of
a deceased person. **211. ostentation:** Ceremony. **IV, VI. Location:** The castle.

(*Enter Sailors.*)

FIRST SAILOR: God bless you sir.

HORATIO: Let him bless thee too.

FIRST SAILOR: 'A shall, sir, an 't please him. There's a letter for you, sir—
it came from th' ambassador that was bound for England—if your
name be Horatio, as I am let to know it is.   [*Gives letter.*] 10

HORATIO [*reads*]: "Horatio, when thou shalt have over-look'd this, give
these fellows some means° to the King; they have letters for him. Ere
we were two days old at sea, a pirate of very warlike appointment°
gave us chase. Finding ourselves too slow of sail, we put on a compell'd valor, and in the grapple I boarded them. On the instant they got 15
clear of our ship, so I alone became their prisoner. They have dealt
with me like thieves of mercy,° but they knew what they did: I am to do
a good turn for them. Let the King have the letters I have sent, and
repair thou to me with as much speed as thou wouldest fly death. I
have words to speak in thine ear will make thee dumb; yet are they 20
much too light for the bore° of the matter. These good fellows will
bring thee where I am. Rosencrantz and Guildenstern hold their
course for England. Of them I have much to tell thee. Farewell.

                                        He that thou knowest thine, Hamlet."

Come, I will give you way for these your letters,   25
And do 't the speedier that you may direct me
To him from whom you brought them.   (*Exeunt.*)

                              [*Scene VII*]°

(*Enter King and Laertes.*)

KING: Now must your conscience my acquittance seal,°
    And you must put me in your heart for friend,
    Sith you have heard, and with a knowing ear,
    That he which hath your noble father slain
    Pursued my life.
LAERTES: It well appears. But tell me   5
    Why you proceeded not against these feats°
    So criminal and so capital° in nature,
    As by your safety, greatness, wisdom, all things else,
    You mainly° were stirr'd up.

---

12. **means:** Means of access.   13. **appointment:** Equipage.   17. **thieves of
mercy:** Merciful thieves.   21. **bore:** Caliber, i.e., importance.   IV, VII. **Location:**
The castle.   1. **my acquittance seal:** Confirm or acknowledge my innocence.
6. **feats:** Acts.   7. **capital:** Punishable by death.   9. **mainly:** Greatly.

KING: O, for two special reasons,
  Which may to you, perhaps, seem much unsinew'd,°   10
  But yet to me th' are strong. The Queen his mother
  Lives almost by his looks, and for myself—
  My virtue or my plague, be it either which—
  She's so conjunctive° to my life and soul
  That, as the star moves not but in his sphere,°   15
  I could not but by her. The other motive,
  Why to a public count° I might not go,
  Is the great love the general gender° bear him,
  Who, dipping all his faults in their affection,
  Would, like the spring° that turneth wood to stone,   20
  Convert his gyves° to graces, so that my arrows,
  Too slightly timber'd° for so loud° a wind,
  Would have reverted to my bow again
  And not where I had aim'd them.
LAERTES: And so have I a noble father lost,   25
  A sister driven into desp'rate terms,°
  Whose worth, if praises may go back° again,
  Stood challenger on mount° of all the age
  For her perfections. But my revenge will come.
KING: Break not your sleeps for that. You must not think   30
  That we are made of stuff so flat and dull
  That we can let our beard be shook with danger
  And think it pastime. You shortly shall hear more.
  I lov'd your father, and we love ourself;
  And that, I hope, will teach you to imagine—   35

(*Enter a Messenger with letters.*)

  [How now? What news?]
MESSENGER: [Letters, my lord, from Hamlet:]
  These to your Majesty, this to the Queen.

                                        [*Gives letters.*]

---

10. unsinew'd: Weak.   **14. conjunctive:** Closely united.   **15. sphere:** The hollow sphere in which, according to Ptolemaic astronomy, the planets moved. **17.   count:** Account, reckoning.   **18.   general gender:** Common people. **20. spring:** A spring with such a concentration of lime that it coats a piece of wood with limestone, in effect gilding it.   **21. gyves:** Fetters (which, gilded by the people's praise, would look like badges of honor).   **22. slightly timber'd:** Light.   **loud:** Strong.   **26.   terms:** State, condition.   **27.   go back:** Recall Ophelia's former virtues.   **28. on mount:** On high.

KING: From Hamlet? Who brought them?
MESSENGER: Sailors, my lord, they say; I saw them not.
　They were given me by Claudio. He receiv'd them   40
　Of him that brought them.
KING: Laertes, you shall hear them.
　Leave us.   [*Exit Messenger.*]
　[*Reads.*] "High and mighty, you shall know I am set naked° on your
　kingdom. Tomorrow shall I beg leave to see your kingly eyes, when I
　shall, first asking your pardon° thereunto, recount the occasion of my   45
　sudden and more strange return.   Hamlet."
　What should this mean? Are all the rest come back?
　Or is it some abuse,° and no such thing?
LAERTES: Know you the hand?
KING: 'Tis Hamlet's character.° "Naked!"
　And in a postscript here, he says "alone."   50
　Can you devise° me?
LAERTES: I am lost in it, my lord. But let him come.
　It warms the very sickness in my heart
　That I shall live and tell him to his teeth,
　"Thus didst thou."
KING: If it be so, Laertes —   55
　As how should it be so? How otherwise?° —
　Will you be ruled by me?
LAERTES: Ay, my lord,
　So° you will not o'errule me to a peace.
KING: To thine own peace. If he be now returned,
　As checking at° his voyage, and that he means   60
　No more to undertake it, I will work him
　To an exploit, now ripe in my device,
　Under the which he shall not choose but fall;
　And for his death no wind of blame shall breathe,
　But even his mother shall uncharge the practice°   65
　And call it accident.
LAERTES: My lord, I will be rul'd,
　The rather if you could devise it so
　That I might be the organ.°

43. **naked:** Destitute, unarmed, without following.   45. **pardon:** Permission.
48. **abuse:** Deceit.   49. **character:** Handwriting.   51. **devise:** Explain to.
56. **As . . . otherwise:** How can this (Hamlet's return) be true? Yet how otherwise
than true (since we have the evidence of his letter).   58. **So:** Provided that.
60. **checking at:** Turning aside from (like a falcon leaving the quarry to fly at a
chance bird).   65. **uncharge the practice:** Acquit the stratagem of being a plot.
68. **organ:** Agent, instrument.

KING: It falls right.
  You have been talk'd of since your travel much,
  And that in Hamlet's hearing, for a quality   70
  Wherein, they say, you shine. Your sum of parts°
  Did not together pluck such envy from him
  As did that one, and that, in my regard,
  Of the unworthiest siege.°
LAERTES: What part is that, my lord?   75
KING: A very riband in the cap of youth,
  Yet needful too, for youth no less becomes
  The light and careless livery that it wears
  Than settled age his sables° and his weeds,°
  Importing health° and graveness. Two months since   80
  Here was a gentleman of Normandy.
  I have seen myself, and serv'd against, the French,
  And they can well° on horseback, but this gallant
  Had witchcraft in 't; he grew unto his seat,
  And to such wondrous doing brought his horse   85
  As had he been incorps'd and demi-natured°
  With the brave beast. So far he topp'd° my thought
  That I, in forgery° of shapes and tricks,
  Come short of what he did.
LAERTES: A Norman was 't?
KING: A Norman.   90
LAERTES: Upon my life, Lamord.
KING: The very same.
LAERTES: I know him well. He is the brooch° indeed
  And gem of all the nation.
KING: He made confession° of you,
  And gave you such a masterly report   95
  For art and exercise in your defense,
  And for your rapier most especial,
  That he cried out, 'twould be a sight indeed,
  If one could match you. The scrimers° of their nation,
  He swore, had neither motion, guard, nor eye,   100
  If you oppos'd them. Sir, this report of his

---

71. **Your . . . parts:** All your other virtues. 74. **unworthiest siege:** Least important rank. 79. **sables:** Rich robes furred with sable. **weeds:** Garments.
80. **Importing health:** Indicating prosperity. 83. **can well:** Are skilled.
86. **incorps'd and demi–natur'd:** Of one body and nearly of one nature (like the
centaur). 87. **topp'd:** Surpassed. 88. **forgery:** Invention. 92. **brooch:** Ornament. 94. **confession:** Admission of superiority. 99. **scrimers:** Fencers.

Did Hamlet so envenom with his envy
That he could nothing do but wish and beg
Your sudden coming o'er to play° with you.
Now, out of this—
LAERTES: What out of this, my lord?   105
KING: Laertes, was your father dear to you?
  Or are you like the painting of a sorrow,
  A face without a heart?
LAERTES: Why ask you this?
KING: Not that I think you did not love your father,
  But that I know love is begun by time,°   110
  And that I see, in passages of proof,°
  Time qualifies° the spark and fire of it.
  There lives within the very flame of love
  A kind of wick or snuff° that will abate it,
  And nothing is at a like goodness still,°   115
  For goodness, growing to a plurisy,°
  Dies in his own too much.° That° we would do,
  We should do when we would; for this "would" changes
  And hath abatements° and delays as many
  As there are tongues, are hands, are accidents,°   120
  And then this "should" is like a spendthrift's sigh,°
  That hurts by easing.° But, to the quick o' th' ulcer;
  Hamlet comes back. What would you undertake
  To show yourself your father's son in deed
  More than in words?
LAERTES: To cut his throat i' th' church!   125
KING: No place, indeed, should murder sanctuarize;°
  Revenge should have no bounds. But, good Laertes,
  Will you do this,° keep close within your chamber.
  Hamlet return'd shall know you are come home.
  We'll put on those° shall praise your excellence   130

---

104. play: Fence.   **110. begun by time:** Subject to change.   **111. passages of proof:** Actual instances.   **112. qualifies:** Weakens.   **114. snuff:** The charred part of a candlewick.   **115. nothing . . . still:** Nothing remains at a constant level of perfection.   **116. plurisy:** Excess, plethora.   **117. in . . . much:** Of its own excess.   **That:** That which.   **119. abatements:** Diminutions.   **120. accidents:** Occurrences, incidents.   **121. spendthrift's sigh:** An allusion to the belief that each sigh cost the heart a drop of blood.   **122. hurts by easing:** Costs the heart blood even while it affords emotional relief.   **126. sanctuarize:** Protect from punishment (alludes to the right of sanctuary with which certain religious places were invested).   **128. Will you do this:** If you wish to do this.   **130. put on those:** Instigate those who.

And set a double varnish on the fame
The Frenchman gave you, bring you in fine° together,
And wager on your heads. He, being remiss,°
Most generous,° and free from all contriving,
Will not peruse the foils, so that, with ease, 135
Or with a little shuffling, you may choose
A sword unbated,° and in a pass of practice°
Requite him for your father.
LAERTES: I will do 't.
And for that purpose I'll anoint my sword.
I bought an unction° of a mountebank° 140
So mortal that, but dip a knife in it,
Where it draws blood no cataplasm° so rare,
Collected from all simples° that have virtue
Under the moon, can save the thing from death
That is but scratch'd withal. I'll touch my point 145
With this contagion, that, if I gall° him slightly,
It may be death.
KING: Let's further think of this,
Weigh what convenience both of time and means
May fit us to our shape.° If this should fail,
And that our drift look through our bad performance,° 150
'Twere better not assay'd. Therefore this project
Should have a back or second, that might hold
If this did blast in proof.° Soft, let me see.
We'll make a solemn wager on your cunnings —
I ha 't! 155
When in your motion you are hot and dry —
As° make your bouts more violent to that end —
And that he calls for drink, I'll have prepar'd him
A chalice for the nonce,° whereon but sipping,
If he by chance escape your venom'd stuck,° 160
Our purpose may hold there. [*A cry within.*] But stay, what noise?

(*Enter Queen.*)

---

132. in fine: Finally. 133. remiss: Negligently unsuspicious. 134. generous:
Noble-minded. 137. unbated: Not blunted, having no button. pass of prac-
tice: Treacherous thrust. 140. unction: Ointment. mountebank: Quack doc-
tor. 142. cataplasm: Plaster or poultice. 143. simples: Herbs. 146. gall:
Graze, wound. 149. shape: Part that we propose to act. 150. drift . . . per-
formance: I.e., intention be disclosed by our bungling. 153. blast in proof:
Burst in the test (like a cannon). 157. As: And you should. 159. nonce:
Occasion. 160. stuck: Thrust (from *stoccado*, a fencing term).

QUEEN: One woe doth tread upon another's heel,
   So fast they follow. Your sister's drowned, Laertes.
LAERTES: Drown'd! O, where?
QUEEN: There is a willow grows askant° the brook   165
   That shows his hoar° leaves in the glassy stream;
   Therewith fantastic garlands did she make
   Of crow-flowers, nettles, daisies, and long purples°
   That liberal° shepherds give a grosser name,
   But our cold° maids do dead men's fingers call them.   170
   There on the pendent boughs her crownet° weeds
   Clamb'ring to hang, an envious sliver° broke,
   When down her weedy° trophies and herself
   Fell in the weeping brook. Her clothes spread wide,
   And mermaid-like awhile they bore her up,   175
   Which time she chanted snatches of old lauds,°
   As one incapable° of her own distress,
   Or like a creature native and indued°
   Unto that element. But long it could not be
   Till that her garments, heavy with their drink,   180
   Pull'd the poor wretch from her melodious lay
   To muddy death.
LAERTES: Alas, then she is drown'd?
QUEEN: Drown'd, drown'd.
LAERTES: Too much of water hast thou, poor Ophelia,
   And therefore I forbid my tears. But yet   185
   It is our trick;° nature her custom holds,
   Let shame say what it will. [*He weeps.*] When these are gone,
   The woman will be out.° Adieu, my lord.
   I have a speech of fire, that fain would blaze,
   But that this folly drowns it.   (*Exit.*)
KING: Let's follow, Gertrude.   190
   How much I had to do to calm his rage!
   Now fear I this will give it start again;
   Therefore let's follow.   (*Exeunt.*)

---

165. askant: Aslant.   **166. hoar:** White or gray.   **168. long purples:** Early purple orchids.   **169. liberal:** Free-spoken.   **170. cold:** Chaste.   **171. crownet:**
Made into a chaplet or coronet.   **172. envious sliver:** Malicious branch.
173. weedy: I.e., of plants.   **176. lauds:** Hymns.   **177. incapable:** Lacking
capacity to apprehend.   **178. indued:** Adapted by nature.   **186. It is our trick:**
Weeping is our natural way (when sad).   **187–88. When . . . out:** When my tears
are all shed, the woman in me will be expended, satisfied.

{ACT V   *Scene I*}°

(*Enter two Clowns*° [*with spades, etc.*])

FIRST CLOWN: Is she to be buried in Christian burial when she willfully
seeks her own salvation?

SECOND CLOWN: I tell thee she is; therefore make her grave straight.° The
crowner° hath sat on her, and finds it Christian burial.

FIRST CLOWN: How can that be, unless she drown'd herself in her own   5
defense?

SECOND CLOWN: Why, 'tis found so.

FIRST CLOWN: It must be "se offendendo";° it cannot be else. For here lies
the point: if I drown myself wittingly, it argues an act, and an act hath
three branches—it is to act, to do, and to perform. Argal,° she   10
drown'd herself wittingly.

SECOND CLOWN: Nay, but hear you, goodman delver—

FIRST CLOWN: Give me leave. Here lies the water; good. Here stands the
man; good. If the man go to this water, and drown himself, it is, will
he,° nill he, he goes, mark you that. But if the water come to him and   15
drown him, he drowns not himself. Argal, he that is not guilty of his
own death shortens not his own life.

SECOND CLOWN: But is this law?

FIRST CLOWN: Ay, marry, is 't—crowner's quest° law.

SECOND CLOWN: Will you ha' the truth on 't? If this had not been a gentle-   20
woman, she should have been buried out o' Christian burial.

FIRST CLOWN: Why, there thou say'st.° And the more pity that great folk
should have count'nance° in this world to drown or hang themselves,
more than their even-Christen.° Come, my spade. There is no ancient
gentlemen but gard'ners, ditchers, and grave-makers. They hold up   25
Adam's profession.

SECOND CLOWN: Was he a gentleman?

FIRST CLOWN: 'A was the first that ever bore arms.

[SECOND CLOWN: Why, he had none.

FIRST CLOWN: What, art a heathen? How dost thou understand the   30
Scripture? The Scripture says "Adam digg'd." Could he dig without

---

V, I. **Location:** A churchyard. [s.d.] *Clowns:* Rustics. **3. straight:** Straightway,
immediately. **4. crowner:** Coroner. **8. se offendendo:** A comic mistake for *se
defendendo,* term used in verdicts of justifiable homicide. **10. Argal:** Corruption
of *ergo,* therefore. **14–15. will he:** Will he not. **19. quest:** Inquest. **22. there
thou say'st:** That's right. **23. count'nance:** Privilege. **24. even-Christen:** Fellow Christian.

arms?] I'll put another question to thee. If thou answerest me not to the purpose, confess thyself° —

SECOND CLOWN: Go to.

FIRST CLOWN: What is he that builds stronger than either the mason, the 35 shipwright, or the carpenter?

SECOND CLOWN: The gallows-maker, for that frame outlives a thousand tenants.

FIRST CLOWN: I like thy wit well, in good faith. The gallows does well, but how does it well? It does well to those that do ill. Now thou dost ill to 40 say the gallows is built stronger than the church. Argal, the gallows may do well to thee. To 't again, come.

SECOND CLOWN: "Who builds stronger than a mason, a shipwright, or a carpenter?"

FIRST CLOWN: Ay, tell me that, and unyoke.°   45

SECOND CLOWN: Marry, now I can tell.

FIRST CLOWN: To 't.

SECOND CLOWN: Mass,° I cannot tell.

(*Enter Hamlet and Horatio [at a distance].*)

FIRST CLOWN: Cudgel thy brains no more about it, for your dull ass will not mend his pace with beating; and, when you are ask'd this question 50 next, say "a grave-maker." The houses he makes lasts till doomsday. Go, get thee in, and fetch me a stoup° of liquor.

[*Exit Second Clown. First Clown digs.*]

(*Song.*)

"In youth, when I did love, did love,°
    Methought it was very sweet,
To contract — O — the time for — a — my behove,°   55
    O, methought there — a — was nothing — a — meet."°

HAMLET: Has this fellow no feeling of his business, that 'a sings at grave-making?

HORATIO: Custom hath made it in him a property of easiness.°

HAMLET: 'Tis e'en so. The hand of little employment hath the daintier 60 sense.°

33. confess thyself: The saying continues, "and be hanged."   **45. unyoke:** After this great effort you may unharness the team of your wits.   **48. Mass:** By the Mass.   **52. stoup:** Two-quart measure.   **53. In . . . love:** This and the two following stanzas, with nonsensical variations, are from a poem attributed to Lord Vaux and printed in *Tottel's Miscellany* (1557). The *O* and *a* (for "ah") seemingly are the grunts of the digger.   **55. To contract . . . behove:** To make a betrothal agreement for my benefit (?).   **56. meet:** Suitable, i.e., more suitable.   **59. property of easiness:** Something he can do easily and without thinking.   **60–61. daintier sense:** More delicate sense of feeling.

(*Song.*)

FIRST CLOWN: "But age, with his stealing steps,
　　Hath claw'd me in his clutch,
　And hath shipped me into the land,°
　　As if I had never been such."   65

[*Throws up a skull.*]

HAMLET: That skull had a tongue in it, and could sing once. How the
knave jowls° it to the ground, as if 'twere Cain's jaw-bone, that did the
first murder! This might be the pate of a politician,° which this ass
now o'erreaches,° one that would circumvent God, might it not?

HORATIO: It might, my lord.   70

HAMLET: Or of a courtier, which could say "Good morrow, sweet lord!
How dost thou, sweet lord?" This might be my Lord Such-a-one, that
prais'd my Lord Such-a-one's horse when 'a meant to beg it, might
it not?

HORATIO: Ay, my lord.   75

HAMLET: Why, e'en so, and now my Lady Worm's, chapless,° and knock'd
about the mazzard° with a sexton's spade. Here's fine revolution,° an°
we had the trick to see 't. Did these bones cost no more the breeding,°
but to play at loggats° with them? Mine ache to think on 't.

(*Song.*)

FIRST CLOWN: "A pick-axe, and a spade, a spade,   80
　　For and° a shrouding sheet;
　O, a pit of clay for to be made
　　For such a guest is meet."

[*Throws up another skull.*]

HAMLET: There's another. Why may not that be the skull of a lawyer?
Where be his quiddities° now, his quillities,° his cases, his tenures,°   85
and his tricks? Why does he suffer this mad knave now to knock him
about the sconce° with a dirty shovel, and will not tell him of his

---

64. into the land: Toward my grave (?) (but note the lack of rhyme in *steps,*
land). **67. jowls:** Dashes. **68. politician:** Schemer, plotter. **69. o'erreaches:**
Circumvents, gets the better of (with a quibble on the literal sense). **76. chap-**
less: Having no lower jaw. **77. mazzard:** Head (literally, a drinking vessel).
revolution: Change. **an:** If. **78. the breeding:** In the breeding, raising.
79. loggats: A game in which pieces of hardwood are thrown to lie as near as possible to a stake. **81. For and:** And moreover. **85. quiddities:** Subtleties,
quibbles (from Latin *quid,* a thing). **quillities:** Verbal niceties, subtle distinc-
tions (variation of *quiddities*). **tenures:** The holding of a piece of property
or office, or the conditions or period of such holding. **87. sconce:** Head.

action of battery? Hum! This fellow might be in 's time a great buyer
of land, with his statutes, his recognizances,° his fines, his double°
vouchers,° his recoveries.° [Is this the fine of his fines, and the recov-   90
ery of his recoveries,] to have his fine pate full of fine dirt?° Will his
vouchers vouch him no more of his purchases, and double [ones too],
than the length and breadth of a pair of indentures?° The very con-
veyances° of his lands will scarcely lie in this box,° and must th' inher-
itor° himself have no more, ha?   95
HORATIO: Not a jot more, my lord.
HAMLET: Is not parchment made of sheep-skins?
HORATIO: Ay, my lord, and of calf-skins too.
HAMLET: They are sheep and calves which seek out assurance in that.° I
will speak to this fellow. — Whose grave's this, sirrah?°   100
FIRST CLOWN: Mine, sir.
[*Sings.*] "O, a pit of clay for to be made
[For such a guest is meet]."
HAMLET: I think it be thine, indeed, for thou liest in 't.
FIRST CLOWN: You lie out on 't, sir, and therefore 'tis not yours. For my 105
part, I do not lie in 't, yet it is mine.
HAMLET: Thou dost lie in 't, to be in 't and say it is thine. 'Tis for the dead,
not for the quick;° therefore thou liest.
FIRST CLOWN: 'Tis a quick lie, sir; 'twill away again from me to you.
HAMLET: What man dost thou dig it for?   110
FIRST CLOWN: For no man, sir.
HAMLET: What woman, then?
FIRST CLOWN: For none, neither.
HAMLET: Who is to be buried in 't?
FIRST CLOWN: One that was a woman, sir, but, rest her soul, she's dead.   115
HAMLET: How absolute° the knave is! We must speak by the card,° or
equivocation° will undo us. By the Lord, Horatio, this three years I

---

89. statutes, recognizances: Legal documents guaranteeing a debt by attaching
land and property.   **89–90. fines, recoveries:** Ways of converting entailed estates
into "fee simple" or freehold.   **89. double:** Signed by two signatories.   **90. vouchers:** Guarantees of the legality of a title to real estate.   **90–91. fine of his fines . . .
fine pate . . . fine dirt:** End of his legal maneuvers . . . elegant head . . . minutely
sifted dirt.   **93. pair of indentures:** Legal document drawn up in duplicate on a
single sheet and then cut apart on a zigzag line so that each pair was uniquely
matched. (Hamlet may refer to two rows of teeth, or dentures.)   **93–94. con-
veyances:** Deeds.   **94. this box:** The skull.   **94–95. inheritor:** Possessor, owner.
99. assurance in that: Safety in legal parchments.   **100. sirrah:** Term of
address to inferiors.   **108. quick:** Living.   **116. absolute:** Positive, decided.
by the card: By the mariner's card on which the points of the compass were
marked, i.e., with precision.   **117. equivocation:** Ambiguity in the use of terms.

have taken note of it: the age is grown so pick'd° that the toe of the
peasant comes so near the heel of the courtier, he galls his kibe.° How
long hast thou been a grave-maker?   120
FIRST CLOWN: Of all the days i' th' year, I came to 't that day that our last
    king Hamlet overcame Fortinbras.
HAMLET: How long is that since?
FIRST CLOWN: Cannot you tell that? Every fool can tell that. It was that
    very day that young Hamlet was born — he that is mad, and sent into 125
    England.
HAMLET: Ay, marry, why was he sent into England?
FIRST CLOWN: Why, because 'a was mad. 'A shall recover his wits there,
    or, if 'a do not, 'tis no great matter there.
HAMLET: Why?   130
FIRST CLOWN: 'Twill not be seen in him there. There the men are as mad
    as he.
HAMLET: How came he mad?
FIRST CLOWN: Very strangely, they say.
HAMLET: How strangely?   135
FIRST CLOWN: Faith, e'en with losing his wits.
HAMLET: Upon what ground?
FIRST CLOWN: Why, here in Denmark. I have been sexton here, man and
    boy, thirty years.
HAMLET: How long will a man lie i' th' earth ere he rot?   140
FIRST CLOWN: Faith, if 'a be not rotten before 'a die — as we have many
    pocky° corses [now-a-days], that will scarce hold the laying in — 'a will
    last you some eight year or nine year. A tanner will last you nine year.
HAMLET: Why he more than another?
FIRST CLOWN: Why, sir, his hide is so tann'd with his trade that 'a will 145
    keep out water a great while, and your water is a sore decayer of your
    whoreson dead body. [*Picks up a skull.*] Here's a skull now hath lain
    you° i' th' earth three and twenty years.
HAMLET: Whose was it?
FIRST CLOWN: A whoreson mad fellow's it was. Whose do you think it 150
    was?
HAMLET: Nay, I know not.
FIRST CLOWN: A pestilence on him for a mad rogue! 'A pour'd a flagon of
    Rhenish° on my head once. This same skull, sir, was Yorick's skull, the
    King's jester.   155

---

118. pick'd: Refined, fastidious.   **119. galls his kibe:** Chafes the courtier's
chilblain (a swelling or sore caused by cold).   **142. pocky:** Rotten, diseased (literally, with the pox, or syphilis).   **147–48. lain you:** Lain.   **154. Rhenish:**
Rhine wine.

HAMLET: This?

FIRST CLOWN: E'en that.

HAMLET: [Let me see.] [*Takes the skull.*] Alas, poor Yorick! I knew him,
Horatio, a fellow of infinite jest, of most excellent fancy. He hath borne
me on his back a thousand times; and now, how abhorr'd in my imagi-   160
nation it is! My gorge rises at it. Here hung those lips that I have kiss'd
I know not how oft. Where be your gibes now? Your gambols, your
songs, your flashes of merriment that were wont to set the table on a
roar? Not one now, to mock your own grinning? Quite chap-fall'n?°
Now get you to my lady's chamber, and tell her, let her paint an inch   165
thick, to this favor° she must come; make her laugh at that. Prithee,
Horatio, tell me one thing.

HORATIO: What's that, my lord?

HAMLET: Dost thou think Alexander look'd o' this fashion i' th' earth?

HORATIO: E'en so.   170

HAMLET: And smelt so? Pah! [*Puts down the skull.*]

HORATIO: E'en so, my lord.

HAMLET: To what base uses we may return, Horatio! Why may not imagination trace the noble dust of Alexander, till 'a find it stopping a bung-
hole?   175

HORATIO: 'twere to consider too curiously,° to consider so.

HAMLET: No, faith, not a jot, but to follow him thither with modesty°
enough, and likelihood to lead it. [As thus]: Alexander died, Alexander
was buried, Alexander returneth to dust; the dust is earth; of earth we
make loam;° and why of that loam, whereto he was converted, might   180
they not stop a beer-barrel?
Imperious° Caesar, dead and turn'd to clay,
Might stop a hole to keep the wind away.
O, that that earth which kept the world in awe
Should patch a wall t' expel the winter's flaw!°   185
But soft, but soft awhile! Here comes the King.

(*Enter King, Queen, Laertes, and the Corse [of Ophelia, in procession, with
Priest, Lords etc.].*)

The Queen, the courtiers. Who is this they follow?
And with such maimed rites? This doth betoken
The corse they follow did with desp'rate hand

---

164. chap-fall'n: (1) Lacking the lower jaw; (2) dejected.   **166. favor:** Aspect,
appearance.   **176. curiously:** Minutely.   **177. modesty:** Moderation.   **180. loam:**
Clay mixture for brickmaking or other clay use.   **182. Imperious:** Imperial.
185. flaw: Gust of wind.

Fordo it° own life. 'Twas of some estate.°   190
Couch° we awhile, and mark.

> [*He and Horatio conceal themselves.*
> *Ophelia's body is taken to the grave.*]

LAERTES: What ceremony else?
HAMLET [*to Horatio*]: That is Laertes, a very noble youth. **Mark.**
LAERTES: What ceremony else?
PRIEST: Her obsequies have been as far enlarg'd   195
  As we have warranty. Her death was doubtful,
  And, but that great command o'ersways the order,
  She should in ground unsanctified been lodg'd
  Till the last trumpet. For° charitable prayers,
  Shards,° flints, and pebbles should be thrown on her.   200
  Yet here she is allow'd her virgin crants,°
  Her maiden strewments,° and the bringing home
  Of bell and burial.°
LAERTES: Must there no more be done?
PRIEST: No more be done.
  We should profane the service of the dead   205
  To sing a requiem and such rest to her
  As to peace-parted souls.
LAERTES: Lay her i' th' earth,
  And from her fair and unpolluted flesh
  May violets° spring! I tell thee, churlish priest,
  A minist'ring angel shall my sister be   210
  When thou liest howling!
HAMLET [*to Horatio*]:   What, the fair Ophelia!
QUEEN [*scattering flowers*]: Sweets to the sweet! Farewell.
  I hoped thou shouldst have been my Hamlet's wife.
  I thought thy bride-bed to have deck'd, sweet maid,
  And not have strew'd thy grave.
LAERTES: O, treble woe   215
  Fall ten times treble on that cursed head
  Whose wicked deed thy most ingenious sense°
  Depriv'd thee of! Hold off the earth awhile,

---

190. Fordo it: Destroy its.   **estate:** Rank.   **191. Couch:** Hide, lurk.   **199. For:**
In place of.   **200. Shards:** Broken bits of pottery.   **201. crants:** Garland.
202. strewments: Traditional strewing of flowers.   **202–03. bringing . . . burial:**
Laying to rest of the body in consecrated ground, to the sound of the bell.
209. violets: See IV, V, 181 and note.   **217. ingenious sense:** Mind endowed
with finest qualities.

Till I have caught her once more in mine arms.

> [*Leaps into the grave and embraces Ophelia.*]

Now pile your dust upon the quick and dead,   220
Till of this flat a mountain you have made
T 'o'ertop old Pelion,° or the skyish head
Of blue Olympus.°

HAMLET [*coming forward*]: What is he whose grief
Bears such an emphasis, whose phrase of sorrow   225
Conjures the wand'ring stars,° and makes them stand
Like wonder-wounded hearers? This is I,
Hamlet the Dane.°

LAERTES: The devil take thy soul!

> [*Grappling with him.*]

HAMLET: Thou pray'st not well.
I prithee, take thy fingers from my throat;   230
For, though I am not splenitive° and rash,
Yet have I in me something dangerous,
Which let thy wisdom fear. Hold off thy hand.

KING: Pluck them asunder.

QUEEN: Hamlet, Hamlet!

ALL: Gentlemen!

HORATIO: Good my lord, be quiet.   235

> [*Hamlet and Horatio are parted.*]

HAMLET: Why, I will fight with him upon this theme
Until my eyelids will no longer wag.

QUEEN: O my son, what theme?

HAMLET: I lov'd Ophelia. Forty thousand brothers
Could not with all their quantity of love   240
Make up my sum. What wilt thou do for her?

KING: O, he is mad, Laertes.

QUEEN: For love of God, forbear him.

HAMLET: 'Swounds,° show me what thou' do.
Woo 't° weep? Woo 't fight? Woo 't fast? Woo 't tear thyself?   245
Woo 't drink up eisel?° Eat a crocodile?
I'll do 't. Dost thou come here to whine?

222, 223. Pelion, Olympus: Mountains in the north of Thessaly; see also *Ossa* at
line 253.   **226. wand'ring stars:** Planets.   **228. the Dane:** This title normally
signifies the king, see I, I, 15 and note.   **231. splenitive:** Quick-tempered.
244. 'Swounds: By His (Christ's) wounds.   **245. Woo 't:** Wilt thou.   **246. eisel:**
Vinegar.

To outface me with leaping in her grave?
Be buried quick° with her, and so will I.
And, if thou prate of mountains, let them throw   250
Millions of acres on us, till our ground,
Singeing his pate° against the burning zone,°
Make Ossa° like a wart! Nay, an thou 'lt mouth,°
I'll rant as well as thou.
QUEEN: This is mere° madness,
And thus a while the fit will work on him;   255
Anon, as patient as the female dove
When that her golden couplets° are disclos'd,°
His silence will sit drooping.
HAMLET: Hear you, sir.
What is the reason that you use me thus?
I lov'd you ever. But it is no matter.   260
Let Hercules himself do what he may,
The cat will mew, and dog will have his day.°
KING: I pray thee, good Horatio, wait upon him.

                                    (*Exit Hamlet and Horatio.*)

[*To Laertes.*] Strengthen your patience in° our last night's speech;
We'll put the matter to the present push.°—   265
Good Gertrude, set some watch over your son.—
This grave shall have a living° monument.
An hour of quiet shortly shall we see;
Till then, in patience our proceeding be.   (*Exeunt.*)

                        {*Scene II*}°

(*Enter Hamlet and Horatio.*)

HAMLET: So much for this, sir; now shall you see the other.°
    You do remember all the circumstance?
HORATIO: Remember it, my lord!
HAMLET: Sir, in my heart there was a kind of fighting

---

249. quick: Alive.   **252. his pate:** Its head, i.e., top.   **burning zone:** Sun's orbit.
253. Ossa: Another mountain in Thessaly. (In their war against the Olympian gods,
the giants attempted to heap Ossa, Pelion, and Olympus on one another to scale
heaven.) **mouth:** Rant.   **254. mere:** Utter.   **257. golden couplets:** Two baby
pigeons, covered with yellow down.   **disclos'd:** Hatched.   **261–62. Let . . . day:**
Despite any blustering attempts at interference every person will sooner or later do
what he must do.   **264. in:** By recalling.   **265. present push:** Immediate test.
267. living: Lasting; also refers (for Laertes' benefit) to the plot against Hamlet.
V, II. Location: The castle.   **1. see the other:** Hear the other news.

That would not let me sleep. Methought I lay   5
Worse than the mutines° in the bilboes.° Rashly,°
And prais'd be rashness for it—let us know,°
Our indiscretion sometime serves us well
When our deep plots do pall,° and that should learn° us
There's a divinity that shapes our ends,   10
Rough-hew° them how we will—

HORATIO: That is most certain.

HAMLET: Up from my cabin,
My sea-gown scarf'd about me, in the dark
Grop'd I to find out them, had my desire,
Finger'd° their packet, and in fine° withdrew   15
To mine own room again, making so bold,
My fears forgetting manners, to unseal
Their grand commission; where I found, Horatio—
Ah, royal knavery!—an exact command,
Larded° with many several sorts of reasons   20
Importing° Denmark's health and England's too,
With, ho, such bugs° and goblins in my life,°
That, on the supervise,° no leisure bated,°
No, not to stay the grinding of the axe,
My head should be struck off.

HORATIO: Is 't possible?   25

HAMLET: Here's the commission; read it at more leisure.

                                     [*Gives document.*]

But wilt thou hear now how I did proceed?

HORATIO: I beseech you.

HAMLET: Being thus benetted round with villainies,
Or I could make a prologue to my brains,
They had begun the play.° I sat me down,   30
Devis'd a new commission, wrote it fair.°
I once did hold it, as our statists° do,

---

6. mutines: Mutineers. **bilboes:** Shackles. **Rashly:** On impulse (this adverb goes with lines 12ff.). **7. know:** Acknowledge. **9. pall:** Fail. **learn:** Teach. **11. Rough-hew:** Shape roughly. **15. Finger'd:** Pilfered, pinched. **in fine:** Finally, in conclusion. **20. Larded:** Enriched. **21. Importing:** Relating to. **22. bugs:** Bugbears, hobgoblins. **in my life:** To be feared if I were allowed to live. **23. supervise:** Reading. **leisure bated:** Delay allowed. **30–31. Or . . . play:** Before I could consciously turn my brain to the matter, it had started working on a plan. (*Or* means *ere*.) **32. fair:** In a clear hand. **33. statists:** Statesmen.

A baseness° to write fair, and labor'd much
How to forget that learning, but, sir, now   35
It did me yeoman's° service. Wilt thou know
Th' effect° of what I wrote?
HORATIO: Ay, good my lord.
HAMLET: An earnest conjuration from the King,
As England was his faithful tributary,
As love between them like the palm might flourish,   40
As peace should still her wheaten garland° wear
And stand a comma° 'tween their amities,
And many such-like as's° of great charge,°
That, on the view and knowing of these contents,
Without debasement further, more or less,   45
He should those bearers put to sudden death,
Not shriving time° allow'd.
HORATIO: How was this seal'd?
HAMLET: Why, even in that was heaven ordinant.°
I had my father's signet° in my purse,
Which was the model of that Danish seal;   50
Folded the writ up in the form of th' other,
Subscrib'd° it, gave 't th' impression,° plac'd it safely,
The changeling° never known. Now, the next day
Was our sea-fight, and what to this was sequent
Thou knowest already.   55
HORATIO: So Guildenstern and Rosencrantz go to 't.
HAMLET: [Why, man, they did make love to this employment.]
They are not near my conscience. Their defeat
Does by their own insinuation° grow.
'Tis dangerous when the baser nature comes   60
Between the pass° and fell° incensed points
Of mighty opposites.
HORATIO: Why, what a king is this!
HAMLET: Does it not, think thee, stand° me now upon—
He that hath killed my king and whor'd my mother,

---

34. baseness: Lower-class trait. **36. yeoman's:** Substantial, workmanlike.
37. effect: Purport. **41. wheaten garland:** Symbolic of fruitful agriculture, of
peace. **42. comma:** Indicating continuity, link. **43. as's:** (1) The "whereases"
of formal document, (2) asses. **charge:** (1) Import, (2) burden. **47. shriving
time:** Time for confession and absolution. **48. ordinant:** Directing.
49. signet: Small seal. **52. Subscrib'd:** Signed. **impression:** With a wax seal.
53. changeling: The substituted letter (literally, a fairy child substituted for a
human one). **59. insinuation:** Interference. **61. pass:** Thrust. **fell:** Fierce.
63. stand: Become incumbent.

Popp'd in between th' election° and my hopes,   65
Thrown out his angle° for my proper° life,
And with such coz'nage°—is 't not perfect conscience
[To quit° him with this arm? And is 't not to be damn'd
To let this canker° of our nature come
In further evil?   70
HORATIO: It must be shortly known to him from England
  What is the issue of the business there.
HAMLET: It will be short. The interim is mine,
  And a man's life 's no more than to say "One."°
  But I am very sorry, good Horatio,   75
  That to Laertes I forgot myself,
  For by the image of my cause I see
  The portraiture of his. I'll court his favors.
  But, sure, the bravery° of his grief did put me
  Into a tow'ring passion.
HORATIO: Peace, who comes here?]   80

(*Enter a Courtier* [*Osric*].)

OSRIC: Your lordship is right welcome back to Denmark.
HAMLET: I humbly thank you, sir. [*To Horatio.*] Dost know this water-fly?
HORATIO: No, my good lord.
HAMLET: Thy state is the more gracious, for 'tis a vice to know him. He
  hath much land, and fertile. Let a beast be lord of beasts, and his crib   85
  shall stand at the King's mess.° 'Tis a chough,° but, as I say, spacious in
  the possession of dirt.
OSRIC: Sweet lord, if your lordship were at leisure, I should impart a
  thing to you from his Majesty.
HAMLET: I will receive it, sir, with all diligence of spirit. Put your bonnet   90
  to his right use; 'tis for the head.
OSRIC: I thank your lordship, it is very hot.
HAMLET: No, believe me, 'tis very cold; the wind is northerly.
OSRIC: It is indifferent° cold, my lord, indeed.
HAMLET: But yet methinks it is very sultry and hot for my complexion.°   95
OSRIC: Exceedingly, my lord; it is very sultry, as 'twere—I cannot tell
  how. My lord, his Majesty bade me signify to you that 'a has laid a
  great wager on your head. Sir, this is the matter—

---

65. election: The Danish monarch was "elected" by a small number of high-
ranking electors. **66. angle:** Fishing line. **proper:** Very. **67. coz'nage:**
Trickery. **68. quit:** Repay. **69. canker:** Ulcer. **74. a man's . . . "One":** To take
a man's life requires no more than to count to one as one duels. **79. bravery:**
Bravado. **85–86. Let . . . mess:** If a man, no matter how beastlike, is as rich
in possessions as Osric, he may eat at the king's table. **86. chough:** Chattering
jackdaw. **94. indifferent:** Somewhat. **95. complexion:** Temperament.

HAMLET: I beseech you, remember—

> [*Hamlet moves him to put on his hat.*]

OSRIC: Nay, good my lord; for my ease,° in good faith. Sir, here is newly 100
come to court Laertes—believe me, an absolute gentleman, full of most
excellent differences,° of very soft society° and great showing.° Indeed,
to speak feelingly° of him, he is the card° or calendar° of gentry,° for you
shall find in him the continent of what part° a gentleman would see.

HAMLET: Sir, his definement° suffers no perdition° in you, though, I 105
know, to divide him inventorially° would dozy° th' arithmetic of memory, and yet but yaw° neither° in respect of° his quick sail. But, in the
verity of extolment,° I take him to be a soul of great article,° and his
infusion° of such dearth and rareness,° as, to make true diction° of
him, his semblable° is his mirror, and who else would trace° him, his 110
umbrage,° nothing more.

OSRIC: Your lordship speaks most infallibly of him.

HAMLET: The concernancy,° sir? Why do we wrap the gentleman in our
more rawer breath?°

OSRIC: Sir? 115

HORATIO: Is 't not possible to understand in another tongue?° You will do
't,° sir, really.

HAMLET: What imports the nomination° of this gentleman?

OSRIC: Of Laertes?

HORATIO [*to Hamlet*]: His purse is empty already; all 's golden words are 120
spent.

HAMLET: Of him, sir.

---

100. for my ease: A conventional reply declining the invitation to put his hat
back on. **102. differences:** Special qualities. **soft society:** Agreeable manners.
great showing: Distinguished appearance. **103. feelingly:** With just perception.
card: Chart, map. **calendar:** Guide. **gentry:** Good breeding. **104. the continent ... part:** One who contains in him all the qualities (a *continent* is that
which contains). **105. definement:** Definition. (Hamlet proceeds to mock Osric
by using his lofty diction back at him.) **perdition:** Loss, diminution.
106. divide him inventorially: Enumerate his graces. **dozy:** Dizzy. **107. yaw:**
To move unsteadily (said of a ship). **neither:** For all that. **in respect of:** In
comparison with. **107–08. in ... extolment:** In true praise (of him).
108. article: Moment or importance. **109. infusion:** Essence, character
imparted by nature. **dearth and rareness:** Rarity. **make true diction:** Speak
truly. **110. semblable:** Only true likeness. **who ... trace:** Any other person
who would wish to follow. **111. umbrage:** Shadow. **113. concernancy:**
Import, relevance. **114. breath:** Speech. **116. to understand ... tongue:** For
Osric to understand when someone else speaks in his manner. (Horatio twits
Osric for not being able to understand the kind of flowery speech he himself uses
when Hamlet speaks in such a vein.) **116–17. You will do't:** You can if you try.
118. nomination: Naming.

OSRIC: I know you are not ignorant—

HAMLET: I would you did, sir; yet, in faith, if you did, it would not much
approve° me. Well, sir?   125

OSRIC: You are not ignorant of what excellence Laertes is—

HAMLET: I dare not confess that, lest I should compare° with him in
excellence; but to know a man well were to know himself.°

OSRIC: I mean, sir, for his weapon; but in the imputation laid on him by
them,° in his meed° he's unfellow'd.°   130

HAMLET: What's his weapon?

OSRIC: Rapier and dagger.

HAMLET: That's two of his weapons—but well.

OSRIC: The King, sir, hath wager'd with him six Barbary horses, against
the which he has impawn'd,° as I take it, six French rapiers and   135
poniards, with their assigns,° as girdle, hangers,° and so. Three of the
carriages,° in faith, are very dear to fancy,° very responsive° to the
hilts, most delicate° carriages, and of very liberal conceit.°

HAMLET: What call you the carriages?

HORATIO [to Hamlet]: I knew you must be edified by the margent° ere you 140
had done.

OSRIC: The carriages, sir, are the hangers.

HAMLET: The phrase would be more germane to the matter if we could
carry a cannon by our sides; I would it might be hangers till then. But,
on: six Barb'ry horses against six French swords, their assigns, and   145
three liberal-conceited carriages; that's the French bet against the
Danish. Why is this impawn'd, as you call it?

OSRIC: The King, sir, hath laid,° sir, that in a dozen passes° between
yourself and him, he shall not exceed you three hits. He hath laid on
twelve for nine, and it would come to immediate trial, if your lordship 150
would vouchsafe the answer.

HAMLET: How if I answer no?

---

125. approve: Commend. **127. compare:** Seem to compete. **128. but . . .
himself:** For, to recognize excellence in another man, one must know
oneself. **129–30. imputation . . . them:** Reputation given him by others.
130. meed: Merit. **unfellow'd:** Unmatched. **135. impawn'd:** Staked, wagered.
136. assigns: Appurtenances. **hangers:** Straps on the sword belt (*girdle*) from
which the sword hung. **137. carriages:** An affected way of saying *hangers;* literally, gun-carriages. **dear to fancy:** Fancifully designed, tasteful. **responsive:**
Corresponding closely, matching. **138. delicate:** I.e., in workmanship. **liberal
conceit:** Elaborate design. **140. margent:** Margin of a book, place for explana-
tory notes. **148. laid:** Wagered. **passes:** Bouts. (The odds of the betting are
hard to explain. Possibly the king bets that Hamlet will win at least five out of
twelve, at which point Laertes raises the odds against himself by betting he will
win nine.)

OSRIC: I mean, my lord, the opposition of your person in trial.

HAMLET: Sir, I will walk here in the hall. If it please his Majesty, it is the breathing time° of day with me. Let the foils be brought, the gentle- 155 man willing, and the King hold his purpose, I will win for him an I can; if not, I will gain nothing but my shame and the odd hits.

OSRIC: Shall I deliver you so?

HAMLET: To this effect, sir—after what flourish your nature will.

OSRIC: I commend my duty to your lordship.   160

HAMLET: Yours, yours. [Exit Osric.] He does well to commend it himself; there are no tongues else for 's turn.

HORATIO: This lapwing° runs away with the shell on his head.

HAMLET: 'A did comply, sir, with his dug,° before 'a suck'd it. Thus has he—and many more of the same breed that I know the drossy° age 165 dotes on—only got the tune° of the time and, out of an habit of encounter,° a kind of yesty° collection,° which carries them through and through the most fann'd and winnow'd° opinions; and do but blow them to their trial, the bubbles are out.°

(Enter a Lord.)

LORD: My lord, his Majesty commended him to you by young Osric, who 170 brings back to him that you attend him in the hall. He sends to know if your pleasure hold to play with Laertes, or that you will take longer time.

HAMLET: I am constant to my purposes; they follow the King's pleasure. If his fitness speaks,° mine is ready; now or whensoever, provided I be 175 so able as now.

LORD: The King and Queen and all are coming down.

HAMLET: In happy time.°

LORD: The Queen desires you to use some gentle entertainment° to Laertes before you fall to play.   180

HAMLET: She well instructs me.   [Exit Lord.]

HORATIO: You will lose, my lord.

---

155. **breathing time:** Exercise period.   163. **lapwing:** A bird that draws intruders away from its nest and was thought to run about when newly hatched with its head in the shell; a seeming reference to Osric's hat.   164. **comply . . . dug:** Observe ceremonious formality toward his mother's teat.   165. **drossy:** Frivolous.   166. **tune:** Temper, mood, manner of speech.   166–67. **habit of encounter:** Demeanor of social intercourse.   167. **yesty:** Yeasty, frothy.   **collection:** I.e., of current phrases.   168. **fann'd and winnow'd:** Select and refined.   169. **blow . . . out:** Put them to the test, and their ignorance is exposed.   175. **If . . . speaks:** If his readiness answers to the time.   178. **In happy time:** A phrase of courtesy indicating acceptance.   179. **entertainment:** Greeting.

HAMLET: I do not think so. Since he went into France, I have been in
   continual practice; I shall win at the odds. But thou wouldst not think
   how ill all's here about my heart; but it is no matter.   185
HORATIO: Nay, good my lord—
HAMLET: It is but foolery, but it is such a kind of gain-giving,° as would
   perhaps trouble a woman.
HORATIO: If your mind dislike anything, obey it. I will forestall their
   repair hither, and say you are not fit.   190
HAMLET: Not a whit, we defy augury. There is special providence in the
   fall of a sparrow. If it be now, 'tis not to come; if it be not to come, it
   will be now, if it be not now, yet it will come. The readiness is all. Since
   no man of aught he leaves knows what is 't to leave betimes,° let be.

(*A table prepar'd.* [*Enter*] *trumpets, drums, and Officers with cushions; King,
Queen,* [*Osric,*] *and all the State; foils, daggers,* [*and wine borne in;*] *and
Laertes.*)

KING: Come, Hamlet, come, and take this hand from me.   195

[*The King puts Laertes' hand into Hamlet's.*]

HAMLET: Give me your pardon, sir. I have done you wrong,
   But pardon 't, as you are a gentleman.
   This presence° knows,
   And you must needs have heard, how I am punish'd
   With a sore distraction. What I have done   200
   That might your nature, honor, and exception°
   Roughly awake, I here proclaim was madness.
   Was 't Hamlet wrong'd Laertes? Never Hamlet.
   If Hamlet from himself be ta'en away,
   And when he's not himself does wrong Laertes,   205
   Then Hamlet does it not, Hamlet denies it.
   Who does it, then? His madness. If 't be so,
   Hamlet is of the faction that is wrong'd;
   His madness is poor Hamlet's enemy.
   [Sir, in this audience,]   210
   Let my disclaiming from a purpos'd evil
   Free me so far in your most generous thoughts
   That I have shot my arrow o'er the house
   And hurt my brother.
LAERTES: I am satisfied in nature,°
   Whose motive in this case should stir me most   215

---

187. **gain-giving:** Misgiving.   194. **what . . . betimes:** What is the best time
to leave it.   198. **presence:** Royal assembly.   201. **exception:** Disapproval.
214. **in nature:** As to my personal feelings.

To my revenge. But in my terms of honor
I stand aloof, and will no reconcilement
Till by some elder masters of known honor
I have a voice° and precedent of peace
To keep my name ungor'd. But till that time,   220
I do receive your offer'd love like love,
And will not wrong it.
HAMLET: I embrace it freely,
And will this brothers' wager frankly play.
Give us the foils. Come on.
LAERTES: Come, one for me.
HAMLET: I'll be your foil,° Laertes. In mine ignorance   225
Your skill shall, like a star i' th' darkest night,
Stick fiery off° indeed.
LAERTES: You mock me, sir.
HAMLET: No, by this hand.
KING: Give them the foils, young Osric. Cousin Hamlet,
You know the wager?
HAMLET: Very well, my lord.   230
Your Grace has laid the odds o' th' weaker side.
KING: I do not fear it; I have seen you both.
But since he is better'd,° we have therefore odds.
LAERTES: This is too heavy, let me see another.

[Exchanges his foil for another.]

HAMLET: This likes me well. These foils have all a length?   235

[They prepare to play.]

OSRIC: Ay, my good lord.
KING: Set me the stoups of wine upon that table.
If Hamlet give the first or second hit,
Or quit° in answer of the third exchange,
Let all the battlements their ordnance fire.   240
The King shall drink to Hamlet's better breath,
And in the cup an union° shall he throw,
Richer than that which four successive kings
In Denmark's crown have worn. Give me the cups,
And let the kettle° to the trumpet speak,   245

219. **voice:** Authoritative pronouncement.   225. **foil:** Thin metal background
which sets a jewel off (with pun on the blunted rapier for fencing).   **227. Stick
fiery off:** Stand out brilliantly.   **233. is better'd:** Has improved; is the odds-on
favorite.   **239. quit:** Repay (with a hit).   **242. union:** Pearl (so called, according to Pliny's *Natural History,* IX, because pearls are *unique,* never identical).
245. kettle: Kettledrum.

The trumpet to the cannoneer without,
The cannons to the heavens, the heaven to earth,
"Now the King drinks to Hamlet." Come, begin.

(Trumpets the while.)

And you, the judges, bear a wary eye.
HAMLET: Come on sir.
LAERTES: Come, my lord.   *[They play. Hamlet scores a hit.]*   250
HAMLET: One.
LAERTES: No.
HAMLET: Judgment.
OSRIC: A hit, a very palpable hit.

*(Drum, trumpets, and shot. Flourish.
A piece goes off.)*

LAERTES: Well, again.   255
KING: Stay, give me drink. Hamlet, this pearl is thine.

[He throws a pearl in Hamlet's cup and drinks.]

Here's to thy health. Give him the cup.
HAMLET: I'll play this bout first, set it by awhile.
Come. *[They play.]* Another hit; what say you?
LAERTES: A touch, a touch. I do confess 't.   260
KING: Our son shall win.
QUEEN: He's fat,° and scant of breath.
Here, Hamlet, take my napkin,° rub thy brows.
The Queen carouses° to thy fortune, Hamlet.
HAMLET: Good madam!
KING: Gertrude, do not drink.   265
QUEEN: I will, my lord; I pray you pardon me.

[Drinks.]

KING *[aside]*: It is the pois'ned cup. It is too late.
HAMLET: I dare not drink yet, madam; by and by.
QUEEN: Come, let me wipe thy face.
LAERTES *[to King]*: My lord, I'll hit him now.
KING: I do not think 't.   270
LAERTES *[aside]*: And yet it is almost against my conscience.
HAMLET: Come, for the third Laertes. You do but dally.
I pray you, pass with your best violence;

---

261. **fat:** Not physically fit, out of training.   262. **napkin:** Handkerchief.
263. **carouses:** Drinks a toast.

I am afeard you make a wanton of me.°
LAERTES: Say you so? Come on.   [*They play.*] 275
OSRIC: Nothing, neither way.
LAERTES: Have at you now!

> [*Laertes wounds Hamlet; then, in scuffling,*
> *they change rapiers,° and Hamlet wounds Laertes.*]

KING: Part them! They are incens'd.
HAMLET: Nay, come, again.   [*The Queen falls.*]
OSRIC: Look to the Queen there, ho!
HORATIO: They bleed on both sides. How is it, my lord?
OSRIC: How is 't, Laertes?   280
LAERTES: Why, as a woodcock° to mine own springe,° Osric;
  I am justly kill'd with mine own treachery.
HAMLET: How does the Queen?
KING: She swoons to see them bleed.
QUEEN: No, no, the drink, the drink—O my dear Hamlet—
  The drink, the drink! I am pois'ned.   [*Dies.*] 285
HAMLET: O villainy! Ho, let the door be lock'd!
  Treachery! Seek it out.   [*Laertes falls.*]
LAERTES: It is here, Hamlet. Hamlet, thou art slain.
  No med'cine in the world can do thee good;
  In thee there is not half an hour's life.   290
  The treacherous instrument is in thy hand,
  Unbated° and envenom'd. The foul practice
  Hath turn'd itself on me. Lo, here I lie,
  Never to rise again. Thy mother's pois'ned.
  I can no more. The King, the King's to blame.   295
HAMLET: The point envenom'd too? Then, venom, to thy work.

> [*Stabs the King.*]

ALL: Treason! Treason!
KING: O, yet defend me, friends; I am but hurt.
HAMLET: Here, thou incestuous, murd'rous, damned Dane,

> [*He forces the King to drink the poisoned cup.*]

---

274. make . . . me: Treat me like a spoiled child, holding back to give me an
advantage. [S.D.] *in scuffling, they change rapiers:* This stage direction occurs
in the Folio. According to a widespread stage tradition, Hamlet receives a scratch,
realizes that Laertes' sword is unbated, and accordingly forces an exchange.
281. woodcock: A bird, a type of stupidity or as a decoy. **springe:** Trap, snare.
292. Unbated: Not blunted with a button.

Drink off this potion. Is thy union° here?   300
Follow my mother.   [*King dies.*]
LAERTES: He is justly serv'd.
It is a poison temper'd° by himself.
Exchange forgiveness with me, noble Hamlet.
Mine and my father's death come not upon thee,
Nor thine on me!   [*Dies.*] 305
HAMLET: Heaven make thee free of it! I follow thee.
I am dead, Horatio. Wretched Queen, adieu!
You that look pale and tremble at this chance,
That are but mutes° or audience to this act,
Had I but time—as this fell° sergeant,° Death,   310
Is strict in his arrest—O, I could tell you—
But let it be. Horatio, I am dead;
Thou livest. Report me and my cause aright
To the unsatisfied.
HORATIO: Never believe it.
I am more an antique Roman° than a Dane.   315
Here's yet some liquor left.

> [*He attempts to drink from the poisoned cup.*
> *Hamlet prevents him.*]

HAMLET: As th' art a man,
Give me the cup! Let go! By heaven, I'll ha 't.
O God, Horatio, what a wounded name,
Things standing thus unknown, shall I leave behind me!
If thou didst ever hold me in thy heart,   320
Absent thee from felicity awhile,
And in this harsh world draw thy breath in pain
To tell my story.

> (*A march afar off* [*and a volley within*].)

What warlike noise is this?
OSRIC: Young Fortinbras, with conquest come from Poland,
To the ambassadors of England gives   325
This warlike volley.
HAMLET: O, I die, Horatio!
The potent poison quite o'ercrows° my spirit.

---

300. union: Pearl (see line 242; with grim puns on the word's other meanings: marriage, shared death[?]). **302. temper'd:** Mixed. **309. mutes:** Silent observers. **310. fell:** Cruel. **sergeant:** Sheriff's officer. **315. Roman:** It was the Roman custom to follow masters in death. **327. o'ercrows:** Triumphs over.

I cannot live to hear the news from England,
But I do prophesy th' election lights
On Fortinbras. He has my dying voice.°   330
So tell him, with th' occurrents° more and less
Which have solicited°—the rest is silence.   [*Dies.*]
HORATIO: Now cracks a noble heart. Good night, sweet prince;
And flights of angels sing thee to thy rest!

                                               [*March within.*]

Why does the drum come hither?   335

(*Enter Fortinbras, with the [English] Ambassadors [with drum, colors, and attendants].*)

FORTINBRAS: Where is this sight?
HORATIO: What is it you would see?
If aught of woe or wonder, cease your search.
FORTINBRAS: This quarry° cries on havoc.° O proud Death.
What feast is toward° in thine eternal cell,
That thou so many princes at a shot   340
So bloodily hast struck?
FIRST AMBASSADOR: The sight is dismal;
And our affairs from England come too late.
The ears are senseless that should give us hearing,
To tell him his commandment is fulfill'd,
That Rosencrantz and Guildenstern are dead.   345
Where should we have our thanks?
HORATIO: Not from his° mouth,
Had it th' ability of life to thank you.
He never gave commandment for their death.
But since, so jump° upon this bloody question,°
You from the Polack wars, and you from England,   350
Are here arriv'd, give order that these bodies
High on a stage° be placed to the view,
And let me speak to th' yet unknowing world
How these things came about. So shall you hear
Of carnal, bloody, and unnatural acts,   355
Of accidental judgments,° casual° slaughters,
Of deaths put on° by cunning and forc'd cause,

---

330. voice: Vote.   **331. occurrents:** Events, incidents.   **332. solicited:** Moved, urged.   **338. quarry:** Heap of dead.   **cries on havoc:** Proclaims a general slaughter.   **339. toward:** In preparation.   **346. his:** Claudius's.   **349. jump:** Precisely.   **question:** Dispute.   **352. stage:** Platform.   **356. judgments:** Retributions.   **casual:** Occurring by chance.   **357. put on:** Instigated.

And, in this upshot, purposes mistook
Fall'n on th' inventors' heads. All this can I
Truly deliver.

FORTINBRAS: Let us haste to hear it,   360
And call the noblest to the audience.
For me, with sorrow I embrace my fortune.
I have some rights of memory° in this kingdom,
Which now to claim my vantage° doth invite me.

HORATIO: Of that I shall have also cause to speak,   365
And from his mouth whose voice will draw on more.°
But let this same be presently° perform'd,
Even while men's minds are wild, lest more mischance
On° plots and errors happen.

FORTINBRAS: Let four captains
Bear Hamlet, like a soldier, to the stage,   370
For he was likely, had he been put on,°
To have prov'd most royal; and, for his passage,°
The soldiers' music and the rite of war
Speak loudly for him.
Take up the bodies. Such a sight as this   375
Becomes the field,° but here shows much amiss.
Go, bid the soldiers shoot.

(*Exeunt* [*marching, bearing off the dead bodies;
a peal of ordnance is shot off*].)

c. 1600

---

363. **of memory:** Traditional, remembered. 364. **vantage:** Presence at this
opportune moment. 366. **voice . . . more:** Vote will influence still others.
367. **presently:** Immediately. 369. **On:** On the basis of. 371. **put on:** Invested
in royal office and so put to the test. 372. **passage:** Death. 376. **field:** I.e., of
battle.

A Doll House

HENRIK IBSEN [1828–1906]

TRANSLATED BY ROLF FJELDE

The Characters
TORVALD HELMER, *a lawyer*
NORA, *his wife*
DR. RANK
MRS. LINDE
NILS KROGSTAD, *a bank clerk*
THE HELMERS' THREE SMALL CHILDREN
ANNE-MARIE, *their nurse*
HELENE, *a maid*
A DELIVERY BOY

The action takes place in Helmer's residence.

ACT I

(*A comfortable room, tastefully but not expensively furnished. A door to the right in the back wall leads to the entryway; another to the left leads to Helmer's study. Between these doors, a piano. Midway in the left-hand wall a door, and further back a window. Near the window a round table with an armchair and a small sofa. In the right-hand wall, toward the rear, a door, and nearer the foreground a porcelain stove with two armchairs and a rocking chair beside it. Between the stove and the side door, a small table. Engravings on the walls. An étagère° with china figures and other small art objects; a small bookcase with richly bound books; the floor carpeted; a fire burning in the stove. It is a winter day.*)

Note: As Fjelde explains in his foreword to the translation, he does not use the possessive "A Doll's House" because "the house is not Nora's, as the possessive implies." Fjelde believes that Ibsen includes Torvald with Nora in the original title, "for the two of them at the play's opening are still posing like the little marzipan bride and groom atop the wedding cake."
[S.D.] *étagère:* Cabinet with shelves.

(*A bell rings in the entryway; shortly after we hear the door being unlocked. Nora comes into the room, humming happily to herself; she is wearing street clothes and carries an armload of packages, which she puts down on the table to the right. She has left the hall door open, and through it a Delivery Boy is seen holding a Christmas tree and a basket, which he gives to the Maid who let them in.*)

NORA: Hide the tree well, Helene. The children mustn't get a glimpse of it till this evening, after it's trimmed. (*To the Delivery Boy, taking out her purse.*) How much?

DELIVERY BOY: Fifty, ma'am.

NORA: There's a crown. No, keep the change. (*The Boy thanks her and leaves. Nora shuts the door. She laughs softly to herself while taking off her street things. Drawing a bag of macaroons from her pocket, she eats a couple, then steals over and listens at her husband's study door.*) Yes, he's home. (*Hums again as she moves to the table right.*)

HELMER (*from the study*): Is that my little lark twittering out there?

NORA (*busy opening some packages*): Yes, it is.

HELMER: Is that my squirrel rummaging around?

NORA: Yes!

HELMER: When did my squirrel get in?

NORA: Just now. (*Putting the macaroon bag in her pocket and wiping her mouth.*) Do come in, Torvald, and see what I've bought.

HELMER: Can't be disturbed. (*After a moment he opens the door and peers in, pen in hand.*) Bought, you say? All that there? Has the little spend-thrift been out throwing money around again?

NORA: Oh, but Torvald, this year we really should let ourselves go a bit. It's the first Christmas we haven't had to economize.

HELMER: But you know we can't go squandering.

NORA: Oh yes, Torvald, we can squander a little now. Can't we? Just a tiny, wee bit. Now that you've got a big salary and are going to make piles and piles of money.

HELMER: Yes — starting New Year's. But then it's a full three months till the raise comes through.

NORA: Pooh! We can borrow that long.

HELMER: Nora! (*Goes over and playfully takes her by the ear.*) Are your scatterbrains off again? What if today I borrowed a thousand crowns, and you squandered them over Christmas week, and then on New Year's Eve a roof tile fell on my head, and I lay there —

NORA (*putting her hand on his mouth*): Oh! Don't say such things!

HELMER: Yes, but what if it happened — then what?

NORA: If anything so awful happened, then it just wouldn't matter if I had debts or not.

HELMER: Well, but the people I'd borrowed from?

NORA: Them? Who cares about them! They're strangers.

HELMER: Nora, Nora, how like a woman! No, but seriously, Nora, you know what I think about that. No debts! Never borrow! Something of freedom's lost—and something of beauty, too—from a home that's founded on borrowing and debt. We've made a brave stand up to now, the two of us; and we'll go right on like that the little while we have to.

NORA (*going toward the stove*): Yes, whatever you say, Torvald.

HELMER (*following her*): Now, now, the little lark's wings mustn't droop. Come on, don't be a sulky squirrel. (*Taking out his wallet.*) Nora, guess what I have here.

NORA (*turning quickly*): Money!

HELMER: There, see. (*Hands her some notes.*) Good grief, I know how costs go up in a house at Christmastime.

NORA: Ten—twenty—thirty—forty. Oh, thank you, Torvald; I can manage no end on this.

HELMER: You really will have to.

NORA: Oh yes, I promise I will! But come here so I can show you everything I bought. And so cheap! Look, new clothes for Ivar here—and a sword. Here a horse and a trumpet for Bob. And a doll and a doll's bed here for Emmy; they're nothing much, but she'll tear them to bits in no time anyway. And here I have dress material and handkerchiefs for the maids. Old Anne-Marie really deserves something more.

HELMER: And what's in that package there?

NORA (*with a cry*): Torvald, no! You can't see that till tonight!

HELMER: I see. But tell me now, you little prodigal, what have you thought of for yourself?

NORA: For myself? Oh, I don't want anything at all.

HELMER: Of course you do. Tell me just what—within reason—you'd most like to have.

NORA: I honestly don't know. Oh, listen, Torvald—

HELMER: Well?

NORA (*fumbling at his coat buttons, without looking at him*): If you want to give me something, then maybe you could—you could—

HELMER: Come on, out with it.

NORA (*hurriedly*): You could give me money, Torvald. No more than you think you can spare; then one of these days I'll buy something with it.

HELMER: But Nora—

NORA: Oh, please, Torvald darling, do that! I beg you, please. Then I could hang the bills in pretty gilt paper on the Christmas tree. Wouldn't that be fun?

HELMER: What are those little birds called that always fly through their fortunes?

NORA: Oh yes, spendthrifts; I know all that. But let's do as I say, Torvald; then I'll have time to decide what I really need most. That's very sensible, isn't it?

HELMER (*smiling*): Yes, very—that is, if you actually hung onto the money I give you, and you actually used it to buy yourself something. But it goes for the house and for all sorts of foolish things, and then I only have to lay out some more.

NORA: Oh, but Torvald—

HELMER: Don't deny it, my dear little Nora. (*Putting his arm around her waist.*) Spendthrifts are sweet, but they use up a frightful amount of money. It's incredible what it costs a man to feed such birds.

NORA: Oh, how can you say that! Really, I save everything I can.

HELMER (*laughing*): Yes, that's the truth. Everything you can. But that's nothing at all.

NORA (*humming, with a smile of quiet satisfaction*): Hm, if you only knew what expenses we larks and squirrels have, Torvald.

HELMER: You're an odd little one. Exactly the way your father was. You're never at a loss for scaring up money; but the moment you have it, it runs right out through your fingers; you never know what you've done with it. Well, one takes you as you are. It's deep in your blood. Yes, these things are hereditary, Nora.

NORA: Ah, I could wish I'd inherited many of Papa's qualities.

HELMER: And I couldn't wish you anything but just what you are, my sweet little lark. But wait; it seems to me you have a very—what should I call it?—a very suspicious look today—

NORA: I do?

HELMER: You certainly do. Look me straight in the eye.

NORA (*looking at him*): Well?

HELMER (*shaking an admonitory finger*): Surely my sweet tooth hasn't been running riot in town today, has she?

NORA: No. Why do you imagine that?

HELMER: My sweet tooth really didn't make a little detour through the confectioner's?

NORA: No, I assure you, Torvald—

HELMER: Hasn't nibbled some pastry?

NORA: No, not at all.

HELMER: Not even munched a macaroon or two?

NORA: No, Torvald, I assure you, really—

HELMER: There, there now. Of course I'm only joking.

NORA (*going to the table, right*): You know I could never think of going against you.

HELMER: No, I understand that; and you *have* given me your word. (*Going over to her.*) Well, you keep your little Christmas secrets to yourself, Nora darling. I expect they'll come to light this evening, when the tree is lit.

NORA: Did you remember to ask Dr. Rank?

HELMER: No. But there's no need for that, it's assumed he'll be dining with us. All the same, I'll ask him when he stops by here this morning.

I've ordered some fine wine. Nora, you can't imagine how I'm looking forward to this evening.

NORA: So am I. And what fun for the children, Torvald!

HELMER: Ah, it's so gratifying to know that one's gotten a safe, secure job, and with a comfortable salary. It's a great satisfaction, isn't it?

NORA: Oh, it's wonderful!

HELMER: Remember last Christmas? Three whole weeks before, you shut yourself in every evening till long after midnight, making flowers for the Christmas tree, and all the other decorations to surprise us. Ugh, that was the dullest time I've ever lived through.

NORA: It wasn't at all dull for me.

HELMER (*smiling*): But the outcome *was* pretty sorry, Nora.

NORA: Oh, don't tease me with that again. How could I help it that the cat came in and tore everything to shreds.

HELMER: No, poor thing, you certainly couldn't. You wanted so much to please us all, and that's what counts. But it's just as well that the hard times are past.

NORA: Yes, it's really wonderful.

HELMER: Now I don't have to sit here alone, boring myself, and you don't have to tire your precious eyes and your fair little delicate hands—

NORA (*clapping her hands*): No, is it really true, Torvald, I don't have to? Oh, how wonderfully lovely to hear! (*Taking his arm.*) Now I'll tell you just how I've thought we should plan things. Right after Christmas— (*The doorbell rings.*) Oh, the bell. (*Straightening the room up a bit.*) Somebody would have to come. What a bore!

HELMER: I'm not at home to visitors, don't forget.

MAID (*from the hall doorway*): Ma'am, a lady to see you—

NORA: All right, let her come in.

MAID (*to Helmer*): And the doctor's just come too.

HELMER: Did he go right to my study?

MAID: Yes, he did.

(*Helmer goes into his room. The Maid shows in Mrs. Linde, dressed in traveling clothes, and shuts the door after her.*)

MRS. LINDE (*in a dispirited and somewhat hesitant voice*): Hello, Nora.

NORA (*uncertain*): Hello—

MRS. LINDE: You don't recognize me.

NORA: No, I don't know—but wait, I think—(*Exclaiming.*) What! Kristine! Is it really you?

MRS. LINDE: Yes, it's me.

NORA: Kristine! To think I didn't recognize you. But then, how could I? (*More quietly.*) How you've changed, Kristine!

MRS. LINDE: Yes, no doubt I have. In nine—ten long years.

NORA: Is it so long since we met! Yes, it's all of that. Oh, these last eight years have been a happy time, believe me. And so now you've come in to town, too. Made the long trip in the winter. That took courage.

MRS. LINDE: I just got here by ship this morning.

NORA: To enjoy yourself over Christmas, of course. Oh, how lovely! Yes, enjoy ourselves, we'll do that. But take your coat off. You're not still cold? (*Helping her.*) There now, let's get cozy here by the stove. No, the easy chair there! I'll take the rocker here. (*Seizing her hands.*) Yes, now you have your old look again; it was only in that first moment. You're a bit more pale, Kristine—and maybe a bit thinner.

MRS. LINDE: And much, much older, Nora.

NORA: Yes, perhaps a bit older; a tiny, tiny bit; not much at all. (*Stopping short; suddenly serious.*) Oh, but thoughtless me, to sit here, chattering away. Sweet, good Kristine, can you forgive me?

MRS. LINDE: What do you mean, Nora?

NORA (*softly*): Poor Kristine, you've become a widow.

MRS. LINDE: Yes, three years ago.

NORA: Oh, I knew it, of course; I read it in the papers. Oh, Kristine, you must believe me; I often thought of writing you then, but I kept postponing it, and something always interfered.

MRS. LINDE: Nora dear, I understand completely.

NORA: No, it was awful of me, Kristine. You poor thing, how much you must have gone through. And he left you nothing?

MRS. LINDE: No.

NORA: And no children?

MRS. LINDE: No.

NORA: Nothing at all, then?

MRS. LINDE: Not even a sense of loss to feed on.

NORA (*looking incredulously at her*): But Kristine, how could that be?

MRS. LINDE (*smiling wearily and smoothing her hair*): Oh, sometimes it happens, Nora.

NORA: So completely alone. How terribly hard that must be for you. I have three lovely children. You can't see them now; they're out with the maid. But now you must tell me everything—

MRS. LINDE: No, no, no, tell me about yourself.

NORA: No, you begin. Today I don't want to be selfish. I want to think only of you today. But there is something I must tell you. Did you hear of the wonderful luck we had recently?

MRS. LINDE: No, what's that?

NORA: My husband's been made manager in the bank, just think!

MRS. LINDE: Your husband? How marvelous!

NORA: Isn't it? Being a lawyer is such an uncertain living, you know, especially if one won't touch any cases that aren't clean and decent. And of course Torvald would never do that, and I'm with him completely there. Oh, we're simply delighted, believe me! He'll join the bank right after New Year's and start getting a huge salary and lots of commissions. From now on we can live quite differently—just as we want. Oh, Kristine, I feel so light and happy! Won't it be lovely to have stacks of money and not a care in the world?

MRS. LINDE: Well, anyway, it would be lovely to have enough for necessities.

NORA: No, not just for necessities, but stacks and stacks of money!

MRS. LINDE (*smiling*): Nora, Nora, aren't you sensible yet? Back in school you were such a free spender.

NORA (*with a quiet laugh*): Yes, that's what Torvald still says. (*Shaking her finger.*) But "Nora, Nora" isn't as silly as you all think. Really, we've been in no position for me to go squandering. We've had to work, both of us.

MRS. LINDE: You too?

NORA: Yes, at odd jobs—needlework, crocheting, embroidery, and such—(*casually*) and other things too. You remember that Torvald left the department when we were married? There was no chance of promotion in his office, and of course he needed to earn more money. But that first year he drove himself terribly. He took on all kinds of extra work that kept him going morning and night. It wore him down, and then he fell deathly ill. The doctors said it was essential for him to travel south.

MRS. LINDE: Yes, didn't you spend a whole year in Italy?

NORA: That's right. It wasn't easy to get away, you know. Ivar had just been born. But of course we had to go. Oh, that was a beautiful trip, and it saved Torvald's life. But it cost a frightful sum, Kristine.

MRS. LINDE: I can well imagine.

NORA: Four thousand, eight hundred crowns it cost. That's really a lot of money.

MRS. LINDE: But it's lucky you had it when you needed it.

NORA: Well, as it was, we got it from Papa.

MRS. LINDE: I see. It was just about the time your father died.

NORA: Yes, just about then. And, you know, I couldn't make that trip out to nurse him. I had to stay here, expecting Ivar any moment, and with my poor sick Torvald to care for. Dearest Papa, I never saw him again, Kristine. Oh, that was the worst time I've known in all my marriage.

MRS. LINDE: I know how you loved him. And then you went off to Italy?

NORA: Yes. We had the means now, and the doctors urged us. So we left a month after.

MRS. LINDE: And your husband came back completely cured?

NORA: Sound as a drum!

MRS. LINDE: But—the doctor?

NORA: Who?

MRS. LINDE: I thought the maid said he was a doctor, the man who came in with me.

NORA: Yes, that was Dr. Rank—but he's not making a sick call. He's our closest friend, and he stops by at least once a day. No, Torvald hasn't had a sick moment since, and the children are fit and strong, and I am, too. (*Jumping up and clapping her hands.*) Oh, dear God, Kristine, what a lovely thing to live and be happy! But how disgusting of me—I'm talking of nothing but my own affairs. (*Sits on a stool close by Kristine, arms resting across her knees.*) Oh, don't be angry with me! Tell me, is it really true that you weren't in love with your husband? Why did you marry him, then?

MRS. LINDE: My mother was still alive, but bedridden and helpless—and I had my two younger brothers to look after. In all conscience, I didn't think I could turn him down.

NORA: No, you were right there. But was he rich at the time?

MRS. LINDE: He was very well off, I'd say. But the business was shaky, Nora. When he died, it all fell apart, and nothing was left.

NORA: And then—?

MRS. LINDE: Yes, so I had to scrape up a living with a little shop and a little teaching and whatever else I could find. The last three years have been like one endless workday without a rest for me. Now, it's over, Nora. My poor mother doesn't need me, for she's passed on. Nor the boys, either; they're working now and can take care of themselves.

NORA: How free you must feel—

MRS. LINDE: No—only unspeakably empty. Nothing to live for now. (*Standing up anxiously.*) That's why I couldn't take it any longer out in that desolate hole. Maybe here it'll be easier to find something to do and keep my mind occupied. If I could only be lucky enough to get a steady job, some office work—

NORA: Oh, but Kristine, that's so dreadfully tiring, and you already look so tired. It would be much better for you if you could go off to a bathing resort.

MRS. LINDE (*going toward the window*): I have no father to give me travel money, Nora.

NORA (*rising*): Oh, don't be angry with me.

MRS. LINDE (*going to her*): Nora dear, don't you be angry with me. The worst of my kind of situation is all the bitterness that's stored away. No one to work for, and yet you're always having to snap up your opportunities. You have to live; and so you grow selfish. When you told me the happy change in your lot, do you know I was delighted less for your sakes than for mine?

NORA: How so? Oh, I see. You think maybe Torvald could do something for you.

MRS. LINDE: Yes, that's what I thought.

NORA: And he will, Kristine! Just leave it to me; I'll bring it up so delicately—find something attractive to humor him with. Oh, I'm so eager to help you.

MRS. LINDE: How very kind of you, Nora, to be so concerned over me—doubly kind, considering you really know so little of life's burdens yourself.

NORA: I—? I know so little—?

MRS. LINDE (*smiling*): Well, my heavens—a little needlework and such—Nora, you're just a child.

NORA (*tossing her head and pacing the floor*): You don't have to act so superior.

MRS. LINDE: Oh?

NORA: You're just like the others. You all think I'm incapable of anything serious—

MRS. LINDE: Come now—

NORA: That I've never had to face the raw world.

MRS. LINDE: Nora dear, you've just been telling me all your troubles.

NORA: Hm! Trivial! (*Quietly.*) I haven't told you the big thing.

MRS. LINDE: Big thing? What do you mean?

NORA: You look down on me so, Kristine, but you shouldn't. You're proud that you worked so long and hard for your mother.

MRS. LINDE: I don't look down on a soul. But it is true: I'm proud—and happy, too—to think it was given to me to make my mother's last days almost free of care.

NORA: And you're also proud thinking of what you've done for your brothers.

MRS. LINDE: I feel I've a right to be.

NORA: I agree. But listen to this, Kristine—I've also got something to be proud and happy for.

MRS. LINDE: I don't doubt it. But whatever do you mean?

NORA: Not so loud. What if Torvald heard! He mustn't, not for anything in the world. Nobody must know, Kristine. No one but you.

MRS. LINDE: But what is it, then?

NORA: Come here. (*Drawing her down beside her on the sofa.*) It's true—I've also got something to be proud and happy for. I'm the one who saved Torvald's life.

MRS. LINDE: Saved—? Saved how?

NORA: I told you about the trip to Italy. Torvald never would have lived if he hadn't gone south—

MRS. LINDE: Of course; your father gave you the means—

NORA (*smiling*): That's what Torvald and all the rest think, but—

MRS. LINDE: But—?

NORA: Papa didn't give us a pin. I was the one who raised the money.

MRS. LINDE: You? That whole amount?

NORA: Four thousand, eight hundred crowns. What do you say to that?

MRS. LINDE: But Nora, how was it possible? Did you win the lottery?

NORA (*disdainfully*): The lottery? Pooh! No art to that.

MRS. LINDE: But where did you get it from then?

NORA (*humming, with a mysterious smile*): Hmm, tra-la-la-la.

MRS. LINDE: Because you couldn't have borrowed it.

NORA: No? Why not?

MRS. LINDE: A wife can't borrow without her husband's consent.

NORA (*tossing her head*): Oh, but a wife with a little business sense, a wife who knows how to manage—

MRS. LINDE: Nora, I simply don't understand—

NORA: You don't have to. Whoever said I *borrowed* the money? I could have gotten it other ways. (*Throwing herself back on the sofa.*) I could have gotten it from some admirer or other. After all, a girl with my ravishing appeal—

MRS. LINDE: You lunatic.

NORA: I'll bet you're eaten up with curiosity, Kristine.

MRS. LINDE: Now listen here, Nora—you haven't done something indiscreet?

NORA (*sitting up again*): Is it indiscreet to save your husband's life?

MRS. LINDE: I think it's indiscreet that without his knowledge you—

NORA: But that's the point: He mustn't know! My Lord, can't you understand? He mustn't ever know the close call he had. It was to *me* the doctors came to say his life was in danger—that nothing could save him but a stay in the south. Didn't I try strategy then! I began talking about how lovely it would be for me to travel abroad like other young wives; I begged and I cried; I told him please to remember my condition, to be kind and indulge me; and then I dropped a hint that he could easily take out a loan. But at that, Kristine, he nearly exploded. He said I was frivolous, and it was his duty as man of the house not to indulge me in whims and fancies—as I think he called them. Aha, I thought, now you'll just have to be saved—and that's when I saw my chance.

MRS. LINDE: And your father never told Torvald the money wasn't from him?

NORA: No, never. Papa died right about then. I'd considered bringing him into my secret and begging him never to tell. But he was too sick at the time—and then, sadly, it didn't matter.

MRS. LINDE: And you've never confided in your husband since?

NORA: For heaven's sake, no! Are you serious? He's so strict on that subject. Besides—Torvald, with all his masculine pride—how painfully humiliating for him if he ever found out he was in debt to me. That would just ruin our relationship. Our beautiful, happy home would never be the same.

MRS. LINDE: Won't you ever tell him?

NORA (*thoughtfully, half smiling*): Yes—maybe sometime years from now, when I'm no longer so attractive. Don't laugh! I only mean when Torvald loves me less than now, when he stops enjoying my dancing and dressing up and reciting for him. Then it might be wise to have something in reserve—(*Breaking off.*) How ridiculous! That'll never happen—Well, Kristine, what do you think of my big secret? I'm capable of something too, hm? You can imagine, of course, how this thing hangs over me. It really hasn't been easy meeting the payments on time. In the business world there's what they call quarterly interest and what they call amortization, and these are always so terribly hard to manage. I've had to skimp a little here and there, wherever I could, you know. I could hardly spare anything from my house allowance, because Torvald has to live well. I couldn't let the children go poorly dressed; whatever I got for them, I felt I had to use up completely—the darlings!

MRS. LINDE: Poor Nora, so it had to come out of your own budget, then?

NORA: Yes, of course. But I was the one most responsible, too. Every time Torvald gave me money for new clothes and such, I never used more than half; always bought the simplest, cheapest outfits. It was a godsend that everything looks so well on me that Torvald never noticed. But it did weigh me down at times, Kristine. It *is* such a joy to wear fine things. You understand.

MRS. LINDE: Oh, of course.

NORA: And then I found other ways of making money. Last winter I was lucky enough to get a lot of copying to do. I locked myself in and sat writing every evening till late in the night. Ah, I was tired so often, dead tired. But still it was wonderful fun, sitting and working like that, earning money. It was almost like being a man.

MRS. LINDE: But how much have you paid off this way so far?

NORA: That's hard to say, exactly. These accounts, you know, aren't easy to figure. I only know that I've paid out all I could scrape together. Time and again I haven't known where to turn. (*Smiling.*) Then I'd sit here dreaming of a rich old gentleman who had fallen in love with me—

MRS. LINDE: What! Who is he?

NORA: Oh, really! And that he'd died, and when his will was opened, there in big letters it said, "All my fortune shall be paid over in cash, immediately, to that enchanting Mrs. Nora Helmer."

MRS. LINDE: But Nora dear—who *was* this gentleman?

NORA: Good grief, can't you understand? The old man never existed; that was only something I'd dream up time and again whenever I was at my wits' end for money. But it makes no difference now; the old fossil can go where he pleases for all I care; I don't need him or his will — because now I'm free. (*Jumping up.*) Oh, how lovely to think of that, Kristine! Carefree! To know you're carefree, utterly carefree; to be able to romp and play with the children, and to keep up a beautiful, charming home — everything just the way Torvald likes it! And think, spring is coming, with big blue skies. Maybe we can travel a little then. Maybe I'll see the ocean again. Oh yes, it *is* so marvelous to live and be happy!

(*The front doorbell rings.*)

MRS. LINDE (*rising*): There's the bell. It's probably best that I go.

NORA: No, stay. No one's expected. It must be for Torvald.

MAID (*from the hall doorway*): Excuse me, ma'am — there's a gentleman here to see Mr. Helmer, but I didn't know — since the doctor's with him —

NORA: Who is the gentleman?

KROGSTAD (*from the doorway*): It's me, Mrs. Helmer.

(*Mrs. Linde starts and turns away toward the window.*)

NORA (*stepping toward him, tense, her voice a whisper*): You? What is it? Why do you want to speak to my husband?

KROGSTAD: Bank business — after a fashion. I have a small job in the investment bank, and I hear now your husband is going to be our chief —

NORA: In other words, it's —

KROGSTAD: Just dry business, Mrs. Helmer. Nothing but that.

NORA: Yes, then please be good enough to step into the study. (*She nods indifferently as she sees him out by the hall door, then returns and begins stirring up the stove.*)

MRS. LINDE: Nora — who was that man?

NORA: That was a Mr. Krogstad — a lawyer.

MRS. LINDE: Then it really was him.

NORA: Do you know that person?

MRS. LINDE: I did once — many years ago. For a time he was a law clerk in our town.

NORA: Yes, he's been that.

MRS. LINDE: How he's changed.

NORA: I understand he had a very unhappy marriage.

MRS. LINDE: He's a widower now.

NORA: With a number of children. There now, it's burning. (*She closes the stove door and moves the rocker a bit to one side.*)

MRS. LINDE: They say he has a hand in all kinds of business.

NORA: Oh? That may be true; I wouldn't know. But let's not think about business. It's so dull.

(*Dr. Rank enters from Helmer's study.*)

RANK (*still in the doorway*): No, no, really—I don't want to intrude, I'd just as soon talk a little while with your wife. (*Shuts the door, then notices Mrs. Linde.*) Oh, beg pardon. I'm intruding here too.

NORA: No, not at all. (*Introducing him.*) Dr. Rank, Mrs. Linde.

RANK: Well now, that's a name much heard in this house. I believe I passed the lady on the stairs as I came.

MRS. LINDE: Yes, I take the stairs very slowly. They're rather hard on me.

RANK: Uh-hm, some touch of internal weakness?

MRS. LINDE: More overexertion, I'd say.

RANK: Nothing else? Then you're probably here in town to rest up in a round of parties?

MRS. LINDE: I'm here to look for work.

RANK: Is that the best cure for overexertion?

MRS. LINDE: One has to live, Doctor.

RANK: Yes, there's a common prejudice to that effect.

NORA: Oh, come on, Dr. Rank—you really do want to live yourself.

RANK: Yes, I really do. Wretched as I am, I'll gladly prolong my torment indefinitely. All my patients feel like that. And it's quite the same, too, with the morally sick. Right at this moment there's one of those moral invalids in there with Helmer—

MRS. LINDE (*softly*): Ah!

NORA: Who do you mean?

RANK: Oh, it's a lawyer, Krogstad, a type you wouldn't know. His character is rotten to the root—but even he began chattering all-importantly about how he had to *live.*

NORA: Oh? What did he want to talk to Torvald about?

RANK: I really don't know. I only heard something about the bank.

NORA: I didn't know that Krog—that this man Krogstad had anything to do with the bank.

RANK: Yes, he's gotten some kind of berth down there. (*To Mrs. Linde.*) I don't know if you also have, in your neck of the woods, a type of person who scuttles about breathlessly, sniffing out hints of moral corruption, and then maneuvers his victim into some sort of key position where he can keep an eye on him. It's the healthy these days that are out in the cold.

MRS. LINDE: All the same, it's the sick who most need to be taken in.

RANK (*with a shrug*): Yes, there we have it. That's the concept that's turning society into a sanatorium.

(*Nora, lost in her thoughts, breaks out into quiet laughter and claps her hands.*)

RANK: Why do you laugh at that? Do you have any real idea of what society is?

NORA: What do I care about dreary old society? I was laughing at something quite different—something terribly funny. Tell me, Doctor—is everyone who works in the bank dependent now on Torvald?

RANK: Is that what you find so terribly funny?

NORA (*smiling and humming*): Never mind, never mind! (*Pacing the floor.*) Yes, that's really immensely amusing: that we—that Torvald has so much power now over all those people. (*Taking the bag out of her pocket.*) Dr. Rank, a little macaroon on that?

RANK: See here, macaroons! I thought they were contraband here.

NORA: Yes, but these are some that Kristine gave me.

MRS. LINDE: What? I—?

NORA: Now, now, don't be afraid. You couldn't possibly know that Torvald had forbidden them. You see, he's worried they'll ruin my teeth. But hmp! Just this once! Isn't that so, Dr. Rank? Help yourself! (*Puts a macaroon in his mouth.*) And you too, Kristine. And I'll also have one, only a little one—or two, at the most. (*Walking about again.*) Now I'm really tremendously happy. Now's there's just one last thing in the world that I have an enormous desire to do.

RANK: Well! And what's that?

NORA: It's something I have such a consuming desire to say so Torvald could hear.

RANK: And why can't you say it?

NORA: I don't dare. It's quite shocking.

MRS. LINDE: Shocking?

RANK: Well, then it isn't advisable. But in front of us you certainly can. What do you have such a desire to say so Torvald could hear?

NORA: I have such a huge desire to say—to hell and be damned!

RANK: Are you crazy?

MRS. LINDE: My goodness, Nora!

RANK: Go on, say it. Here he is.

NORA (*hiding the macaroon bag*): Shh, shh, shh!

(*Helmer comes in from his study, hat in hand, overcoat over his arm.*)

NORA (*going toward him*): Well, Torvald dear, are you through with him?

HELMER: Yes, he just left.

NORA: Let me introduce you—this is Kristine, who's arrived here in town.

HELMER: Kristine—? I'm sorry, but I don't know—

NORA: Mrs. Linde, Torvald dear. Mrs. Kristine Linde.

HELMER: Of course. A childhood friend of my wife's, no doubt?

MRS. LINDE: Yes, we knew each other in those days.

NORA: And just think, she made the long trip down here in order to talk with you.

HELMER: What's this?

MRS. LINDE: Well, not exactly—

NORA: You see, Kristine is remarkably clever in office work, and so she's terribly eager to come under a capable man's supervision and add more to what she already knows—

HELMER: Very wise, Mrs. Linde.

NORA: And then when she heard that you'd become a bank manager— the story was wired out to the papers—then she came in as fast as she could and—Really, Torvald, for my sake you can do a little something for Kristine, can't you?

HELMER: Yes, it's not at all impossible. Mrs. Linde, I suppose you're a widow?

MRS. LINDE: Yes.

HELMER: Any experience in office work?

MRS. LINDE: Yes, a good deal.

HELMER: Well, it's quite likely that I can make an opening for you—

NORA (*clapping her hands*): You see, you see!

HELMER: You've come at a lucky moment, Mrs. Linde.

MRS. LINDE: Oh, how can I thank you?

HELMER: Not necessary. (*Putting his overcoat on.*) But today you'll have to excuse me—

RANK: Wait, I'll go with you. (*He fetches his coat from the hall and warms it at the stove.*)

NORA: Don't stay out long, dear.

HELMER: An hour; no more.

NORA: Are you going too, Kristine?

MRS. LINDE (*putting on her winter garments*): Yes, I have to see about a room now.

HELMER: Then perhaps we can all walk together.

NORA (*helping her*): What a shame we're so cramped here, but it's quite impossible for us to—

MRS. LINDE: Oh, don't even think of it! Good-bye, Nora dear, and thanks for everything.

NORA: Good-bye for now. Of course you'll be back this evening. And you too, Dr. Rank. What? If you're well enough? Oh, you've got to be! Wrap up tight now.

(*In a ripple of small talk the company moves out into the hall; children's voices are heard outside on the steps.*)

NORA: There they are! There they are! (*She runs to open the door. The children come in with their nurse, Anne-Marie.*) Come in, come in! (*Bends down and kisses them.*) Oh, you darlings—! Look at them, Kristine. Aren't they lovely!

RANK: No loitering in the draft here.

HELMER: Come, Mrs. Linde—this place is unbearable now for anyone but mothers.

(*Dr. Rank, Helmer, and Mrs. Linde go down the stairs. Anne-Marie goes into the living room with the children. Nora follows, after closing the hall door.*)

NORA: How fresh and strong you look. Oh, such red cheeks you have! Like apples and roses. (*The children interrupt her throughout the following.*) And it was so much fun? That's wonderful. Really? You pulled both Emmy and Bob on the sled? Imagine, all together! Yes, you're a clever boy, Ivar. Oh, let me hold her a bit, Anne-Marie. My sweet little doll baby! (*Takes the smallest from the nurse and dances with her.*) Yes, yes, Mama will dance with Bob as well. What? Did you throw snowballs? Oh, if I'd only been there! No, don't bother, Anne-Marie—I'll undress them myself. Oh yes, let me. It's such fun. Go in and rest; you look half frozen. There's hot coffee waiting for you on the stove. (*The nurse goes into the room to the left. Nora takes the children's winter things off, throwing them about, while the children talk to her all at once.*) Is that so? A big dog chased you? But it didn't bite? No, dogs never bite little, lovely doll babies. Don't peek in the packages, Ivar! What is it? Yes, wouldn't you like to know. No, no, it's an ugly something. Well? Shall we play? What shall we play? Hide-and-seek? Yes, let's play hide-and-seek. Bob must hide first. I must? Yes, let me hide first. (*Laughing and shouting, she and the children play in and out of the living room and the adjoining room to the right. At last Nora hides under the table. The children come storming in, search, but cannot find her, then hear her muffled laughter, dash over to the table, lift the cloth up and find her. Wild shouting. She creeps forward as if to scare them. More shouts. Meanwhile, a knock at the hall door; no one has noticed it. Now the door half opens, and Krogstad appears. He waits a moment; the game goes on.*)

KROGSTAD: Beg pardon, Mrs. Helmer—

NORA (*with a strangled cry, turning and scrambling to her knees*): Oh! What do you want?

KROGSTAD: Excuse me. The outer door was ajar; it must be someone forgot to shut it—

NORA (*rising*): My husband isn't home, Mr. Krogstad.

KROGSTAD: I know that.

NORA: Yes—then what do you want here?

KROGSTAD: A word with you.

NORA: With—? (*To the children, quietly.*) Go in to Anne-Marie. What? No, the strange man won't hurt Mama. When he's gone, we'll play some more. (*She leads the children into the room to the left and shuts the door after them. Then, tense and nervous:*) You want to speak to me?

KROGSTAD: Yes, I want to.

NORA: Today? But it's not yet the first of the month—

KROGSTAD: No, it's Christmas Eve. It's going to be up to you how merry a Christmas you have.

NORA: What is it you want? Today I absolutely can't—

KROGSTAD: We won't talk about that till later. This is something else. You do have a moment to spare, I suppose?

NORA: Oh yes, of course—I do, except—

KROGSTAD: Good. I was sitting over at Olsen's Restaurant when I saw your husband go down the street—

NORA: Yes?

KROGSTAD: With a lady.

NORA: Yes. So?

KROGSTAD: If you'll pardon my asking: Wasn't that lady a Mrs. Linde?

NORA: Yes.

KROGSTAD: Just now come into town?

NORA: Yes, today.

KROGSTAD: She's a good friend of yours?

NORA: Yes, she is. But I don't see—

KROGSTAD: I also knew her once.

NORA: I'm aware of that.

KROGSTAD: Oh? You know all about it. I thought so. Well, then let me ask you short and sweet: Is Mrs. Linde getting a job in the bank?

NORA: What makes you think you can cross-examine me, Mr. Krogstad— you, one of my husband's employees? But since you ask, you might as well know—yes, Mrs. Linde's going to be taken on at the bank. And I'm the one who spoke for her, Mr. Krogstad. Now you know.

KROGSTAD: So I guessed right.

NORA (*pacing up and down*): Oh, one does have a tiny bit of influence, I should hope. Just because I am a woman, don't think it means that— When one has a subordinate position, Mr. Krogstad, one really ought to be careful about pushing somebody who—hm—

KROGSTAD: Who has influence?

NORA: That's right.

KROGSTAD (*in a different tone*): Mrs. Helmer, would you be good enough to use your influence on my behalf?

NORA: What? What do you mean?

KROGSTAD: Would you please make sure that I keep my subordinate position in the bank?

NORA: What does that mean? Who's thinking of taking away your position?

KROGSTAD: Oh, don't play the innocent with me. I'm quite aware that your friend would hardly relish the chance of running into me again; and I'm also aware now whom I can thank for being turned out.

NORA: But I promise you—

KROGSTAD: Yes, yes, yes, to the point: There's still time, and I'm advising you to use your influence to prevent it.

NORA: But Mr. Krogstad, I have absolutely no influence.

KROGSTAD: You haven't? I thought you were just saying—

NORA: You shouldn't take me so literally. I! How can you believe that I have any such influence over my husband?

KROGSTAD: Oh, I've known your husband from our student days. I don't think the great bank manager's more steadfast than any other married man.

NORA: You speak insolently about my husband, and I'll show you the door.

KROGSTAD: The lady has spirit.

NORA: I'm not afraid of you any longer. After New Year's, I'll soon be done with the whole business.

KROGSTAD: (*restraining himself*): Now listen to me, Mrs. Helmer. If necessary, I'll fight for my little job in the bank as if it were life itself.

NORA: Yes, so it seems.

KROGSTAD: It's not just a matter of income; that's the least of it. It's something else—All right, out with it! Look, this is the thing. You know, just like all the others, of course, that once, a good many years ago, I did something rather rash.

NORA: I've heard rumors to that effect.

KROGSTAD: The case never got into court; but all the same, every door was closed in my face from then on. So I took up those various activities you know about. I had to grab hold somewhere; and I dare say I haven't been among the worst. But now I want to drop all that. My boys are growing up. For their sakes, I'll have to win back as much respect as possible here in town. That job in the bank was like the first rung in my ladder. And now your husband wants to kick me right back down in the mud again.

NORA: But for heaven's sake, Mr. Krogstad, it's simply not in my power to help you.

KROGSTAD: That's because you haven't the will to—but I have the means to make you.

NORA: You certainly won't tell my husband that I owe you money?

KROGSTAD: Hm—what if I told him that?

NORA: That would be shameful of you. (*Nearly in tears.*) This secret — my joy and my pride — that he should learn it in such a crude and disgusting way — learn it from you. You'd expose me to the most horrible unpleasantness —

KROGSTAD: Only unpleasantness?

NORA (*vehemently*): But go on and try. It'll turn out the worse for you, because then my husband will really see what a crook you are, and then you'll never be able to hold your job.

KROGSTAD: I asked if it was just domestic unpleasantness you were afraid of?

NORA: If my husband finds out, then of course he'll pay what I owe at once, and then we'd be through with you for good.

KROGSTAD (*a step closer*): Listen, Mrs. Helmer — you've either got a very bad memory, or else no head at all for business. I'd better put you a little more in touch with the facts.

NORA: What do you mean?

KROGSTAD: When your husband was sick, you came to me for a loan of four thousand, eight hundred crowns.

NORA: Where else could I go?

KROGSTAD: I promised to get you that sum —

NORA: And you got it.

KROGSTAD: I promised to get you that sum, on certain conditions. You were so involved in your husband's illness, and so eager to finance your trip, that I guess you didn't think out all the details. It might just be a good idea to remind you. I promised you the money on the strength of a note I drew up.

NORA: Yes, and that I signed.

KROGSTAD: Right. But at the bottom I added some lines for your father to guarantee the loan. He was supposed to sign down there.

NORA: Supposed to? He did sign.

KROGSTAD: I left the date blank. In other words, your father would have dated his signature himself. Do you remember that?

NORA: Yes, I think —

KROGSTAD: Then I gave you the note for you to mail to your father. Isn't that so?

NORA: Yes.

KROGSTAD: And naturally you sent it at once — because only some five, six days later you brought me the note, properly signed. And with that, the money was yours.

NORA: Well, then; I've made my payments regularly, haven't I?

KROGSTAD: More or less. But — getting back to the point — those were hard times for you then, Mrs. Helmer.

NORA: Yes, they were.

KROGSTAD: Your father was very ill, I believe.

NORA: He was near the end.

KROGSTAD: He died soon after?

NORA: Yes.

KROGSTAD: Tell me, Mrs. Helmer, do you happen to recall the date of your father's death? The day of the month, I mean.

NORA: Papa died the twenty-ninth of September.

KROGSTAD: That's quite correct; I've already looked into that. And now we come to a curious thing—(*taking out a paper*) which I simply cannot comprehend.

NORA: Curious thing? I don't know—

KROGSTAD: This is the curious thing: that your father co-signed the note for your loan three days after his death.

NORA: How—? I don't understand.

KROGSTAD: Your father died the twenty-ninth of September. But look. Here your father dated his signature October second. Isn't that curious, Mrs. Helmer? (*Nora is silent.*) Can you explain it to me? (*Nora remains silent.*) It's also remarkable that the words "October second" and the year aren't written in your father's hand, but rather in one that I think I know. Well, it's easy to understand. Your father forgot perhaps to date his signature, and then someone or other added it, a bit sloppily, before anyone knew of his death. There's nothing wrong in that. It all comes down to the signature. And there's no question about *that*, Mrs. Helmer. It really *was* your father who signed his own name here, wasn't it?

NORA (*after a short silence, throwing her head back and looking squarely at him*): No, it wasn't. *I* signed Papa's name.

KROGSTAD: Wait, now—are you fully aware that this is a dangerous confession?

NORA: Why? You'll soon get your money.

KROGSTAD: Let me ask you a question—why didn't you send the paper to your father?

NORA: That was impossible. Papa was so sick. If I'd asked him for his signature, I also would have had to tell him what the money was for. But I couldn't tell him, sick as he was, that my husband's life was in danger. That was just impossible.

KROGSTAD: Then it would have been better if you'd given up the trip abroad.

NORA: I couldn't possibly. The trip was to save my husband's life. I couldn't give that up.

KROGSTAD: But didn't you ever consider that this was a fraud against me?

NORA: I couldn't let myself be bothered by that. You weren't any concern of mine. I couldn't stand you, with all those cold complications you made, even though you knew how badly off my husband was.

KROGSTAD: Mrs. Helmer, obviously you haven't the vaguest idea of what you've involved yourself in. But I can tell you this: It was nothing more and nothing worse that I once did—and it wrecked my whole reputation.

NORA: You? Do you expect me to believe that you ever acted bravely to save your wife's life?

KROGSTAD: Laws don't inquire into motives.

NORA: Then they must be very poor laws.

KROGSTAD: Poor or not—if I introduce this paper in court, you'll be judged according to law.

NORA: This I refuse to believe. A daughter hasn't a right to protect her dying father from anxiety and care? A wife hasn't a right to save her husband's life? I don't know much about laws, but I'm sure that somewhere in the books these things are allowed. And you don't know anything about it—you who practice the law? You must be an awful lawyer, Mr. Krogstad.

KROGSTAD: Could be. But business—the kind of business we two are mixed up in—don't you think I know about that? All right. Do what you want now. But I'm telling you *this:* If I get shoved down a second time, you're going to keep me company. (*He bows and goes out through the hall.*)

NORA (*pensive for a moment, then tossing her head*): Oh, really! Trying to frighten me! I'm not so silly as all that. (*Begins gathering up the children's clothes, but soon stops.*) But—? No, but that's impossible! I did it out of love.

THE CHILDREN (*in the doorway, left*): Mama, that strange man's gone out the door.

NORA: Yes, yes, I know it. But don't tell anyone about the strange man. Do you hear? Not even Papa!

THE CHILDREN: No, Mama. But now will you play again?

NORA: No, not now.

THE CHILDREN: Oh, but Mama, you promised.

NORA: Yes, but I can't now. Go inside; I have too much to do. Go in, go in, my sweet darlings. (*She herds them gently back in the room and shuts the door after them. Settling on the sofa, she takes up a piece of embroidery and makes some stitches, but soon stops abruptly.*) No! (*Throws the work aside, rises, goes to the hall door and calls out.*) Helene! Let me have the tree in here. (*Goes to the table, left, opens the table drawer, and stops again.*) No, but that's utterly impossible!

MAID (*with the Christmas tree*): Where should I put it, ma'am?

NORA: There. The middle of the floor.

MAID: Should I bring anything else?

NORA: No, thanks. I have what I need.

(*The Maid, who has set the tree down, goes out.*)

NORA (*absorbed in trimming the tree*): Candles here—and flowers here. That terrible creature! Talk, talk, talk! There's nothing to it at all. The tree's going to be lovely. I'll do anything to please you Torvald. I'll sing for you, dance for you—

(*Helmer comes in from the hall, with a sheaf of papers under his arm.*)

NORA: Oh! You're back so soon?

HELMER: Yes. Has anyone been here?

NORA: Here? No.

HELMER: That's odd. I saw Krogstad leaving the front door.

NORA: So? Oh yes, that's true. Krogstad was here a moment.

HELMER: Nora, I can see by your face that he's been here, begging you to put in a good word for him.

NORA: Yes.

HELMER: And it was supposed to seem like your own idea? You were to hide it from me that he'd been here. He asked you that, too, didn't he?

NORA: Yes, Torvald, but—

HELMER: Nora, Nora, and you could fall for that? Talk with that sort of person and promise him anything? And then in the bargain, tell me an untruth.

NORA: An untruth—?

HELMER: Didn't you say that no one had been here? (*Wagging his finger.*) My little songbird must never do that again. A songbird needs a clean beak to warble with. No false notes. (*Putting his arm about her waist.*) That's the way it should be, isn't it? Yes, I'm sure of it. (*Releasing her.*) And so, enough of that. (*Sitting by the stove.*) Ah, how snug and cozy it is here. (*Leafing among his papers.*)

NORA (*busy with the tree, after a short pause*): Torvald!

HELMER: Yes.

NORA: I'm so much looking forward to the Stenborgs' costume party, day after tomorrow.

HELMER: And I can't wait to see what you'll surprise me with.

NORA: Oh, that stupid business!

HELMER: What?

NORA: I can't find anything that's right. Everything seems so ridiculous, so inane.

HELMER: So my little Nora's come to *that* recognition?

NORA (*going behind his chair, her arms resting on its back*): Are you very busy, Torvald?

HELMER: Oh—

NORA: What papers are those?

HELMER: Bank matters.

NORA: Already?

HELMER: I've gotten full authority from the retiring management to make all necessary changes in personnel and procedure. I'll need Christmas week for that. I want to have everything in order by New Year's.

NORA: So that was the reason this poor Krogstad—

HELMER: Hm.

NORA (*still leaning on the chair and slowly stroking the nape of his neck*): If you weren't so very busy, I would have asked you an enormous favor, Torvald.

HELMER: Let's hear. What is it?

NORA: You know, there isn't anyone who has your good taste—and I want so much to look well at the costume party. Torvald, couldn't you take over and decide what I should be and plan my costume?

HELMER: Ah, is my stubborn little creature calling for a lifeguard?

NORA: Yes, Torvald, I can't get anywhere without your help.

HELMER: All right—I'll think it over. We'll hit on something.

NORA: Oh, how sweet of you. (*Goes to the tree again. Pause.*) Aren't the red flowers pretty—? But tell me, was it really such a crime that this Krogstad committed?

HELMER: Forgery. Do you have any idea what that means?

NORA: Couldn't he have done it out of need?

HELMER: Yes, or thoughtlessness, like so many others. I'm not so heartless that I'd condemn a man categorically for just one mistake.

NORA: No, of course not, Torvald!

HELMER: Plenty of men have redeemed themselves by openly confessing their crimes and taking their punishment.

NORA: Punishment—?

HELMER: But now Krogstad didn't go that way. He got himself out by sharp practices, and that's the real cause of his moral breakdown.

NORA: Do you really think that would—?

HELMER: Just imagine how a man with that sort of guilt in him has to lie and cheat and deceive on all sides, has to wear a mask even with the nearest and dearest he has, even with his own wife and children. And with the children, Nora—that's where it's most horrible.

NORA: Why?

HELMER: Because that kind of atmosphere of lies infects the whole life of a home. Every breath the children take in is filled with the germs of something degenerate.

NORA (*coming closer behind him*): Are you sure of that?

HELMER: Oh, I've seen it often enough as a lawyer. Almost everyone who goes bad early in life has a mother who's a chronic liar.

NORA: Why just—the mother?

HELMER: It's usually the mother's influence that's dominant, but the father's works in the same way, of course. Every lawyer is quite familiar with it. And still this Krogstad's been going home year in, year out, poisoning his own children with lies and pretense; that's why I call him morally lost. (*Reaching his hands out toward her.*) So my sweet little Nora must promise me never to plead his cause. Your hand on it. Come, come, what's this? Give me your hand. There, now. All settled. I can tell you it'd be impossible for me to work alongside of him. I literally feel physically revolted when I'm anywhere near such a person.

NORA (*withdraws her hand and goes to the other side of the Christmas tree*): How hot it is here! And I've got so much to do.

HELMER (*getting up and gathering his papers*): Yes, and I have to think about getting some of these read through before dinner. I'll think about your costume, too. And something to hang on the tree in gilt paper, I may even see about that. (*Putting his hand on her head.*) Oh you, my darling little songbird. (*He goes into his study and closes the door after him.*)

NORA (*softly, after a silence*): Oh, really! It isn't so. It's impossible. It must be impossible.

ANNE-MARIE (*in the doorway left*): The children are begging so hard to come in to Mama.

NORA: No, no, no, don't let them in to me! You stay with them, Anne-Marie.

ANNE-MARIE: Of course, ma'am. (*Closes the door.*)

NORA (*pale with terror*): Hurt my children—! Poison my home? (*A moment's pause; then she tosses her head.*) That's not true. Never. Never in all the world.

ACT II

(*Same room. Beside the piano the Christmas tree now stands stripped of ornament, burned-down candle stubs on its ragged branches. Nora's street clothes lie on the sofa. Nora, alone in the room, moves restlessly about; at last she stops at the sofa and picks up her coat.*)

NORA (*dropping the coat again*): Someone's coming! (*Goes toward the door, listens.*) No—there's no one. Of course—nobody's coming today, Christmas Day—or tomorrow, either. But maybe—(*Opens the door and looks out.*) No, nothing in the mailbox. Quite empty. (*Coming forward.*) What nonsense! He won't do anything serious. Nothing terrible could happen. It's impossible. Why, I have three small children.

(*Anne-Marie, with a large carton, comes in from the room to the left.*)

ANNE-MARIE: Well, at last I found the box with the masquerade clothes.

NORA: Thanks. Put it on the table.

ANNE-MARIE (*does so*): But they're all pretty much of a mess.

NORA: Ahh! I'd love to rip them in a million pieces!

ANNE-MARIE: Oh, mercy, they can be fixed right up. Just a little patience.

NORA: Yes, I'll go get Mrs. Linde to help me.

ANNE-MARIE: Out again now? In this nasty weather? Miss Nora will catch cold—get sick.

NORA: Oh, worse things could happen—How are the children?

ANNE-MARIE: The poor mites are playing with their Christmas presents, but—

NORA: Do they ask for me much?

ANNE-MARIE: They're so used to having Mama around, you know.

NORA: Yes, but Anne-Marie, I *can't* be together with them as much as I was.

ANNE-MARIE: Well, small children get used to anything.

NORA: You think so? Do you think they'd forget their mother if she was gone for good?

ANNE-MARIE: Oh, mercy—gone for good!

NORA: Wait, tell me. Anne-Marie—I've wondered so often—how could you ever have the heart to give your child over to strangers?

ANNE-MARIE: But I had to, you know, to become little Nora's nurse.

NORA: Yes, but how could you *do* it?

ANNE-MARIE: When I could get such a good place? A girl who's poor and who's gotten in trouble is glad enough for that. Because that slippery fish, he didn't do a thing for me, you know.

NORA: But your daughter's surely forgotten you.

ANNE-MARIE: Oh, she certainly has not. She's written to me, both when she was confirmed and when she was married.

NORA (*clasping her about the neck*): You old Anne-Marie, you were a good mother for me when I was little.

ANNE-MARIE: Poor little Nora, with no other mother but me.

NORA: And if the babies didn't have one, then I know that you'd—What silly talk! (*Opening the carton.*) Go in to them. Now I'll have to— Tomorrow you can see how lovely I'll look.

ANNE-MARIE: Oh, there won't be anyone at the party as lovely as Miss Nora. (*She goes off into the room, left.*)

NORA (*begins unpacking the box, but soon throws it aside*): Oh, if I dared to go out. If only nobody would come. If only nothing would happen here while I'm out. What craziness—nobody's coming. Just don't think. This muff—needs a brushing. Beautiful gloves, beautiful gloves. Let it go. Let it go! One, two, three, four, five, six—(*With a cry.*) Oh, there they are! (*Poises to move toward the door, but remains irresolutely standing. Mrs. Linde enters from the hall, where she has removed her street clothes.*)

NORA: Oh, it's you, Kristine. There's no one else out there? How good that you've come.

MRS. LINDE: I hear you were up asking for me.

NORA: Yes, I just stopped by. There's something you really can help me with. Let's get settled on the sofa. Look, there's going to be a costume party tomorrow evening at the Stenborgs' right above us, and now Torvald wants me to go as a Neapolitan peasant girl and dance the tarantella that I learned in Capri.

MRS. LINDE: Really, are you giving a whole performance?

NORA: Torvald says yes, I should. See, here's the dress. Torvald had it made for me down there; but now it's all so tattered that I just don't know—

MRS. LINDE: Oh, we'll fix that up in no time. It's nothing more than the trimmings—they're a bit loose here and there. Needle and thread? Good, now we have what we need.

NORA: Oh, how sweet of you!

MRS. LINDE (*sewing*): So you'll be in disguise tomorrow, Nora. You know what? I'll stop by then for a moment and have a look at you all dressed up. But listen, I've absolutely forgotten to thank you for that pleasant evening yesterday.

NORA (*getting up and walking about*): I don't think it was as pleasant as usual yesterday. You should have come to town a bit sooner, Kristine— Yes, Torvald really knows how to give a home elegance and charm.

MRS. LINDE: And you do, too, if you ask me. You're not your father's daughter for nothing. But tell me, is Dr. Rank always so down in the mouth as yesterday?

NORA: No, that was quite an exception. But he goes around critically ill all the time—tuberculosis of the spine, poor man. You know, his father was a disgusting thing who kept mistresses and so on—and that's why the son's been sickly from birth.

MRS. LINDE (*lets her sewing fall to her lap*): But my dearest Nora, how do you know about such things?

NORA (*walking more jauntily*): Hmp! When you've had three children, then you've had a few visits from—from women who know something of medicine, and they tell you this and that.

MRS. LINDE (*resumes sewing; a short pause*): Does Dr. Rank come here every day?

NORA: Every blessed day. He's Torvald's best friend from childhood, and *my* good friend, too. Dr. Rank almost belongs to this house.

MRS. LINDE: But tell me—is he quite sincere? I mean, doesn't he rather enjoy flattering people?

NORA: Just the opposite. Why do you think that?

MRS. LINDE: When you introduced us yesterday, he was proclaiming that he'd often heard my name in this house; but later I noticed that your husband hadn't the slightest idea who I really was. So how could Dr. Rank—?

NORA: But it's all true, Kristine. You see, Torvald loves me beyond words, and, as he puts it, he'd like to keep me all to himself. For a long time he'd almost be jealous if I even mentioned any of my old friends back home. So of course I dropped that. But with Dr. Rank I talk a lot about such things because he likes hearing about them.

MRS. LINDE: Now listen, Nora; in many ways you're still like a child. I'm a good deal older than you, with a little more experience. I'll tell you something: You ought to put an end to all this with Dr. Rank.

NORA: What should I put an end to?

MRS. LINDE: Both parts of it, I think. Yesterday you said something about a rich admirer who'd provide you with money—

NORA: Yes, one who doesn't exist—worse luck. So?

MRS. LINDE: Is Dr. Rank well off?

NORA: Yes, he is.

MRS. LINDE: With no dependents?

NORA: No, no one. But—

MRS. LINDE: And he's over here every day?

NORA: Yes, I told you that.

MRS. LINDE: How can a man of such refinement be so grasping?

NORA: I don't follow you at all.

MRS. LINDE: Now don't try to hide it, Nora. You think I can't guess who loaned you the forty-eight hundred crowns?

NORA: Are you out of your mind? How could you think such a thing! A friend of ours, who comes here every single day. What an intolerable situation that would have been!

MRS. LINDE: Then it really wasn't him.

NORA: No, absolutely not. It never even crossed my mind for a moment—And he had nothing to lend in those days; his inheritance came later.

MRS. LINDE: Well, I think that was a stroke of luck for you, Nora dear.

NORA: No, it never would have occurred to me to ask Dr. Rank—Still, I'm quite sure that if I had asked him—

MRS. LINDE: Which you won't, of course.

NORA: No, of course not. I can't see that I'd ever need to. But I'm quite positive that if I talked to Dr. Rank—

MRS. LINDE: Behind your husband's back?

NORA: I've got to clear up this other thing; *that's* also behind his back. I've *got* to clear it all up.

MRS. LINDE: Yes, I was saying that yesterday, but—

NORA (*pacing up and down*): A man handles these problems so much better than a woman—

MRS. LINDE: One's husband does, yes.

NORA: Nonsense. (*Stopping.*) When you pay everything you owe, then you get your note back, right?

MRS. LINDE: Yes, naturally.

NORA: And can rip it into a million pieces and burn it up—that filthy scrap of paper!

MRS. LINDE (*looking hard at her, laying her sewing aside, and rising slowly*): Nora, you're hiding something from me.

NORA: You can see it in my face?

MRS. LINDE: Something's happened to you since yesterday morning. Nora, what is it?

NORA (*hurrying toward her*): Kristine! (*Listening.*) Shh! Torvald's home. Look, go in with the children a while. Torvald can't bear all this snipping and stitching. Let Anne-Marie help you.

MRS. LINDE (*gathering up some of the things*): All right, but I'm not leaving here until we've talked this out. (*She disappears into the room, left, as Torvald enters from the hall.*)

NORA: Oh, how I've been waiting for you, Torvald dear.

HELMER: Was that the dressmaker?

NORA: No, that was Kristine. She's helping me fix up my costume. You know, it's going to be quite attractive.

HELMER: Yes, wasn't that a bright idea I had?

NORA: Brilliant! But then wasn't I good as well to give in to you?

HELMER: Good—because you give in to your husband's judgment? All right, you little goose, I know you didn't mean it like that. But I won't disturb you. You'll want to have a fitting, I suppose.

NORA: And you'll be working?

HELMER: Yes. (*Indicating a bundle of papers.*) See. I've been down to the bank. (*Starts toward his study.*)

NORA: Torvald.

HELMER (*stops*): Yes.

NORA: If your little squirrel begged you, with all her heart and soul, for something—?

HELMER: What's that?

NORA: Then would you do it?

HELMER: First, naturally, I'd have to know what it was.

NORA: Your squirrel would scamper about and do tricks, if you'd only be sweet and give in.

HELMER: Out with it.

NORA: Your lark would be singing high and low in every room—

HELMER: Come on, she does that anyway.

NORA: I'd be a wood nymph and dance for you in the moonlight.

HELMER: Nora—don't tell me it's that same business from this morning?

NORA (*coming closer*): Yes, Torvald, I beg you, please!

HELMER: And you actually have the nerve to drag that up again?

NORA: Yes, yes, you've got to give in to me; you *have* to let Krogstad keep his job in the bank.

HELMER: My dear Nora, I've slated his job for Mrs. Linde.

NORA: That's awfully kind of you. But you could just fire another clerk instead of Krogstad.

HELMER: This is the most incredible stubbornness! Because you go and give an impulsive promise to speak up for him, I'm expected to—

NORA: That's not the reason, Torvald. It's for your own sake. That man does writing for the worst papers; you said it yourself. He could do you any amount of harm. I'm scared to death of him—

HELMER: Ah, I understand. It's the old memories haunting you.

NORA: What do you mean by that?

HELMER: Of course, you're thinking about your father.

NORA: Yes, all right. Just remember how those nasty gossips wrote in the papers about Papa and slandered him so cruelly. I think they'd have had him dismissed if the department hadn't sent you up to investigate, and if you hadn't been so kind and open-minded toward him.

HELMER: My dear Nora, there's a notable difference between your father and me. Your father's official career was hardly above reproach. But mine is; and I hope it'll stay that way as long as I hold my position.

NORA: Oh, who can ever tell what vicious minds can invent? We could be so snug and happy now in our quiet, carefree home—you and I and the children, Torvald! That's why I'm pleading with you so—

HELMER: And just by pleading for him you make it impossible for me to keep him on. It's already known at the bank that I'm firing Krogstad. What if it's rumored around now that the new bank manager was vetoed by his wife—

NORA: Yes, what then—?

HELMER: Oh yes—as long as our little bundle of stubbornness gets her way—! I should go and make myself ridiculous in front of the whole office—give people the idea I can be swayed by all kinds of outside pressure. Oh, you can bet I'd feel the effects of that soon enough! Besides—there's something that rules Krogstad right out at the bank as long as I'm the manager.

NORA: What's that?

HELMER: His moral failings I could maybe overlook if I had to—

NORA: Yes, Torvald, why not?

HELMER: And I hear he's quite efficient on the job. But he was a crony of mine back in my teens—one of those rash friendships that crop up again and again to embarrass you later in life. Well, I might as well say it straight out: We're on a first-name basis. And that tactless fool makes no effort at all to hide it in front of others. Quite the contrary— he thinks that entitles him to take a familiar air around me, and so every other second he comes booming out with his, "Yes, Torvald!" and "Sure thing, Torvald!" I tell you, it's been excruciating for me. He's out to make my place in the bank unbearable.

NORA: Torvald, you can't be serious about all this.

HELMER: Oh no? Why not?

NORA: Because these are such petty considerations.

HELMER: What are you saying? Petty? You think I'm petty!

NORA: No, just the opposite, Torvald dear. That's exactly why—

HELMER: Never mind. You call my motives petty; then I might as well be just that. Petty! All right! We'll put a stop to this for good. (*Goes to the hall door and calls.*) Helene!

NORA: What do you want?

HELMER (*searching among his papers*): A decision. (*The Maid comes in.*) Look here; take this letter; go out with it at once. Get hold of a messenger and have him deliver it. Quick now. It's already addressed. Wait, here's some money.

MAID: Yes, sir. (*She leaves with the letter.*)

HELMER (*straightening his papers*): There, now, little Miss Willful.

NORA (*breathlessly*): Torvald, what was that letter?

HELMER: Krogstad's notice.

NORA: Call it back, Torvald! There's still time. Oh, Torvald, call it back! Do it for my sake—for your sake, for the children's sake! Do you hear, Torvald; do it! You don't know how this can harm us.

HELMER: Too late.

NORA: Yes, too late.

HELMER: Nora, dear, I can forgive you this panic, even though basically you're insulting me. Yes, you are! Or isn't it an insult to think that *I* should be afraid of a courtroom hack's revenge? But I forgive you anyway, because this shows so beautifully how much you love me. (*Takes her in his arms.*) This is the way it should be, my darling Nora. Whatever comes, you'll see: When it really counts, I have strength and courage enough as a man to take on the whole weight myself.

NORA (*terrified*): What do you mean by that?

HELMER: The whole weight, I said.

NORA (*resolutely*): No, never in all the world.

HELMER: Good. So we'll share it, Nora, as man and wife. That's as it
should be. (*Fondling her.*) Are you happy now? There, there, there—not
these frightened dove's eyes. It's nothing at all but empty fantasies—
Now you should run through your tarantella and practice your tambourine. I'll go to the inner office, and shut both doors, so I won't hear a
thing; you can make all the noise you like. (*Turning in the doorway.*) And
when Rank comes, just tell him where he can find me. (*He nods to her
and goes with his papers into the study, closing the door.*)

NORA (*standing as though rooted, dazed with fright, in a whisper*): He really
could do it. He will do it. He'll do it in spite of everything. No, not that,
never, never! Anything but that! Escape! A way out—(*The doorbell
rings.*) Dr. Rank! Anything but that! *Anything*, whatever it is! (*Her hands
pass over her face, smoothing it; she pulls herself together, goes over and
opens the hall door. Dr. Rank stands outside, hanging his fur coat up. During
the following scene, it begins getting dark.*)

NORA: Hello, Dr. Rank. I recognized your ring. But you mustn't go in to
Torvald yet; I believe he's working.

RANK: And you?

NORA: For you, I always have an hour to spare—you know that. (He has
entered, and she shuts the door after him.)

RANK: Many thanks. I'll make use of these hours while I can.

NORA: What do you mean by that? While you can?

RANK: Does that disturb you?

NORA: Well, it's such an odd phrase. Is anything going to happen?

RANK: What's going to happen is what I've been expecting so long—but
I honestly didn't think it would come so soon.

NORA (*gripping his arm*): What is it you've found out? Dr. Rank, you have
to tell me!

RANK (*sitting by the stove*): It's all over with me. There's nothing to be
done about it.

NORA (*breathing easier*): Is it you—then—?

RANK: Who else? There's no point in lying to one's self. I'm the most miserable of all my patients, Mrs. Helmer. These past few days I've been
auditing my internal accounts. Bankrupt! Within a month I'll probably
be laid out and rotting in the churchyard.

NORA: Oh, what a horrible thing to say.

RANK: The thing itself is horrible. But the worst of it is all the other
horror before it's over. There's only one final examination left; when I'm
finished with that, I'll know about when my disintegration will begin.
There's something I want to say. Helmer with his sensitivity has such a
sharp distaste for anything ugly. I don't want him near my sickroom.

NORA: Oh, but Dr. Rank—

RANK: I won't have him in there. Under no condition. I'll lock my door to him—As soon as I'm completely sure of the worst, I'll send you my calling card marked with a black cross, and you'll know then the wreck has started to come apart.

NORA: No, today you're completely unreasonable. And I wanted you so much to be in a really good humor.

RANK: With death up my sleeve? And then to suffer this way for somebody else's sins. Is there any justice in that? And in every single family, in some way or another, this inevitable retribution of nature goes on—

NORA (*her hands pressed over her ears*): Oh, stuff! Cheer up! Please— be gay!

RANK: Yes, I'd just as soon laugh at it all. My poor, innocent spine, serving time for my father's gay army days.

NORA (*by the table, left*): He was so infatuated with asparagus tips and pâté de foie gras, wasn't that it?

RANK: Yes—and with truffles.

NORA: Truffles, yes. And then with oysters, I suppose?

RANK: Yes, tons of oysters, naturally.

NORA: And then the port and champagne to go with it. It's so sad that all these delectable things have to strike at our bones.

RANK: Especially when they strike at the unhappy bones that never shared in the fun.

NORA: Ah, that's the saddest of all.

RANK (*looks searchingly at her*): Hm.

NORA (*after a moment*): Why did you smile?

RANK: No, it was you who laughed.

NORA: No, it was you who smiled, Dr. Rank!

RANK (*getting up*): You're even a bigger tease than I'd thought.

NORA: I'm full of wild ideas today.

RANK: That's obvious.

NORA (*putting both hands on his shoulders*): Dear, dear Dr. Rank, you'll never die for Torvald and me.

RANK: Oh, that loss you'll easily get over. Those who go away are soon forgotten.

NORA (*looks fearfully at him*): You believe that?

RANK: One makes new connections, and then—

NORA: Who makes new connections?

RANK: Both you and Torvald will when I'm gone. I'd say you're well under way already. What was that Mrs. Linde doing here last evening?

NORA: Oh, come—you can't be jealous of poor Kristine?

RANK: Oh yes, I am. She'll be my successor here in the house. When I'm down under, that woman will probably—

NORA: Shh! Not so loud. She's right in there.

RANK: Today as well. So you see.

NORA: Only to sew on my dress. Good gracious, how unreasonable you
are. (*Sitting on the sofa.*) Be nice now, Dr. Rank. Tomorrow you'll see
how beautifully I'll dance; and you can imagine then that I'm dancing
only for you—yes, and of course for Torvald, too—that's understood.
(*Takes various items out of the carton.*) Dr. Rank, sit over here and I'll
show you something.

RANK (*sitting*): What's that?

NORA: Look here. Look.

RANK: Silk stockings.

NORA: Flesh-colored. Aren't they lovely? Now it's so dark here, but
tomorrow—No, no, no, just look at the feet. Oh well, you might as
well look at the rest.

RANK: Hm—

NORA: Why do you look so critical? Don't you believe they'll fit?

RANK: I've never had any chance to form an opinion on that.

NORA (*glancing at him a moment*): Shame on you. (*Hits him lightly on the
ear with the stockings.*) That's for you. (*Puts them away again.*)

RANK: And what other splendors am I going to see now?

NORA: Not the least bit more, because you've been naughty. (*She hunts a
little and rummages among her things.*)

RANK (*after a short silence*): When I sit here together with you like this,
completely easy and open, then I don't know—I simply can't imagine—
whatever would have become of me if I'd never come into this house.

NORA (*smiling*): Yes, I really think you feel completely at ease with us.

RANK (*more quietly, staring straight ahead*): And then to have to go away
from it all—

NORA: Nonsense, you're not going away.

RANK (*his voice unchanged*):—and not even be able to leave some poor
show of gratitude behind, scarcely a fleeting regret—no more than a
vacant place that anyone can fill.

NORA: And if I asked you now for—No—

RANK: For what?

NORA: For a great proof of your friendship—

RANK: Yes, yes?

NORA: No, I mean—for an exceptionally big favor—

RANK: Would you really, for once, make me so happy?

NORA: Oh, you haven't the vaguest idea what it is.

RANK: All right, then tell me.

NORA: No, but I can't, Dr. Rank—it's all out of reason. It's advice and
help, too—and a favor—

RANK: So much the better. I can't fathom what you're hinting at. Just
speak out. Don't you trust me?

Nora: Of course. More than anyone else. You're my best and truest friend, I'm sure. That's why I want to talk to you. All right, then, Dr. Rank: There's something you can help me prevent. You know how deeply, how inexpressibly dearly Torvald loves me; he'd never hesitate a second to give up his life for me.

Rank (*leaning close to her*): Nora—do you think he's the only one—

Nora (*with a slight start*): Who—?

Rank: Who'd gladly give up his life for you.

Nora (*heavily*): I see.

Rank: I swore to myself you should know this before I'm gone. I'll never find a better chance. Yes, Nora, now you know. And also you know now that you can trust me beyond anyone else.

Nora (*rising, natural and calm*): Let me by.

Rank (*making room for her, but still sitting*): Nora—

Nora (*in the hall doorway*): Helene, bring the lamp in. (*Goes over to the stove.*) Ah, dear Dr. Rank, that was really mean of you.

Rank (*getting up*): That I've loved you just as deeply as somebody else? Was *that* mean?

Nora: No, but that you came out and told me. That was quite unnecessary—

Rank: What do you mean? Have you known—?

(*The Maid comes in with the lamp, sets it on the table, and goes out again.*)

Rank: Nora—Mrs. Helmer—I'm asking you: Have you known about it?

Nora: Oh, how can I tell what I know or don't know? Really, I don't know what to say—Why did you have to be so clumsy, Dr. Rank! Everything was so good.

Rank: Well, in any case, you now have the knowledge that my body and soul are at your command. So won't you speak out?

Nora (*looking at him*): After that?

Rank: Please, just let me know what it is.

Nora: You can't know anything now.

Rank: I have to. You mustn't punish me like this. Give me the chance to do whatever is humanly possible for you.

Nora: Now there's nothing you can do for me. Besides, actually, I don't need any help. You'll see—it's only my fantasies. That's what it is. Of course! (*Sits in the rocker, looks at him, and smiles.*) What a nice one you are, Dr. Rank. Aren't you a little bit ashamed, now that the lamp is here?

Rank: No, not exactly. But perhaps I'd better go—for good?

Nora: No, you certainly can't do that. You must come here just as you always have. You know Torvald can't do without you.

Rank: Yes, but *you*?

NORA: You know how much I enjoy it when you're here.

RANK: That's precisely what threw me off. You're a mystery to me. So many times I've felt you'd almost rather be with me than with Helmer.

NORA: Yes—you see, there are some people that one loves most and other people that one would almost prefer being with.

RANK: Yes, there's something to that.

NORA: When I was back home, of course I loved Papa most. But I always thought it was so much fun when I could sneak down to the maids' quarters, because they never tried to improve me, and it was always so amusing, the way they talked to each other.

RANK: Aha, so it's their place that I've filled.

NORA (*jumping up and going to him*): Oh, dear, sweet Dr. Rank, that's not what I meant at all. But you can understand that with Torvald it's just the same as with Papa—

(*The Maid enters from the hall.*)

MAID: Ma'am—please! (*She whispers to Nora and hands her a calling card.*)

NORA (*glancing at the card*): Ah! (*Slips it into her pocket.*)

RANK: Anything wrong?

NORA: No, no, not at all. It's only some—it's my new dress—

RANK: Really? But—there's your dress.

NORA: Oh, that. But this is another one—I ordered it—Torvald mustn't know—

RANK: Ah, now we have the big secret.

NORA: That's right. Just go in with him—he's back in the inner study. Keep him there as long as—

RANK: Don't worry. He won't get away. (*Goes into the study.*)

NORA (*to the Maid*): And he's standing waiting in the kitchen?

MAID: Yes, he came up by the back stairs.

NORA: But didn't you tell him somebody was here?

MAID: Yes, but that didn't do any good.

NORA: He won't leave?

MAID: No, he won't go till he's talked with you, ma'am.

NORA: Let him come in, then—but quietly. Helene, don't breathe a word about this. It's a surprise for my husband.

MAID: Yes, yes, I understand—(*Goes out.*)

NORA: This horror—it's going to happen. No, no, no, it can't happen, it mustn't. (*She goes and bolts Helmer's door. The Maid opens the hall door for Krogstad and shuts it behind him. He is dressed for travel in a fur coat, boots, and a fur cap.*)

NORA (*going toward him*): Talk softly. My husband's home.

KROGSTAD: Well, good for him.

NORA: What do you want?

KROGSTAD: Some information.

NORA: Hurry up, then. What is it?

KROGSTAD: You know, of course, that I got my notice.

NORA: I couldn't prevent it, Mr. Krogstad. I fought for you to the bitter end, but nothing worked.

KROGSTAD: Does your husband's love for you run so thin? He knows everything I can expose you to, and all the same he dares to—

NORA: How can you imagine he knows anything about this?

KROGSTAD: Ah, no—I can't imagine it either, now. It's not at all like my fine Torvald Helmer to have so much guts—

NORA: Mr. Krogstad, I demand respect for my husband!

KROGSTAD: Why, of course—all due respect. But since the lady's keeping it so carefully hidden, may I presume to ask if you're also a bit better informed than yesterday about what you've actually done?

NORA: More than you ever could teach me.

KROGSTAD: Yes, I *am* such an awful lawyer.

NORA: What is it you want from me?

KROGSTAD: Just a glimpse of how you are, Mrs. Helmer. I've been think-ing about you all day long. A cashier, a night-court scribbler, a—well, a type like me also has a little of what they call a heart, you know.

NORA: Then show it. Think of my children.

KROGSTAD: Did you or your husband ever think of mine? But never mind. I simply wanted to tell you that you don't need to take this thing too seriously. For the present, I'm not proceeding with any action.

NORA: Oh no, really! Well—I knew that.

KROGSTAD: Everything can be settled in a friendly spirit. It doesn't have to get around town at all; it can stay just among us three.

NORA: My husband must never know anything of this.

KROGSTAD: How can you manage that? Perhaps you can pay me the balance?

NORA: No, not right now.

KROGSTAD: Or you know some way of raising the money in a day or two?

NORA: No way that I'm willing to use.

KROGSTAD: Well, it wouldn't have done you any good, anyway. If you stood in front of me with a fistful of bills, you still couldn't buy your signature back.

NORA: Then tell me what you're going to do with it.

KROGSTAD: I'll just hold onto it—keep it on file. There's no outsider who'll even get wind of it. So if you've been thinking of taking some desperate step—

NORA: I have.

KROGSTAD: Been thinking of running away from home—

NORA: I have!

KROGSTAD: Or even of something worse —

NORA: How could you guess that?

KROGSTAD: You can drop those thoughts.

NORA: How could you guess I was thinking of *that*?

KROGSTAD: Most of us think about *that* at first. I thought about it too, but I discovered I hadn't the courage —

NORA (*lifelessly*): I don't either.

KROGSTAD (*relieved*): That's true, you haven't the courage? You too?

NORA: I don't have it — I don't have it.

KROGSTAD: It would be terribly stupid, anyway. After that first storm at home blows out, why, then — I have here in my pocket a letter for your husband —

NORA: Telling everything?

KROGSTAD: As charitably as possible.

NORA (*quickly*): He mustn't ever get that letter. Tear it up. I'll find some way to get money.

KROGSTAD: Beg pardon, Mrs. Helmer, but I think I just told you —

NORA: Oh, I don't mean the money I owe you. Let me know how much you want from my husband, and I'll manage it.

KROGSTAD: I don't want any money from your husband.

NORA: What do you want, then?

KROGSTAD: I'll tell you what. I want to recoup, Mrs. Helmer; I want to get on in the world — and there's where your husband can help me. For a year and a half I've kept myself clean of anything disreputable — all that time struggling with the worst conditions; but I was satisfied, working my way up step by step. Now I've been written right off, and I'm just not in the mood to come crawling back. I tell you, I want to move on. I want to get back in the bank — in a better position. Your husband can set up a job for me —

NORA: He'll never do that!

KROGSTAD: He'll do it. I know him. He won't dare breathe a word of protest. And once I'm in there together with him, you just wait and see! Inside of a year, I'll be the manager's right-hand man. It'll be Nils Krogstad, not Torvald Helmer, who runs the bank.

NORA: You'll never see the day!

KROGSTAD: Maybe you think you can —

NORA: I have the courage now — for *that*.

KROGSTAD: Oh, you don't scare me. A smart, spoiled lady like you —

NORA: You'll see; you'll see!

KROGSTAD: Under the ice, maybe? Down in the freezing, coal-black water? There, till you float up in the spring, ugly unrecognizable, with your hair falling out —

NORA: You don't frighten me.

KROGSTAD: Nor do you frighten me. One doesn't do these things, Mrs. Helmer. Besides what good would it be? I'd still have him safe in my pocket.

NORA: Afterwards? When I'm no longer—?

KROGSTAD: Are you forgetting that *I'll* be in control then over your final reputation? (*Nora stands speechless, staring at him.*) Good; now I've warned you. Don't do anything stupid. When Helmer's read my letter, I'll be waiting for his reply. And bear in mind that it's your husband himself who's forced me back to my old ways. I'll never forgive him for that. Good-bye, Mrs. Helmer. (*He goes out through the hall.*)

NORA (*goes to the hall door, opens it a crack, and listens*): He's gone. Didn't leave the letter. Oh no, no, that's impossible too! (*Opening the door more and more.*) What's that? He's standing outside—not going downstairs. He's thinking it over? Maybe he'll—? (*A letter falls in the mailbox; then Krogstad's footsteps are heard, dying away down a flight of stairs. Nora gives a muffled cry and runs over toward the sofa table. A short pause.*) In the mailbox. (*Slips warily over to the hall door.*) It's lying there. Torvald, Torvald—now we're lost!

MRS. LINDE (*entering with the costume from the room, left*): There now, I can't see anything else to mend. Perhaps you'd like to try—

NORA (*in a hoarse whisper*): Kristine, come here.

MRS. LINDE (*tossing the dress on the sofa*): What's wrong? You look upset.

NORA: Come here. See that letter? There! Look—through the glass in the mailbox.

MRS. LINDE: Yes, yes, I see it.

NORA: That letter's from Krogstad—

MRS. LINDE: Nora—it's Krogstad who loaned you the money!

NORA: Yes, and now Torvald will find out everything.

MRS. LINDE: Believe me, Nora, it's best for both of you.

NORA: There's more you don't know. I forged a name.

MRS. LINDE: But for heaven's sake—?

NORA: I only want to tell you that, Kristine, so that you can be my witness.

MRS. LINDE: Witness? Why should I—?

NORA: If I should go out of my mind—it could easily happen—

MRS. LINDE: Nora!

NORA: Or anything else occurred—so I couldn't be present here—

MRS. LINDE: Nora, Nora, you aren't yourself at all!

NORA: And someone should try to take on the whole weight, all of the guilt, you follow me—

MRS. LINDE: Yes, of course, but why do you think—?

NORA: Then you're the witness that it isn't true, Kristine. I'm very much myself; my mind right now is perfectly clear; and I'm telling you:

Nobody else has known about this; I alone did everything. Remember that.

MRS. LINDE: I will. But I don't understand all this.

NORA: Oh, how could you ever understand it? It's the miracle now that's going to take place.

MRS. LINDE: The miracle?

NORA: Yes, the miracle. But it's so awful, Kristine. It mustn't take place, not for anything in the world.

MRS. LINDE: I'm going right over and talk with Krogstad.

NORA: Don't go near him; he'll do you some terrible harm!

MRS. LINDE: There was a time once when he'd gladly have done anything for me.

NORA: He?

MRS. LINDE: Where does he live?

NORA: Oh, how do I know? Yes. (*Searches in her pocket.*) Here's his card. But the letter, the letter—!

HELMER (*from the study, knocking on the door*): Nora!

NORA (*with a cry of fear*): Oh! What is it? What do you want?

HELMER: Now, now, don't be so frightened. We're not coming in. You locked the door—are you trying on the dress?

NORA: Yes, I'm trying it. I'll look just beautiful, Torvald.

MRS. LINDE (*who has read the card*): He's living right around the corner.

NORA: Yes, but what's the use? We're lost. The letter's in the box.

MRS. LINDE: And your husband has the key?

NORA: Yes, always.

MRS. LINDE: Krogstad can ask for his letter back unread; he can find some excuse—

NORA: But it's just this time that Torvald usually—

MRS. LINDE: Stall him. Keep him in there. I'll be back as quick as I can. (*She hurries out through the hall entrance.*)

NORA (*goes to Helmer's door, opens it, and peers in*): Torvald!

HELMER (*from the inner study*): Well—does one dare set foot in one's own living room at last? Come on, Rank, now we'll get a look—(*In the doorway.*) But what's this?

NORA: What, Torvald dear?

HELMER: Rank had me expecting some grand masquerade.

RANK (*in the doorway*): That was my impression, but I must have been wrong.

NORA: No one can admire me in my splendor—not till tomorrow.

HELMER: But Nora dear, you look so exhausted. Have you practiced too hard?

NORA: No, I haven't practiced at all yet.

HELMER: You know, it's necessary—

NORA: Oh, it's absolutely necessary, Torvald. But I can't get anywhere without your help. I've forgotten the whole thing completely.

HELMER: Ah, we'll soon take care of that.

NORA: Yes, take care of me, Torvald, please! Promise me that? Oh, I'm so nervous. That big party—You must give up everything this evening for me. No business—don't even touch your pen. Yes? Dear Torvald, promise?

HELMER: It's a promise. Tonight I'm totally at your service—you little helpless thing. Hm—but first there's one thing I want to—(*Goes toward the hall door.*)

NORA: What are you looking for?

HELMER: Just to see if there's any mail.

NORA: No, no, don't do that, Torvald!

HELMER: Now what?

NORA: Torvald, please. There isn't any.

HELMER: Let me look, though. (*Starts out. Nora, at the piano, strikes the first notes of the tarantella. Helmer, at the door, stops.*) Aha!

NORA: I can't dance tomorrow if I don't practice with you.

HELMER (*going over to her*): Nora dear, are you really so frightened?

NORA: Yes, so terribly frightened. Let me practice right now; there's still time before dinner. Oh, sit down and play for me, Torvald. Direct me. Teach me, the way you always have.

HELMER: Gladly, if it's what you want. (*Sits at the piano.*)

NORA (*snatches the tambourine up from the box, then a long, varicolored shawl, which she throws around herself, whereupon she springs forward and cries out*): Play for me now! Now I'll dance!

(*Helmer plays and Nora dances. Rank stands behind Helmer at the piano and looks on.*)

HELMER (*as he plays*): Slower. Slow down.

NORA: Can't change it.

HELMER: Not so violent, Nora!

NORA: Has to be just like this.

HELMER (*stopping*): No, no, that won't do at all.

NORA (*laughing and swinging her tambourine*): Isn't that what I told you?

RANK: Let me play for her.

HELMER (*getting up*): Yes, go on. I can teach her more easily then.

(*Rank sits at the piano and plays, Nora dances more and more wildly. Helmer has stationed himself by the stove and repeatedly gives her directions; she seems not to hear them; her hair loosens and falls over her shoulders; she does not notice, but goes on dancing. Mrs. Linde enters.*)

MRS. LINDE (*standing dumbfounded at the door*): Ah—!

NORA (*still dancing*): See what fun, Kristine!

HELMER: But Nora darling, you dance as if your life were at stake.

NORA: And it is.

HELMER: Rank, stop! This is pure madness. Stop it, I say!

(*Rank breaks off playing, and Nora halts abruptly.*)

HELMER (*going over to her*): I never would have believed it. You've forgotten everything I taught you.

NORA (*throwing away the tambourine*): You see for yourself.

HELMER: Well, there's certainly room for instruction here.

NORA: Yes, you see how important it is. You've got to teach me to the very last minute. Promise me that, Torvald?

HELMER: You can bet on it.

NORA: You mustn't, either today or tomorrow, think about anything else but me; you mustn't open any letters — or the mailbox —

HELMER: Ah, it's still the fear of that man —

NORA: Oh yes, yes, that too.

HELMER: Nora, it's written all over you — there's already a letter from him out there.

NORA: I don't know. I guess so. But you mustn't read such things now; there mustn't be anything ugly between us before it's all over.

RANK (*quietly to Helmer*): You shouldn't deny her.

HELMER (*putting his arm around her*): The child can have her way. But tomorrow night, after you've danced —

NORA: Then you'll be free.

MAID (*in the doorway, right*): Ma'am, dinner is served.

NORA: We'll be wanting champagne, Helene.

MAID: Very good, ma'am. (*Goes out.*)

HELMER: So — a regular banquet, hm?

NORA: Yes, a banquet — champagne till daybreak! (*Calling out.*) And some macaroons, Helene. Heaps of them — just this once.

HELMER (*taking her hands*): Now, now, now — no hysterics. Be my own little lark again.

NORA: Oh, I will soon enough. But go on in — and you, Dr. Rank. Kristine, help me put up my hair.

RANK (*whispering, as they go*): There's nothing wrong — really wrong, is there?

HELMER: Oh, of course not. It's nothing more than this childish anxiety I was telling you about. (*They go out, right.*)

NORA: Well?

MRS. LINDE: Left town.

NORA: I could see by your face.

MRS. LINDE: He'll be home tomorrow evening. I wrote him a note.

NORA: You shouldn't have. Don't try to stop anything now. After all, it's a wonderful joy, this waiting here for the miracle.

MRS. LINDE: What is it you're waiting for?

NORA: Oh, you can't understand that. Go in to them; I'll be along in a moment.

(*Mrs. Linde goes into the dining room. Nora stands a short while as if composing herself; then she looks at her watch.*)

NORA: Five. Seven hours to midnight. Twenty-four hours to the midnight after, and then the tarantella's done. Seven and twenty-four? Thirty-one hours to live.

HELMER (*in the doorway, right*): What's become of the little lark?

NORA (*going toward him with open arms*): Here's your lark!

ACT III

(*Same scene. The table, with chairs around it, has been moved to the center of the room. A lamp on the table is lit. The hall door stands open. Dance music drifts down from the floor above. Mrs. Linde sits at the table, absently paging through a book, trying to read, but apparently unable to focus her thoughts. Once or twice she pauses, tensely listening for a sound at the outer entrance.*)

MRS. LINDE (*glancing at her watch*): Not yet—and there's hardly any time left. If only he's not—(*Listening again.*) Ah, there it is. (*She goes out in the hall and cautiously opens the outer door. Quiet footsteps are heard on the stairs. She whispers.*) Come in. Nobody's here.

KROGSTAD (*in the doorway*): I found a note from you at home. What's back of all this?

MRS. LINDE: I just *had* to talk to you.

KROGSTAD: Oh? And it just *had* to be here in this house?

MRS. LINDE: At my place it was impossible; my room hasn't a private entrance. Come in, we're all alone. The maid's asleep, and the Helmers are at the dance upstairs.

KROGSTAD (*entering the room*): Well, well, the Helmers are dancing tonight? Really?

MRS. LINDE: Yes, why not?

KROGSTAD: How true—why not?

MRS. LINDE: All right, Krogstad, let's talk.

KROGSTAD: Do we two have anything more to talk about?

MRS. LINDE: We have a great deal to talk about.

KROGSTAD: I wouldn't have thought so.

MRS. LINDE: No, because you've never understood me, really.

KROGSTAD: Was there anything more to understand—except what's all too common in life? A calculating woman throws over a man the moment a better catch comes by.

MRS. LINDE: You think I'm so thoroughly calculating? You think I broke it off lightly?

KROGSTAD: Didn't you?

MRS. LINDE: Nils—is that what you really thought?

KROGSTAD: If you cared, then why did you write me the way you did?

MRS. LINDE: What else could I do? If I had to break off with you, then it was my job as well to root out everything you felt for me.

KROGSTAD (*wringing his hands*): So that was it. And this—all this, simply for money!

MRS. LINDE: Don't forget I had a helpless mother and two small brothers. We couldn't wait for you, Nils; you had such a long road ahead of you then.

KROGSTAD: That may be; but you still hadn't the right to abandon me for somebody else's sake.

MRS. LINDE: Yes—I don't know. So many, many times I've asked myself if I did have that right.

KROGSTAD (*more softly*): When I lost you, it was as if all the solid ground dissolved from under my feet. Look at me; I'm a half-drowned man now, hanging onto a wreck.

MRS. LINDE: Help may be near.

KROGSTAD: It was near—but then you came and blocked it off.

MRS. LINDE: Without my knowing it, Nils. Today for the first time I learned that it's you I'm replacing at the bank.

KROGSTAD: All right—I believe you. But now that you know, will you step aside?

MRS. LINDE: No, because that wouldn't benefit you in the slightest.

KROGSTAD: Not "benefit" me, hm! I'd step aside anyway.

MRS. LINDE: I've learned to be realistic. Life and hard, bitter necessity have taught me that.

KROGSTAD: And life's taught me never to trust fine phrases.

MRS. LINDE: Then life's taught you a very sound thing. But you do have to trust in actions, don't you?

KROGSTAD: What does that mean?

MRS. LINDE: You said you were hanging on like a half-drowned man to a wreck.

KROGSTAD: I've good reason to say that.

MRS. LINDE: I'm also like a half-drowned woman on a wreck. No one to suffer with; no one to care for.

KROGSTAD: You made your choice.

MRS. LINDE: There wasn't any choice then.

KROGSTAD: So—what of it?

MRS. LINDE: Nils, if only we two shipwrecked people could reach across to each other.

KROGSTAD: What are you saying?

MRS. LINDE: Two on one wreck are at least better off than each on his own.

KROGSTAD: Kristine!

MRS. LINDE: Why do you think I came into town?

KROGSTAD: Did you really have some thought of me?

MRS. LINDE: I have to work to go on living. All my born days, as long as I can remember, I've worked, and it's been my best and my only joy. But now I'm completely alone in the world; it frightens me to be so empty and lost. To work for yourself—there's no joy in that. Nils, give me something—someone to work for.

KROGSTAD: I don't believe all this. It's just some hysterical feminine urge to go out and make a noble sacrifice.

MRS. LINDE: Have you ever found me to be hysterical?

KROGSTAD: Can you honestly mean this? Tell me—do you know everything about my past?

MRS. LINDE: Yes.

KROGSTAD: And you know what they think I'm worth around here.

MRS. LINDE: From what you were saying before, it would seem that with me you could have been another person.

KROGSTAD: I'm positive of that.

MRS. LINDE: Couldn't it happen still?

KROGSTAD: Kristine—you're saying this in all seriousness? Yes, you are! I can see it in you. And do you really have the courage, then—?

MRS. LINDE: I need to have someone to care for, and your children need a mother. We both need each other. Nils, I have faith that you're good at heart—I'll risk everything together with you.

KROGSTAD (*gripping her hands*): Kristine, thank you, thank you—Now I know I can win back a place in their eyes. Yes—but I forgot—

MRS. LINDE (*listening*): Shh! The tarantella. Go now! Go on!

KROGSTAD: Why? What is it?

MRS. LINDE: Hear the dance up there? When that's over, they'll be coming down.

KROGSTAD: Oh, then I'll go. But—it's all pointless. Of course, you don't know the move I made against the Helmers.

MRS. LINDE: Yes, Nils, I know.

KROGSTAD: And all the same, you have the courage to—?

MRS. LINDE: I know how far despair can drive a man like you.

KROGSTAD: Oh, if I only could take it all back.

MRS. LINDE: You easily could—your letter's still lying in the mailbox.

KROGSTAD: Are you sure of that?

MRS. LINDE: Positive. But—

KROGSTAD (*looks at her searchingly*): Is that the meaning of it, then? You'll save your friend at any price. Tell me straight out. Is that it?

MRS. LINDE: Nils—anyone who's sold herself for somebody else once isn't going to do it again.

KROGSTAD: I'll demand my letter back.

MRS. LINDE: No, no.

KROGSTAD: Yes, of course. I'll stay here till Helmer comes down; I'll tell him to give me my letter again—that it only involves my dismissal— that he shouldn't read it—

MRS. LINDE: No, Nils, don't call the letter back.

KROGSTAD: But wasn't that exactly why you wrote me to come here?

MRS. LINDE: Yes, in that first panic. But it's been a whole day and night since then, and in that time I've seen such incredible things in this house. Helmer's got to learn everything; this dreadful secret has to be aired; those two have to come to a full understanding; all these lies and evasions can't go on.

KROGSTAD: Well, then, if you want to chance it. But at least there's one thing I can do, and do right away—

MRS. LINDE (*listening*): Go now, go, quick! The dance is over. We're not safe another second.

KROGSTAD: I'll wait for you downstairs.

MRS. LINDE: Yes, please do; take me home.

KROGSTAD: I can't believe it; I've never been so happy. (*He leaves by way of the outer door; the door between the room and the hall stays open.*)

MRS. LINDE (*straightening up a bit and getting together her street clothes*): How different now! How different! Someone to work for, to live for— a home to build. Well, it is worth the try! Oh, if they'd only come! (*Listening.*) Ah, there they are. Bundle up. (*She picks up her hat and coat. Nora's and Helmer's voices can be heard outside; a key turns in the lock, and Helmer brings Nora into the hall almost by force. She is wearing the Italian costume with a large black shawl about her; he has on evening dress, with a black domino open over it.*)

NORA (*struggling in the doorway*): No, no, no, not inside! I'm going up again. I don't want to leave so soon.

HELMER: But Nora dear—

NORA: Oh, I beg you, please, Torvald. From the bottom of my heart, *please*—only an hour more!

HELMER: Not a single minute, Nora darling. You know our agreement. Come on, in we go; you'll catch cold out here. (*In spite of her resistance, he gently draws her into the room.*)

MRS. LINDE: Good evening.

NORA: Kristine!

HELMER: Why, Mrs. Linde—are you here so late?

MRS. LINDE: Yes, I'm sorry, but I did want to see Nora in costume.

NORA: Have you been sitting here, waiting for me?

MRS. LINDE: Yes. I didn't come early enough; you were all upstairs; and then I thought I really couldn't leave without seeing you.

HELMER (*removing Nora's shawl*): Yes, take a good look. She's worth looking at, I can tell you that, Mrs. Linde. Isn't she lovely?

MRS. LINDE: Yes, I should say—

HELMER: A dream of loveliness, isn't she? That's what everyone thought at the party, too. But she's horribly stubborn—this sweet little thing. What's to be done with her? Can you imagine, I almost had to use force to pry her away.

NORA: Oh, Torvald, you're going to regret you didn't indulge me, even for just a half hour more.

HELMER: There, you see. She danced her tarantella and got a tumultuous hand—which was well earned, although the performance may have been a bit too naturalistic—I mean it rather overstepped the proprieties of art. But never mind—what's important is, she made a success, an overwhelming success. You think I could let her stay on after that and spoil the effect? Oh no; I took my lovely little Capri girl—my capricious little Capri girl, I should say—took her under my arm; one quick tour of the ballroom, a curtsy to every side, and then—as they say in novels—the beautiful vision disappeared. An exit should always be effective, Mrs. Linde, but that's what I can't get Nora to grasp. Phew, It's hot in here. (*Flings the domino on a chair and opens the door to his room.*) Why's it dark in here? Oh yes, of course. Excuse me. (*He goes in and lights a couple of candles.*)

NORA (*in a sharp, breathless whisper*): So?

MRS. LINDE (*quietly*): I talked with him.

NORA: And—?

MRS. LINDE: Nora—you must tell your husband everything.

NORA (*dully*): I knew it.

MRS. LINDE: You've got nothing to fear from Krogstad, but you have to speak out.

NORA: I won't tell.

MRS. LINDE: Then the letter will.

NORA: Thanks, Kristine. I know now what's to be done. Shh!

HELMER (*reentering*): Well, then, Mrs. Linde—have you admired her?

MRS. LINDE: Yes, and now I'll say good night.

HELMER: Oh, come, so soon? Is this yours, this knitting?

MRS. LINDE: Yes, thanks. I nearly forgot it.

HELMER: Do you knit, then?

MRS. LINDE: Oh yes.

HELMER: You know what? You should embroider instead.

MRS. LINDE: Really? Why?

HELMER: Yes, because it's a lot prettier. See here, one holds the embroidery so, in the left hand, and then one guides the needle with the right—so—in an easy, sweeping curve—right?

MRS. LINDE: Yes, I guess that's—

HELMER: But, on the other hand, knitting—it can never be anything but ugly. Look, see here, the arms tucked in, the knitting needles going up and down—there's something Chinese about it. Ah, that was really a glorious champagne they served.

MRS. LINDE: Yes, good night, Nora, and don't be stubborn anymore.

HELMER: Well put, Mrs. Linde!

MRS. LINDE: Good night, Mr. Helmer.

HELMER (*accompanying her to the door*): Good night, good night. I hope you get home all right. I'd be very happy to—but you don't have far to go. Good night, good night. (*She leaves. He shuts the door after her and returns.*) There, now, at last we got her out the door. She's a deadly bore, that creature.

NORA: Aren't you pretty tired, Torvald?

HELMER: No, not a bit.

NORA: You're not sleepy?

HELMER: Not at all. On the contrary, I'm feeling quite exhilarated. But you? Yes, you really look tired and sleepy.

NORA: Yes, I'm very tired. Soon now I'll sleep.

HELMER: See! You see! I was right all along that we shouldn't stay longer.

NORA: Whatever you do is always right.

HELMER (*kissing her brow*): Now my little lark talks sense. Say, did you notice what a time Rank was having tonight?

NORA: Oh, was he? I didn't get to speak with him.

HELMER: I scarcely did either, but it's a long time since I've seen him in such high spirits. (*Gazes at her a moment, then comes nearer her.*) Hm— it's marvelous, though, to be back home again—to be completely alone with you. Oh, you bewitchingly lovely young woman!

NORA: Torvald, don't look at me like that!

HELMER: Can't I look at my richest treasure? At all that beauty that's mine, mine alone—completely and utterly.

NORA (*moving around to the other side of the table*): You mustn't talk to me that way tonight.

HELMER (*following her*): The tarantella is still in your blood. I can see— and it makes you even more enticing. Listen. The guests are beginning to go. (*Dropping his voice.*) Nora—it'll soon be quiet through this whole house.

NORA: Yes, I hope so.

HELMER: You do, don't you, my love? Do you realize—when I'm out at a party like this with you—do you know why I talk to you so little, and keep such a distance away; just send you a stolen look now and then— you know why I do it? It's because I'm imagining then that you're my secret darling, my secret young bride-to-be, and that no one suspects there's anything between us.

NORA: Yes, yes; oh, yes, I know you're always thinking of me.

HELMER: And then when we leave and I place the shawl over those fine young rounded shoulders—over that wonderful curving neck—then I pretend that you're my young bride, that we're just coming from the wedding, that for the first time I'm bringing you into my house—that for the first time I'm alone with you—completely alone with you, your trembling young beauty! All this evening I've longed for nothing but you. When I saw you turn and sway in the tarantella—my blood was pounding till I couldn't stand it—that's why I brought you down here so early—

NORA: Go away, Torvald! Leave me alone. I don't want all this.

HELMER: What do you mean? Nora, you're teasing me. You will, won't you? Aren't I your husband—?

(*A knock at the outside door.*)

NORA (*startled*): What's that?

HELMER (*going toward the hall*): Who is it?

RANK (*outside*): It's me. May I come in a moment?

HELMER (*with quiet irritation*): Oh, what does he want now? (*Aloud.*) Hold on. (*Goes and opens the door.*) Oh, how nice that you didn't just pass us by!

RANK: I thought I heard your voice, and then I wanted so badly to have a look in. (*Lightly glancing about.*) Ah, me, these old familiar haunts. You have it snug and cozy in here, you two.

HELMER: You seemed to be having it pretty cozy upstairs, too.

RANK: Absolutely. Why shouldn't I? Why not take in everything in life? As much as you can, anyway, and as long as you can. The wine was superb—

HELMER: The champagne especially.

RANK: You noticed that too? It's amazing how much I could guzzle down.

NORA: Torvald also drank a lot of champagne this evening.

RANK: Oh?

NORA: Yes, and that always makes him so entertaining.

RANK: Well, why shouldn't one have a pleasant evening after a well-spent day?

HELMER: Well spent? I'm afraid I can't claim that.

RANK (*slapping him on the back*): But I can, you see!

NORA: Dr. Rank, you must have done some scientific research today.

RANK: Quite so.

HELMER: Come now—little Nora talking about scientific research!

NORA: And can I congratulate you on the results?

RANK: Indeed you may.

NORA: Then they were good?

RANK: The best possible for both doctor and patient—certainty.

NORA (*quickly and searchingly*): Certainty?

RANK: Complete certainty. So don't I owe myself a gay evening afterwards?

NORA: Yes, you're right, Dr. Rank.

HELMER: I'm with you—just so long as you don't have to suffer for it in the morning.

RANK: Well, one never gets something for nothing in life.

NORA: Dr. Rank—are you very fond of masquerade parties?

RANK: Yes, if there's a good array of odd disguises—

NORA: Tell me, what should we two go as at the next masquerade?

HELMER: You little featherhead—already thinking of the next!

RANK: We two? I'll tell you what: You must go as Charmed Life—

HELMER: Yes, but find a costume for that!

RANK: Your wife can appear just as she looks every day.

HELMER: That was nicely put. But don't you know what you're going to be?

RANK: Yes, Helmer, I've made up my mind.

HELMER: Well?

RANK: At the next masquerade I'm going to be invisible.

HELMER: That's a funny idea.

RANK: They say there's a hat—black, huge—have you never heard of the hat that makes you invisible? You put it on, and then no one on earth can see you.

HELMER (*suppressing a smile*): Ah, of course.

RANK: But I'm quite forgetting what I came for. Helmer, give me a cigar, one of the dark Havanas.

HELMER: With the greatest pleasure. (*Holds out his case.*)

RANK: Thanks. (*Takes one and cuts off the tip.*)

NORA (*striking a match*): Let me give you a light.

RANK: Thank you. (*She holds the match for him; he lights the cigar.*) And now good-bye.

HELMER: Good-bye, good-bye, old friend.

NORA: Sleep well, Doctor.

RANK: Thanks for that wish.

NORA: Wish me the same.

RANK: You? All right, if you like—Sleep well. And thanks for the light. (*He nods to them both and leaves.*)

HELMER (*his voice subdued*): He's been drinking heavily.

NORA (*absently*): Could be. (*Helmer takes his keys from his pocket and goes out in the hall.*) Torvald—what are you after?

HELMER: Got to empty the mailbox; it's nearly full. There won't be room for the morning papers.

NORA: Are you working tonight?

HELMER: You know I'm not. Why—what's this? Someone's been at the lock.

NORA: At the lock—?

HELMER: Yes, I'm positive. What do you suppose—? I can't imagine one of the maids—? Here's a broken hairpin. Nora, it's yours—

NORA (*quickly*): Then it must be the children—

HELMER: You'd better break them of that. Hm, hm—well, opened it after all. (*Takes the contents out and calls into the kitchen.*) Helene! Helene, would you put out the lamp in the hall. (*He returns to the room, shutting the hall door, then displays the handful of mail.*) Look how it's piled up. (*Sorting through them.*) Now what's this?

NORA (*at the window*): The letter! Oh, Torvald, no!

HELMER: Two calling cards—from Rank.

NORA: From Dr. Rank?

HELMER (*examining them*): "Dr. Rank, Consulting Physician." They were on top. He must have dropped them in as he left.

NORA: Is there anything on them?

HELMER: There's a black cross over the name. See? That's a gruesome notion. He could almost be announcing his own death.

NORA: That's just what he's doing.

HELMER: What! You've heard something? Something he's told you?

NORA: Yes. That when those cards came, he'd be taking his leave of us. He'll shut himself in now and die.

HELMER: Ah, my poor friend! Of course I knew he wouldn't be here much longer. But so soon—And then to hide himself away like a wounded animal.

NORA: If it has to happen, then it's best it happens in silence—don't you think so, Torvald?

HELMER (*pacing up and down*): He's grown right into our lives. I simply can't imagine him gone. He with his suffering and loneliness—like a dark cloud setting off our sunlit happiness. Well, maybe it's best this way. For him, at least. (*Standing still.*) And maybe for us too, Nora. Now we're thrown back on each other, completely. (*Embracing her.*) Oh you, my darling wife, how can I hold you close enough? You know what, Nora—time and again I've wished you were in some terrible danger, just so I could stake my life and soul and everything, for your sake.

NORA (*tearing herself away, her voice firm and decisive*): Now you must read your mail, Torvald.

HELMER: No, no, not tonight. I want to stay with you, dearest.

NORA: With a dying friend on your mind?

HELMER: You're right. We've both had a shock. There's ugliness between us—these thoughts of death and corruption. We'll have to get free of them first. Until then—we'll stay apart.

NORA (*clinging about his neck*): Torvald—good night! Good night!

HELMER (*kissing her on the cheek*): Good night, little songbird. Sleep well, Nora. I'll be reading my mail now. (*He takes the letters into his room and shuts the door after him.*)

NORA (*with bewildered glances, groping about, seizing Helmer's domino, throwing it around her, and speaking in short, hoarse, broken whispers*): Never see him again. Never, never. (*Putting her shawl over her head.*) Never see the children either—them, too. Never, never. Oh, the freezing black water! The depths—down—Oh, I wish it were over—He has it now; he's reading it—now. Oh no, no, not yet. Torvald, goodbye, you and the children—(*She starts for the hall; as she does, Helmer throws open his door and stands with an open letter in his hand.*)

HELMER: Nora!

NORA (*screams*): Oh—!

HELMER: What is this? You know what's in this letter?

NORA: Yes, I know. Let me go! Let me out!

HELMER (*holding her back*): Where are you going?

NORA (*struggling to break loose*): You can't save me, Torvald!

HELMER (*slumping back*): True! Then it's true what he writes? How horrible! No, no, it's impossible—it can't be true.

NORA: It *is* true. I've loved you more than all this world.

HELMER: Ah, none of your slippery tricks.

NORA (*taking one step toward him*): Torvald—!

HELMER: What *is* this you've blundered into!

NORA: Just let me loose. You're not going to suffer for my sake. You're not going to take on my guilt.

HELMER: No more playacting. (*Locks the hall door.*) You stay right here and give me a reckoning. You understand what you've done? Answer! You understand?

NORA (*looking squarely at him, her face hardening*): Yes. I'm beginning to understand everything now.

HELMER (*striding about*): Oh, what an awful awakening! In all these eight years—she who was my pride and joy—a hypocrite, a liar—worse, worse—a criminal! How infinitely disgusting it all is! The shame!

(*Nora says nothing and goes on looking straight at him. He stops in front of her.*) I should have suspected something of the kind. I should have known. All your father's flimsy values—Be still! All your father's flimsy values have come out in you. No religion, no morals, no sense of duty—Oh, how I'm punished for letting him off! I did it for your sake, and you repay me like this.

NORA: Yes, like this.

HELMER: Now you've wrecked all my happiness—ruined my whole future. Oh, it's awful to think of. I'm in a cheap little grafter's hands; he can do anything he wants with me, ask for anything, play with me like a puppet—and I can't breathe a word. I'll be swept down miserably into the depths on account of a featherbrained woman.

NORA: When I'm gone from this world, you'll be free.

HELMER: Oh, quit posing. Your father had a mess of those speeches too. What good would that ever do me if you were gone from this world, as you say? Not the slightest. He can still make the whole thing known; and if he does, I could be falsely suspected as your accomplice. They might even think that I was behind it—that I put you up to it. And all that I can thank you for—you that I've coddled the whole of our marriage. Can you see now what you've done to me?

NORA (*icily calm*): Yes.

HELMER: It's so incredible, I just can't grasp it. But we'll have to patch up whatever we can. Take off the shawl. I said, take it off! I've got to appease him somehow or other. The thing has to be hushed up at any cost. And as for you and me, it's got to seem like everything between us is just as it was—to the outside world, that is. You'll go right on living in this house, of course. But you can't be allowed to bring up the children; I don't dare trust you with them—Oh, to have to say this to someone I've loved so much! Well, that's done with. From now on happiness doesn't matter; all that matters is saving the bits and pieces, the appearance—(*The doorbell rings. Helmer starts.*) What's that? And so late. Maybe the worst—? You think he'd—? Hide, Nora! Say you're sick. (*Nora remains standing motionless. Helmer goes and opens the door.*)

MAID (*half dressed, in the hall*): A letter for Mrs. Helmer.

HELMER: I'll take it. (*Snatches the letter and shuts the door.*) Yes, it's from him. You don't get it; I'm reading it myself.

NORA: Then read it.

HELMER (*by the lamp*): I hardly dare. We may be ruined, you and I. But— I've got to know. (*Rips open the letter, skims through a few lines, glances at an enclosure, then cries out joyfully.*) Nora! (*Nora looks inquiringly at him.*) Nora! Wait—better check it again—Yes, yes, it's true. I'm saved. Nora, I'm saved!

NORA: And I?

HELMER: You too, of course. We're both saved, both of us. Look. He's sent back your note. He says he's sorry and ashamed—that a happy development in his life—oh, who cares what he says! Nora, we're saved! No one can hurt you. Oh, Nora, Nora—but first, this ugliness all has to go. Let me see—(*Takes a look at the note.*) No, I don't want to see it; I want the whole thing to fade like a dream. (*Tears the note and both letters to pieces, throws them into the stove and watches them burn.*) There—now there's nothing left—He wrote that since Christmas Eve you—Oh, they must have been three terrible days for you, Nora.

NORA: I fought a hard fight.

HELMER: And suffered pain and saw no escape but—No, we're not going to dwell on anything unpleasant. We'll just be grateful and keep on repeating: It's over now, it's over! You hear me, Nora? You don't seem to realize—it's over. What's it mean—that frozen look? Oh, poor little Nora, I understand. You can't believe I've forgiven you. But I have, Nora; I swear I have. I know that what you did, you did out of love for me.

NORA: That's true.

HELMER: You loved me the way a wife ought to love her husband. It's simply the means that you couldn't judge. But you think I love you any the less for not knowing how to handle your affairs? No, no—just lean on me; I'll guide you and teach you. I wouldn't be a man if this feminine helplessness didn't make you twice as attractive to me. You mustn't mind those sharp words I said—that was all in the first confusion of thinking my world had collapsed. I've forgiven you, Nora; I swear I've forgiven you.

NORA: My thanks for your forgiveness. (*She goes out through the door, right.*)

HELMER: No, wait—(*Peers in.*) What are you doing in there?

NORA (*inside*): Getting out of my costume.

HELMER (*by the open door*): Yes, do that. Try to calm yourself and collect your thoughts again, my frightened little songbird. You can rest easy now; I've got wide wings to shelter you with. (*Walking about close by the door.*) How snug and nice our home is, Nora. You're safe here; I'll keep you like a hunted dove I've rescued out of a hawk's claws. I'll bring peace to your poor, shuddering heart. Gradually it'll happen, Nora; you'll see. Tomorrow all this will look different to you; then everything will be as it was. I won't have to go on repeating I forgive you; you'll feel it for yourself. How can you imagine I'd ever conceivably want to disown you—or even blame you in any way? Ah, you don't know a man's heart, Nora. For a man there's something indescribably sweet and satisfying in knowing he's forgiven his wife—and forgiven her out of a full and open heart. It's as if she belongs to him in two ways now: In a sense he's given her fresh into the world again, and she's become his wife and his child as well. From now on that's what you'll be to me—you little, bewildered, helpless thing. Don't be afraid of anything, Nora; just open your heart to me, and I'll be conscience and will to you both—(*Nora enters in her regular clothes.*) What's this? Not in bed? You've changed your dress?

NORA: Yes, Torvald, I've changed my dress.

HELMER: But why now, so late?

NORA: Tonight I'm not sleeping.

HELMER: But Nora dear—

NORA (*looking at her watch*): It's still not so very late. Sit down, Torvald; we have a lot to talk over. (*She sits at one side of the table.*)

HELMER: Nora—what is this? That hard expression—

NORA: Sit down. This'll take some time. I have a lot to say.

HELMER (*sitting at the table directly opposite her*): You worry me, Nora. And I don't understand you.

NORA: No, that's exactly it. You don't understand me. And I've never understood you either—until tonight. No, don't interrupt. You can just listen to what I say. We're closing out accounts, Torvald.

HELMER: How do you mean that?

NORA (*after a short pause*): Doesn't anything strike you about our sitting here like this?

HELMER: What's that?

NORA: We've been married now eight years. Doesn't it occur to you that this is the first time we two, you and I, man and wife, have ever talked seriously together?

HELMER: What do you mean—seriously?

NORA: In eight whole years—longer even—right from our first acquaintance, we've never exchanged a serious word on any serious thing.

HELMER: You mean I should constantly go and involve you in problems you couldn't possibly help me with?

NORA: I'm not talking of problems. I'm saying that we've never sat down seriously together and tried to get to the bottom of anything.

HELMER: But dearest, what good would that ever do you?

NORA: That's the point right there: You've never understood me. I've been wronged greatly, Torvald—first by Papa, and then by you.

HELMER: What! By us—the two people who've loved you more than anyone else?

NORA (*shaking her head*): You never loved me. You've thought it fun to be in love with me, that's all.

HELMER: Nora, what a thing to say!

NORA: Yes, it's true now, Torvald. When I lived at home with Papa, he told me all his opinions, so I had the same ones too; or if they were different I hid them, since he wouldn't have cared for that. He used to call me his doll-child, and he played with me the way I played with my dolls. Then I came into your house —

HELMER: How can you speak of our marriage like that?

NORA (*unperturbed*): I mean, then I went from Papa's hands into yours. You arranged everything to your own taste, and so I got the same taste as you — or I pretended to; I can't remember. I guess a little of both, first one, then the other. Now when I look back, it seems as if I'd lived here like a beggar — just from hand to mouth. I've lived by doing tricks for you, Torvald. But that's the way you wanted it. It's a great sin what you and Papa did to me. You're to blame that nothing's become of me.

HELMER: Nora, how unfair and ungrateful you are! Haven't you been happy here?

NORA: No, never. I thought so — but I never have.

HELMER: Not — not happy!

NORA: No, only lighthearted. And you've always been so kind to me. But our home's been nothing but a playpen. I've been your doll-wife here, just as at home I was Papa's doll-child. And in turn the children have been my dolls. I thought it was fun when you played with me, just as they thought it fun when I played with them. That's been our marriage, Torvald.

HELMER: There's some truth in what you're saying — under all the raving exaggeration. But it'll all be different after this. Playtime's over; now for the schooling.

NORA: Whose schooling — mine or the children's?

HELMER: Both yours and the children's, dearest.

NORA: Oh, Torvald, you're not the man to teach me to be a good wife to you.

HELMER: And you can say that?

NORA: And I — how am I equipped to bring up children?

HELMER: Nora!

NORA: Didn't you say a moment ago that that was no job to trust me with?

HELMER: In a flare of temper! Why fasten on that?

NORA: Yes, but you were so very right. I'm not up to the job. There's another job I have to do first. I have to try to educate myself. You can't help me with that. I've got to do it alone. And that's why I'm leaving you now.

HELMER (*jumping up*): What's that?

NORA: I have to stand completely alone, if I'm ever going to discover myself and the world out there. So I can't go on living with you.

HELMER: Nora, Nora!

NORA: I want to leave right away. Kristine should put me up for the night—

HELMER: You're insane! You've no right! I forbid you!

NORA: From here on, there's no use forbidding me anything. I'll take with me whatever is mine. I don't want a thing from you, either now or later.

HELMER: What kind of madness is this!

NORA: Tomorrow I'm going home—I mean, home where I came from. It'll be easier up there to find something to do.

HELMER: Oh, you blind, incompetent child!

NORA: I must learn to be competent, Torvald.

HELMER: Abandon your home, your husband, your children! And you're not even thinking what people will say.

NORA: I can't be concerned about that. I only know how essential this is.

HELMER: Oh, it's outrageous. So you'll run out like this on your most sacred vows.

NORA: What do you think are my most sacred vows?

HELMER: And I have to tell you that! Aren't they your duties to your husband and children?

NORA: I have other duties equally sacred.

HELMER: That isn't true. What duties are they?

NORA: Duties to myself.

HELMER: Before all else, you're a wife and a mother.

NORA: I don't believe in that anymore. I believe that before all else, I'm a human being, no less than you—or anyway, I ought to try to become one. I know the majority thinks you're right, Torvald, and plenty of books agree with you, too. But I can't go on believing what the majority says, or what's written in books. I have to think over these things myself and try to understand them.

HELMER: Why can't you understand your place in your own home? On a point like that, isn't there one everlasting guide you can turn to? Where's your religion?

NORA: Oh, Torvald, I'm really not sure what religion is.

HELMER: What—?

NORA: I only know what the minister said when I was confirmed. He told me religion was this thing and that. When I get clear and away by myself, I'll go into that problem too. I'll see if what the minister said was right, or, in any case, if it's right for me.

HELMER: A young woman your age shouldn't talk like that. If religion can't move you, I can try to rouse your conscience. You do have some moral feeling? Or, tell me—has that gone too?

NORA: It's not easy to answer that, Torvald. I simply don't know. I'm all confused about these things. I just know I see them so differently from you. I find out for one thing, that the law's not at all what I'd thought— but I can't get it through my head that the law is fair. A woman hasn't a right to protect her dying father or save her husband's life! I can't believe that.

HELMER: You talk like a child. You don't know anything of the world you live in.

NORA: No, I don't. But now I'll begin to learn for myself. I'll try to discover who's right, the world or I.

HELMER: Nora, you're sick; you've got a fever. I almost think you're out of your head.

NORA: I've never felt more clearheaded and sure in my life.

HELMER: And—clearheaded and sure—you're leaving your husband and children?

NORA: Yes.

HELMER: Then there's only one possible reason.

NORA: What?

HELMER: You no longer love me.

NORA: No. That's exactly it.

HELMER: Nora! You can't be serious!

NORA: Oh, this is so hard, Torvald—you've been so kind to me always. But I can't help it. I don't love you anymore.

HELMER (*struggling for composure*): Are you also clearheaded and sure about that?

NORA: Yes, completely. That's why I can't go on staying here.

HELMER: Can you tell me what I did to lose your love?

NORA: Yes, I can tell you. It was this evening when the miraculous thing didn't come—then I knew you weren't the man I'd imagined.

HELMER: Be more explicit; I don't follow you.

NORA: I've waited now so patiently eight long years—for, my Lord, I know miracles don't come every day. Then this crisis broke over me, and such a certainty filled me: *Now* the miraculous event would occur. While Krogstad's letter was lying out there, I never for an instant dreamed that you could give in to his terms. I was so utterly sure you'd say to him: Go on, tell your tale to the whole wide world. And when he'd done that—

HELMER: Yes, what then? When I'd delivered my own wife into shame and disgrace—!

NORA: When he'd done that, I was so utterly sure that you'd step forward, take the blame on yourself and say: I am the guilty one.

HELMER: Nora—!

NORA: You're thinking I'd never accept such a sacrifice from you? No, of course not. But what good would my protests be against you? That was the miracle I was waiting for, in terror and hope. And to stave that off, I would have taken my life.

HELMER: I'd gladly work for you day and night, Nora—and take on pain and deprivation. But there's no one who gives up honor for love.

NORA: Millions of women have done just that.

HELMER: Oh, you think and talk like a silly child.

NORA: Perhaps. But you neither think nor talk like the man I could join myself to. When your big fright was over—and it wasn't from any threat against me, only for what might damage you—when all the danger was past, for you it was just as if nothing had happened. I was exactly the same, your little lark, your doll, that you'd have to handle with double care now that I'd turned out so brittle and frail. (*Gets up.*) Torvald—in that instant it dawned on me that for eight years I've been living here with a stranger, and that I'd even conceived three children—oh, I can't stand the thought of it! I could tear myself to bits.

HELMER (*heavily*): I see. There's a gulf that's opened between us—that's clear. Oh, but Nora, can't we bridge it somehow?

NORA: The way I am now, I'm no wife for you.

HELMER: I have the strength to make myself over.

NORA: Maybe—if your doll gets taken away.

HELMER: But to part! To part from you! No, Nora, no—I can't imagine it.

NORA (*going out, right*): All the more reason why it has to be. (*She reenters with her coat and a small overnight bag, which she puts on a chair by the table.*)

HELMER: Nora, Nora, not now! Wait till tomorrow.

NORA: I can't spend the night in a strange man's room.

HELMER: But couldn't we live here like brother and sister—

NORA: You know very well how long that would last. (*Throws her shawl about her.*) Good-bye, Torvald. I won't look in on the children. I know they're in better hands than mine. The way I am now, I'm no use to them.

HELMER: But someday, Nora—someday—?

NORA: How can I tell? I haven't the least idea what'll become of me.

HELMER: But you're my wife, now and wherever you go.

NORA: Listen, Torvald—I've heard that when a wife deserts her husband's house just as I'm doing, then the law frees him from all responsibility. In any case, I'm freeing you from being responsible. Don't feel yourself bound, any more than I will. There has to be absolute freedom for us both. Here, take your ring back. Give me mine.

HELMER: That too?

NORA: That too.

HELMER: There it is.

NORA: Good. Well, now it's all over. I'm putting the keys here. The maids know all about keeping up the house—better than I do. Tomorrow, after I've left town, Kristine will stop by to pack up everything that's mine from home. I'd like those things shipped up to me.

HELMER: Over! All over! Nora, won't you ever think about me?

NORA: I'm sure I'll think of you often, and about the children and the house here.

HELMER: May I write you?

NORA: No—never. You're not to do that.

HELMER: Oh, but let me send you—

NORA: Nothing. Nothing.

HELMER: Or help you if you need it.

NORA: No. I accept nothing from strangers.

HELMER: Nora—can I never be more than a stranger to you?

NORA (*picking up the overnight bag*): Ah, Torvald—it would take the greatest miracle of all—

HELMER: Tell me the greatest miracle!

NORA: You and I both would have to transform ourselves to the point that—Oh, Torvald, I've stopped believing in miracles.

HELMER: But I'll believe. Tell me! Transform ourselves to the point that—?

NORA: That our living together could be a true marriage. (*She goes out down the hall.*)

HELMER (*sinks down on a chair by the door, face buried in his hands*): Nora! Nora! (*Looking about and rising.*) Empty. She's gone. (*A sudden hope leaps in him.*) The greatest miracle—?

(*From below, the sound of a door slamming shut.*)

1879

The Cherry Orchard

A Comedy in Four Acts

ANTON CHEKHOV [1860–1904]

TRANSLATED BY CAROL ROCAMORA

Cast of Characters°
RANEVSKAYA, Lyubov Andreevna, *a landowner*
ANYA, *her daughter, aged seventeen*
VARYA, *her adopted daughter, aged twenty-four*
GAEV, Leonid Andreevich, *Ranevskaya's brother*
LOPAKHIN, Yermolai Alekseevich, *a merchant*
TROFIMOV, Pyotr Sergeevich, *a student*
SIMEONOV-PISHCHIK, Boris Borisovich, *a landowner*
CHARLOTTA IVANOVNA, *a governess*
YEPIKHODOV, Semyon Panteleevich, *a clerk*
DUNYASHA, *a maid*
FIRS, *a servant, an old man of eighty-seven*
YASHA, *a young servant*
A PASSERBY
A STATIONMASTER
A POST OFFICE CLERK
Guests, servants

The action takes place on the estate of Lyubov Andreevna Ranevskaya.

Cast of Characters: The pronunciations given here approximate the sounds of the original Russian. Accented syllables are indicated in all capitals:

Lyubov Andreevna Ranevskaya (Ly-oo-BOF Ahn-DRAY-ev-na Rah-NYEF-sky-a)
Anya (AHN-ya)
Varya (VAR-ya)
Leonid Andreevich Gaev (Lee-o-NEED Ahn-DRAY-e-veech GA-yef)
Yermolai Alekseevich Lopakhin (Yer-mo-LIE Ah-lek-SAY-e-veech Lo-PA-keen)
Pyotr Sergeevich Trofimov (P'YO-tir Sehr-GAY-e-veech Tro-FEE-mof)
Boris Borisovich Simeonov-Pishchik (Bo-REES Bo-REE-so-veech Si-MEE-o-nof-
PEESH-cheek)

272

ACT ONE

A room which is still called the nursery. One of the doors leads to Anya's room. It is dawn, just before sunrise. It is already May, the cherry trees are all in bloom, but outside it is still cold; there is an early morning frost in the orchard. The windows in the room are closed.

Enter Dunyasha, carrying a candle, and Lopakhin with a book in his hand.

LOPAKHIN: The train's arrived, thank God. What time is it?

DUNYASHA: Almost two. (*Puts out the candle.*) It's already getting light out.

LOPAKHIN: So how late is the train, then? A couple of hours, at least. (*Yawns and stretches.*) Well, I've made a fool of myself, then, haven't I! Hm? Came all the way out here, just to meet the train, and fell fast asleep . . . Sat here waiting and dozed right off. Annoying, isn't it . . . You should have woken me up.

DUNYASHA: I thought you'd already gone. (*Listens.*) Listen, I think they're here.

LOPAKHIN: (*Listens.*) No . . . They've got to get their baggage first, you know, that sort of thing . . .

Pause.

Lyubov Andreevna, she's been living abroad for five years, I don't know, I can't even imagine what's become of her now . . . She's a fine person, you know . . . a warm, kind person. I remember, once, when I was a boy, oh, about fifteen years old, say, and my father—he had a shop here in the village then—my father, he hit me in the face with his fist, blood was pouring from my nose . . . We'd come out into the courtyard together, somehow, and he was drunk. And there was Lyubov Andreevna, I remember her so vividly, so young then, so graceful, so slender, she took me by the hand, brought me over to the washstand, right into this very room, into the nursery. "Don't cry, little peasant," she said, "it will heal before your wedding day . . ."

Pause.

Little peasant . . . yes, my father was a peasant, it's true enough, and here I am in a three-piece suit and fancy shoes. A silk purse from a sow's ear, or something like that, isn't that how the expression goes . . .

Charlotta Ivanovna (Shar-LO-ta Ee-VAN-ov-na)
Semyon Panteleevich Yepikhodov (Sem-YON Pahn-te-LAY-veech Yep-ee-KOH-dof)
Dunyasha (Doon-YAH-sha)
Firs (Feers)
Yasha (YAH-sha)

Yes . . . The only difference is, now I'm rich, I've got a lot of money, but don't look too closely, once a peasant . . . (*Leafs through the book.*) Look at me, I read through this entire book and didn't understand a word of it. Read it and dozed right off.

Pause.

DUNYASHA: The dogs didn't sleep at all last night, they can sense their masters are coming home.

LOPAKHIN: What's wrong with you, Dunyasha . . .

DUNYASHA: My hands are trembling. I'm going to faint, I know I am.

LOPAKHIN: You're much too high-strung, Dunyasha. And look at you, all dressed up like a young lady, hair done up, too. You mustn't do that. Remember who you are.

Enter Yepikhodov with a bouquet; he is wearing a jacket and highly polished boots, which squeak loudly; upon entering, he drops the bouquet.

YEPIKHODOV: (*Picks up the bouquet.*) Look what the gardener sent. Put them on the dining room table. That's what he said. (*Gives the bouquet to Dunyasha.*)

LOPAKHIN: Bring me some kvass, will you?

DUNYASHA: Yes, sir. (*Leaves.*)

YEPIKHODOV: We have an early morning frost, we have three degrees below zero, and we have the cherry blossoms all in bloom. I don't approve of our climate. (*Sighs.*) Really, I don't. Our climate doesn't work, it just doesn't work. It's not conducive. And would you like to hear more, Yermolai Alekseich, well, then you will, because the day before yesterday, I bought these boots, and, trust me, they squeak so much, that they are beyond hope. Now how can I oil them? Tell me? How?

LOPAKHIN: Enough. You're getting on my nerves.

YEPIKHODOV: Every day some new disaster befalls me. A new day, a new disaster. But do I grumble, do I complain, no, I don't, I accept it, look, I'm smiling, even.

Dunyasha enters, gives Lopakhin some kvass.

I'm going now. (*Stumbles against a chair, which falls down.*) There . . . (*As if vindicated.*) You see? I mean, that's the situation, and excuse me for saying so . . . Remarkable, even . . . isn't it! (*Exits.*)

DUNYASHA: Yermolai Alekseich, I have something to tell you . . . Yepikhodov has proposed to me.

LOPAKHIN: Ah!

DUNYASHA: But I don't know, really . . . He's a nice enough fellow, you know, quiet and all, it's just that whenever he starts to talk, I can't understand a word he's saying. I mean, it all sounds so sweet and sincere, only it just doesn't make any sense. I like him, I mean, I think I like him. And he? He adores me. But he's such an unfortunate fellow, you know, really, every day it's something else. They even have a name for him, do you know what they call him: "Mister Disaster" . . .

LOPAKHIN: (*Listens.*) I think they're coming . . .

DUNYASHA: They're coming! What's happening to me . . . I'm freezing, look, I'm shivering all over.

LOPAKHIN: They're really coming! Let's go meet them. Will she recognize me? We haven't seen each other in five years.

DUNYASHA: (*Agitated.*) I'm going to faint, I know I am . . . Look, I'm fainting!

Two carriages are heard pulling up to the house. Lopakhin and Dunyasha exit quickly. The stage is empty. Then there is noise in the adjacent rooms. Firs hurries across the stage to meet Lyubov Andreevna; he is leaning on a cane, and is dressed in old-fashioned livery and a high hat; he mutters something to himself, but it is impossible to make out a single word. The offstage noise crescendos. A voice calls out: "Let's go this way, through here . . ." Enter Lyubov Andreevna, Anya, and Charlotta Ivanovna with a little dog on a leash; they are all dressed in traveling clothes. Enter Varya, wearing a coat and a shawl, Gaev, Simeonov-Pishchik, Lopakhin, Dunyasha carrying a bundle and an umbrella, Servants carrying luggage — they all come through the room.

ANYA: This way! Mama, do you remember what room this is?

LYUBOV ANDREEVNA: (*Ecstatic, in tears.*) The nursery!

VARYA: How cold it is, my hands are numb. (*To Lyubov Andreevna.*) Look, Mamochka, your rooms, violet and white, just as you left them.

LYUBOV ANDREEVNA: My nursery, my darling nursery, my beautiful room . . . I slept here, when I was a child . . . (*Weeps.*) And now, I'm a child again . . . (*Kisses her brother, Varya, and her brother again.*) And Varya looks the same as ever, just like a little nun. And Dunyasha I recognize, of course . . . (*Kisses Dunyasha.*)

GAEV: The train was two hours late. How do you like that? How's that for efficiency!

CHARLOTTA: (*To Pishchik.*) My dog eats walnuts, too.

PISHCHIK: (*Amazed.*) Imagine that!

They all exit, except for Anya and Dunyasha.

DUNYASHA: We've been waiting forever . . . (*Takes Anya's coat and hat.*)

ANYA: I didn't sleep one moment the whole journey long, four whole nights . . . and now I'm absolutely frozen!

DUNYASHA: You left during Lent, we had snow then, and frost, and now! My darling! (*Bursts out laughing, kisses her.*) I've waited forever for you, my precious, my joy . . . And I've got something to tell you, I can't wait one minute longer . . .

ANYA: (*Listlessly.*) Now what . . .

DUNYASHA: Yepikhodov, the clerk, proposed to me just after Easter.

ANYA: Not again . . . (*Adjusts her hair.*) I've lost all my hairpins . . . (*She is exhausted; she almost sways on her feet.*)

DUNYASHA: No, really, I don't know what to think any more. He adores me, God, how he adores me!

ANYA: (*Gazes at the door to her room, tenderly.*) My very own room, my windows, it's as if I never left. I'm home! And tomorrow I'll wake up, and I'll run out into the orchard . . . Oh, if only I could rest! I'm so exhausted—I didn't sleep one moment the whole way, I was so worried.

DUNYASHA: Pyotr Sergeich arrived the day before yesterday.

ANYA: (*Overjoyed.*) Petya!

DUNYASHA: He's out in the bathhouse, asleep, that's where he's staying. "I'm afraid of being in the way," he said. (*Glances at her pocket watch.*) We ought to wake him up, but Varvara Mikhailovna gave us strict orders not to. "Don't you dare wake him up," she said.

Enter Varya, a bunch of keys hanging from her belt.

VARYA: Dunyasha, go, quickly, bring the coffee . . . Mamochka wants coffee.

DUNYASHA: Right away. (*Exits.*)

VARYA: So, thank God, you're here. You're home at last! (*Embracing her.*) My darling's home! My angel is home.

ANYA: I've been through so much.

VARYA: I can imagine.

ANYA: I left during Holy Week, it was so cold then, remember? And Charlotta Ivanovna talked the whole way, talked and played card tricks. How could you have stuck me with Charlotta! . . .

VARYA: You can't travel alone, darling. At seventeen!

ANYA: When we arrived in Paris, it was cold there, too, and snowing. My French is terrible. Mama lived on the fifth floor, and when I finally got there, the flat was filled with all sorts of French people, ladies, an old Catholic priest with a little book, and, oh, it was so uncomfortable there, so stuffy, the room was filled with smoke. And suddenly I felt sorry for Mama, so very sorry, I threw my arms around her neck, I held her so tight, I couldn't let go. And Mama kept clinging to me, and weeping . . .

VARYA: (*In tears.*) Enough, enough . . .

ANYA: She had already sold the dacha near Menton, she had nothing left, nothing at all. And neither did I, not a single kopek, we hardly had enough money to get home. And Mama just doesn't understand it, still! There we are, sitting in the station restaurant, and she orders the most expensive thing on the menu, she gives the waiter a ruble tip for

tea. Charlotta, too. And Yasha orders a complete dinner, it's simply terrible. Yasha is Mama's butler, you know. We brought him with us . . .

VARYA: I've seen him, the devil . . .

ANYA: So, tell me! Have we paid the interest yet?

VARYA: With what?

ANYA: Dear God, dear God . . .

VARYA: And in August, the estate will be sold . . .

ANYA: Dear God . . .

LOPAKHIN: (*Peeks through the door and makes a "bleating" sound.*) Ba-a-a . . .
(*Exits.*)

VARYA: (*In tears.*) I'd like to give him such a . . . (*Makes a threatening gesture with her fist.*)

ANYA: (*Embraces Varya, softly.*) Varya, has he proposed yet? (*Varya shakes
her head "no."*) But he loves you, he does . . . Why don't you talk about
it, what are you two waiting for?

VARYA: I know nothing will ever come of it, nothing. He's so busy, he has
no time for me, really . . . he pays no attention to me at all. Well, God
bless him, but it's too painful for me even to look at him . . . Everyone
talks about our wedding, everyone congratulates us, but the fact is,
there's absolutely nothing to it, it's all a dream . . . (*Changes tone.*) Your
brooch looks just like a little bee.

ANYA: (*Sadly.*) Mama bought it. (*She goes to her room, speaking in a gay,
childlike voice.*) And in Paris, I went up in a hot air balloon!

VARYA: My darling's home! My angel is home!

Dunyasha has already returned with the coffee pot and prepares the coffee.

(*Stands by the doorway.*) All day long, darling, I go about my business, I
run the household, I do my chores, but all the time I'm thinking,
dreaming. If only we could marry you off to a rich man, then I'd
find peace, I'd go to a cloister, and then on a pilgrimage to Kiev, to
Moscow, and on and on, from one holy place to the next . . . on and on.
A blessing!

ANYA: The birds are singing in the orchard. What time is it?

VARYA: After two, it must be . . . Time for you to sleep, darling. (*Goes into
Anya's room.*) Yes, a blessing!

Yasha enters with a rug, and a traveling bag.

YASHA: (*Crosses the stage, discreetly.*) May I?

DUNYASHA: I wouldn't have recognized you, Yasha. How you've changed,
since you've been abroad.

YASHA: Hm . . . And who are you?

DUNYASHA: When you left, I was about "so" high . . . (*Indicates.*) Dunyasha,
Fyodor Kozoedov's daughter. Don't you remember!

YASHA: Hm . . . Ripe as a cucumber! (*Glances around, and then grabs her and embraces her; she screams and drops a saucer. Yasha exits quickly.*)

VARYA: (*In the doorway, displeased.*) What's going on here?

DUNYASHAZ: (*In tears.*) I broke a saucer . . .

VARYA: That means good luck.

ANYA: (*Coming out of her room.*) We'd better warn Mama: Petya's here . . .

VARYA: I gave strict orders not to wake him up.

ANYA: (*Deep in thought.*) Father died six years ago, and one month later my little brother Grisha drowned in the river, a lovely little seven-year-old boy. Mama couldn't endure it, she ran away, she ran away without once looking back . . . (*Shudders.*) How well I understand her, if only she knew! And Petya Trofimov was Grisha's tutor, he might remind her of it all . . .

Enter Firs, in a jacket and white waistcoat.

FIRS: (*Goes to the coffee pot, anxiously.*) The mistress will take her coffee here . . . (*Puts on white gloves.*) Is the coffee ready? (*Sternly, to Dunyasha.*) You! Where is the cream?

DUNYASHA: Oh, my God! (*Rushes out.*)

FIRS: (*Fusses with the coffee pot.*) Pathetic fool . . . . . . (*Mutters to himself under his breath.*) They've just returned from Paris . . . Now in the old days, the master used to go to Paris, too . . . by horse and carriage . . . (*Bursts out laughing.*)

VARYA: What is it, Firs?

FIRS: Yes, and what may I do for you? (*Overjoyed.*) My mistress has come home! I've waited for so long! Now I can die . . . (*Weeps with joy.*)

Enter Lyubov Andreevna, Gaev, Lopakhin, and Simeonov-Pishchik; Simeonov-Pishchik wears a lightweight coat, fitted at the waist, and wide trousers. As he walks, Gaev gestures, as if he were playing a game of billiards.

LYUBOV ANDREEVNA: How does it go? Wait — don't tell me, let me think . . . "Yellow into the corner pocket! Double into the middle!"

GAEV: "Cut shot into the corner!" Once upon a time, sister dearest, we slept in this very room, you and I, and now I'm fifty-one years old, strange, isn't it? . . .

LOPAKHIN: Yes, time flies.

GAEV: Beg pardon?

LOPAKHIN: As I was saying, time flies.

GAEV: It smells of patchouli in here.

ANYA: I'm going to bed. Good night, Mama. (*Kisses her mother.*)

LYUBOV ANDREEVNA: My beloved child. (*Kisses her hands.*) Are you glad you're home? I simply can't get hold of myself.

ANYA: Good night, Uncle.

GAEV: (*Kisses her face, hands.*) God bless you. You are the image of your mother! (*To his sister.*) Lyuba, you looked exactly like this at her age.

Anya gives her hand to Lopakhin and Pishchik; she exits, and closes the door behind her.

LYUBOV ANDREEVNA: She's exhausted, really.

PISHCHIK: A tiring journey, no doubt.

VARYA: (*To Lopakhin and Pishchik.*) So, gentlemen? It's almost three o'clock in the morning, let's not overstay our welcome.

LYUBOV ANDREEVNA: (*Laughs.*) You're the same as ever, Varya. (*Draws her close and kisses her.*) First I'll have my coffee, then we'll all go, yes?

Firs places a cushion under her feet.

Thank you, dearest. I've gotten so used to coffee. I drink it day and night. Thank you, my darling old man. (*Kisses Firs.*)

VARYA: I'll go see if they've brought everything in . . . (*Exits.*)

LYUBOV ANDREEVNA: Am I really sitting here? (*Bursts out laughing.*) I feel like jumping up and down, and waving my arms in the air! (*Covers her face with her hands.*) No, really, I must be dreaming! God knows, I love my country, I love it passionately, I couldn't even see out of the train window, I wept the whole way. (*In tears.*) Never mind, we must have our coffee. Thank you, Firs, thank you, my darling old man. I'm so glad you're still alive.

FIRS: The day before yesterday.

GAEV: He's hard of hearing.

LOPAKHIN: I'd better be going; I leave for Kharkov at five this morning. What a nuisance! I only wanted to see you, that's all, to talk to you a little . . . You're as lovely as ever . . .

PISHCHIK: (*Sighs heavily.*) Even lovelier . . . All dressed up, Parisian style . . . I'm head-over-heels, as they say!

LOPAKHIN: People like Leonid Andreich here, they say all sorts of things about me, call me a boor, a kulak, but really, it doesn't matter, I couldn't care less. Let them say whatever they like. I only want you to believe in me, as you always did, to look at me with those beautiful, soulful eyes, as you used to, once. Merciful God! My father was a serf, he belonged to your grandfather and then to your father, but it was you, yes, you, who did so much for me once, so much, and I've forgotten everything now, I love you like my own flesh and blood . . . more, even, than my own flesh and blood.

LYUBOV ANDREEVNA: I can't sit still, I'm in such a state . . . (*Jumps up and walks around the room, agitated.*) I simply can't bear all this joy . . . Go ahead, laugh at me, I'm being foolish, I know it . . . My dear little bookcase . . . (*Kisses the bookcase.*) My own little table.

GAEV: Nanny died while you were gone.

LYUBOV ANDREEVNA: (*Sits and drinks coffee.*) Yes, God rest her soul. They wrote me.

GAEV: Anastasy died, too. And cross-eyed Petrushka—you remember him—he ran away, he lives in town now, at the district superintendent's. (*Takes a box of fruit drops out of his pocket, pops one into his mouth.*)

PISHCHIK: My daughter, Dashenka . . . she sends her regards . . .

LOPAKHIN: I'd like to tell you some good news, if I may, some cheerful news, all right? (*Looks at his watch.*) I've got to go, there's no time to talk . . . so, very briefly, then. As you already know, your cherry orchard is being sold to pay off the debts, the auction date has been set for the twenty-second of August, but don't you worry, my dear, you don't have to lose any sleep over this, rest assured, there is a way out . . . Here's my plan. Your attention, please! Your estate is located only thirteen miles from town, roughly, a railroad runs nearby, so if the cherry orchard and the land along the river are divided up into plots and then leased for summer homes, why then you'll receive at least 25,000 in yearly income.

GAEV: Forgive me, but what nonsense!

LYUBOV ANDREEVNA: I don't quite understand you, Yermolai Alekseich.

LOPAKHIN: You'll receive at least twenty-five rubles a year per three acre plot from the summer tenants, and if you advertise right away, I'll guarantee you, by autumn, there won't be a single plot left, they'll all be bought up. In a word, congratulations, you're saved. The site is marvelous, the river is deep. Only, of course, you'll have to clear it out, get rid of some things . . . for example, let us say, tear down all the old buildings, and this house, too, which isn't much good for anything any more, cut down the old cherry orchard . . .

LYUBOV ANDREEVNA: Cut it down? Forgive me, my darling, but you have no idea what you're talking about. If there is one thing in the entire province that's of interest, that's remarkable, even, why it's our own cherry orchard.

LOPAKHIN: The only thing remarkable about this orchard is that it's so big. There's a cherry crop once every two years, and yes, there are a lot of them, but what good are they, nobody buys them.

GAEV: There is a reference to this cherry orchard in the Encyclopaedia.

LOPAKHIN: (*Looks at his watch.*) Unless we come up with a plan, unless we reach a decision, then on the twenty-second of August the cherry orchard and the entire estate will be auctioned off. Make up your minds, will you, please! There is no other way, I swear to you. None. Absolutely none.

FIRS: Once upon a time, forty—fifty years ago, they used to dry the cherries, soak them, marinate them, preserve them, and often . . .

GAEV: Hush, Firs.

FIRS: And often, they would send cart loads of dried cherries to Moscow and Kharkov. Brought in heaps of money! And those dried cherries, oh, how soft they were, soft, sweet, plump, juicy, fragrant . . . They knew the recipe in those days . . .

LYUBOV ANDREEVNA: Yes, where is that recipe now?

FIRS: Forgotten. No one remembers it any more.

PISHCHIK: (*To Lyubov Andreevna.*) Tell us! What is it like in Paris? Did you eat frogs' legs?

LYUBOV ANDREEVNA: I ate crocodile.

PISHCHIK: Imagine that . . .

LOPAKHIN: Up until now, we've only had landowners and peasants living in our countryside, but now, the summer people are starting to appear among us. All the towns, even the smallest ones, are surrounded by summer homes now. And, it's possible to predict that, in twenty years or so, the summer population will multiply beyond our wildest dreams. Now they're just sitting out on their balconies, drinking their tea, but just wait, soon it will come to pass, you'll see, they'll start cultivating their little plots of land, and your cherry orchard will bloom again with wealth, prosperity, happiness . . .

GAEV: (*Indignant.*) What nonsense!

Enter Varya and Yasha.

VARYA: Two telegrams came for you, Mamochka. (*Takes keys and unlocks the antique bookcase; the keys make a clinking sound.*) Here they are.

LYUBOV ANDREEVNA: From Paris. (*Rips them up, without reading them.*) I'm through with Paris.

GAEV: And do you know, Lyuba, how old this bookcase is? Only one week ago, I pull out the bottom drawer, I look, and what do I see—a mark burned into it, a number. This bookcase was built exactly one hundred years ago. How do you like that? Eh? We may now celebrate the jubilee anniversary of this bookcase, ladies and gentlemen. Yes, it's an inanimate object, of course, but nevertheless, it is still a *book* case.

PISHCHIK: (*Amazed.*) One hundred years old. Imagine that! . . .

GAEV: Yes . . . a work of art . . . (*Touching the bookcase.*) O venerable bookcase! I salute thy existence. For over a century, thou hast sought the pure ideals of truth and justice; thy silent exhortation for fruitful labor has not yet faltered these one hundred years, inspiring courage and hope for the brightest future (*in tears*) in generation after generation of our kin, and fostering in us the noble ideals of charity and good.

Pause.

LOPAKHIN: Yes . . .

LYUBOV ANDREEVNA: You haven't changed a bit, Lyonya.

GAEV: (*A bit embarrassed.*) "Off the ball . . . right-hand corner! Cut shot into the middle."

LOPAKHIN: (*Glances at his watch.*) Time for me to go.

YASHA: (*Gives Lyubov Andreevna medicine.*) Perhaps you'll take your pills now . . .

PISHCHIK: Why bother taking medicine, lovely lady . . . doesn't do any harm, doesn't do any good either . . . Do let me have them . . . dearest lady. (*Takes the pills, pours them into the palm of his hand, blows on them, puts them in his mouth, and washes them down with kvass.*) There!

LYUBOV ANDREEVNA: (*Frightened.*) You've gone mad!

PISHCHIK: Took them all.

LOPAKHIN: There's an appetite.

Everyone laughs.

FIRS: When he was here during Holy Week, he ate half a bucket of cucumbers . . . (*Mutters to himself.*)

LYUBOV ANDREEVNA: What is he saying?

VARYA: He's been muttering like that for three years now. We're used to it.

YASHA: Old age.

Enter Charlotta Ivanovna wearing a white dress; she is very thin and tightly laced, with a lorgnette on her belt; she crosses the stage.

LOPAKHIN: Forgive me, Charlotta Ivanovna, I didn't have the chance to greet you. (*Goes to kiss her hand.*)

CHARLOTTA IVANOVA: (*Takes her hand away.*) If I let you kiss my hand, next you'll want to kiss my elbow, then my shoulder . . .

LOPAKHIN: Not my lucky day.

Everyone laughs.

So, Charlotta Ivanovna, show us a trick!

LYUBOV ANDREEVNA: Yes, Charlotta, show us a trick!

CHARLOTTA: I don't want to. I wish to sleep. (*Exits.*)

LOPAKHIN: We'll see each other again in three weeks. (*Kisses Lyubov Andreevna's hand.*) Farewell for now. Time to go. (*To Gaev.*) A very goodbye to you. (*Kisses Pishchik.*) And to you. (*Shakes hands with Varya, then with Firs and Yasha.*) I don't feel like going. (*To Lyubov Andreevna.*) If you make up your mind about the summer homes, if you decide to proceed, just let me know, I'll lend you 50,000. Think about it, seriously.

VARYA: (*Angrily.*) So go, then!

LOPAKHIN: I'm going, I'm going. . . . (*Exits.*)

GAEV: What a boor. Oh, wait, "pardon" . . . Our Varya's going to marry him. That's our Varya's fiancé.

VARYA: Don't talk so much, Uncle.

LYUBOV ANDREEVNA: Why not, Varya, I'd be so pleased. He's a good man.

PISHCHIK: And a most worthy man, as they say, truth be told . . . Now my Dashenka . . . she also says, that . . . well, she says a variety of things. (*Snores, then suddenly awakes with a start.*) Nevertheless, dearest lady, oblige me, would you, please . . . lend me two hundred and forty rubles . . . tomorrow I must pay off the interest on my mortgage.

VARYA: (*Startled.*) We have no money! None!

LYUBOV ANDREEVNA: As a matter of fact, I don't, I have nothing, really.

PISHCHIK: Some will turn up, you'll see! (*Bursts out laughing.*) I never lose hope. There, I say to myself, all is lost, all is ruined, and then suddenly, what do you know—they build a railroad right through my land, and . . . they pay me for it! So just wait and see, something will happen, if not today, then tomorrow. My Dashenka is going to win 200,000 . . . she has a lottery ticket.

LYUBOV ANDREEVNA: The coffee's finished, now we can go to bed.

FIRS: (*Brushes Gaev's clothes, scolding him.*) And you've gone and put on the wrong trousers again. What am I going to do with you?

VARYA: (*Softly.*) Anya's sleeping. (*Quietly opens the window.*) The sun is up now, it isn't cold any more. Look, Mamochka: what glorious trees! My God, the air! And the starlings are singing!

GAEV: (*Opens another window.*) The orchard is all in white. You haven't forgotten, Lyuba, have you? Look—that long row of trees stretching on and on, like a silver cord, on and on, do you remember, how it gleams on moonlit nights? You haven't forgotten, have you?

LYUBOV ANDREEVNA: (*Looks out the window onto the orchard.*) O, my childhood, my innocence! Once I slept in this very nursery, I'd look out on the orchard, right from here, and happiness would awaken with me, every morning, every morning, and look, it's all the same, nothing has changed. (*Laughs with joy.*) White, all white! O, my orchard! After the dark, dreary autumn, the cold winter, you're young again, blooming with joy, the heavenly angels have not forsaken you . . . If only this terrible weight could be lifted from my soul, if only I could forget my past!

GAEV: Yes, and the orchard will be sold to pay off our debts, strange, isn't it . . .

LYUBOV ANDREEVNA: Look, there's my mother, walking through the orchard . . . all in white! (*Laughs with joy.*) There she is.

GAEV: Where?

VARYA: God bless you, Mamochka.

LYUBOV ANDREEVNA: There's no one there, I only dreamed it . . . Look, to the right, on the way to the summer-house, a white sapling, bowing low, I thought it was a woman . . .

Trofimov enters, wearing a shabby, threadbare student's uniform, and spectacles.

What an astonishing orchard! Masses of white blossoms, radiant blue sky . . .

TROFIMOV: Lyubov Andreevna!

She turns and looks at him.

I only came to pay my respects, I'll go, right away. (*Kisses her hand passionately.*) They told me I had to wait till morning, but I couldn't bear it any longer . . .

Lyubov Andreevna looks at him with bewilderment.

VARYA: (*In tears.*) It's Petya Trofimov . . .

TROFIMOV: Petya Trofimov, former tutor to your Grisha . . . Have I really changed that much?

Lyubov Andreevna embraces him and weeps softly.

GAEV: (*Embarrassed.*) Now, now, Lyuba.

VARYA: (*Weeps.*) You see, Petya, didn't I tell you to wait till tomorrow.

LYUBOV ANDREEVNA: My Grisha . . . my little boy . . . Grisha . . . son . . .

VARYA: But what can we do, Mamochka. It's God's will.

TROFIMOV: (*Gently, in tears.*) There, there . . .

LYUBOV ANDREEVNA: (*Weeps softly.*) My little boy . . . lost . . . drowned . . . Why? Why, my friend? (*Softer.*) Anya's sleeping, and here I am, raising my voice . . . carrying on . . . So, now, Petya, tell me! Why have you grown so ugly? And so old, too!

TROFIMOV: There was an old peasant woman on the train once, she called me "a shabby-looking gentleman."

LYUBOV ANDREEVNA: You were just a boy then, a sweet, young student, and now look at you, you're hair's gotten thin, you wear glasses . . . Don't tell me you're still a student? (*Goes to the door.*)

TROFIMOV: And I shall be an eternal student, so it seems.

LYUBOV ANDREEVNA: (*Kisses her brother, then Varya.*) Better go to bed now . . . You've gotten old, too, Leonid.

PISHCHIK: (*Follows her.*) Yes, time for bed . . . Ach, this gout of mine . . . I'll stay the night with you . . . Lyubov Andreevna, lovely lady, tomorrow morning, if only you would . . . two hundred and forty rubles . . .

GAEV: He never gives up.

PISHCHIK: Two hundred and forty rubles . . . to pay the interest on the mortgage.

LYUBOV ANDREEVNA: But I don't have any money, really, my sweet, I don't.

PISHCHIK: I'll pay you back, charming lady . . . Such a small amount . . .

LYUBOV ANDREEVNA: Oh, all right, Leonid will give it to you . . . Give it to him, Leonid.

GAEV: I should give it to him? Don't hold your pockets open.

LYUBOV ANDREEVNA: Give it to him, what else can we do . . . He needs it . . . He'll pay it back.

Exeunt Lyubov Andreevna, Trofimov, Pishchik, and Firs. Gaev, Varya, and Yasha remain.

GAEV: My sister just can't seem to hold on to her money. (*To Yasha.*) Move away, good fellow, you smell like a chicken coop.

YASHA: (*With a grin.*) And you, Leonid Andreich, you haven't changed a bit.

GAEV: Beg pardon? (*To Varya.*) What did he say?

VARYA: (*To Yasha.*) Your mother's come from the village to see you, she's been waiting since yesterday in the servants' quarters . . .

YASHA: Good for her!

VARYA: Shame on you!

YASHA: Who needs her? She could have waited till tomorrow to come. (*Exits.*)

VARYA: Mamochka's the same as she's always been, she hasn't changed at all. If she could, she'd give away everything.

GAEV: Yes . . .

Pause.

If there are many remedies offered for a disease, then that means the disease is incurable. Now, I've been thinking, wracking my brain, and I've got lots of remedies, oh yes, lots and lots of remedies, and you know what that means, don't you, in essence, that means I don't have any. Wouldn't it be nice, for example, if we received a large inheritance from somebody or other, wouldn't it be nice to marry our Anya off to a very rich fellow, wouldn't it be nice to go to Yaroslavl and try and get some money from our aunt, the countess. Our aunty's very very rich, you know.

VARYA: (*Weeps.*) If only God would help us.

GAEV: Stop weeping. The old lady's very rich, it's true, but the fact is, she doesn't like us. For one thing, my dear sister went off and married a lawyer, and not a gentleman . . .

Anya appears in the doorway.

She didn't marry a gentleman, and you can't really say she's led a particularly conventional life. I mean, she's a good, kind person, a splendid person, and I love her very very much, of course, but, whatever the extenuating circumstances may have been, let's face it, she hasn't exactly been the model of virtue. Why, you can sense it in everything about her, her slightest gesture, her movements.

VARYA: (*In a whisper.*) Anya's standing in the doorway.

GAEV: Beg pardon?

Pause.

Amazing, there's something in my right eye . . . I can't see a thing. And on Thursday, when I was at the district court . . .

Anya enters.

VARYA: Why aren't you in bed, Anya?

ANYA: I can't fall asleep. I just can't.

GAEV: My little one. (*Kisses Anya's face, hands.*) My child . . . (*In tears.*) You're not my niece, you're my angel, you're everything to me. Believe me, believe me . . .

ANYA: I believe you, Uncle, I do. Everyone loves you, everyone reveres you . . . but, darling Uncle, you must try to be quiet, really, just be quiet. What were you saying just now about my Mama, about your own sister? Why would you say such a thing?

GAEV: Yes, yes . . . (*Covers his face with her hand.*) As a matter of fact, it's terrible! My God! My God, save me! And today, I made a speech before a bookcase . . . how foolish of me! And it was only after I'd finished, that I realized how foolish it was.

VARYA: It's true, Uncle dear, you should try to be quiet. Just be very quiet, that's all.

ANYA: And if you're quiet, you'll feel much better, really.

GAEV: I'll be quiet. (*Kisses Anya's and Varya's hands.*) I'll be quiet. Just one small matter. On Thursday I was at the circuit court, and, well, some people got together and started talking, you know, about this, that, the other thing, and so on and so on, and one thing led to another, and so it seems that a loan might be arranged, to pay off the interest to the bank.

VARYA: God willing!

GAEV: And, on Tuesday, I'm going to have another little talk with them again. (*To Varya.*) Stop weeping. (*To Anya.*) Your mama will have a word with Lopakhin; he won't refuse her, of course . . . As for you, as soon as you've had your rest, off you'll go to Yaroslavl to see the countess, your great-aunt. So that way, we'll mount a three-pronged attack—and presto! it's in the bag. We'll pay off that interest, I'm sure of it . . . (*Pops a fruit drop into his mouth.*) On my honor, I swear to you, if you like, this estate will not be sold! (*Excited.*) I swear on my happiness! I give you my hand, call me a worthless good-for-nothing, a dishonorable fellow, if I allow it to go up for auction! I swear on my entire being!

ANYA: (*She regains her composure; she is happy.*) How good you are, Uncle, how wise! (*Embraces her uncle.*) Now I'm content! I'm content! I'm happy, now!

Enter Firs.

FIRS: (*Reproachfully.*) Leonid Andreich, have you no fear of God in you? When are you going to bed?

GAEV: In a minute, in a minute. Go on, Firs. Yes, it's all right, I'm quite capable of undressing myself. So, children dear, night-night . . . Details tomorrow, but now, it's time for bed. (*Kisses Anya and Varya.*) I am a man of the eighties . . . These are not laudable times, but nevertheless, I can say that I've suffered greatly for my convictions in this life. It's not without reason that the peasants love me. One must give the peasant his due! Give him his due, for . . .

ANYA: You're off again, Uncle!

VARYA: Uncle, be quiet!

FIRS: (*Angrily.*) Leonid Andreich!

GAEV: I'm coming, I'm coming . . . And so, to bed. "Off two cushions into the middle. Pocket the white . . . clean shot." (*Exits, with Firs shuffling behind him.*)

ANYA: Now, I'm content. I don't want to go to Yaroslavl, not really, I don't like my great-aunt that much, but, all the same, I'm content. Thanks to Uncle. (*Sits.*)

VARYA: We must get to bed. I know I'm going to . . . Oh, an awful thing happened here while you were gone. You remember the old servants' quarters, well, only the old ones live there now: you know, Yefimyushka, Polya, Yevstigney, oh, and don't forget Karp . . . Anyway, they started letting some homeless folks stay the night with them—I didn't say anything at first. But then, I hear, they're spreading this rumor, that I'd been giving orders to feed them nothing but dried peas. Because I was being stingy, you see . . . And all this coming from Yevstigney . . . So I say to myself, fine. If that's the way you want it, I say, just you wait and see. So I call for Yevstigney . . . (*Yawns.*) And he comes in . . . And I say to him, how dare you, Yevstigney . . . you're such a fool . . . (*Looks at Anya.*) Anyechka!

Pause.

She's asleep! (*Takes Anya by the arm.*) Come to bed . . . Come! . . . (*Leads her.*) My darling's sleeping! Come . . .

They go.

Far beyond the orchard, a shepherd plays on a pipe. Trofimov enters, crosses the stage, and, seeing Varya and Anya, stops.

VARYA: Shh . . . she's asleep . . . fast asleep . . . Come, my precious.

ANYA: (*Softly, half-asleep.*) I'm so tired . . . do you hear the bells . . . Dearest Uncle . . . Mama and Uncle . . .

VARYA: Come, my precious, come . . . (*Exits into Anya's room.*)

TROFIMOV: (*Tenderly.*) My sunlight! My springtime!

CURTAIN

ACT TWO

A field. There is a small, dilapidated old chapel, long deserted, and beside it, a well, an old bench, and several large stones, once apparently gravestones. The road to Gaev's country estate is visible. To the side, towering poplar trees loom darkly, where the cherry orchard begins. In the distance, there is a row of telegraph poles, and far beyond that, on the horizon, is the indistinct outline of a large town, visible only in very clear, fine weather. Soon, it will be sunset. Charlotta, Yasha, and Dunyasha sit on the bench; Yepikhodov stands nearby and plays the guitar; all are lost in thought. Charlotta is wearing an old, peaked military cap; she removes the rifle from her shoulder and adjusts the buckle on the rifle sling.

CHARLOTTA: (*Deep in thought.*) I have no passport, no real one . . . no one ever told me how old I was, not really . . . but I always have this feeling that I'm still very young. When I was a little girl, Papa and Mama traveled in a circus, they were acrobats, good ones. And I performed the "salto-mortale," the dive of death, and all kinds of tricks. And when Papa and Mama died, a German lady took me in, she raised me, gave me lessons. "Gut." I grew up, I became a governess. But where I am from, and who I am—I don't know . . . Who were my parents, were they ever married . . . I don't know. (*Takes a cucumber out of her pocket and eats it.*) I don't know anything.

Pause.

So now I feel like talking, but to whom . . . I have no one to talk to.

YEPIKHODOV: (*Plays guitar and sings.*) "What care I for worldly woe, / What care I for friend and foe . . ." How pleasant it is to play upon the mandolin!

DUNYASHA: That's a guitar, not a mandolin. (*Looks in a little mirror and powders her nose.*)

YEPIKHODOV: For the man, who is mad with love, it's a mandolin. (*Sings.*) "If my true love were requited, / It would set my heart aglow . . ."

Yasha joins in, harmonizing.

CHARLOTTA: These people sing terribly . . . Phooey! Like jackals.

DUNYASHA: (*To Yasha.*) How blissful, to have been abroad.

YASHA: Well, of course. I'm not going to disagree with you on that one. (*Yawns, then lights a cigar.*)

YEPIKHODOV: But we know that already. Everything abroad is very well organized, and has been so for a long long time.

YASHA: Right.

YEPIKHODOV: I am a man of the world. I am. I read many many remarkable books. But, speaking for myself, personally, I have no clue, no clue as to what direction I, personally, want my life to take, I mean: Do I want to live, or do I want to shoot myself, in the head . . . So just in case, I always carry a revolver around with me. Here it is . . . (*Shows them a revolver.*)

CHARLOTTA: I'm finished. And now, I'm leaving. (*Puts on the rifle.*) You, Yepikhodov, you are a very intelligent man and also a very dangerous one; women must be mad for you. Brrr! (*Starts to leave.*) These clever people, they're all such fools, no one for me to talk to . . . Alone, all alone, I have no one . . . and who I am, why I am on this earth, no one knows . . . (*Exits, without hurrying.*)

YEPIKHODOV: Now. Speaking for myself, personally, again, putting all else aside, that is, if I may, when it comes to me, I mean, personally, again, I ask myself: Does fate care? No, fate doesn't care, very much as a terrible storm doesn't care about a tiny boat upon the sea. Now. Let us assume I am wrong in this regard, so then, tell me, would you, please, why is it that this morning, yes, this morning, I wake up, just to give you an example, I look up, and there, sitting right on my chest, is this huge and terrifying spider . . . About "so" big. (*Indicates with both hands.*) And then, to give you yet another example, I go to pick up a glass of kvass, you know, to drink it, I look inside it, and what do I see? Possibly the most offensive species on the face of this earth—like a cockroach.

Pause.

Have you ever read Buckle?°

Pause.

May I trouble you, Avdotya Fyodorovna, for a word or two.

DUNYASHA: Speak.

Buckle: Thomas Henry Buckle (1821–1862), an English radical historian and economist.

YEPIKHODOV: It would be far more desirable to speak to you in private . . .
(*Sighs.*)

DUNYASHA: (*Embarrassed.*) Oh, all right . . . only first, bring me my
cloak . . . I left it near the cupboard . . . it's a bit chilly out . . .

YEPIKHODOV: Of course . . . Right away . . . Of course. Now I know what
to do with my revolver . . . (*Takes the guitar and exits, strumming.*)

YASHA: Mister Disaster! He's hopeless, just between you and me.
(*Yawns.*)

DUNYASHA: God forbid he should shoot himself.

Pause.

I'm so nervous, I worry all the time. I was just a girl when they took me
in, you know, I'm not used to the simple life any more, look at my
hands, how lily-white they are, like a young lady's. Can't you see, I've
become so delicate, so fragile, so . . . so sensitive, every little thing
upsets me . . . It's just awful. And if you deceive me, Yasha, I just don't
know what will happen to my nerves.

YASHA: (*Kisses her.*) My little cucumber! Of course, a girl should know
how to behave, I can't stand a girl who doesn't know how to behave.

DUNYASHA: I've fallen madly in love with you, you are so refined, you can
talk about anything.

Pause.

YASHA: (*Yawns.*) Right! . . . Now, in my opinion, if a girl falls in love, that
means she's immoral.

Pause.

Nice, isn't it, to smoke a cigar in the fresh, open air . . . (*Listens.*)
Someone's coming . . . It's the ladies and gentlemen . . .

Dunyasha embraces him impetuously.

Go home, pretend you've gone for a swim in the river, take that path
there, or else they'll run into you and think I arranged this little ren-
dezvous. I can't have that.

DUNYASHA: (*Coughs quietly.*) I've got a headache from all this cigar
smoke . . . (*Exits.*)

*Yasha remains; he sits by the chapel. Enter Lyubov Andreevna, Gaev, and
Lopakhin.*

LOPAKHIN: You must decide, once and for all—time waits for no one.
The question's quite simple, you know. Will you or won't you agree to
lease your land for conversion into summer homes? Answer in one
word: yes or no? One word, that's all!

LYUBOV ANDREEVNA: Who has been smoking those disgusting cigars here . . . (*Sits.*)

GAEV: Since they've built the railroad, it's all become so convenient. (*Sits down.*) We took a little ride into town, we had our lunch . . . "yellow into the middle pocket!" Now, if only I'd gone home first and played one little game . . .

LYUBOV ANDREEVNA: You'll have plenty of time.

LOPAKHIN: One word, that's all! (*Entreating.*) Give me your answer!

GAEV: (*Yawns.*) Beg pardon?

LYUBOV ANDREEVNA: (*Looks in her purse.*) Yesterday I had so much money, and today I have hardly any at all. My poor, thrifty Varya feeds everyone milk soup, the old folks in the kitchen get nothing but dried peas to eat, and I manage to let money slip right through my fingers. (*Drops her purse, gold coins scatter.*) There, you see, now I've gone and spilled it . . . (*She is annoyed.*)

YASHA: I'll get them, allow me. (*Collects the coins.*)

LYUBOV ANDREEVNA: Please do, Yasha. And why on earth did I go out to lunch . . . That ridiculous restaurant of yours with the music, and the tablecloths that smell of soap . . . And why drink so much, Lyonya? Why eat so much? Why talk so much? Today in the restaurant you went on and on again, on and on . . . About the seventies, about the decadents. And to whom? Talking to the waiters about the decadents!

LOPAKHIN: Yes.

GAEV: (*Waves his hand.*) I'm incorrigible, it's obvious . . . (*Irritably, to Yasha.*) What is it with you, you're always disturbing my line of vision . . .

YASHA: (*Laughs.*) I can't hear the sound of your voice without laughing.

GAEV: (*To his sister.*) It's either him or me . . .

LYUBOV ANDREEVNA: Go away, Yasha, go on . . .

YASHA: (*Gives Lyubov Andreevna her purse.*) Right away. (*Barely contains his laughter.*) At once . . . (*Exits.*)

LOPAKHIN: Your estate is going to be bought by that millionaire, Deriganov. He's coming to the auction himself, they say, in person.

LYUBOV ANDREEVNA: And where did you hear that?

LOPAKHIN: They were talking about it in town.

GAEV: Our aunty from Yaroslavl promised to send us something, but when and how much she will send, who knows . . .

LOPAKHIN: How much is she sending? One hundred thousand? Two hundred thousand?

LYUBOV ANDREEVNA: Oh, well, . . . ten—fifteen thousand, at most, and that much we can be thankful for . . .

LOPAKHIN: Forgive me, but such frivolous people as you, my friends, such strange, impractical people, I have never before met in my entire life. I'm speaking to you in the Russian language, I'm telling you that your estate is about to be sold, and you simply don't understand.

LYUBOV ANDREEVNA: But what on earth are we to do? Tell us, what?

LOPAKHIN: Every day I've been telling you. Every day I've been repeating the same thing, over and over again. The cherry orchard and the land must be leased for summer homes, it must be done immediately, as soon as possible—the auction is imminent! Do you understand! As soon as you decide, once and for all, about the summer homes, you'll have as much money as you'll ever want, and then you will be saved.

LYUBOV ANDREEVNA: Summer homes, summer people—forgive me, please, it all sounds so vulgar.

GAEV: I agree with you, absolutely.

LOPAKHIN: Either I'm going to burst out sobbing, or screaming, or else I'm going to fall on the ground, right here in front of you. I can't stand it any more! You're driving me mad! (*To Gaev.*) And you, you act like an old woman!

GAEV: Beg pardon?

LOPAKHIN: An old woman! (*Wants to leave.*)

LYUBOV ANDREEVNA: (*Frightened.*) No, don't go, please, stay, dearest. I beg of you. Who knows, perhaps we'll think of something!

LOPAKHIN: What's there to think of!

LYUBOV ANDREEVNA: Don't go, I beg of you. It's so much more cheerful when you're here . . .

Pause.

I keep waiting for something to happen, as if the house were going to tumble down on top of us.

GAEV: (*Deep in thought.*) "Double into the corner pocket . . . Croisé into the middle . . ."

LYUBOV ANDREEVNA: How we have sinned . . .

LOPAKHIN: What are you talking about, what sins . . .

GAEV: (*Pops a fruit drop in his mouth.*) They say I've squandered an entire fortune on fruit drops . . . (*Laughs.*)

LYUBOV ANDREEVNA: O my sins, my sins . . . I've always thrown money around, uncontrollably, like a madwoman, and I married a man, who did nothing but keep us in debt. My husband died from too much champagne—he drank himself to death,—then, for my next misfortune, I fell in love with another man, I began living with him . . . and just at that time, there came my first great punishment, and what a blow it dealt me—right here in this river . . . my little boy drowned, and so I fled, abroad, I simply fled, never to return, never to see this river again . . . I closed my eyes and I ran, not knowing where I was going, what I was doing, and *he* following after . . . ruthlessly, relentlessly. I bought a dacha near Menton, *he* had fallen ill there, and for three years I knew no rest, neither day nor night; his illness exhausted me, wasted me, my soul withered away. And then last year, when the dacha was sold to pay off the debts, I fled again, to Paris, and there he robbed me, he left me for another woman, I tried to poison myself . . . How stupid, how shameful . . . And suddenly I felt drawn again to Russia, to my homeland, to my daughter . . . (*Wipes away her tears.*) Dear God, dear God, be merciful, forgive me my sins! Don't punish me any longer! (*Pulls a telegram from her pocket.*) Today, I received this from Paris . . . He begs my forgiveness, beseeches me to return . . . (*Rips up the telegram.*) There's music playing, somewhere. (*Listens.*)

GAEV: It's our celebrated Jewish orchestra. Don't you remember, four violins, flute, and contrabass.

LYUBOV ANDREEVNA: Does it still exist? We ought to invite them sometime, plan a little soirée.

LOPAKHIN: (*Listens.*) I don't hear anything. (*Hums softly.*)
"An enterprising man, the Prussian,
He'll make a Frenchman from a Russian!"
(*Laughs.*) What a play I saw at the theatre last night, it was very funny, really.

LYUBOV ANDREEVNA: There probably wasn't anything funny about it. Why go to the theatre to see a play! Better to see yourselves more often. How grey your lives are, how endlessly you talk.

LOPAKHIN: It's the truth. And the truth must be told, our lives are foolish . . .

Pause.

My papa was a peasant, an ignorant fool, he understood nothing, taught me nothing, he only beat me when he was drunk, and always with a stick. And the fact of the matter is, I'm the same kind of ignorant fool that he was. I never learned anything, I'm ashamed of my own handwriting, it's not even human, it's more like a hoof-mark than a signature.

LYUBOV ANDREEVNA: You ought to get married, my friend.

LOPAKHIN: Yes . . . It's the truth.

LYUBOV ANDREEVNA: Why not to our Varya? She's a good girl.

LOPAKHIN: Yes.

LYUBOV ANDREEVNA: She's of simple origin, she works all day long, but the important thing is, she loves you. And you've been fond of her for a long time now.

LOPAKHIN: Well . . . I have nothing against it . . . She's a good girl.

Pause.

GAEV: They've offered me a job at the bank. 6,000 a year . . . Have you heard?

LYUBOV ANDREEVNA: You, in a bank! Stay where you are . . .

Firs enters; he is carrying a coat.

FIRS: (*To Gaev.*) Please, sir, better put this on . . . it's chilly out.

GAEV: (*Puts on the coat.*) You get on my nerves, old man.

FIRS: Now, there's no need for that . . . You went out this morning, without telling anyone. (*Looks him over.*)

LYUBOV ANDREEVNA: How old you've grown, Firs!

FIRS: Yes, what may I do for you?

LOPAKHIN: She said: How old you've grown!

FIRS: Well, I've lived a long time. They were marrying me off, and your papa wasn't even in this world yet . . . (*Laughs.*) Then, when the emancipation came, I was already head valet . . . I didn't want my freedom, so I stayed with my masters . . .

Pause.

I remember how glad everyone was, but what they were glad about, they didn't even know themselves.

LOPAKHIN: Ah yes, the good old days. At least there was flogging.

FIRS: (*Not hearing.*) I'll say. The servants belonged to the masters, the masters belonged to the servants, but now everything's all mixed up, you can't tell one from the other.

GAEV: Hush, Firs. Tomorrow I've got to go to town. They've promised to introduce me to some general, he might give us a loan on a promissory note.

LOPAKHIN: Nothing will come of it. And you won't pay off the interest, rest assured.

LYUBOV ANDREEVNA: He's delirious. There are no generals, they don't exist.

Enter Trofimov, Anya, and Varya.

GAEV: Ah, here they come.

ANYA: Here's Mama.

LYUBOV ANDREEVNA: (*Tenderly.*) Come, come . . . My darling children . . . (*Embraces Anya and Varya.*) If you only knew how much I love you both. Sit here, right next to me.

They all get settled.

LOPAKHIN: Our eternal student is always in the company of the young ladies.

TROFIMOV: Mind your own business.

LOPAKHIN: And when he's fifty, he'll still be a student.

TROFIMOV: Stop your foolish joking.

LOPAKHIN: You're such a peculiar fellow! Why are you so angry with me, anyway?

TROFIMOV: Because you won't stop bothering me.

LOPAKHIN: (*Laughs.*) Permit me to ask you, if I may, what do you think of me?

TROFIMOV: Here is what I think of you, Yermolai Alekseich: You are a rich man, soon you'll be a millionaire. So, in the general scheme of things, that is, according to the laws of nature, we need you, we need predatory beasts, who devour everything which stands in their path, so in that sense you are a necessary evil.

All laugh.

VARYA: Petya, you do better when you talk about astronomy.

LYUBOV ANDREEVNA: No, let's continue yesterday's conversation.

TROFIMOV: What about?

GAEV: About pride. Pride in man.

TROFIMOV: That. We talked about that forever, but we did not come to any conclusion. According to your way of thinking, there is something mystical about the proud man, an aura, almost. Perhaps you are correct in your beliefs, but if you analyze the issue clearly, without complicating things, then why does this pride even exist, what reason can there be for pride, if a man is not physically distinguished, if the vast majority of mankind is coarse, stupid, or profoundly miserable. There is no time for the admiration of self. There is only time for work.

GAEV: We're all going to die, anyway, so what difference does it make?

TROFIMOV: Who knows? And what does it really mean—to die? For all we know, man is endowed with a hundred sensibilities, and when he dies, only the five known to us perish along with him, while the other ninety-five remain alive.

LYUBOV ANDREEVNA: How intelligent you are, Petya! . . .

LOPAKHIN: (*Ironically.*) Yes, terribly!

TROFIMOV: Mankind marches onward, ever onward, strengthening his skills, his capacities. All that has up until now been beyond his reach may one day be attainable, only he must work, indeed, he must do everything in his power to help those who seek the truth. In Russia, however, very few people actually do work. The vast majority of the intelligentsia, as I know them, do nothing, pursue nothing, and, meanwhile, have no predisposition whatsoever to work, they're completely incapable of it. They call themselves "the intelligentsia," and yet they address their servants with disrespect, they treat the peasants as if they were animals, they're dismal students, they're poorly educated, they never read serious literature, they're absolutely idle, they don't do a thing except sit around talking about science and art, about which they know nothing at all. And they're all so grim looking, they have tense, taut faces, they only talk about "important things," they spend all their time philosophizing, and meanwhile, right before their very eyes, the workers live atrociously, eat abominably, sleep without bedding, thirty-forty to a room, together with bedbugs, stench, dankness, depravity . . . And so it seems that all this lofty talk is simply meant to conceal the truth from themselves and others. Show me, please, where are the day nurseries, about which they speak so much and so often, where are the public reading rooms? They only write about them in novels, they never become a reality, never. There is only filth, vulgarity, barbarism . . . I dread their serious countenances, their serious conversations, I despise them. Better to be silent!

LOPAKHIN: You know, I get up before five every morning, I work from dawn until night, I deal with money, constantly, mine and others, and yes, I see how people really are. You only have to try to get something done to realize how few honest, decent people there are in this world. Sometimes, when I can't fall asleep, I lie there thinking: "Dear Lord, you have given us the vast forests, the boundless plains, the endless horizons, and we who live here on this earth, we should be true giants . . ."

LYUBOV ANDREEVNA: What good are giants . . . They're very nice in fairy tales, you know, but in true life, they're terrifying.

Yepikhodov crosses upstage, playing the guitar.

(*Pensively.*) There goes Yepikhodov.

ANYA: (*Pensively.*) There goes Yepikhodov.

GAEV: The sun has set, ladies and gentlemen.

TROFIMOV: Yes.

GAEV: (*Softly, as if reciting.*) O nature, wondrous nature, you shine on, radiant and eternal, beauteous and indifferent, you whom we call mother, you embody birth and death, you create and you destroy, you . . .

VARYA: (*Imploring.*) Uncle, dear!

ANYA: Not again, Uncle!

TROFIMOV: You're better off "pocketing the yellow . . ."

GAEV: I'll be quiet, I'll be quiet.

All sit, deep in thought. Silence. Only Firs's muttering can be heard. Suddenly from far, far away, a sound is heard, as if coming from the sky, the sound of a breaking string, dying away in the distance, a mournful sound.

LYUBOV ANDREEVNA: What was that?

LOPAKHIN: Don't know. Somewhere far away, deep in the mines, a bucket broke loose and fell . . . But somewhere very far away.

GAEV: Or a bird of some kind . . . a heron, perhaps.

TROFIMOV: Or an owl . . .

LYUBOV ANDREEVNA: (*Shudders.*) Disturbing, somehow.

Pause.

FIRS: Right before the time of trouble, it was the same thing: The owl screeched, and the samovar hissed, it never stopped.

GAEV: What time of trouble?

FIRS: Why, before the emancipation of the serfs.

Pause.

LYUBOV ANDREEVNA: Let's go, dear friends, shall we, it's getting dark. (*To Anya.*) You've got tears in your eyes . . . What is it, my pet? (*Embraces her.*)

ANYA: I'm fine, Mama. It's nothing.

TROFIMOV: Someone's coming.

A passerby appears in a shabby, white cap and a coat; he is slightly drunk.

PASSERBY: Permit me to inquire, may I pass through here to get to the train station?

GAEV: You may. Go down that road.

PASSERBY: I'm deeply grateful. (*Coughs.*) What superb weather we're having . . . (*Recites.*) "My brother, my suffering brother . . . Come down to the Volga, whose moan . . ." (*To Varya.*) Mademoiselle, please, give a poor starving Russian thirty kopeks . . .

Varya cries out in fear.

LOPAKHIN: (*Angrily.*) This has gone too far!

LYUBOV ANDREEVNA: (*Stunned.*) Here . . . take this . . . (*Searches in her purse.*) I have no silver . . . Never mind, here's a gold piece . . .

PASSERBY: I'm deeply grateful! (*Exits.*)

Laughter.

VARYA: (*Frightened.*) I'm leaving . . . I'm leaving . . . Oh, Mamochka, the servants at home have nothing to eat, and you gave him a gold piece.

LYUBOV ANDREEVNA: What are you going to do with me, I'm such a silly fool! I'll give you everything I have. Yermolai Alekseich, please, lend me some more money! . . .

LOPAKHIN: Yes, madam.

LYUBOV ANDREEVNA: Come, ladies and gentlemen, time to go. Oh, yes, Varya, we've just made a match for you. Congratulations.

VARYA: (*In tears.*) Mama, you mustn't joke about that.

LOPAKHIN: "Oh-phel-i-a, get thee to a nunnery . . ."

GAEV: It's been so long since I've played a game of billiards, my hands are shaking.

LOPAKHIN: "Oh-phel-i-a, o nymph, remember me in thy prayers!"

LYUBOV ANDREEVNA: Come, ladies and gentlemen. It's almost suppertime.

VARYA: How he frightened me. My heart is pounding.

LOPAKHIN: May I remind you, ladies and gentlemen: On the twenty-second of August, the cherry orchard will be sold. Think about it! Think! . . .

They all leave, except Trofimov and Anya.

ANYA: (*Laughing.*) The stranger frightened Varya off, thank goodness, now we're alone.

TROFIMOV: Varya's afraid we'll fall madly in love, she hasn't let us out of her sight for days. She's so narrow-minded, she can't understand we're above love. To overcome all obstacles, real and imagined, which stand in the path of freedom and happiness,—that is our quest in life. Onward! We set forth, undaunted, toward that star, burning bright in the distance! Onward! Don't fall behind, my friends!

ANYA: (*Clasps her hands.*) How beautifully you talk!

Pause.

It's glorious here today!

TROFIMOV: Yes, the weather is amazing.

ANYA: What have you done to me, Petya, why don't I love the cherry orchard, as I did, once? I loved it so tenderly, I couldn't imagine any other place on earth more lovely than our orchard.

TROFIMOV: All Russia is our orchard. The land is vast and beautiful, there are many marvelous places on it.

Pause.

Just think, Anya: Your grandfather, your great-grandfather, and his forefathers before him, all were serf-owners, they all owned living souls, so isn't it possible, then, that in every blossom, every leaf, every tree trunk in the orchard, a human soul now gazes down upon us, can't you hear their voices . . . To own human souls—can't you see how this has transformed each and every one of us, those who have lived before and those who live today, so that you, your mother, your uncle, all of you, are no longer aware that you are alive at the expense of others, at the expense of those whom you would not even permit beyond your front hall . . . We have fallen behind, by two hundred years or so, at least, we have nothing left, absolutely nothing, no clear understanding of the past, we only philosophize, complain about our boredom, or drink vodka. And it's all so clear, can't you see, that to begin a new life, to live in the present, we must first redeem our past, put an end to it, and redeem it we shall, but only with suffering, only with extraordinary, everlasting toil and suffering. You must understand this, Anya.

ANYA: The house, in which we live, is no longer our house, and I shall leave it, I give you my word.

TROFIMOV: If you have the key, throw it in the well and run, run far, far away. Be free, like the wind.

ANYA: (*Ecstatic.*) How wonderfully you say it!

TROFIMOV: Believe me, Anya, believe me! I'm not even thirty yet, I'm young, I'm still a student, and yet, I've endured so much! Come winter, I'm hungry, sick, anxiety-ridden, poverty-stricken, like a beggar, and wherever fate carries me, there I shall be! And yet, all the while, every waking moment, day and night, my soul is filled with an indescribable premonition, a vision. A vision of happiness, Anya, I can see it now . . .

ANYA: (*Pensively.*) The moon is rising.

Yepikhodov is heard playing the guitar, the same melancholy song as before. The moon is rising. Somewhere near the poplars, Varya is looking for Anya and calling: "Anya! Where are you?"

TROFIMOV: Yes, the moon is rising.

Pause.

Here comes happiness, here it comes, closer and closer, I can already hear its footsteps. And if we don't see it, if we don't recognize it, then what does it matter? Others will!

Varya's voice: "Anya! Where are you?"

Varya, again! (*Angrily.*) It's disgraceful!

ANYA: I know! Let's go down to the river. It's lovely there.

TROFIMOV: Let's go.

They go.

Varya's voice: "Anya! Anya!"

CURTAIN

ACT THREE

The drawing room, separated from the ballroom by an archway. A chandelier burns brightly. A Jewish orchestra, the same one referred to in Act Two, is heard playing in the entrance hall. It is evening. In the ballroom, the crowd is dancing the "grand-rond." The voice of Simeonov-Pishchik is heard: "Promenade à une paire!"° The couples dance through the drawing room, as follows: first Pishchik and Charlotta Ivanovna; then Trofimov and Lyubov Andreevna; then Anya and the Post Office Clerk; then Varya and the Stationmaster, and so on. Varya is weeping quietly and wipes away her tears as she dances. Dunyasha is in the last couple. They dance around the drawing room. Pishchik calls out: "Grand-rond, balancez!" and "Les cavaliers à genoux et remerciez vos dames!"°

Firs, wearing a tailcoat, carries a tray with seltzer water. Pishchik and Trofimov enter the drawing room.

PISHCHIK: I have high blood pressure, I've had two strokes already, it's difficult for me to dance, but, you know what they say: "If you run in a pack, whether you bark or not, you'd better wag your tail." Never you mind, I'm as healthy as a horse. My dear departed father, joker that he was, God rest his soul, always used to say, on the subject of our ancestry, that the Simeonov-Pishchiks are descended from the same horse that Caligula° appointed to the Senate . . . (*Sits.*) The only trouble is: We don't have any money! And you know what they say: "A hungry dog believes only in meat . . ." (*Snores and suddenly wakes up.*) And that's my problem . . . all I ever dream about is money . . .

TROFIMOV: As a matter of fact, you do bear some resemblance to a horse.

PISHCHIK: And why not . . . a horse is a good animal . . . you can get a very good price for a horse, you know . . .

In the next room, the sound of a billiard game is heard. Varya appears in the archway to the hall.

TROFIMOV: (*Teasing.*) Madame Lopakhina! Madame Lopakhina! . . .

VARYA: (*Angrily.*) The shabby-looking gentleman!

TROFIMOV: Yes, I'm a shabby-looking gentleman, and proud of it!

VARYA: (*Bitterly.*) We've gone and hired the musicians, now how are we going to pay for them? (*Exits.*)

TROFIMOV: (*To Pishchik.*) Think about it: The energy you've wasted your whole life through in search of money to pay off the interest on your debts, if only you'd spent that energy elsewhere, then, no doubt, you could have changed the world.

PISHCHIK: Nietzsche . . . the philosopher . . . the supreme, the exalted . . . a man of the greatest genius, this man once said, in his own writings, that it's all right to forge banknotes.

TROFIMOV: Have you ever read Nietzsche?

"Promenade à une paire!": Instructions in the dance: "Walk in a pair!" (French).
"Grand-rond . . . dames!": "Large circle!" and "Gentlemen, kneel down and thank your ladies!" (French).
Caligula: Flamboyant and controversial Roman emperor (A.D. 37–41).

PISHCHIK: Well . . . Dashenka told me that one. And anyway, given my situation, even if I could forge banknotes . . . Day after tomorrow, I owe a payment of three hundred and ten rubles . . . I've already scraped up one hundred and thirty so far . . . (*Searches in his pockets, anxiously.*) My money's gone! I've lost my money! (*In tears.*) Where is my money? (*Overjoyed.*) Here it is, in the lining . . . Look, I even broke into a sweat . . .

Enter Lyubov Andreevna and Charlotta Ivanovna.

LYUBOV ANDREEVNA: (*Humming the "lezginka."*)° Why has Leonid been gone so long? What is he doing in town? (*To Dunyasha.*) Dunyasha, offer the musicians some tea . . .

TROFIMOV: The auction didn't take place, in all probability.

LYUBOV ANDREEVNA: And of all times to invite the musicians and give a ball . . . Oh well, never mind . . . (*Sits and hums softly.*)

CHARLOTTA: (*Gives Pishchik a deck of cards.*) Here is a deck of cards, think of a card, any card.

PISHCHIK: I've got one.

CHARLOTTA: Now shuffle the deck. Give it to me, oh my dear Mr. Pishchik, Eins, zwei, drei!° Now go look, it's in your side pocket . . .

PISHCHIK: (*Takes a card from his side pocket.*) The eight of spades, you're absolutely right! (*Amazed.*) Imagine that!

CHARLOTTA: (*Holds out the deck of cards in her palm to Trofimov.*) Tell me, quickly, which card is the top card?

TROFIMOV: What? Oh, the queen of spades.

CHARLOTTA: Right! (*To Pishchik.*): So? Which card is the top card?

PISHCHIK: The ace of hearts.

CHARLOTTA: Right! (*Claps her hands, and the deck of cards disappears.*) My, what lovely weather we're having today.

A mysterious female voice answers her as if coming from underneath the floor: "Oh yes, the weather is splendid, dear lady."

You are the image of perfection . . .

Voice: "And you I like very much too, dear lady."

STATIONMASTER: (*Applauds.*) Madame Ventriloquist, bravo!

PISHCHIK: (*Amazed.*) Imagine that! Most enchanting Charlotta Ivanovna . . . I'm head-over-heels in love . . .

CHARLOTTA: In love? (*Shrugs her shoulders.*) How could you possibly be in love? "Guter Mensch, aber schlechter Musikant."°

lezginka: Russian dance tune.
Eins, zwei, drei!: "One, two, three!" (German).
"Guter Mensch, aber schlechter Musikant": "A good man, but a poor musician" (German).

TROFIMOV: (*Claps Pishchik on the shoulder.*) Well done, old horse . . .

CHARLOTTA: Your attention please, for one more trick. (*Gets a lap robe from a chair.*) Here's a very lovely lap robe, I wish to sell it . . . (*Shakes it.*) Doesn't anyone wish to buy it?

PISHCHIK: (*Amazed.*) Imagine that!

CHARLOTTA: Eins, zwei, drei! (*Quickly lifts the lap robe.*)

Anya appears behind the lap robe; she curtsies, runs to her mother, embraces her, and runs out into the ballroom, amidst general delight.

LYUBOV ANDREEVNA: (*Applauds.*) Bravo, bravo! . . .

CHARLOTTA: Once more. Eins, zwei, drei! (*Lifts the lap robe.*)

Varya appears behind the lap robe; she bows.

PISHCHIK: (*Amazed.*) Imagine that!

CHARLOTTA: The end! (*Throws the lap robe over Pishchik, curtsies, and runs out into the ballroom.*)

PISHCHIK: (*Hurries after her.*) Sorceress . . . how did you do it? How? (*Exits.*)

LYUBOV ANDREEVNA: And Leonid is still not back. What can he be doing in town this long, I don't understand it! Surely everything is over by now, either the estate has been sold or else the auction never took place, one or the other, so why must we be kept in the dark forever!

VARYA: (*Attempting to console her.*) Uncle has bought it, I'm sure of it.

TROFIMOV: (*Sarcastically.*) Yes.

VARYA: Great-aunt sent him power of attorney to buy the estate in her name and transfer the mortgage to her. She did it for Anya. And Uncle will buy it, with God's help, I'm sure of it.

LYUBOV ANDREEVNA: Great-aunt in Yaroslavl sent 50,000 to buy the estate in her name because she doesn't trust us, — and that wasn't even enough to pay the interest. (*Covers her face with her hands.*) Today my destiny will be decided, my destiny . . .

TROFIMOV: (*Teasing Varya.*) Madame Lopakhina!

VARYA: (*Angrily.*) The eternal student! Twice you've been expelled from the university.

LYUBOV ANDREEVNA: Why are you so angry, Varya? He's teasing you about Lopakhin, but what does it matter? If you want to — marry Lopakhin he's a fine man, a fascinating man. And if you don't want to — don't; no one is forcing you to, darling . . .

VARYA: I take this matter very seriously, Mamochka, I must tell you. He is a good man, I like him, I do.

LYUBOV ANDREEVNA: Then marry him. What are you waiting for, I don't understand.

VARYA: But Mamochka, I can't propose to him myself. For two years now everyone's been talking to me about him, everyone, and either he says nothing, or else he jokes about it. I understand. He's busy getting rich, he's preoccupied with his affairs, he has no time for me. Oh, if only I had money, only a little, a hundred rubles even, I'd give up everything, I'd run away as far as I could. I'd enter a convent.

TROFIMOV: Blessings on you!

VARYA: (*To Trofimov.*) A student's supposed to be intelligent! (*Gently, in tears.*) How ugly you've grown, Petya, and how old, too! (*To Lyubov Andreevna, no longer crying.*) I simply can't live without work, Mamochka. I must be doing something, every minute.

Enter Yasha.

YASHA: (*Hardly able to contain his laughter.*) Yepikhodov has broken a billiard cue! . . . (*Exits.*)

VARYA: Why is Yepikhodov here? Who allowed him to play billiards? I don't understand these people . . . (*Exits.*)

LYUBOV ANDREEVNA: Don't tease her, Petya, can't you see how miserable she is.

TROFIMOV: She's overbearing, that's what she is . . . always poking her nose into other people's business. She hasn't given Anya and me a moment's peace all summer, she's afraid we might fall in love. What business is it of hers, anyway? And how could she even think that of me, I'm far beyond such vulgarity. We are above love!

LYUBOV ANDREEVNA: And I suppose that means I must be beneath love. (*Tremendously agitated.*) Why isn't Leonid back yet? I only want to know: Is the estate sold or isn't it? This terrible business has gone too far, I don't know what to think any more, I'm at my wits' end . . . I might scream any minute . . . I might do something foolish. Save me, Petya. Say something, anything . . .

TROFIMOV: Whether the estate is sold today or not—does it really matter? It's over, it's been so for a long time, there's no turning back again, that path is long overgrown. Face it, dear friend. You mustn't delude yourself any longer, for once in your life you must look the truth straight in the eye.

LYUBOV ANDREEVNA: What truth? Oh, yes, of course, you see what is true and what is not true, while I have lost my vision, I see nothing. You boldly solve all the problems of the world, don't you, but tell me, my darling, isn't that because you're still so young, because you haven't even suffered through one of life's problems yet, not even one? You boldly look to the future, but isn't that because you see nothing so terrible lying ahead, because life is still safely hidden from your young eyes? You have more courage, more character, more honesty than any of us, so then why not have compassion, find it, somewhere in a corner of your heart, have mercy on me. I was born here, my mother and

father lived here, my grandfather, too, I love this house, I can't comprehend a life without the cherry orchard, and if it must be sold, then
sell me with it . . . (*Embraces Trofimov, kisses him on the forehead.*) My
son drowned here . . . (*Weeps.*) Have pity on me, my good, kind fellow.

TROFIMOV: You know I do, with all my heart.

LYUBOV ANDREEVNA: Yes, but there must be another way to say it, another
way . . . (*Takes out a handkerchief, a telegram falls on the floor.*) My soul is
so heavy today, you can't possibly imagine. There is such a din here, I'm
trembling with each and every sound, trembling all over, but I can't be
alone, the silence would be terrifying. Don't judge me, Petya . . . I love
you, as if you were my own child. And I'd gladly let you marry Anya, I
would, I swear to you, only first you must finish your education, darling, get your degree. You don't do a thing, you just let fate carry you
from place to place, and that's such a strange way to live . . . Isn't it?
Well? And you simply must do something about that beard, to make it
grow, somehow . . . (*Bursts out laughing.*) How funny-looking you are!

TROFIMOV: (*Picks up the telegram.*) I don't wish to be handsome.

LYUBOV ANDREEVNA: It's a telegram from Paris. Every day I receive one.
Yesterday, and today, too. That terrible man is ill again, he's in trouble
again . . . He begs my forgiveness, he beseeches me to return to him, I
really ought to be going to Paris, to be near him. You should see your
face now, Petya, so severe, so judgmental, but, really, what am I to do,
darling, tell me, what can I do, he's ill, he's alone, unhappy, and who
will take care of him, who will keep him from harm, who will nurse
him through his illness? Oh, why hide it, why keep silent, I love him,
it's the truth. I love him, I love him . . . He is the stone around my
neck, and I shall sink with him to the bottom, and how I love this
stone, I can't live without it! (*Presses Trofimov's hand.*) Don't think ill of
me, Petya, and don't speak, please, not a word . . .

TROFIMOV: (*In tears.*) Forgive me for saying it, but for God's sake: This
man robbed you, he cleaned you out!

LYUBOV ANDREEVNA: No, no, no, you mustn't talk like that . . . (*Covers her
ears.*)

TROFIMOV: He's an absolute scoundrel, and you're the only one who
doesn't know it! A petty thief, a good-for-nothing . . .

LYUBOV ANDREEVNA: (*With controlled anger.*) And you're twenty-six or
twenty-seven years old, and still a schoolboy!

TROFIMOV: So be it!

LYUBOV ANDREEVNA: You're supposed to be a man, at your age you're
supposed to understand how lovers behave. Why don't you know this
by now . . . why haven't you fallen in love yourself? (*Angrily.*) Yes, yes!
You and all your talk about purity . . . why, you're nothing but a prude,
that's what you are, an eccentric, a freak . . .

TROFIMOV: (*Horrified.*) What is she saying!

LYUBOV ANDREEVNA: "I am above love!" You're not above love, no, as Firs says, you're pathetic! At your age, not to have a lover! . . .

TROFIMOV: (*Horrified.*) This is terrible! What is she saying?! (*Rushes out into the ballroom, holding his head.*) This is terrible . . . I can't bear it, I'm leaving . . . (*Exits, but returns again immediately.*) It's all over between us! (*Exits into the front hall.*)

LYUBOV ANDREEVNA: (*Calls after him.*) Petya, wait! Don't be silly, I was only joking! Petya!

In the front hall, someone is heard dashing down the stairs, and suddenly falling the rest of the way with a crash. Anya and Varya cry out, but then, almost immediately, laughter is heard.

What happened?

Anya runs in.

ANYA: (*Laughing.*) Petya fell down the stairs! (*Runs out.*)

LYUBOV ANDREEVNA: What a peculiar fellow that Petya is . . .

The Stationmaster stands in the middle of the ballroom, and starts to recite a poem: "The Fallen Woman" by Alexey Konstantinovich Tolstoy. Everyone stops to listen, but after a few lines, the strains of a waltz are heard coming from the front hall, and the recitation is interrupted. Everyone dances. Trofimov, Anya, Varya, and Lyubov Andreevna pass through from the entrance hall.

Petya . . . my pure Petya . . . I beg your forgiveness . . . Come, dance with me . . . (*Dances with him.*)

Anya and Varya dance together. Firs enters, and places his cane near the side door. Yasha also enters, and watches the dancing.

YASHA: So, what's new, grandpa?

FIRS: I don't feel very well. In the old days, we used to have generals, barons, admirals dancing at our balls; nowadays we have to send for the postal clerk and the stationmaster, and even they come reluctantly. And I'm getting weaker, somehow. In the old days, when anyone of us fell ill, my old master—that would be their grandfather—he would treat us all with sealing wax. I've taken a dose of sealing wax every day for twenty years now, even more, who knows; perhaps that's why I'm still alive.

YASHA: You get on my nerves, grandpa. (*Yawns.*) Maybe it's time for you to kick the bucket.

FIRS: And you're a pathetic fool, that's what you are. (*Mumbles.*)

Trofimov and Lyubov Andreevna dance in the ballroom, and then in the drawing room.

LYUBOV ANDREEVNA: "Merci." Let me sit down . . . (*Sits.*) I'm exhausted.

Enter Anya.

ANYA: (*Agitated.*) There's a man out in the kitchen, he was just saying that the cherry orchard was sold today.

LYUBOV ANDREEVNA: To whom?

ANYA: He didn't say. He left. (*Dances with Trofimov.*)

Both exit into the ballroom.

YASHA: Some old fellow jabbering, that's all. A stranger.

FIRS: And Leonid Andreich is still not here, he's still not back yet. All he has on is a lightweight overcoat, one for in-between seasons, he's bound to catch cold. Oh, these young people nowadays!

LYUBOV ANDREEVNA: I think I'm going to die. Go, Yasha, hurry, find out to whom it was sold.

YASHA: Oh, he left a long time ago, that old fellow. (*Laughs.*)

LYUBOV ANDREEVNA: (*Slightly annoyed.*) And what are you laughing about? What's so funny?

YASHA: That Yepikhodov, he's a clown. The man is pitiful. "Mister Disaster."

LYUBOV ANDREEVNA: Firs, if the estate is sold, where will you go?

FIRS: Wherever you tell me, that's where I'll go.

LYUBOV ANDREEVNA: Why do you look like that? Are you ill? You should be in bed, you know . . .

FIRS: Yes . . . (*With a grin.*) I'll go to bed, and who will serve, who will manage everything? Hm? One servant for the whole household.

YASHA: (*To Lyubov Andreevna.*) Lyubov Andreevna! One small request, allow me, please! If you go to Paris again, take me with you, I beg of you. I can't stay here any more, it's absolutely impossible. (*Looks around, in a low voice.*) What can I say, you see for yourself, this is an ignorant country, the people are immoral, and anyway, life here is boring, the food they give you in the kitchen is disgusting, and you have Firs wandering around everywhere, muttering all kinds of nonsense. Take me with you, I beg of you!

Enter Pishchik.

PISHCHIK: May I have the pleasure . . . a little waltz, most charming lady . . .

Lyubov Andreevna joins him.

But, don't forget, one hundred eighty rubles, enchanting lady . . . That, I'll take . . . (*They dance.*) One hundred and eighty sweet little rubles . . .

They cross into the ballroom.

YASHA: (*Sings softly.*) "O, do you know how my heart is yearning . . ."

In the ballroom, a figure in a grey top hat and checkered trousers waves her hands and jumps up and down; there are cries of: "Bravo, Charlotta Ivanovna!"

DUNYASHA: (*Stops to powder her face.*) The mistress told me to dance — too many gentlemen, too few ladies, — but now my head is spinning from too much waltzing, my heart is pounding, and, do you know what else, Firs Nikolaevich, the postmaster just told me something that took my breath away.

The music dies down.

FIRS: What did he say?

DUNYASHA: "You," he said, "are like a little flower."

YASHA: (*Yawns.*) What ignorance . . . (*Exits.*)

DUNYASHA: "A little flower" . . . I'm such a sensitive young woman, you know, I adore a few tender words.

FIRS: You'll get yourself into a lot of trouble.

Enter Yepikhodov.

YEPIKHODOV: Avdotya Fyodorovna, you keep avoiding me . . . what am I, some sort of insect? (*Sighs.*) Ach, life!

DUNYASHA: Yes, what may I do for you?

YEPIKHODOV: And no doubt, probably, you're right. Of course. (*Sighs.*) Who can blame you. And yet, look at it from my point, of view, I mean, if I may say so myself, and I shall, so excuse me, but you have reduced me to a complete state of mind. Now I know my destiny in life, every day some new disaster befalls me, and have I accepted this? — yes, I have, I look upon my fate with a smile. You have given me your word, and though . . .

DUNYASHA: Can we have our little talk later, please? Leave me alone now. I'm in a fantasy. (*Plays with her fan.*)

YEPIKHODOV: A new day, a new disaster, and excuse me, I just keep smiling, I even laugh, sometimes.

Enter Varya from the ballroom.

VARYA: You still haven't left yet, Semyon? Who do you think you are, really. (*To Dunyasha.*) Get out of here, Dunyasha. (*To Yepikhodov.*) First you play billiards and you break a cue, then you parade around the drawing room like a guest.

YEPIKHODOV: You should not reprimand me. Excuse me.

VARYA: I'm not reprimanding you, I'm telling you. All you do is float from one place to the next, you don't do a blessed bit of work. Why we keep you as clerk, God only knows.

YEPIKHODOV: (*Offended.*) Whether I work, or float, or eat, or play billiards, for that matter, excuse me, but that's a subject of discussion only for our elders.

VARYA: How dare you speak to me like that! (*Enraged.*) How dare you? Do you mean to tell me I don't know what I'm doing? Get out of here! This minute!

YEPIKHODOV: (*Cowering.*) Excuse me, may I ask that you express yourself in a more delicate fashion?

VARYA: (*Beside herself.*) Get out, this minute! Out!

He goes to the door, she follows him.

"Mister Disaster!" Never set foot in here again, do you hear! I never want to lay eyes on you!

Yepikhodov has exited; from behind the door, his voice is heard: "I am going to file a complaint against you."

So, you think you're coming back, eh? (*Grabs the cane, which Firs has left by the door.*) Come on . . . come on . . . come on, I'll show you . . . So, are you coming back? Are you? This is for you, then . . . (*Swings the cane.*)

Just at this moment Lopakhin enters.

LOPAKHIN: I humbly thank you.

VARYA: (*Angrily and sarcastically.*) Sorry!

LOPAKHIN: Please, it's nothing. I'm most grateful for the warm reception.

VARYA: Don't mention it. (*She turns to go, then looks around and asks, meekly.*) I didn't hurt you, did I?

LOPAKHIN: No, of course not, it's nothing. Just a bump, an enormous one, that's all.

Voices in the ballroom: "Lopakhin has returned! Yermolai Alekseich!"

PISHCHIK: Well, well, well, and speaking of the devil! . . . (*Kisses Lopakhin.*) I smell a touch of brandy, my dear, good fellow, yes, I do! And we've been celebrating here, too!

Enter Lyubov Andreevna.

LYUBOV ANDREEVNA: Yermolai Alekseich, you're back. Why did it take you so long? Where is Leonid?

LOPAKHIN: Leonid Andreich returned with me, he's coming . . .

LYUBOV ANDREEVNA: (*Upset.*) So? Was there an auction? Tell me!

LOPAKHIN: (*Disconcerted, afraid to reveal his excitement.*) The auction was over at four o'clock . . . We missed the train, we had to wait till nine-thirty. (*Sighs heavily.*) Oh! My head is spinning . . .

Enter Gaev. In his right hand he carries some packages; he wipes away the tears with his left hand.

LYUBOV ANDREEVNA: Lyonya, what is it? Lyonya? (*Impatiently, in tears.*) Tell me, quickly, for God's sake . . .

GAEV: (*Doesn't answer her, simply waves his hands; weeping, to Firs.*) Here, take it . . . anchovies, and some kerch herring . . . I haven't had a thing to eat all day . . . What I have lived through!

The door of the billiard room is open; the clicking of billiard balls is heard and Yasha's voice: "Seven and eighteen!" Gaev's expression changes; he is no longer crying.

I'm terribly tired. Help me change my clothes, Firs. (*Exits through the ballroom to his room, Firs follows behind.*)

PISHCHIK: What happened at the auction? Tell us! Please!

LYUBOV ANDREEVNA: Is the cherry orchard sold?

LOPAKHIN: It is sold.

LYUBOV ANDREEVNA: Who bought it?

LOPAKHIN: I bought it.

Pause. Lyubov Andreevna is stunned; she might have fallen, were she not standing near an armchair and table. Varya takes the keys off her belt, throws them on the floor in the middle of the drawing room, and exits.

I bought it! Wait, ladies and gentlemen, bear with me, please, my head is spinning, I can't speak . . . (*Laughs.*) We arrived at the auction, and Deriganov was already there. Leonid Andreich only had 15,000, so right away Deriganov bid 30,000 over and above the debt on the mortgage. I saw how it was going, so I decided to take him on, I bid forty. And he bid forty-five. Then I bid fifty-five. You see—he'd raise it by five, I'd raise it by ten . . . And then, it was all over. I bid ninety over and above the debt, and that was it, it went to me. And now, the cherry orchard is mine! Mine! (*Roars with laughter.*) My God, ladies and gentlemen, the cherry orchard is mine! Tell me that I'm drunk, that I'm out of my mind, that I've made it all up . . . (*Stamps his feet.*) Don't you laugh at me! If only my father and my grandfather could get up from their graves and witness all these events, how their Yermolai, their ignorant little Yermolai, the one who was beaten, the one who ran barefoot in the bitter winter, how this same little Yermolai bought the estate, the most beautiful estate in the world. I bought the estate, where my grandfather and my father were slaves, where they were forbidden to set foot in the kitchen. No, I'm dreaming, I'm hallucinating, it's only an illusion . . . a figment of the imagination, shrouded in a cloak of mystery . . . (*Picks up the keys, smiles tenderly.*) She threw down the keys, she's saying she's not the mistress of the house any more . . . (*Jingles the keys.*) Ah, well, what does it matter.

The orchestra can be heard tuning up.

Eh, musicians, play, I want to hear you play! Everyone, come and see, how Yermolai Lopakhin will take an axe out into the cherry orchard, and all the trees will come crashing to the ground! And we'll build summer homes, and our grandchildren and great grandchildren will see a new life . . . Let's have music, play!

The music plays. Lyubov Andreevna lowers herself into a chair and weeps bitterly.

(*Reproachfully.*) Why, why didn't you listen to me? My, poor, dear friend, you'll never get it back now, never. (*In tears.*) Oh, the sooner all this is behind us, the sooner we can change our chaotic lives, our absurd, unhappy lives.

PISHCHIK: (*Takes him by the hand, in a low voice.*) She is weeping. Come into the ballroom, let's leave her alone . . . Come . . . (*Takes him by the hand and leads him into the ballroom.*)

LOPAKHIN: What's going on here? Let there be music? Loud, the way I want it! Let everything be the way I want it! (*With irony.*) Here comes the new master, the owner of the cherry orchard! (*Accidentally shoves against a table, almost turning over a candelabra.*) I can pay for it all, for everything! (*Exits with Pishchik.*)

There is no one left in the ballroom or the drawing room, except Lyubov Andreevna, who is sitting, huddled over, weeping bitterly. The music plays softly. Anya and Trofimov rush in. Anya goes to her mother and kneels before her. Trofimov stays at the entrance to the ballroom.

ANYA: Mama! . . . Mama, are you crying? My dear, good, kind Mama, my beautiful Mama, I love you . . . I bless you. The cherry orchard is sold, it's gone, it's true, it's true, but don't cry, Mama, you still have your whole life before you to live, and your pure and beautiful soul . . . Come with me, come, my darling, away from here, come! . . . We'll plant a new orchard, more glorious than this one, you'll see, you'll understand, and joy, a deep, peaceful, gentle joy will settle into your soul, like the warm, evening sun, and you will smile, Mama! Come, darling! Come! . . .

CURTAIN

ACT FOUR

The same setting as Act One. There are no curtains on the windows, no pictures on the walls; only a few pieces of furniture remain, stacked in a corner, as if for sale. There is a feeling of emptiness. There are suitcases, travel bags, etc., piled high upstage by the door leading to the outside. The door to stage left is open, from which the voices of Varya and Anya can be heard. Lopakhin stands there, waiting. Yasha holds a tray of glasses, filled with champagne. In the entrance hall, Yepikhodov is packing a case. Offstage, voices are heard—the peasants have come to say good-bye. Gaev's voice is heard: "Thank you, my friends, I thank you."

YASHA: The peasants have come to say good-bye. Now here's my opinion on that subject, Yermolai Alekseich: The people are good, but what do *they* know.

The noise dies down. Lyubov Andreevna and Gaev enter through the entrance hall; she is no longer crying, but she is very pale: she is trembling, and it is difficult for her to speak.

GAEV: You gave them everything in your purse, Lyuba. No! You mustn't do that!

LYUBOV ANDREEVNA: I couldn't help it! I couldn't help it!

Both exit.

LOPAKHIN: (*At the door, following after them.*) Please, I humbly beg you! A farewell toast! I didn't think to bring any from town . . . and I could only find one bottle at the station. Please!

Pause.

So, my friends! You don't want any? (*Steps away from the door.*) If I'd known, I wouldn't have bought it. Never mind, I won't have any, either.

Yasha carefully places the tray on the table.

Drink up, Yasha, why don't you.

YASHA: To those who are leaving! And to those who are staying behind! (*Drinks.*) This isn't real champagne, that much I can tell you.

LOPAKHIN: Eight rubles a bottle.

Pause.

Wickedly cold in here, isn't it.

YASHA: They didn't stoke up the stoves today, what's the point, every-body's leaving. (*Laughs.*)

LOPAKHIN: What are you laughing about?

YASHA: I'm happy.

LOPAKHIN: It's October, but outside it's sunny and mild, like summertime. Good weather for construction. (*Looks at his watch, at the door.*) Ladies and gentlemen, bear in mind, only forty-six minutes left until the train departs! That means we have to leave for the station in twenty minutes. Hurry, everyone!

Trofimov enters from the outside, wearing a coat.

TROFIMOV: I think it's time to go now. They've already brought the horses around. Where are my galoshes, damn it! They've disappeared. (*At the door.*) Anya, my galoshes aren't here! I can't find them!

LOPAKHIN: And I've got to get to Kharkov. I'll go with you as far as the station. I'm going to spend the winter in Kharkov. Yes. Here I am, standing around, talking to you, I'm lost when I'm not working. I can't live without work, I don't know what to do with my hands; isn't it strange, look, they're hanging there, as if they belonged to someone else.

TROFIMOV: We'll be leaving momentarily, and you'll return to all your worthy enterprises.

LOPAKHIN: Have a glass of with me.

TROFIMOV: I can't.

LOPAKHIN: So, it's off to Moscow, then?

TROFIMOV: Yes, that's right, I'll go with them into town, and tomorrow, it's off to Moscow.

LOPAKHIN: Yes . . . Well, the professors haven't started their lectures yet, no doubt they're all waiting for you!

TROFIMOV: That's none of your business.

LOPAKHIN: How many years is it, then, since you've been at the university?

TROFIMOV: Think up something new, why don't you? That's a stale and feeble joke, it's not funny any more. (*Searches for his galoshes.*) It's very likely we may never see each other again, you know, so allow me, please, to give you some parting advice. Don't wave your arms around so much! Try to get out of the habit of waving your arms when you talk, if you can. All this planning of yours, you know, building summer houses, creating a new generation of independent landowners, and so on and so forth,—why, that's just another form of waving your arms . . . Oh, well, never mind, all things considered, I like you . . . I do. You have delicate, sensitive fingers, the fingers of an artist . . . you have a delicate, sensitive soul . . .

LOPAKHIN: (*Embraces him.*) Good-bye, my friend. Thanks for everything. Just in case, here, take some money for the journey.

TROFIMOV: Why should I? I don't need it.

LOPAKHIN: But you don't have any!

TROFIMOV: Yes, I do, thank you very much. I've just received some money for a translation. Here it is, right here, in my pocket. (*Anxiously.*) Now where are my galoshes!

VARYA: (*From the other room.*) Here, take the filthy things! (*Tosses a pair of rubber galoshes on the stage.*)

TROFIMOV: Why are you so angry, Varya? Hm . . . These are not my galoshes!

LOPAKHIN: This spring I planted almost 3,000 acres of poppies, and made a clean profit of 40,000. And when my poppies bloomed, now what a sight that was! So, here's what I'm saying, I've just made 40,000 rubles, and I'm offering you a loan because I can afford to. Why do you look down your nose at me? I'm a peasant . . . what do you expect?

TROFIMOV: Your father was a peasant, mine was a chemist, none of it means a thing.

Lopakhin takes out his wallet.

Stop that, stop . . . Even if you were to give me 200,000, I wouldn't take it. I am a free man. And everything that is so sacred and dear to all of you, rich and poor alike, hasn't the slightest significance to me, it's all dust, adrift in the wind. I can survive without you, I can even surpass you, I am proud and strong. Mankind is on a quest to seek the highest truth, the greatest happiness possible on this earth, and I am in the front ranks!

LOPAKHIN: And will you reach your destination?

TROFIMOV: Yes, I shall.

Pause.

I shall, or else I'll show others the way.

In the distance, the sound is heard of an axe falling on a tree.

LOPAKHIN: So, good-bye, my friend. Time to go. Here we are, looking down our noses at one another, and all the while, life goes on, in spite of any of us. When I work, for days on end, without any rest, that's when my thoughts come most clearly, that's when I know why I am on this earth, why I exist. And how many of us are there in Russia, my friend, who still don't know why they exist. Ah well, what does it matter, that's not the point, is it. They say that Leonid Andreich has taken a position at a bank, 6,000 a year . . . He won't be able to keep it, though, he's too lazy . . .

ANYA: (*At the door.*) Mama asks you not to cut down the orchard till after she's gone.

TROFIMOV: Isn't it possible to show some tact . . . (*Exits through the entrance hall.*)

LOPAKHIN: Yes, yes, right away . . . Really.

ANYA: Have they sent Firs to the hospital yet?

YASHA: I told them about it this morning. I'm sure they did.

ANYA: (*To Yepikhodov, who is walking through the hall.*) Semyon Pante-leich, please, go find out, would you, if they've taken Firs to the hospi-tal yet.

YASHA: (*Offended.*) I told Yegor this morning. Why ask the same question over and over!

YEPIKHODOV: The ancient Firs, in my final opinion, is beyond repair; he should return to his forefathers. And I can only envy him. (*Places the suitcase on a hat box, and crushes it.*) Oh, well, of course. I knew it. (*Exits.*)

YASHA: (*Mocking.*) "Mister Disaster" . . .

VARYA: (*From behind the door.*) Have they taken Firs to the hospital?

ANYA: Yes, they have.

VARYA: Why didn't they bring the letter to the doctor?

ANYA: We'll just have to send it along . . . (*Exits.*)

VARYA: (*From the adjacent room.*) Where's Yasha? Tell him his mother's here, she wants to say good-bye to him.

YASHA: (*Waves his hand.*) I'm losing my patience.

During this, Dunyasha has been busying herself with the luggage; now that Yasha is alone, she goes up to him.

DUNYASHA: Just one last look, Yasha. You're leaving . . . you're abandon-ing me . . . (*Weeps and throws her arms around his neck.*)

YASHA: What's there to cry about? (*Drinks champagne.*) In six days, I'll be in Paris again. Tomorrow we'll board an express train, and off we'll go, that's the last you'll ever see of us. I just can't believe it. "Vive la France!" . . . This place is not for me, I can't live here . . . and that's all there is to it. I've seen a lot of ignorance—and I've had enough. (*Drinks champagne.*) What's there to cry about? Behave yourself prop-erly, then you won't cry so much.

DUNYASHA: (*Powders her face, looks at herself in the mirror.*) Send me a letter from Paris. You know how much I have loved you, Yasha, I have loved you very, very much! I'm a sensitive creature, Yasha!

YASHA: They're coming. (*Busies himself with the luggage, hums softly.*)

Enter Lyubov Andreevna, Gaev, Anya, and Charlotta Ivanovna.

GAEV: We really ought to be going. There's hardly any time left. (*Looks at Yasha.*) Who smells of herring in here?

LYUBOV ANDREEVNA: In ten minutes time we'll be getting into the car-riages . . . (*Glances around the room.*) Good-bye, beloved home, home of my forefathers. Winter will pass, spring will come, and you'll no longer be here, they will have destroyed you. How much these walls have seen! (*Kisses her daughter passionately.*) My treasure, you're radiant, your eyes are sparkling, like two diamonds. Are you happy? Very happy?

ANYA: Very! We're starting a new life, Mama!

GAEV: (*Cheerfully.*) Everything's turned out quite well, as a matter of fact, yes, indeed. Before the cherry orchard was sold, we were all upset, we suffered a great deal, but then, when everything was settled, once and for all, finally and irrevocably, we all calmed down, we were even glad . . . And now I'm a bank official, a financier . . . "yellow into the middle pocket," and you, Lyuba, for all that we've been through, you're looking better than ever, no doubt about it.

LYUBOV ANDREEVNA: Yes, I'm calmer, it's true.

She is given her hat and coat.

I can sleep better now. Take my things out, Yasha. It's time. (*To Anya.*) My darling child, we shall see each other again, soon . . . I am going to Paris, I shall live there on the money your great-aunt from Yaroslavl sent to buy the estate—God bless great-aunt!—but that money won't last very long.

ANYA: You'll come home soon, Mama, soon . . . won't you? And I'll study, take my examinations, and then I'll work, I'll take care of you. And we'll read all sorts of marvelous books together, Mama . . . Won't we? (*Kisses her mother's hands.*) We'll read through the long autumn evenings, we'll read so many books, and a wonderful new world will open before us . . . (*Dreaming.*) Come home, Mama . . .

LYUBOV ANDREEVNA: I'll come, my jewel. (*Embraces her daughter.*)

Enter Lopakhin, and Charlotta, who is softly humming a tune.

GAEV: Charlotta is happy: she's singing!

CHARLOTTA: (*Picks up a bundle, resembling an infant in swaddling clothes.*) "My sweet little baby, 'bye, 'bye . . ."

The child's cry: "Wa, wa! . . ." can be heard.

"Hushabye, baby, my sweet little boy."

The child's cry: "Wa! . . . wa! . . ."

Poor baby! I feel so sorry for you! (*Throws the bundle down.*) Now, please, find me another job. I can't go on like this.

LOPAKHIN: We shall, Charlotta Ivanovna, don't worry.

GAEV: We're all being cast out, Varya's going away . . . suddenly no one needs us any more.

CHARLOTTA: There's nowhere for me to live in town. I must go away . . . (*Hums.*) It doesn't matter . . .

Enter Pishchik.

LOPAKHIN: One of nature's wonders! . . .

PISHCHIK: (*Out of breath.*) Oy, let me catch my breath . . . I'm all worn out . . . Most honorable friends . . . Give me some water . . .

GAEV: Looking for money, by any chance? I remain your humble servant, but, forgive me, I really must avoid the temptation . . . (*Exits.*)

PISHCHIK: I haven't been here in such a long, long, time . . . loveliest lady . . . (*To Lopakhin.*) And you are here, too . . . so good to see you . . . a man of the highest intelligence . . . here, take it . . . it's yours . . . (*Gives Lopakhin some money.*) Four hundred rubles . . . I still owe you eight hundred and forty . . .

LOPAKHIN: (*Shrugs his shoulders in amazement.*): I must be dreaming . . . Where on earth did you get this?

PISHCHIK: Wait . . . So hot . . . Most extraordinary circumstances. Some Englishmen came to visit my estate, and what do you know, they found white clay in the earth . . . whatever that is . . . (*To Lyubov Andreevna.*) And here's four hundred for you . . . elegant, exquisite lady . . . (*Gives her some money.*) The rest will come later. (*Drinks the water.*) Just now, a young man on the train was telling us about this great philosopher . . . how he's advising everyone to jump off the roof . . . "Jump!" — he says, and that will solve everything. (*Amazed.*) Imagine that! Water! . . .

LOPAKHIN: What Englishmen are you talking about?

PISHCHIK: I leased them a plot of the land with the white clay for twenty-four years . . . But now, forgive me, please, I've run out of time . . . a long ride ahead . . . I'm going to the Znoykovs . . . to the Kardamonovs . . . I owe everybody . . . (*Drinks.*) Good day to you all . . . I'll drop by again on Thursday . . .

LYUBOV ANDREEVNA: We're just moving into town now, and tomorrow I'm going abroad . . .

PISHCHIK: What? (*Anxiously.*) Why to town? What's this I see . . . furniture . . . suitcases . . . Well, never mind . . . (*In tears.*) Never mind . . . Very very smart people, these Englishmen . . . people of the highest intelligence . . . Never mind . . . I wish you happiness . . . God will watch over you . . . Never mind . . . Everything on this earth must come to an end . . . (*Kisses Lyubov Andreevna's hand.*) And when you hear the news that my own end has come, remember this good old horse, won't you, and say: "Once upon a time there lived an old so-and-so . . . Simeonov-Pishchik . . . God rest his soul" . . . Magnificent weather we're having . . . Yes . . . (*Exits in great confusion, and immediately returns and speaks from the doorway.*) Dashenka sends her regards. (*Exits.*)

LYUBOV ANDREEVNA: And now we can go. But I'm leaving with two worries. The first is Firs—he's ill. (*Looks at her watch.*) We still have five minutes . . .

ANYA: Mama, they've already sent Firs to the hospital. Yasha sent him this morning.

LYUBOV ANDREEVNA: My second sorrow is Varya. She's used to getting up early and working, and now, without work, she's like a fish out of water. She's grown thin and pale, she weeps all the time, poor thing . . .

Pause.

You know very well, Yermolai Alekseich, I have dreamed . . . that one day she would marry you, in fact, it was obvious to everyone that you would be married. (*She whispers to Anya, who motions to Charlotta, and both exit.*) She loves you, you seem to be fond of her, and I don't know why, I simply don't know why it is that you go out of your way to avoid one another. I don't understand it!

LOPAKHIN: I don't understand it myself, to tell the truth. It's all so strange, somehow . . . If there's still time, then I'm ready to do it now . . . Basta!° Let's settle it once and for all; without you here, I don't think I could possibly propose to her.

LYUBOV ANDREEVNA: Excellent! It only takes a minute, you know. I'll call her in right away . . .

LOPAKHIN: Oh yes, and there's champagne, too. (*Looks at glasses.*) It's empty, someone drank it all up.

Yasha coughs.

Or, should I say, lapped it all up . . .

LYUBOV ANDREEVNA: (*Excited.*) Splendid. We're leaving . . . Yasha, "allez!"° I'll call her . . . (*At the door.*) Varya, stop what you're doing, and come here. Come! (*Exits with Yasha.*)

LOPAKHIN: (*Looks at his watch.*): Yes . . .

Pause.

Muffled laughter and whispering is heard from behind the door; finally, Varya enters.

VARYA: (*In a lengthy search for something.*) That's strange, I can't find it anywhere . . .

LOPAKHIN: What are you looking for?

VARYA: I put it away myself, I can't remember where.

Pause.

Basta!: "Enough!" (Italian).
"allez!": "Go!" (French).

LOPAKHIN: So where will you go now, Varvara Mikhailovna?

VARYA: Me? To the Ragulins'... I've agreed to work for them ... you know ... as a housekeeper.

LOPAKHIN: Aren't they in Yashnevo? That's about forty-five miles from here.

Pause.

And so, life has come to an end in this house ...

VARYA: (*Searching among the things.*) Where can it be ... Perhaps I put it in the trunk ... Yes, life has come to an end in this house ... and will be no more ...

LOPAKHIN: And I'm off to Kharkov now ... on the same train. I've got a lot of business there. But I'm leaving Yepikhodov here to look after things ... I've hired him, you know.

VARYA: Really!

LOPAKHIN: Last year at this time it was already snowing, if you remember, and now it's so sunny and calm. Only it's quite cold ... Three degrees of frost, almost.

VARYA: I hadn't noticed.

Pause.

Anyway, our thermometer's broken ...

Pause.

A voice is heard calling from outside: "Yermolai Alekseich! ..."

LOPAKHIN: (*As if he'd long been waiting for this call.*) Coming! (*He hurries out.*)

Varya sits on the floor, puts her head on a bundle of clothing, and sobs quietly. The door opens, and Lyubov Andreevna enters cautiously.

LYUBOV ANDREEVNA: So?

Pause.

We'd better go.

VARYA: (*No longer weeping, wipes her eyes.*) Yes, Mamochka, it's time. If I don't miss the train, I might even get to the Raqulins' today ...

LYUBOV ANDREEVNA: (*At the door.*) Anya, put your coat on!

Enter Anya, then Gaev, Charlotta Ivanovna. Gaev is wearing a warm coat with a hood. The servants and carriage drivers assemble. Yepikhodov is busy with the luggage.

Now, we can be on our way.

ANYA: (*Overjoyed.*) We're on our way!

GAEV: My friends, my dear, kind friends! Upon leaving this house forever, how can I be silent, how can I refrain, upon this our departure, from expressing those feelings, which now fill my very being ...

ANYA: (*Imploring.*) Uncle!

VARYA: Uncle, must you!

GAEV: (*Dejected.*) "Double the yellow into the middle . . ." I'll be quiet . . .

Enter Trofimov, then Lopakhin.

TROFIMOV: All right, ladies and gentlemen, time to depart.

LOPAKHIN: Yepikhodov, my coat!

LYUBOV ANDREEVNA: I want to sit for just one minute longer. I never really noticed before, what walls this house has, what ceilings, and now I look at them with such longing, with such tender love . . .

GAEV: I remember, when I was six, on Trinity Sunday, I sat at this window and watched my father walking to church . . .

LYUBOV ANDREEVNA: Have they taken everything out?

LOPAKHIN: I think so. (*To Yepikhodov, who is putting on his coat.*) Yepikhodov, see to it that everything's been taken care of.

YEPIKHODOV: (*Speaking in a hoarse voice.*) Don't you worry, Yermolai Alekseich.

LOPAKHIN: What's the matter with your voice?

YEPIKHODOV: I just drank some water, and I must have swallowed something.

YASHA: (*Contemptuously.*) What ignorance . . .

LYUBOV ANDREEVNA: We're leaving—and not a soul will be left here . . .

LOPAKHIN: Until springtime.

VARYA: (*Pulls an umbrella out of a bundle—it appears as if she were about to strike someone; Lopakhin pretends to be frightened.*) What's wrong with you? . . . I wouldn't think of it . . .

TROFIMOV: Ladies and gentlemen, please, let's get into the carriages now . . . It's time to go! The train will arrive any minute!

VARYA: Petya, here they are, your galoshes, beside the suitcase. (*In tears.*) Look how old and muddy they are . . .

TROFIMOV: (*Putting on his galoshes.*) We're off, ladies and gentlemen!

GAEV: (*Very confused, afraid of bursting into tears.*) Train . . . station . . . "Croisé into the middle pocket, Double the white into the corner . . ."

LYUBOV ANDREEVNA: We're off!

LOPAKHIN: Is everyone here? No one left behind? (*Locks the side door stage left.*) There are some things stored in here, better lock up. We're off!

ANYA: Good-bye, house! Good-bye, old life!

TROFIMOV: Hello, new life! . . . (*Exits with Anya.*)

Varya glances around the room and exits without hurrying. Exit Yasha, and Charlotta, with the little dog,

LOPAKHIN: And so, until springtime. Come now, ladies and gentlemen, we'd better be going . . . Once more, a very good-bye!! . . . (*Exits.*)

Lyubov Andreevna and Gaev are left alone together. It is as if they have been waiting for this moment; they throw themselves into each others' arms and sob quietly, with restraint, fearing they might be heard.

GAEV: (*In despair.*) My sister, my sister . . .

LYUBOV ANDREEVNA: O my precious orchard, my sweet, lovely orchard! . . . My life, my youth, my happiness, farewell! . . . Farewell! . . .

Anya's voice calls out, merrily: "Mama! . . ."

Trofimov's voice calls out, gaily, excitedly: "A-oo! . . ."

LYUBOV ANDREEVNA: For the last time, let me look at these walls, these windows . . . how my mother loved to walk about this room . . .

GAEV: My sister, my sister! . . .

Anya's voice: "Mama! . . ."

Trofimov's voice: "A-oo . . ."

LYUBOV ANDREEVNA: We're off! . . .

They exit.

The stage is empty. There is the sound of all the doors being locked, and then of the carriages pulling away. It grows very still. Through the stillness comes the remote sound of the axe falling on a tree, a lonely, melancholy sound. Footsteps are heard. Firs appears at the door, stage right. He is dressed, as always, in a jacket and a white waistcoat, with slippers on his feet. He is ill.

FIRS: (*Goes to the door, tries the handle.*) Locked! They've gone . . . (*Sits on the sofa.*) They've forgotten about me . . . Never mind . . . I'll sit here for just a bit . . . And Leonid Andreich, most likely, didn't put his fur coat on, went off wearing his light one . . . (*Sighs, anxiously.*) Just slipped my notice . . . These young people nowadays! (*Mutters something incomprehensible.*) And life has passed by, somehow, as if I never lived it at all. (*Lies down.*) I'll lie down for just a bit . . . Don't have too much strength left, now, do you, no, not much, not much at all . . . You pathetic old fool, you! . . . (*Lies there, immobile.*)

A distant sound is heard, as if coming from the sky, the sound of a breaking string, dying away, a mournful sound. Silence falls, and all that is heard, far off in the orchard, is the sound of the axe falling on a tree.

CURTAIN

1903

Trifles

SUSAN GLASPELL [1882–1948]

Characters
GEORGE HENDERSON, *county attorney*
HENRY PETERS, *sheriff*
LEWIS HALE, *a neighboring farmer*
MRS. PETERS
MRS. HALE

Scene: *The kitchen in the now abandoned farmhouse of John Wright, a gloomy kitchen, and left without having been put in order—the walls covered with a faded wall paper. Down right is a door leading to the parlor. On the right wall above this door is a built-in kitchen cupboard with shelves in the upper portion and drawers below. In the rear wall at right, up two steps is a door opening onto stairs leading to the second floor. In the rear wall at left is a door to the shed and from there to the outside. Between these two doors is an old-fashioned black iron stove. Running along the left wall from the shed door is an old iron sink and sink shelf, in which is set a hand pump. Downstage of the sink is an uncurtained window. Near the window is an old wooden rocker. Center stage is an unpainted wooden kitchen table with straight chairs on either side. There is a small chair down right. Unwashed pans under the sink, a loaf of bread outside the breadbox, a dish towel on the table—other signs of incompleted work. At the rear the shed door opens and the Sheriff comes in followed by the County Attorney and Hale. The Sheriff and Hale are men in middle life, the County Attorney is a young man; all are much bundled up and go at once to the stove. They are followed by the two women—the Sheriff's wife, Mrs. Peters, first: she is a slight wiry woman, a thin nervous face. Mrs. Hale is larger and would ordinarily be called more comfortable looking, but she is disturbed now and looks fearfully about as she enters. The women have come in slowly, and stand close together near the door.*

COUNTY ATTORNEY (*at stove rubbing his hands*): This feels good. Come up to the fire, ladies.
MRS. PETERS (*after taking a step forward*): I'm not—cold.
SHERIFF (*unbuttoning his overcoat and stepping away from the stove to right of table as if to mark the beginning of official business*): Now, Mr. Hale,

before we move things about, you explain to Mr. Henderson just what you saw when you came here yesterday morning.

COUNTY ATTORNEY (*crossing down to left of the table*): By the way, has anything been moved? Are things just as you left them yesterday?

SHERIFF (*looking about*): It's just about the same. When it dropped below zero last night I thought I'd better send Frank out this morning to make a fire for us—(*sits right of center table*) no use getting pneumonia with a big case on, but I told him not to touch anything except the stove—and you know Frank.

COUNTY ATTORNEY: Somebody should have been left here yesterday.

SHERIFF: Oh—yesterday. When I had to send Frank to Morris Center for that man who went crazy—I want you to know I had my hands full yesterday. I knew you could get back from Omaha by today and as long as I went over everything here myself———

COUNTY ATTORNEY: Well, Mr. Hale, tell just what happened when you came here yesterday morning.

HALE (*crossing down to above table*): Harry and I had started to town with a load of potatoes. We came along the road from my place and as I got here I said, "I'm going to see if I can't get John Wright to go in with me on a party telephone." I spoke to Wright about it once before and he put me off, saying folks talked too much anyway, and all he asked was peace and quiet—I guess you know about how much he talked himself; but I thought maybe if I went to the house and talked about it before his wife, though I said to Harry that I didn't know as what his wife wanted made much difference to John———

COUNTY ATTORNEY: Let's talk about that later, Mr. Hale. I do want to talk about that, but tell now just what happened when you got to the house.

HALE: I didn't hear or see anything; I knocked at the door, and still it was all quiet inside. I knew they must be up, it was past eight o'clock. So I knocked again, and I thought I heard someone say, "Come in." I wasn't sure, I'm not sure yet, but I opened the door—this door (*indicating the door by which the two women are still standing*) and there in that rocker—(*pointing to it*) sat Mrs. Wright. (*They all look at the rocker down left.*)

COUNTY ATTORNEY: What—was she doing?

HALE: She was rockin' back and forth. She had her apron in her hand and was kind of—pleating it.

COUNTY ATTORNEY: And how did she—look?

HALE: Well, she looked queer.

COUNTY ATTORNEY: How do you mean—queer?

HALE: Well, as if she didn't know what she was going to do next. And kind of done up.

COUNTY ATTORNEY (*takes out notebook and pencil and sits left of center table*): How did she seem to feel about your coming?

HALE: Why, I don't think she minded—one way or other. She didn't pay much attention. I said, "How do, Mrs. Wright, it's cold, ain't it?" And she said, "Is it?"—and went on kind of pleating at her apron. Well, I was surprised: she didn't ask me to come up to the stove, or to set down, but just sat there, not even looking at me, so I said, "I want to see John." And then she—laughed. I guess you would call it a laugh. I thought of Harry and the team outside, so I said a little sharp: "Can't I see John?" "No," she says, kind o' dull like. "Ain't he home?" says I. "Yes," says she, "he's home." "Then why can't I see him?" I asked her, out of patience. "'Cause he's dead," says she. "*Dead?*" says I. She just nodded her head, not getting a bit excited, but rockin' back and forth. "Why—where is he?" says I, not knowing what to say. She just pointed upstairs—like that. (*Himself pointing to the room above.*) I started for the stairs, with the idea of going up there. I walked from there to here—then I says, "Why, what did he die of?" "He died of a rope round his neck," says she, and just went on pleatin' at her apron. Well, I went out and called Harry. I thought I might—need help. We went upstairs and there he was lyin'——

COUNTY ATTORNEY: I think I'd rather have you go into that upstairs, where you can point it all out. Just go on now with the rest of the story.

HALE: Well, my first thought was to get that rope off. It looked . . . (*stops: his face twitches*) . . . but Harry, he went up to him, and he said, "No, he's dead all right, and we'd better not touch anything." So we went right back downstairs. She was still sitting that same way. "Has anybody been notified?" I asked. "No," says she, unconcerned. "Who did this, Mrs. Wright?" said Harry. He said it businesslike—and she stopped pleatin' of her apron. "I don't know," she says. "You don't *know?*" says Harry. "No," says she. "Weren't you sleepin' in the bed with him?" says Harry. "Yes," says she, "but I was on the inside." "Somebody slipped a rope round his head and strangled him and you didn't wake up?" says Harry. "I didn't wake up," she said after him. We must 'a' looked as if we didn't see how that could be, for after a minute she said, "I sleep sound." Harry was going to ask her more questions but I said maybe we ought to let her tell her story first to the coroner, or the sheriff, so Harry went fast as he could to Rivers' place, where there's a telephone.

COUNTY ATTORNEY: And what did Mrs. Wright do when she knew that you had gone for the coroner?

HALE: She moved from the rocker to that chair over there (*pointing to a small chair in the down right corner*) and just sat there with her hands held together and looking down. I got a feeling that I ought to make some conversation, so I said I had come in to see if John wanted to put in a telephone, and at that she started to laugh, and then she stopped and looked at me—scared. (*The County Attorney, who has had his notebook out, makes a note.*) I dunno, maybe it wasn't scared. I wouldn't like to say it was. Soon Harry got back, and then Dr. Lloyd came and you, Mr. Peters, and so I guess that's all I know that you don't.

COUNTY ATTORNEY (*rising and looking around*): I guess we'll go upstairs first—and then out to the barn and around there. (*To the Sheriff.*) You're convinced that there was nothing important here—nothing that would point to any motive?

SHERIFF: Nothing here but kitchen things. (*The County Attorney, after again looking around the kitchen, opens the door of a cupboard closet in right wall. He brings a small chair from right—gets on it and looks on a shelf. Pulls his hand away, sticky.*)

COUNTY ATTORNEY: Here's a nice mess. (*The women draw nearer up to center.*)

MRS. PETERS (*to the other woman*): Oh, her fruit; it did freeze. (*To the Lawyer.*) She worried about that when it turned so cold. She said the fire'd go out and her jars would break.

SHERIFF (*rises*): Well, can you beat the woman! Held for murder and worryin' about her preserves.

COUNTY ATTORNEY (*getting down from chair*): I guess before we're through she may have something more serious than preserves to worry about. (*Crosses down right center.*)

HALE: Well, women are used to worrying over trifles. (*The two women move a little closer together.*)

COUNTY ATTORNEY (*with the gallantry of a young politician*): And yet, for all their worries, what would we do without the ladies? (*The women do not unbend. He goes below the center table to the sink, takes a dipperful of water from the pail, and pouring it into a basin, washes his hands. While he is doing this the Sheriff and Hale cross to cupboard, which they inspect. The County Attorney starts to wipe his hands on the roller towel, turns it for a cleaner place.*) Dirty towels! (*Kicks his foot against the pans under the sink.*) Not much of a housekeeper, would you say, ladies?

MRS. HALE (*stiffly*): There's a great deal of work to be done on a farm.

COUNTY ATTORNEY: To be sure. And yet (*with a little bow to her*) I know there are some Dickson County farmhouses which do not have such roller towels. (*He gives it a pull to expose its full-length again.*)

MRS. HALE: Those towels get dirty awful quick. Men's hands aren't always clean as they might be.

COUNTY ATTORNEY: Ah, loyal to your sex, I see. But you and Mrs. Wright were neighbors. I suppose you were friends, too.

MRS. HALE (*shaking her head*): I've not seen much of her of late years. I've not been in this house—it's more than a year.

COUNTY ATTORNEY (*crossing to women up center*): And why was that? You didn't like her?

MRS. HALE: I liked her all well enough. Farmer's wives have their hands full, Mr. Henderson. And then——

COUNTY ATTORNEY: Yes——?

MRS. HALE (*looking about*): It never seemed a very cheerful place.

COUNTY ATTORNEY: No—it's not cheerful. I shouldn't say she had the homemaking instinct.

MRS. HALE: Well, I don't know as Wright had, either.

COUNTY ATTORNEY: You mean that they didn't get on very well?

MRS. HALE: No, I don't mean anything. But I don't think a place'd be any cheerfuller for John Wright's being in it.

COUNTY ATTORNEY: I'd like to talk more of that a little later. I want to get the lay of things upstairs now. (*He goes past the women to up right where the steps lead to a stair door.*)

SHERIFF: I suppose anything Mrs. Peters does'll be all right. She was to take in some clothes for her, you know, and a few little things. We left in such a hurry yesterday.

COUNTY ATTORNEY: Yes, but I would like to see what you take, Mrs. Peters, and keep an eye out for anything that might be of use to us.

MRS. PETERS: Yes, Mr. Henderson. (*The men leave by up right door to stairs. The women listen to the men's steps on the stairs, then look about the kitchen.*)

MRS. HALE (*crossing left to sink*): I'd hate to have men coming into my kitchen, snooping around and criticizing. (*She arranges the pans under sink which the lawyer had shoved out of place.*)

MRS. PETERS: Of course it's no more than their duty. (*Crosses to cupboard up right.*)

MRS. HALE: Duty's all right, but I guess that deputy sheriff that came out to make the fire might have got a little of this on. (*Gives the roller towel a pull.*) Wish I'd though of that sooner. Seems mean to talk about her for not having things slicked up when she had to come away in such a hurry. (*Crosses right to Mrs. Peters at cupboard.*)

MRS. PETERS (*who has been looking through cupboard, lifts one end of towel that covers a pan*): She had bread set. (*Stands still.*)

MRS. HALE (*eyes fixed on a loaf of bread beside the breadbox, which is on a low shelf of the cupboard*): She was going to put this in there. (*Picks up loaf, abruptly drops it. In a manner of returning to familiar things.*) It's a shame about her fruit. I wonder if it's all gone. (*Gets up on chair and looks.*) I think there's some here that's all right, Mrs. Peters. Yes — here; (*holding it toward the window*) this is cherries, too. (*Looking again.*) I declare I believe that's the only one. (*Gets down, jar in hand. Goes to the sink and wipes it off on the outside.*) She'll feel awful bad after all her hard work in the hot weather. I remember the afternoon I put up my cherries last summer. (*She puts the jar on the big kitchen table, center of the room. With a sigh, is about to sit down in the rocking chair. Before she is seated realizes what chair it is; with a slow look at it, steps back. The chair which she has touched rocks back and forth. Mrs. Peters moves to center table and they both watch the chair rock for a moment or two.*)

MRS. PETERS (*shaking off the mood which the empty rocking chair has evoked. Now in a businesslike manner she speaks*): Well I must get those things from the front room closet. (*She goes to the door at the right but, after looking into the other room, steps back.*) You coming with me, Mrs. Hale? You could help me carry them. (*They go in the other room; reappear, Mrs. Peters carrying a dress, petticoat, and skirt, Mrs. Hale following with a pair of shoes.*) My, it's cold in there. (*She puts the clothes on the big table and hurries to the stove.*)

MRS. HALE (*right of center table examining the skirt*): Wright was close. I think maybe that's why she kept so much to herself. She didn't even belong to the Ladies' Aid. I suppose she felt she couldn't do her part, and then you don't enjoy things when you feel shabby. I heard she used to wear pretty clothes and be lively, when she was Minnie Foster, one of the town girls singing in the choir. But that — oh, that was thirty years ago. This all you want to take in?

MRS. PETERS: She said she wanted an apron. Funny thing to want, for there isn't much to get you dirty in jail, goodness knows. But I suppose just to make her feel more natural. (*Crosses to cupboard.*) She said they was in the top drawer in this cupboard. Yes, here. And then her little shawl that always hung behind the door. (*Opens stair door and looks.*) Yes, here it is. (*Quickly shuts door leading upstairs.*)

MRS. HALE (*abruptly moving toward her*): Mrs. Peters?

MRS. PETERS: Yes, Mrs. Hale? (*At up right door.*)

MRS. HALE: Do you think she did it?

MRS. PETERS (*in a frightened voice*): Oh, I don't know.

MRS. HALE: Well, I don't think she did. Asking for an apron and her little shawl. Worrying about her fruit.

MRS. PETERS (*starts to speak, glances up, where footsteps are heard in the room above. In a low voice*): Mr. Peters says it looks bad for her. Mr.

Henderson is awful sarcastic in a speech and he'll make fun of her sayin' she didn't wake up.

MRS. HALE: Well, I guess John Wright didn't wake when they was slipping that rope under his neck.

MRS. PETERS (*crossing slowly to table and placing shawl and apron on table with other clothing*): No, it's strange. It must have been done awful crafty and still. They say it was such a—funny way to kill a man, rigging it all up like that.

MRS. HALE (*crossing to left of Mrs. Peters at table*): That's just what Mr. Hale said. There was a gun in the house. He says that's what he can't understand.

MRS. PETERS: Mr. Henderson said coming out that what was needed for the case was a motive: something to show anger, or—sudden feeling.

MRS. HALE (*who is standing by the table*): Well, I don't see any signs of anger around here. (*She puts her hand on the dish towel, which lies on the table, stands looking down at table, one-half of which is clean, the other half messy.*) It's wiped to here. (*Makes a move as if to finish work, then turns and looks at loaf of bread outside the breadbox. Drops towel. In that voice of coming back to familiar things.*) Wonder how they are finding things upstairs. (*Crossing below table to down right.*) I hope she had it a little more red-up up there. You know, it seems kind of *sneaking*. Locking her up in town and then coming out here and trying to get her own house to turn against her!

MRS. PETERS: But, Mrs. Hale, the law is the law.

MRS. HALE: I s'pose 'tis. (*Unbuttoning her coat.*) Better loosen up your things, Mrs. Peters. You won't feel them when you go out. (*Mrs. Peters takes off her fur tippet, goes to hang it on chair back left of table, stands looking at the work basket on floor near down left window.*)

MRS. PETERS: She was piecing a quilt. (*She brings the large sewing basket to the center table and they look at the bright pieces, Mrs. Hale above the table and Mrs. Peters left of it.*)

MRS. HALE: It's a log cabin pattern. Pretty, isn't it? I wonder if she was goin' to quilt it or just knot it? (*Footsteps have been heard coming down the stairs. The Sheriff enters followed by Hale and the County Attorney.*)

SHERIFF: They wonder if she was going to quilt it or just knot it! (*The men laugh, the women look abashed.*)

COUNTY ATTORNEY (*rubbing his hands over the stove*): Frank's fire didn't do much up there, did it? Well, let's go out to the barn and get that cleared up. (*The men go outside by up left door.*)

MRS. HALE (*resentfully*): I don't know as there's anything so strange, our takin' up our time with little things while we're waiting for them to get the evidence. (*She sits in chair right of table smoothing out a block with decision.*) I don't see as it's anything to laugh about.

MRS. PETERS (*apologetically*): Of course they've got awful important things on their minds. (*Pulls up a chair and joins Mrs. Hale at the left of the table.*)

MRS. HALE (*examining another block*): Mrs. Peters, look at this one. Here, this is the one she was working on, and look at the sewing! All the rest of it has been so nice and even. And look at this! It's all over the place! Why, it looks as if she didn't know what she was about! (*After she has said this they look at each other, then start to glance back at the door. After an instant Mrs. Hale has pulled at a knot and ripped the sewing.*)

MRS. PETERS: Oh, what are you doing, Mrs. Hale?

MRS. HALE (*mildly*): Just pulling out a stitch or two that's not sewed very good. (*Threading a needle.*) Bad sewing always made me fidgety.

MRS. PETERS (*with a glance at the door, nervously*): I don't think we ought to touch things.

MRS. HALE: I'll just finish up this end. (*Suddenly stopping and leaning forward.*) Mrs. Peters?

MRS. PETERS: Yes, Mrs. Hale?

MRS. HALE: What do you suppose she was so nervous about?

MRS. PETERS: Oh—I don't know. I don't know as she was nervous. I sometimes sew awful queer when I'm just tired. (*Mrs. Hale starts to say something, looks at Mrs. Peters, then goes on sewing.*) Well, I must get these things wrapped up. They may be through sooner than we think. (*Putting apron and other things together.*) I wonder where I can find a piece of paper, and string. (*Rises.*)

MRS. HALE: In that cupboard, maybe.

MRS. PETERS (*crosses right looking in cupboard*): Why, here's a bird-cage. (*Holds it up.*) Did she have a bird, Mrs. Hale?

MRS. HALE: Why, I don't know whether she did or not—I've not been here for so long. There was a man around last year selling canaries cheap, but I don't know as she took one; maybe she did. She used to sing real pretty herself.

MRS. PETERS (*glancing around*): Seems funny to think of a bird here. But she must have had one, or why would she have a cage? I wonder what happened to it?

MRS. HALE: I s'pose maybe the cat got it.

MRS. PETERS: No, she didn't have a cat. She's got that feeling some people have about cats—being afraid of them. My cat got in her room and she was real upset and asked me to take it out.

MRS. HALE: My sister Bessie was like that. Queer, ain't it?

MRS. PETERS (*examining the cage*): Why, look at this door. It's broke. One hinge is pulled apart. (*Takes a step down to Mrs. Hale's right.*)

MRS. HALE (*looking too*): Looks as if someone must have been rough with it.

MRS. PETERS: Why, yes. (*She brings the cage forward and puts it on the table.*)

MRS. HALE (*glancing toward up left door*): I wish if they're going to find any evidence they'd be about it. I don't like this place.

MRS. PETERS: But I'm awful glad you came with me, Mrs. Hale. It would be lonesome for me sitting here alone.

MRS. HALE: It would, wouldn't it? (*Dropping her sewing.*) But I tell you what I do wish, Mrs. Peters. I wish I had come over sometimes when *she* was here. I—(*looking around the room*)—wish I had.

MRS. PETERS: But of course you were awful busy, Mrs. Hale—your house and your children.

MRS. HALE (*rises and crosses left*): I could've come. I stayed away because it weren't cheerful—and that's why I ought to have come. I—(*looking out left window*)—I've never liked this place. Maybe it's because it's down in a hollow and you don't see the road. I dunno what it is, but it's a lonesome place and always was. I wish I had come over to see Minnie Foster sometimes. I can see now—(*Shakes her head.*)

MRS. PETERS (*left of table and above it*): Well, you mustn't reproach yourself, Mrs. Hale. Somehow we just don't see how it is with other folks until—something turns up.

MRS. HALE: Not having children makes less work—but it makes a quiet house, and Wright out to work all day, and no company when he did come in. (*Turning from window.*) Did you know John Wright, Mrs. Peters?

MRS. PETERS: Not to know him; I've seen him in town. They say he was a good man.

MRS. HALE: Yes—good; he didn't drink, and kept his word as well as most, I guess, and paid his debts. But he was a hard man, Mrs. Peters. Just to pass the time of day with him—(*Shivers.*) Like a raw wind that gets to the bone. (*Pauses, her eye falling on the cage.*) I should think she would 'a' wanted a bird. But what do you suppose went with it?

MRS. PETERS: I don't know, unless it got sick and died. (*She reaches over and swings the broken door, swings it again, both women watch it.*)

MRS. HALE: You weren't raised round here, were you? (*Mrs. Peters shakes her head.*) You didn't know—her?

MRS. PETERS: Not till they brought her yesterday.

MRS. HALE: She—come to think of it, she was kind of like a bird herself—real sweet and pretty, but kind of timid and—fluttery. How—she—did—change. (*Silence: then as if struck by a happy thought and relieved to get back to everyday things. Crosses right above Mrs. Peters to cupboard, replaces small chair used to stand on to its original place down right.*) Tell you what, Mrs. Peters, why don't you take the quilt in with you? It might take up her mind.

MRS. PETERS: Why, I think that's a real nice idea, Mrs. Hale. There couldn't possibly be any objection to it could there? Now, just what would I take? I wonder if her patches are in here—and her things. (*They look in the sewing basket.*)

MRS. HALE (*crosses to right of table*): Here's some red. I expect this has got sewing things in it. (*Brings out a fancy box.*) What a pretty box. Looks like something somebody would give you. Maybe her scissors are in here. (*Opens box. Suddenly puts her hand to her nose.*) Why———(*Mrs. Peters bends nearer, then turns her face away.*) There's something wrapped up in this piece of silk.

MRS. PETERS: Why, this isn't her scissors.

MRS. HALE (*lifting the silk*): Oh, Mrs. Peters—it's———(*Mrs. Peters bends closer.*)

MRS. PETERS: It's the bird.

MRS. HALE: But, Mrs. Peters—look at it! Its neck! Look at its neck! It's all—other side *to.*

MRS. PETERS: Somebody—wrung—its—neck. (*Their eyes meet. A look of growing comprehension, of horror. Steps are heard outside. Mrs. Hale slips box under quilt pieces, and sinks into her chair. Enter Sheriff and County Attorney. Mrs. Peters steps down left and stands looking out of window.*)

COUNTY ATTORNEY (*as one turning from serious things to little pleasantries*): Well, ladies, have you decided whether she was going to quilt it or knot it? (*Crosses to center above table.*)

MRS. PETERS: We think she was going to—knot it. (*Sheriff crosses to right of stove, lifts stove lid, and glances at fire, then stands warming hands at stove.*)

COUNTY ATTORNEY: Well, that's interesting, I'm sure. (*Seeing the bird-cage.*) Has the bird flown?

MRS. HALE (*putting more quilt pieces over the box*): We think the—cat got it.

COUNTY ATTORNEY (*preoccupied*): Is there a cat? (*Mrs. Hale glances in a quick covert way at Mrs. Peters.*)

MRS. PETERS (*turning from window takes a step in*): Well, not *now.* They're superstitious, you know. They leave.

COUNTY ATTORNEY (*to Sheriff Peters, continuing an interrupted conversation*): No sign at all of anyone having come from the outside. Their own rope. Now let's go up again and go over it piece by piece. (*They start upstairs.*) It would have to have been someone who knew just the ———(*Mrs. Peters sits down left of table. The two women sit there not looking at one another, but as if peering into something and at the same time holding back. When they talk now it is in the manner of feeling their way over strange ground, as if afraid of what they are saying, but as if they cannot help saying it.*)

MRS. HALE (*hesistatively and in hushed voice*): She liked the bird. She was going to bury it in that pretty box.

MRS. PETERS (*in a whisper*): When I was a girl — my kitten — there was a boy took a hatchet, and before my eyes — and before I could get there —— (*Covers her face an instant.*) If they hadn't held me back I would have — (*catches herself, looks upstairs where steps are heard, falters weakly*) — hurt him.

MRS. HALE (*with a slow look around her*): I wonder how it would seem never to have had any children around. (*Pause.*) No, Wright wouldn't like the bird — a thing that sang. She used to sing. He killed that, too.

MRS. PETERS (*moving uneasily*): We don't know who killed the bird.

MRS. HALE: I knew John Wright.

MRS. PETERS: It was an awful thing was done in this house that night, Mrs. Hale. Killing a man while he slept, slipping a rope around his neck that choked the life out of him.

MRS. HALE: His neck. Choked the life out of him. (*Her hand goes out and rests on the bird-cage.*)

MRS. PETERS (*with rising voice*): We don't know who killed him. We don't know.

MRS. HALE (*her own feelings not interrupted*): If there'd been years and years of nothing, then a bird to sing to you, it would be awful — still, after the bird was still.

MRS. PETERS (*something within her speaking*): I know what stillness is. When we homesteaded in Dakota, and my first baby died — after he was two years old, and me with no other then ——

MRS. HALE (*moving*): How soon do you suppose they'll be through looking for the evidence?

MRS. PETERS: I know what stillness is. (*Pulling herself back.*) The law has got to punish crimes, Mrs. Hale.

MRS. HALE (*not as if answering that*): I wish you'd seen Minnie Foster when she wore a white dress with blue ribbons and stood up there in the choir and sang. (*A look around the room.*) Oh, I *wish* I'd come over here once in a while! That was a crime! That was a crime! Who's going to punish that?

MRS. PETERS (*looking upstairs*): We mustn't — take on.

MRS. HALE: I might have known she needed help! I know how things can be — for women. I tell you, it's queer, Mrs. Peters. We live close together and we live far apart. We all go through the same things — it's all just a different kind of the same thing. (*Brushes her eyes, noticing the jar of fruit, reaches out for it.*) If I was you I wouldn't tell her her fruit was gone. Tell her it *ain't*. Tell her it's all right. Take this in to prove it to her. She — she may never know whether it was broke or not.

MRS. PETERS (*takes the jar, looks about for something to wrap it in; takes petti-coat from the clothes brought from the other room, very nervously begins winding this around the jar. In a false voice*): My, it's a good thing the men couldn't hear us. Wouldn't they just laugh! Getting all stirred up over a little thing like a—dead canary. As if that could have anything to do with—with—wouldn't they *laugh!* (*The men are heard coming downstairs.*)

MRS. HALE (*under her breath*): Maybe they would—maybe they wouldn't.

COUNTY ATTORNEY: No, Peters, it's all perfectly clear except a reason for doing it. But you know juries when it comes to women. If there was some definite thing. (*Crosses slowly to above table. Sheriff crosses down right. Mrs. Hale and Mrs. Peters remain seated at either side of table.*) Something to show—something to make a story about—a thing that would connect up with this strange way of doing it———(*The women's eyes meet for an instant. Enter Hale from outer door.*)

HALE (*remaining by door*): Well, I've got the team around. Pretty cold out there.

COUNTY ATTORNEY: I'm going to stay awhile by myself. (*To the Sheriff.*) You can send Frank out for me, can't you? I want to go over every-thing. I'm not satisfied that we can't do better.

SHERIFF: Do you want to see what Mrs. Peters is going to take in? (*The Lawyer picks up the apron, laughs.*)

COUNTY ATTORNEY: Oh, I guess they're not very dangerous things the ladies have picked out. (*Moves a few things about, disturbing the quilt pieces which cover the box. Steps back.*) No, Mrs. Peters doesn't need supervising. For that matter a sheriff's wife is married to the law. Ever think of it that way, Mrs. Peters?

MRS. PETERS: Not—just that way.

SHERIFF (*chuckling*): Married to the law. (*Moves to down right door to the other room.*) I just want you to come in here a minute, George. We ought to take a look at these windows.

COUNTY ATTORNEY (*scoffingly*): Oh, windows!

SHERIFF: We'll be right out, Mr. Hale. (*Hale goes outside. The Sheriff follows the County Attorney into the room. Then Mrs. Hale rises, hands tight together, looking intensely at Mrs. Peters, whose eyes make a slow turn, finally meeting Mrs. Hale's. A moment Mrs. Hale holds her, then her own eyes point the way to where the box is concealed. Suddenly Mrs. Peters throws back quilt pieces and tries to put the box in the bag she is carrying. It is too big. She opens box, starts to take bird out, cannot touch it, goes to pieces, stands there helpless. Sound of a knob turning in the other room. Mrs. Hale snatches the box and puts it in the pocket of her big coat. Enter County Attorney and Sheriff, who remains down right.*)

COUNTY ATTORNEY (*crosses to up left door facetiously*): Well, Henry, at least we found out that she was not going to quilt it. She was going to— what is it you call it, ladies?

MRS. HALE (*standing center below table facing front, her hand against her pocket*): We call it—knot it, Mr. Henderson.

1916

The Glass Menagerie

TENNESSEE WILLIAMS [1911–1983]

nobody, not even the rain, has such small hands — E. E. CUMMINGS

Production Notes by Tennessee Williams

Being a "memory play," *The Glass Menagerie* can be presented with unusual freedom of convention. Because of its considerably delicate or tenuous material, atmospheric touches and subtleties of direction play a particularly important part. Expressionism and all other unconventional techniques in drama have only one valid aim, and this is a closer approach to truth. When a play employs unconventional techniques, it is not, or certainly shouldn't be, trying to escape its responsibility of dealing with reality, or interpreting experience, but is actually or should be attempting to find a closer approach, or more penetrating and vivid expression of things as they are. The straight realistic play with its genuine frigidaire and authentic ice cubes, its characters that speak exactly as its audience speaks, corresponds to the academic landscape and has the same virtue of a photographic likeness. Everyone should know nowadays the unimportance of the photographic in art: that truth, life, or reality is an organic thing which the poetic imagination can represent or suggest, in essence, only through transformation, through changing into other forms than those which were merely present in appearance.

These remarks are not meant as a preface only to this particular play. They have to do with a conception of a new, plastic theatre which must take the place of the exhausted theatre of realistic conventions if the theatre is to resume vitality as a part of our culture.

The Screen Device: There is *only one important difference between the original and acting version of the play* and that is the *omission* in the latter of the device which I tentatively included in my *original* script. This device was the use of a screen on which were projected magic-lantern slides bearing images or titles. I do not regret the omission of this device from the present Broadway production. The extraordinary power of Miss Taylor's performance made it suitable to have the utmost simplicity in the physical production. But I think it may be interesting to some readers to see how this device was conceived. So I am putting it into the published manuscript. These images and legends, projected from behind, were cast on a section of wall between the front-room and dining-room areas, which should be indistin-guishable from the rest when not in use.

The purpose of this will probably be apparent. It is to give accent to cer-tain values in each scene. Each scene contains a particular point (or several) which is structurally the most important. In an episodic play, such as this, the basic structure or narrative line may be obscured from the audience; the effect may seem fragmentary rather than architectural. This may not be the fault of the play so much as a lack of attention in the audience. The legend or image upon the screen will strengthen the effect of what is merely allusion in the writing and allow the primary point to be made more simply and lightly than if the entire responsibility were on the spoken lines. Aside from this structural value, I think the screen will have a definite emotional appeal, less definable but just as important. An imaginative producer or director may invent many other uses for this device than those indicated in the present script. In fact the possibilities of the device seem much larger to me than the instance of this play can possibly utilize.

The Music: Another extra-literary accent in this play is provided by the use of music. A single recurring tune, "The Glass Menagerie," is used to give emotional emphasis to suitable passages. This tune is like circus music, not when you are on the grounds or in the immediate vicinity of the parade, but when you are at some distance and very likely thinking of something else. It seems under those circumstances to continue almost interminably and it weaves in and out of your preoccupied consciousness; then it is the lightest, most delicate music in the world and perhaps the saddest. It expresses the surface vivacity of life with the underlying strain of immutable and inex-pressible sorrow. When you look at a piece of delicately spun glass you think of two things: how beautiful it is and how easily it can be broken. Both of those ideas should be woven into the recurring tune, which dips in and out of the play as if it were carried on a wind that changes. It serves as a thread of connection and allusion between the narrator with his separate point in time and space and the subject of his story. Between each episode it returns as reference to the emotion, nostalgia, which is the first condition of the play. It is primarily Laura's music and therefore comes out most clearly when the play focuses upon her and the lovely fragility of glass which is her image.

The Lighting: The lighting in the play is not realistic. In keeping with the atmosphere of memory, the stage is dim. Shafts of light are focused on selected areas or actors, sometimes in contradistinction to what is the appar-ent center. For instance, in the quarrel scene between Tom and Amanda, in which Laura has no active part, the clearest pool of light is on her figure. This is also true of the supper scene, when her silent figure on the sofa should remain the visual center. The light upon Laura should be distinct from the others, having a peculiar pristine clarity such as light used in early religious portraits of female saints or madonnas. A certain correspondence to light in religious paintings, such as El Greco's, where the figures are radiant in atmosphere that is relatively dusky, could be effectively used throughout the play. (It will also permit a more effective use of the screen.) A free, imaginative use of light can be of enormous value in giving a mobile, plastic quality to plays of a more or less static nature.

Characters

AMANDA WINGFIELD, *the mother. A little woman of great but confused vitality clinging frantically to another time and place. Her characterization must be carefully created, not copied from type. She is not paranoiac, but her life is paranoia. There is much to admire in Amanda, and as much to love and pity as there is to laugh at. Certainly she has endurance and a kind of heroism, and though her foolishness makes her unwittingly cruel at times, there is tenderness in her slight person.*

LAURA WINGFIELD, *her daughter. Amanda, having failed to establish contact with reality, continues to live vitally in her illusions, but Laura's situation is even graver. A childhood illness has left her crippled, one leg slightly shorter than the other, and held in a brace. This defect need not be more than suggested on the stage. Stemming from this, Laura's separation increases till she is like a piece of her own glass collection, too exquisitely fragile to move from the shelf.*

TOM WINGFIELD, *her son. And the narrator of the play. A poet with a job in a warehouse. His nature is not remorseless, but to escape from a trap he has to act without pity.*

JIM O'CONNOR, *the gentleman caller. A nice, ordinary, young man.*

Scene: *An alley in St. Louis.*
Part I: *Preparation for a Gentleman Caller.*
Part II: *The Gentleman Calls.*
Time: *Now and the Past.*

SCENE 1

(The Wingfield apartment is in the rear of the building, one of those vast hive-like conglomerations of cellular living-units that flower as warty growths in over-crowded urban centers of lower middle-class population and are symptomatic of the impulse of this largest and fundamentally enslaved section of American society to avoid fluidity and differentiation and to exist and function as one interfused mass of automatism.)

(*The apartment faces an alley and is entered by a fire escape, a structure whose name is a touch of accidental poetic truth, for all of these huge buildings are always burning with the slow and implacable fires of human desperation. The fire escape is included in the set—that is, the landing of it and steps descending from it.*)

(*The scene is memory and is therefore nonrealistic. Memory takes a lot of poetic license. It omits some details; others are exaggerated, according to the emotional value of the articles it touches, for memory is seated predominantly in the heart. The interior is therefore rather dim and poetic.*)

(*At the rise of the curtain, the audience is faced with the dark, grim rear wall of the Wingfield tenement. This building, which runs parallel to the footlights, is flanked on both sides by dark, narrow alleys which run into murky canyons of tangled clotheslines, garbage cans, and the sinister latticework of neighboring fire escapes. It is up and down these side alleys that exterior entrances and exits are made, during the play. At the end of Tom's opening commentary, the dark tenement wall slowly reveals* [*by means of a transparency*] *the interior of the ground floor Wingfield apartment.*)

(*Downstage is the living room, which also serves as a sleeping room for Laura, the sofa unfolding to make her bed. Upstage, center, and divided by a wide arch or second proscenium with transparent faded portieres* [*or second curtain*]*, is the dining room. In an old-fashioned what-not in the living room are seen scores of transparent glass animals. A blown-up photograph of the father hangs on the wall of the living room, facing the audience, to the left of the archway. It is the face of a very handsome young man in a doughboy's First World War cap. He is gallantly smiling, ineluctably smiling, as if to say, "I will be smiling forever."*)

(*The audience hears and sees the opening scene in the dining room through both the transparent fourth wall of the building and the transparent gauze portieres of the dining-room arch. It is during this revealing scene that the fourth wall slowly ascends, out of sight. This transparent exterior wall is not brought down again until the very end of the play, during Tom's final speech.*)

(*The narrator is an undisguised convention of the play. He takes whatever license with dramatic convention as is convenient to his purposes.*)

(*Tom enters dressed as a merchant sailor from alley, stage left, and strolls across the front of the stage to the fire escape. There he stops and lights a cigarette. He addresses the audience.*)

Tom: Yes, I have tricks in my pocket, I have things up my sleeve. But I am the opposite of a stage magician. He gives you illusion that has the appearance of truth. I give you truth in the pleasant disguise of illusion. To begin with, I turn back time. I reverse it to that quaint period, the thirties, when the huge middle class of America was matriculating in a school for the blind. Their eyes had failed them, or they had failed their eyes, and so they were having their fingers pressed forcibly down on the fiery Braille alphabet of a dissolving economy. In Spain there was revolution. Here there was only shouting and confusion. In Spain there was Guernica. Here there were disturbances of labor, sometimes pretty violent, in otherwise peaceful cities such as Chicago, Cleveland, Saint Louis. . . . This is the social background of the play.

(*Music.*)

The play is memory. Being a memory play, it is dimly lighted, it is sentimental, it is not realistic. In memory everything seems to happen to music. That explains the fiddle in the wings. I am the narrator of the play, and also a character in it. The other characters are my mother, Amanda, my sister, Laura, and a gentleman caller who appears in the final scenes. He is the most realistic character in the play, being an emissary from a world of reality that we were somehow set apart from. But since I have a poet's weakness for symbols, I am using this character also as a symbol; he is the long delayed but always expected something that we live for. There is a fifth character in the play who doesn't appear except in this larger-than-life photograph over the mantel. This is our father who left us a long time ago. He was a telephone man who fell in love with long distances; he gave up his job with the telephone company and skipped the light fantastic out of town . . . The last we heard of him was a picture postcard from Mazatlan, on the Pacific coast of Mexico, containing a message of two words— "Hello—Good-bye!" and no address. I think the rest of the play will explain itself. . . .

(*Amanda's voice becomes audible through the portieres.*)
    (*Legend on Screen: "Où Sont les Neiges."*)°
    (*He divides the portieres and enters the upstage area.*)
    (*Amanda and Laura are seated at a drop-leaf table. Eating is indicated by gestures without food or utensils. Amanda faces the audience. Tom and Laura are seated in profile.*)
    (*The interior has lit up softly and through the scrim we see Amanda and Laura seated at the table in the upstage area.*)

AMANDA (*calling*): Tom?
TOM: Yes, Mother.
AMANDA: We can't say grace until you come to the table!
TOM: Coming, Mother. (*He bows slightly and withdraws, reappearing a few moments later in his place at the table.*)
AMANDA (*to her son*): Honey, don't *push* with your *fingers*. If you have to push with something, the thing to push with is a crust of bread. And

"*Où sont les neiges*": "Où sont les neiges d'antan?" ("Where are the snows of yesteryear?") is a line from a poem by fifteenth-century French poet François Villon.

chew—chew! Animals have sections in their stomachs which enable them to digest food without mastication, but human beings are supposed to chew their food before they swallow it down. Eat food leisurely, son, and really enjoy it. A well-cooked meal has lots of delicate flavors that have to be held in the mouth for appreciation. So chew your food and give your salivary glands a chance to function!

(*Tom deliberately lays his imaginary fork down and pushes his chair back from the table.*)

TOM: I haven't enjoyed one bite of this dinner because of your constant directions on how to eat it. It's you that makes me rush through meals with your hawk-like attention to every bite I take. Sickening—spoils my appetite—all this discussion of animals' secretion—salivary glands—mastication!

AMANDA (*lightly*): Temperament like a Metropolitan° star! (*He rises and crosses downstage.*) You're not excused from the table.

TOM: I'm getting a cigarette.

AMANDA: You smoke too much.

(*Laura rises.*)

LAURA: I'll bring in the blancmange.

(*He remains standing with his cigarette by the portieres during the following.*)

AMANDA (*rising*): No, sister, no, sister—you be the lady this time and I'll be the darky.

LAURA: I'm already up.

AMANDA: Resume your seat, little sister—I want you to stay fresh and pretty—for gentlemen callers!

LAURA: I'm not expecting any gentlemen callers.

AMANDA (*crossing out to kitchenette. Airily*): Sometimes they come when they are least expected! Why, I remember one Sunday afternoon in Blue Mountain—(*Enters kitchenette.*)

TOM: I know what's coming!

LAURA: Yes. But let her tell it.

TOM: Again?

LAURA: She loves to tell it.

(*Amanda returns with bowl of dessert.*)

AMANDA: One Sunday afternoon in Blue Mountain—your mother received—*seventeen!*—gentlemen callers! Why, sometimes there weren't chairs enough to accommodate them all. We had to send the nigger over to bring in folding chairs from the parish house.

Metropolitan: Metropolitan Opera.

TOM (*remaining at portieres*): How did you entertain those gentlemen callers?

AMANDA: I understood the art of conversation!

TOM: I bet you could talk.

AMANDA: Girls in those days *knew* how to talk, I can tell you.

TOM: Yes?

(*Image: Amanda as a girl on a porch greeting callers.*)

AMANDA: They knew how to entertain their gentlemen callers. It wasn't enough for a girl to be possessed of a pretty face and a graceful figure—although I wasn't slighted in either respect. She also needed to have a nimble wit and a tongue to meet all occasions.

TOM: What did you talk about?

AMANDA: Things of importance going on in the world! Never anything coarse or common or vulgar. (*She addresses Tom as though he were seated in the vacant chair at the table though he remains by portieres. He plays this scene as though he held the book.*) My callers were gentlemen—all! Among my callers were some of the most prominent young planters of the Mississippi Delta—planters and sons of planters!

(*Tom motions for music and a spot of light on Amanda.*)
(*Her eyes lift, her face glows, her voice becomes rich and elegiac.*)
(*Screen legend: "Où Sont les Neiges."*)

There was young Champ Laughlin who later became vice-president of the Delta Planters Bank. Hadley Stevenson who was drowned in Moon Lake and left his widow one hundred and fifty thousand in Government bonds. There were the Cutrere brothers, Wesley and Bates. Bates was one of my bright particular beaux! He got in a quarrel with that wild Wainright boy. They shot it out on the floor of Moon Lake Casino. Bates was shot through the stomach. Died in the ambulance on his way to Memphis. His widow was also well-provided for, came into eight or ten thousand acres, that's all. She married him on the rebound—never loved her—carried my picture on him the night he died! And there was that boy that every girl in the Delta had set her cap for! That beautiful, brilliant young Fitzhugh boy from Greene County!

TOM: What did he leave his widow?

AMANDA: He never married! Gracious, you talk as though all of my old admirers had turned up their toes to the daisies!

TOM: Isn't this the first you mentioned that still survives?

AMANDA: That Fitzhugh boy went North and made a fortune—came to be known as the Wolf of Wall Street! He had the Midas touch, whatever he touched turned to gold! And I could have been Mrs. Duncan J. Fitzhugh, mind you! But—I picked your *father!*

LAURA (*rising*): Mother, let me clear the table.

AMANDA: No, dear, you go in front and study your typewriter chart. Or practice your shorthand a little. Stay fresh and pretty!—It's almost time for our gentlemen callers to start arriving. (*She flounces girlishly toward the kitchenette.*) How many do you suppose we're going to entertain this afternoon?

(*Tom throws down the paper and jumps up with a groan.*)

LAURA (*alone in the dining room*): I don't believe we're going to receive any, Mother.

AMANDA (*reappearing, airily*): What? No one—not one? You must be joking! (*Laura nervously echoes her laugh. She slips in a fugitive manner through the half-open portieres and draws them gently behind her. A shaft of very clear light is thrown on her face against the faded tapestry of the curtains. Music: "The Glass Menagerie" under faintly. Lightly.*) Not one gentleman caller? It can't be true! There must be a flood, there must have been a tornado!

LAURA: It isn't a flood, it's not a tornado, Mother. I'm just not popular like you were in Blue Mountain. . . . (*Tom utters another groan. Laura glances at him with a faint, apologetic smile. Her voice catching a little.*) Mother's afraid I'm going to be an old maid.

(*The scene dims out with "Glass Menagerie" music.*)

SCENE 2

(*"Laura, Haven't You Ever Liked Some Boy?"*)
  (*On the dark stage the screen is lighted with the image of blue roses.*)
  (*Gradually Laura's figure becomes apparent and the screen goes out.*)
  (*The music subsides.*)
  (*Laura is seated in the delicate ivory chair at the small clawfoot table.*)
  (*She wears a dress of soft violet material for a kimono—her hair tied back from her forehead with a ribbon.*)
  (*She is washing and polishing her collection of glass.*)
  (*Amanda appears on the fire escape steps. At the sound of her ascent, Laura catches her breath, thrusts the bowl of ornaments away and seats herself stiffly before the diagram of the typewriter keyboard as though it held her spellbound. Something has happened to Amanda. It is written in her face as she climbs to the landing: a look that is grim and hopeless and a little absurd.*)
  (*She has on one of those cheap or imitation velvety-looking cloth coats with imitation fur collar. Her hat is five or six years old, one of those dreadful cloche hats that were worn in the late twenties, and she is clasping an enormous black*

patent-leather pocketbook with nickel clasp and initials. This is her full-dress outfit, the one she usually wears to the D.A.R.°)

(*Before entering she looks through the door.*)

(*She purses her lips, opens her eyes wide, rolls them upward and shakes her head.*)

(*Then she slowly lets herself in the door. Seeing her mother's expression Laura touches her lips with a nervous gesture.*)

LAURA: Hello, Mother, I was—(*She makes a nervous gesture toward the chart on the wall. Amanda leans against the shut door and stares at Laura with a martyred look.*)

AMANDA: Deception? Deception? (*She slowly removes her hat and gloves, continuing the swift suffering stare. She lets the hat and gloves fall on the floor—a bit of acting.*)

LAURA (*shakily*): How was the D.A.R. meeting? (*Amanda slowly opens her purse and removes a dainty white handkerchief which she shakes out delicately and delicately touches to her lips and nostrils.*) Didn't you go to the D.A.R. meeting, Mother?

AMANDA (*faintly, almost inaudibly*):—No.—No. (*Then more forcibly*). I did not have the strength—to go to the D.A.R. In fact, I did not have the courage! I wanted to find a hole in the ground and hide myself in it forever! (*She crosses slowly to the wall and removes the diagram of the typewriter keyboard. She holds it in front of her for a second, staring at it sweetly and sorrowfully—then bites her lips and tears it in two pieces.*)

LAURA (*faintly*): Why did you do that, Mother? (*Amanda repeats the same procedure with the chart of the Gregg Alphabet.*) Why are you—

AMANDA: Why? Why? How old are you, Laura?

LAURA: Mother, you know my age.

AMANDA: I thought that you were an adult; it seems that I was mistaken. (*She crosses slowly to the sofa and sinks down and stares at Laura.*)

LAURA: Please don't stare at me, Mother.

(*Amanda closes her eyes and lowers her head. Count ten.*)

AMANDA: What are we going to do, what is going to become of us, what is the future?

(*Count ten.*)

LAURA: Has something happened, Mother? (*Amanda draws a long breath and takes out the handkerchief again. Dabbing process.*) Mother, has—something happened?

D.A.R.: Daughters of the American Revolution is a patriotic organization for women whose ancestors were part of the American War of Independence.

AMANDA: I'll be all right in a minute. I'm just bewildered — (*Count five.*) — by life. . . .

LAURA: Mother, I wish that you would tell me what's happened.

AMANDA: As you know, I was supposed to be inducted into my office at the D.A.R. this afternoon. (*Image: a swarm of typewriters.*) But I stopped off at Rubicam's Business College to speak to your teachers about your having a cold and ask them what progress they thought you were making down there.

LAURA: Oh. . . .

AMANDA: I went to the typing instructor and introduced myself as your mother. She didn't know who you were. Wingfield, she said. We don't have any such student enrolled at the school! I assured her she did, that you had been going to classes since early in January. "I wonder," she said, "if you could be talking about that terribly shy little girl who dropped out of school after only a few days' attendance?" "No," I said, "Laura, my daughter, has been going to school every day for the past six weeks!" "Excuse me," she said. She took the attendance book out and there was your name, unmistakably printed, and all the dates you were absent until they decided that you had dropped out of school. I still said, "No, there must have been some mistake! There must have been some mix-up in the records!" And she said, "No—I remember her perfectly now. Her hands shook so that she couldn't hit the right keys! The first time we gave a speed test, she broke down completely — was sick at the stomach and almost had to be carried into the washroom! After that morning she never showed up any more. We phoned the house but never got any answer"—while I was working at Famous and Barr, I suppose, demonstrating those—Oh! I felt so weak I could barely keep on my feet. I had to sit down while they got me a glass of water! Fifty dollars' tuition, all of our plans—my hopes and ambitions for you—just gone up the spout, just gone up the spout like that. (*Laura draws a long breath and gets awkwardly to her feet. She crosses to the victrola and winds it up.*) What are you doing?

LAURA: Oh! (*She releases the handle and returns to her seat.*)

AMANDA: Laura, where have you been going when you've gone out pretending that you were going to business college?

LAURA: I've just been going out walking.

AMANDA: That's not true.

LAURA: It is. I just went walking.

AMANDA: Walking? Walking? In winter? Deliberately courting pneumonia in that light coat? Where did you walk to, Laura?

LAURA: All sorts of places—mostly in the park.

AMANDA: Even after you'd started catching that cold?

LAURA: It was the lesser of two evils, Mother. (*Image: winter scene in park.*)
I couldn't go back up. I—threw up—on the floor!

AMANDA: From half past seven till after five every day you mean to tell
me you walked around in the park, because you wanted to make me
think that you were still going to Rubicam's Business College?

LAURA: It wasn't as bad as it sounds. I went inside places to get warmed up.

AMANDA: Inside where?

LAURA: I went in the art museum and the bird houses at the Zoo. I visited the penguins every day! Sometimes I did without lunch and went
to the movies. Lately I've been spending most of my afternoons in the
Jewel-box, that big glass house where they raise the tropical flowers.

AMANDA: You did all this to deceive me, just for the deception? (*Laura
looks down.*) Why?

LAURA: Mother, when you're disappointed, you get that awful suffering
look on your face, like the picture of Jesus' mother in the museum!

AMANDA: Hush!

LAURA: I couldn't face it.

(*Pause. A whisper of strings.*)
(*Legend: "The Crust of Humility."*)

AMANDA (*hopelessly fingering the huge pocketbook*): So what are we going to
do the rest of our lives? Stay home and watch the parades go by?
Amuse ourselves with the glass menagerie, darling? Eternally play
those worn-out phonograph records your father left as a painful
reminder of him? We won't have a business career—we've given that
up because it gave us nervous indigestion! (*Laughs wearily.*) What is
there left but dependency all our lives? I know so well what becomes of
unmarried women who aren't prepared to occupy a position. I've seen
such pitiful cases in the South—barely tolerated spinsters living upon
the grudging patronage of sister's husband or brother's wife!—stuck
away in some little mousetrap of a room—encouraged by one in-law to
visit another—little birdlike women without any nest—eating the
crust of humility all their life! Is that the future that we've mapped out
for ourselves? I swear it's the only alternative I can think of! It isn't a
very pleasant alternative, is it? Of course—some girls do *marry*. (*Laura
twists her hands nervously.*) Haven't you ever liked some boy?

LAURA: Yes. I liked one once. (*Rises.*) I came across his picture a while ago.

AMANDA (*with some interest*): He gave you his picture?

LAURA: No, it's in the yearbook.

AMANDA (*disappointed*): Oh—a high-school boy.

(*Screen image: Jim as high school hero bearing a silver cup.*)

LAURA: Yes. His name was Jim. (*Laura lifts the heavy annual from the claw-foot table.*) Here he is in *The Pirates of Penzance.*

AMANDA (*absently*): The what?

LAURA: The operetta the senior class put on. He had a wonderful voice and we sat across the aisle from each other Mondays, Wednesdays, and Fridays in the Aud. Here he is with the silver cup for debating! See his grin?

AMANDA (*absently*): He must have had a jolly disposition.

LAURA: He used to call me—Blue Roses.

(*Image: blue roses.*)

AMANDA: Why did he call you such a name as that?

LAURA: When I had that attack of pleurosis—he asked me what was the matter when I came back. I said pleurosis—he thought that I said Blue Roses! So that's what he always called me after that. Whenever he saw me, he'd holler, "Hello, Blue Roses!" I didn't care for the girl that he went out with. Emily Meisenbach. Emily was the best-dressed girl at Soldan. She never struck me, though, as being sincere . . . It says in the Personal Section—they're engaged. That's—six years ago! They must be married by now.

AMANDA: Girls that aren't cut out for business careers usually wind up married to some nice man. (*Gets up with a spark of revival.*) Sister, that's what you'll do!

(*Laura utters a startled, doubtful laugh. She reaches quickly for a piece of glass.*)

LAURA: But, Mother—

AMANDA: Yes? (*Crossing to photograph.*)

LAURA (*in a tone of frightened apology*): I'm—crippled!

(*Image: screen.*)

AMANDA: Nonsense! Laura, I've told you never, never to use that word. Why, you're not crippled, you just have a little defect—hardly notice-able, even! When people have some slight disadvantage like that, they cultivate other things to make up for it—develop charm—and vivac-ity—and—*charm*! That's all you have to do! (*She turns again to the pho-tograph.*) One thing your father had *plenty of*—was *charm!*

(*Tom motions to the fiddle in the wings.*)
(*The scene fades out with music.*)

SCENE 3

(*Legend on screen: "After the Fiasco—"*)
(*Tom speaks from the fire escape landing.*)

TOM: After the fiasco at Rubicam's Business College, the idea of getting a
gentleman caller for Laura began to play a more important part in
Mother's calculations. It became an obsession. Like some archetype of
the universal unconscious, the image of the gentleman caller haunted
our small apartment.... (*Image: young man at door with flowers.*) An
evening at home rarely passed without some allusion to this image, this
specter, this hope.... Even when he wasn't mentioned, his presence
hung in Mother's preoccupied look and in my sister's frightened, apologetic manner—hung like a sentence passed upon the Wingfields!
Mother was a woman of action as well as words. She began to take logi-
cal steps in the planned direction. Late that winter and in the early
spring—realizing that extra money would be needed to properly feather
the nest and plume the bird—she conducted a vigorous campaign on
the telephone, roping in subscribers to one of those magazines for
matrons called *The Home-maker's Companion,* the type of journal that
features the serialized sublimations of ladies of letters who think in
terms of delicate cuplike breasts, slim, tapering waists, rich, creamy
thighs, eyes like wood smoke in autumn, fingers that soothe and caress
like strains of music, bodies as powerful as Etruscan sculpture.

(*Screen image: glamor magazine cover.*)
(*Amanda enters with phone on long extension cord. She is spotted in the dim
stage.*)

AMANDA: Ida Scott? This is Amanda Wingfield! We *missed* you at the
D.A.R. last Monday! I said to myself: She's probably suffering with
that sinus condition! How is that sinus condition? Horrors! Heaven
have mercy!—You're a Christian martyr, yes, that's what you are, a
Christian martyr! Well I just now happened to notice that your subscription to the *Companion's* about to expire! Yes, it expires with the
next issue, honey!—just when that wonderful new serial by Bessie
Mae Hopper is getting off to such an exciting start. Oh, honey, it's
something that you can't miss! You remember how *Gone with the
Wind* took everybody by storm? You simply couldn't go out if you
hadn't read it. All everybody *talked* was Scarlett O'Hara. Well, this is
a book that critics already compare to *Gone with the Wind.* It's the
Gone with the Wind of the post–World War generation!—What?—
Burning?—Oh, honey, don't let them burn, go take a look in the oven
and I'll hold the wire! Heavens—I think she's hung up!

(*Dim out.*)

(*Legend on screen: "You Think I'm in Love with Continental Shoemakers?"*)

(*Before the stage is lighted, the violent voices of Tom and Amanda are heard.*)

(*They are quarreling behind the portieres. In front of them stands Laura with clenched hands and panicky expression.*)

(*A clear pool of light on her figure throughout this scene.*)

Tom: What in Christ's name am I—

Amanda (*shrilly*): Don't you use that—

Tom: Supposed to do!

Amanda: Expression! Not in my—

Tom: Ohhh!

Amanda: Presence! Have you gone out of your senses?

Tom: I have, that's true, *driven* out!

Amanda: What is the matter with you, you—big—big—IDIOT!

Tom: Look—I've got *no thing*, no single thing—

Amanda: Lower your voice!

Tom: In my life here that I can call my OWN! Everything is—

Amanda: Stop that shouting!

Tom: Yesterday you confiscated my books! You had the nerve to—

Amanda: I took that horrible novel back to the library—yes! That hideous book by that insane Mr. Lawrence. (*Tom laughs wildly.*) I cannot control the output of diseased minds or people who cater to them—(*Tom laughs still more wildly.*) BUT I WON'T ALLOW SUCH FILTH BROUGHT INTO MY HOUSE! No, no, no, no, no!

Tom: House, house! Who pays rent on it, who makes a slave of himself to—

Amanda (*fairly screeching*): Don't you DARE to—

Tom: No, no, *I* mustn't say things! *I've* got to just—

Amanda: Let me tell you—

Tom: I don't want to hear any more! (*He tears the portieres open. The upstage area is lit with a turgid smoky red glow.*)

(*Amanda's hair is in metal curlers and she wears a very old bathrobe, much too large for her slight figure, a relic of the faithless Mr. Wingfield.*)

(*An upright typewriter and a wild disarray of manuscripts are on the dropleaf table. The quarrel was probably precipitated by Amanda's interruption of his creative labor. A chair lying overthrown on the floor.*)

(*Their gesticulating shadows are cast on the ceiling by the fiery glow.*)

Amanda: You *will* hear more, you—

Tom: No, I won't hear more, I'm going out!

Amanda: You come right back in—

Tom: Out, out out! Because I'm—

Amanda: Come back here, Tom Wingfield! I'm not through talking to you!

TOM: Oh, go—

LAURA (*desperately*): Tom!

AMANDA: You're going to listen, and no more insolence from you! I'm at the end of my patience! (*He comes back toward her.*)

TOM: What do you think I'm at? Aren't I supposed to have any patience to reach the end of, Mother? I know, I know. It seems unimportant to you, what I'm *doing*—what I *want* to do—having a little *difference* between them! You don't think that—

AMANDA: I think you've been doing things that you're ashamed of. That's why you act like this. I don't believe that you go every night to the movies. Nobody goes to the movies night after night. Nobody in their right minds goes to the movies as often as you pretend to. People don't go to the movies at nearly midnight, and movies don't let out at two A.M. Come in stumbling. Muttering to yourself like a maniac! You get three hours' sleep and then go to work. Oh, I can picture the way you're doing down there. Moping, doping, because you're in no condition.

TOM (*wildly*): No, I'm in no condition!

AMANDA: What right have you got to jeopardize your job? Jeopardize the security of us all? How do you think we'd manage if you were—

TOM: Listen! You think I'm crazy *about* the *warehouse*? (*He bends fiercely toward her slight figure.*) You think I'm in love with the Continental Shoemakers? You think I want to spend fifty-five *years* down there in that—*celotex interior!* with—*fluorescent*—*tubes!* Look! I'd rather somebody picked up a crowbar and battered out my brains—than go back mornings! I *go!* Every time you come in yelling that God damn *"Rise and Shine!" "Rise and Shine!"* I say to myself, *"How lucky dead people are!"* But I get up. I *go!* For sixty-five dollars a month I give up all that I dream of doing and being *ever!* And you say self—*self's* all I ever think of. Why, listen, if self is what I thought of, Mother, I'd be where he is—GONE! (*Pointing to father's picture.*) As far as the system of transportation reaches! (*He starts past her. She grabs his arm.*) Don't grab at me, Mother!

AMANDA: Where are you going?

TOM: I'm going to the *movies!*

AMANDA: I don't believe that lie!

TOM (*Crouching toward her, overtowering her tiny figure. She backs away, gasping.*): I'm going to opium dens! Yes, opium dens, dens of vice and criminals' hangouts, Mother. I've joined the Hogan gang, I'm a hired assassin, I carry a tommy-gun in a violin case! I run a string of cathouses in the Valley! They call me Killer, Killer Wingfield, I'm leading a double life, a simple, honest warehouse worker by day, by night, a dynamic *czar* of the *underworld, Mother.* I go to gambling casinos, I spin away fortunes on the roulette table! I wear a patch over one eye and a false mustache, sometimes I put on green whiskers. On those occasions they call me—*El Diablo!* Oh, I could tell you things to make you sleepless! My enemies plan to dynamite this place. They're going to blow us all skyhigh some night! I'll be glad, very happy, and so will you! You'll go up, up on a broomstick, over Blue Mountain with seventeen gentlemen callers! You ugly—babbling old—*witch*. . . . (*He goes through a series of violent, clumsy movements, seizing his overcoat, lunging to the door, pulling it fiercely open. The women watch him, aghast. His arm catches in the sleeve of the coat as he struggles to pull it on. For a moment he is pinioned by the bulky garment. With an outraged groan he tears the coat off again, splitting the shoulders of it, and hurls it across the room. It strikes against the shelf of Laura's glass collection, there is a tinkle of shattering glass. Laura cries out as if wounded.*)

(*Music legend: "The Glass Menagerie."*)

LAURA (*shrilly*): My glass!—menagerie. . . . (*She covers her face and turns away.*)

(*But Amanda is still stunned and stupefied by the "ugly witch" so that she barely notices this occurrence. Now she recovers her speech.*)

AMANDA (*in an awful voice*): I won't speak to you—until you apologize! (*She crosses through portieres and draws them together behind her. Tom is left with Laura. Laura clings weakly to the mantel with her face averted. Tom stares at her stupidly for a moment. Then he crosses to shelf. Drops awkwardly to his knees to collect the fallen glass, glancing at Laura as if he would speak but couldn't.*)

(*"The Glass Menagerie" steals in as the scene dims out.*)

SCENE 4

(*The interior is dark. Faint light in the alley.*)

(*A deep-voiced bell in a church is tolling the hour of five as the scene commences.*)

(*Tom appears at the top of the alley. After each solemn boom of the bell in the tower, he shakes a little noisemaker or rattle as if to express the tiny spasm of man in contrast to the sustained power and dignity of the Almighty. This and the unsteadiness of his advance make it evident that he has been drinking.*)

(*As he climbs the few steps to the fire escape landing light steals up inside. Laura appears in nightdress, observing Tom's empty bed in the front room.*)

(*Tom fishes in his pockets for the door key, removing a motley assortment of articles in the search, including a perfect shower of movie ticket stubs and an empty bottle. At last he finds the key, but just as he is about to insert it, it slips from his fingers. He strikes a match and crouches below the door.*)

TOM (*bitterly*): One crack—and it falls through!

(*Laura opens the door.*)

LAURA: Tom! Tom, what are you doing?
TOM: Looking for a door key.
LAURA: Where have you been all this time?
TOM: I have been to the movies.
LAURA: All this time at the movies?
TOM: There was a very long program. There was a Garbo picture and a Mickey Mouse and a travelogue and a newsreel and a preview of coming attractions. And there was an organ solo and a collection for the milk fund—simultaneously—which ended up in a terrible fight between a fat lady and an usher!
LAURA (*innocently*): Did you have to stay through everything?
TOM: Of course! And, oh, I forgot! There was a big stage show! The headliner on this stage show was Malvolio the Magician. He performed wonderful tricks, many of them, such as pouring water back and forth between pitchers. First it turned to wine and then it turned to beer and then it turned to whiskey. I know it was whiskey it finally turned into because he needed somebody to come up out of the audience to help him, and I came up—both shows! It was Kentucky Straight Bourbon. A very generous fellow, he gave souvenirs. (*He pulls from his back pocket a shimmering rainbow-colored scarf.*) He gave me this. This is his magic scarf. You can have it, Laura. You wave it over a canary cage and you get a bowl of goldfish. You wave it over the goldfish bowl and they fly away canaries. . . . But the wonderfullest trick of all was the coffin trick. We nailed him into a coffin and he got out of the coffin without removing one nail. (*He has come inside.*) There is a trick that would come in handy for me—get me out of this 2 by 4 situation! (*Flops onto bed and starts removing shoes.*)
LAURA: Tom—Shhh!
TOM: What you shushing me for?
LAURA: You'll wake up Mother.
TOM: Goody, goody! Pay 'er back for all those "Rise an' Shines." (*Lies down, groaning.*) You know it don't take much intelligence to get yourself into a nailed-up coffin, Laura. But who in hell ever got himself out of one without removing one nail?

(*As if in answer, the father's grinning photograph lights up.*)
(*Scene dims out.*)

(*Immediately following: The church bell is heard striking six. At the sixth stroke the alarm clock goes off in Amanda's room, and after a few moments we hear her calling: "Rise and Shine! Rise and Shine! Laura, go tell your brother to rise and shine!"*)

TOM (*sitting up slowly*): I'll rise—but I won't shine.

(*The light increases.*)

AMANDA: Laura, tell your brother his coffee is ready.

(*Laura slips into front room.*)

LAURA: Tom! it's nearly seven. Don't make Mother nervous. (*He stares at her stupidly. Beseechingly.*) Tom, speak to Mother this morning. Make up with her, apologize, speak to her!
TOM: She won't to me. It's her that started not speaking.
LAURA: If you just say you're sorry she'll start speaking.
TOM: Her not speaking—is that such a tragedy?
LAURA: Please—please!
AMANDA (*calling from kitchenette*): Laura, are you going to do what I asked you to do, or do I have to get dressed and go out myself?
LAURA: Going, going—soon as I get on my coat! (*She pulls on a shapeless felt hat with nervous, jerky movement, pleadingly glancing at Tom. Rushes awkwardly for coat. The coat is one of Amanda's, inaccurately made over, the sleeves too short for Laura.*) Butter and what else?
AMANDA (*entering upstage*): Just butter. Tell them to charge it.
LAURA: Mother, they make such faces when I do that.
AMANDA: Sticks and stones may break my bones, but the expression on Mr. Garfinkel's face won't harm us! Tell your brother his coffee is getting cold.
LAURA (*at door*): Do what I asked you, will you, will you, Tom?

(*He looks sullenly away.*)

AMANDA: Laura, go now or just don't go at all!
LAURA (*rushing out*): Going—going! (*A second later she cries out. Tom springs up and crosses to the door. Amanda rushes anxiously in. Tom opens the door.*)
TOM: Laura?
LAURA: I'm all right. I slipped, but I'm all right.
AMANDA (*peering anxiously after her*): If anyone breaks a leg on those fire escape steps, the landlord ought to be sued for every cent he possesses! (*She shuts door. Remembers she isn't speaking and returns to other room.*)

(*As Tom enters listlessly for his coffee, she turns her back to him and stands rigidly facing the window on the gloomy gray vault of the areaway. Its light on her face with its aged but childish features is cruelly sharp, satirical as a Daumier print.)*

(Music under: "Ave Maria.")

(Tom glances sheepishly but sullenly at her averted figure and slumps at the table. The coffee is scalding hot; he sips it and gasps and spits it back in the cup. At his gasp, Amanda catches her breath and half turns. Then catches herself and turns back to window.)

(Tom blows on his coffee, glancing sidewise at his mother. She clears her throat. Tom clears his. He starts to rise. Sinks back down again, scratches his head, clears his throat again. Amanda coughs. Tom raises his cup in both hands to blow on it, his eyes staring over the rim of it at his mother for several moments. Then he slowly sets the cup down and awkwardly and hesitantly rises from the chair.)

TOM (*hoarsely*): Mother. I—I apologize. Mother. (*Amanda draws a quick, shuddering breath. Her face works grotesquely. She breaks into childlike tears.*) I'm sorry for what I said, for everything that I said, I didn't mean it.

AMANDA (*sobbingly*): My devotion has made me a witch and so I make myself hateful to my children!

TOM: *No,* you *don't.*

AMANDA: I worry so much, don't sleep, it makes me nervous!

TOM (*gently*): I understand that.

AMANDA: I've had to put up a solitary battle all these years. But you're my right-hand bower! Don't fall down, don't fail!

TOM (*gently*): I try, Mother.

AMANDA (*with great enthusiasm*): Try and you will SUCCEED! (*The notion makes her breathless.*) Why, you—you're just *full* of natural endowments! Both of my children—they're *unusual* children! Don't you think I know it? I'm so—*proud!* Happy and—feel I've—so much to be thankful for but—Promise me one thing, son!

TOM: What, Mother?

AMANDA: Promise, son, you'll—never be a drunkard!

TOM (*turns to her grinning*): I will never be a drunkard, Mother.

AMANDA: That's what frightened me so, that you'd be drinking! Eat a bowl of Purina!

TOM: Just coffee, Mother.

AMANDA: Shredded wheat biscuit?

TOM: No, no, Mother, just coffee.

AMANDA: You can't put in a day's work on an empty stomach. You've got ten minutes—don't gulp! Drinking too-hot liquids makes cancer of the stomach. . . . Put cream in.

TOM: No, thank you.

AMANDA: To cool it.

TOM: No! No, thank you, I want it black.

AMANDA: I know, but it's not good for you. We have to do all that we can to build ourselves up. In these trying times we live in, all that we have to cling to is—each other. . . . That's why it's so important to—Tom, I—I sent out your sister so I could discuss something with you. If you hadn't spoken I would have spoken to you. (*Sits down.*)

TOM (*gently*): What is it, Mother, that you want to discuss?

AMANDA: *Laura!*

(*Tom puts his cup down slowly.*)
   (*Legend on screen: "Laura."*)
   (*Music: "The Glass Menagerie."*)

TOM: —Oh.—Laura . . .

AMANDA (*touching his sleeve*): You know how Laura is. So quiet but— still water runs deep! She notices things and I think she—broods about them. (*Tom looks up.*) A few days ago I came in and she was crying.

TOM: What about?

AMANDA: You.

TOM: Me?

AMANDA: She has an idea that you're not happy here.

TOM: What gave her that idea?

AMANDA: What gives her any idea? However, you do act strangely. I—I'm not criticizing, understand *that!* I know your ambitions do not lie in the warehouse, that like everybody in the whole wide world—you've had to—make sacrifices, but—Tom—Tom—life's not easy, it calls for—Spartan endurance! There's so many things in my heart that I cannot describe to you! I've never told you but I—*loved your father.* . . .

TOM (*gently*): I know that, Mother.

AMANDA: And you—when I see you taking after his ways! Staying out late—and—well, you *had* been drinking the night you were in that— terrifying condition! Laura says that you hate the apartment and that you go out nights to get away from it! Is that true, Tom?

TOM: No. You say there's so much in your heart that you can't describe to me. That's true of me, too. There's so much in my heart that I can't describe to *you!* So let's respect each other's—

AMANDA: But, why—*why*, Tom—are you always so *restless?* Where do you go to, nights?

TOM: I—go to the movies.

AMANDA: Why do you go to the movies so much, Tom?

TOM: I go to the movies because—I like adventure. Adventure is some- thing I don't have much of at work, so I go to the movies.

AMANDA: But, Tom, you go to the movies *entirely* too *much!*

Tom: I like a lot of adventure.

(*Amanda looks baffled, then hurt. As the familiar inquisition resumes he becomes hard and impatient again. Amanda slips back into her querulous attitude toward him.*)
   (*Image on screen: sailing vessel with Jolly Roger.°*)

Amanda: Most young men find adventure in their careers.

Tom: Then most young men are not employed in a warehouse.

Amanda: The world is full of young men employed in warehouses and offices and factories.

Tom: Do all of them find adventure in their careers?

Amanda: They do or they do without it! Not everybody has a craze for adventure.

Tom: Man is by instinct a lover, a hunter, a fighter, and none of those instincts are given much play at the warehouse!

Amanda: Man is by instinct! Don't quote instinct to me! Instinct is something that people have got away from! It belongs to animals! Christian adults don't want it!

Tom: What do Christian adults want, then, Mother?

Amanda: Superior things! Things of the mind and the spirit! Only animals have to satisfy instincts! Surely your aims are somewhat higher than theirs! Than monkeys—pigs—

Tom: I reckon they're not.

Amanda: You're joking. However, that isn't what I wanted to discuss.

Tom (*rising*): I haven't much time.

Amanda (*pushing his shoulders*): Sit down.

Tom: You want me to punch in red at the warehouse, Mother?

Amanda: You have five minutes. I want to talk about Laura.

(*Legend: "Plans and Provisions."*)

Tom: All right! What about Laura?

Amanda: We have to be making plans and provisions for her. She's older than you, two years, and nothing has happened. She just drifts along doing nothing. It frightens me terribly how she just drifts along.

Tom: I guess she's the type that people call home girls.

Amanda: There's no such type, and if there is, it's a pity! That is unless the home is hers, with a husband!

Tom: What?

Amanda: Oh, I can see the handwriting on the wall as plain as I see the nose in front of my face! It's terrifying! More and more you remind me

___

Jolly Roger: A black flag with a white skull and crossbones formerly used by pirates.

of your father! He was out all hours without explanation—Then *left!*
Good-bye! And me with a bag to hold. I saw that letter you got from
the Merchant Marine. I know what you're dreaming of. I'm not standing here blindfolded. Very well, then. Then *do* it! But not till there's
somebody to take your place.

Tom: What do you mean?

Amanda: I mean that as soon as Laura has got somebody to take care of
her, married, a home of her own, independent—why, then you'll be
free to go wherever you please, on land, on sea, whichever way the
wind blows you! But until that time you've got to look out for your sister. I don't say me because I'm old and don't matter! I say for your sister because she's young and dependent. I put her in business college—
a dismal failure! Frightened her so it made her sick to her stomach. I
took her over to the Young People's League at the church. Another
fiasco. She spoke to nobody, nobody spoke to her. Now all she does is
fool with those pieces of glass and play those worn-out records. What
kind of a life is that for a girl to lead!

Tom: What can I do about it?

Amanda: Overcome selfishness! Self, self, self is all that you ever think
of! (*Tom springs up and crosses to get his coat. It is ugly and bulky. He
pulls on a cap with earmuffs.*) Where is your muffler? Put your wool
muffler on! (*He snatches it angrily from the closet and tosses it around his
neck and pulls both ends tight.*) Tom! I haven't said what I had in mind to
ask you.

Tom: I'm too late to—

Amanda (*Catching his arms—very importunately. Then shyly*): Down at the
warehouse, aren't there some—nice young men?

Tom: No!

Amanda: There *must* be—*some* . . .

Tom: Mother—

(*Gesture.*)

Amanda: Find out one that's clean-living—doesn't drink and—ask him
out for sister!

Tom: What?

Amanda: For *sister!* To *meet!* Get *acquainted!*

Tom (*stamping to door*): Oh, my *go-osh!*

Amanda: Will you? (*He opens door. Imploringly.*) Will you? (*He starts down.*)
Will you? *Will* you, dear?

Tom (*calling back*): YES!

(*Amanda closes the door hesitantly and with a troubled but faintly hopeful
expression.*)

(*Screen image: glamor magazine cover.*)
(*Spot° Amanda at phone.*)

AMANDA: Ella Cartwright? This is Amanda Wingfield! How are you, honey? How is that kidney condition? (*Count five.*) Horrors! (*Count five.*) You're a Christian martyr, yes, honey, that's what you are, a Christian martyr! Well, I just happened to notice in my little red book that your subscription to the *Companion* has just run out! I knew that you wouldn't want to miss out on the wonderful serial starting in this new issue. It's by Bessie Mae Hopper, the first thing she's written since *Honeymoon for Three*. Wasn't that a strange and interesting story? Well, this one is even lovelier, I believe. It has a sophisticated society background. It's all about the horsey set on Long Island!

(*Fade out.*)

SCENE 5

(*Legend on screen "Annunciation." Fade with music.*)

(*It is early dusk of a spring evening. Supper has just been finished in the Wingfield apartment. Amanda and Laura in light colored dresses are removing dishes from the table, in the upstage area, which is shadowy, their movements formalized almost as a dance or ritual, their moving forms as pale and silent as moths.*)

(*Tom, in white shirt and trousers, rises from the table and crosses toward the fire escape.*)

AMANDA (*as he passes her*): Son, will you do me a favor?

TOM: What?

AMANDA: Comb your hair! You look so pretty when your hair is combed! (*Tom slouches on sofa with evening paper. Enormous caption "Franco Triumphs."*) There is only one respect in which I would like you to emulate your father.

TOM: What respect is that?

AMANDA: The care he always took of his appearance. He never allowed himself to look untidy. (*He throws down the paper and crosses to fire escape.*) Where are you going?

TOM: I'm going out to smoke.

AMANDA: You smoke too much. A pack a day at fifteen cents a pack. How much would that amount to in a month? Thirty times fifteen is how much, Tom? Figure it out and you will be astounded at what you could

Spot: Spotlight.

save. Enough to give you a night school course in accounting at Washington U! Just think what a wonderful thing that would be for you, son!

(*Tom is unmoved by the thought.*)

TOM: I'd rather smoke. (*He steps out on landing, letting the screen door slam.*)

AMANDA (*sharply*): I know! That's the tragedy of it. . . . (*Alone, she turns to look at her husband's picture.*)

(*Dance music: "All the World is Waiting for the Sunrise!"*)

TOM (*to the audience*): Across the alley from us was the Paradise Dance Hall. On evenings in spring the windows and doors were open and the music came outdoors. Sometimes the lights were turned out except for a large glass sphere that hung from the ceiling. It would turn slowly about and filter the dusk with delicate rainbow colors. Then the orchestra played a waltz or a tango, something that had a slow and sensuous rhythm. Couples would come outside, to the relative privacy of the alley. You could see them kissing behind ash-pits and telephone poles. This was the compensation for lives that passed like mine, without any change or adventure. Adventure and change were imminent in this year. They were waiting around the corner for all these kids. Suspended in the mist over Berchtesgaden, caught in the folds of Chamberlain's umbrella—In Spain there was Guernica!° But here there was only hot swing music and liquor, dance halls, bars, and movies, and sex that hung in the gloom like a chandelier and flooded the world with brief, deceptive rainbows. . . . All the world was waiting for bombardments!

(*Amanda turns from the picture and comes outside.*)

AMANDA (*sighing*): A fire escape landing's a poor excuse for a porch. (*She spreads a newspaper on a step and sits down, gracefully and demurely as if she were settling into a swing on a Mississippi veranda.*) What are you looking at?

TOM: The moon.

AMANDA: Is there a moon this evening?

TOM: It's rising over Garfinkel's Delicatessen.

AMANDA: So it is! A little silver slipper of a moon. Have you made a wish on it yet?

Berchtesgaden . . . Chamberlain's . . . Guernica: All World War II references. Berchtesgaden was Hitler's summer home. Neville Chamberlain was a British prime minister who tried to avoid war with Hitler through the Munich Pact. Guernica was a Spanish town bombed by Germany during the Spanish Civil War.

Tom: Um-hum.

Amanda: What did you wish for?

Tom: That's a secret.

Amanda: A secret, huh? Well, I won't tell mine either. I will be just as mysterious as you.

Tom: I bet I can guess what yours is.

Amanda: Is my head so transparent?

Tom: You're not a sphinx.

Amanda: No, I don't have secrets. I'll tell you what I wished for on the moon. Success and happiness for my precious children! I wish for that whenever there's a moon, and when there isn't a moon, I wish for it, too.

Tom: I thought perhaps you wished for a gentleman caller.

Amanda: Why do you say that?

Tom: Don't you remember asking me to fetch one?

Amanda: I remember suggesting that it would be nice for your sister if you brought home some nice young man from the warehouse. I think I've made that suggestion more than once.

Tom: Yes, you have made it repeatedly.

Amanda: Well?

Tom: We are going to have one.

Amanda: *What?*

Tom: A gentleman caller!

(*The annunciation is celebrated with music.*)
    (*Amanda rises.*)
    (*Image on screen: caller with bouquet.*)

Amanda: You mean you have asked some nice young man to come over?

Tom: Yep. I've asked him to dinner.

Amanda: You really did?

Tom: I did!

Amanda: You did, and did he—*accept?*

Tom: He did!

Amanda: Well, well—well, well! That's—lovely!

Tom: I thought that you would be pleased.

Amanda: It's definite, then?

Tom: Very definite.

Amanda: Soon?

Tom: Very soon.

Amanda: For heaven's sake, stop putting on and tell me some things, will you?

Tom: What things do you want me to tell you?

Amanda: *Naturally* I would like to know when he's *coming!*

Tom: He's coming tomorrow.

Amanda: *Tomorrow?*

Tom: Yep. Tomorrow.

Amanda: But, Tom!

Tom: Yes, Mother?

Amanda: Tomorrow gives me no time!

Tom: Time for what?

Amanda: Preparations! Why didn't you phone me at once, as soon as you asked him, the minute that he accepted? Then, don't you see, I could have been getting ready!

Tom: You don't have to make any fuss.

Amanda: Oh, Tom, Tom, Tom, of course I have to make a fuss! I want things nice, not sloppy! Not thrown together. I'll certainly have to do some fast thinking, won't I?

Tom: I don't see why you have to think at all.

Amanda: You just don't know. We can't have a gentleman caller in a pigsty! All my wedding silver has to be polished, the monogrammed table linen ought to be laundered! The windows have to be washed and fresh curtains put up. And how about clothes? We have to *wear* something, don't we?

Tom: Mother, this boy is no one to make a fuss over!

Amanda: Do you realize he's the first young man we've introduced to your sister? It's terrible, dreadful, disgraceful that poor little sister has never received a single gentleman caller! Tom, come inside! (*She opens the screen door.*)

Tom: What for?

Amanda: I want to ask you some things.

Tom: If you're going to make such a fuss, I'll call it off, I'll tell him not to come.

Amanda: You certainly won't do anything of the kind. Nothing offends people worse than broken engagements. It simply means I'll have to work like a Turk! We won't be brilliant, but we'll pass inspection. Come on inside. (*Tom follows, groaning.*) Sit down.

Tom: Any particular place you would like me to sit?

Amanda: Thank heavens I've got that new sofa! I'm also making payments on a floor lamp I'll have sent out! And put the chintz covers on, they'll brighten things up! Of course I'd hoped to have these walls repapered. . . . What is the young man's name?

Tom: His name is O'Connor.

Amanda: That, of course, means fish—tomorrow is Friday!° I'll have that salmon loaf—with Durkee's dressing! What does he do? He works at the warehouse?

Tom: Of course! How else would I—

---

fish . . . Friday: Reference to the religious doctrine that prohibited Catholics from eating meat on Fridays.

AMANDA: Tom, he—doesn't drink?

TOM: Why do you ask me that?

AMANDA: Your father *did!*

TOM: Don't get started on that!

AMANDA: He *does* drink, then?

TOM: Not that I know of!

AMANDA: Make sure, be certain! The last thing I want for my daughter's a boy who drinks!

TOM: Aren't you being a little premature? Mr. O'Connor has not yet appeared on the scene!

AMANDA: But will tomorrow. To meet your sister, and what do I know about his character? Nothing! Old maids are better off than wives of drunkards!

TOM: Oh, my God!

AMANDA: Be still!

TOM (*leaning forward to whisper*): Lots of fellows meet girls whom they don't marry!

AMANDA: Oh, talk sensibly, Tom—and don't be sarcastic! (*She has gotten a hairbrush.*)

TOM: What are you doing?

AMANDA: I'm brushing that cowlick down! What is this young man's position at the warehouse?

TOM (*submitting grimly to the brush and the interrogation*): This young man's position is that of a shipping clerk, Mother.

AMANDA: Sounds to me like a fairly responsible job, the sort of a job *you* would be in if you just had more *get-up.* What is his salary? Have you got any idea.

TOM: I would judge it to be approximately eighty-five dollars a month.

AMANDA: Well—not princely, but—

TOM: Twenty more than I make.

AMANDA: Yes, how well I know! But for a family man, eighty-five dollars a month is not much more than you can just get by on. . . .

TOM: Yes, but Mr. O'Connor is not a family man.

AMANDA: He might be, mightn't he? Some time in the future?

TOM: I see. Plans and provisions.

AMANDA: You are the only young man that I know of who ignores the fact that the future becomes the present, the present the past, and the past turns into everlasting regret if you don't plan for it!

TOM: I will think that over and see what I can make of it.

AMANDA: Don't be supercilious with your mother! Tell me some more about this—what do you call him?

TOM: James D. O'Connor. The D. is for Delaney.

AMANDA: Irish on *both* sides! *Gracious!* And doesn't drink?

TOM: Shall I call him up and ask him right this minute?

AMANDA: The only way to find out about those things is to make discreet inquiries at the proper moment. When I was a girl in Blue Mountain and it was suspected that a young man drank, the girl whose attentions he had been receiving, if any girl *was,* would sometimes speak to the minister of his church, or rather her father would if her father was living, and sort of feel him out on the young man's character. That is the way such things are discreetly handled to keep a young woman from making a tragic mistake!

TOM: Then how did you happen to make a tragic mistake?

AMANDA: That innocent look of your father's had everyone fooled! He *smiled* — the world was *enchanted!* No girl can do worse than put herself at the mercy of a handsome appearance! I hope that Mr. O'Connor is not too good-looking.

TOM: No, he's not too good-looking. He's covered with freckles and hasn't too much of a nose.

AMANDA: He's not right-down homely, though?

TOM: Not right-down homely. Just medium homely, I'd say.

AMANDA: Character's what to look for in a man.

TOM: That's what I've always said, Mother.

AMANDA: You've never said anything of the kind and I suspect you would never give it a thought.

TOM: Don't be suspicious of me.

AMANDA: At least I hope he's the type that's up and coming.

TOM: I think he really goes in for self-improvement.

AMANDA: What reason have you to think so?

TOM: He goes to night school.

AMANDA (*beaming*): Splendid! What does he do, I mean study?

TOM: Radio engineering and public speaking!

AMANDA: Then he has visions of being advanced in the world! Any young man who studies public speaking is aiming to have an executive job some day! And radio engineering? A thing for the future! Both of these facts are very illuminating. Those are the sort of things that a mother should know concerning any young man who comes to call on her daughter. Seriously or — not.

TOM: One little warning. He doesn't know about Laura. I didn't let on that we had dark ulterior motives. I just said, why don't you come have dinner with us? He said okay and that was the whole conversation.

AMANDA: I bet it was! You're eloquent as an oyster. However, he'll know about Laura when he gets here. When he sees how lovely and sweet and pretty she is, he'll thank his lucky stars he was asked to dinner.

TOM: Mother, you mustn't expect too much of Laura.

AMANDA: What do you mean?

TOM: Laura seems all those things to you and me because she's ours and we love her. We don't even notice she's crippled anymore.

AMANDA: Don't say crippled! You know that I never allow that word to be used!

TOM: But face facts, Mother. She is and—that's not all—

AMANDA: What do you mean not all?

TOM: Laura is very different from other girls.

AMANDA: I think the difference is all to her advantage.

TOM: Not quite all—in the eyes of others—strangers—she's terribly shy and lives in a world of her own and those things make her seem a little peculiar to people outside the house.

AMANDA: Don't say peculiar.

TOM: Face the facts. She is.

(*The dance-hall music changes to a tango that has a minor and somewhat ominous tone.*)

AMANDA: In what way is she peculiar—may I ask?

TOM (*gently*): She lives in a world of her own—a world of—little glass ornaments, Mother. . . . (*Gets up. Amanda remains holding brush, looking at him, troubled.*) She plays old phonograph records and—that's about all—(*He glances at himself in the mirror and crosses to door.*)

AMANDA (*sharply*): Where are you going?

TOM: I'm going to the movies. (*Out screen door.*)

AMANDA: Not to the movies, every night to the movies! (*Follows quickly to screen door.*) I don't believe you always go to the movies! (*He is gone. Amanda looks worriedly after him for a moment. Then vitality and optimism return and she turns from the door. Crossing to portieres.*) Laura! Laura! (*Laura answers from kitchenette.*)

LAURA: Yes, Mother.

AMANDA: Let those dishes go and come in front! (*Laura appears with dish towel. Gaily.*) Laura, come here and make a wish on the moon!

LAURA (*entering*): Moon—moon?

AMANDA: A little silver slipper of a moon. Look over your left shoulder, Laura, and make a wish! (*Laura looks faintly puzzled as if called out of sleep. Amanda seizes her shoulders and turns her at an angle by the door.*) Now! Now, darling, *wish!*

LAURA: What shall I wish for, Mother?

AMANDA (*her voice trembling and her eyes suddenly filling with tears*): Happiness! Good Fortune!

(*The violin rises and the stage dims out.*)

SCENE 6

(*Image: high school hero.*)

TOM: And so the following evening I brought Jim home to dinner. I had
known Jim slightly in high school. In high school Jim was a hero. He
had tremendous Irish good nature and vitality with the scrubbed and
polished look of white chinaware. He seemed to move in a continual
spotlight. He was a star in basketball, captain of the debating club,
president of the senior class and the glee club and he sang the male
lead in the annual light operas. He was always running or bounding,
never just walking. He seemed always at the point of defeating the law
of gravity. He was shooting with such velocity through his adolescence
that you would logically expect him to arrive at nothing short of the
White House by the time he was thirty. But Jim apparently ran into
more interference after his graduation from Soldan. His speed had
definitely slowed. Six years after he left high school he was holding a
job that wasn't much better than mine.

(*Image: clerk.*)

   He was the only one at the warehouse with whom I was on friendly
terms. I was valuable to him as someone who could remember his former glory, who had seen him win basketball games and the silver cup
in debating. He knew of my secret practice of retiring to a cabinet of
the washroom to work on poems when business was slack in the warehouse. He called me Shakespeare. And while the other boys in the
warehouse regarded me with suspicious hostility, Jim took a humorous attitude toward me. Gradually his attitude affected the others,
their hostility wore off and they also began to smile at me as people
smile at an oddly fashioned dog who trots across their path at some
distance.
   I knew that Jim and Laura had known each other at Soldan, and I
had heard Laura speak admiringly of his voice. I didn't know if Jim
remembered her or not. In high school Laura had been as unobtrusive
as Jim had been astonishing. If he did remember Laura, it was not as
my sister, for when I asked him to dinner, he grinned and said, "You
know, Shakespeare, I never thought of you as having folks!"
   He was about to discover that I did. . . .

(*Light up stage.*)
   (*Legend on screen: "The Accent of a Coming Foot."*)
   (*Friday evening. It is about five o'clock of a late spring evening which comes
"scattering poems in the sky."*)
   (*A delicate lemony light is in the Wingfield apartment.*)

(*Amanda has worked like a Turk in preparation for the gentleman caller. The results are astonishing. The new floor lamp with its rose-silk shade is in place, a colored paper lantern conceals the broken light fixture in the ceiling, new billowing white curtains are at the windows, chintz covers are on chairs and sofa, a pair of new sofa pillows make their initial appearance.*)

(*Open boxes and tissue paper are scattered on the floor.*)

(*Laura stands in the middle with lifted arms while Amanda crouches before her, adjusting the hem of the new dress, devout and ritualistic. The dress is colored and designed by memory. The arrangement of Laura's hair is changed; it is softer and more becoming. A fragile, unearthly prettiness has come out in Laura: she is like a piece of translucent glass touched by light, given a momentary radiance, not actual, not lasting.*)

AMANDA (*impatiently*): Why are you trembling?

LAURA: Mother, you've made me so nervous!

AMANDA: How have I made you nervous?

LAURA: By all this fuss! You make it seem so important!

AMANDA: I don't understand you, Laura. You couldn't be satisfied with just sitting home, and yet whenever I try to arrange something for you, you seem to resist it. (*She gets up.*) Now take a look at yourself. No, wait! Wait just a moment—I have an idea!

LAURA: What is it now?

(*Amanda produces two powder puffs which she wraps in handkerchiefs and stuffs in Laura's bosom.*)

LAURA: Mother, what are you doing?

AMANDA: They call them "Gay Deceivers"!

LAURA: I won't wear them!

AMANDA: You will!

LAURA: Why should I?

AMANDA: Because, to be painfully honest, your chest is flat.

LAURA: You make it seem like we were setting a trap.

AMANDA: All pretty girls are a trap, a pretty trap, and men expect them to be. (*Legend: "A Pretty Trap."*) Now look at yourself, young lady. This is the prettiest you will ever be! I've got to fix myself now! You're going to be surprised by your mother's appearance! (*She crosses through portieres, humming gaily.*)

(*Laura moves slowly to the long mirror and stares solemnly at herself.*)

(*A wind blows the white curtains inward in a slow, graceful motion and with a faint, sorrowful sighing.*)

AMANDA (*offstage*): It isn't dark enough yet. (*She turns slowly before the mirror with a troubled look.*)

(*Legend on screen: "This Is My Sister: Celebrate Her with Strings!" Music.*)

AMANDA (*laughing, off*): I'm going to show you something. I'm going to make a spectacular appearance!

LAURA: What is it, Mother?

AMANDA: Possess your soul in patience—you will see! Something I've resurrected from that old trunk! Styles haven't changed so terribly much after all. . . . (*She parts the portieres.*) Now just look at your mother! (*She wears a girlish frock of yellowed voile with a blue silk sash. She carries a bunch of jonquils—the legend of her youth is nearly revived. Feverishly.*) This is the dress in which I led the cotillion. Won the cakewalk twice at Sunset Hill, wore one spring to the Governor's ball in Jackson! See how I sashayed around the ballroom, Laura? (*She raises her skirt and does a mincing step around the room.*) I wore it on Sundays for my gentlemen callers! I had it on the day I met your father—I had malaria fever all that spring. The change of climate from East Tennessee to the Delta—weakened resistance—I had a little temperature all the time—not enough to be serious—just enough to make me restless and giddy! Invitations poured in—parties all over the Delta!—"Stay in bed," said Mother, "you have fever!"—but I just wouldn't.—I took quinine but kept on going, going!—Evenings, dances!—Afternoons, long, long rides! Picnics—lovely!—So lovely, that country in May.—All lacy with dogwood, literally flooded with jonquils!—That was the spring I had the craze for jonquils. Jonquils became an absolute obsession. Mother said, "Honey, there's no more room for jonquils." And still I kept on bringing in more jonquils. Whenever, wherever I saw them, I'd say, "Stop! Stop! I see jonquils!" I made the young men help me gather the jonquils! It was a joke, Amanda and her jonquils! Finally there were no more vases to hold them, every available space was filled with jonquils. No vases to hold them? All right, I'll hold them myself! And then I— (*She stops in front of the picture. Music.*) met your father! Malaria fever and jonquils and then—this—boy. . . . (*She switches on the rose-colored lamp.*) I hope they get here before it starts to rain. (*She crosses upstage and places the jonquils in bowl on table.*) I gave your brother a little extra change so he and Mr. O'Connor could take the service car home.

LAURA (*with altered look*): What did you say his name was?

AMANDA: O'Connor.

LAURA: What is his first name?

AMANDA: I don't remember. Oh, yes, I do. It was—Jim!

(*Laura sways slightly and catches hold of a chair.*)
(*Legend on screen: "Not Jim!"*)

LAURA (*faintly*): Not—Jim!

AMANDA: Yes, that was it, it was Jim! I've never known a Jim that wasn't nice!

(*Music: ominous.*)

LAURA: Are you sure his name is Jim O'Connor?

AMANDA: Yes. Why?

LAURA: Is he the one that Tom used to know in high school?

AMANDA: He didn't say so. I think he just got to know him at the warehouse.

LAURA: There was a Jim O'Connor we both knew in high school—(*Then, with effort.*) If that is the one that Tom is bringing to dinner—you'll have to excuse me, I won't come to the table.

AMANDA: What sort of nonsense is this?

LAURA: You asked me once if I'd ever liked a boy. Don't you remember I showed you this boy's picture?

AMANDA: You mean the boy you showed me in the yearbook?

LAURA: Yes, that boy.

AMANDA: Laura, Laura, were you in love with that boy?

LAURA: I don't know, Mother. All I know is I couldn't sit at the table if it was him!

AMANDA: It won't be him! It isn't the least bit likely. But whether it is or not, you will come to the table. You will not be excused.

LAURA: I'll have to be, Mother.

AMANDA: I don't intend to humor your silliness, Laura. I've had too much from you and your brother, both! So just sit down and compose yourself till they come. Tom has forgotten his key so you'll have to let them in, when they arrive.

LAURA (*panicky*): Oh, Mother—*you* answer the door!

AMANDA (*lightly*): I'll be in the kitchen—busy!

LAURA: Oh, Mother, please answer the door, don't make me do it!

AMANDA (*crossing into kitchenette*): I've got to fix the dressing for the salmon. Fuss, fuss—silliness!—over a gentleman caller!

(*Door swings shut. Laura is left alone.*)

(*Legend: "Terror!"*)

(*She utters a low moan and turns off the lamp—sits stiffly on the edge of the sofa, knotting her fingers together.*)

(*Legend on screen: "The Opening of a Door!"*)

(*Tom and Jim appear on the fire escape steps and climb to landing. Hearing their approach, Laura rises with a panicky gesture. She retreats to the portieres.*)

(*The doorbell. Laura catches her breath and touches her throat. Low drums.*)

AMANDA (*calling*): Laura, sweetheart! The door!

(*Laura stares at it without moving.*)

JIM: I think we just beat the rain.

TOM: Uh-huh. (*He rings again, nervously. Jim whistles and fishes for a cigarette.*)

AMANDA (*very, very gaily*): Laura, that is your brother and Mr. O'Connor! Will you let them in, darling?

(*Laura crosses toward kitchenette door.*)

LAURA (*breathlessly*): Mother—you go to the door!

(*Amanda steps out of kitchenette and stares furiously at Laura. She points imperiously at the door.*)

LAURA: Please, please!

AMANDA (*in a fierce whisper*): What is the matter with you, you silly thing?

LAURA (*desperately*): Please, you answer it, *please!*

AMANDA: I told you I wasn't going to humor you, Laura. Why have you chosen this moment to lose your mind?

LAURA: Please, please, please, you go!

AMANDA: You'll have to go to the door because I can't!

LAURA (*despairingly*): I can't either!

AMANDA: *Why?*

LAURA: I'm *sick!*

AMANDA: I'm sick, too—of your nonsense! Why can't you and your brother be normal people? Fantastic whims and behavior! (*Tom gives a long ring.*) Preposterous goings on! Can you give me one reason— (*Calls out lyrically.*) COMING! JUST ONE SECOND!—why should you be afraid to open a door? Now you answer it, Laura!

LAURA: Oh, oh, oh . . . (*She returns through the portieres. Darts to the victrola and winds it frantically and turns it on.*)

AMANDA: Laura Wingfield, you march right to that door!

LAURA: Yes—yes, Mother!

(*A faraway, scratchy rendition of "Dardanella" softens the air and gives her strength to move through it. She slips to the door and draws it cautiously open.*)
(*Tom enters with the caller, Jim O'Connor.*)

TOM: Laura, this is Jim. Jim, this is my sister, Laura.

JIM (*stepping inside*): I didn't know that Shakespeare had a sister!

LAURA (*retreating stiff and trembling from the door*): How—how do you do?

JIM (*heartily extending his hand*): Okay!

(*Laura touches it hesitantly with hers.*)

JIM: Your hand's *cold,* Laura!

LAURA: Yes, well—I've been playing the victrola. . . .

JIM: Must have been playing classical music on it! You ought to play a little hot swing music to warm you up!

LAURA: Excuse me—I haven't finished playing the victrola. . . .

(*She turns awkwardly and hurries into the front room. She pauses a second by the victrola. Then catches her breath and darts through the portieres like a frightened deer.*)

JIM (*grinning*): What was the matter?

TOM: Oh—with Laura? Laura is—terribly shy.

JIM: Shy, huh? It's unusual to meet a shy girl nowadays. I don't believe you ever mentioned you had a sister.

TOM: Well, now you know. I have one. Here is the *Post Dispatch*. You want a piece of it?

JIM: Uh-huh.

TOM: What piece? The comics?

JIM: Sports! (*Glances at it.*) Ole Dizzy Dean is on his bad behavior.

TOM (*disinterest*): Yeah? (*Lights cigarette and crosses back to fire escape door.*)

JIM: Where are *you* going?

TOM: I'm going out on the terrace.

JIM (*goes after him*): You know, Shakespeare—I'm going to sell you a bill of goods!

TOM: What goods?

JIM: A course I'm taking.

TOM: Huh?

JIM: In public speaking! You and me, we're not the warehouse type.

TOM: Thanks—that's good news. But what has public speaking got to do with it?

JIM: It fits you for—executive positions!

TOM: Awww.

JIM: I tell you it's done a helluva lot for me.

(*Image: executive at desk.*)

TOM: In what respect?

JIM: In every! Ask yourself what is the difference between you an' me and men in the office down front? Brains?—No!—Ability?—No! Then what? Just one little thing—

TOM: What is that one little thing?

JIM: Primarily it amounts to—social poise! Being able to square up to people and hold your own on any social level!

AMANDA (*offstage*): Tom?

TOM: Yes, Mother?

AMANDA: Is that you and Mr. O'Connor?

TOM: Yes, Mother.

AMANDA: Well, you just make yourselves comfortable in there.

TOM: Yes, Mother.

AMANDA: Ask Mr. O'Connor if he would like to wash his hands.

JIM: Aw,—no—no—thank you—I took care of that at the warehouse. Tom—

TOM: Yes?

JIM: Mr. Mendoza was speaking to me about you.

TOM: Favorably?

JIM: What do you think?

TOM: Well—

JIM: You're going to be out of a job if you don't wake up.

TOM: I am waking up—

JIM: You show no signs.

TOM: The signs are interior.

(*Image on screen: the sailing vessel with Jolly Roger again.*)

TOM: I'm planning to change. (*He leans over the rail speaking with quiet exhilaration. The incandescent marquees and signs of the first-run movie houses light his face from across the alley. He looks like a voyager.*) I'm right at the point of committing myself to a future that doesn't include the warehouse and Mr. Mendoza or even a night school course in public speaking.

JIM: What are you gassing about?

TOM: I'm tired of the movies.

JIM: Movies!

TOM: Yes, movies! Look at them—(*A wave toward the marvels of Grand Avenue.*) All of those glamorous people—having adventures—hogging it all, gobbling the whole thing up! You know what happens? People go to the *movies* instead of *moving!* Hollywood characters are supposed to have all the adventures for everybody in America, while everybody in America sits in a dark room and watches them have them! Yes, until there's a war. That's when adventure becomes available to the masses! *Everyone's* dish, not only Gable's! Then the people in the dark room come out of the dark room to have some adventures themselves—Goody, goody!—It's our turn now, to go to the South Sea Island—to make a safari—to be exotic, far-off!—But I'm not patient. I don't want to wait till then. I'm tired of the *movies* and I am *about* to *move!*

JIM (*incredulously*): Move?

TOM: Yes.

JIM: When?

TOM: Soon!

JIM: Where? Where?

(*Theme three music seems to answer the question, while Tom thinks it over. He searches among his pockets.*)

TOM: I'm starting to boil inside. I know I seem dreamy, but inside— well, I'm boiling! Whenever I pick up a shoe, I shudder a little thinking how short life is and what I am doing!—Whatever that means. I know it doesn't mean shoes—except as something to wear on a traveler's feet! (*Finds paper.*) Look—

JIM: What?

TOM: I'm a member.

JIM (*reading*): The Union of Merchant Seamen.

TOM: I paid my dues this month, instead of the light bill.

JIM: You will regret it when they turn the lights off.

TOM: I won't be here.

JIM: How about your mother?

TOM: I'm like my father. The bastard son of a bastard! See how he grins! And he's been absent going on sixteen years!

JIM: You're just talking, you drip. How does your mother feel about it?

TOM: Shhh!—Here comes Mother! Mother is not acquainted with my plans!

AMANDA (*enters portieres*): Where are you all?

TOM: On the terrace, Mother.

(*They start inside. She advances to them. Tom is distinctly shocked at her appearance. Even Jim blinks a little. He is making his first contact with girlish Southern vivacity and in spite of the night school course in public speaking is somewhat thrown off the beam by the unexpected outlay of social charm.*)

(*Certain responses are attempted by Jim but are swept aside by Amanda's gay laughter and chatter. Tom is embarrassed but after the first shock Jim reacts very warmly. Grins and chuckles, is altogether won over.*)

(*Image: Amanda as a girl.*)

AMANDA (*coyly smiling, shaking her girlish ringlets*): Well, well, well, so this is Mr. O'Connor. Introductions entirely unnecessary. I've heard so much about you from my boy. I finally said to him, Tom—good gracious!—why don't you bring this paragon to supper? I'd like to meet this nice young man at the warehouse!—Instead of just hearing him sing your praises so much! I don't know why my son is so standoffish— that's not Southern behavior! Let's sit down and—I think we could stand a little more air in here! Tom, leave the door open. I felt a nice fresh breeze a moment ago. Where has it gone to? Mmm, so warm already! And not quite summer, even. We're going to burn up when summer really gets started. However, we're having—we're having a very light supper. I think light things are better fo' this time of year. The same as light clothes are. Light clothes an' light food are what warm weather calls fo'. You know our blood gets so thick during th' winter—it takes a while fo' us to *adjust* ou'selves!—when the season changes . . . It's come so quick this year. I wasn't prepared. All of a sudden—heavens! Already summer!—I ran to the trunk an' pulled out this light dress—Terribly old! Historical almost! But feels so good—so good an' co-ol, y'know. . . .

TOM: Mother—

AMANDA: Yes, honey?

TOM: How about—supper?

AMANDA: Honey, you go ask Sister if supper is ready! You know that Sister is in full charge of supper! Tell her you hungry boys are waiting for it. (*To Jim.*) Have you met Laura?

JIM: She—

AMANDA: Let you in? Oh, good, you've met already! It's rare for a girl as sweet an' pretty as Laura to be domestic! But Laura is, thank heavens, not only pretty but also very domestic. I'm not at all. I never was a bit. I never could make a thing but angel food cake. Well, in the South we had so many servants. Gone, gone, gone. All vestiges of gracious living! Gone completely! I wasn't prepared for what the future brought me. All of my gentlemen callers were sons of planters and so of course I assumed that I would be married to one and raise my family on a large piece of land with plenty of servants. But man proposes—and woman accepts the proposal!—To vary that old, old saying a little bit—I married no planter! I married a man who worked for the telephone company!—That gallantly smiling gentleman over there! (*Points to the picture.*) A telephone man who—fell in love with long distance!—Now he travels and I don't even know where!—But what am I going on for about my—tribulations! Tell me yours—I hope you don't have any! Tom?

TOM (*returning*): Yes, Mother?

AMANDA: Is supper nearly ready?

TOM: It looks to me like supper is on the table.

AMANDA: Let me look—(*She rises prettily and looks through portieres.*) Oh, lovely!—But where is Sister?

TOM: Laura is not feeling well and she says that she thinks she'd better not come to the table.

AMANDA: What?—Nonsense!—Laura? Oh, Laura!

LAURA (*offstage, faintly*): Yes, Mother.

AMANDA: You really must come to the table. We won't be seated until you come to the table! Come in, Mr. O'Connor. You sit over there, and I'll—Laura? Laura Wingfield! You're keeping us waiting, honey! We can't say grace until you come to the table!

(The back door is pushed weakly open and Laura comes in. She is obviously quite faint, her lips trembling, her eyes wide and staring. She moves unsteadily toward the table.)

(Legend: "Terror!")

(Outside a summer storm is coming abruptly. The white curtains billow inward at the windows and there is a sorrowful murmur and deep blue dusk.)

(Laura suddenly stumbles — she catches at a chair with a faint moan.)

TOM: Laura!

AMANDA: Laura! *(There is a clap of thunder.) (Legend: "Ah!") (Despairingly.)* Why, Laura, you *are* sick, darling! Tom, help your sister into the living room, dear! Sit in the living room, Laura—rest on the sofa. Well! *(To the gentleman caller.)* Standing over the hot stove made her ill!—I told her that it was just too warm this evening, but—*(Tom comes back in. Laura is on the sofa.)* Is Laura all right now?

TOM: Yes.

AMANDA: What *is* that? Rain? A nice cool rain has come up! *(She gives the gentleman caller a frightened look.)* I think we may—have grace—now . . . *(Tom looks at her stupidly.)*Tom, honey—you say grace!

TOM: Oh . . . "For these and all thy mercies—" *(They bow their heads, Amanda stealing a nervous glance at Jim. In the living room Laura, stretched on the sofa, clenches her hand to her lips, to hold back a shuddering sob.)* God's Holy Name be praised—

(The scene dims out.)

SCENE 7

(A Souvenir)

(Half an hour later. Dinner is just being finished in the upstage area which is concealed by the drawn portieres.)

(As the curtain rises Laura is still huddled upon the sofa, her feet drawn under her, her head resting on a pale blue pillow, her eyes wide and mysteriously watchful. The new floor lamp with its shade of rose-colored silk gives a soft, becoming light to her face, bringing out the fragile, unearthly prettiness which usually escapes attention. There is a steady murmur of rain, but it is slackening and stops soon after the scene begins; the air outside becomes pale and luminous as the moon breaks out.)

(A moment after the curtain rises, the lights in both rooms flicker and go out.)

JIM: Hey, there, Mr. Light Bulb!

(Amanda laughs nervously.)

(Legend: "Suspension of a Public Service.")

AMANDA: Where was Moses when the lights went out? Ha-ha. Do you know the answer to that one, Mr. O'Connor?

JIM: No, Ma'am, what's the answer?

AMANDA: In the dark! (*Jim laughs appreciably.*) Everybody sit still. I'll light the candles. Isn't it lucky we have them on the table? Where's a match? Which of you gentlemen can provide a match?

JIM: Here.

AMANDA: Thank you, sir.

JIM: Not at all, Ma'am!

AMANDA: I guess the fuse has burnt out. Mr. O'Connor, can you tell a burnt-out fuse? I know I can't and Tom is a total loss when it comes to mechanics. (*Sound: getting up: voices recede a little to kitchenette.*) Oh, be careful you don't bump into something. We don't want our gentleman caller to break his neck. Now wouldn't that be a fine howdy-do?

JIM: Ha-ha! Where is the fuse box?

AMANDA: Right here next to the stove. Can you see anything?

JIM: Just a minute.

AMANDA: Isn't electricity a mysterious thing? Wasn't it Benjamin Franklin who tied a key to a kite? We live in such a mysterious universe, don't we? Some people say that science clears up all the mysteries for us. In my opinion it only creates more! Have you found it yet?

JIM: No, Ma'am. All these fuses look okay to me.

AMANDA: Tom!

TOM: Yes, Mother?

AMANDA: That light bill I gave you several days ago. The one I told you we got the notices about?

TOM: Oh. — Yeah.

(*Legend: "Ha!"*)

AMANDA: You didn't neglect to pay it by any chance?

TOM: Why, I —

AMANDA: Didn't! I might have known it!

JIM: Shakespeare probably wrote a poem on that light bill, Mrs. Wingfield.

AMANDA: I might have known better than to trust him with it! There's such a high price for negligence in this world!

JIM: Maybe the poem will win a ten-dollar prize.

AMANDA: We'll just have to spend the remainder of the evening in the nineteenth century, before Mr. Edison made the Mazda lamp!

JIM: Candlelight is my favorite kind of light.

AMANDA: That shows you're romantic! But that's no excuse for Tom. Well, we got through dinner. Very considerate of them to let us get through dinner before they plunged us into everlasting darkness, wasn't it, Mr. O'Connor?

JIM: Ha-ha!

AMANDA: Tom, as a penalty for your carelessness you can help me with the dishes.

JIM: Let me give you a hand.

AMANDA: Indeed you will not!

JIM: I ought to be good for something.

AMANDA: Good for something? (*Her tone is rhapsodic.*) *You?* Why, Mr. O'Connor, nobody, *nobody's* given me this much entertainment in years—as you have!

JIM: Aw, now, Mrs. Wingfield!

AMANDA: I'm not exaggerating, not one bit! But Sister is all by her lonesome. You go keep her company in the parlor! I'll give you this lovely old candelabrum that used to be on the altar at the church of the Heavenly Rest. It was melted a little out of shape when the church burnt down. Lightning struck it one spring. Gypsy Jones was holding a revival at the time and he intimated that the church was destroyed because the Episcopalians gave card parties.

JIM: Ha-ha.

AMANDA: And how about coaxing Sister to drink a little wine? I think it would be good for her! Can you carry both at once?

JIM: Sure. I'm Superman!

AMANDA: Now, Thomas, get into this apron!

(*The door of kitchenette swings closed on Amanda's gay laughter; the flickering light approaches the portieres.*)

(*Laura sits up nervously as he enters. Her speech at first is low and breathless from the almost intolerable strain of being alone with a stranger.*)

(*The legend: "I Don't Suppose You Remember Me at All!"*)

(*In her first speeches in this scene, before Jim's warmth overcomes her paralyzing shyness, Laura's voice is thin and breathless as though she has just run up a steep flight of stairs.*)

(*Jim's attitude is gently humorous. In playing this scene it should be stressed that while the incident is apparently unimportant, it is to Laura the climax of her secret life.*)

JIM: Hello, there, Laura.

LAURA (*faintly*): Hello. (*She clears her throat.*)

JIM: How are you feeling now? Better?

LAURA: Yes. Yes, thank you.

JIM: This is for you. A little dandelion wine. (*He extends it toward her with extravagant gallantry.*)

LAURA: Thank you.

JIM: Drink it—but don't get drunk! (*He laughs heartily. Laura takes the glass uncertainly; laughs shyly.*) Where shall I set the candles?

LAURA: Oh—oh, anywhere . . .

JIM: How about here on the floor? Any objections?

LAURA: No.

JIM: I'll spread a newspaper under to catch the drippings. I like to sit on the floor. Mind if I do?

LAURA: Oh, no.

JIM: Give me a pillow?

LAURA: What?

JIM: A pillow!

LAURA: Oh . . . (*Hands him one quickly.*)

JIM: How about you? Don't you like to sit on the floor?

LAURA: Oh—yes.

JIM: Why don't you, then?

LAURA: I—will.

JIM: Take a pillow! (*Laura does. Sits on the other side of the candelabrum. Jim crosses his legs and smiles engagingly at her.*) I can't hardly see you sitting way over there.

LAURA: I can—see you.

JIM: I know, but that's not fair, I'm in the limelight. (*Laura moves her pillow closer.*) Good! Now I can see you! Comfortable?

LAURA: Yes.

JIM: So am I. Comfortable as a cow. Will you have some gum?

LAURA: No, thank you.

JIM: I think that I will indulge, with your permission. (*Musingly unwraps it and holds it up.*) Think of the fortune made by the guy that invented the first piece of chewing gum. Amazing, huh? The Wrigley Building is one of the sights of Chicago.—I saw it summer before last when I went up to the Century of Progress. Did you take in the Century of Progress?

LAURA: No, I didn't.

JIM: Well, it was quite a wonderful exposition. What impressed me most was the Hall of Science. Gives you an idea of what the future will be in America, even more wonderful than the present time is! (*Pause. Smiling at her.*) Your brother tells me you're shy. Is that right, Laura?

LAURA: I—don't know.

JIM: I judge you to be an old-fashioned type of girl. Well, I think that's a pretty good type to be. Hope you don't think I'm being too personal—do you?

LAURA (*hastily, out of embarrassment*): I believe I *will* take a piece of gum, if you—don't mind. (*Clearing her throat.*) Mr. O'Connor, have you—kept up with your singing?

JIM: Singing? Me?

LAURA: Yes. I remember what a beautiful voice you had.

JIM: When did you hear me sing?

(*Voice offstage in the pause.*)

VOICE: (*offstage*): O blow, ye winds, heigh-ho,
   A-roving I will go!
      I'm off to my love
      With a boxing glove —
   Ten thousand miles away!

JIM: You say you've heard me sing?

LAURA: Oh, yes! Yes, very often . . . I — don't suppose you remember me — at all?

JIM (*smiling doubtfully*): You know I have an idea I've seen you before. I had that idea soon as you opened the door. It seemed almost like I was about to remember your name. But the name that I started to call you — wasn't a name! And so I stopped myself before I said it.

LAURA: Wasn't it — Blue Roses?

JIM (*Springs up. Grinning.*): Blue Roses! My gosh, yes — Blue Roses! That's what I had on my tongue when you opened the door! Isn't it funny what tricks your memory plays? I didn't connect you with the high school somehow or other. But that's where it was; it was high school. I didn't even know you were Shakespeare's sister! Gosh, I'm sorry.

LAURA: I didn't expect you to. You — barely knew me!

JIM: But we did have a speaking acquaintance, huh?

LAURA: Yes, we — spoke to each other.

JIM: When did you recognize me?

LAURA: Oh, right away!

JIM: Soon as I came in the door?

LAURA: When I heard your name I thought it was probably you. I knew that Tom used to know you a little in high school. So when you came in the door — Well, then I was — sure.

JIM: Why didn't you *say* something, then?

LAURA (*breathlessly*): I didn't know what to say, I was — too surprised!

JIM: For goodness' sakes! You know, this sure is funny!

LAURA: Yes! Yes, isn't it, though . . .

JIM: Didn't we have a class in something together?

LAURA: Yes, we did.

JIM: What class was that?

LAURA: It was — singing — Chorus!

JIM: Aw!

LAURA: I sat across the aisle from you in the Aud.

JIM: Aw.

LAURA: Mondays, Wednesdays, and Fridays.

JIM: Now I remember—you always came in late.

LAURA: Yes, it was so hard for me, getting upstairs. I had that brace on my leg—it clumped so loud!

JIM: I never heard any clumping.

LAURA (*wincing at the recollection*): To me it sounded like—thunder!

JIM: Well, well, well, I never even noticed.

LAURA: And everybody was seated before I came in. I had to walk in front of all those people. My seat was in the back row. I had to go clumping all the way up the aisle with everyone watching!

JIM: You shouldn't have been self-conscious.

LAURA: I know, but I was. It was always such a relief when the singing started.

JIM: Aw, yes, I've placed you now! I used to call you Blue Roses. How was it that I got started calling you that?

LAURA: I was out of school a little while with pleurosis. When I came back you asked me what was the matter. I said I had pleurosis—you thought I said Blue Roses. That's what you always called me after that!

JIM: I hope you didn't mind.

LAURA: Oh, no—I liked it. You see, I wasn't acquainted with many— people . . .

JIM: As I remember you sort of stuck by yourself.

LAURA: I—I—never had much luck at—making friends.

JIM: I don't see why you wouldn't.

LAURA: Well, I—started out badly.

JIM: You mean being—

LAURA: Yes, it sort of—stood between me—

JIM: You shouldn't have let it!

LAURA: I know, but it did, and—

JIM: You were shy with people!

LAURA: I tried not to be but never could—

JIM: Overcome it?

LAURA: No, I—I never could!

JIM: I guess being shy is something you have to work out of kind of gradually.

LAURA (*sorrowfully*): Yes—I guess it—

JIM: Takes time!

LAURA: Yes—

JIM: People are not so dreadful when you know them. That's what you have to remember! And everybody has problems, not just you, but practically everybody has got some problems. You think of yourself as having the only problems, as being the only one who is disappointed. But just look around you and you will see lots of people as disappointed as

you are. For instance, I hoped when I was going to high school that I
would be further along at this time, six years later, than I am now—You
remember that wonderful write-up I had in *The Torch*?

LAURA: Yes! (*She rises and crosses to table.*)

JIM: It said I was bound to succeed in anything I went into! (*Laura
returns with the annual.*) Holy Jeez! The Torch! (*He accepts it reverently.
They smile across it with mutual wonder. Laura crouches beside him
and they begin to turn through it. Laura's shyness is dissolving in his
warmth.*)

LAURA: Here you are in *Pirates of Penzance!*

JIM (*wistfully*): I sang the baritone lead in that operetta.

LAURA (*rapidly*): So—*beautifully!*

JIM (*protesting*): Aw—

LAURA: Yes, yes—beautifully—beautifully!

JIM: You heard me?

LAURA: All three times!

JIM: No!

LAURA: Yes!

JIM: All three performances?

LAURA (*looking down*): Yes.

JIM: Why?

LAURA: I—wanted to ask you to—autograph my program.

JIM: Why didn't you ask me to?

LAURA: You were always surrounded by your own friends so much that I
never had a chance to.

JIM: You should have just—

LAURA: Well, I—thought you might think I was—

JIM: Thought I might think you was—what?

LAURA: Oh—

JIM (*with reflective relish*): I was beleaguered by females in those days.

LAURA: You were terribly popular!

JIM: Yeah—

LAURA: You had such a—friendly way—

JIM: I was spoiled in high school.

LAURA: Everybody—liked you!

JIM: Including you?

LAURA: I—yes, I—I did, too—(*She gently closes the book in her lap.*)

JIM: Well, well, well!—Give me that program, Laura. (*She hands it
to him. He signs it with a flourish.*) There you are—better late than
never!

LAURA: Oh, I—what a—surprise!

JIM: My signature isn't worth very much right now. But some day—
maybe—it will increase in value! Being disappointed is one thing and

being discouraged is something else. I am disappointed but I am not discouraged. I'm twenty-three years old. How old are you?

LAURA: I'll be twenty-four in June.

JIM: That's not old age!

LAURA: No, but—

JIM: You finished high school?

LAURA (*with difficulty*): I didn't go back.

JIM: You mean you dropped out?

LAURA: I made bad grades in my final examinations. (*She rises and replaces the book and the program. Her voice strained.*) How is—Emily Meisenbach getting along?

JIM: Oh, that kraut-head!

LAURA: Why do you call her that?

JIM: That's what she was.

LAURA: You're not still—going with her?

JIM: I never see her.

LAURA: It said in the Personal Section that you were—engaged!

JIM: I know, but I wasn't impressed by that—propaganda!

LAURA: It wasn't—the truth?

JIM: Only in Emily's optimistic opinion!

LAURA: Oh—

(*Legend: "What Have You Done since High School?"*)

(*Jim lights a cigarette and leans indolently back on his elbows smiling at Laura with a warmth and charm which lights her inwardly with altar candles. She remains by the table and turns in her hands a piece of glass to cover her tumult.*)

JIM (*after several reflective puffs on a cigarette*): What have you done since high school? (*She seems not to hear him.*) Huh? (*Laura looks up.*) I said what have you done since high school, Laura?

LAURA: Nothing much.

JIM: You must have been doing something these six long years.

LAURA: Yes.

JIM: Well, then, such as what?

LAURA: I took a business course at business college—

JIM: How did that work out?

LAURA: Well, not very—well—I had to drop out, it gave me—indigestion—

(*Jim laughs gently.*)

JIM: What are you doing now?

LAURA: I don't do anything—much. Oh, please don't think I sit around doing nothing! My glass collection takes up a good deal of my time. Glass is something you have to take good care of.

JIM: What did you say—about glass?

LAURA: Collection I said—I have one—(*She clears her throat and turns away again, acutely shy.*)

JIM (*abruptly*): You know what I judge to be the trouble with you? Inferiority complex! Know what that is? That's what they call it when someone low-rates himself! I understand it because I had it, too. Although my case was not so aggravated as yours seems to be. I had it until I took up public speaking, developed my voice, and learned that I had an aptitude for science. Before that time I never thought of myself as being outstanding in any way whatsoever! Now I've never made a regular study of it, but I have a friend who says I can analyze people better than doctors that make a profession of it. I don't claim that to be necessarily true, but I can sure guess a person's psychology, Laura! (*Takes out his gum.*) Excuse me, Laura. I always take it out when the flavor is gone. I'll use this scrap of paper to wrap it in. I know how it is to get it stuck on a shoe. Yep—that's what I judge to be your principal trouble. A lack of confidence in yourself as a person. You don't have the proper amount of faith in yourself. I'm basing that fact on a number of your remarks and also on certain observations I've made. For instance that clumping you thought was so awful in high school. You say that you even dreaded to walk into class. You see what you did? You dropped out of school, you gave up an education because of a clump, which as far as I know was practically nonexistent! A little physical defect is what you have. Hardly noticeable even! Magnified thousands of times by imagination! You know what my strong advice to you is? Think of yourself as *superior* in some way!

LAURA: In what way would I think?

JIM: Why, man alive, Laura! Just look about you a little. What do you see? A world full of common people! All of 'em born and all of 'em going to die! Which of them has one-tenth of your good points! Or mine! Or anyone else's, as far as that goes—Gosh! Everybody excels in some one thing. Some in many! (*Unconsciously glances at himself in the mirror.*) All you've got to do is discover in what! Take me, for instance. (*He adjusts his tie at the mirror.*) My interest happens to lie in electrodynamics. I'm taking a course in radio engineering at night school, Laura, on top of a fairly responsible job at the warehouse. I'm taking that course and studying public speaking.

LAURA: Ohhhh.

JIM: Because I believe in the future of television! (*Turning back to her.*) I wish to be ready to go up right along with it. Therefore I'm planning to get in on the ground floor. In fact, I've already made the right connections and all that remains is for the industry itself to get under way! Full steam—(*His eyes are starry.*) *Knowledge*—Zzzzzp! *Money*—

Zzzzzzp!—*Power!* That's the cycle democracy is built on! (*His attitude is convincingly dynamic. Laura stares at him, even her shyness eclipsed in her absolute wonder. He suddenly grins.*) I guess you think I think a lot of myself!

LAURA: No—o-o-o, I—

JIM: Now how about you? Isn't there something you take more interest in than anything else?

LAURA: Well, I do—as I said—have my—glass collection—

(*A peal of girlish laughter from the kitchen.*)

JIM: I'm not right sure I know what you're talking about. What kind of glass is it?

LAURA: Little articles of it, they're ornaments mostly! Most of them are little animals made out of glass, the tiniest little animals in the world. Mother calls them a glass menagerie! Here's an example of one, if you'd like to see it! This one is one of the oldest. It's nearly thirteen. (*He stretches out his hand.*) (*Music: "The Glass Menagerie."*) Oh, be careful—if you breathe, it breaks!

JIM: I'd better not take it. I'm pretty clumsy with things.

LAURA: Go on, I trust you with him! (*Places it in his palm.*) There now—you're holding him gently! Hold him over the light, he loves the light! You see how the light shines through him?

JIM: It sure does shine!

LAURA: I shouldn't be partial, but he is my favorite one.

JIM: What kind of a thing is this one supposed to be?

LAURA: Haven't you noticed the single horn on his forehead?

JIM: A unicorn, huh?

LAURA: Mmm-hmmm!

JIM: Unicorns, aren't they extinct in the modern world?

LAURA: I know!

JIM: Poor little fellow, he must feel sort of lonesome.

LAURA (*smiling*): Well, if he does he doesn't complain about it. He stays on a shelf with some horses that don't have horns and all of them seem to get along nicely together.

JIM: How do you know?

LAURA (*lightly*): I haven't heard any arguments among them!

JIM (*grinning*): No arguments, huh? Well, that's a pretty good sign! Where shall I set him?

LAURA: Put him on the table. They all like a change of scenery once in a while!

JIM (*stretching*): Well, well, well, well—Look how big my shadow is when I stretch!

LAURA: Oh, oh, yes—it stretches across the ceiling!

JIM (*crossing to door*): I think it's stopped raining. (*Opens fire escape door.*)
Where does the music come from?

LAURA: From the Paradise Dance Hall across the alley.

JIM: How about cutting the rug a little, Miss Wingfield?

LAURA: Oh, I—

JIM: Or is your program filled up? Let me have a look at it. (*Grasps imaginary card.*) Why, every dance is taken! I'll just have to scratch some out. (*Waltz music: "La Golondrina."*) Ahhh, a waltz! (*He executes some sweeping turns by himself then holds his arms toward Laura.*)

LAURA (*breathlessly*): I—can't dance!

JIM: There you go, that inferiority stuff!

LAURA: I've never danced in my life!

JIM: Come on, try!

LAURA: Oh, but I'd step on you!

JIM: I'm not made out of glass.

LAURA: How—how—how do we start?

JIM: Just leave it to me. You hold your arms out a little.

LAURA: Like this?

JIM: A little bit higher. Right. Now don't tighten up, that's the main thing about it—relax.

LAURA (*laughing breathlessly*): It's hard not to.

JIM: Okay.

LAURA: I'm afraid you can't budge me.

JIM: What do you bet I can't? (*He swings her into motion.*)

LAURA: Goodness, yes, you can!

JIM: Let yourself go, now, Laura, just let yourself go.

LAURA: I'm—

JIM: Come on!

LAURA: Trying!

JIM: Not so stiff—Easy does it!

LAURA: I know but I'm—

JIM: Loosen th' backbone! There now, that's a lot better.

LAURA: Am I?

JIM: Lots, lots better! (*He moves her about the room in a clumsy waltz.*)

LAURA: Oh, my!

JIM: Ha-ha!

LAURA: Oh, my goodness!

JIM: Ha-ha-ha! (*They suddenly bump into the table. Jim stops.*) What did we hit on?

LAURA: Table.

JIM: Did something fall off it? I think—

LAURA: Yes.

JIM: I hope that it wasn't the little glass horse with the horn!

LAURA: Yes.

JIM: Aw, aw, aw. Is it broken?

LAURA: Now it is just like all the other horses.

JIM: It's lost its—

LAURA: Horn! It doesn't matter. Maybe it's a blessing in disguise.

JIM: You'll never forgive me. I bet that that was your favorite piece of glass.

LAURA: I don't have favorites much. It's no tragedy, Freckles. Glass breaks so easily. No matter how careful you are. The traffic jars the shelves and things fall off them.

JIM: Still I'm awfully sorry that I was the cause.

LAURA (*smiling*): I'll just imagine he had an operation. The horn was removed to make him feel less—freakish! (*They both laugh.*) Now he will feel more at home with the other horses, the ones that don't have horns . . .

JIM: Ha-ha, that's very funny! (*Suddenly serious.*) I'm glad to see that you have a sense of humor. You know—you're—well—very different! Surprisingly different from anyone else I know! (*His voice becomes soft and hesitant with a genuine feeling.*) Do you mind me telling you that? (*Laura is abashed beyond speech.*) I mean it in a nice way . . . (*Laura nods shyly, looking away.*) You make me feel sort of—I don't know how to put it! I'm usually pretty good at expressing things, but—This is something that I don't know how to say! (*Laura touches her throat and clears it—turns the broken unicorn in her hands.*) (*Even softer.*) Has anyone ever told you that you were pretty? (*Pause: Music.*) (*Laura looks up slowly, with wonder, and shakes her head.*) Well, you are! In a very different way from anyone else. And all the nicer because of the difference, too. (*His voice becomes low and husky. Laura turns away, nearly faint with the novelty of her emotions.*) I wish that you were my sister. I'd teach you to have some confidence in yourself. The different people are not like other people, but being different is nothing to be ashamed of. Because other people are not such wonderful people. They're one hundred times one thousand. You're one times one! They walk all over the earth. You just stay here. They're common as—weeds, but—you— well, you're—*Blue Roses!*

(*Image on screen: blue roses.*)
(*Music changes.*)

LAURA: But blue is wrong for—roses . . .

JIM: It's right for you—You're—pretty!

LAURA: In what respect am I pretty?

JIM: In all respects—believe me! Your eyes—your hair—are pretty! Your hands are pretty! (*He catches hold of her hand.*) You think I'm making this up because I'm invited to dinner and have to be nice. Oh, I could do that! I could put on an act for you, Laura, and say lots of things without being very sincere. But this time I am. I'm talking to you sincerely. I happened to notice you had this inferiority complex that keeps you from feeling comfortable with people. Somebody needs to build your confidence up and make you proud instead of shy and turning away and—blushing—Somebody ought to—Ought to—*kiss* you, Laura! (*His hand slips slowly up her arm to her shoulder.*) (*Music swells tumultuously.*) (*He suddenly turns her about and kisses her on the lips. When he releases her Laura sinks on the sofa with a bright, dazed look. Jim backs away and fishes in his pocket for a cigarette.*) (*Legend on screen: "Souvenir."*) Stumble-john! (*He lights the cigarette, avoiding her look. There is a peal of girlish laughter from Amanda in the kitchen. Laura slowly raises and opens her hand. It still contains the little broken glass animal. She looks at it with a tender, bewildered expression.*) Stumble-john! I shouldn't have done that—That was way off the beam. You don't smoke, do you? (*She looks up, smiling, not hearing the question. He sits beside her a little gingerly. She looks at him speechlessly—waiting. He coughs decorously and moves a little farther aside as he considers the situation and senses her feelings, dimly, with perturbation. Gently.*) Would you—care for a—mint? (*She doesn't seem to hear him but her look grows brighter even.*) Peppermint—Life Saver? My pocket's a regular drugstore—wherever I go . . . (*He pops a mint in his mouth. Then gulps and decides to make a clean breast of it. He speaks slowly and gingerly.*) Laura, you know, if I had a sister like you, I'd do the same thing as Tom. I'd bring out fellows and—introduce her to them. The right type of boys of a type to—appreciate her. Only— well—he made a mistake about me. Maybe I've got no call to be saying this. That may not have been the idea in having me over. But what if it was? There's nothing wrong about that. The only trouble is that in my case—I'm not in a situation to—do the right thing. I can't take down your number and say I'll phone. I can't call up next week and— ask for a date. I thought I had better explain the situation in case you misunderstood it and—hurt your feelings. . . . (*Pause. Slowly, very slowly, Laura's look changes, her eyes returning slowly from his to the ornament in her palm.*)

(*Amanda utters another gay laugh in the kitchen.*)

LAURA (*faintly*): You—won't—call again?

JIM: No, Laura, I can't. (*He rises from the sofa.*) As I was just explaining, I've—got strings on me, Laura, I've—been going steady! I go out all the time with a girl named Betty. She's a home-girl like you, and Catholic, and Irish, and in a great many ways we—get along fine. I

met her last summer on a moonlight boat trip up the river to Alton, on the *Majestic*. Well — right away from the start it was — love! (*Legend: Love!*) (*Laura sways slightly forward and grips the arm of the sofa. He fails to notice, now enrapt in his own comfortable being.*) Being in love has made a new man of me! (*Leaning stiffly forward, clutching the arm of the sofa, Laura struggles visibly with her storm. But Jim is oblivious, she is a long way off.*) The power of love is really pretty tremendous! Love is something that — changes the whole world, Laura! (*The storm abates a little and Laura leans back. He notices her again.*) It happened that Betty's aunt took sick, she got a wire and had to go to Centralia. So Tom — when he asked me to dinner — I naturally just accepted the invitation, not knowing that you — that he — that I — (*He stops awkwardly.*) Huh — I'm a stumble-john! (*He flops back on the sofa. The holy candles in the altar of Laura's face have been snuffed out! There is a look of almost infinite desolation. Jim glances at her uneasily.*) I wish that you would — say something. (*She bites her lip which was trembling and then bravely smiles. She opens her hand again on the broken glass ornament. Then she gently takes his hand and raises it level with her own. She carefully places the unicorn in the palm of his hand, then pushes his fingers closed upon it.*) What are you — doing that for? You want me to have him? — Laura? (*She nods.*) What for?
LAURA: A — souvenir . . .

(*She rises unsteadily and crouches beside the victrola to wind it up.*)
(*Legend on screen: "Things Have a Way of Turning out so Badly."*)
(*Or Image: "Gentleman Caller Waving Good-bye! — Gaily."*)
(*At this moment Amanda rushes brightly back in the front room. She bears a pitcher of fruit punch in an old-fashioned cut-glass pitcher and a plate of macaroons. The plate has a gold border and poppies painted on it.*)

AMANDA: Well, well, well! Isn't the air delightful after the shower? I've made you children a little liquid refreshment. (*Turns gaily to the gentleman caller.*) Jim, do you know that song about lemonade?
    "Lemonade, lemonade
        Made in the shade and stirred with a spade —
    Good enough for any old maid!"
JIM (*uneasily*): Ha-ha! No — I never heard it.
AMANDA: Why, Laura! You look so serious!
JIM: We were having a serious conversation.
AMANDA: Good! Now you're better acquainted!
JIM (*uncertainly*): Ha-ha! Yes.
AMANDA: You modern young people are much more serious-minded than my generation. I was so gay as a girl!
JIM: You haven't changed, Mrs. Wingfield.

AMANDA: Tonight I'm rejuvenated! The gaiety of the occasion, Mr. O'Connor! (*She tosses her head with a peal of laughter. Spills lemonade.*) Oooo! I'm baptizing myself!

JIM: Here—let me—

AMANDA (*setting the pitcher down*): There now. I discovered we had some maraschino cherries. I dumped them in, juice and all!

JIM: You shouldn't have gone to that trouble, Mrs. Wingfield.

AMANDA: Trouble, trouble? Why it was loads of fun! Didn't you hear me cutting up in the kitchen? I bet your ears were burning! I told Tom how out-done with him I was for keeping you to himself so long a time! He should have brought you over much, much sooner! Well, now that you've found your way, I want you to be a very frequent caller! Not just occasional but all the time. Oh, we're going to have a lot of gay times together! I see them coming! Mmm, just breathe that air! So fresh, and the moon's so pretty! I'll skip back out—I know where my place is when young folks are having a—serious conversation!

JIM: Oh, don't go out, Mrs. Wingfield. The fact of the matter is I've got to be going.

AMANDA: Going, now? You're joking! Why, it's only the shank of the evening, Mr. O'Connor!

JIM: Well, you know how it is.

AMANDA: You mean you're a young workingman and have to keep workingmen's hours. We'll let you off early tonight. But only on the condition that next time you stay later. What's the best night for you? Isn't Saturday night the best night for you workingmen?

JIM: I have a couple of time clocks to punch, Mrs. Wingfield. One at morning, another one at night!

AMANDA: My, but you *are* ambitious! You work at night, too?

JIM: No, Ma'am, not work but—Betty! (*He crosses deliberately to pick up his hat. The band at the Paradise Dance Hall goes into a tender waltz.*)

AMANDA: Betty? Betty? Who's—Betty! (*There is an ominous cracking sound in the sky.*)

JIM: Oh, just a girl. The girl I go steady with! (*He smiles charmingly. The sky falls.*)

(*Legend: "The Sky Falls."*)

AMANDA (*a long-drawn exhalation*): Ohhhh . . . Is it a serious romance, Mr. O'Connor?

JIM: We're going to be married the second Sunday in June.

AMANDA: Ohhhh—how nice! Tom didn't mention that you were engaged to be married.

JIM: The cat's not out of the bag at the warehouse yet. You know how they are. They call you Romeo and stuff like that. (*He stops at the oval mirror to put on his hat. He carefully shapes the brim and the crown to give a discreetly dashing effect.*) It's been a wonderful evening, Mrs. Wingfield. I guess this is what they mean by Southern hospitality.

AMANDA: It really wasn't anything at all.

JIM: I hope it don't seem like I'm rushing off. But I promised Betty I'd pick her up at the Wabash depot, an' by the time I get my jalopy down there her train'll be in. Some women are pretty upset if you keep 'em waiting.

AMANDA: Yes, I know—The tyranny of women! (*Extends her hand.*) Good-bye, Mr. O'Connor. I wish you luck—and happiness—and success! All three of them, and so does Laura!—Don't you, Laura?

LAURA: Yes!

JIM (*taking her hand*): Good-bye, Laura. I'm certainly going to treasure that souvenir. And don't you forget the good advice I gave you. (*Raises his voice to a cheery shout.*) So long, Shakespeare! Thanks again, ladies—Good night!

(*He grins and ducks jauntily out.*)

(*Still bravely grimacing, Amanda closes the door on the gentleman caller. Then she turns back to the room with a puzzled expression. She and Laura don't dare to face each other. Laura crouches beside the victrola to wind it.*)

AMANDA (*faintly*): Things have a way of turning out so badly. I don't believe that I would play the victrola. Well, well—well—Our gentleman caller was engaged to be married! Tom!

TOM (*from back*): Yes, Mother?

AMANDA: Come in here a minute. I want to tell you something awfully funny.

TOM (*enters with macaroon and a glass of the lemonade*): Has the gentleman caller gotten away already?

AMANDA: The gentleman caller has made an early departure. What a wonderful joke you played on us!

TOM: How do you mean?

AMANDA: You didn't mention that he was engaged to be married.

TOM: Jim? Engaged?

AMANDA: That's what he just informed us.

TOM: I'll be jiggered! I didn't know about that.

AMANDA: That seems very peculiar.

TOM: What's peculiar about it?

AMANDA: Didn't you call him your best friend down at the warehouse?

TOM: He is, but how did I know?

AMANDA: It seems extremely peculiar that you wouldn't know your best friend was going to be married!

TOM: The warehouse is where I work, not where I know things about people!

AMANDA: You don't know things anywhere! You live in a dream; you manufacture illusions! (*He crosses to door.*) Where are you going?

TOM: I'm going to the movies.

AMANDA: That's right, now that you've had us make such fools of ourselves. The effort, the preparations, all the expense! The new floor lamp, the rug, the clothes for Laura! All for what? To entertain some other girl's fiancé! Go to the movies, go! Don't think about us, a mother deserted, an unmarried sister who's crippled and has no job! Don't let anything interfere with your selfish pleasure! Just go, go, go — to the movies!

TOM: All right, I will! The more you shout about my selfishness to me the quicker I'll go, and I won't go to the movies!

AMANDA: Go, then! Then go to the moon — you selfish dreamer!

(*Tom smashes his glass on the floor. He plunges out on the fire escape, slamming the door. Laura screams — cut by door.*)

(*Dance hall music up. Tom goes to the rail and grips it desperately, lifting his face in the chill white moonlight penetrating the narrow abyss of the alley.*)

(*Legend on screen: "And so Good-bye . . . "*)

(*Tom's closing speech is timed with the interior pantomime. The interior scene is played as though viewed through soundproof glass. Amanda appears to be making a comforting speech to Laura who is huddled upon the sofa. Now that we cannot hear the mother's speech, her silliness is gone and she has dignity and tragic beauty. Laura's dark hair hides her face until at the end of the speech she lifts it to smile at her mother. Amanda's gestures are slow and graceful, almost dancelike, as she comforts the daughter. At the end of her speech she glances a moment at the father's picture — then withdraws through the portieres. At close of Tom's speech, Laura blows out the candles, ending the play.*)

TOM: I didn't go to the moon, I went much further — for time is the longest distance between two places — Not long after that I was fired for writing a poem on the lid of a shoebox. I left Saint Louis. I descended the steps of this fire escape for a last time and followed, from then on, in my father's footsteps, attempting to find in motion what was lost in space — I traveled around a great deal. The cities swept about me like dead leaves, leaves that were brightly colored but torn away from the branches. I would have stopped, but I was pursued by something. It always came upon me unawares, taking me altogether by surprise. Perhaps it was a familiar bit of music. Perhaps it was only a piece of transparent glass — Perhaps I am walking along a street at night, in some strange city, before I have found companions. I pass the lighted window of a shop where perfume is sold. The window is filled with pieces of colored glass, tiny transparent bottles in delicate colors, like bits of a shattered rainbow. Then all at once my sister touches my shoulder. I turn around and look into her eyes . . . Oh, Laura, Laura, I tried to leave you behind me, but I am more faithful than I intended to be! I reach for a cigarette, I cross the street, I run into the movies or a bar, I buy a drink, I speak to the nearest stranger—anything that can blow your candles out! (*Laura bends over the candles.*)—for nowadays the world is lit by lightning! Blow out your candles, Laura—and so good-bye. . . .

(*She blows the candles out.*)
(*The scene dissolves.*)

1944

Death of a Salesman

Certain Private Conversations in Two Acts and a Requiem

ARTHUR MILLER [b. 1915]

Characters
WILLY LOMAN
LINDA
BIFF
HAPPY
BERNARD
THE WOMAN
CHARLEY
UNCLE BEN
HOWARD WAGNER
JENNY
STANLEY
MISS FORSYTHE
LETTA

The action takes place in Willy Loman's house and yard and in various places he visits in the New York and Boston of today.

(Throughout the play, in the stage directions, left and right mean stage left and stage right.)

ACT I

(A melody is heard, played upon a flute. It is small and fine, telling of grass and trees and the horizon. The curtain rises.)

(Before us is the Salesman's house. We are aware of towering, angular shapes behind it, surrounding it on all sides. Only the blue light of the sky falls upon the house and forestage; the surrounding area shows an angry glow of orange. As more light appears, we see a solid vault of apartment houses around the small, fragile-seeming home. An air of the dream clings to the place, a dream rising out of reality. The kitchen at center seems actual enough, for there is a kitchen table

with three chairs, and a refrigerator. But no other fixtures are seen. At the back of the kitchen there is a draped entrance, which leads to the living room. To the right of the kitchen, on a level raised two feet, is a bedroom furnished only with a brass bedstead and a straight chair. On a shelf over the bed a silver athletic trophy stands. A window opens onto the apartment house at the side.)

(Behind the kitchen, on a level raised six and a half feet, is the boys' bedroom, at present barely visible. Two beds are dimly seen, and at the back of the room a dormer window. [This bedroom is above the unseen living room.] At the left a stairway curves up to it from the kitchen.)

(The entire setting is wholly or, in some places, partially transparent. The roofline of the house is one-dimensional; under and over it we see the apartment buildings. Before the house lies an apron, curving beyond the forestage into the orchestra. This forward area serves as the back yard as well as the locale of all Willy's imaginings and of his city scenes. Whenever the action is in the present the actors observe the imaginary wall-lines, entering the house only through its door at the left. But in the scenes of the past these boundaries are broken, and characters enter or leave a room by stepping "through" a wall onto the forestage.)

(From the right, Willy Loman, the Salesman, enters, carrying two large sample cases. The flute plays on. He hears but is not aware of it. He is past sixty years of age, dressed quietly. Even as he crosses the stage to the doorway of the house, his exhaustion is apparent. He unlocks the door, comes into the kitchen, and thankfully lets his burden down, feeling the soreness of his palms. A word-sigh escapes his lips — it might be "Oh, boy, oh, boy." He closes the door then carries his cases out into the living room, through the draped kitchen doorway.)

(Linda, his wife, has stirred in her bed at the right. She gets out and puts on a robe, listening. Most often jovial, she has developed an iron repression of her exceptions to Willy's behavior — she more than loves him, she admires him, as though his mercurial nature, his temper, his massive dreams and little cruelties, served her only as sharp reminders of the turbulent longings within him, longings which she shares but lacks the temperament to utter and follow to their end.)

LINDA (*hearing Willy outside the bedroom, calls with some trepidation*): Willy!

WILLY: It's all right. I came back.

LINDA: Why? What happened? (*Slight pause.*) Did something happen, Willy?

WILLY: No, nothing happened.

LINDA: You didn't smash the car, did you?

WILLY (*with casual irritation*): I said nothing happened. Didn't you hear me?

LINDA: Don't you feel well?

WILLY: I'm tired to the death. (*The flute has faded away. He sits on the bed beside her, a little numb.*) I couldn't make it. I just couldn't make it, Linda.

LINDA (*very carefully, delicately*): Where were you all day? You look terrible.

WILLY: I got as far as a little above Yonkers. I stopped for a cup of coffee. Maybe it was the coffee.

LINDA: What?

WILLY (*after a pause*): I suddenly couldn't drive anymore. The car kept going off onto the shoulder, y'know?

LINDA (*helpfully*): Oh. Maybe it was the steering again. I don't think Angelo knows the Studebaker.

WILLY: No, it's me, it's me. Suddenly I realize I'm goin' sixty miles an hour and I don't remember the last five minutes. I'm—I can't seem to—keep my mind to it.

LINDA: Maybe it's your glasses. You never went for your new glasses.

WILLY: No, I see everything. I came back ten miles an hour. It took me nearly four hours from Yonkers.

LINDA (*resigned*): Well, you'll just have to take a rest, Willy, you can't continue this way.

WILLY: I just got back from Florida.

LINDA: But you didn't rest your mind. Your mind is overactive, and the mind is what counts, dear.

WILLY: I'll start out in the morning. Maybe I'll feel better in the morning. (*She is taking off his shoes.*) These goddam arch supports are killing me.

LINDA: Take an aspirin. Should I get you an aspirin? It'll soothe you.

WILLY (*with wonder*): I was driving along, you understand? And I was fine. I was even observing the scenery. You can imagine, me looking at scenery, on the road every week of my life. But it's so beautiful up there, Linda, the trees are so thick, and the sun is warm. I opened the windshield and just let the warm air bathe over me. And then all of a sudden I'm goin' off the road! I'm tellin' ya, I absolutely forgot I was driving. If I'd've gone the other way over the white line I might've killed somebody. So I went on again—and five minutes later I'm dreamin' again, and I nearly—(*He presses two fingers against his eyes.*) I have such thoughts, I have such strange thoughts.

LINDA: Willy, dear. Talk to them again. There's no reason why you can't work in New York.

WILLY: They don't need me in New York. I'm the New England man. I'm vital in New England.

LINDA: But you're sixty years old. They can't expect you to keep traveling every week.

WILLY: I'll have to send a wire to Portland. I'm supposed to see Brown and Morrison tomorrow morning at ten o'clock to show the line. Goddammit, I could sell them! (*He starts putting on his jacket.*)

LINDA (*taking the jacket from him*): Why don't you go down to the place tomorrow and tell Howard you've simply got to work in New York? You're too accommodating, dear.

WILLY: If old man Wagner was alive I'd a been in charge of New York now! That man was a prince, he was a masterful man. But that boy of his, that Howard, he don't appreciate. When I went north the first time, the Wagner Company didn't know where New England was!

LINDA: Why don't you tell those things to Howard, dear?

WILLY (*encouraged*): I will, I definitely will. Is there any cheese?

LINDA: I'll make you a sandwich.

WILLY: No, go to sleep. I'll take some milk. I'll be up right away. The boys in?

LINDA: They're sleeping. Happy took Biff on a date tonight.

WILLY (*interested*): That so?

LINDA: It was so nice to see them shaving together, one behind the other, in the bathroom. And going out together. You notice? The whole house smells of shaving lotion.

WILLY: Figure it out. Work a lifetime to pay off a house. You finally own it, and there's nobody to live in it.

LINDA: Well, dear, life is a casting off. It's always that way.

WILLY: No, no, some people—some people accomplish something. Did Biff say anything after I went this morning?

LINDA: You shouldn't have criticized him, Willy, especially after he just got off the train. You mustn't lose your temper with him.

WILLY: When the hell did I lose my temper? I simply asked him if he was making any money. Is that a criticism?

LINDA: But, dear, how could he make any money?

WILLY (*worried and angered*): There's such an undercurrent in him. He became a moody man. Did he apologize when I left this morning?

LINDA: He was crestfallen, Willy. You know how he admires you. I think if he finds himself, then you'll both be happier and not fight any more.

WILLY: How can he find himself on a farm? Is that a life? A farmhand? In the beginning, when he was young, I thought, well, a young man, it's good for him to tramp around, take a lot of different jobs. But it's more than ten years now and he has yet to make thirty-five dollars a week!

LINDA: He's finding himself, Willy.

WILLY: Not finding yourself at the age of thirty-four is a disgrace!

LINDA: Shh!

WILLY: The trouble is he's lazy, goddammit!

LINDA: Willy, please!

WILLY: Biff is a lazy bum!

LINDA: They're sleeping. Get something to eat. Go on down.

WILLY: Why did he come home? I would like to know what brought him home.

LINDA: I don't know. I think he's still lost, Willy. I think he's very lost.

WILLY: Biff Loman is lost. In the greatest country in the world a young
man with such—personal attractiveness, gets lost. And such a hard
worker. There's one thing about Biff—he's not lazy.

LINDA: Never.

WILLY (*with pity and resolve*): I'll see him in the morning; I'll have a nice
talk with him. I'll get him a job selling. He could be big in no time. My
God! Remember how they used to follow him around in high school?
When he smiled at one of them their faces lit up. When he walked
down the street . . . (*He loses himself in reminiscences.*)

LINDA (*trying to bring him out of it*): Willy, dear, I got a new kind of
American-type cheese today. It's whipped.

WILLY: Why do you get American when I like Swiss?

LINDA: I just thought you'd like a change—

WILLY: I don't want a change! I want Swiss cheese. Why am I always
being contradicted?

LINDA (*with a covering laugh*): I thought it would be a surprise.

WILLY: Why don't you open a window in here, for God's sake?

LINDA (*with infinite patience*): They're all open, dear.

WILLY: The way they boxed us in here. Bricks and windows, windows
and bricks.

LINDA: We should've bought the land next door.

WILLY: The street is lined with cars. There's not a breath of fresh air in
the neighborhood. The grass don't grow anymore, you can't raise a
carrot in the back yard. They should've had a law against apartment
houses. Remember those two beautiful elm trees out there? When I
and Biff hung the swing between them?

LINDA: Yeah, like being a million miles from the city.

WILLY: They should've arrested the builder for cutting those down. They
massacred the neighborhood. (*Lost.*) More and more I think of those
days, Linda. This time of year it was lilac and wisteria. And then the
peonies would come out, and the daffodils. What fragrance in this room!

LINDA: Well, after all, people had to move somewhere.

WILLY: No, there's more people now.

LINDA: I don't think there's more people. I think—

WILLY: There's more people! That's what's ruining this country!
Population is getting out of control. The competition is maddening!
Smell the stink from that apartment house! And another one on the
other side . . . How can they whip cheese?

(*On Willy's last line, Biff and Happy raise themselves up in their beds, listening.*)

LINDA: Go down, try it. And be quiet.

WILLY (*turning to Linda, guiltily*): You're not worried about me, are you,
sweetheart?

BIFF: What's the matter?

HAPPY: Listen!

LINDA: You've got too much on the ball to worry about.

WILLY: You're my foundation and my support, Linda.

LINDA: Just try to relax, dear. You make mountains out of molehills.

WILLY: I won't fight with him any more. If he wants to go back to Texas, let him go.

LINDA: He'll find his way.

WILLY: Sure. Certain men just don't get started till later in life. Like Thomas Edison, I think. Or B. F. Goodrich. One of them was deaf. (*He starts for the bedroom doorway.*) I'll put my money on Biff.

LINDA: And Willy—if it's warm Sunday we'll drive in the country. And we'll open the windshield, and take lunch.

WILLY: No, the windshields don't open on the new cars.

LINDA: But you opened it today.

WILLY: Me? I didn't. (*He stops.*) Now isn't that peculiar! Isn't that a remarkable—(*He breaks off in amazement and fright as the flute is heard distantly.*)

LINDA: What, darling?

WILLY: That is the most remarkable thing.

LINDA: What, dear?

WILLY: I was thinking of the Chevvy. (*Slight pause.*) Nineteen twenty-eight . . . when I had that red Chevvy—(*Breaks off.*) That funny? I coulda sworn I was driving that Chevvy today.

LINDA: Well, that's nothing. Something must've reminded you.

WILLY: Remarkable. Ts. Remember those days? The way Biff used to simonize that car? The dealer refused to believe there was eighty thousand miles on it. (*He shakes his head.*) Heh! (*To Linda.*) Close your eyes, I'll be right up. (*He walks out of the bedroom.*)

HAPPY (*to Biff*): Jesus, maybe he smashed up the car again!

LINDA (*calling after Willy*): Be careful on the stairs, dear! The cheese is on the middle shelf! (*She turns, goes over to the bed, takes his jacket, and goes out of the bedroom.*)

(*Light has risen on the boys' room. Unseen, Willy is heard talking to himself, "Eighty thousand miles," and a little laugh. Biff gets out of bed, comes downstage a bit, and stands attentively. Biff is two years older than his brother Happy, well built, but in these days bears a worn air and seems less self-assured. He has succeeded less, and his dreams are stronger and less acceptable than Happy's. Happy is tall, powerfully made. Sexuality is like a visible color on him, or a scent that many women have discovered. He, like his brother, is lost, but in a different way, for he has never allowed himself to turn his face toward defeat and is thus more confused and hard-skinned, although seemingly more content.*)

HAPPY (*getting out of bed*): He's going to get his license taken away if he keeps that up. I'm getting nervous about him, y'know, Biff?

BIFF: His eyes are going.

HAPPY: No, I've driven with him. He sees all right. He just doesn't keep his mind on it. I drove into the city with him last week. He stops at a green light and then it turns red and he goes. (*He laughs.*)

BIFF: Maybe he's color-blind.

HAPPY: Pop? Why he's got the finest eye for color in the business. You know that.

BIFF (*sitting down on his bed*): I'm going to sleep.

HAPPY: You're not still sour on Dad, are you, Biff?

BIFF: He's all right, I guess.

WILLY (*underneath them, in the living room*): Yes, sir, eighty thousand miles—eighty-two thousand!

BIFF: You smoking?

HAPPY (*holding out a pack of cigarettes*): Want one?

BIFF (*taking a cigarette*): I can never sleep when I smell it.

WILLY: What a simonizing job, heh!

HAPPY (*with deep sentiment*): Funny, Biff, y'know? Us sleeping in here again? The old beds. (*He pats his bed affectionately.*) All the talk that went across those two beds, huh? Our whole lives.

BIFF: Yeah. Lotta dreams and plans.

HAPPY (*with a deep and masculine laugh*): About five hundred women would like to know what was said in this room.

(*They share a soft laugh.*)

BIFF: Remember that big Betsy something—what the hell was her name—over on Bushwick Avenue?

HAPPY (*combing his hair*): With the collie dog!

BIFF: That's the one. I got you in there, remember?

HAPPY: Yeah, that was my first time—I think. Boy, there was a pig. (*They laugh, almost crudely.*) You taught me everything I know about women. Don't forget that.

BIFF: I bet you forgot how bashful you used to be. Especially with girls.

HAPPY: Oh, I still am, Biff.

BIFF: Oh, go on.

HAPPY: I just control it, that's all. I think I got less bashful and you got more so. What happened, Biff? Where's the old humor, the old confidence? (*He shakes Biff's knee. Biff gets up and moves restlessly about the room.*) What's the matter?

BIFF: Why does Dad mock me all the time?

HAPPY: He's not mocking you, he—

BIFF: Everything I say there's a twist of mockery on his face. I can't get near him.

HAPPY: He just wants you to make good, that's all. I wanted to talk to you about Dad for a long time, Biff. Something's—happening to him. He—talks to himself.

BIFF: I noticed that this morning. But he always mumbled.

HAPPY: But not so noticeable. It got so embarrassing I sent him to Florida. And you know something? Most of the time he's talking to you.

BIFF: What's he say about me?

HAPPY: I can't make it out.

BIFF: What's he say about me?

HAPPY: I think the fact that you're not settled, that you're still kind of up in the air . . .

BIFF: There's one or two other things depressing him, Happy.

HAPPY: What do you mean?

BIFF: Never mind. Just don't lay it all to me.

HAPPY: But I think if you just got started—I mean—is there any future for you out there?

BIFF: I tell ya, Hap, I don't know what the future is. I don't know—what I'm supposed to want.

HAPPY: What do you mean?

BIFF: Well, I spent six or seven years after high school trying to work myself up. Shipping clerk, salesman, business of one kind or another. And it's a measly manner of existence. To get on that subway on the hot mornings in summer. To devote your whole life to keeping stock, or making phone calls, or selling or buying. To suffer fifty weeks of the year for the sake of a two-week vacation, when all you really desire is to be outdoors, with your shirt off. And always to have to get ahead of the next fella. And still—that's how you build a future.

HAPPY: Well, you really enjoy it on a farm? Are you content out there?

BIFF (*with rising agitation*): Hap, I've had twenty or thirty different kinds of jobs since I left home before the war, and it always turns out the same. I just realized it lately. In Nebraska when I herded cattle, and the Dakotas, and Arizona, and now in Texas. It's why I came home now, I guess, because I realized it. This farm I work on, it's spring there now, see? And they've got about fifteen new colts. There's nothing more inspiring or—beautiful than the sight of a mare and a new colt. And it's cool there now, see? Texas is cool now, and it's spring. And whenever spring comes to where I am, I suddenly get the feeling, my God, I'm not gettin' anywhere! What the hell am I doing, playing around with horses, twenty-eight dollars a week! I'm thirty-four years old, I oughta be makin' my future. That's when I come running home. And now, I get here, and I don't know what to do with myself. (*After a pause.*) I've always made a point of not wasting my life, and every time I come back here I know that all I've done is to waste my life.

HAPPY: You're a poet, you know that, Biff? You're a—you're an idealist!

BIFF: No, I'm mixed up very bad. Maybe I oughta get married. Maybe I oughta get stuck into something. Maybe that's my trouble. I'm like a boy. I'm not married, I'm not in business, I just—I'm like a boy. Are you content, Hap? You're a success, aren't you? Are you content?

HAPPY: Hell, no!

BIFF: Why? You're making money, aren't you?

HAPPY (*moving about with energy, expressiveness*): All I can do now is wait for the merchandise manager to die. And suppose I get to be merchandise manager? He's a good friend of mine, and he just built a terrific estate on Long Island. And he lived there about two months and sold it, and now he's building another one. He can't enjoy it once it's finished. And I know that's just what I would do. I don't know what the hell I'm workin' for. Sometimes I sit in my apartment—all alone. And I think of the rent I'm paying. And it's crazy. But then, it's what I always wanted. My own apartment, a car, and plenty of women. And still, goddammit, I'm lonely.

BIFF (*with enthusiasm*): Listen, why don't you come out West with me?

HAPPY: You and I, heh?

BIFF: Sure, maybe we could buy a ranch. Raise cattle, use our muscles. Men built like we are should be working out in the open.

HAPPY (*avidly*): The Loman Brothers, heh?

BIFF (*with vast affection*): Sure, we'd be known all over the counties!

HAPPY (*enthralled*): That's what I dream about, Biff. Sometimes I want to just rip my clothes off in the middle of the store and outbox that goddam merchandise manager. I mean I can outbox, outrun and outlift anybody in that store, and I have to take orders from those common, petty sons-of-bitches till I can't stand it anymore.

BIFF: I'm tellin' you, kid, if you were with me I'd be happy out there.

HAPPY (*enthused*): See, Biff, everybody around me is so false that I'm constantly lowering my ideals . . .

BIFF: Baby, together we'd stand up for one another, we'd have someone to trust.

HAPPY: If I were around you—

BIFF: Hap, the trouble is we weren't brought up to grub for money. I don't know how to do it.

HAPPY: Neither can I!

BIFF: Then let's go!

HAPPY: The only thing is—what can you make out there?

BIFF: But look at your friend. Builds an estate and then hasn't the peace of mind to live in it.

HAPPY: Yeah, but when he walks into the store the waves part in front of him. That's fifty-two thousand dollars a year coming through the revolving door, and I got more in my pinky finger than he's got in his head.

BIFF: Yeah, but you just said—

HAPPY: I gotta show some of those pompous, self-important executives over there that Hap Loman can make the grade. I want to walk into the store the way he walks in. Then I'll go with you, Biff. We'll be together yet, I swear. But take those two we had tonight. Now weren't they gorgeous creatures?

BIFF: Yeah, yeah, most gorgeous I've had in years.

HAPPY: I get that any time I want, Biff. Whenever I feel disgusted. The only trouble is, it gets like bowling or something. I just keep knockin' them over and it doesn't mean anything. You still run around a lot?

BIFF: Naa. I'd like to find a girl—steady, somebody with substance.

HAPPY: That's what I long for.

BIFF: Go on! You'd never come home.

HAPPY: I would! Somebody with character, with resistance! Like Mom, y'know? You're gonna call me a bastard when I tell you this. That girl Charlotte I was with tonight is engaged to be married in five weeks. (*He tries on his new hat.*)

BIFF: No kiddin'!

HAPPY: Sure, the guy's in line for the vice-presidency of the store. I don't know what gets into me, maybe I just have an overdeveloped sense of competition or something, but I went and ruined her, and furthermore I can't get rid of her. And he's the third executive I've done that to. Isn't that a crummy characteristic? And to top it all, I go to their weddings! (*Indignantly, but laughing.*) Like I'm not supposed to take bribes. Manufacturers offer me a hundred-dollar bill now and then to throw an order their way. You know how honest I am, but it's like this girl, see. I hate myself for it. Because I don't want the girl, and, still, I take it and—I love it!

BIFF: Let's go to sleep.

HAPPY: I guess we didn't settle anything, heh?

BIFF: I just got one idea that I think I'm going to try.

HAPPY: What's that?

BIFF: Remember Bill Oliver?

HAPPY: Sure, Oliver is very big now. You want to work for him again?

BIFF: No, but when I quit he said something to me. He put his arm on my shoulder, and he said, "Biff, if you ever need anything, come to me."

HAPPY: I remember that. That sounds good.

BIFF: I think I'll go to see him. If I could get ten thousand or even seven or eight thousand dollars I could buy a beautiful ranch.

HAPPY: I bet he'd back you. 'Cause he thought highly of you, Biff. I mean, they all do. You're well liked, Biff. That's why I say to come back here, and we both have the apartment. And I'm tellin' you, Biff, any babe you want . . .

BIFF: No, with a ranch I could do the work I like and still be something. I just wonder though. I wonder if Oliver still thinks I stole that carton of basketballs.

HAPPY: Oh, he probably forgot that long ago. It's almost ten years. You're too sensitive. Anyway, he didn't really fire you.

BIFF: Well, I think he was going to. I think that's why I quit. I was never sure whether he knew or not. I know he thought the world of me, though. I was the only one he'd let lock up the place.

WILLY (*below*): You gonna wash the engine, Biff?

HAPPY: Shh!

(*Biff looks at Happy, who is gazing down, listening. Willy is mumbling in the parlor.*)

HAPPY: You hear that?

(*They listen. Willy laughs warmly.*)

BIFF (*growing angry*): Doesn't he know Mom can hear that?

WILLY: Don't get your sweater dirty, Biff!

(*A look of pain crosses Biff's face.*)

HAPPY: Isn't that terrible? Don't leave again, will you? You'll find a job here. You gotta stick around. I don't know what to do about him, it's getting embarrassing.

WILLY: What a simonizing job!

BIFF: Mom's hearing that!

WILLY: No kiddin', Biff, you got a date? Wonderful!

HAPPY: Go on to sleep. But talk to him in the morning, will you?

BIFF (*reluctantly getting into bed*): With her in the house. Brother!

HAPPY (*getting into bed*): I wish you'd have a good talk with him.

(*The light on their room begins to fade.*)

BIFF (*to himself in bed*): That selfish, stupid . . .

HAPPY: Sh . . . Sleep, Biff.

(*Their light is out. Well before they have finished speaking, Willy's form is dimly seen below in the darkened kitchen. He opens the refrigerator, searches in there, and takes out a bottle of milk. The apartment houses are fading out, and the entire house and surroundings become covered with leaves. Music insinuates itself as the leaves appear.*)

WILLY: Just wanna be careful with those girls, Biff, that's all. Don't make any promises. No promises of any kind. Because a girl, y'know, they always believe what you tell 'em, and you're very young, Biff, you're too young to be talking seriously to girls.

(*Light rises on the kitchen. Willy, talking, shuts the refrigerator door and comes downstage to the kitchen table. He pours milk into a glass. He is totally immersed in himself, smiling faintly.*)

WILLY: Too young entirely, Biff. You want to watch your schooling first. Then when you're all set, there'll be plenty of girls for a boy like you. (*He smiles broadly at a kitchen chair.*) That so? The girls pay for you? (*He laughs.*) Boy, you must really be makin' a hit.

(*Willy is gradually addressing—physically—a point offstage, speaking through the wall of the kitchen, and his voice has been rising in volume to that of a normal conversation.*)

WILLY: I been wondering why you polish the car so careful. Ha! Don't leave the hubcaps, boys. Get the chamois to the hubcaps. Happy, use newspaper on the windows, it's the easiest thing. Show him how to do it, Biff! You see, Happy? Pad it up, use it like a pad. That's it, that's it, good work. You're doin' all right, Hap. (*He pauses, then nods in approbation for a few seconds, then looks upward.*) Biff, first thing we gotta do when we get time is clip that big branch over the house. Afraid it's gonna fall in a storm and hit the roof. Tell you what. We get a rope and sling her around, and then we climb up there with a couple of saws and take her down. Soon as you finish the car, boys, I wanna see ye. I got a surprise for you, boys.

BIFF (*offstage*): Whatta ya got, Dad?

WILLY: No, you finish first. Never leave a job till you're finished— remember that. (*Looking toward the "big trees."*) Biff, up in Albany I saw a beautiful hammock. I think I'll buy it next trip, and we'll hang it right between those two elms. Wouldn't that be something? Just swingin' there under those branches. Boy, that would be . . .

(*Young Biff and Young Happy appear from the direction Willy was addressing. Happy carries rags and a pail of water. Biff, wearing a sweater with a block "S," carries a football.*)

BIFF (*pointing in the direction of the car offstage*): How's that, Pop, professional?

WILLY: Terrific. Terrific job, boys. Good work, Biff.

HAPPY: Where's the surprise, Pop?

WILLY: In the back seat of the car.

HAPPY: Boy! (*He runs off.*)

BIFF: What is it, Dad? Tell me, what'd you buy?

WILLY (*laughing, cuffs him*): Never mind, something I want you to have.

BIFF (*turns and starts off*): What is it, Hap?

HAPPY (*offstage*): It's a punching bag!

BIFF: Oh, Pop!

WILLY: It's got Gene Tunney's signature on it!

(*Happy runs onstage with a punching bag.*)

BIFF: Gee, how'd you know we wanted a punching bag?

WILLY: Well, it's the finest thing for the timing.

HAPPY (*lies down on his back and pedals with his feet*): I'm losing weight, you notice, Pop?

WILLY (*to Happy*): Jumping rope is good too.

BIFF: Did you see the new football I got?

WILLY (*examining the ball*): Where'd you get a new ball?

BIFF: The coach told me to practice my passing.

WILLY: That so? And he gave you the ball, heh?

BIFF: Well, I borrowed it from the locker room. (*He laughs confidentially.*)

WILLY (*laughing with him at the theft*): I want you to return that.

HAPPY: I told you he wouldn't like it!

BIFF (*angrily*): Well, I'm bringing it back!

WILLY (*stopping the incipient argument, to Happy*): Sure, he's gotta practice with a regulation ball, doesn't he? (*To Biff.*) Coach'll probably congratulate you on your initiative!

BIFF: Oh, he keeps congratulating my initiative all the time, Pop.

WILLY: That's because he likes you. If somebody else took that ball there'd be an uproar. So what's the report, boys, what's the report?

BIFF: Where'd you go this time, Dad? Gee we were lonesome for you.

WILLY (*pleased, puts an arm around each boy and they come down to the apron*): Lonesome, heh?

BIFF: Missed you every minute.

WILLY: Don't say? Tell you a secret, boys. Don't breathe it to a soul. Someday I'll have my own business, and I'll never have to leave home anymore.

HAPPY: Like Uncle Charley, heh?

WILLY: Bigger than Uncle Charley! Because Charley is not—liked. He's liked, but he's not—well liked.

BIFF: Where'd you go this time, Dad?

WILLY: Well, I got on the road, and I went north to Providence. Met the Mayor.

BIFF: The Mayor of Providence!

WILLY: He was sitting in the hotel lobby.

BIFF: What'd he say?

WILLY: He said, "Morning!" And I said, "You got a fine city here, Mayor." And then he had coffee with me. And then I went to Waterbury. Waterbury is a fine city. Big clock city, the famous Waterbury clock. Sold a nice bill there. And then Boston—Boston is the cradle of the Revolution. A fine city. And a couple of other towns in Mass., and on to Portland and Bangor and straight home!

BIFF: Gee, I'd love to go with you sometime, Dad.

WILLY: Soon as summer comes.

HAPPY: Promise?

WILLY: You and Hap and I, and I'll show you all the towns. America is full of beautiful towns and fine, upstanding people. And they know me, boys, they know me up and down New England. The finest people. And when I bring you fellas up, there'll be open sesame for all of us, 'cause one thing, boys: I have friends. I can park my car in any street in New England, and the cops protect it like their own. This summer, heh?

BIFF AND HAPPY (*together*): Yeah! You bet!

WILLY: We'll take our bathing suits.

HAPPY: We'll carry your bags, Pop!

WILLY: Oh, won't that be something! Me comin' into the Boston stores with you boys carryin' my bags. What a sensation!

(*Biff is prancing around, practicing passing the ball.*)

WILLY: You nervous, Biff, about the game?

BIFF: Not if you're gonna be there.

WILLY: What do they say about you in school, now that they made you captain?

HAPPY: There's a crowd of girls behind him every time the classes change.

BIFF (*taking Willy's hand*): This Saturday, Pop, this Saturday—just for you, I'm going to break through for a touchdown.

HAPPY: You're supposed to pass.

BIFF: I'm takin' one play for Pop. You watch me, Pop, and when I take off my helmet, that means I'm breakin' out. Then you watch me crash through that line!

WILLY (*kisses Biff*): Oh, wait'll I tell this in Boston!

(*Bernard enters in knickers. He is younger than Biff, earnest and loyal, a worried boy.*)

BERNARD: Biff, where are you? You're supposed to study with me today.

WILLY: Hey, looka Bernard. What're you lookin' so anemic about, Bernard?

BERNARD: He's gotta study, Uncle Willy. He's got Regents next week.

HAPPY (*tauntingly, spinning Bernard around*): Let's box, Bernard!

BERNARD: Biff! (*He gets away from Happy.*) Listen, Biff, I heard Mr. Birnbaum say that if you don't start studyin' math he's gonna flunk you, and you won't graduate. I heard him!

WILLY: You better study with him, Biff. Go ahead now.

BERNARD: I heard him!

BIFF: Oh, Pop, you didn't see my sneakers! (*He holds up a foot for Willy to look at.*)

WILLY: Hey, that's a beautiful job of printing!

BERNARD (*wiping his glasses*): Just because he printed University of Virginia on his sneakers doesn't mean they've got to graduate him, Uncle Willy!

WILLY (*angrily*): What're you talking about? With scholarships to three universities they're gonna flunk him?

BERNARD: But I heard Mr. Birnbaum say—

WILLY: Don't be a pest, Bernard! (*To his boys.*) What an anemic!

BERNARD: Okay, I'm waiting for you in my house, Biff.

(*Bernard goes off. The Lomans laugh.*)

WILLY: Bernard is not well liked, is he?

BIFF: He's liked, but he's not well liked.

HAPPY: That's right, Pop.

WILLY: That's just what I mean. Bernard can get the best marks in school, y'understand, but when he gets out in the business world, y'understand, you are going to be five times ahead of him. That's why I thank Almighty God you're both built like Adonises. Because the man who makes an appearance in the business world, the man who creates personal interest, is the man who gets ahead. Be liked and you will never want. You take me, for instance. I never have to wait in line to see a buyer. "Willy Loman is here!" That's all they have to know, and I go right through.

BIFF: Did you knock them dead, Pop?

WILLY: Knocked 'em cold in Providence, slaughtered 'em in Boston.

HAPPY (*on his back, pedaling again*): I'm losing weight, you notice, Pop?

(*Linda enters as of old, a ribbon in her hair, carrying a basket of washing.*)

LINDA (*with youthful energy*): Hello, dear!

WILLY: Sweetheart!

LINDA: How'd the Chevvy run?

WILLY: Chevrolet, Linda, is the greatest car ever built. (*To the boys.*) Since when do you let your mother carry wash up the stairs?

BIFF: Grab hold there, boy!

HAPPY: Where to, Mom?

LINDA: Hang them up on the line. And you better go down to your friends, Biff. The cellar is full of boys. They don't know what to do with themselves.

BIFF: Ah, when Pop comes home they can wait!

WILLY (*laughs appreciatively*): You better go down and tell them what to do, Biff.

BIFF: I think I'll have them sweep out the furnace room.

WILLY: Good work, Biff.

BIFF (*goes through wall-line of kitchen to doorway at back and calls down*): Fellas! Everybody sweep out the furnace room! I'll be right down!

VOICES: All right! Okay, Biff.

BIFF: George and Sam and Frank, come out back! We're hangin' up the wash! Come on, Hap, on the double! (*He and Happy carry out the basket.*)

LINDA: The way they obey him!

WILLY: Well, that's training, the training. I'm tellin' you, I was sellin' thousands and thousands, but I had to come home.

LINDA: Oh, the whole block'll be at that game. Did you sell anything?

WILLY: I did five hundred gross in Providence and seven hundred gross in Boston.

LINDA: No! Wait a minute, I've got a pencil. (*She pulls pencil and paper out of her apron pocket.*) That makes your commission . . . Two hundred— my God! Two hundred and twelve dollars!

WILLY: Well, I didn't figure it yet, but . . .

LINDA: How much did you do?

WILLY: Well, I—I did—about a hundred and eighty gross in Providence. Well, no—it came to—roughly two hundred gross on the whole trip.

LINDA (*without hesitation*): Two hundred gross. That's . . . (*She figures.*)

WILLY: The trouble was that three of the stores were half-closed for inventory in Boston. Otherwise I woulda broke records.

LINDA: Well, it makes seventy dollars and some pennies. That's very good.

WILLY: What do we owe?

LINDA: Well, on the first there's sixteen dollars on the refrigerator—

WILLY: Why sixteen?

LINDA: Well, the fan belt broke, so it was a dollar eighty.

WILLY: But it's brand new.

LINDA: Well, the man said that's the way it is. Till they work themselves in, y'know.

(*They move through the wall-line into the kitchen.*)

WILLY: I hope we didn't get stuck on that machine.

LINDA: They got the biggest ads of any of them!

WILLY: I know, it's a fine machine. What else?

LINDA: Well, there's nine-sixty for the washing machine. And for the vacuum cleaner there's three and a half due on the fifteenth. Then the roof, you got twenty-one dollars remaining.

WILLY: It don't leak, does it?

LINDA: No, they did a wonderful job. Then you owe Frank for the carburetor.

WILLY: I'm not going to pay that man! That goddam Chevrolet, they ought to prohibit the manufacture of that car!

LINDA: Well, you owe him three and a half. And odds and ends, comes to around a hundred and twenty dollars by the fifteenth.

WILLY: A hundred and twenty dollars! My God, if business don't pick up I don't know what I'm gonna do!

LINDA: Well, next week you'll do better.

WILLY: Oh, I'll knock 'em dead next week. I'll go to Hartford. I'm very well liked in Hartford. You know, the trouble is, Linda, people don't seem to take to me.

(*They move onto the forestage.*)

LINDA: Oh, don't be foolish.

WILLY: I know it when I walk in. They seem to laugh at me.

LINDA: Why? Why would they laugh at you? Don't talk that way, Willy.

(*Willy moves to the edge of the stage. Linda goes into the kitchen and starts to darn stockings.*)

WILLY: I don't know the reason for it, but they just pass me by. I'm not noticed.

LINDA: But you're doing wonderful, dear. You're making seventy to a hundred dollars a week.

WILLY: But I gotta be at it ten, twelve hours a day. Other men—I don't know—they do it easier. I don't know why—I can't stop myself—I talk too much. A man oughta come in with a few words. One thing about Charley. He's a man of few words, and they respect him.

LINDA: You don't talk too much, you're just lively.

WILLY (*smiling*): Well, I figure, what the hell, life is short, a couple of jokes. (*To himself.*) I joke too much! (*The smile goes.*)

LINDA: Why? You're—

WILLY: I'm fat. I'm very—foolish to look at, Linda. I didn't tell you, but Christmas time I happened to be calling on F. H. Stewarts, and a salesman I know, as I was going in to see the buyer I heard him say something about—walrus. And I—I cracked him right across the face. I won't take that. I simply will not take that. But they do laugh at me. I know that.

LINDA: Darling . . .

WILLY: I gotta overcome it. I know I gotta overcome it. I'm not dressing to advantage, maybe.

LINDA: Willy, darling, you're the handsomest man in the world—

WILLY: Oh, no, Linda.

LINDA: To me you are. (*Slight pause.*) The handsomest.

(*From the darkness is heard the laughter of a woman. Willy doesn't turn to it, but it continues through Linda's lines.*)

LINDA: And the boys, Willy. Few men are idolized by their children the way you are.

(*Music is heard as behind a scrim, to the left of the house, The Woman, dimly seen, is dressing.*)

WILLY (*with great feeling*): You're the best there is, Linda, you're a pal, you know that? On the road—on the road I want to grab you sometimes and just kiss the life outa you.

(*The laughter is loud now, and he moves into a brightening area at the left, where The Woman has come from behind the scrim and is standing, putting on her hat, looking into a "mirror" and laughing.*)

WILLY: 'Cause I get so lonely—especially when business is bad and there's nobody to talk to. I get the feeling that I'll never sell anything again, that I won't make a living for you, or a business, a business for the boys. (*He talks through The Woman's subsiding laughter; The Woman primps at the "mirror."*) There's so much I want to make for—

THE WOMAN: Me? You didn't make me, Willy. I picked you.

WILLY (*pleased*): You picked me?

THE WOMAN (*who is quite proper-looking, Willy's age*): I did. I've been sitting at that desk watching all the salesmen go by, day in, day out. But you've got such a sense of humor, and we do have such a good time together, don't we?

WILLY: Sure, sure. (*He takes her in his arms.*) Why do you have to go now?

THE WOMAN: It's two o'clock . . .

WILLY: No, come on in! (*He pulls her.*)

THE WOMAN: . . . my sisters'll be scandalized. When'll you be back?

WILLY: Oh, two weeks about. Will you come up again?

THE WOMAN: Sure thing. You do make me laugh. It's good for me. (*She squeezes his arm, kisses him.*) And I think you're a wonderful man.

WILLY: You picked me, heh?

THE WOMAN: Sure. Because you're so sweet. And such a kidder.

WILLY: Well, I'll see you next time I'm in Boston.

THE WOMAN: I'll put you right through to the buyers.

WILLY (*slapping her bottom*): Right. Well, bottoms up!

THE WOMAN (*slaps him gently and laughs*): You just kill me, Willy. (*He suddenly grabs her and kisses her roughly.*) You kill me. And thanks for the stockings. I love a lot of stockings. Well, good night.

WILLY: Good night. And keep your pores open!

THE WOMAN: Oh, Willy!

(*The Woman bursts out laughing, and Linda's laughter blends in. The Woman disappears into the dark. Now the area at the kitchen table brightens. Linda is sitting where she was at the kitchen table, but now is mending a pair of her silk stockings.*)

LINDA: You are, Willy. The handsomest man. You've got no reason to feel that—

WILLY (*coming out of The Woman's dimming area and going over to Linda*): I'll make it all up to you, Linda, I'll—

LINDA: There's nothing to make up, dear. You're doing fine, better than—

WILLY (*noticing her mending*): What's that?

LINDA: Just mending my stockings. They're so expensive—

WILLY (*angrily, taking them from her*): I won't have you mending stockings in this house! Now throw them out!

(*Linda puts the stockings in her pocket.*)

BERNARD (*entering on the run*): Where is he? If he doesn't study!

WILLY (*moving to the forestage, with great agitation*): You'll give him the answers!

BERNARD: I do, but I can't on a Regents! That's a state exam! They're liable to arrest me!

WILLY: Where is he? I'll whip him, I'll whip him!

LINDA: And he'd better give back that football, Willy, it's not nice.

WILLY: Biff! Where is he? Why is he taking everything?

LINDA: He's too rough with the girls, Willy. All the mothers are afraid of him!

WILLY: I'll whip him!

BERNARD: He's driving the car without a license!

(*The Woman's laugh is heard.*)

WILLY: Shut up!

LINDA: All the mothers —

WILLY: Shut up!

BERNARD (*backing quietly away and out*): Mr. Birnbaum says he's stuck up.

WILLY: Get outa here!

BERNARD: If he doesn't buckle down he'll flunk math! (*He goes off.*)

LINDA: He's right, Willy, you've gotta —

WILLY (*exploding at her*): There's nothing the matter with him! You want him to be a worm like Bernard? He's got spirit, personality . . .

(*As he speaks, Linda, almost in tears, exits into the living room. Willy is alone in the kitchen, wilting and staring. The leaves are gone. It is night again, and the apartment houses look down from behind.*)

WILLY: Loaded with it. Loaded! What is he stealing? He's giving it back, isn't he? Why is he stealing? What did I tell him? I never in my life told him anything but decent things.

(*Happy in pajamas has come down the stairs; Willy suddenly becomes aware of Happy's presence.*)

HAPPY: Let's go now, come on.

WILLY (*sitting down at the kitchen table*): Huh! Why did she have to wax the floors herself? Everytime she waxes the floors she keels over. She knows that!

HAPPY: Shh! Take it easy. What brought you back tonight?

WILLY: I got an awful scare. Nearly hit a kid in Yonkers. God! Why didn't I go to Alaska with my brother Ben that time! Ben! That man was a genius, that man was success incarnate! What a mistake! He begged me to go.

HAPPY: Well, there's no use in —

WILLY: You guys! There was a man started with the clothes on his back and ended up with diamond mines!

HAPPY: Boy, someday I'd like to know how he did it.

WILLY: What's the mystery? The man knew what he wanted and went out and got it! Walked into a jungle, and comes out, the age of twenty-one, and he's rich! The world is an oyster, but you don't crack it open on a mattress!

HAPPY: Pop, I told you I'm gonna retire you for life.

WILLY: You'll retire me for life on seventy goddam dollars a week? And your women and your car and your apartment, and you'll retire me for life! Christ's sake, I couldn't get past Yonkers today! Where are you guys, where are you? The woods are burning! I can't drive a car!

(*Charley has appeared in the doorway. He is a large man, slow of speech, laconic, immovable. In all he says, despite what he says, there is pity, and, now,*) *trepidation. He has a robe over pajamas, slippers on his feet. He enters the kitchen.*)

CHARLEY: Everything all right?

HAPPY: Yeah, Charley, everything's . . .

WILLY: What's the matter?

CHARLEY: I heard some noise. I thought something happened. Can't we do something about the walls? You sneeze in here, and in my house hats blow off.

HAPPY: Let's go to bed, Dad. Come on.

(*Charley signals to Happy to go.*)

WILLY: You go ahead, I'm not tired at the moment.

HAPPY (*to Willy*): Take it easy, huh? (*He exits.*)

WILLY: What're you doin' up?

CHARLEY (*sitting down at the kitchen table opposite Willy*): Couldn't sleep good. I had a heartburn.

WILLY: Well, you don't know how to eat.

CHARLEY: I eat with my mouth.

WILLY: No, you're ignorant. You gotta know about vitamins and things like that.

CHARLEY: Come on, let's shoot. Tire you out a little.

WILLY (*hesitantly*): All right. You got cards?

CHARLEY (*taking a deck from his pocket*): Yeah, I got them. Someplace. What is it with those vitamins?

WILLY (*dealing*): They build up your bones. Chemistry.

CHARLEY: Yeah, but there's no bones in a heartburn.

WILLY: What are you talkin' about? Do you know the first thing about it?

CHARLEY: Don't get insulted.

WILLY: Don't talk about something you don't know anything about.

(*They are playing. Pause.*)

CHARLEY: What're you doin' home?

WILLY: A little trouble with the car.

CHARLEY: Oh. (*Pause.*) I'd like to take a trip to California.

WILLY: Don't say.

CHARLEY: You want a job?

WILLY: I got a job, I told you that. (*After a slight pause.*) What the hell are you offering me a job for?

CHARLEY: Don't get insulted.

WILLY: Don't insult me.

CHARLEY: I don't see no sense in it. You don't have to go on this way.

WILLY: I got a good job. (*Slight pause.*) What do you keep comin' in here for?

CHARLEY: You want me to go?

WILLY (*after a pause, withering*): I can't understand it. He's going back to Texas again. What the hell is that?

CHARLEY: Let him go.

WILLY: I got nothin' to give him, Charley, I'm clean, I'm clean.

CHARLEY: He won't starve. None a them starve. Forget about him.

WILLY: Then what have I got to remember?

CHARLEY: You take it too hard. To hell with it. When a deposit bottle is broken you don't get your nickel back.

WILLY: That's easy enough for you to say.

CHARLEY: That ain't easy for me to say.

WILLY: Did you see the ceiling I put up in the living room?

CHARLEY: Yeah, that's a piece of work. To put up a ceiling is a mystery to me. How do you do it?

WILLY: What's the difference?

CHARLEY: Well, talk about it.

WILLY: You gonna put up a ceiling?

CHARLEY: How could I put up a ceiling?

WILLY: Then what the hell are you bothering me for?

CHARLEY: You're insulted again.

WILLY: A man who can't handle tools is not a man. You're disgusting.

CHARLEY: Don't call me disgusting, Willy.

(*Uncle Ben, carrying a valise and an umbrella, enters the forestage from around the right corner of the house. He is a stolid man, in his sixties, with a mustache and an authoritative air. He is utterly certain of his destiny, and there is an aura of far places about him. He enters exactly as Willy speaks.*)

WILLY: I'm getting awfully tired, Ben.

(*Ben's music is heard. Ben looks around at everything.*)

CHARLEY: Good, keep playing; you'll sleep better. Did you call me Ben?

(*Ben looks at his watch.*)

WILLY: That's funny. For a second there you reminded me of my brother Ben.

BEN: I only have a few minutes. (*He strolls, inspecting the place. Willy and Charley continue playing.*)

CHARLEY: You never heard from him again, heh? Since that time?

WILLY: Didn't Linda tell you? Couple of weeks ago we got a letter from his wife in Africa. He died.

CHARLEY: That so.

BEN (*chuckling*): So this is Brooklyn, eh?

CHARLEY: Maybe you're in for some of his money.

WILLY: Naa, he had seven sons. There's just one opportunity I had with that man . . .

BEN: I must make a train, William. There are several properties I'm looking at in Alaska.

WILLY: Sure, sure! If I'd gone with him to Alaska that time, everything would've been totally different.

CHARLIE: Go on, you'd froze to death up there.

WILLY: What're you talking about?

BEN: Opportunity is tremendous in Alaska, William. Surprised you're not up there.

WILLY: Sure, tremendous.

CHARLEY: Heh?

WILLY: There was the only man I ever met who knew the answers.

CHARLEY: Who?

BEN: How are you all?

WILLY (*taking a pot, smiling*): Fine, fine.

CHARLEY: Pretty sharp tonight.

BEN: Is Mother living with you?

WILLY: No, she died a long time ago.

CHARLEY: Who?

BEN: That's too bad. Fine specimen of a lady, Mother.

WILLY (*to Charley*): Heh?

BEN: I'd hoped to see the old girl.

CHARLEY: Who died?

BEN: Heard anything from Father, have you?

WILLY (*unnerved*): What do you mean, who died?

CHARLEY (*taking a pot*): What're you talkin' about?

BEN (*looking at his watch*): William, it's half-past eight!

WILLY (*as though to dispel his confusion he angrily stops Charley's hand*): That's my build!

CHARLEY: I put the ace—

WILLY: If you don't know how to play the game I'm not gonna throw my money away on you!

CHARLEY (*rising*): It was my ace, for God's sake!

WILLY: I'm through, I'm through!

BEN: When did Mother die?

WILLY: Long ago. Since the beginning you never knew how to play cards.

CHARLEY (*picks up the cards and goes to the door*): All right! Next time I'll bring a deck with five aces.

WILLY: I don't play that kind of game!

CHARLEY (*turning to him*): You ought to be ashamed of yourself!

WILLY: Yeah?

CHARLEY: Yeah! (*He goes out.*)

WILLY (*slamming the door after him*): Ignoramus!

BEN (*as Willy comes toward him through the wall-line of the kitchen*): So you're William.

WILLY (*shaking Ben's hand*): Ben! I've been waiting for you so long! What's the answer? How did you do it?

BEN: Oh, there's a story in that.

(*Linda enters the forestage, as of old, carrying the wash basket.*)

LINDA: Is this Ben?

BEN (*gallantly*): How do you do, my dear.

LINDA: Where've you been all these years? Willy's always wondered why you—

WILLY (*pulling Ben away from her impatiently*): Where is Dad? Didn't you follow him? How did you get started?

BEN: Well, I don't know how much you remember.

WILLY: Well, I was just a baby, of course, only three or four years old—

BEN: Three years and eleven months.

WILLY: What a memory, Ben!

BEN: I have many enterprises, William, and I have never kept books.

WILLY: I remember I was sitting under the wagon in—was it Nebraska?

BEN: It was South Dakota, and I gave you a bunch of wild flowers.

WILLY: I remember you walking away down some open road.

BEN (*laughing*): I was going to find Father in Alaska.

WILLY: Where is he?

BEN: At that age I had a very faulty view of geography, William. I discovered after a few days that I was heading due south, so instead of Alaska, I ended up in Africa.

LINDA: Africa!

WILLY: The Gold Coast!

BEN: Principally diamond mines.

LINDA: Diamond mines!

BEN: Yes, my dear. But I've only a few minutes—

WILLY: No! Boys! Boys! (*Young Biff and Happy appear.*) Listen to this. This is your Uncle Ben, a great man! Tell my boys, Ben!

BEN: Why, boys, when I was seventeen I walked into the jungle, and when I was twenty-one I walked out. (*He laughs.*) And by God I was rich.

WILLY (*to the boys*): You see what I been talking about? The greatest things can happen!

BEN (*glancing at his watch*): I have an appointment in Ketchikan Tuesday week.

WILLY: No, Ben! Please tell about Dad. I want my boys to hear. I want them to know the kind of stock they spring from. All I remember is a man with a big beard, and I was in Mamma's lap, sitting around a fire, and some kind of high music.

BEN: His flute. He played the flute.

WILLY: Sure, the flute, that's right!

(*New music is heard, a high, rollicking tune.*)

BEN: Father was a very great and a very wild-hearted man. We would start in Boston, and he'd toss the whole family into the wagon, and then he'd drive the team right across the country; through Ohio, and Indiana, Michigan, Illinois, and all the Western states. And we'd stop in the towns and sell the flutes that he'd made on the way. Great inventor Father. With one gadget he made more in a week than a man like you could make in a lifetime.

WILLY: That's just the way I'm bringing them up, Ben—rugged, well liked, all-around.

BEN: Yeah? (*To Biff.*) Hit that, boy—hard as you can. (*He pounds his stomach.*)

BIFF: Oh, no, sir!

BEN (*taking boxing stance*): Come on, get to me! (*He laughs.*)

WILLY: Go to it, Biff! Go ahead, show him!

BIFF: Okay! (*He cocks his fists and starts in.*)

LINDA (*to Willy*): Why must he fight, dear?

BEN (*sparring with Biff*): Good boy! Good boy!

WILLY: How's that, Ben, heh?

HAPPY: Give him the left, Biff!

LINDA: Why are you fighting?

BEN: Good boy! (*Suddenly comes in, trips Biff, and stands over him, the point of his umbrella poised over Biff's eye.*)

LINDA: Look out, Biff!

BIFF: Gee!

BEN (*patting Biff's knee*): Never fight fair with a stranger, boy. You'll never get out of the jungle that way. (*Taking Linda's hand and bowing.*) It was an honor and a pleasure to meet you, Linda.

LINDA (*withdrawing her hand coldly, frightened*): Have a nice—trip.

BEN (*to Willy*): And good luck with your—what do you do?

WILLY: Selling.

BEN: Yes. Well . . . (*He raises his hand in farewell to all.*)

WILLY: No, Ben, I don't want you to think . . . (*He takes Ben's arm to show him.*) It's Brooklyn, I know, but we hunt too.

BEN: Really, now.

WILLY: Oh, sure, there's snakes and rabbits and—that's why I moved out here. Why, Biff can fell any one of these trees in no time! Boys! Go right over to where they're building the apartment house and get some sand. We're gonna rebuild the entire front stoop right now! Watch this, Ben!

BIFF: Yes, sir! On the double, Hap!

HAPPY (*as he and Biff run off*): I lost weight, Pop, you notice?

(*Charley enters in knickers, even before the boys are gone.*)

CHARLEY: Listen, if they steal any more from that building the watch-man'll put the cops on them!

LINDA (*to Willy*): Don't let Biff . . .

(*Ben laughs lustily.*)

WILLY: You shoulda seen the lumber they brought home last week. At least a dozen six-by-tens worth all kinds a money.

CHARLEY: Listen, if that watchman—

WILLY: I gave them hell, understand. But I got a couple of fearless char-acters there.

CHARLEY: Willy, the jails are full of fearless characters.

BEN (*clapping Willy on the back, with a laugh at Charley*): And the stock exchange, friend!

WILLY (*joining in Ben's laughter*): Where are the rest of your pants?

CHARLEY: My wife bought them.

WILLY: Now all you need is a golf club and you can go upstairs and go to sleep. (*To Ben.*) Great athlete! Between him and his son Bernard they can't hammer a nail!

BERNARD (*rushing in*): The watchman's chasing Biff!

WILLY (*angrily*): Shut up! He's not stealing anything!

LINDA (*alarmed, hurrying off left*): Where is he? Biff, dear! (*She exits.*)

WILLY (*moving toward the left, away from Ben*): There's nothing wrong. What's the matter with you?

BEN: Nervy boy. Good!

WILLY (*laughing*): Oh, nerves of iron, that Biff!

CHARLEY: Don't know what it is. My New England man comes back and he's bleedin', they murdered him up there.

WILLY: It's contacts, Charley, I got important contacts!

CHARLEY (*sarcastically*): Glad to hear it, Willy. Come in later, we'll shoot a little casino. I'll take some of your Portland money. (*He laughs at Willy and exits.*)

WILLY (*turning to Ben*): Business is bad, it's murderous. But not for me, of course.

BEN: I'll stop by on my way back to Africa.

WILLY (*longingly*): Can't you stay a few days? You're just what I need, Ben, because I—I have a fine position here, but I—well, Dad left when I was such a baby and I never had a chance to talk to him and I still feel—kind of temporary about myself.

BEN: I'll be late for my train.

(*They are at opposite ends of the stage.*)

WILLY: Ben, my boys—can't we talk? They'd go into the jaws of hell for me, see, but I—

BEN: William, you're being first-rate with your boys. Outstanding, manly chaps!

WILLY (*hanging on to his words*): Oh, Ben, that's good to hear! Because sometimes I'm afraid that I'm not teaching them the right kind of— Ben, how should I teach them?

BEN (*giving great weight to each word, and with a certain vicious audacity*): William, when I walked into the jungle, I was seventeen. When I walked out I was twenty-one. And, by God, I was rich! (*He goes off into darkness around the right corner of the house.*)

WILLY: . . . was rich! That's just the spirit I want to imbue them with! To walk into a jungle! I was right! I was right! I was right!

(*Ben is gone, but Willy is still speaking to him as Linda, in nightgown and robe, enters the kitchen, glances around for Willy, then goes to the door of the house, looks out and sees him. Comes down to his left. He looks at her.*)

LINDA: Willy, dear? Willy?

WILLY: I was right!

LINDA: Did you have some cheese? (*He can't answer.*) It's very late, darling. Come to bed, heh?

WILLY (*looking straight up*): Gotta break your neck to see a star in this yard.

LINDA: You coming in?

WILLY: Whatever happened to that diamond watch fob? Remember? When Ben came from Africa that time? Didn't he give me a watch fob with a diamond in it?

LINDA: You pawned it, dear. Twelve, thirteen years ago. For Biff's radio correspondence course.

WILLY: Gee, that was a beautiful thing. I'll take a walk.

LINDA: But you're in your slippers.

WILLY (*starting to go around the house at the left*): I was right! I was! (*Half to Linda, as he goes, shaking his head.*) What a man! There was a man worth talking to. I was right!

LINDA (*calling after Willy*): But in your slippers, Willy!

(*Willy is almost gone when Biff, in his pajamas, comes down the stairs and enters the kitchen.*)

BIFF: What is he doing out there?

LINDA: Sh!

BIFF: God Almighty, Mom, how long has he been doing this?

LINDA: Don't, he'll hear you.

BIFF: What the hell is the matter with him?

LINDA: It'll pass by morning.

BIFF: Shouldn't we do anything?

LINDA: Oh, my dear, you should do a lot of things, but there's nothing to do, so go to sleep.

(*Happy comes down the stair and sits on the steps.*)

HAPPY: I never heard him so loud, Mom.

LINDA: Well, come around more often, you'll hear him. (*She sits down at the table and mends the lining of Willy's jacket.*)

BIFF: Why didn't you ever write me about this, Mom?

LINDA: How would I write to you? For over three months you had no address.

BIFF: I was on the move. But you know I thought of you all the time. You know that, don't you, pal?

LINDA: I know, dear, I know. But he likes to have a letter. Just to know that there's still a possibility for better things.

BIFF: He's not like this all the time, is he?

LINDA: It's when you come home he's always the worst.

BIFF: When I come home?

LINDA: When you write you're coming, he's all smiles and talks about the future, and—he's just wonderful. And then the closer you seem to come, the more shaky he gets, and then, by the time you get here, he's arguing, and he seems angry at you. I think it's just that maybe he can't bring himself to—to open up to you. Why are you so hateful to each other? Why is that?

BIFF (*evasively*): I'm not hateful, Mom.

LINDA: But you no sooner come in the door than you're fighting!

BIFF: I don't know why. I mean to change. I'm tryin', Mom, you understand?

LINDA: Are you home to stay now?

BIFF: I don't know. I want to look around, see what's goin'.

LINDA: Biff, you can't look around all your life, can you?

BIFF: I just can't take hold, Mom. I can't take hold of some kind of a life.

LINDA: Biff, a man is not a bird, to come and go with the springtime.

BIFF: Your hair . . . (*He touches her hair.*) Your hair got so gray.

LINDA: Oh, it's been gray since you were in high school. I just stopped dyeing it, that's all.

BIFF: Dye it again, will ye? I don't want my pal looking old. (*He smiles.*)

LINDA: You're such a boy! You think you can go away for a year and . . . You've got to get it into your head now that one day you'll knock on this door and there'll be strange people here—

BIFF: What are you talking about? You're not even sixty, Mom.

LINDA: But what about your father?

BIFF (*lamely*): Well, I meant him too.

HAPPY: He admires Pop.

LINDA: Biff, dear, if you don't have any feeling for him, then you can't have any feeling for me.

BIFF: Sure I can, Mom.

LINDA: No. You can't just come to see me, because I love him. (*With a threat, but only a threat, of tears.*) He's the dearest man in the world to me, and I won't have anyone making him feel unwanted and low and blue. You've got to make up your mind now, darling, there's no leeway any more. Either he's your father and you pay him that respect, or else you're not to come here. I know he's not easy to get along with—nobody knows that better than me—but . . .

WILLY (*from the left, with a laugh*): Hey, hey, Biffo!

BIFF (*starting to go out after Willy*): What the hell is the matter with him? (*Happy stops him.*)

LINDA: Don't—don't go near him!

BIFF: Stop making excuses for him! He always, always wiped the floor with you. Never had an ounce of respect for you.

HAPPY: He's always had respect for—

BIFF: What the hell do you know about it?

HAPPY (*surlily*): Just don't call him crazy!

BIFF: He's got no character—Charley wouldn't do this. Not in his own house—spewing out that vomit from his mind.

HAPPY: Charley never had to cope with what he's got to.

BIFF: People are worse off than Willy Loman. Believe me, I've seen them!

LINDA: Then make Charley your father, Biff. You can't do that, can you? I don't say he's a great man. Willy Loman never made a lot of money. His name was never in the paper. He's not the finest character that ever lived. But he's a human being, and a terrible thing is happening to him. So attention must be paid. He's not to be allowed to fall into his grave like an old dog. Attention, attention must be finally paid to such a person. You called him crazy—

BIFF: I didn't mean—

LINDA: No, a lot of people think he's lost his—balance. But you don't have to be very smart to know what his trouble is. The man is exhausted.

HAPPY: Sure!

LINDA: A small man can be just as exhausted as a great man. He works for a company thirty-six years this March, opens up unheard-of territories to their trademark, and now in his old age they take his salary away.

HAPPY (*indignantly*): I didn't know that, Mom.

LINDA: You never asked, my dear! Now that you get your spending money someplace else you don't trouble your mind with him.

HAPPY: But I gave you money last—

LINDA: Christmas time, fifty dollars! To fix the hot water it cost ninety-seven fifty! For five weeks he's been on straight commission, like a beginner, an unknown!

BIFF: Those ungrateful bastards!

LINDA: Are they any worse than his sons? When he brought them business, when he was young, they were glad to see him. But now his old friends, the old buyers that loved him so and always found some order to hand him in a pinch—they're all dead, retired. He used to be able to make six, seven calls a day in Boston. Now he takes his valises out of the car and puts them back and takes them out again and he's exhausted. Instead of walking he talks now. He drives seven hundred miles, and when he gets there no one knows him anymore, no one welcomes him. And what goes through a man's mind, driving seven hundred miles home without having earned a cent? Why shouldn't he talk to himself? Why? When he has to go to Charley and borrow fifty dollars a week and pretend to me that it's his pay? How long can that go on? How long? You see what I'm sitting here and waiting for? And you tell me he has no character? The man who never worked a day but for your benefit? When does he get the medal for that? Is this his reward—to turn around at the age of sixty-three and find his sons, who he loved better than his life, one a philandering bum—

HAPPY: Mom!

LINDA: That's all you are, my baby! (*To Biff.*) And you! What happened to the love you had for him? You were such pals! How you used to talk to him on the phone every night! How lonely he was till he could come home to you!

BIFF: All right, Mom. I'll live here in my room, and I'll get a job. I'll keep away from him, that's all.

LINDA: No, Biff. You can't stay here and fight all the time.

BIFF: He threw me out of this house, remember that.

LINDA: Why did he do that? I never knew why.

BIFF: Because I know he's a fake and he doesn't like anybody around who knows!

LINDA: Why a fake? In what way? What do you mean?

BIFF: Just don't lay it all at my feet. It's between me and him—that's all I have to say. I'll chip in from now on. He'll settle for half my pay check. He'll be all right. I'm going to bed. (*He starts for the stairs.*)

LINDA: He won't be all right.

BIFF (*turning on the stairs, furiously*): I hate this city and I'll stay here. Now what do you want?

LINDA: He's dying, Biff.

(Happy turns quickly to her, shocked.)

BIFF *(after a pause)*: Why is he dying?

LINDA: He's been trying to kill himself.

BIFF *(with great horror)*: How?

LINDA: I live from day to day.

BIFF: What're you talking about?

LINDA: Remember I wrote you that he smashed up the car again? In February?

BIFF: Well?

LINDA: The insurance inspector came. He said that they have evidence. That all these accidents in the last year—weren't—weren't—accidents.

HAPPY: How can they tell that? That's a lie.

LINDA: It seems there's a woman . . . *(She takes a breath as)*

BIFF *(sharply but contained)*: ⎤ What woman?

LINDA *(simultaneously)*: ⎦ . . . and this woman . . .

LINDA: What?

BIFF: Nothing. Go ahead.

LINDA: What did you say?

BIFF: Nothing. I just said what woman?

HAPPY: What about her?

LINDA: Well, it seems she was walking down the road and saw his car. She says that he wasn't driving fast at all, and that he didn't skid. She says he came to that little bridge, and then deliberately smashed into the railing, and it was only the shallowness of the water that saved him.

BIFF: Oh, no, he probably just fell asleep again.

LINDA: I don't think he fell asleep.

BIFF: Why not?

LINDA: Last month . . . *(With great difficulty.)* Oh, boys, it's so hard to say a thing like this! He's just a big stupid man to you, but I tell you there's more good in him than in many other people. *(She chokes, wipes her eyes.)* I was looking for a fuse. The lights blew out, and I went down the cellar. And behind the fuse box—it happened to fall out—was a length of rubber pipe—just short.

HAPPY: No kidding!

LINDA: There's a little attachment on the end of it. I knew right away. And sure enough, on the bottom of the water heater there's a new little nipple on the gas pipe.

HAPPY *(angrily)*: That—jerk.

BIFF: Did you have it taken off?

LINDA: I'm—I'm ashamed to. How can I mention it to him? Every day I go down and take away that little rubber pipe. But, when he comes home, I put it back where it was. How can I insult him that way? I don't know what to do. I live from day to day, boys. I tell you, I know every thought in his mind. It sounds so old-fashioned and silly, but I tell you he put his whole life into you and you've turned your backs on him. (*She is bent over in the chair, weeping, her face in her hands.*) Biff, I swear to God! Biff, his life is in your hands!

HAPPY (*to Biff*): How do you like that damned fool!

BIFF (*kissing her*): All right, pal, all right. It's all settled now. I've been remiss. I know that, Mom. But now I'll stay, and I swear to you, I'll apply myself. (*Kneeling in front of her, in a fever of self-reproach.*) It's just—you see, Mom, I don't fit in business. Not that I won't try. I'll try, and I'll make good.

HAPPY: Sure you will. The trouble with you in business was you never tried to please people.

BIFF: I know, I—

HAPPY: Like when you worked for Harrison's. Bob Harrison said you were tops, and then you go and do some damn fool thing like whistling whole songs in the elevator like a comedian.

BIFF (*against Happy*): So what? I like to whistle sometimes.

HAPPY: You don't raise a guy to a responsible job who whistles in the elevator!

LINDA: Well, don't argue about it now.

HAPPY: Like when you'd go off and swim in the middle of the day instead of taking the line around.

BIFF (*his resentment rising*): Well, don't you run off? You take off sometimes, don't you? On a nice summer day?

HAPPY: Yeah, but I cover myself!

LINDA: Boys!

HAPPY: If I'm going to take a fade the boss can call any number where I'm supposed to be and they'll swear to him that I just left. I'll tell you something that I hate to say, Biff, but in the business world some of them think you're crazy.

BIFF (*angered*): Screw the business world!

HAPPY: All right, screw it! Great, but cover yourself!

LINDA: Hap, Hap!

BIFF: I don't care what they think! They've laughed at Dad for years, and you know why? Because we don't belong in this nuthouse of a city! We should be mixing cement on some open plain, or—or carpenters. A carpenter is allowed to whistle!

(*Willy walks in from the entrance of the house, at left.*)

WILLY: Even your grandfather was better than a carpenter. (*Pause. They watch him.*) You never grew up. Bernard does not whistle in the elevator, I assure you.

BIFF (*as though to laugh Willy out of it*): Yeah, but you do, Pop.

WILLY: I never in my life whistled in an elevator! And who in the business world thinks I'm crazy?

BIFF: I didn't mean it like that, Pop. Now don't make a whole thing out of it, will ye?

WILLY: Go back to the West! Be a carpenter, a cowboy, enjoy yourself!

LINDA: Willy, he was just saying—

WILLY: I heard what he said!

HAPPY (*trying to quiet Willy*): Hey, Pop, come on now . . .

WILLY (*continuing over Happy's line*): They laugh at me, heh? Go to Filene's, go to the Hub, go to Slattery's, Boston. Call out the name Willy Loman and see what happens! Big shot!

BIFF: All right, Pop.

WILLY: Big!

BIFF: All right!

WILLY: Why do you always insult me?

BIFF: I didn't say a word. (*To Linda.*) Did I say a word?

LINDA: He didn't say anything, Willy.

WILLY (*going to the doorway of the living room*): All right, good night, good night.

LINDA: Willy, dear, he just decided . . .

WILLY (*to Biff*): If you get tired hanging around tomorrow, paint the ceiling I put up in the living room.

BIFF: I'm leaving early tomorrow.

HAPPY: He's going to see Bill Oliver, Pop.

WILLY (*interestedly*): Oliver? For what?

BIFF (*with reserve, but trying, trying*): He always said he'd stake me. I'd like to go into business, so maybe I can take him up on it.

LINDA: Isn't that wonderful?

WILLY: Don't interrupt. What's wonderful about it? There's fifty men in the City of New York who'd stake him. (*To Biff.*) Sporting goods?

BIFF: I guess so. I know something about it and—

WILLY: He knows something about it! You know sporting goods better than Spalding, for God's sake! How much is he giving you?

BIFF: I don't know, I didn't even see him yet, but—

WILLY: Then what're you talkin' about?

BIFF (*getting angry*): Well, all I said was I'm gonna see him, that's all!

WILLY (*turning away*): Ah, you're counting your chickens again.

BIFF (*starting left for the stairs*): Oh, Jesus, I'm going to sleep!

WILLY (*calling after him*): Don't curse in this house!

BIFF (*turning*): Since when did you get so clean?

HAPPY (*trying to stop them*): Wait a . . .

WILLY: Don't use that language to me! I won't have it!

HAPPY (*grabbing Biff, shouts*): Wait a minute! I got an idea. I got a feasible idea. Come here, Biff, let's talk this over now, let's talk some sense here. When I was down in Florida last time, I thought of a great idea to sell sporting goods. It just came back to me. You and I, Biff—we have a line, the Loman Line. We train a couple of weeks, and put on a couple of exhibitions, see?

WILLY: That's an idea!

HAPPY: Wait! We form two basketball teams, see? Two water polo teams. We play each other. It's a million dollars' worth of publicity. Two brothers, see? The Loman Brothers. Displays in the Royal Palms—all the hotels. And banners over the ring and the basketball court: "Loman Brothers." Baby, we could sell sporting goods!

WILLY: That is a one-million-dollar idea!

LINDA: Marvelous!

BIFF: I'm in great shape as far as that's concerned.

HAPPY: And the beauty of it is, Biff, it wouldn't be like a business. We'd be out playin' ball again . . .

BIFF (*enthused*): Yeah, that's . . .

WILLY: Million-dollar . . .

HAPPY: And you wouldn't get fed up with it, Biff. It'd be the family again. There'd be the old honor, and comradeship, and if you wanted to go off for a swim or somethin'—well, you'd do it! Without some smart cooky gettin' up ahead of you!

WILLY: Lick the world! You guys together could absolutely lick the civilized world.

BIFF: I'll see Oliver tomorrow. Hap, if we could work that out . . .

LINDA: Maybe things are beginning to—

WILLY (*wildly enthused, to Linda*): Stop interrupting! (*To Biff.*) But don't wear sport jacket and slacks when you see Oliver.

BIFF: No, I'll—

WILLY: A business suit, and talk as little as possible, and don't crack any jokes.

BIFF: He did like me. Always liked me.

LINDA: He loved you!

WILLY (*to Linda*): Will you stop! (*To Biff.*) Walk in very serious. You are not applying for a boy's job. Money is to pass. Be quiet, fine, and serious. Everybody likes a kidder, but nobody lends him money.

HAPPY: I'll try to get some myself, Biff. I'm sure I can.

WILLY: I see great things for you kids, I think your troubles are over. But remember, start big and you'll end big. Ask for fifteen. How much you gonna ask for?

BIFF: Gee, I don't know—

WILLY: And don't say "Gee." "Gee" is a boy's word. A man walking in for fifteen thousand dollars does not say "Gee!"

BIFF: Ten, I think, would be top though.

WILLY: Don't be so modest. You always started too low. Walk in with a big laugh. Don't look worried. Start off with a couple of your good stories to lighten things up. It's not what you say, it's how you say it—because personality always wins the day.

LINDA: Oliver always thought the highest of him—

WILLY: Will you let me talk?

BIFF: Don't yell at her, Pop, will ye?

WILLY (angrily): I was talking, wasn't I?

BIFF: I don't like you yelling at her all the time, and I'm tellin' you, that's all.

WILLY: What're you, takin' over this house?

LINDA: Willy—

WILLY (turning to her): Don't take his side all the time, goddammit!

BIFF (furiously): Stop yelling at her!

WILLY (suddenly pulling on his cheek, beaten down, guilt ridden): Give my best to Bill Oliver—he may remember me. (He exits through the living room doorway.)

LINDA (her voice subdued): What'd you have to start that for? (Biff turns away.) You see how sweet he was as soon as you talked hopefully? (She goes over to Biff.) Come up and say good night to him. Don't let him go to bed that way.

HAPPY: Come on, Biff, let's buck him up.

LINDA: Please, dear. Just say good night. It takes so little to make him happy. Come. (She goes through the living room doorway, calling upstairs from within the living room.) Your pajamas are hanging in the bathroom, Willy!

HAPPY (looking toward where Linda went out): What a woman! They broke the mold when they made her. You know that, Biff?

BIFF: He's off salary. My God, working on commission!

HAPPY: Well, let's face it: he's no hot-shot selling man. Except that sometimes, you have to admit, he's a sweet personality.

BIFF (deciding): Lend me ten bucks, will ye? I want to buy some new ties.

HAPPY: I'll take you to a place I know. Beautiful stuff. Wear one of my striped shirts tomorrow.

BIFF: She got gray. Mom got awful old. Gee, I'm gonna go in to Oliver tomorrow and knock him for a—

HAPPY: Come on up. Tell that to Dad. Let's give him a whirl. Come on.

BIFF (steamed up): You know, with ten thousand bucks, boy!

HAPPY (as they go into the living room): That's the talk, Biff, that's the first time I've heard the old confidence out of you! (From within the living *room, fading off.*) You're gonna live with me, kid, and any babe you want just say the word . . . (*The last lines are hardly heard. They are mounting the stairs to their parents' bedroom.*)

LINDA (*entering her bedroom and addressing Willy, who is in the bathroom. She is straightening the bed for him.*): Can you do anything about the shower? It drips.

WILLY (*from the bathroom*): All of a sudden everything falls to pieces. Goddam plumbing, oughta be sued, those people. I hardly finished putting it in and the thing . . . (*His words rumble off.*)

LINDA: I'm just wondering if Oliver will remember him. You think he might?

WILLY (*coming out of the bathroom in his pajamas*): Remember him? What's the matter with you, you crazy? If he'd've stayed with Oliver he'd be on top by now! Wait'll Oliver gets a look at him. You don't know the average caliber any more. The average young man today— (*he is getting into bed*)—is got a caliber of zero. Greatest thing in the world for him was to bum around.

(*Biff and Happy enter the bedroom. Slight pause.*)

WILLY (*stops short, looking at Biff*): Glad to hear it, boy.

HAPPY: He wanted to say good night to you, sport.

WILLY (*to Biff*): Yeah. Knock him dead, boy. What'd you want to tell me?

BIFF: Just take it easy, Pop. Good night. (*He turns to go.*)

WILLY (*unable to resist*): And if anything falls off the desk while you're talking to him—like a package or something—don't you pick it up. They have office boys for that.

LINDA: I'll make a big breakfast—

WILLY: Will you let me finish? (*To Biff.*) Tell him you were in the business in the West. Not farm work.

BIFF: All right, Dad.

LINDA: I think everything—

WILLY (*going right through her speech*): And don't undersell yourself. No less than fifteen thousand dollars.

BIFF (*unable to bear him*): Okay. Good night, Mom. (*He starts moving.*)

WILLY: Because you got a greatness in you, Biff, remember that. You got all kinds of greatness . . . (*He lies back, exhausted. Biff walks out.*)

LINDA (*calling after Biff*): Sleep well, darling!

HAPPY: I'm gonna get married, Mom. I wanted to tell you.

LINDA: Go to sleep, dear.

HAPPY (*going*): I just wanted to tell you.

WILLY: Keep up the good work. (*Happy exits.*) God . . . remember that Ebbets Field game? The championship of the city?

LINDA: Just rest. Should I sing to you?

WILLY: Yeah. Sing to me. (*Linda hums a soft lullaby.*) When that team came out—he was the tallest, remember?
LINDA: Oh, yes. And in gold.

(*Biff enters the darkened kitchen, takes a cigarette, and leaves the house. He comes downstage into a golden pool of light. He smokes, staring at the night.*)

WILLY: Like a young god. Hercules—something like that. And the sun, the sun all around him. Remember how he waved to me? Right up from the field, with the representatives of three colleges standing by? And the buyers I brought, and the cheers when he came out—Loman, Loman, Loman! God Almighty, he'll be great yet. A star like that, magnificent, can never really fade away!

(*The light on Willy is fading. The gas heater begins to glow through the kitchen wall, near the stairs, a blue flame beneath red coils.*)

LINDA (*timidly*): Willy dear, what has he got against you?
WILLY: I'm so tired. Don't talk anymore.

(*Biff slowly returns to the kitchen. He stops, stares toward the heater.*)

LINDA: Will you ask Howard to let you work in New York?
WILLY: First thing in the morning. Everything'll be all right.

(*Biff reaches behind the heater and draws out a length of rubber tubing. He is horrified and turns his head toward Willy's room, still dimly lit, from which the strains of Linda's desperate but monotonous humming rise.*)

WILLY (*staring through the window into the moonlight*): Gee, look at the moon moving between the buildings!

(*Biff wraps the tubing around his hand and quickly goes up the stairs.*)

ACT II

(*Music is heard, gay and bright. The curtain rises as the music fades away. Willy, in shirt sleeves is sitting at the kitchen table, sipping coffee, his hat in his lap. Linda is filling his cup when she can.*)

WILLY: Wonderful coffee. Meal in itself.
LINDA: Can I make you some eggs?
WILLY: No. Take a breath.
LINDA: You look so rested, dear.
WILLY: I slept like a dead one. First time in months. Imagine, sleeping till ten on a Tuesday morning. Boys left nice and early, heh?
LINDA: They were out of here by eight o'clock.
WILLY: Good work!

LINDA: It was so thrilling to see them leaving together. I can't get over the shaving lotion in this house!

WILLY (*smiling*): Mmm—

LINDA: Biff was very changed this morning. His whole attitude seemed to be hopeful. He couldn't wait to get downtown to see Oliver.

WILLY: He's heading for a change. There's no question, there simply are certain men that take longer to get—solidified. How did he dress?

LINDA: His blue suit. He's so handsome in that suit. He could be a—anything in that suit!

(*Willy gets up from the table. Linda holds his jacket for him.*)

WILLY: There's no question, no question at all. Gee, on the way home tonight I'd like to buy some seeds.

LINDA (*laughing*): That'd be wonderful. But not enough sun gets back there. Nothing'll grow any more.

WILLY: You wait, kid, before it's all over we're gonna get a little place out in the country, and I'll raise some vegetables, a couple of chickens . . .

LINDA: You'll do it yet, dear.

(*Willy walks out of his jacket. Linda follows him.*)

WILLY: And they'll get married, and come for a weekend. I'd build a little guest house. 'Cause I got so many fine tools, all I'd need would be a little lumber and some peace of mind.

LINDA (*joyfully*): I sewed the lining . . .

WILLY: I could build two guest houses, so they'd both come. Did he decide how much he's going to ask Oliver for?

LINDA (*getting him into the jacket*): He didn't mention it, but I imagine ten or fifteen thousand. You going to talk to Howard today?

WILLY: Yeah. I'll put it to him straight and simple. He'll just have to take me off the road.

LINDA: And Willy, don't forget to ask for a little advance, because we've got the insurance premium. It's the grace period now.

WILLY: That's a hundred . . . ?

LINDA: A hundred and eight, sixty-eight. Because we're a little short again.

WILLY: Why are we short?

LINDA: Well, you had the motor job on the car . . .

WILLY: That goddam Studebaker!

LINDA: And you got one more payment on the refrigerator . . .

WILLY: But it just broke again!

LINDA: Well, it's old, dear.

WILLY: I told you we should've bought a well-advertised machine. Charley bought a General Electric and it's twenty years old and it's still good, that son-of-a-bitch.

LINDA: But, Willy—

WILLY: Whoever heard of a Hastings refrigerator? Once in my life I would like to own something outright before it's broken! I'm always in a race with the junkyard! I just finished paying for the car and it's on its last legs. The refrigerator consumes belts like a goddamn maniac. They time those things. They time them so when you finally paid for them, they're used up.

LINDA (*buttoning up his jacket as he unbuttons it*): All told, about two hundred dollars would carry us, dear. But that includes the last payment on the mortgage. After this payment, Willy, the house belongs to us.

WILLY: It's twenty-five years!

LINDA: Biff was nine years old when we bought it.

WILLY: Well, that's a great thing. To weather a twenty-five year mortgage is—

LINDA: It's an accomplishment.

WILLY: All the cement, the lumber, the reconstruction I put in this house! There ain't a crack to be found in it anymore.

LINDA: Well, it served its purpose.

WILLY: What purpose? Some stranger'll come along, move in, and that's that. If only Biff would take this house, and raise a family . . . (*He starts to go.*) Good-by, I'm late.

LINDA (*suddenly remembering*): Oh, I forgot! You're supposed to meet them for dinner.

WILLY: Me?

LINDA: At Frank's Chop House on Forty-eighth near Sixth Avenue.

WILLY: Is that so! How about you?

LINDA: No, just the three of you. They're gonna blow you to a big meal!

WILLY: Don't say! Who thought of that?

LINDA: Biff came to me this morning, Willy, and he said, "Tell Dad, we want to blow him to a big meal." Be there six o'clock. You and your two boys are going to have dinner.

WILLY: Gee whiz! That's really somethin'. I'm gonna knock Howard for a loop, kid. I'll get an advance, and I'll come home with a New York job. Goddammit, now I'm gonna do it!

LINDA: Oh, that's the spirit, Willy!

WILLY: I will never get behind a wheel the rest of my life!

LINDA: It's changing, Willy, I can feel it changing!

WILLY: Beyond a question. G'by, I'm late. (*He starts to go again.*)

LINDA (*calling after him as she runs to the kitchen table for a handkerchief*): You got your glasses?

WILLY (*feels for them, then comes back in*): Yeah, yeah, got my glasses.

LINDA (*giving him the handkerchief*): And a handkerchief.

WILLY: Yeah, handkerchief.

LINDA: And your saccharine?
WILLY: Yeah, my saccharine.
LINDA: Be careful on the subway stairs.

(*She kisses him, and a silk stocking is seen hanging from her hand. Willy notices it.*)

WILLY: Will you stop mending stockings? At least while I'm in the house. It gets me nervous. I can't tell you. Please.

(*Linda hides the stocking in her hand as she follows Willy across the forestage in front of the house.*)

LINDA: Remember, Frank's Chop House.
WILLY (*passing the apron*): Maybe beets would grow out there.
LINDA (*laughing*): But you tried so many times.
WILLY: Yeah. Well, don't work hard today. (*He disappears around the right corner of the house.*)
LINDA: Be careful!

(*As Willy vanishes, Linda waves to him. Suddenly the phone rings. She runs across the stage and into the kitchen and lifts it.*)

LINDA: Hello? Oh, Biff! I'm so glad you called, I just . . . Yes, sure, I just told him. Yes, he'll be there for dinner at six o'clock, I didn't forget. Listen, I was just dying to tell you. You know that little rubber pipe I told you about? That he connected to the gas heater? I finally decided to go down the cellar this morning and take it away and destroy it. But it's gone! Imagine? He took it away himself, it isn't there! (*She listens.*) When? Oh, then you took it. Oh—nothing, it's just that I'd hoped he'd taken it away himself. Oh, I'm not worried, darling, because this morning he left in such high spirits, it was like the old days! I'm not afraid any more. Did Mr. Oliver see you? . . . Well, you wait there then. And make a nice impression on him, darling. Just don't perspire too much before you see him. And have a nice time with Dad. He may have big news too! . . . That's right, a New York job. And be sweet to him tonight, dear. Be loving to him. Because he's only a little boat looking for a harbor. (*She is trembling with sorrow and joy.*) Oh, that's wonderful, Biff, you'll save his life. Thanks, darling. Just put your arm around him when he comes into the restaurant. Give him a smile. That's the boy . . . Good-by, dear. . . . You got your comb? . . . That's fine. Good-by, Biff dear.

(*In the middle of her speech, Howard Wagner, thirty-six, wheels in a small typewriter table on which is a wire-recording machine and proceeds to plug it in. This is on the left forestage. Light slowly fades on Linda as it rises on Howard. Howard is intent on threading the machine and only glances over his shoulder as Willy appears.*)

WILLY: Pst! Pst!

HOWARD: Hello, Willy, come in.

WILLY: Like to have a little talk with you, Howard.

HOWARD: Sorry to keep you waiting. I'll be with you in a minute.

WILLY: What's that, Howard?

HOWARD: Didn't you ever see one of these? Wire recorder.

WILLY: Oh. Can we talk a minute?

HOWARD: Records things. Just got delivery yesterday. Been driving me crazy, the most terrific machine I ever saw in my life. I was up all night with it.

WILLY: What do you do with it?

HOWARD: I bought it for dictation, but you can do anything with it. Listen to this. I had it home last night. Listen to what I picked up. The first one is my daughter. Get this. (*He flicks the switch and "Roll out the Barrel" is heard being whistled.*) Listen to that kid whistle.

WILLY: That is lifelike, isn't it?

HOWARD: Seven years old. Get that tone.

WILLY: Ts, ts. Like to ask a little favor if you . . .

(*The whistling breaks off, and the voice of Howard's daughter is heard.*)

HIS DAUGHTER: Now you, Daddy.

HOWARD: She's crazy for me! (*Again the same song is whistled.*) That's me! Ha! (*He winks.*)

WILLY: You're very good!

(*The whistling breaks off again. The machine runs silent for a moment.*)

HOWARD: Sh! Get this now, this is my son.

HIS SON: "The capital of Alabama is Montgomery; the capital of Arizona is Phoenix; the capital of Arkansas is Little Rock; the capital of California is Sacramento . . ." (*and on, and on.*)

HOWARD (*holding up five fingers*): Five years old, Willy!

WILLY: He'll make an announcer some day!

HIS SON (*continuing*): "The capita . . ."

HOWARD: Get that—alphabetical order! (*The machine breaks off suddenly.*) Wait a minute. The maid kicked the plug out.

WILLY: It certainly is a—

HOWARD: Sh, for God's sake!

HIS SON: "It's nine o'clock, Bulova watch time. So I have to go to sleep."

WILLY: That really is—

HOWARD: Wait a minute! The next is my wife.

(*They wait.*)

HOWARD'S VOICE: "Go on, say something." (*Pause.*) "Well, you gonna talk?"

HIS WIFE: "I can't think of anything."

HOWARD'S VOICE: "Well, talk—it's turning."

HIS WIFE (*shyly, beaten*): "Hello." (*Silence.*) "Oh, Howard, I can't talk into this . . ."

HOWARD (*snapping the machine off*): That was my wife.

WILLY: That is a wonderful machine. Can we—

HOWARD: I tell you, Willy, I'm gonna take my camera, and my bandsaw, and all my hobbies, and out they go. This is the most fascinating relaxation I ever found.

WILLY: I think I'll get one myself.

HOWARD: Sure, they're only a hundred and a half. You can't do without it. Supposing you wanna hear Jack Benny, see? But you can't be at home at that hour. So you tell the maid to turn the radio on when Jack Benny comes on, and this automatically goes on with the radio . . .

WILLY: And when you come home you . . .

HOWARD: You can come home twelve o'clock, one o'clock, any time you like, and you get yourself a Coke and sit yourself down, throw the switch, and there's Jack Benny's program in the middle of the night!

WILLY: I'm definitely going to get one. Because lots of times I'm on the road, and I think to myself, what I must be missing on the radio!

HOWARD: Don't you have a radio in the car?

WILLY: Well, yeah, but who ever thinks of turning it on?

HOWARD: Say, aren't you supposed to be in Boston?

WILLY: That's what I want to talk to you about, Howard. You got a minute? (*He draws a chair in from the wing.*)

HOWARD: What happened? What're you doing here?

WILLY: Well . . .

HOWARD: You didn't crack up again, did you?

WILLY: Oh, no. No . . .

HOWARD: Geez, you had me worried there for a minute. What's the trouble?

WILLY: Well, tell you the truth, Howard. I've come to the decision that I'd rather not travel anymore.

HOWARD: Not travel! Well, what'll you do?

WILLY: Remember, Christmas time, when you had the party here? You said you'd try to think of some spot for me here in town.

HOWARD: With us?

WILLY: Well, sure.

HOWARD: Oh, yeah, yeah. I remember. Well, I couldn't think of anything for you, Willy.

WILLY: I tell ya, Howard. The kids are all grown up, y'know. I don't need much anymore. If I could take home—well, sixty-five dollars a week, I could swing it.

HOWARD: Yeah, but Willy, see I—

WILLY: I tell ya why, Howard. Speaking frankly and between the two of us, y'know—I'm just a little tired.

HOWARD: Oh, I could understand that, Willy. But you're a road man, Willy, and we do a road business. We've only got a half-dozen salesmen on the floor here.

WILLY: God knows, Howard, I never asked a favor of any man. But I was with the firm when your father used to carry you in here in his arms.

HOWARD: I know that, Willy, but—

WILLY: Your father came to me the day you were born and asked me what I thought of the name Howard, may he rest in peace.

HOWARD: I appreciate that, Willy, but there just is no spot here for you. If I had a spot I'd slam you right in, but I just don't have a single solitary spot.

(*He looks for his lighter. Willy has picked it up and gives it to him. Pause.*)

WILLY (*with increasing anger*): Howard, all I need to set my table is fifty dollars a week.

HOWARD: But where am I going to put you, kid?

WILLY: Look, it isn't a question of whether I can sell merchandise, is it?

HOWARD: No, but it's business, kid, and everybody's gotta pull his own weight.

WILLY (*desperately*): Just let me tell you a story, Howard—

HOWARD: 'Cause you gotta admit, business is business.

WILLY (*angrily*): Business is definitely business, but just listen for a minute. You don't understand this. When I was a boy—eighteen, nineteen—I was already on the road. And there was a question in my mind as to whether selling had a future for me. Because in those days I had a yearning to go to Alaska. See, there were three gold strikes in one month in Alaska, and I felt like going out. Just for the ride, you might say.

HOWARD (*barely interested*): Don't say.

WILLY: Oh, yeah, my father lived many years in Alaska. He was an adventurous man. We've got quite a little streak of self-reliance in our family. I thought I'd go out with my older brother and try to locate him, and maybe settle in the North with the old man. And I was almost decided to go, when I met a salesman in the Parker House. His name was Dave Singleman. And he was eighty-four years old, and he'd drummed merchandise in thirty-one states. And old Dave, he'd go up to his room, y'understand, put on his green velvet slippers—I'll never forget—and pick up his phone and call the buyers, and without ever leaving his room, at the age of eighty-four, he made his living. And when I saw that, I realized that selling was the greatest career a man could want. 'Cause what could be more satisfying than to be able to go, at the age of eighty-four, into twenty or thirty different cities, and pick up a phone, and be remembered and loved and helped by so many different people? Do you know? When he died—and by the way he died the death of a salesman, in his green velvet slippers in the smoker of the New York, New Haven and Hartford, going into Boston—when he died, hundreds of salesmen and buyers were at his funeral. Things were sad on a lotta trains for months after that. (*He stands up. Howard has not looked at him.*) In those days there was personality in it, Howard. There was respect and comradeship, and gratitude in it. Today, it's all cut and dried, and there's no chance for bringing friendship to bear—or personality. You see what I mean? They don't know me any more.

HOWARD (*moving away, to the right*): That's just the thing, Willy.

WILLY: If I had forty dollars a week—that's all I'd need. Forty dollars, Howard.

HOWARD: Kid, I can't take blood from a stone, I—

WILLY (*desperation is on him now*): Howard, the year Al Smith was nominated, your father came to me and—

HOWARD (*starting to go off*): I've got to see some people, kid.

WILLY (*stopping him*): I'm talking about your father! There were promises made across this desk! You mustn't tell me you've got people to see—I put thirty-four years into this firm, Howard, and now I can't pay my insurance! You can't eat the orange and throw the peel away— a man is not a piece of fruit! (*After a pause.*) Now pay attention. Your father—in 1928 I had a big year. I averaged a hundred and seventy dollars a week in commissions.

HOWARD (*impatiently*): Now, Willy, you never averaged—

WILLY (*banging his hand on the desk*): I averaged a hundred and seventy dollars a week in the year of 1928! And your father came to me—or rather I was in the office here—it was right over this desk—and he put his hand on my shoulder—

HOWARD (*getting up*): You'll have to excuse me, Willy, I gotta see some people. Pull yourself together. (*Going out.*) I'll be back in a little while.

(*On Howard's exit, the light on his chair grows very bright and strange.*)

WILLY: Pull myself together! What the hell did I say to him? My God, I was yelling at him! How could I? (*Willy breaks off, staring at the light, which occupies the chair, animating it. He approaches this chair, standing across the desk from it.*) Frank, Frank, don't you remember what you told me that time? How you put your hand on my shoulder, and Frank . . . (*He leans on the desk and as he speaks the dead man's name he accidentally switches on the recorder, and instantly*)

HOWARD'S SON: ". . . of New York is Albany. The capital of Ohio is Cincinnati, the capital of Rhode Island is . . . " (*The recitation continues.*)

WILLY (*leaping away with fright, shouting*): Ha! Howard! Howard! Howard!

HOWARD (*rushing in*): What happened?

WILLY (*pointing at the machine, which continues nasally, childishly, with the capital cities*): Shut it off! Shut it off!

HOWARD (*pulling the plug out*): Look, Willy . . .

WILLY (*pressing his hands to his eyes*): I gotta get myself some coffee. I'll get some coffee . . .

(*Willy starts to walk out. Howard stops him.*)

HOWARD (*rolling up the cord*): Willy, look . . .

WILLY: I'll go to Boston.

HOWARD: Willy, you can't go to Boston for us.

WILLY: Why can't I go?

HOWARD: I don't want you to represent us. I've been meaning to tell you for a long time now.

WILLY: Howard, are you firing me?

HOWARD: I think you need a good long rest, Willy.

WILLY: Howard—

HOWARD: And when you feel better, come back, and we'll see if we can work something out.

WILLY: But I gotta earn money, Howard. I'm in no position to—

HOWARD: Where are your sons? Why don't your sons give you a hand?

WILLY: They're working on a very big deal.

HOWARD: This is no time for false pride, Willy. You go to your sons and you tell them that you're tired. You've got two great boys, haven't you?

WILLY: Oh, no question, no question, but in the meantime . . .

HOWARD: Then that's that, heh?

WILLY: All right, I'll go to Boston tomorrow.

HOWARD: No, no.

WILLY: I can't throw myself on my sons. I'm not a cripple!

HOWARD: Look, kid, I'm busy this morning.

WILLY (*grasping Howard's arm*): Howard, you've got to let me go to Boston!

HOWARD (*hard, keeping himself under control*): I've got a line of people to see this morning. Sit down, take five minutes, and pull yourself together, and then go home, will ya? I need the office, Willy. (*He starts to go, turns, remembering the recorder, starts to push off the table holding the recorder.*) Oh, yeah. Whenever you can this week, stop by and drop off the samples. You'll feel better, Willy, and then come back and we'll talk. Pull yourself together, kid, there's people outside.

(*Howard exits, pushing the table off left. Willy stares into space, exhausted. Now the music is heard—Ben's music—first distantly, then closer, closer. As Willy speaks, Ben enters from the right. He carries valise and umbrella.*)

WILLY: Oh, Ben, how did you do it? What is the answer? Did you wind up the Alaska deal already?

BEN: Doesn't take much time if you know what you're doing. Just a short business trip. Boarding ship in an hour. Wanted to say good-by.

WILLY: Ben, I've got to talk to you.

BEN (*glancing at his watch*): Haven't the time, William.

WILLY (*crossing the apron to Ben*): Ben, nothing's working out. I don't know what to do.

BEN: Now, look here, William. I've bought timberland in Alaska and I need a man to look after things for me.

WILLY: God, timberland! Me and my boys in those grand outdoors!

BEN: You've a new continent at your doorstep, William. Get out of these cities, they're full of talk and time payments and courts of law. Screw on your fists and you can fight for a fortune up there.

WILLY: Yes, yes! Linda, Linda!

(*Linda enters as of old, with the wash.*)

LINDA: Oh, you're back?

BEN: I haven't much time.

WILLY: No, wait! Linda, he's got a proposition for me in Alaska.

LINDA: But you've got—(*To Ben.*) He's got a beautiful job here.

WILLY: But in Alaska, kid, I could—

LINDA: You're doing well enough, Willy!

BEN (*to Linda*): Enough for what, my dear?

LINDA (*frightened of Ben and angry at him*): Don't say those things to him! Enough to be happy right here, right now. (*To Willy, while Ben laughs.*) Why must everybody conquer the world? You're well liked, and the boys love you, and someday—(*To Ben*)—why, old man Wagner told him just the other day that if he keeps it up he'll be a member of the firm, didn't he, Willy?

WILLY: Sure, sure. I am building something with this firm, Ben, and if a man is building something he must be on the right track, mustn't he?

BEN: What are you building? Lay your hand on it. Where is it?

WILLY (*hesitantly*): That's true, Linda, there's nothing.

LINDA: Why? (*To Ben.*) There's a man eighty-four years old—

WILLY: That's right, Ben, that's right. When I look at that man I say, what is there to worry about?

BEN: Bah!

WILLY: It's true, Ben. All he has to do is go into any city, pick up the phone, and he's making his living and you know why?

BEN (*picking up his valise*): I've got to go.
WILLY (*holding Ben back*): Look at this boy!

(*Biff, in his high school sweater, enters carrying suitcase. Happy carries Biff's shoulder guards, gold helmet, and football pants.*)

WILLY: Without a penny to his name, three great universities are begging for him, and from there the sky's the limit, because it's not what you do, Ben. It's who you know and the smile on your face! It's contacts, Ben, contacts! The whole wealth of Alaska passes over the lunch table at the Commodore Hotel, and that's the wonder, the wonder of this country, that a man can end with diamonds here on the basis of being liked! (*He turns to Biff.*) And that's why when you get out on that field today it's important. Because thousands of people will be rooting for you and loving you. (*To Ben, who has again begun to leave.*) And Ben! when he walks into a business office his name will sound out like a bell and all the doors will open to him! I've seen it, Ben, I've seen it a thousand times! You can't feel it with your hand like timber, but it's there!
BEN: Good-by, William.
WILLY: Ben, am I right? Don't you think I'm right? I value your advice.
BEN: There's a new continent at your doorstep, William. You could walk out rich. Rich! (*He is gone.*)
WILLY: We'll do it here, Ben! You hear me? We're gonna do it here!

(*Young Bernard rushes in. The gay music of the Boys is heard.*)

BERNARD: Oh, gee, I was afraid you left already!
WILLY: Why? What time is it?
BERNARD: It's half-past one!
WILLY: Well, come on, everybody! Ebbets Field next stop! Where's the pennants? (*He rushes through the wall-line of the kitchen and out into the living room.*)
LINDA (*to Biff*): Did you pack fresh underwear?
BIFF (*who has been limbering up*): I want to go!
BERNARD: Biff, I'm carrying your helmet, ain't I?
HAPPY: No, I'm carrying the helmet.
BERNARD: Oh, Biff, you promised me.
HAPPY: I'm carrying the helmet.
BERNARD: How am I going to get in the locker room?
LINDA: Let him carry the shoulder guards. (*She puts her coat and hat on in the kitchen.*)
BERNARD: Can I, Biff? 'Cause I told everybody I'm going to be in the locker room.
HAPPY: In Ebbets Field it's the clubhouse.
BERNARD: I meant the clubhouse. Biff!

HAPPY: Biff!

BIFF (*grandly, after a slight pause*): Let him carry the shoulder guards.

HAPPY (*as he gives Bernard the shoulder guards*): Stay close to us now.

(*Willy rushes in with the pennants.*)

WILLY (*handing them out*): Everybody wave when Biff comes out on the field. (*Happy and Bernard run off.*) You set now, boy?

(*The music has died away.*)

BIFF: Ready to go, Pop. Every muscle is ready.

WILLY (*at the edge of the apron*): You realize what this means?

BIFF: That's right, Pop.

WILLY (*feeling Biff's muscles*): You're comin' home this afternoon captain of the All-Scholastic Championship Team of the City of New York.

BIFF: I got it, Pop. And remember, pal, when I take off my helmet, that touchdown is for you.

WILLY: Let's go! (*He is starting out, with his arm around Biff, when Charley enters, as of old, in knickers.*) I got no room for you, Charley.

CHARLEY: Room? For what?

WILLY: In the car.

CHARLEY: You goin' for a ride? I wanted to shoot some casino.

WILLY (*furiously*): Casino! (*Incredulously.*) Don't you realize what today is?

LINDA: Oh, he knows, Willy. He's just kidding you.

WILLY: That's nothing to kid about!

CHARLEY: No, Linda, what's goin' on?

LINDA: He's playing in Ebbets Field.

CHARLEY: Baseball in this weather?

WILLY: Don't talk to him. Come on, come on! (*He is pushing them out.*)

CHARLEY: Wait a minute, didn't you hear the news?

WILLY: What?

CHARLEY: Don't you listen to the radio? Ebbets Field just blew up.

WILLY: You go to hell! (*Charley laughs. Pushing them out.*) Come on, come on! We're late.

CHARLEY (*as they go*): Knock a homer, Biff, knock a homer!

WILLY (*the last to leave, turning to Charley*): I don't think that was funny, Charley. This is the greatest day of his life.

CHARLEY: Willy, when are you going to grow up?

WILLY: Yeah, heh? When this game is over, Charley, you'll be laughing out of the other side of your face. They'll be calling him another Red Grange. Twenty-five thousand a year.

CHARLEY (*kidding*): Is that so?

WILLY: Yeah, that's so.

CHARLEY: Well, then, I'm sorry, Willy. But tell me something.

WILLY: What?
CHARLEY: Who is Red Grange?
WILLY: Put up your hands. Goddam you, put up your hands!

(*Charley, chuckling, shakes his head and walks away, around the left corner of the stage. Willy follows him. The music rises to a mocking frenzy.*)

WILLY: Who the hell do you think you are, better than everybody else? You don't know everything, you big, ignorant, stupid . . . Put up your hands!

(*Light rises, on the right side of the forestage, on a small table in the reception room of Charley's office. Traffic sounds are heard. Bernard, now mature, sits whistling to himself. A pair of tennis rackets and an overnight bag are on the floor beside him.*)

WILLY (*offstage*): What are you walking away for? Don't walk away! If you're going to say something say it to my face! I know you laugh at me behind my back. You'll laugh out of the other side of your goddam face after this game. Touchdown! Touchdown! Eighty thousand people! Touchdown! Right between the goal posts.

(*Bernard is a quiet, earnest, but self-assured young man. Willy's voice is coming from right upstage now. Bernard lowers his feet off the table and listens. Jenny, his father's secretary, enters.*)

JENNY (*distressed*): Say, Bernard, will you go out in the hall?
BERNARD: What is that noise? Who is it?
JENNY: Mr. Loman. He just got off the elevator.
BERNARD (*getting up*): Who's he arguing with?
JENNY: Nobody. There's nobody with him. I can't deal with him anymore, and your father gets all upset everytime he comes. I've got a lot of typing to do, and your father's waiting to sign it. Will you see him?
WILLY (*entering*): Touchdown! Touch—(*He sees Jenny.*) Jenny, Jenny, good to see you. How're ya? Workin'? Or still honest?
JENNY: Fine. How've you been feeling?
WILLY: Not much any more, Jenny. Ha, ha! (*He is surprised to see the rackets.*)
BERNARD: Hello, Uncle Willy.
WILLY (*almost shocked*): Bernard! Well, look who's here! (*He comes quickly, guiltily, to Bernard and warmly shakes his hand.*)
BERNARD: How are you? Good to see you.
WILLY: What are you doing here?
BERNARD: Oh, just stopped by to see Pop. Get off my feet till my train leaves. I'm going to Washington in a few minutes.
WILLY: Is he in?

BERNARD: Yes, he's in his office with the accountant. Sit down.

WILLY (*sitting down*): What're you going to do in Washington?

BERNARD: Oh, just a case I've got there, Willy.

WILLY: That so? (*Indicating the rackets.*) You going to play tennis there?

BERNARD: I'm staying with a friend who's got a court.

WILLY: Don't say. His own tennis court. Must be fine people, I bet.

BERNARD: They are, very nice. Dad tells me Biff's in town.

WILLY (*with a big smile*): Yeah, Biff's in. Working on a very big deal, Bernard.

BERNARD: What's Biff doing?

WILLY: Well, he's been doing very big things in the West. But he decided to establish himself here. Very big. We're having dinner. Did I hear your wife had a boy?

BERNARD: That's right. Our second.

WILLY: Two boys! What do you know!

BERNARD: What kind of a deal has Biff got?

WILLY: Well, Bill Oliver—very big sporting-goods man—he wants Biff very badly. Called him in from the West. Long distance, carte blanche, special deliveries. Your friends have their own private tennis court?

BERNARD: You still with the old firm, Willy?

WILLY (*after a pause*): I'm—I'm overjoyed to see how you made the grade, Bernard, overjoyed. It's an encouraging thing to see a young man really—really—Looks very good for Biff—very—(*He breaks off, then.*) Bernard—(*He is so full of emotion, he breaks off again.*)

BERNARD: What is it, Willy?

WILLY (*small and alone*): What—what's the secret?

BERNARD: What secret?

WILLY: How—how did you? Why didn't he ever catch on?

BERNARD: I wouldn't know that, Willy.

WILLY (*confidentially, desperately*): You were his friend, his boyhood friend. There's something I don't understand about it. His life ended after that Ebbets Field game. From the age of seventeen nothing good ever happened to him.

BERNARD: He never trained himself for anything.

WILLY: But he did, he did. After high school he took so many correspondence courses. Radio mechanics; television; God knows what, and never made the slightest mark.

BERNARD (*taking off his glasses*): Willy, do you want to talk candidly?

WILLY (*rising, faces Bernard*): I regard you as a very brilliant man, Bernard. I value your advice.

BERNARD: Oh, the hell with the advice, Willy. I couldn't advise you. There's just one thing I've always wanted to ask you. When he was supposed to graduate, and the math teacher flunked him—

WILLY: Oh, that son-of-a-bitch ruined his life.

BERNARD: Yeah, but, Willy, all he had to do was go to summer school and make up that subject.

WILLY: That's right, that's right.

BERNARD: Did you tell him not to go to summer school?

WILLY: Me? I begged him to go. I ordered him to go!

BERNARD: Then why wouldn't he go?

WILLY: Why? Why! Bernard, that question has been trailing me like a ghost for the last fifteen years. He flunked the subject, and laid down and died like a hammer hit him!

BERNARD: Take it easy, kid.

WILLY: Let me talk to you—I got nobody to talk to. Bernard, Bernard, was it my fault? Y'see? It keeps going around in my mind, maybe I did something to him. I got nothing to give him.

BERNARD: Don't take it so hard.

WILLY: Why did he lay down? What is the story there? You were his friend!

BERNARD: Willy, I remember, it was June, and our grades came out. And he'd flunked math.

WILLY: That son-of-a-bitch!

BERNARD: No, it wasn't right then. Biff just got very angry, I remember, and he was ready to enroll in summer school.

WILLY (*surprised*): He was?

BERNARD: He wasn't beaten by it at all. But then, Willy, he disappeared from the block for almost a month. And I got the idea that he'd gone up to New England to see you. Did he have a talk with you then?

(*Willy stares in silence.*)

BERNARD: Willy?

WILLY (*with a strong edge of resentment in his voice*): Yeah, he came to Boston. What about it?

BERNARD: Well, just that when he came back—I'll never forget this, it always mystifies me. Because I'd thought so well of Biff, even though he'd always taken advantage of me. I loved him, Willy, y'know? And he came back after that month and took his sneakers—remember those sneakers with "University of Virginia" printed on them? He was so proud of those, wore them every day. And he took them down in the cellar, and burned them up in the furnace. We had a fist fight. It lasted at least half an hour. Just the two of us, punching each other down the cellar, and crying right through it. I've often thought of how strange it was that I knew he'd given up his life. What happened in Boston, Willy?

(*Willy looks at him as at an intruder.*)

BERNARD: I just bring it up because you asked me.

WILLY (*angrily*): Nothing. What do you mean, "What happened?" What's that got to do with anything?

BERNARD: Well, don't get sore.

WILLY: What are you trying to do, blame it on me? If a boy lays down is that my fault?

BERNARD: Now, Willy, don't get—

WILLY: Well, don't—don't talk to me that way! What does that mean, "What happened?"

(*Charley enters. He is in his vest, and he carries a bottle of bourbon.*)

CHARLEY: Hey, you're going to miss that train. (*He waves the bottle.*)

BERNARD: Yeah, I'm going. (*He takes the bottle.*) Thanks, Pop. (*He picks up his rackets and bag.*) Good-by, Willy, and don't worry about it. You know, "If at first you don't succeed . . ."

WILLY: Yes, I believe in that.

BERNARD: But sometimes, Willy, it's better for a man just to walk away.

WILLY: Walk away?

BERNARD: That's right.

WILLY: But if you can't walk away?

BERNARD (*after a slight pause*): I guess that's when it's tough. (*Extending his hand.*) Good-by, Willy.

WILLY (*shaking Bernard's hand*): Good-by, boy.

CHARLEY (*an arm on Bernard's shoulder*): How do you like this kid? Gonna argue a case in front of the Supreme Court.

BERNARD (*protesting*): Pop!

WILLY (*genuinely shocked, pained, and happy*): No! The Supreme Court!

BERNARD: I gotta run. 'By, Dad!

CHARLEY: Knock 'em dead, Bernard!

(*Bernard goes off.*)

WILLY (*as Charley takes out his wallet*): The Supreme Court! And he didn't even mention it!

CHARLEY (*counting out money on the desk*): He don't have to—he's gonna do it.

WILLY: And you never told him what to do, did you? You never took any interest in him.

CHARLEY: My salvation is that I never took any interest in anything. There's some money—fifty dollars. I got an accountant inside.

WILLY: Charley, look . . . (*With difficulty.*) I got my insurance to pay. If you can manage it—I need a hundred and ten dollars.

(*Charley doesn't reply for a moment; merely stops moving.*)

WILLY: I'd draw it from my bank but Linda would know, and I . . .

CHARLEY: Sit down, Willy.

WILLY (*moving toward the chair*): I'm keeping an account of everything, remember. I'll pay every penny back. (*He sits.*)

CHARLEY: Now listen to me, Willy.

WILLY: I want you to know I appreciate . . .

CHARLEY (*sitting down on the table*): Willy, what're you doin'? What the hell is goin' on in your head?

WILLY: Why? I'm simply . . .

CHARLEY: I offered you a job. You make fifty dollars a week. And I won't send you on the road.

WILLY: I've got a job.

CHARLEY: Without pay? What kind of a job is a job without pay? (*He rises.*) Now, look, kid, enough is enough. I'm no genius but I know when I'm being insulted.

WILLY: Insulted!

CHARLEY: Why don't you want to work for me?

WILLY: What's the matter with you? I've got a job.

CHARLEY: Then what're you walkin' in here every week for?

WILLY (*getting up*): Well, if you don't want me to walk in here—

CHARLEY: I'm offering you a job.

WILLY: I don't want your goddam job!

CHARLEY: When the hell are you going to grow up?

WILLY (*furiously*): You big ignoramus, if you say that to me again I'll rap you one! I don't care how big you are! (*He's ready to fight.*)

(*Pause.*)

CHARLEY (*kindly, going to him*): How much do you need, Willy?

WILLY: Charley, I'm strapped. I'm strapped. I don't know what to do. I was just fired.

CHARLEY: Howard fired you?

WILLY: That snotnose. Imagine that? I named him. I named him Howard.

CHARLEY: Willy, when're you gonna realize that them things don't mean anything? You named him Howard, but you can't sell that. The only thing you got in this world is what you can sell. And the funny thing is that you're a salesman, and you don't know that.

WILLY: I've always tried to think otherwise, I guess. I always felt that if a man was impressive, and well liked, that nothing—

CHARLEY: Why must everybody like you? Who liked J. P. Morgan?° Was he impressive? In a Turkish bath he'd look like a butcher. But with his

---

J. P. Morgan: (1837–1913), a wealthy American businessman who made his money primarily from investments in banking, railroads, and steel and who collected art.

pockets on he was very well liked. Now listen, Willy, I know you don't like me, and nobody can say I'm in love with you, but I'll give you a job because—just for the hell of it, put it that way. Now what do you say?

WILLY: I—I just can't work for you, Charley.

CHARLEY: What're you, jealous of me?

WILLY: I can't work for you, that's all, don't ask me why.

CHARLEY (*angered, takes out more bills*): You been jealous of me all your life, you dammed fool! Here, pay your insurance. (*He puts the money in Willy's hand.*)

WILLY: I'm keeping strict accounts.

CHARLEY: I've got some work to do. Take care of yourself. And pay your insurance.

WILLY (*moving to the right*): Funny, y'know? After all the highways, and the trains, and the appointments, and the years, you end up worth more dead than alive.

CHARLEY: Willy, nobody's worth nothin' dead. (*After a slight pause.*) Did you hear what I said?

(*Willy stands still, dreaming.*)

CHARLEY: Willy!

WILLY: Apologize to Bernard for me when you see him. I didn't mean to argue with him. He's a fine boy. They're all fine boys, and they'll end up big—all of them. Someday they'll all play tennis together. Wish me luck, Charley. He saw Bill Oliver today.

CHARLEY: Good luck.

WILLY (*on the verge of tears*): Charley, you're the only friend I got. Isn't that a remarkable thing? (*He goes out.*)

CHARLEY: Jesus!

(*Charley stares after him a moment and follows. All light blacks out. Suddenly raucous music is heard, and a red glow rises behind the screen at right. Stanley, a young waiter, appears, carrying a table, followed by Happy, who is carrying two chairs.*)

STANLEY (*putting the table down*): That's all right, Mr. Loman, I can handle it myself. (*He turns and takes the chairs from Happy and places them at the table.*)

HAPPY (*glancing around*): Oh, this is better.

STANLEY: Sure, in the front there you're in the middle of all kinds of noise. Whenever you got a party, Mr. Loman, you just tell me and I'll put you back here. Y'know, there's a lotta people they don't like it private, because when they go out they like to see a lotta action around them because they're sick and tired to stay in the house by theirself. But I know you, you ain't from Hackensack. You know what I mean?

HAPPY (*sitting down*): So how's it coming, Stanley?

STANLEY: Ah, it's a dog life. I only wish during the war they'd a took me in the Army. I coulda been dead by now.

HAPPY: My brother's back, Stanley.

STANLEY: Oh, he come back, heh? From the Far West.

HAPPY: Yeah, big cattle man, my brother, so treat him right. And my father's coming too.

STANLEY: Oh, your father too!

HAPPY: You got a couple of nice lobsters?

STANLEY: Hundred percent, big.

HAPPY: I want them with the claws.

STANLEY: Don't worry, I don't give you no mice. (*Happy laughs.*) How about some wine? It'll put a head on the meal.

HAPPY: No. You remember, Stanley, that recipe I brought you from overseas? With the champagne in it?

STANLEY: Oh, yeah, sure. I still got it tacked up yet in the kitchen. But that'll have to cost a buck apiece anyways.

HAPPY: That's all right.

STANLEY: What'd you, hit a number or somethin'?

HAPPY: No, it's a little celebration. My brother is—I think he pulled off a big deal today. I think we're going into business together.

STANLEY: Great! That's the best for you. Because a family business, you know what I mean?—that's the best.

HAPPY: That's what I think.

STANLEY: 'Cause what's the difference? Somebody steals? It's in the family. Know what I mean? (*Sotto voce.°*) Like this bartender here. The boss is goin' crazy what kinda leak he's got in the cash register. You put it in but it don't come out.

HAPPY (*raising his head*): Sh!

STANLEY: What?

HAPPY: You notice I wasn't lookin' right or left, was I?

STANLEY: No.

HAPPY: And my eyes are closed.

STANLEY: So what's the—?

HAPPY: Strudel's comin'.

STANLEY (*catching on, looks around*): Ah, no, there's no—

(*He breaks off as a furred, lavishly dressed girl enters and sits at the next table. Both follow her with their eyes.*)

STANLEY: Geez, how'd ya know?

HAPPY: I got radar or something. (*Staring directly at her profile.*) Oooooooo . . . Stanley.

Sotto voce: "In a soft voice," i.e., stage whisper.

STANLEY: I think that's for you, Mr. Loman.

HAPPY: Look at that mouth. Oh, God. And the binoculars.

STANLEY: Geez, you got a life, Mr. Loman.

HAPPY: Wait on her.

STANLEY (*going to the girl's table*): Would you like a menu, ma'am?

GIRL: I'm expecting someone, but I'd like a—

HAPPY: Why don't you bring her—excuse me, miss, do you mind? I sell champagne, and I'd like you to try my brand. Bring her a champagne, Stanley.

GIRL: That's awfully nice of you.

HAPPY: Don't mention it. It's all company money. (*He laughs.*)

GIRL: That's a charming product to be selling, isn't it?

HAPPY: Oh, gets to be like everything else. Selling is selling, y'know.

GIRL: I suppose.

HAPPY: You don't happen to sell, do you?

GIRL: No, I don't sell.

HAPPY: Would you object to a compliment from a stranger? You ought to be on a magazine cover.

GIRL (*looking at him a little archly*): I have been.

(*Stanley comes in with a glass of champagne.*)

HAPPY: What'd I say before, Stanley? You see? She's a cover girl.

STANLEY: Oh, I could see, I could see.

HAPPY (*to the Girl*): What magazine?

GIRL: Oh, a lot of them. (*She takes the drink.*) Thank you.

HAPPY: You know what they say in France, don't you? "Champagne is the drink of the complexion"—Hya, Biff!

(*Biff has entered and sits with Happy.*)

BIFF: Hello, kid. Sorry I'm late.

HAPPY: I just got here. Uh, Miss—?

GIRL: Forsythe.

HAPPY: Miss Forsythe, this is my brother.

BIFF: Is Dad here?

HAPPY: His name is Biff. You might've heard of him. Great football player.

GIRL: Really? What team?

HAPPY: Are you familiar with football?

GIRL: No, I'm afraid I'm not.

HAPPY: Biff is quarterback with the New York Giants.

GIRL: Well, that is nice, isn't it? (*She drinks.*)

HAPPY: Good health.

GIRL: I'm happy to meet you.

HAPPY: That's my name. Hap. It's really Harold, but at West Point they called me Happy.

GIRL (*now really impressed*): Oh, I see. How do you do? (*She turns her profile.*)

BIFF: Isn't Dad coming?

HAPPY: You want her?

BIFF: Oh, I could never make that.

HAPPY: I remember the time that idea would never come into your head. Where's the old confidence, Biff?

BIFF: I just saw Oliver—

HAPPY: Wait a minute. I've got to see that old confidence again. Do you want her? She's on call.

BIFF: Oh, no. (*He turns to look at the Girl.*)

HAPPY: I'm telling you. Watch this. (*Turning to the Girl*): Honey? (*She turns to him.*) Are you busy?

GIRL: Well, I am . . . but I could make a phone call.

HAPPY: Do that, will you, honey? And see if you can get a friend. We'll be here for a while. Biff is one of the greatest football players in the country.

GIRL (*standing up*): Well, I'm certainly happy to meet you.

HAPPY: Come back soon.

GIRL: I'll try.

HAPPY: Don't try, honey, try hard.

(*The Girl exits. Stanley follows, shaking his head in bewildered admiration.*)

HAPPY: Isn't that a shame now? A beautiful girl like that? That's why I can't get married. There's not a good woman in a thousand. New York is loaded with them, kid!

BIFF: Hap, look—

HAPPY: I told you she was on call!

BIFF (*strangely unnerved*): Cut it out, will ya? I want to say something to you.

HAPPY: Did you see Oliver?

BIFF: I saw him all right. Now look, I want to tell Dad a couple of things and I want you to help me.

HAPPY: What? Is he going to back you?

BIFF: Are you crazy? You're out of your goddam head, you know that?

HAPPY: Why? What happened?

BIFF (*breathlessly*): I did a terrible thing today, Hap. It's been the strangest day I ever went through. I'm all numb, I swear.

HAPPY: You mean he wouldn't see you?

BIFF: Well, I waited six hours for him, see? All day. Kept sending my name in. Even tried to date his secretary so she'd get me to him, but no soap.

HAPPY: Because you're not showin' the old confidence Biff. He remembered you, didn't he?

BIFF (*stopping Happy with a gesture*): Finally, about five o'clock, he comes out. Didn't remember who I was or anything. I felt like such an idiot, Hap.

HAPPY: Did you tell him my Florida idea?

BIFF: He walked away. I saw him for one minute. I got so mad I could've torn the walls down! How the hell did I ever get the idea I was a salesman there? I even believed myself that I'd been a salesman for him! And then he gave me one look and—I realized what a ridiculous lie my whole life has been! We've been talking in a dream for fifteen years. I was a shipping clerk.

HAPPY: What'd you do?

BIFF (*with great tension and wonder*): Well, he left, see. And the secretary went out. I was all alone in the waiting room. I don't know what came over me, Hap. The next thing I know I'm in his office—paneled walls, everything. I can't explain it. I—Hap, I took his fountain pen.

HAPPY: Geez, did he catch you?

BIFF: I ran out. I ran down all eleven flights. I ran and ran and ran.

HAPPY: That was an awful dumb—what'd you do that for?

BIFF (*agonized*): I don't know, I just—wanted to take something, I don't know. You gotta help me, Hap. I'm gonna tell Pop.

HAPPY: You crazy? What for?

BIFF: Hap, he's got to understand that I'm not the man somebody lends that kind of money to. He thinks I've been spiting him all these years and it's eating him up.

HAPPY: That's just it. You tell him something nice.

BIFF: I can't.

HAPPY: Say you got a lunch date with Oliver tomorrow.

BIFF: So what do I do tomorrow?

HAPPY: You leave the house tomorrow and come back at night and say Oliver is thinking it over. And he thinks it over for a couple of weeks, and gradually it fades away and nobody's the worse.

BIFF: But it'll go on forever!

HAPPY: Dad is never so happy as when he's looking forward to something!

(*Willy enters.*)

HAPPY: Hello, scout!

WILLY: Gee, I haven't been here in years!

(*Stanley has followed Willy in and sets a chair for him. Stanley starts off but Happy stops him.*)

HAPPY: Stanley!

(*Stanley stands by, waiting for an order.*)

BIFF (*going to Willy with guilt, as to an invalid*): Sit down, Pop. You want a drink?

WILLY: Sure, I don't mind.

BIFF: Let's get a load on.

WILLY: You look worried.

BIFF: N-no. (*To Stanley.*) Scotch all around. Make it doubles.

STANLEY: Doubles, right. (*He goes.*)

WILLY: You had a couple already, didn't you?

BIFF: Just a couple, yeah.

WILLY: Well, what happened, boy? (*Nodding affirmatively, with a smile.*) Everything go all right?

BIFF (*takes a breath, then reaches out and grasps Willy's hand*): Pal . . . (*He is smiling bravely, and Willy is smiling too.*) I had an experience today.

HAPPY: Terrific, Pop.

WILLY: That so? What happened?

BIFF (*high, slightly alcoholic, above the earth*): I'm going to tell you everything from first to last. It's been a strange day. (*Silence. He looks around, composes himself as best he can, but his breath keeps breaking the rhythm of his voice.*) I had to wait quite a while for him, and—

WILLY: Oliver?

BIFF: Yeah, Oliver. All day, as a matter of cold fact. And a lot of— instances—facts, Pop, facts about my life came back to me. Who was it, Pop? Who ever said I was a salesman with Oliver?

WILLY: Well, you were.

BIFF: No, Dad, I was a shipping clerk.

WILLY: But you were practically—

BIFF (*with determination*): Dad, I don't know who said it first, but I was never a salesman for Bill Oliver.

WILLY: What're you talking about?

BIFF: Let's hold on to the facts tonight, Pop. We're not going to get anywhere bullin' around. I was a shipping clerk.

WILLY (*angrily*): All right, now listen to me—

BIFF: Why don't you let me finish?

WILLY: I'm not interested in stories about the past or any crap of that kind because the woods are burning, boys, you understand? There's a big blaze going on all around. I was fired today.

BIFF (*shocked*): How could you be?

WILLY: I was fired, and I'm looking for a little good news to tell your mother, because the woman has waited and the woman has suffered. The gist of it is that I haven't got a story left in my head, Biff. So don't give me a lecture about facts and aspects. I am not interested. Now what've you got to say to me?

(*Stanley enters with three drinks. They wait until he leaves.*)

WILLY: Did you see Oliver?

BIFF: Jesus, Dad!

WILLY: You mean you didn't go up there?

HAPPY: Sure he went up there.

BIFF: I did. I—saw him. How could they fire you?

WILLY (*on the edge of his chair*): What kind of a welcome did he give you?

BIFF: He won't even let you work on commission?

WILLY: I'm out! (*Driving.*) So tell me, he gave you a warm welcome?

HAPPY: Sure, Pop, sure!

BIFF (*driven*): Well, it was kind of—

WILLY: I was wondering if he'd remember you. (*To Happy.*) Imagine, man doesn't see him for ten, twelve years and gives him that kind of a welcome!

HAPPY: Damn right!

BIFF (*trying to return to the offensive*): Pop, look—

WILLY: You know why he remembered you, don't you? Because you impressed him in those days.

BIFF: Let's talk quietly and get this down to the facts, huh?

WILLY (*as though Biff had been interrupting*): Well, what happened? It's great news, Biff. Did he take you into his office or'd you talk in the waiting room?

BIFF: Well, he came in, see, and—

WILLY (*with a big smile*): What'd he say? Betcha he threw his arm around you.

BIFF: Well, he kinda—

WILLY: He's a fine man. (*To Happy.*) Very hard man to see, y'know.

HAPPY (*agreeing*): Oh, I know.

WILLY (*to Biff*): Is that where you had the drinks?

BIFF: Yeah, he gave me a couple of—no, no!

HAPPY (*cutting in*): He told him my Florida idea.

WILLY: Don't interrupt. (*To Biff.*) How'd he react to the Florida idea?

BIFF: Dad, will you give me a minute to explain?

WILLY: I've been waiting for you to explain since I sat down here! What happened? He took you into his office and what?

BIFF: Well—I talked. And—and he listened, see.

WILLY: Famous for the way he listens, y'know. What was his answer?

BIFF: His answer was—(*He breaks off, suddenly angry.*) Dad, you're not letting me tell you what I want to tell you!

WILLY (*accusing, angered*): You didn't see him, did you?

BIFF: I did see him!

WILLY: What'd you insult him or something? You insulted him, didn't you?

BIFF: Listen, will you let me out of it, will you just let me out of it!
HAPPY: What the hell!
WILLY: Tell me what happened!
BIFF (*to Happy*): I can't talk to him!

(*A single trumpet note jars the ear. The light of green leaves stains the house, which holds the air of night and a dream. Young Bernard enters and knocks on the door of the house.*)

YOUNG BERNARD (*frantically*): Mrs. Loman, Mrs. Loman!
HAPPY: Tell him what happened!
BIFF (*to Happy*): Shut up and leave me alone!
WILLY: No, no! You had to go and flunk math!
BIFF: What math? What're you talking about?
YOUNG BERNARD: Mrs. Loman, Mrs. Loman!

(*Linda appears in the house, as of old.*)

WILLY (*wildly*): Math, math, math!
BIFF: Take it easy, Pop!
YOUNG BERNARD: Mrs. Loman!
WILLY (*furiously*): If you hadn't flunked you'd've been set by now!
BIFF: Now, look, I'm gonna tell you what happened, and you're going to listen to me.
YOUNG BERNARD: Mrs. Loman!
BIFF: I waited six hours—
HAPPY: What the hell are you saying?
BIFF: I kept sending in my name but he wouldn't see me. So finally he . . . (*He continues unheard as light fades low on the restaurant.*)
YOUNG BERNARD: Biff flunked math!
LINDA: No!
YOUNG BERNARD: Birnbaum flunked him! They won't graduate him!
LINDA: But they have to. He's gotta go to the university. Where is he? Biff! Biff!
YOUNG BERNARD: No, he left. He went to Grand Central.
LINDA: Grand—You mean he went to Boston!
YOUNG BERNARD: Is Uncle Willy in Boston?
LINDA: Oh, maybe Willy can talk to the teacher. Oh, the poor, poor boy!

(*Light on house area snaps out.*)

BIFF (*at the table, now audible, holding up a gold fountain pen*): . . . so I'm washed up with Oliver, you understand? Are you listening to me?
WILLY (*at a loss*): Yeah, sure. If you hadn't flunked—
BIFF: Flunked what? What're you talking about?
WILLY: Don't blame everything on me! I didn't flunk math—you did! What pen?

HAPPY: That was awful dumb, Biff, a pen like that is worth—

WILLY (*seeing the pen for the first time*): You took Oliver's pen?

BIFF (*weakening*): Dad, I just explained it to you.

WILLY: You stole Bill Oliver's fountain pen!

BIFF: I didn't exactly steal it! That's just what I've been explaining to you!

HAPPY: He had it in his hand and just then Oliver walked in, so he got nervous and stuck it in his pocket!

WILLY: My God, Biff!

BIFF: I never intended to do it, Dad!

OPERATOR'S VOICE: Standish Arms, good evening!

WILLY (*shouting*): I'm not in my room!

BIFF (*frightened*): Dad, what's the matter? (*He and Happy stand up.*)

OPERATOR: Ringing Mr. Loman for you!

WILLY: I'm not there, stop it!

BIFF (*horrified, gets down on one knee before Willy*): Dad, I'll make good, I'll make good. (*Willy tries to get to his feet. Biff holds him down.*) Sit down now.

WILLY: No, you're no good, you're no good for anything.

BIFF: I am, Dad, I'll find something else, you understand? Now don't worry about anything. (*He holds up Willy's face.*) Talk to me, Dad.

OPERATOR: Mr. Loman does not answer. Shall I page him?

WILLY (*attempting to stand, as though to rush and silence the Operator*): No, no, no!

HAPPY: He'll strike something, Pop.

WILLY: No, no . . .

BIFF (*desperately, standing over Willy*): Pop, listen! Listen to me! I'm telling you something good. Oliver talked to his partner about the Florida idea. You listening? He—he talked to his partner, and he came to me . . . I'm going to be all right, you hear? Dad, listen to me, he said it was just a question of the amount!

WILLY: Then you . . . got it?

HAPPY: He's gonna be terrific, Pop!

WILLY (*trying to stand*): Then you got it, haven't you? You got it! You got it!

BIFF (*agonized, holds Willy down*): No, no. Look, Pop. I'm supposed to have lunch with them tomorrow. I'm just telling you this so you'll know that I can still make an impression, Pop. And I'll make good somewhere, but I can't go tomorrow, see?

WILLY: Why not? You simply—

BIFF: But the pen, Pop!

WILLY: You give it to him and tell him it was an oversight!

HAPPY: Sure, have lunch tomorrow!

BIFF: I can't say that—

WILLY: You were doing a crossword puzzle and accidentally used his pen!

BIFF: Listen, kid, I took those balls years ago, now I walk in with his fountain pen? That clinches it, don't you see? I can't face him like that! I'll try elsewhere.

PAGE'S VOICE: Paging Mr. Loman!

WILLY: Don't you want to be anything?

BIFF: Pop, how can I go back?

WILLY: You don't want to be anything, is that what's behind it?

BIFF (now angry at Willy for not crediting his sympathy): Don't take it that way! You think it was easy walking into that office after what I'd done to him? A team of horses couldn't have dragged me back to Bill Oliver!

WILLY: Then why'd you go?

BIFF: Why did I go? Why did I go! Look at you! Look at what's become of you!

(Off left, The Woman laughs.)

WILLY: Biff, you're going to go to that lunch tomorrow, or—

BIFF: I can't go. I've got no appointment!

HAPPY: Biff, for . . . !

WILLY: Are you spiting me?

BIFF: Don't take it that way! Goddammit!

WILLY (strikes Biff and falters away from the table): You rotten little louse! Are you spiting me?

THE WOMAN: Someone's at the door, Willy!

BIFF: I'm no good, can't you see what I am?

HAPPY (separating them): Hey, you're in a restaurant! Now cut it out, both of you! (The girls enter.) Hello, girls, sit down.

(The Woman laughs, off left.)

MISS FORSYTHE: I guess we might as well. This is Letta.

THE WOMAN: Willy, are you going to wake up?

BIFF (ignoring Willy): How're ya, miss, sit down. What do you drink?

MISS FORSYTHE: Letta might not be able to stay long.

LETTA: I gotta get up very early tomorrow. I got jury duty. I'm so excited! Were you fellows ever on a jury?

BIFF: No, but I been in front of them! (The girls laugh.) This is my father.

LETTA: Isn't he cute? Sit down with us, Pop.

HAPPY: Sit him down, Biff!

BIFF (going to him): Come on, slugger, drink us under the table. To hell with it! Come on, sit down, pal.

(On Biff's last insistence, Willy is about to sit.)

THE WOMAN (now urgently): Willy, are you going to answer the door!

(The Woman's call pulls Willy back. He starts right, befuddled.)

BIFF: Hey, where are you going?

WILLY: Open the door.

BIFF: The door?

WILLY: The washroom . . . the door . . . where's the door?

BIFF *(leading Willy to the left)*: Just go straight down.

(Willy moves left.)

THE WOMAN: Willy, Willy, are you going to get up, get up, get up, get up?

(Willy exits left.)

LETTA: I think it's sweet you bring your daddy along.

MISS FORSYTHE: Oh, he isn't really your father!

BIFF *(at left, turning to her resentfully)*: Miss Forsythe, you've just seen a prince walk by. A fine, troubled prince. A hard-working, unappreciated prince. A pal, you understand? A good companion. Always for his boys.

LETTA: That's so sweet.

HAPPY: Well, girls, what's the program? We're wasting time. Come on, Biff. Gather round. Where would you like to go?

BIFF: Why don't you do something for him?

HAPPY: Me!

BIFF: Don't you give a damn for him, Hap?

HAPPY: What're you talking about? I'm the one who—

BIFF: I sense it, you don't give a good goddam about him. *(He takes the rolled-up hose from his pocket and puts it on the table in front of Happy.)* Look what I found in the cellar, for Christ's sake. How can you bear to let it go on?

HAPPY: Me? Who goes away? Who runs off and—

BIFF: Yeah, but he doesn't mean anything to you. You could help him— I can't! Don't you understand what I'm talking about? He's going to kill himself, don't you know that?

HAPPY: Don't I know it! Me!

BIFF: Hap, help him! Jesus . . . help him . . . Help me, help me, I can't bear to look at his face! *(Ready to weep, he hurries out, up right.)*

HAPPY *(starting after him)*: Where are you going?

MISS FORSYTHE: What's he so mad about?

HAPPY: Come on, girls, we'll catch up with him.

MISS FORSYTHE *(as Happy pushes her out)*: Say, I don't like that temper of his!

HAPPY: He's just a little overstrung, he'll be all right!

WILLY *(off left, as The Woman laughs)*: Don't answer! Don't answer!

LETTA: Don't you want to tell your father—

HAPPY: No, that's not my father. He's just a guy. Come on, we'll catch Biff, and, honey, we're going to paint this town! Stanley, where's the check! Hey, Stanley!

(*They exit. Stanley looks toward left.*)

STANLEY (*calling to Happy indignantly*): Mr. Loman! Mr. Loman!

(*Stanley picks up a chair and follows them off. Knocking is heard off left. The Woman enters, laughing. Willy follows her. She is in a black slip; he is buttoning his shirt. Raw, sensuous music accompanies their speech.*)

WILLY: Will you stop laughing? Will you stop?

THE WOMAN: Aren't you going to answer the door? He'll wake the whole hotel.

WILLY: I'm not expecting anybody.

THE WOMAN: Whyn't you have another drink, honey, and stop being so damn self-centered?

WILLY: I'm so lonely.

THE WOMAN: You know you ruined me, Willy? From now on, whenever you come to the office, I'll see that you go right through to the buyers. No waiting at my desk anymore, Willy. You ruined me.

WILLY: That's nice of you to say that.

THE WOMAN: Gee, you are self-centered! Why so sad? You are the saddest, self-centeredest soul I ever did see-saw. (*She laughs. He kisses her.*) Come on inside, drummer boy. It's silly to be dressing in the middle of the night. (*As knocking is heard.*) Aren't you going to answer the door?

WILLY: They're knocking on the wrong door.

THE WOMAN: But I felt the knocking. And he heard us talking in here. Maybe the hotel's on fire!

WILLY (*his terror rising*): It's a mistake.

THE WOMAN: Then tell him to go away!

WILLY: There's nobody there.

THE WOMAN: It's getting on my nerves, Willy. There's somebody standing out there and it's getting on my nerves!

WILLY (*pushing her away from him*): All right, stay in the bathroom here, and don't come out. I think there's a law in Massachusetts about it, so don't come out. It may be that new room clerk. He looked very mean. So don't come out. It's a mistake, there's no fire.

(*The knocking is heard again. He takes a few steps away from her, and she vanishes into the wing. The light follows him, and now he is facing Young Biff, who carries a suitcase. Biff steps toward him. The music is gone.*)

BIFF: Why didn't you answer?

WILLY: Biff! What are you doing in Boston?

BIFF: Why didn't you answer? I've been knocking for five minutes, I called you on the phone—

WILLY: I just heard you. I was in the bathroom and had the door shut. Did anything happen home?

BIFF: Dad—I let you down.

WILLY: What do you mean?

BIFF: Dad . . .

WILLY: Biffo, what's this about? (*Putting his arm around Biff.*) Come on, let's go downstairs and get you a malted.

BIFF: Dad, I flunked math.

WILLY: Not for the term?

BIFF: The term. I haven't got enough credits to graduate.

WILLY: You mean to say Bernard wouldn't give you the answers?

BIFF: He did, he tried, but I only got a sixty-one.

WILLY: And they wouldn't give you four points?

BIFF: Birnbaum refused absolutely. I begged him, Pop, but he won't give me those points. You gotta talk to him before they close the school. Because if he saw the kind of man you are, and you just talked to him in your way, I'm sure he'd come through for me. The class came right before practice, see, and I didn't go enough. Would you talk to him? He'd like you, Pop. You know the way you could talk.

WILLY: You're on. We'll drive right back.

BIFF: Oh, Dad, good work! I'm sure he'll change it for you!

WILLY: Go downstairs and tell the clerk I'm checkin' out. Go right down.

BIFF: Yes, sir! See, the reason he hates me, Pop—one day he was late for class so I got up at the blackboard and imitated him. I crossed my eyes and talked with a lithp.

WILLY (*laughing*): You did? The kids like it?

BIFF: They nearly died laughing!

WILLY: Yeah? What'd you do?

BIFF: The thquare root of thixthy twee is . . . (*Willy bursts out laughing; Biff joins.*) And in the middle of it he walked in!

(*Willy laughs and The Woman joins in offstage.*)

WILLY (*without hesitation*): Hurry downstairs and—

BIFF: Somebody in there?

WILLY: No, that was next door.

(*The Woman laughs offstage.*)

BIFF: Somebody got in your bathroom!

WILLY: No, it's the next room, there's a party—

THE WOMAN (*enters, laughing. She lisps this.*): Can I come in? There's something in the bathtub, Willy, and it's moving!

(*Willy looks at Biff, who is staring open-mouthed and horrified at The Woman.*)

WILLY: Ah—you better go back to your room. They must be finished painting by now. They're painting her room so I let her take a shower here. Go back, go back . . . (*He pushes her.*)

THE WOMAN (*resisting*): But I've got to get dressed, Willy, I can't—

WILLY: Get out of here! Go back, go back . . . (*Suddenly striving for the ordinary.*) This is Miss Francis, Biff, she's a buyer. They're painting her room. Go back, Miss Francis, go back . . .

THE WOMAN: But my clothes, I can't go out naked in the hall!

WILLY (*pushing her offstage*): Get outa here! Go back, go back!

(*Biff slowly sits down on his suitcase as the argument continues offstage.*)

THE WOMAN: Where's my stockings? You promised me stockings, Willy!

WILLY: I have no stockings here!

THE WOMAN: You had two boxes of size nine sheers for me, and I want them!

WILLY: Here, for God's sake, will you get outa here!

THE WOMAN (*enters holding a box of stockings*): I just hope there's nobody in the hall. That's all I hope. (*To Biff.*) Are you football or baseball?

BIFF: Football.

THE WOMAN (*angry, humiliated*): That's me too. G'night. (*She snatches her clothes from Willy, and walks out.*)

WILLY (*after a pause*): Well, better get going. I want to get to the school first thing in the morning. Get my suits out of the closet. I'll get my valise. (*Biff doesn't move.*) What's the matter! (*Biff remains motionless, tears falling.*) She's a buyer. Buys for J. H. Simmons. She lives down the hall—they're painting. You don't imagine—(*He breaks off. After a pause.*) Now listen, pal, she's just a buyer. She sees merchandise in her room and they have to keep it looking just so . . . (*Pause. Assuming command.*) All right, get my suits. (*Biff doesn't move.*) Now stop crying and do as I say. I gave you an order. Biff, I gave you an order! Is that what you do when I give you an order? How dare you cry! (*Putting his arm around Biff.*) Now look, Biff, when you grow up you'll understand about these things. You mustn't—you mustn't overemphasize a thing like this. I'll see Birnbaum first thing in the morning.

BIFF: Never mind.

WILLY (*getting down beside Biff*): Never mind! He's going to give you those points. I'll see to it.

BIFF: He wouldn't listen to you.

WILLY: He certainly will listen to me. You need those points for the U. of Virginia.

BIFF: I'm not going there.

WILLY: Heh? If I can't get him to change that mark you'll make it up in summer school. You've got all summer to—

BIFF (*his weeping breaking from him*): Dad . . .

WILLY (*infected by it*): Oh, my boy . . .

BIFF: Dad . . .

WILLY: She's nothing to me, Biff. I was lonely, I was terribly lonely.

BIFF: You—you gave her Mama's stockings! (*His tears break through and he rises to go.*)

WILLY (*grabbing for Biff*): I gave you an order!

BIFF: Don't touch me, you—liar!

WILLY: Apologize for that!

BIFF: You fake! You phony little fake! You fake! (*Overcome, he turns quickly and weeping fully goes out with his suitcase. Willy is left on the floor on his knees.*)

WILLY: I gave you an order! Biff, come back here or I'll beat you! Come back here! I'll whip you!

(*Stanley comes quickly in from the right and stands in front of Willy.*)

WILLY (*shouts at Stanley*): I gave you an order . . .

STANLEY: Hey, let's pick it up, pick it up, Mr. Loman. (*He helps Willy to his feet.*) Your boys left with the chippies. They said they'll see you home.

(*A second waiter watches some distance away.*)

WILLY: But we were supposed to have dinner together.

(*Music is heard, Willy's theme.*)

STANLEY: Can you make it?

WILLY: I'll—sure, I can make it. (*Suddenly concerned about his clothes.*) Do I—I look all right?

STANLEY: Sure, you look all right. (*He flicks a speck off Willy's lapel.*)

WILLY: Here—here's a dollar.

STANLEY: Oh, your son paid me. It's all right.

WILLY (*putting it in Stanley's hand*): No, take it. You're a good boy.

STANLEY: Oh, no, you don't have to . . .

WILLY: Here—here's some more, I don't need it anymore. (*After a slight pause.*) Tell me—is there a seed store in the neighborhood?

STANLEY: Seeds? You mean like to plant?

(*As Willy turns, Stanley slips the money back into his jacket pocket.*)

WILLY: Yes. Carrots, peas . . .

STANLEY: Well, there's hardware stores on Sixth Avenue, but it may be too late now.

WILLY (*anxiously*): Oh, I'd better hurry. I've got to get some seeds. (*He starts off to the right.*) I've got to get some seeds, right away. Nothing's planted. I don't have a thing in the ground.

(*Willy hurries out as the light goes down. Stanley moves over to the right after him, watches him off. The other waiter has been staring at Willy.*)

STANLEY (*to the waiter*): Well, whatta you looking at?

(*The waiter picks up the chairs and moves off right. Stanley takes the table and follows him. The light fades on this area. There is a long pause, the sound of the flute coming over. The light gradually rises on the kitchen, which is empty. Happy appears at the door of the house, followed by Biff. Happy is carrying a large bunch of long-stemmed roses. He enters the kitchen, looks around for Linda. Not seeing her, he turns to Biff, who is just outside the house door, and makes a gesture with his hands, indicating "Not here, I guess." He looks into the living room and freezes. Inside, Linda, unseen, is seated, Willy's coat on her lap. She rises ominously and quietly and moves toward Happy, who backs up into the kitchen, afraid.*)

HAPPY: Hey, what're you doing up? (*Linda says nothing but moves toward him implacably.*) Where's Pop? (*He keeps backing to the right, and now Linda is in full view in the doorway to the living room.*) Is he sleeping?
LINDA: Where were you?
HAPPY (*trying to laugh it off*): We met two girls, Mom, very fine types. Here, we brought you some flowers. (*Offering them to her.*) Put them in your room, Ma.

(*She knocks them to the floor at Biff's feet. He has now come inside and closed the door behind him. She stares at Biff, silent.*)

HAPPY: Now what'd you do that for? Mom, I want you to have some flowers—
LINDA (*cutting Happy off, violently to Biff*): Don't you care whether he lives or dies?
HAPPY (*going to the stairs*): Come upstairs, Biff.
BIFF (*with a flare of disgust, to Happy*): Go away from me! (*To Linda.*) What do you mean, lives or dies? Nobody's dying around here, pal.
LINDA: Get out of my sight! Get out of here!
BIFF: I wanna see the boss.
LINDA: You're not going near him!
BIFF: Where is he? (*He moves into the living room and Linda follows.*)
LINDA (*shouting after Biff*): You invite him for dinner. He looks forward to it all day—(*Biff appears in his parents' bedroom, looks around, and exits*)—and then you desert him there. There's no stranger you'd do that to!

HAPPY: Why? He had a swell time with us. Listen, when I—(*Linda comes back into the kitchen*)—desert him I hope I don't outlive the day!

LINDA: Get out of here!

HAPPY: Now look, Mom . . .

LINDA: Did you have to go to women tonight? You and your lousy rotten whores!

(*Biff reenters the kitchen.*)

HAPPY: Mom, all we did was follow Biff around trying to cheer him up! (*To Biff.*) Boy, what a night you gave me!

LINDA: Get out of here, both of you, and don't come back! I don't want you tormenting him any more. Go on now, get your things together! (*To Biff.*) You can sleep in his apartment. (*She starts to pick up the flowers and stops herself.*) Pick up this stuff, I'm not your maid anymore. Pick it up, you bum, you!

(*Happy turns his back to her in refusal. Biff slowly moves over and gets down on his knees, picking up the flowers.*)

LINDA: You're a pair of animals! Not one, not another living soul would have had the cruelty to walk out on that man in a restaurant!

BIFF (*not looking at her*): Is that what he said?

LINDA: He didn't have to say anything. He was so humiliated he nearly limped when he came in.

HAPPY: But, Mom, he had a great time with us—

BIFF (*cutting him off violently*): Shut up!

(*Without another word, Happy goes upstairs.*)

LINDA: You! You didn't even go in to see if he was all right!

BIFF (*still on the floor in front of Linda, the flowers in his hand; with self-loathing*): No. Didn't. Didn't do a damned thing. How do you like that, heh? Left him babbling in a toilet.

LINDA: You louse. You . . .

BIFF: Now you hit it on the nose! (*He gets up, throws the flowers in the wastebasket.*) The scum of the earth, and you're looking at him!

LINDA: Get out of here!

BIFF: I gotta talk to the boss, Mom. Where is he?

LINDA: You're not going near him. Get out of this house!

BIFF (*with absolute assurance, determination*): No. We're gonna have an abrupt conversation, him and me.

LINDA: You're not talking to him.

(*Hammering is heard from outside the house, off right. Biff turns toward the noise.*)

LINDA (*suddenly pleading*): Will you please leave him alone?
BIFF: What's he doing out there?
LINDA: He's planting the garden!
BIFF (*quietly*): Now? Oh, my God!

(*Biff moves outside, Linda following. The light dies down on them and comes up on the center of the apron as Willy walks into it. He is carrying a flashlight, a hoe, and a handful of seed packets. He raps the top of the hoe sharply to fix it firmly, and then moves to the left, measuring off the distance with his foot. He holds the flashlight to look at the seed packets, reading off the instructions. He is in the blue of night.*)

WILLY: Carrots . . . quarter-inch apart. Rows . . . one-foot rows. (*He measures it off.*) One foot. (*He puts down a package and measures off.*) Beets. (*He puts down another package and measures again.*) Lettuce. (*He reads the package, puts it down.*) One foot—(*He breaks off as Ben appears at the right and moves slowly down to him.*) What a proposition, ts, ts. Terrific, terrific. 'Cause she's suffered, Ben, the woman has suffered. You understand me? A man can't go out the way he came in, Ben, a man has got to add up to something. You can't, you can't—(*Ben moves toward him as though to interrupt.*) You gotta consider, now. Don't answer so quick. Remember, it's a guaranteed twenty-thousand-dollar proposition. Now look, Ben, I want you to go through the ins and outs of this thing with me. I've got nobody to talk to, Ben, and the woman has suffered, you hear me?
BEN (*standing still, considering*): What's the proposition?
WILLY: It's twenty thousand dollars on the barrelhead. Guaranteed, gilt-edged, you understand?
BEN: You don't want to make a fool of yourself. They might not honor the policy.
WILLY: How can they dare refuse? Didn't I work like a coolie to meet every premium on the nose? And now they don't pay off? Impossible!
BEN: It's called a cowardly thing, William.
WILLY: Why? Does it take more guts to stand here the rest of my life ringing up a zero?
BEN (*yielding*): That's a point, William. (*He moves, thinking, turns.*) And twenty thousand—that is something one can feel with the hand, it is there.
WILLY (*now assured, with rising power*): Oh, Ben, that's the whole beauty of it! I see it like a diamond, shining in the dark, hard and rough, that I can pick up and touch in my hand. Not like—like an appointment! This would not be another damned-fool appointment, Ben, and it changes all the aspects. Because he thinks I'm nothing, see, and so he spites me. But the funeral—(*Straightening up.*) Ben, that funeral will

be massive! They'll come from Maine, Massachusetts, Vermont, New Hampshire! All the old-timers with the strange license plates—that boy will be thunderstruck, Ben, because he never realized—I am known! Rhode Island, New York, New Jersey—I am known, Ben and he'll see it with his eyes once and for all. He'll see what I am, Ben! He's in for a shock, that boy!

BEN (*coming down to the edge of the garden*): He'll call you a coward.

WILLY (*suddenly fearful*): No, that would be terrible.

BEN: Yes. And a damned fool.

WILLY: No, no, he mustn't, I won't have that! (*He is broken and desperate.*)

BEN: He'll hate you, William.

(*The gay music of the Boys is heard.*)

WILLY: Oh, Ben, how do we get back to all the great times? Used to be so full of light, and comradeship, the sleigh-riding in winter, and the ruddiness on his cheeks. And always some kind of good news coming up, always something nice coming up ahead. And never even let me carry the valises in the house, and simonizing, simonizing that little red car! Why, why can't I give him something and not have him hate me?

BEN: Let me think about it. (*He glances at his watch.*) I still have a little time. Remarkable proposition, but you've got to be sure you're not making a fool of yourself.

(*Ben drifts off upstage and goes out of sight. Biff comes down from the left.*)

WILLY (*suddenly conscious of Biff, turns and looks up at him, then begins picking up the packages of seeds in confusion*): Where the hell is that seed? (*Indignantly.*) You can't see nothing out here! They boxed in the whole goddam neighborhood!

BIFF: There are people all around here. Don't you realize that?

WILLY: I'm busy. Don't bother me.

BIFF (*taking the hoe from Willy*): I'm saying good-by to you, Pop. (*Willy looks at him, silent, unable to move.*) I'm not coming back any more.

WILLY: You're not going to see Oliver tomorrow?

BIFF: I've got no appointment, Dad.

WILLY: He put his arm around you, and you've got no appointment?

BIFF: Pop, get this now, will you? Everytime I've left it's been a fight that sent me out of here. Today I realized something about myself and I tried to explain it to you and I—I think I'm just not smart enough to make any sense out of it for you. To hell with whose fault it is or anything like that. (*He takes Willy's arm.*) Let's just wrap it up, heh? Come on in, we'll tell Mom. (*He gently tries to pull Willy to left.*)

WILLY (*frozen, immobile, with guilt in his voice*): No, I don't want to see her.

BIFF: Come on! (*He pulls again, and Willy tries to pull away.*)

WILLY (*highly nervous*): No, no, I don't want to see her.

BIFF (*tries to look into Willy's face, as if to find the answer there*): Why don't you want to see her?

WILLY (*more harshly now*): Don't bother me, will you?

BIFF: What do you mean, you don't want to see her? You don't want them calling you yellow, do you? This isn't your fault; it's me, I'm a bum. Now come inside! (*Willy strains to get away.*) Did you hear what I said to you?

(*Willy pulls away and quickly goes by himself into the house. Biff follows.*)

LINDA (*to Willy*): Did you plant, dear?

BIFF (*at the door, to Linda*): All right, we had it out. I'm going and I'm not writing any more.

LINDA (*going to Willy in the kitchen*): I think that's the best way, dear. 'Cause there's no use drawing it out, you'll just never get along.

(*Willy doesn't respond.*)

BIFF: People ask where I am and what I'm doing, you don't know, and you don't care. That way it'll be off your mind and you can start brightening up again. All right? That clears it, doesn't it? (*Willy is silent, and Biff goes to him.*) You gonna wish me luck, scout? (*He extends his hand.*) What do you say?

LINDA: Shake his hand, Willy.

WILLY (*turning to her, seething with hurt*): There's no necessity to mention the pen at all, y'know.

BIFF (*gently*): I've got no appointment, Dad.

WILLY (*erupting fiercely*): He put his arm around . . . ?

BIFF: Dad, you're never going to see what I am, so what's the use of arguing? If I strike oil I'll send you a check. Meantime forget I'm alive.

WILLY (*to Linda*): Spite, see?

BIFF: Shake hands, Dad.

WILLY: Not my hand.

BIFF: I was hoping not to go this way.

WILLY: Well, this is the way you're going. Good-by.

(*Biff looks at him a moment, then turns sharply and goes to the stairs.*)

WILLY (*stops him with*): May you rot in hell if you leave this house!

BIFF (*turning*): Exactly what is it that you want from me?

WILLY: I want you to know, on the train, in the mountains, in the valleys, wherever you go, that you cut down your life for spite!

BIFF: No, no.

WILLY: Spite, spite, is the word of your undoing! And when you're down and out, remember what did it. When you're rotting somewhere beside the railroad tracks, remember, and don't you dare blame it on me!

BIFF: I'm not blaming it on you!

WILLY: I won't take the rap for this, you hear?

(*Happy comes down the stairs and stands on the bottom step, watching.*)

BIFF: That's just what I'm telling you!

WILLY (*sinking into a chair at a table, with full accusation*): You're trying to put a knife in me—don't think I don't know what you're doing!

BIFF: All right, phony! Then let's lay it on the line. (*He whips the rubber tube out of his pocket and puts it on the table.*)

HAPPY: You crazy . . .

LINDA: Biff! (*She moves to grab the hose, but Biff holds it down with his hand.*)

BIFF: Leave it there! Don't move it!

WILLY (*not looking at it*): What is that?

BIFF: You know goddam well what that is.

WILLY (*caged, wanting to escape*): I never saw that.

BIFF: You saw it. The mice didn't bring it into the cellar! What is this supposed to do, make a hero out of you? This supposed to make me sorry for you?

WILLY: Never heard of it.

BIFF: There'll be no pity for you, you hear it? No pity!

WILLY (*to Linda*): You hear the spite!

BIFF: No, you're going to hear the truth—what you are and what I am!

LINDA: Stop it!

WILLY: Spite!

HAPPY (*coming down toward Biff*): You cut it now!

BIFF (*to Happy*): The man don't know who we are! The man is gonna know! (*To Willy.*) We never told the truth for ten minutes in this house!

HAPPY: We always told the truth!

BIFF (*turning on him*): You big blow, are you the assistant buyer? You're one of the two assistants to the assistant, aren't you?

HAPPY: Well, I'm practically . . .

BIFF: You're practically full of it! We all are! and I'm through with it. (*To Willy.*) Now hear this, Willy, this is me.

WILLY: I know you!

BIFF: You know why I had no address for three months? I stole a suit in Kansas City and I was in jail. (*To Linda, who is sobbing.*) Stop crying. I'm through with it.

(*Linda turns away from them, her hands covering her face.*)

WILLY: I suppose that's my fault!

BIFF: I stole myself out of every good job since high school!

WILLY: And whose fault is that?

BIFF: And I never got anywhere because you blew me so full of hot air I could never stand taking orders from anybody! That's whose fault it is!

WILLY: I hear that!

LINDA: Don't, Biff!

BIFF: It's goddam time you heard that! I had to be boss big shot in two weeks, and I'm through with it!

WILLY: Then hang yourself! For spite, hang yourself!

BIFF: No! Nobody's hanging himself, Willy! I ran down eleven flights with a pen in my hand today. And suddenly I stopped, you hear me? And in the middle of that office building, do you hear this? I stopped in the middle of that building and I saw — the sky. I saw the things that I love in this world. The work and the food and time to sit and smoke. And I looked at the pen and said to myself, what the hell am I grabbing this for? Why am I trying to become what I don't want to be? What am I doing in an office, making a contemptuous begging fool of myself, when all I want is out there, waiting for me the minute I say I know who I am! Why can't I say that, Willy? (*He tries to make Willy face him, but Willy pulls away and moves to the left.*)

WILLY (*with hatred, threateningly*): The door of your life is wide open!

BIFF: Pop! I'm a dime a dozen, and so are you!

WILLY (*turning on him now in an uncontrolled outburst*): I am not a dime a dozen! I am Willy Loman, and you are Biff Loman!

(*Biff starts for Willy, but is blocked by Happy. In his fury, Biff seems on the verge of attacking his father.*)

BIFF: I am not a leader of men, Willy, and neither are you. You were never anything but a hard-working drummer who landed in the ash can like all the rest of them! I'm one dollar an hour, Willy! I tried seven states and couldn't raise it. A buck an hour! Do you gather my meaning? I'm not bringing home any prizes any more, and you're going to stop waiting for me to bring them home!

WILLY (*directly to Biff*): You vengeful, spiteful mutt!

(*Biff breaks from Happy. Willy, in fright, starts up the stairs. Biff grabs him.*)

BIFF (*at the peak of his fury*): Pop, I'm nothing! I'm nothing, Pop. Can't you understand that? There's no spite in it any more. I'm just what I am, that's all.

(*Biff's fury has spent itself and he breaks down, sobbing, holding on to Willy, who dumbly fumbles for Biff's face.*)

WILLY (*astonished*): What're you doing? What're you doing? (*To Linda.*) Why is he crying?

BIFF (*crying, broken*): Will you let me go, for Christ's sake? Will you take that phony dream and burn it before something happens? (*Struggling to contain himself he pulls away and moves to the stairs.*) I'll go in the morning. Put him — put him to bed. (*Exhausted, Biff moves up the stairs to his room.*)

WILLY (*after a long pause, astonished, elevated*): Isn't that — isn't that remarkable? Biff — he likes me!

LINDA: He loves you, Willy!

HAPPY (*deeply moved*): Always did, Pop.

WILLY: Oh, Biff! (*Staring wildly.*) He cried! Cried to me. (*He is choking with his love, and now cries out his promise.*) That boy — that boy is going to be magnificent!

(*Ben appears in the light just outside the kitchen.*)

BEN: Yes, outstanding, with twenty thousand behind him.

LINDA (*sensing the racing of his mind, fearfully, carefully*): Now come to bed, Willy. It's all settled now.

WILLY (*finding it difficult not to rush out of the house*): Yes, we'll sleep. Come on. Go to sleep, Hap.

BEN: And it does take a great kind of a man to crack the jungle.

(*In accents of dread, Ben's idyllic music starts up.*)

HAPPY (*his arm around Linda*): I'm getting married, Pop, don't forget it. I'm changing everything. I'm gonna run that department before the year is up. You'll see, Mom. (*He kisses her.*)

BEN: The jungle is dark but full of diamonds, Willy.

(*Willy turns, moves, listening to Ben.*)

LINDA: Be good. You're both good boys, just act that way, that's all.

HAPPY: 'Night, Pop. (*He goes upstairs.*)

LINDA (*to Willy*): Come, dear.

BEN (*with greater force*): One must go in to fetch a diamond out.

WILLY (*to Linda, as he moves slowly along the edge of kitchen, toward the door*): I just want to get settled down, Linda. Let me sit alone for a little.

LINDA (*almost uttering her fear*): I want you upstairs.

WILLY (*taking her in his arms*): In a few minutes, Linda. I couldn't sleep right now. Go on, you look awful tired. (*He kisses her.*)

BEN: Not like an appointment at all. A diamond is rough and hard to the touch.

WILLY: Go on now. I'll be right up.

LINDA: I think this is the only way, Willy.

WILLY: Sure, it's the best thing.

BEN: Best thing!

WILLY: The only way. Everything is gonna be—go on, kid, get to bed. You look so tired.

LINDA: Come right up.

WILLY: Two minutes.

(*Linda goes into the living room, then reappears in her bedroom. Willy moves just outside the kitchen door.*)

WILLY: Loves me. (*Wonderingly.*) Always loved me. Isn't that a remarkable thing? Ben, he'll worship me for it!

BEN (*with promise*): It's dark there, but full of diamonds.

WILLY: Can you imagine that magnificence with twenty thousand dollars in his pocket?

LINDA (*calling from her room*): Willy! Come up!

WILLY (*calling into the kitchen*): Yes! yes. Coming! It's very smart, you realize that, don't you, sweetheart? Even Ben sees it. I gotta go, baby. 'By! 'By! (*Going over to Ben, almost dancing.*) Imagine? When the mail comes he'll be ahead of Bernard again!

BEN: A perfect proposition all around.

WILLY: Did you see how he cried to me? Oh, if I could kiss him, Ben!

BEN: Time, William, time!

WILLY: Oh, Ben, I always knew one way or another we were gonna make it, Biff and I!

BEN (*looking at his watch*): The boat. We'll be late. (*He moves slowly off into the darkness.*)

WILLY (*elegiacally, turning to the house*): Now when you kick off, boy, I want a seventy-yard boot, and get right down the field under the ball, and when you hit, hit low and hit hard, because it's important, boy. (*He swings around and faces the audience.*) There's all kinds of important people in the stands, and the first thing you know . . . (*Suddenly realizing he is alone.*) Ben! Ben, where do I . . . ? (*He makes a sudden movement of search.*) Ben, how do I . . . ?

LINDA (*calling*): Willy, you coming up?

WILLY (*uttering a gasp of fear, whirling about as if to quiet her*): Sh! (*He turns around as if to find his way; sounds, faces, voices, seem to be swarming in upon him and he flicks at them, crying, Sh! Sh! Suddenly music, faint and high, stops him. It rises in intensity, almost to an unbearable scream. He goes up and down on his toes, and rushes off around the house.*) Shhh!

LINDA: Willy?

(*There is no answer. Linda waits. Biff gets up off his bed. He is still in his clothes. Happy sits up. Biff stands listening.*)

LINDA (*with real fear*): Willy, answer me! Willy!

(*There is the sound of a car starting and moving away at full speed.*)

LINDA: No!

BIFF (*rushing down the stairs*): Pop!

(*As the car speeds off, the music crashes down in a frenzy of sound, which becomes the soft pulsation of a single cello string. Biff slowly returns to his bedroom. He and Happy gravely don their jackets. Linda slowly walks out of her room. The music has developed into a dead march. The leaves of day are appearing over everything. Charley and Bernard, somberly dressed, appear and knock on the kitchen door. Biff and Happy slowly descend the stairs to the kitchen as Charley and Bernard enter. All stop a moment when Linda, in clothes of mourning, bearing a little bunch of roses, comes through the draped doorway into the kitchen. She goes to Charley and takes his arm. Now all move toward the audience, through the wall-line of the kitchen. At the limit of the apron, Linda lays down the flowers, kneels, and sits back on her heels. All stare down at the grave.*)

REQUIEM

CHARLEY: It's getting dark, Linda.

(*Linda doesn't react. She stares at the grave.*)

BIFF: How about it, Mom? Better get some rest, heh? They'll be closing the gate soon.

(*Linda makes no move. Pause.*)

HAPPY (*deeply angered*): He had no right to do that. There was no necessity for it. We would've helped him.

CHARLEY (*grunting*): Hmmm.

BIFF: Come along, Mom.

LINDA: Why didn't anybody come?

CHARLEY: It was a very nice funeral.

LINDA: But where are all the people he knew? Maybe they blame him.

CHARLEY: Naa. It's a rough world, Linda. They wouldn't blame him.

LINDA: I can't understand it. At this time especially. First time in thirty-five years we were just about free and clear. He only needed a little salary. He was even finished with the dentist.

CHARLEY: No man only needs a little salary.

LINDA: I can't understand it.

BIFF: There were a lot of nice days. When he'd come home from a trip; or on Sundays, making the stoop; finishing the cellar; putting on the new porch; when he built the extra bathroom; and put up the garage. You know something, Charley, there's more of him in that front stoop than in all the sales he ever made.

CHARLEY: Yeah. He was a happy man with a batch of cement.

LINDA: He was so wonderful with his hands.

BIFF: He had the wrong dreams. All, all, wrong.

HAPPY (*almost ready to fight Biff*): Don't say that!

BIFF: He never knew who he was.

CHARLEY (*stopping Happy's movement and reply. To Biff*): Nobody dast blame this man. You don't understand: Willy was a salesman. And for a salesman, there is no rock bottom to the life. He don't put a bolt to a nut, he don't tell you the law or give you medicine. He's a man way out there in the blue, riding on a smile and a shoeshine. And when they start not smiling back—that's an earthquake. And then you get yourself a couple of spots on your hat, and you're finished. Nobody dast blame this man. A salesman is got to dream, boy. It comes with the territory.

BIFF: Charley, the man didn't know who he was.

HAPPY (*infuriated*): Don't say that!

BIFF: Why don't you come with me, Happy?

HAPPY: I'm not licked that easily. I'm staying right in this city, and I'm gonna beat this racket! (*He looks at Biff, his chin set.*) The Loman Brothers!

BIFF: I know who I am, kid.

HAPPY: All right, boy. I'm gonna show you and everybody else that Willy Loman did not die in vain. He had a good dream. It's the only dream you can have—to come out number-one man. He fought it out here, and this is where I'm gonna win it for him.

BIFF (*with a hopeless glance at Happy, bends toward his mother*): Let's go, Mom.

LINDA: I'll be with you in a minute. Go on, Charley. (*He hesitates.*) I want to, just for a minute. I never had a chance to say good-by.

(*Charley moves away, followed by Happy. Biff remains a slight distance up and left of Linda. She sits there, summoning herself. The flute begins, not far away, playing behind her speech.*)

LINDA: Forgive me, dear. I can't cry. I don't know what it is, but I can't cry. I don't understand it. Why did you ever do that? Help me, Willy, I can't cry. It seems to me that you're just on another trip. I keep expecting you. Willy, dear, I can't cry. Why did you do it? I search and search and I search, and I can't understand it, Willy. I made the last payment on the house today. Today, dear. And there'll be nobody home. (*A sob rises in her throat.*) We're free and clear. (*Sobbing more fully, released.*) We're free. (*Biff comes slowly toward her.*) We're free . . . We're free . . .

(*Biff lifts her to her feet and moves out up right with her in his arms. Linda sobs quietly. Bernard and Charley come together and follow them, followed by Happy. Only the music of the flute is left on the darkening stage as over the house the hard towers of the apartment buildings rise into sharp focus, and the curtain falls.*)

1949

Endgame

A Play in One Act

SAMUEL BECKETT [1906–1989]

The Characters
NAGG
NELL
HAMM
CLOV

(*Bare interior.*)
   (*Gray light.*)
   (*Left and right back, high up, two small windows, curtains drawn.*)
   (*Front right, a door. Hanging near door, its face to wall, a picture.*)
   (*Front left, touching each other, covered with an old sheet, two ashbins.*°)
   (*Center, in an armchair on casters, covered with an old sheet, Hamm.*)
   (*Motionless by the door, his eyes fixed on Hamm, Clov. Very red face.*)
   (*Brief tableau.*)

(*Clov goes and stands under window left. Stiff, staggering walk. He looks up at window left. He turns and looks at window right. He goes and stands under window right. He looks up at window right. He turns and looks at window left. He goes out, comes back immediately with a small stepladder, carries it over and sets it down under window left, gets up on it, draws back curtain. He gets down, takes six steps (for example) towards window right, goes back for ladder, carries it over and sets it down under window right, gets up on it, draws back curtain. He gets down, takes three steps towards window left, goes back for ladder, carries it over and sets it down under window left, gets up on it, looks out of window. Brief laugh. He gets down, takes one step towards window right, goes back for ladder, carries it over and sets it down under window right, gets up on it, looks out of window. Brief laugh. He gets down, goes with ladder towards ashbins, halts, turns, carries back ladder and sets it down under window right, goes to ashbins, removes sheet covering them, folds it over his arm. He raises one lid, stoops and looks into bin. Brief laugh. He closes lid. Same with other bin. He goes to Hamm, removes sheet covering him, folds it over his*)

ashbins: Trash cans.

470

arm. In a dressing gown, a stiff toque° on his head, a large bloodstained hand-
kerchief over his face, a whistle hanging from his neck, a rug over his knees,
thick socks on his feet, Hamm seems to be asleep. Clov looks over him. Brief
laugh. He goes to door, halts, turns towards auditorium.)

CLOV (*fixed gaze, tonelessly*): Finished, it's finished, nearly finished, it
must be nearly finished.

(*Pause.*)

Grain upon grain, one by one, and one day, suddenly, there's a heap, a
little heap, the impossible heap.

(*Pause.*)

I can't be punished anymore.

(*Pause.*)

I'll go now to my kitchen, ten feet by ten feet by ten feet, and wait for
him to whistle me.

(*Pause.*)

Nice dimensions, nice proportions, I'll lean on the table, and look at
the wall, and wait for him to whistle me.

(*He remains a moment motionless, then goes out. He comes back immediately,*
goes to window right, takes up the ladder and carries it out. Pause. Hamm stirs.
He yawns under the handkerchief. He removes the handkerchief from his face.
Very red face. Black glasses.)

HAMM: Me—(*he yawns*)—to play.

(*He holds the handkerchief spread out before him.*)

Old stancher!

(*He takes off his glasses, wipes his eyes, his face, the glasses, puts them on*
again, folds the handkerchief and puts it back neatly in the breast pocket of his
dressing gown. He clears his throat, joins the tips of his fingers.)

Can there be misery—(*he yawns*)—loftier than mine? No doubt.
Formerly. But now?

(*Pause.*)

My father?

(*Pause.*)

toque: A small, soft hat with a narrow brim.

My mother?

(*Pause.*)

My . . . dog?

(*Pause.*)

Oh I am willing to believe they suffer as much as such creatures can suffer. But does that mean their sufferings equal mine? No doubt.

(*Pause.*)

No, all is a—(*he yawns*)—bsolute, (*proudly*) the bigger a man is the fuller he is.

(*Pause. Gloomily.*)

And the emptier.

(*He sniffs.*)

Clov!

(*Pause.*)

No, alone.

(*Pause.*)

What dreams! Those forests!

(*Pause.*)

Enough, it's time it ended, in the shelter too.

(*Pause.*)

And yet I hesitate, I hesitate to . . . to end. Yes there it is, it's time it ended and yet I hesitate to—(*he yawns*)—to end.

(*Yawns.*)

God, I'm tired, I'd be better off in bed.

(*He whistles. Enter Clov immediately. He halts beside the chair.*)

You pollute the air!

(*Pause.*)

Get me ready, I'm going to bed.
CLOV: I've just got you up.
HAMM: And what of it?
CLOV: I can't be getting you up and putting you to bed every five minutes, I have things to do.

(*Pause.*)

HAMM: Did you ever see my eyes?
CLOV: No.
HAMM: Did you never have the curiosity, while I was sleeping, to take off
   my glasses and look at my eyes?
CLOV: Pulling back the lids?

(*Pause.*)

   No.
HAMM: One of these days I'll show them to you.

(*Pause.*)

   It seems they've gone all white.

(*Pause.*)

   What time is it?
CLOV: The same as usual.
HAMM (*gesture towards window right*): Have you looked?
CLOV: Yes.
HAMM: Well?
CLOV: Zero.
HAMM: It'd need to rain.
CLOV: It won't rain.

(*Pause.*)

HAMM: Apart from that, how do you feel?
CLOV: I don't complain.
HAMM: You feel normal?
CLOV (*irritably*): I tell you I don't complain.
HAMM: I feel a little queer.

(*Pause.*)

   Clov!
CLOV: Yes.
HAMM: Have you not had enough?
CLOV: Yes!

(*Pause.*)

   Of what?
HAMM: Of this . . . this . . . thing.
CLOV: I always had.

(*Pause.*)

Not you?

HAMM (*gloomily*): Then there's no reason for it to change.

CLOV: It may end.

(*Pause.*)

All life long the same questions, the same answers.

HAMM: Get me ready.

(*Clov does not move.*)

Go and get the sheet.

(*Clov does not move.*)

Clov!

CLOV: Yes.

HAMM: I'll give you nothing more to eat.

CLOV: Then we'll die.

HAMM: I'll give you just enough to keep you from dying. You'll be hungry all the time.

CLOV: Then we won't die.

(*Pause.*)

I'll go and get the sheet.

(*He goes towards the door.*)

HAMM: No!

(*Clov halts.*)

I'll give you one biscuit per day.

(*Pause.*)

One and a half.

(*Pause.*)

Why do you stay with me?

CLOV: Why do you keep me?

HAMM: There's no one else.

CLOV: There's nowhere else.

(*Pause.*)

HAMM: You're leaving me all the same.

CLOV: I'm trying.

HAMM: You don't love me.

CLOV: No.

HAMM: You loved me once.
CLOV: Once!
HAMM: I've made you suffer too much.

(*Pause.*)

Haven't I?
CLOV: It's not that.
HAMM (*shocked*): I haven't made you suffer too much?
CLOV: Yes!
HAMM (*relieved*): Ah you gave me a fright!

(*Pause. Coldly.*)

Forgive me.

(*Pause. Louder.*)

I said, Forgive me.
CLOV: I heard you.

(*Pause.*)

Have you bled?
HAMM: Less.

(*Pause.*)

Is it not time for my painkiller?
CLOV: No.

(*Pause.*)

HAMM: How are your eyes?
CLOV: Bad.
HAMM: How are your legs?
CLOV: Bad.
HAMM: But you can move.
CLOV: Yes.
HAMM (*violently*): Then move!

(*Clov goes to back wall, leans against it with his forehead and hands.*)

Where are you?
CLOV: Here.
HAMM: Come back!

(*Clov returns to his place beside the chair.*)

Where are you?
CLOV: Here.

HAMM: Why don't you kill me?
CLOV: I don't know the combination of the cupboard.

(*Pause.*)

HAMM: Go and get two bicycle wheels.
CLOV: There are no more bicycle wheels.
HAMM: What have you done with your bicycle?
CLOV: I never had a bicycle.
HAMM: The thing is impossible.
CLOV: When there were still bicycles I wept to have one. I crawled at your feet. You told me to go to hell. Now there are none.
HAMM: And your rounds? When you inspected my paupers. Always on foot?
CLOV: Sometimes on horse.

(*The lid of one of the bins lifts and the hands of Nagg appear, gripping the rim. Then his head emerges. Nightcap. Very white face. Nagg yawns, then listens.*)

I'll leave you, I have things to do.
HAMM: In your kitchen?
CLOV: Yes.
HAMM: Outside of here it's death.

(*Pause.*)

All right, be off.

(*Exit Clov. Pause.*)

We're getting on.
NAGG: Me pap!
HAMM: Accursed progenitor!
NAGG: Me pap!
HAMM: The old folks at home! No decency left! Guzzle, guzzle, that's all they think of.

(*He whistles. Enter Clov. He halts beside the chair.*)

Well! I thought you were leaving me.
CLOV: Oh not just yet, not just yet.
NAGG: Me pap!
HAMM: Give him his pap.
CLOV: There's no more pap.
HAMM (*to Nagg*): Do you hear that? There's no more pap. You'll never get any more pap.
NAGG: I want me pap!
HAMM: Give him a biscuit.

(*Exit Clov.*)

Accursed fornicator! How are your stumps?
NAGG: Never mind me stumps.

(*Enter Clov with biscuit.*)

CLOV: I'm back again, with the biscuit.

(*He gives biscuit to Nagg who fingers it, sniffs it.*)

NAGG (*plaintively*): What is it?
CLOV: Spratt's medium.
NAGG (*as before*): It's hard! I can't!
HAMM: Bottle him!

(*Clov pushes Nagg back into the bin, closes the lid.*)

CLOV (*returning to his place beside the chair*): If age but knew!
HAMM: Sit on him!
CLOV: I can't sit.
HAMM: True. And I can't stand.
CLOV: So it is.
HAMM: Every man his speciality.

(*Pause.*)

No phone calls?

(*Pause.*)

Don't we laugh?
CLOV (*after reflection*): I don't feel like it.
HAMM (*after reflection*): Nor I.

(*Pause.*)

Clov!
CLOV: Yes.
HAMM: Nature has forgotten us.
CLOV: There's no more nature.
HAMM: No more nature! You exaggerate.
CLOV: In the vicinity.
HAMM: But we breathe, we change! We lose our hair, our teeth! Our
    bloom! Our ideals!
CLOV: Then she hasn't forgotten us.
HAMM: But you say there is none.
CLOV (*sadly*): No one that ever lived ever thought so crooked as we.
HAMM: We do what we can.
CLOV: We shouldn't.

(*Pause.*)

HAMM: You're a bit of all right, aren't you?
CLOV: A smithereen.

(*Pause.*)

HAMM: This is slow work.

(*Pause.*)

Is it not time for my painkiller?
CLOV: No.

(*Pause.*)

I'll leave you, I have things to do.
HAMM: In your kitchen?
CLOV: Yes.
HAMM: What, I'd like to know.
CLOV: I look at the wall.
HAMM: The wall! And what do you see on your wall? Mene, mene?° Naked bodies?
CLOV: I see my light dying.
HAMM: Your light dying! Listen to that! Well, it can die just as well here, *your* light. Take a look at me and then come back and tell me what you think of *your* light.

(*Pause.*)

CLOV: You shouldn't speak to me like that.

(*Pause.*)

HAMM (*coldly*): Forgive me.

(*Pause. Louder.*)

I said, Forgive me.
CLOV: I heard you.

(*The lid of Nagg's bin lifts. His hands appear, gripping the rim. Then his head emerges. In his mouth the biscuit. He listens.*)

HAMM: Did your seeds come up?
CLOV: No.
HAMM: Did you scratch round them to see if they had sprouted?

Mene, mene: "Mene, Mene, Tekel, Upharsin" (Aramaic; literally, "It has been counted and counted, weighed and divided"). In the Bible, this was the riddle written on a wall that revealed the end of King Belshazzar's reign.

CLOV: They haven't sprouted.
HAMM: Perhaps it's still too early.
CLOV: If they were going to sprout they would have sprouted.

(*Violently.*)

They'll never sprout!

(*Pause. Nagg takes biscuit in his hand.*)

HAMM: This is not much fun.

(*Pause.*)

But that's always the way at the end of the day, isn't it, Clov?
CLOV: Always.
HAMM: It's the end of the day like any other day, isn't it, Clov?
CLOV: Looks like it.

(*Pause.*)

HAMM (*anguished*): What's happening, what's happening?
CLOV: Something is taking its course.

(*Pause.*)

HAMM: All right, be off.

(*He leans back in his chair, remains motionless. Clov does not move, heaves a great groaning sigh. Hamm sits up.*)

I thought I told you to be off.
CLOV: I'm trying.

(*He goes to door, halts.*)

Ever since I was whelped.

(*Exit Clov.*)

HAMM: We're getting on.

(*He leans back in his chair, remains motionless. Nagg knocks on the lid of the other bin. Pause. He knocks harder. The lid lifts and the hands of Nell appear, gripping the rim. Then her head emerges. Lace cap. Very white face.*)

NELL: What is it, my pet?

(*Pause.*)

Time for love?
NAGG: Were you asleep?
NELL: Oh no!
NAGG: Kiss me.

NELL: We can't.
NAGG: Try.

(*Their heads strain towards each other, fail to meet, fall apart again.*)

NELL: Why this farce, day after day?

(*Pause.*)

NAGG: I've lost me tooth.
NELL: When?
NAGG: I had it yesterday.
NELL (*elegiac*): Ah yesterday!

(*They turn painfully towards each other.*)

NAGG: Can you see me?
NELL: Hardly. And you?
NAGG: What?
NELL: Can you see me?
NAGG: Hardly.
NELL: So much the better, so much the better.
NAGG: Don't say that.

(*Pause.*)

   Our sight has failed.
NELL: Yes.

(*Pause. They turn away from each other.*)

NAGG: Can you hear me?
NELL: Yes. And you?
NAGG: Yes.

(*Pause.*)

   Our hearing hasn't failed.
NELL: Our what?
NAGG: Our hearing.
NELL: No.

(*Pause.*)

   Have you anything else to say to me?
NAGG: Do you remember—
NELL: No.
NAGG: When we crashed on our tandem and lost our shanks.

(*They laugh heartily.*)

NELL: It was in the Ardennes.

(*They laugh less heartily.*)

NAGG: On the road to Sedan.

(*They laugh still less heartily.*)

Are you cold?
NELL: Yes, perished. And you?
NAGG:

(*Pause.*)

I'm freezing.

(*Pause.*)

Do you want to go in?
NELL: Yes.
NAGG: Then go in.

(*Nell does not move.*)

Why don't you go in?
NELL: I don't know.

(*Pause.*)

NAGG: Has he changed your sawdust?
NELL: It isn't sawdust.

(*Pause. Wearily.*)

Can you not be a little accurate, Nagg?
NAGG: Your sand then. It's not important.
NELL: It is important.

(*Pause.*)

NAGG: It was sawdust once.
NELL: Once!
NAGG: And now it's sand.

(*Pause.*)

From the shore.

(*Pause. Impatiently.*)

Now it's sand he fetches from the shore.
NELL: Now it's sand.
NAGG: Has he changed yours?
NELL: No.
NAGG: Nor mine.

(*Pause.*)

I won't have it!

(*Pause. Holding up the biscuit.*)

Do you want a bit?
NELL: No.

(*Pause.*)

Of what?
NAGG: Biscuit. I've kept you half.

(*He looks at the biscuit. Proudly.*)

Three quarters. For you. Here.

(*He proffers the biscuit.*)

No?

(*Pause.*)

Do you not feel well?
HAMM (*wearily*): Quiet, quiet, you're keeping me awake.

(*Pause.*)

Talk softer.

(*Pause.*)

If I could sleep I might make love. I'd go into the woods. My eyes
would see . . . the sky, the earth. I'd run, run, they wouldn't catch me.

(*Pause.*)

Nature!

(*Pause.*)

There's something dripping in my head.

(*Pause.*)

A heart, a heart in my head.

(*Pause.*)

NAGG (*soft*): Do you hear him? A heart in his head!

(*He chuckles cautiously.*)

NELL: One mustn't laugh at those things, Nagg. Why must you always
laugh at them?

NAGG: Not so loud!

NELL (*without lowering her voice*): Nothing is funnier than unhappiness, I grant you that. But—

NAGG (*shocked*): Oh!

NELL: Yes, yes, it's the most comical thing in the world. And we laugh, we laugh, with a will, in the beginning. But it's always the same thing. Yes, it's like the funny story we have heard too often, we still find it funny, but we don't laugh anymore.

(*Pause.*)

Have you anything else to say to me?

NAGG: No.

NELL: Are you quite sure?

(*Pause.*)

Then I'll leave you.

NAGG: Do you not want your biscuit?

(*Pause.*)

I'll keep it for you.

(*Pause.*)

I thought you were going to leave me.

NELL: I am going to leave you.

NAGG: Could you give me a scratch before you go?

NELL: No.

(*Pause.*)

Where?

NAGG: In the back.

NELL: No.

(*Pause.*)

Rub yourself against the rim.

NAGG: It's lower down. In the hollow.

NELL: What hollow?

NAGG: The hollow!

(*Pause.*)

Could you not?

(*Pause.*)

Yesterday you scratched me there.

NELL (*elegiac*): Ah yesterday!
NAGG: Could you not?

(*Pause.*)

Would you like me to scratch you?

(*Pause.*)

Are you crying again?
NELL: I was trying.

(*Pause.*)

HAMM: Perhaps it's a little vein.

(*Pause.*)

NAGG: What was that he said?
NELL: Perhaps it's a little vein.
NAGG: What does that mean?

(*Pause.*)

That means nothing.

(*Pause.*)

Will I tell you the story of the tailor?
NELL: No.

(*Pause.*)

What for?
NAGG: To cheer you up.
NELL: It's not funny.
NAGG: It always made you laugh.

(*Pause.*)

The first time I thought you'd die.
NELL: It was on Lake Como.

(*Pause.*)

One April afternoon.

(*Pause.*)

Can you believe it?
NAGG: What?
NELL: That we once went out rowing on Lake Como.

(*Pause.*)

One April afternoon.

NAGG: We had got engaged the day before.

NELL: Engaged!

NAGG: You were in such fits that we capsized. By rights we should have been drowned.

NELL: It was because I felt happy.

NAGG (*indignant*): It was not, it was not, it was my story and nothing else. Happy! Don't you laugh at it still? Every time I tell it. Happy!

NELL: It was deep, deep. And you could see down to the bottom. So white. So clean.

NAGG: Let me tell it again.

(*Raconteur's voice.*)

An Englishman, needing a pair of striped trousers in a hurry for the New Year festivities, goes to his tailor who takes his measurements.

(*Tailor's voice.*)

"That's the lot, come back in four days, I'll have it ready." Good. Four days later.

(*Tailor's voice.*)

"So sorry, come back in a week, I've made a mess of the seat." Good, that's all right, a neat seat can be very ticklish. A week later.

(*Tailor's voice.*)

"Frightfully sorry, come back in ten days, I've made a hash of the crotch." Good, can't be helped, a snug crotch is always a teaser. Ten days later.

(*Tailor's voice.*)

"Dreadfully sorry, come back in a fortnight, I've made a balls of the fly." Good, at a pinch, a smart fly is a stiff proposition.

(*Pause. Normal voice.*)

I never told it worse.

(*Pause. Gloomy.*)

I tell this story worse and worse.

(*Pause. Raconteur's voice.*)

Well, to make it short, the bluebells are blowing and he ballockses the buttonholes.

(*Customer's voice.*)

"God damn you to hell, Sir, no, it's indecent, there are limits! In six days, do you hear me, six days, God made the world. Yes Sir, no less

Sir, the WORLD! And you are not bloody well capable of making me a pair of trousers in three months!"

(*Tailor's voice, scandalized.*)

"But my dear Sir, my dear Sir, look—(*disdainful gesture, disgustedly*)—at the world—(*pause*) and look—(*loving gesture, proudly*)—at my TROUSERS!"

(*Pause. He looks at Nell who has remained impassive, her eyes unseeing, breaks into a high forced laugh, cuts it short, pokes his head towards Nell, launches his laugh again.*)

HAMM: Silence!

(*Nagg starts, cuts short his laugh.*)

NELL: You could see down to the bottom.
HAMM (*exasperated*): Have you not finished? Will you never finish?

(*With sudden fury.*)

Will this never finish?

(*Nagg disappears into his bin, closes the lid behind him. Nell does not move. Frenziedly.*)

My kingdom for a nightman!

(*He whistles. Enter Clov.*)

Clear away this muck! Chuck it in the sea!

(*Clov goes to bins, halts.*)

NELL: So white.
HAMM: What? What's she blathering about?

(*Clov stoops, takes Nell's hand, feels her pulse.*)

NELL (*to Clov*): Desert!

(*Clov lets go her hand, pushes her back in the bin, closes the lid.*)

CLOV (*returning to his place beside the chair*): She has no pulse.
HAMM: What was she driveling about?
CLOV: She told me to go away, into the desert.
HAMM: Damn busybody! Is that all?
CLOV: No.
HAMM: What else?
CLOV: I didn't understand.
HAMM: Have you bottled her?
CLOV: Yes.

HAMM: Are they both bottled?
CLOV: Yes.
HAMM: Screw down the lids.

(*Clov goes towards door.*)

   Time enough.

(*Clov halts.*)

   My anger subsides, I'd like to pee.
CLOV (*with alacrity*): I'll go and get the catheter.

(*He goes towards door.*)

HAMM: Time enough.

(*Clov halts.*)

   Give me my painkiller.
CLOV: It's too soon.

(*Pause.*)

   It's too soon on top of your tonic, it wouldn't act.
HAMM: In the morning they brace you up and in the evening they calm
   you down. Unless it's the other way round.

(*Pause.*)

   That old doctor, he's dead naturally?
CLOV: He wasn't old.
HAMM: But he's dead?
CLOV: Naturally.

(*Pause.*)

   You ask *me* that?

(*Pause.*)

HAMM: Take me for a little turn.

(*Clov goes behind the chair and pushes it forward.*)

   Not too fast!

(*Clov pushes chair.*)

   Right round the world!

(*Clov pushes chair.*)

   Hug the walls, then back to the center again.

(*Clov pushes chair.*)

I was right in the center, wasn't I?
CLOV (*pushing*): Yes.
HAMM: We'd need a proper wheelchair. With big wheels. Bicycle wheels!

(*Pause.*)

Are you hugging?
CLOV (*pushing*): Yes.
HAMM (*groping for wall*): It's a lie! Why do you lie to me?
CLOV (*bearing closer to wall*): There! There!
HAMM: Stop!

(*Clov stops chair close to back wall. Hamm lays his hand against wall.*)

Old wall!

(*Pause.*)

Beyond is the . . . other hell.

(*Pause. Violently.*)

Closer! Closer! Up against!
CLOV: Take away your hand.

(*Hamm withdraws his hand. Clov rams chair against wall.*)

There!

(*Hamm leans towards wall, applies his ear to it.*)

HAMM: Do you hear?

(*He strikes the wall with his knuckles.*)

Do you hear? Hollow bricks!

(*He strikes again.*)

All that's hollow!

(*Pause. He straightens up. Violently.*)

That's enough. Back!
CLOV: We haven't done the round.
HAMM: Back to my place!

(*Clov pushes chair back to center.*)

Is that my place?
CLOV: Yes, that's your place.
HAMM: Am I right in the center?

CLOV: I'll measure it.
HAMM: More or less! More or less!
CLOV (*moving chair slightly*): There!
HAMM: I'm more or less in the center?
CLOV: I'd say so.
HAMM: You'd say so! Put me right in the center!
CLOV: I'll go and get the tape.
HAMM: Roughly! Roughly!

(*Clov moves chair slightly.*)

Bang in the center!
CLOV: There!

(*Pause.*)

HAMM: I feel a little too far to the left.

(*Clov moves chair slightly.*)

Now I feel a little too far to the right.

(*Clov moves chair slightly.*)

I feel a little too far forward.

(*Clov moves chair slightly.*)

Now I feel a little too far back.

(*Clov moves chair slightly.*)

Don't stay there (*i.e., behind the chair*), you give me the shivers.

(*Clov returns to his place beside the chair.*)

CLOV: If I could kill him I'd die happy.

(*Pause.*)

HAMM: What's the weather like?
CLOV: As usual.
HAMM: Look at the earth.
CLOV: I've looked.
HAMM: With the glass?
CLOV: No need of the glass.
HAMM: Look at it with the glass.
CLOV: I'll go and get the glass.

(*Exit Clov.*)

HAMM: No need of the glass!

(*Enter Clov with telescope.*)

CLOV: I'm back again, with the glass.

(*He goes to window right, looks up at it.*)

I need the steps.
HAMM: Why? Have you shrunk?

(*Exit Clov with telescope.*)

I don't like that, I don't like that.

(*Enter Clov with ladder, but without telescope.*)

CLOV: I'm back again, with the steps.

(*He sets down ladder under window right, gets up on it, realizes he has not the telescope, gets down.*)

I need the glass.

(*He goes towards door.*)

HAMM (*violently*): But you have the glass!
CLOV (*halting, violently*): No, I haven't the glass!

(*Exit Clov.*)

HAMM: This is deadly.

(*Enter Clov with telescope. He goes towards ladder.*)

CLOV: Things are livening up.

(*He gets up on ladder, raises the telescope, lets it fall.*)

I did it on purpose.

(*He gets down, picks up the telescope, turns it on auditorium.*)

I see . . . a multitude . . . in transports . . . of joy.

(*Pause.*)

That's what I call a magnifier.

(*He lowers the telescope, turns towards Hamm.*)

Well? Don't we laugh?
HAMM (*after reflection*): I don't.
CLOV (*after reflection*): Nor I.

(*He gets up on ladder, turns the telescope on the without.*)

Let's see.

(*He looks, moving the telescope.*)

Zero . . . (*he looks*) . . . zero . . . (*he looks*) . . . and zero.
HAMM: Nothing stirs. All is —
CLOV: Zer—
HAMM (*violently*): Wait till you're spoken to!

(*Normal voice.*)

All is . . . all is . . . all is what?

(*Violently.*)

All is what?
CLOV: What all is? In a word? Is that what you want to know? Just a
  moment.

(*He turns the telescope on the without, looks, lowers the telescope, turns
towards Hamm.*)

Corpsed.

(*Pause.*)

Well? Content?
HAMM: Look at the sea.
CLOV: It's the same.
HAMM: Look at the ocean!

(*Clov gets down, takes a few steps towards window left, goes back for ladder,
carries it over and sets it down under window left, gets up on it, turns the telescope on the without, looks at length. He starts, lowers the telescope, examines
it, turns it again on the without.*)

CLOV: Never seen anything like that!
HAMM (*anxious*): What? A sail? A fin? Smoke?
CLOV (*looking*): The light is sunk.
HAMM (*relieved*): Pah! We all knew that.
CLOV (*looking*): There was a bit left.
HAMM: The base.
CLOV (*looking*): Yes.
HAMM: And now?
CLOV (*looking*): All gone.
HAMM: No gulls?
CLOV (*looking*): Gulls!
HAMM: And the horizon? Nothing on the horizon?
CLOV (*lowering the telescope, turning towards Hamm, exasperated*): What in
  God's name could there be on the horizon?

(*Pause.*)

HAMM: The waves, how are the waves?
CLOV: The waves?

(*He turns the telescope on the waves.*)

Lead.
HAMM: And the sun?
CLOV (*looking*): Zero.
HAMM: But it should be sinking. Look again.
CLOV (*looking*): Damn the sun.
HAMM: Is it night already then?
CLOV (*looking*): No.
HAMM: Then what is it?
CLOV (*looking*): Gray.

(*Lowering the telescope, turning towards Hamm, louder.*)

Gray!

(*Pause. Still louder.*)

GRRAY!

(*Pause. He gets down, approaches Hamm from behind, whispers in his ear.*)

HAMM (*starting*): Gray! Did I hear you say gray?
CLOV: Light black. From pole to pole.
HAMM: You exaggerate.

(*Pause.*)

Don't stay there, you give me the shivers.

(*Clov returns to his place beside the chair.*)

CLOV: Why this farce, day after day?
HAMM: Routine. One never knows.

(*Pause.*)

Last night I saw inside my breast. There was a big sore.
CLOV: Pah! You saw your heart.
HAMM: No, it was living.

(*Pause. Anguished.*)

Clov!
CLOV: Yes.
HAMM: What's happening?
CLOV: Something is taking its course.

(*Pause.*)

HAMM: Clov!
CLOV (*impatiently*): What is it?
HAMM: We're not beginning to . . . to . . . mean something?
CLOV: Mean something! You and I, mean something!

(*Brief laugh.*)

Ah that's a good one!
HAMM: I wonder.

(*Pause.*)

Imagine if a rational being came back to earth, wouldn't he be liable to get ideas into his head if he observed us long enough.

(*Voice of rational being.*)

Ah, good, now I see what it is, yes, now I understand what they're at!

(*Clov starts, drops the telescope and begins to scratch his belly with both hands. Normal voice.*)

And without going so far as that, we ourselves . . . (*with emotion*) . . . we ourselves . . . at certain moments . . .

(*Vehemently.*)

To think perhaps it won't all have been for nothing!
CLOV (*anguished, scratching himself*): I have a flea!
HAMM: A flea! Are there still fleas?
CLOV: On me there's one.

(*Scratching.*)

Unless it's a crablouse.
HAMM (*very perturbed*): But humanity might start from there all over again! Catch him, for the love of God!
CLOV: I'll go and get the powder.

(*Exit Clov.*)

HAMM: A flea! This is awful! What a day!

(*Enter Clov with a sprinkling tin.*)

CLOV: I'm back again, with the insecticide.
HAMM: Let him have it!

(*Clov loosens the top of his trousers, pulls it forward and shakes powder into the aperture. He stoops, looks, waits, starts, frenziedly shakes more powder, stoops, looks, waits.*)

CLOV: The bastard!

HAMM: Did you get him?
CLOV: Looks like it.

(*He drops the tin and adjusts his trousers.*)

Unless he's laying doggo.°
HAMM: Laying! Lying you mean. Unless he's *lying* doggo.
CLOV: Ah? One says lying? One doesn't say laying?
HAMM: Use your head, can't you. If he was laying we'd be bitched.
CLOV: Ah.

(*Pause.*)

What about that pee?
HAMM: I'm having it.
CLOV: Ah that's the spirit, that's the spirit!

(*Pause.*)

HAMM (*with ardor*): Let's go from here, the two of us! South! You can
    make a raft and the currents will carry us away, far away, to
    other . . . mammals!
CLOV: God forbid!
HAMM: Alone, I'll embark alone! Get working on that raft immediately.
    Tomorrow I'll be gone forever.
CLOV (*hastening towards door*): I'll start straight away.
HAMM: Wait!

(*Clov halts.*)

Will there be sharks, do you think?
CLOV: Sharks? I don't know. If there are there will be.

(*He goes towards door.*)

HAMM: Wait!

(*Clov halts.*)

Is it not yet time for my painkiller?
CLOV (*violently*): No!

(*He goes towards door.*)

HAMM: Wait!

(*Clov halts.*)

How are your eyes?
CLOV: Bad.

laying doggo: Lying low; keeping still.

HAMM: But you can see.
CLOV: All I want.
HAMM: How are your legs
CLOV: Bad.
HAMM: But you can walk.
CLOV: I come . . . and go.
HAMM: In my house.

(*Pause. With prophetic relish.*)

One day you'll be blind, like me. You'll be sitting there, a speck in the void, in the dark, forever, like me.

(*Pause.*)

One day you'll say to yourself, I'm tired, I'll sit down, and you'll go and sit down. Then you'll say, I'm hungry, I'll get up and get something to eat. But you won't get up. You'll say, I shouldn't have sat down, but since I have I'll sit on a little longer, then I'll get up and get something to eat. But you won't get up and you won't get anything to eat.

(*Pause.*)

You'll look at the wall a while, then you'll say, I'll close my eyes, perhaps have a little sleep, after that I'll feel better, and you'll close them. And when you open them again there'll be no wall anymore.

(*Pause.*)

Infinite emptiness will be all around you, all the resurrected dead of all the ages wouldn't fill it, and there you'll be like a little bit of grit in the middle of the steppe.

(*Pause.*)

Yes, one day you'll know what it is, you'll be like me, except that you won't have anyone with you, because you won't have had pity on anyone and because there won't be anyone left to have pity on.

(*Pause.*)

CLOV: It's not certain.

(*Pause.*)

And there's one thing you forget.
HAMM: Ah?
CLOV: I can't sit down.
HAMM (*impatiently*): Well you'll lie down then, what the hell! Or you'll come to a standstill, simply stop and stand still, the way you are now. One day you'll say, I'm tired, I'll stop. What does the attitude matter?

(*Pause.*)

CLOV: So you all want me to leave you.
HAMM: Naturally.
CLOV: Then I'll leave you.
HAMM: You can't leave us.
CLOV: Then I won't leave you.

(*Pause.*)

HAMM: Why don't you finish us?

(*Pause.*)

   I'll tell you the combination of the cupboard if you promise to finish me.
CLOV: I couldn't finish you.
HAMM: Then you won't finish me.

(*Pause.*)

CLOV: I'll leave you, I have things to do.
HAMM: Do you remember when you came here?
CLOV: No. Too small, you told me.
HAMM: Do you remember your father?
CLOV (*wearily*): Same answer.

(*Pause.*)

   You've asked me these questions millions of times.
HAMM: I love the old questions.

(*With fervor.*)

   Ah the old questions, the old answers, there's nothing like them!

(*Pause.*)

   It was I was a father to you.
CLOV: Yes.

(*He looks at Hamm fixedly.*)

   You were that to me.
HAMM: My house a home for you.
CLOV: Yes.

(*He looks about him.*)

   This was that for me.
HAMM (*proudly*): But for me (*gesture towards himself*), no father. But for
   Hamm (*gesture towards surroundings*), no home.

(*Pause.*)

CLOV: I'll leave you.
HAMM: Did you ever think of one thing?
CLOV: Never.
HAMM: That here we're down in a hole.

(*Pause.*)

But beyond the hills? Eh? Perhaps it's still green. Eh?

(*Pause.*)

Flora! Pomona!

(*Ecstatically.*)

Ceres!°

(*Pause.*)

Perhaps you won't need to go very far.
CLOV: I can't go very far.

(*Pause.*)

I'll leave you.
HAMM: Is my dog ready?
CLOV: He lacks a leg.
HAMM: Is he silky?
CLOV: He's a kind of Pomeranian.
HAMM: Go and get him.
CLOV: He lacks a leg.
HAMM: Go and get him!

(*Exit Clov.*)

We're getting on.

(*Enter Clov holding by one of its three legs a black toy dog.*)

CLOV: Your dogs are here.

(*He hands the dog to Hamm who feels it, fondles it.*)

HAMM: He's white, isn't he?
CLOV: Nearly.
HAMM: What do you mean, nearly? Is he white or isn't he?

Flora . . . Ceres: All Roman goddesses: Flora is the goddess of flowers; Pomona is the goddess of fruit; Ceres is the goddess of agriculture.

CLOV: He isn't.

(*Pause.*)

HAMM: You've forgotten the sex.
CLOV (*vexed*): But he isn't finished. The sex goes on at the end.

(*Pause.*)

HAMM: You haven't put on his ribbon.
CLOV (*angrily*): But he isn't finished, I tell you! First you finish your dog and then you put on his ribbon!

(*Pause.*)

HAMM: Can he stand?
CLOV: I don't know.
HAMM: Try.

(*He hands the dog to Clov who places it on the ground.*)

Well?
CLOV: Wait!

(*He squats down and tries to get the dog to stand on its three legs, fails, lets it go. The dog falls on its side.*)

HAMM (*impatiently*): Well?
CLOV: He's standing.
HAMM (*groping for the dog*): Where? Where is he?

(*Clov holds up the dog in a standing position.*)

CLOV: There.

(*He takes Hamm's hand and guides it towards the dog's head.*)

HAMM (*his hand on the dog's head*): Is he gazing at me?
CLOV: Yes.
HAMM (*proudly*): As if he were asking me to take him for a walk?
CLOV: If you like.
HAMM (*as before*): Or as if he were begging me for a bone.

(*He withdraws his hand.*)

Leave him like that, standing there imploring me.

(*Clov straightens up. The dog falls on its side.*)

CLOV: I'll leave you.
HAMM: Have you had your visions?
CLOV: Less.

HAMM: Is Mother Pegg's light on?
CLOV: Light! How could anyone's light be on?
HAMM: Extinguished!
CLOV: Naturally it's extinguished. If it's not on it's extinguished.
HAMM: No, I mean Mother Pegg.
CLOV: But naturally she's extinguished!

(*Pause.*)

   What's the matter with you today?
HAMM: I'm taking my course.

(*Pause.*)

   Is she buried?
CLOV: Buried! Who would have buried her?
HAMM: You.
CLOV: Me! Haven't I enough to do without burying people?
HAMM: But you'll bury me.
CLOV: No I won't bury you.

(*Pause.*)

HAMM: She was bonny once, like a flower of the field.

(*With reminiscent leer.*)

   And a great one for the men!
CLOV: We too were bonny—once. It's a rare thing not to have been bonny—once.

(*Pause.*)

HAMM: Go and get the gaff.

(*Clov goes to door, halts.*)

CLOV: Do this, do that, and I do it. I never refuse. Why?
HAMM: You're not able to.
CLOV: Soon I won't do it anymore.
HAMM: You won't be able to anymore.

(*Exit Clov.*)

   Ah the creatures, the creatures, everything has to be explained to them.

(*Enter Clov with gaff.*)

CLOV: Here's your gaff. Stick it up.

(*He gives the gaff to Hamm who, wielding it like a puntpole, tries to move his chair.*)

HAMM: Did I move?
CLOV: No.

(*Hamm throws down the gaff.*)

HAMM: Go and get the oilcan.
CLOV: What for?
HAMM: To oil the casters.
CLOV: I oiled them yesterday.
HAMM: Yesterday! What does that mean? Yesterday!
CLOV (*violently*): That means that bloody awful day, long ago, before this bloody awful day. I use the words you taught me. If they don't mean anything anymore, teach me others. Or let me be silent.

(*Pause.*)

HAMM: I once knew a madman who thought the end of the world had come. He was a painter—and engraver. I had a great fondness for him. I used to go and see him, in the asylum. I'd take him by the hand and drag him to the window. Look! There! All that rising corn! And there! Look! The sails of the herring fleet! All that loveliness!

(*Pause.*)

He'd snatch away his hand and go back into his corner. Appalled. All he had seen was ashes.

(*Pause.*)

He alone had been spared.

(*Pause.*)

Forgotten.

(*Pause.*)

It appears the case is . . . was not so . . . so unusual.
CLOV: A madman? When was that?
HAMM: Oh way back, way back, you weren't in the land of the living.
CLOV: God be with the days!

(*Pause. Hamm raises his toque.*)

HAMM: I had a great fondness for him.

(*Pause. He puts on his toque again.*)

He was a painter—and engraver.
CLOV: There are so many terrible things.
HAMM: No, no, there are not so many now.

(*Pause.*)

  Clov!

CLOV: Yes.

HAMM: Do you not think this has gone on long enough?

CLOV: Yes!

(*Pause.*)

  What?

HAMM: This . . . this . . . thing.

CLOV: I've always thought so.

(*Pause.*)

  You not?

HAMM (*gloomily*): Then it's a day like any other day.

CLOV: As long as it lasts.

(*Pause.*)

  All life long the same inanities.

HAMM: I can't leave you.

CLOV: I know. And you can't follow me.

(*Pause.*)

HAMM: If you leave me how shall I know?

CLOV (*briskly*): Well you simply whistle me and if I don't come running it
  means I've left you.

(*Pause.*)

HAMM: You won't come and kiss me good-bye?

CLOV: Oh I shouldn't think so.

(*Pause.*)

HAMM: But you might be merely dead in your kitchen.

CLOV: The result would be the same.

HAMM: Yes, but how would I know, if you were merely dead in your
  kitchen?

CLOV: Well . . . sooner or later I'd start to stink.

HAMM: You stink already. The whole place stinks of corpses.

CLOV: The whole universe.

HAMM (*angrily*): To hell with the universe.

(*Pause.*)

  Think of something.

CLOV: What?

HAMM: An idea, have an idea.

(*Angrily.*)

A bright idea!
CLOV: Ah good.

(*He starts pacing to and fro, his eyes fixed on the ground, his hands behind his back. He halts.*)

The pains in my legs! It's unbelievable! Soon I won't be able to think anymore.
HAMM: You won't be able to leave me.

(*Clov resumes his pacing.*)

What are you doing?
CLOV: Having an idea.

(*He paces.*)

Ah!

(*He halts.*)

HAMM: What a brain!

(*Pause.*)

Well?
CLOV: Wait!

(*He meditates. Not very convinced.*)

Yes . . .

(*Pause. More convinced.*)

Yes!

(*He raises his head.*)

I have it! I set the alarm.

(*Pause.*)

HAMM: This is perhaps not one of my bright days, but frankly—
CLOV: You whistle me. I don't come. The alarm rings. I'm gone. It doesn't ring. I'm dead.

(*Pause.*)

HAMM: Is it working?

(*Pause. Impatiently.*)

The alarm, is it working?

CLOV: Why wouldn't it be working?

HAMM: Because it's worked too much.

CLOV: But it's hardly worked at all.

HAMM (*angrily*): Then because it's worked too little!

CLOV: I'll go and see.

(*Exit Clov. Brief ring of alarm off. Enter Clov with alarm clock. He holds it against Hamm's ear and releases alarm. They listen to it ringing to the end. Pause.*)

Fit to wake the dead! Did you hear it?

HAMM: Vaguely.

CLOV: The end is terrific!

HAMM: I prefer the middle.

(*Pause.*)

Is it not time for my painkiller?

CLOV: No!

(*He goes to door, turns.*)

I'll leave you.

HAMM: It's time for my story. Do you want to listen to my story?

CLOV: No.

HAMM: Ask my father if he wants to listen to my story.

(*Clov goes to bins, raises the lid of Nagg's, stoops, looks into it. Pause. He straightens up.*)

CLOV: He's asleep.

HAMM: Wake him.

(*Clov stoops, wakes Nagg with the alarm. Unintelligible words. Clov straightens up.*)

CLOV: He doesn't want to listen to your story.

HAMM: I'll give him a bonbon.

(*Clov stoops. As before.*)

CLOV: He wants a sugarplum.

HAMM: He'll get a sugarplum.

(*Clov stoops. As before.*)

CLOV: It's a deal.

(*He goes towards door. Nagg's hands appear, gripping the rim. Then the head emerges. Clov reaches door, turns.*)

Do you believe in the life to come?

HAMM: Mine was always that.

(*Exit Clov.*)

Got him that time!
NAGG: I'm listening.
HAMM: Scoundrel! Why did you engender me?
NAGG: I didn't know.
HAMM: What? What didn't you know?
NAGG: That it'd be you.

(*Pause.*)

You'll give me a sugarplum?
HAMM: After the audition.
NAGG: You swear?
HAMM: Yes.
NAGG: On what?
HAMM: My honor.

(*Pause. They laugh heartily.*)

NAGG: Two.
HAMM: One.
NAGG: One for me and one for—
HAMM: One! Silence!

(*Pause.*)

Where was I?

(*Pause. Gloomily.*)

It's finished, we're finished.

(*Pause.*)

Nearly finished.

(*Pause.*)

There'll be no more speech.

(*Pause.*)

Something dripping in my head, ever since the fontanelles.°

(*Stifled hilarity of Nagg.*)

Splash, splash, always on the same spot.

---

fontanelles: Soft membranes that link the incompletely developed skull bones in a baby's head.

(*Pause.*)

Perhaps it's a little vein.

(*Pause.*)

A little artery.

(*Pause. More animated.*)

Enough of that, it's story time, where was I?

(*Pause. Narrative tone.*)

The man came crawling towards me, on his belly. Pale, wonderfully pale and thin, he seemed on the point of—

(*Pause. Normal tone.*)

No, I've done that bit.

(*Pause. Narrative tone.*)

I calmly filled my pipe—the meerschaum, lit it with . . . let us say a vesta,° drew a few puffs. Aah!

(*Pause.*)

Well, what is it *you* want?

(*Pause.*)

It was an extraordinarily bitter day, I remember, zero by the thermometer. But considering it was Christmas Eve there was nothing . . . extraordinary about that. Seasonable weather, for once in a way.

(*Pause.*)

Well, what ill wind blows you my way? He raised his face to me, black with mingled dirt and tears.

(*Pause. Normal tone.*)

That should do it.

(*Narrative tone.*)

No no, don't look at me, don't look at me. He dropped his eyes and mumbled something, apologies I presume.

(*Pause.*)

---

vesta: A small wooden match.

I'm a busy man, you know, the final touches, before the festivities, you know what it is.

(*Pause. Forcibly.*)

Come on now, what is the object of this invasion?

(*Pause.*)

It was a glorious bright day, I remember, fifty by the heliometer,° but already the sun was sinking down into the . . . down among the dead.

(*Normal tone.*)

Nicely put, that.

(*Narrative tone.*)

Come on now, come on, present your petition and let me resume my labors.

(*Pause. Normal tone.*)

There's English for you. Ah well . . .

(*Narrative tone.*)

It was then he took the plunge. It's my little one, he said. Tsstss, a little one, that's bad. My little boy, he said, as if the sex mattered. Where did he come from? He named the hole. A good half-day, on horse. What are you insinuating? That the place is still inhabited? No, no, not a soul, except himself and the child—assuming he existed. Good. I inquired about the situation at Kov, beyond the gulf. Not a sinner. Good. And you expect me to believe you have left your little one back there, all alone, and alive into the bargain? Come now!

(*Pause.*)

It was a howling wild day, I remember, a hundred by the anemometer.° The wind was tearing up the dead pines and sweeping them . . . away.

(*Pause. Normal tone.*)

A bit feeble, that.

(*Narrative tone.*)

Come on, man, speak up, what is you want from me, I have to put up my holly.

---

heliometer: A telescope that measures the apparent diameter of the sun.
anemometer: A device that measures wind speed.

(*Pause.*)

Well to make it short it finally transpired that what he wanted from me was . . . bread for his brat? Bread? But I have no bread, it doesn't agree with me. Good. Then perhaps a little corn?

(*Pause. Normal tone.*)

That should do it.

(*Narrative tone.*)

Corn, yes, I have corn, it's true, in my granaries. But use your head. I give you some corn, a pound, a pound and a half, you bring it back to your child and you make him—if he's still alive—a nice pot of porridge, (*Nagg reacts*) a nice pot and a half of porridge, full of nourishment. Good. The colors come back into his little cheeks—perhaps. And then?

(*Pause.*)

I lost patience.

(*Violently.*)

Use your head, can't you, use your head, you're on earth, there's no cure for that!

(*Pause.*)

It was an exceedingly dry day, I remember, zero by the hygrometer.° Ideal weather, for my lumbago.

(*Pause. Violently.*)

But what in God's name do you imagine? That the earth will awake in spring? That the rivers and seas will run with fish again? That there's manna in heaven still for imbeciles like you?

(*Pause.*)

Gradually I cooled down, sufficiently at least to ask him how long he had taken on the way. Three whole days. Good. In what condition he had left the child. Deep in sleep.

(*Forcibly.*)

But deep in what sleep, deep in what sleep already?

(*Pause.*)

hygrometer: An instrument that measures humidity.

Well to make it short I finally offered to take him into my service. He had touched a chord. And then I imagined already that I wasn't much longer for this world.

(*He laughs. Pause.*)

Well?

(*Pause.*)

Well? Here if you were careful you might die a nice natural death, in peace and comfort.

(*Pause.*)

Well?

(*Pause.*)

In the end he asked me would I consent to take in the child as well—if he were still alive.

(*Pause.*)

It was the moment I was waiting for.

(*Pause.*)

Would I consent to take in the child . . .

(*Pause.*)

I can see him still, down on his knees, his hands flat on the ground, glaring at me with his mad eyes, in defiance of my wishes.

(*Pause. Normal tone.*)

I'll soon have finished with this story.

(*Pause.*)

Unless I bring in other characters.

(*Pause.*)

But where would I find them?

(*Pause.*)

Where would I look for them?

(*Pause. He whistles. Enter Clov.*)

Let us pray to God.
NAGG: Me sugarplum!

CLOV: There's a rat in the kitchen!

HAMM: A rat! Are there still rats?

CLOV: In the kitchen there's one.

HAMM: And you haven't exterminated him?

CLOV: Half. You disturbed us.

HAMM: He can't get away?

CLOV: No.

HAMM: You'll finish him later. Let us pray to God.

CLOV: Again!

NAGG: Me sugarplum!

HAMM: God first!

(*Pause.*)

Are you right?

CLOV (*resigned*): Off we go.

HAMM (*to Nagg*): And you?

NAGG (*clasping his hands, closing his eyes, in a gabble*): Our Father which art—

HAMM: Silence! In silence! Where are your manners?

(*Pause.*)

Off we go.

(*Attitudes of prayer. Silence. Abandoning his attitude, discouraged.*)

Well?

CLOV (*abandoning his attitude*): What a hope! And you?

HAMM: Sweet damn all!

(*To Nagg.*)

And you?

NAGG: Wait!

(*Pause. Abandoning his attitude.*)

Nothing doing!

HAMM: The bastard! He doesn't exist!

CLOV: Not yet.

NAGG: Me sugarplum!

HAMM: There are no more sugarplums!

(*Pause.*)

NAGG: It's natural. After all I'm your father. It's true if it hadn't been me it would have been someone else. But that's no excuse.

(*Pause.*)

Turkish Delight,° for example, which no longer exists, we all know that, there is nothing in the world I love more. And one day I'll ask you for some, in return for a kindness, and you'll promise it to me. One must live with the times.

(*Pause.*)

Whom did you call when you were a tiny boy, and were frightened, in the dark? Your mother? No. Me. We let you cry. Then we moved you out of earshot, so that we might sleep in peace.

(*Pause.*)

I was asleep, as happy as a king, and you woke me up to have me listen to you. It wasn't indispensable, you didn't really need to have me listen to you.

(*Pause.*)

I hope the day will come when you'll really need to have me listen to you, and need to hear my voice, any voice.

(*Pause.*)

Yes, I hope I'll live till then, to hear you calling me like when you were a tiny boy, and were frightened, in the dark, and I was your only hope.

(*Pause. Nagg knocks on lid of Nell's bin. Pause.*)

Nell!

(*Pause. He knocks louder. Pause. Louder.*)

Nell!

(*Pause. Nagg sinks back into his bin, closes the lid behind him. Pause.*)

HAMM: Our revels now are ended.

(*He gropes for the dog.*)

The dog's gone.
CLOV: He's not a real dog, he can't go.
HAMM (*groping*): He's not there.
CLOV: He's lain down.
HAMM: Give him up to me.

(*Clov picks up the dog and gives it to Hamm. Hamm holds it in his arms. Pause. Hamm throws away the dog.*)

Dirty brute!

Turkish Delight: A jellylike candy cut into cubes and dusted in sugar.

(*Clov begins to pick up the objects lying on the ground.*)

What are you doing?
CLOV: Putting things in order.

(*He straightens up. Fervently.*)

I'm going to clear everything away!

(*He starts picking up again.*)

HAMM: Order!
CLOV (*straightening up*): I love order. It's my dream. A world where all would be silent and still and each thing in its last place, under the last dust.

(*He starts picking up again.*)

HAMM (*exasperated*): What in God's name do you think you are doing?
CLOV (*straightening up*): I'm doing my best to create a little order.
HAMM: Drop it!

(*Clov drops the objects he has picked up.*)

CLOV: After all, there or elsewhere.

(*He goes towards door.*)

HAMM (*irritably*): What's wrong with your feet?
CLOV: My feet?
HAMM: Tramp! Tramp!
CLOV: I must have put on my boots.
HAMM: Your slippers were hurting you?

(*Pause.*)

CLOV: I'll leave you.
HAMM: No!
CLOV: What is there to keep me here?
HAMM: The dialogue.

(*Pause.*)

I've got on with my story.

(*Pause.*)

I've got on with it well.

(*Pause. Irritably.*)

Ask me where I've got to.
CLOV: Oh, by the way, your story?

HAMM (*surprised*): What story?
CLOV: The one you've been telling yourself all your days.
HAMM: Ah you mean my chronicle?
CLOV: That's the one.

(*Pause.*)

HAMM (*angrily*): Keep going, can't you, keep going!
CLOV: You've got on with it, I hope.
HAMM (*modestly*): Oh not very far, not very far.

(*He sighs.*)

There are days like that, one isn't inspired.

(*Pause.*)

Nothing you can do about it, just wait for it to come.

(*Pause.*)

No forcing, no forcing, it's fatal.

(*Pause.*)

I've got on with it a little all the same.

(*Pause.*)

Technique, you know.

(*Pause. Irritably.*)

I say I've got on with it a little all the same.
CLOV (*admiringly*): Well I never! In spite of everything you were able to
get on with it!
HAMM (*modestly*): Oh not very far, you know, not very far, but neverthe-
less, better than nothing.
CLOV: Better than nothing! Is it possible?
HAMM: I'll tell you how it goes. He comes crawling on his belly —
CLOV: Who?
HAMM: What?
CLOV: Who do you mean, he?
HAMM: Who do I mean! Yet another.
CLOV: Ah him! I wasn't sure.
HAMM: Crawling on his belly, whining for bread for his brat. He's offered
a job as gardener. Before —

(*Clov bursts out laughing.*)

What is there so funny about that?

CLOV: A job as gardener!
HAMM: Is that what tickles you?
CLOV: It must be that.
HAMM: It wouldn't be the bread?
CLOV: Or the brat.

(*Pause.*)

HAMM: The whole thing is comical, I grant you that. What about having a good guffaw the two of us together?
CLOV (*after reflection*): I couldn't guffaw again today.
HAMM (*after reflection*): Nor I.

(*Pause.*)

I continue then. Before accepting with gratitude he asks if he may have his little boy with him.
CLOV: What age?
HAMM: Oh tiny.
CLOV: He would have climbed the trees.
HAMM: All the little odd jobs.
CLOV: And then he would have grown up.
HAMM: Very likely.

(*Pause.*)

CLOV: Keep going, can't you, keep going!
HAMM: That's all. I stopped there.

(*Pause.*)

CLOV: Do you see how it goes on.
HAMM: More or less.
CLOV: Will it not soon be the end?
HAMM: I'm afraid it will.
CLOV: Pah! You'll make up another.
HAMM: I don't know.

(*Pause.*)

I feel rather drained.

(*Pause.*)

The prolonged creative effort.

(*Pause.*)

If I could drag myself down to the sea! I'd make a pillow of sand for my head and the tide would come.

CLOV: There's no more tide.

(*Pause.*)

HAMM: Go and see is she dead.

(*Clov goes to bins, raises the lid of Nell's, stoops, looks into it. Pause.*)

CLOV: Looks like it.

(*He closes the lid, straightens up. Hamm raises his toque. Pause. He puts it on again.*)

HAMM (*with his hand to his toque*): And Nagg?

(*Clov raises lid of Nagg's bin, stoops, looks into it. Pause.*)

CLOV: Doesn't look like it.

(*He closes the lid, straightens up.*)

HAMM (*letting go his toque*): What's he doing?

(*Clov raises lid of Nagg's bin, stoops, looks into it. Pause.*)

CLOV: He's crying.

(*He closes lid, straightens up.*)

HAMM: Then he's living.

(*Pause.*)

Did you ever have an instant of happiness?
CLOV: Not to my knowledge.

(*Pause.*)

HAMM: Bring me under the window.

(*Clov goes towards chair.*)

I want to feel the light on my face.

(*Clov pushes chair.*)

Do you remember, in the beginning, when you took me for a turn? You used to hold the chair too high. At every step you nearly tipped me out.

(*With senile quaver.*)

Ah great fun, we had, the two of us, great fun.

(*Gloomily.*)

And then we got into the way of it.

(*Clov stops the chair under window right.*)

There already?

(*Pause. He tilts back his head.*)

Is it light?
CLOV: It isn't dark.
HAMM (*angrily*): I'm asking you is it light.
CLOV: Yes.

(*Pause.*)

HAMM: The curtain isn't closed?
CLOV: No.
HAMM: What window is it?
CLOV: The earth.
HAMM: I knew it!

(*Angrily.*)

But there's no light there! The other!

(*Clov pushes chair towards window left.*)

The earth!

(*Clov stops the chair under window left. Hamm tilts back his head.*)

That's what I call light!

(*Pause.*)

Feels like a ray of sunshine.

(*Pause.*)

No?
CLOV: No.
HAMM: It isn't a ray of sunshine I feel on my face?
CLOV: No.

(*Pause.*)

HAMM: Am I very white?

(*Pause. Angrily.*)

I'm asking you am I very white!
CLOV: Not more so than usual.

(*Pause.*)

HAMM: Open the window.

CLOV: What for?
HAMM: I want to hear the sea.
CLOV: You wouldn't hear it.
HAMM: Even if you opened the window?
CLOV: No.
HAMM: Then it's not worthwhile opening it?
CLOV: No.
HAMM (*violently*): Then open it!

(*Clov gets up on the ladder, opens the window. Pause.*)

Have you opened it?
CLOV: Yes.

(*Pause.*)

HAMM: You swear you've opened it?
CLOV: Yes.

(*Pause.*)

HAMM: Well . . . !

(*Pause.*)

It must be very calm.

(*Pause. Violently.*)

I'm asking you is it very calm!
CLOV: Yes.
HAMM: It's because there are no more navigators.

(*Pause.*)

You haven't much conversation all of a sudden. Do you not feel well?
CLOV: I'm cold.
HAMM: What month are we?

(*Pause.*)

Close the window, we're going back.

(*Clov closes the window, gets down, pushes the chair back to its place, remains standing behind it, head bowed.*)

Don't stay there, you give me the shivers!

(*Clov returns to his place beside the chair.*)

Father!

(*Pause. Louder.*)

Father!

(*Pause.*)

Go and see did he hear me.

(*Clov goes to Nagg's bin, raises the lid, stoops. Unintelligible words. Clov straightens up.*)

CLOV: Yes.
HAMM: Both times?

(*Clov stoops. As before.*)

CLOV: Once only.
HAMM: The first time or the second?

(*Clov stoops. As before.*)

CLOV: He doesn't know.
HAMM: It must have been the second.
CLOV: We'll never know.

(*He closes lid.*)

HAMM: Is he still crying?
CLOV: No.
HAMM: The dead go fast.

(*Pause.*)

What's he doing?
CLOV: Sucking his biscuit.
HAMM: Life goes on.

(*Clov returns to his place beside the chair.*)

Give me a rug,° I'm freezing.
CLOV: There are no more rugs.

(*Pause.*)

HAMM: Kiss me.

(*Pause.*)

Will you not kiss me?
CLOV: No.
HAMM: On the forehead.
CLOV: I won't kiss you anywhere.

---

rug: A blanket for the lower half of the body.

(*Pause.*)

HAMM (*holding out his hand*): Give me your hand at least.

(*Pause.*)

Will you not give me your hand?
CLOV: I won't touch you.

(*Pause.*)

HAMM: Give me the dog.

(*Clov looks round for the dog.*)

No!
CLOV: Do you not want your dog?
HAMM: No.
CLOV: Then I'll leave you.
HAMM (*head bowed, absently*): That's right.

(*Clov goes to door, turns.*)

CLOV: If I don't kill that rat he'll die.
HAMM (*as before*): That's right.

(*Exit Clov. Pause.*)

Me to play.

(*He takes out his handkerchief, unfolds it, holds it spread out before him.*)

We're getting on.

(*Pause.*)

You weep, and weep, for nothing, so as not to laugh, and little by
little . . . you begin to grieve.

(*He folds the handkerchief, puts it back in his pocket, raises his head.*)

All those I might have helped.

(*Pause.*)

Helped!

(*Pause.*)

Saved.

(*Pause.*)

Saved!

(*Pause.*)

The place was crawling with them!

(*Pause. Violently.*)

Use your head, can't you, use your head, you're on earth, there's no cure for that!

(*Pause.*)

Get out of here and love one another! Lick your neighbor as yourself!

(*Pause. Calmer.*)

When it wasn't bread they wanted it was crumpets.

(*Pause. Violently.*)

Out of my sight and back to your petting parties!

(*Pause.*)

All that, all that!

(*Pause.*)

Not even a real dog!

(*Calmer.*)

The end is in the beginning and yet you go on.

(*Pause.*)

Perhaps I could go on with my story, end it and begin another.

(*Pause.*)

Perhaps I could throw myself out on the floor.

(*He pushes himself painfully off his seat, falls back again.*)

Dig my nails into the cracks and drag myself forward with my fingers.

(*Pause.*)

It will be the end and there I'll be, wondering what can have brought it on and wondering what can have ... (*he hesitates*) ... why it was so long coming.

(*Pause.*)

There I'll be, in the old shelter, alone against the silence and ... (*he hesitates*) ... the stillness. If I can hold my peace, and sit quiet, it will be all over with sound, and motion, all over and done with.

(*Pause.*)

I'll have called my father and I'll have called my ... (*he hesitates*) ... my son. And even twice, or three times, in case they shouldn't have heard me, the first time, or the second.

(*Pause.*)

I'll say to myself, He'll come back.

(*Pause.*)

And then?

(*Pause.*)

And then?

(*Pause.*)

He couldn't, he has gone too far.

(*Pause.*)

And then?

(*Pause. Very agitated.*)

All kinds of fantasies! That I'm being watched! A rat! Steps! Breath held and then . . .

(*He breathes out.*)

Then babble, babble, words, like the solitary child who turns himself into children, two, three, so as to be together, and whisper together, in the dark.

(*Pause.*)

Moment upon moment, pattering down, like the millet grains of . . . (*he hesitates*) . . . that old Greek,° and all life long you wait for that to mount up to a life.

(*Pause. He opens his mouth to continue, renounces.*)

Ah let's get it over!

(*He whistles. Enter Clov with alarm clock. He halts beside the chair.*)

What? Neither gone nor dead?
CLOV: In spirit only.
HAMM: Which?
CLOV: Both.
HAMM: Gone from me you'd be dead.
CLOV: And vice versa.

---

millet grains of . . . that old Greek: a reference to the mathematical problem known as "Zeno's paradox." The problem exhibits the concept of deceleration: If you continually fill a container with millet grains by half of the previous amount added, the container will never become full.

HAMM: Outside of here it's death!

(*Pause.*)

   And the rat?
CLOV: He's got away.
HAMM: He can't go far.

(*Pause. Anxious.*)

   Eh?
CLOV: He doesn't need to go far.

(*Pause.*)

HAMM: Is it not time for my painkiller?
CLOV: Yes.
HAMM: Ah! At last! Give it to me! Quick!

(*Pause.*)

CLOV: There's no more painkiller.

(*Pause.*)

HAMM (*appalled*): Good . . . !

(*Pause.*)

   No more painkiller!
CLOV: No more painkiller. You'll never get any more painkiller.

(*Pause.*)

HAMM: But the little round box. It was full!
CLOV: Yes. But now it's empty.

(*Pause. Clov starts to move about the room. He is looking for a place to put down the alarm clock.*)

HAMM (*soft*): What'll I do?

(*Pause. In a scream.*)

   What'll I do?

(*Clov sees the picture, takes it down, stands it on the floor with its face to the wall, hangs up the alarm clock in its place.*)

   What are you doing?
CLOV: Winding up.
HAMM: Look at the earth.
CLOV: Again!

HAMM: Since it's calling to you.
CLOV: Is your throat sore?

(*Pause.*)

Would you like a lozenge?

(*Pause.*)

No.

(*Pause.*)

Pity.

(*Clov goes, humming, towards window right, halts before it, looks up at it.*)

HAMM: Don't sing.
CLOV (*turning towards Hamm*): One hasn't the right to sing anymore?
HAMM: No.
CLOV: Then how can it end?
HAMM: You want it to end?
CLOV: I want to sing.
HAMM: I can't prevent you.

(*Pause. Clov turns towards window right.*)

CLOV: What did I do with that steps?

(*He looks around for ladder.*)

You didn't see that steps?

(*He sees it.*)

Ah, about time.

(*He goes towards window left.*)

Sometimes I wonder if I'm in my right mind. Then it passes over and I'm as lucid as before.

(*He gets up on ladder, looks out of window.*)

Christ, she's under water!

(*He looks.*)

How can that be?

(*He pokes forward his head, his hand above his eyes.*)

It hasn't rained.

(*He wipes the pane, looks. Pause.*)

Ah what a fool I am! I'm on the wrong side!

(*He gets down, takes a few steps towards window right.*)

Under water!

(*He goes back for ladder.*)

What a fool I am!

(*He carries ladder towards window right.*)

Sometimes I wonder if I'm in my right senses. Then it passes off and I'm as intelligent as ever.

(*He sets down ladder under window right, gets up on it, looks out of window. He turns towards Hamm.*)

Any particular sector you fancy? Or merely the whole thing?
HAMM: Whole thing.
CLOV: The general effect? Just a moment.

(*He looks out of window. Pause.*)

HAMM: Clov.
CLOV (*absorbed*): Mmm.
HAMM: Do you know what it is?
CLOV (*as before*): Mmm.
HAMM: I was never there.

(*Pause.*)

Clov!
CLOV (*turning towards Hamm, exasperated*): What is it?
HAMM: I was never there.
CLOV: Lucky for you.

(*He looks out of window.*)

HAMM: Absent, always. It all happened without me. I don't know what's happened.

(*Pause.*)

Do you know what's happened?

(*Pause.*)

Clov!
CLOV (*turning towards Hamm, exasperated*): Do you want me to look at this muckheap, yes or no?
HAMM: Answer me first.
CLOV: What?

HAMM: Do you know what's happened?

CLOV: When? Where?

HAMM (*violently*): When! What's happened? Use your head, can't you! What has happened?

CLOV: What for Christ's sake does it matter?

(*He looks out of window.*)

HAMM: I don't know.

(*Pause. Clov turns towards Hamm.*)

CLOV (*harshly*): When old Mother Pegg asked you for oil for her lamp and you told her to get out to hell, you knew what was happening then, no?

(*Pause.*)

You know what she died of, Mother Pegg? Of darkness.

HAMM (*feebly*): I hadn't any.

CLOV (*as before*): Yes, you had.

(*Pause.*)

HAMM: Have you the glass?

CLOV: No, it's clear enough as it is.

HAMM: Go and get it.

(*Pause. Clov casts up his eyes, brandishes his fists. He loses balance, clutches on to the ladder. He starts to get down, halts.*)

CLOV: There's one thing I'll never understand.

(*He gets down.*)

Why I always obey you. Can you explain that to me?

HAMM: No. . . . Perhaps it's compassion.

(*Pause.*)

A kind of great compassion.

(*Pause.*)

Oh you won't find it easy, you won't find it easy.

(*Pause. Clov begins to move about the room in search of the telescope.*)

CLOV: I'm tired of our goings on, very tired.

(*He searches.*)

You're not sitting on it?

(*He moves the chair, looks at the place where it stood, resumes his search.*)

HAMM (*anguished*): Don't leave me there!

(*Angrily Clov restores the chair to its place.*)

Am I right in the center?
CLOV: You'd need a microscope to find this —

(*He sees the telescope.*)

Ah, about time.

(*He picks up the telescope, gets up on the ladder, turns the telescope on the without.*)

HAMM: Give me the dog.
CLOV (*looking*): Quiet!
HAMM (*angrily*): Give me the dog!

(*Clov drops the telescope, clasps his hands to his head. Pause. He gets down precipitately, looks for the dog, sees it, picks it up, hastens towards Hamm and strikes him violently on the head with the dog.*)

CLOV: There's your dog for you!

(*The dog falls to the ground. Pause.*)

HAMM: He hit me!
CLOV: You drive me mad, I'm mad!
HAMM: If you must hit me, hit me with the axe.

(*Pause.*)

Or with the gaff, hit me with the gaff. Not with the dog. With the gaff. Or with the axe.

(*Clov picks up the dog and gives it to Hamm who takes it in his arms.*)

CLOV (*imploringly*): Let's stop playing!
HAMM: Never!

(*Pause.*)

Put me in my coffin.
CLOV: There are no more coffins.
HAMM: Then let it end!

(*Clov goes towards ladder.*)

With a bang!

(*Clov gets up on ladder, gets down again, looks for telescope, sees it, picks it up, gets up ladder, raises telescope.*)

Of darkness! And me? Did anyone ever have pity on me?

CLOV (*lowering the telescope, turning towards Hamm*): What?

(*Pause.*)

Is it me you're referring to?

HAMM (*angrily*): An aside, ape! Did you never hear an aside before?

(*Pause.*)

I'm warming up for my last soliloquy.

CLOV: I warn you. I'm going to look at this filth since it's an order. But it's the last time.

(*He turns the telescope on the without.*)

Let's see.

(*He moves the telescope.*)

Nothing . . . nothing . . . good . . . good . . . nothing . . . goo—

(*He starts, lowers the telescope, examines it, turns it again on the without. Pause.*)

Bad luck to it!

HAMM: More complications!

(*Clov gets down.*)

Not an underplot, I trust.

(*Clov moves ladder nearer window, gets up on it, turns telescope on the without.*)

CLOV (*dismayed*): Looks like a small boy!

HAMM (*sarcastic*): A small . . . boy!

CLOV: I'll go and see.

(*He gets down, drops the telescope, goes towards door, turns.*)

I'll take the gaff.

(*He looks for the gaff, sees it, picks it up, hastens towards door.*)

HAMM: No!

(*Clov halts.*)

CLOV: No? A potential procreator?

HAMM: If he exists he'll die there or he'll come here. And if he doesn't . . .

(*Pause.*)

CLOV: You don't believe me? You think I'm inventing?

(*Pause.*)

HAMM: It's the end, Clov, we've come to the end. I don't need you any-more.

(*Pause.*)

CLOV: Lucky for you.

(*He goes towards door.*)

HAMM: Leave me the gaff.

(*Clov gives him the gaff, goes towards door, halts, looks at alarm clock, takes it down, looks round for a better place to put it, goes to bins, puts it on lid of Nagg's bin. Pause.*)

CLOV: I'll leave you.

(*He goes towards door.*)

HAMM: Before you go . . .

(*Clov halts near door.*)

. . . say something.
CLOV: There is nothing to say.
HAMM: A few words . . . to ponder . . . in my heart.
CLOV: Your heart!
HAMM: Yes.

(*Pause. Forcibly.*)

Yes!

(*Pause.*)

With the rest, in the end, the shadows, the murmurs, all the trouble, to end up with.

(*Pause.*)

Clov. . . . He never spoke to me. Then, in the end, before he went, with-out my having asked him, he spoke to me. He said . . .
CLOV (*despairingly*): Ah . . . !
HAMM: Something . . . from your heart.
CLOV: My heart!
HAMM: A few words . . . from your heart.

(*Pause.*)

CLOV (*fixed gaze, tonelessly, towards auditorium*): They said to me, That's love, yes, yes, not a doubt, now you see how —
HAMM: Articulate!

CLOV (*as before*): How easy it is. They said to me, That's friendship, yes, yes, no question, you've found it. They said to me, Here's the place, stop, raise your head and look at all that beauty. That order! They said to me, Come now, you're not a brute beast, think upon these things and you'll see how all becomes clear. And simple! They said to me, What skilled attention they get, all these dying of their wounds.

HAMM: Enough!

CLOV (*as before*): I say to myself—sometimes, Clov, you must learn to suffer better than that if you want them to weary of punishing you—one day. I say to myself—sometimes, Clov, you must be there better than that if you want them to let you go—one day. But I feel too old, and too far, to form new habits. Good, it'll never end, I'll never go.

(*Pause.*)

Then one day, suddenly, it ends, it changes, I don't understand, it dies, or it's me, I don't understand, that either. I ask the words that remain—sleeping, waking, morning, evening. They have nothing to say.

(*Pause.*)

I open the door of the cell and go. I am so bowed I only see my feet, if I open my eyes, and between my legs a little trail of black dust. I say to myself that the earth is extinguished, though I never saw it lit.

(*Pause.*)

It's easy going.

(*Pause.*)

When I fall I'll weep for happiness.

(*Pause. He goes towards door.*)

HAMM: Clov!

(*Clov halts, without turning.*)

Nothing.

(*Clov moves on.*)

Clov!

(*Clov halts, without turning.*)

CLOV: This is what we call making an exit.

HAMM: I'm obliged to you, Clov. For your services.

CLOV (*turning, sharply*): Ah pardon, it's I am obliged to you.

HAMM: It's we are obliged to each other.

(*Pause. Clov goes towards door.*)

One thing more.

(*Clov halts.*)

A last favor.

(*Exit Clov.*)

Cover me with the sheet.

(*Long pause.*)

No? Good.

(*Pause.*)

Me to play.

(*Pause. Wearily.*)

Old endgame lost of old, play and lose and have done with losing.

(*Pause. More animated.*)

Let me see.

(*Pause.*)

Ah yes!

(*He tries to move the chair, using the gaff as before. Enter Clov, dressed for the road. Panama hat, tweed coat, raincoat over his arm, umbrella, bag. He halts by the door and stands there, impassive and motionless, his eyes fixed on Hamm, till the end. Hamm gives up.*)

Good.

(*Pause.*)

Discard.

(*He throws away the gaff, makes to throw away the dog, thinks better of it.*)

Take it easy.

(*Pause.*)

And now?

(*Pause.*)

Raise hat.

(*He raises his toque.*)

Peace to our . . . arses.

(*Pause.*)

And put on again.

(*He puts on his toque.*)

Deuce.

(*Pause. He takes off his glasses.*)

Wipe.

(*He takes out his handkerchief and, without unfolding it, wipes his glasses.*)

And put on again.

(*He puts on his glasses, puts back the handkerchief in his pocket.*)

We're coming. A few more squirms like that and I'll call.

(*Pause.*)

A little poetry.

(*Pause.*)

You prayed —

(*Pause. He corrects himself.*)

You CRIED for night; it comes —

(*Pause. He corrects himself.*)

It FALLS: now cry in darkness.

(*He repeats, chanting.*)

You cried for night; it falls: now cry in darkness.

(*Pause.*)

Nicely put, that.

(*Pause.*)

And now?

(*Pause.*)

Moments for nothing, now as always, time was never and time is over, reckoning closed and story ended.

(*Pause. Narrative tone.*)

If he could have his child with him. . . .

(*Pause.*)

It was the moment I was waiting for.

(*Pause.*)

You don't want to abandon him? You want him to bloom while you are withering? Be there to solace your last million last moments?

(*Pause.*)

He doesn't realize, all he knows is hunger, and cold, and death to crown it all. But you! You ought to know what the earth is like, nowadays. Oh I put him before his responsibilities!

(*Pause. Normal tone.*)

Well, there we are, there I am, that's enough.

(*He raises the whistle to his lips, hesitates, drops it. Pause.*)

Yes, truly!

(*He whistles. Pause. Louder. Pause.*)

Good.

(*Pause.*)

Father!

(*Pause. Louder.*)

Father!

(*Pause.*)

Good.

(*Pause.*)

We're coming.

(*Pause.*)

And to end up with?

(*Pause.*)

Discard.

(*He throws away the dog. He tears the whistle from his neck.*)

With my compliments.

(*He throws whistle towards auditorium. Pause. He sniffs. Soft.*)

Clov!

(*Long pause.*)

No? Good.

(*He takes out the handkerchief.*)

Since that's the way we're playing it . . . (*he unfolds handkerchief*) . . . let's play it that way . . . (*he unfolds*) . . . and speak no more about it . . . (*he finishes unfolding*) . . . speak no more.

(*He holds handkerchief spread out before him.*)

Old stancher!

(*Pause.*)

You . . . remain.

(*Pause. He covers his face with handkerchief, lowers his arms to armrests, remains motionless.*)

(*Brief tableau.*)

1955

Top Girls

CARYL CHURCHILL [b. 1938]

Characters
MARLENE
WAITRESS/KIT/SHONA
ISABELLA BIRD/JOYCE/MRS. KIDD
LADY NIJO/WIN
DULL GRET/ANGIE
POPE JOAN/LOUISE
PATIENT GRISELDA/NELL/JEANINE

Act I
Scene I: *A Restaurant.*
Scene II: *Top Girls' Employment Agency, London.*
Scene III: *Joyce's backyard in Suffolk.*

Act II
Scene I: *Top Girls' Employment Agency.*
Scene II: *A Year Earlier. Joyce's kitchen.*

Production Note: *The seating order for Act I, Scene I, in the original production at the Royal Court Theatre was (from right) Gret, Nijo, Marlene, Joan, Griselda, Isabella.*

The Characters
ISABELLA BIRD (1831–1904): *Lived in Edinburgh, traveled extensively between the ages of forty and seventy.*
LADY NIJO (B. 1258): *Japanese, was an Emperor's courtesan and later a Buddhist nun who traveled on foot through Japan.*
DULL GRET: *Is the subject of the Brueghel painting* DULLE GRIET, *in which a woman in an apron and armor leads a crowd of women charging through hell and fighting the devils.*
POPE JOAN: *Disguised as a man, is thought to have been pope between 854 and 856.*
PATIENT GRISELDA: *Is the obedient wife whose story is told by Chaucer in "The Clerk's Tale" of* THE CANTERBURY TALES.

The Layout: *A speech usually follows the one immediately before it but:*
(1) When one character starts speaking before the other has finished, the point
of interruption is marked /. E.g.,

ISABELLA: This is the Emperor of Japan? / I once met the Emperor of
    Morocco.
NIJO: In fact he was the ex-Emperor.

(2) A character sometimes continues speaking right through another's speech.
E.g.,

ISABELLA: When I was forty I thought my life was over. / Oh I was pitiful.
    I was
NIJO: I didn't say I felt it for twenty years. Not every minute.
ISABELLA: sent on a cruise for my health and felt even worse. Pains in my
    bones, pins and needles . . . etc.

(3) Sometimes a speech follows on from a speech earlier than the one immedi-
ately before it, and continuity is marked*. E.g.,

GRISELDA: I'd seen him riding by, we all had. And he'd seen me in the
    fields with the sheep.*
ISABELLA: I would have been well suited to minding sheep.
NIJO: And Mr. Nugent went riding by.
ISABELLA: Of course not, Nijo, I mean a healthy life in the open air.
JOAN: *He just rode up while you were minding the sheep and asked you
    to marry him?

where "in the fields with the sheep" is the cue to both "I would have been" and
"He just rode up."

ACT I   *Scene 1*

(Restaurant. Saturday night. There is a table with a white cloth set for dinner
with six places. The lights come up on Marlene and the Waitress.)

MARLENE: Excellent, yes, table for six. One of them's going to be late but
    we won't wait. I'd like a bottle of Frascati straight away if you've got
    one really cold. *(The Waitress goes. Isabella Bird arrives.)* Here we are.
    Isabella.
ISABELLA: Congratulations, my dear.
MARLENE: Well, it's a step. It makes for a party. I haven't time for a holi-
    day. I'd like to go somewhere exotic like you but I can't get away. I
    don't know how you could bear to leave Hawaii. / I'd like to lie
ISABELLA: I did think of settling.

MARLENE: in the sun forever, except of course I can't bear sitting still.

ISABELLA: I sent for my sister Hennie to come and join me. I said, Hennie we'll live here forever and help the natives. You can buy two sirloins of beef for what a pound of chops cost in Edinburgh. And Hennie wrote back, the dear, that yes, she would come to Hawaii if I wished, but I said she had far better stay where she was. Hennie was suited to life in Tobermory.

MARLENE: Poor Hennie.

ISABELLA: Do you have a sister?

MARLENE: Yes in fact.

ISABELLA: Hennie was happy. She was good. I did miss its face, my own pet. But I couldn't stay in Scotland. I loathed the constant murk.

(*Lady Nijo arrives.*)

MARLENE (*seeing her*): Ah! Nijo! (*The Waitress enters with the wine.*)

NIJO: Marlene! (*To Isabella.*) So excited when Marlene told me / you were coming.

ISABELLA: I'm delighted / to meet you.

MARLENE: I think a drink while we wait for the others. I think a drink anyway. What a week. (*Marlene seats Nijo. The Waitress pours the wine.*)

NIJO: It was always the men who used to get so drunk. I'd be one of the maidens, passing the sake.

ISABELLA: I've had sake. Small hot drink. Quite fortifying after a day in the wet.

NIJO: One night my father proposed three rounds of three cups, which was normal, and then the Emperor should have said three rounds of three cups, but he said three rounds of nine cups, so you can imagine. Then the Emperor passed his sake cup to my father and said, "Let the wild goose come to me this spring."

MARLENE: Let the what?

NIJO: It's a literary allusion to a tenth-century epic, / His Majesty was very cultured.

ISABELLA: This is the Emperor of Japan? / I once met the Emperor of Morocco.

NIJO: In fact he was the ex-Emperor.

MARLENE: But he wasn't old? / Did you, Isabella?

NIJO: Twenty-nine.

ISABELLA: Oh it's a long story.

MARLENE: Twenty-nine's an excellent age.

NIJO: Well I was only fourteen and I knew he meant something but I didn't know what. He sent me an eight-layered gown and I sent it back. So when the time came I did nothing but cry. My thin gowns were badly ripped. But even that morning when he left / he'd a green

MARLENE: Are you saying he raped you?

NIJO: robe with a scarlet lining and very heavily embroidered trousers, I already felt different about him. It made me uneasy. No, of course not, Marlene, I belonged to him, it was what I was brought up for from a baby. I soon found I was sad if he stayed away. It was depressing day after day not knowing when he would come. I never enjoyed taking other women to him.

ISABELLA: I certainly never saw my father drunk. He was a clergyman. / And I didn't get married till I was fifty. (*The Waitress brings the menus.*)

NIJO: Oh, my father was a very religious man. Just before he died he said to me, "Serve His Majesty, be respectful, if you lose his favor enter holy orders."

MARLENE: But he meant stay in a convent, not go wandering round the country.

NIJO: Priests were often vagrants, so why not a nun? You think I shouldn't? / I still did what my father wanted.

MARLENE: No no, I think you should. / I think it was wonderful.

(*Dull Gret arrives.*)

ISABELLA: I tried to do what my father wanted.

MARLENE: Gret, good. Nijo. Gret / I know Griselda's going to be late, but should we wait for Joan? / Let's get you a drink.

ISABELLA: Hello, Gret! (*She continues to Nijo.*) I tried to be a clergyman's daughter. Needlework, music, charitable schemes. I had a tumor removed from my spine and spent a great deal of time on the sofa. I studied the metaphysical poets and hymnology. / I thought I enjoyed intellectual pursuits.

NIJO: Ah, you like poetry. I come of a line of eight generations of poets. Father had a poem / in the anthology.

ISABELLA: My father taught me Latin although I was a girl. / But really I was

MARLENE: They didn't have Latin at my school.

ISABELLA: more suited to manual work. Cooking, washing, mending, riding horses. / Better than reading

NIJO: Oh but I'm sure you're very clever.

ISABELLA: books, eh Gret? A rough life in the open air.

NIJO: I can't say I enjoyed my rough life. What I enjoyed most was being the Emperor's favorite / and wearing thin silk.

ISABELLA: Did you have any horses, Gret?

GRET: Pig.

(*Pope Joan arrives.*)

MARLENE: Oh Joan, thank God, we can order. Do you know everyone? We were just talking about learning Latin and being clever girls. Joan was by way of an infant prodigy. Of course you were. What excited you when you were ten?

JOAN: Because angels are without matter they are not individuals. Every angel is a species.

MARLENE: There you are. (*They laugh. They look at the menus.*)

ISABELLA: Yes, I forgot all my Latin. But my father was the mainspring of my life and when he died I was so grieved. I'll have the chicken, please, / and the soup.

NIJO: Of course you were grieved. My father was saying his prayers and he dozed off in the sun. So I touched his knee to rouse him. "I wonder what will happen," he said, and then he was dead before he finished the sentence. / If he'd

MARLENE: What a shock.

NIJO: died saying his prayers he would have gone straight to heaven. / Waldorf salad.

JOAN: Death is the return of all creatures to God.

NIJO: I shouldn't have woken him.

JOAN: Damnation only means ignorance of the truth. I was always attracted by the teachings of John the Scot, though he was inclined to confuse / God and the world.

ISABELLA: Grief always overwhelmed me at the time.

MARLENE: What I fancy is a rare steak. Gret?

ISABELLA: I am of course a member of the / Church of England.

MARLENE: Gret?

GRET: Potatoes.

MARLENE: I haven't been to church for years. / I like Christmas carols.

ISABELLA: Good works matter more than church attendance.

MARLENE: Make that two steaks and a lot of potatoes. Rare. But I don't do good works either.

JOAN: Canelloni, please, / and a salad.

ISABELLA: Well, I tried, but oh dear. Hennie did good works.

NIJO: The first half of my life was all sin and the second / all repentance.*

MARLENE: Oh what about starters?

GRET: Soup.

JOAN: *And which did you like best?

MARLENE: Were your travels just a penance? Avocado vinaigrette. Didn't you / enjoy yourself?

JOAN: Nothing to start with for me, thank you.

NIJO: Yes, but I was very unhappy. / It hurt to remember the past.

MARLENE: And the wine list.

NIJO: I think that was repentance.

MARLENE: Well I wonder.

NIJO: I might have just been homesick.

MARLENE: Or angry.

NIJO: Not angry, no, / why angry?

GRET: Can we have some more bread?

MARLENE: Don't you get angry? I get angry.

NIJO: But what about?

MARLENE: Yes let's have two more Frascati. And some more bread, please. (*The Waitress exits.*)

ISABELLA: I tried to understand Buddhism when I was in Japan but all this birth and death succeeding each other through eternities just filled me with the most profound melancholy. I do like something more active.

NIJO: You couldn't say I was inactive. I walked every day for twenty years.

ISABELLA: I don't mean walking. / I mean in the head.

NIJO: I vowed to copy five Mahayana sutras.° / Do you know how long they are?

MARLENE: I don't think religious beliefs are something we have in common. Activity yes. (*Gret empties the bread basket into her apron.*)

NIJO: My head was active. / My head ached.

JOAN: It's no good being active in heresy.

ISABELLA: What heresy? She's calling the Church of England / a heresy.

JOAN: There are some very attractive / heresies.

NIJO: I had never heard of Christianity. Never / heard of it. Barbarians.

MARLENE: Well I'm not a Christian. / And I'm not a Buddhist.

ISABELLA: You have heard of it?

MARLENE: We don't all have to believe the same.

ISABELLA: I knew coming to dinner with a Pope we should keep off religion.

JOAN: I always enjoy a theological argument. But I won't try to convert you, I'm not a missionary. Anyway I'm a heresy myself.

ISABELLA: There are some barbaric practices in the east.

NIJO: Barbaric?

ISABELLA: Among the lower classes.

NIJO: I wouldn't know.

ISABELLA: Well theology always made my head ache.

MARLENE: Oh good, some food. (*The Waitress brings the first course, serves it during the following, then exits.*)

NIJO: How else could I have left the court if I wasn't a nun? When father died I had only His Majesty. So when I fell out of favor I had nothing. Religion is a kind of nothing / and I dedicated what was left of me to nothing.

Mahayana sutras: Buddhist scriptures.

ISABELLA: That's what I mean about Buddhism. It doesn't brace.

MARLENE: Come on, Nijo, have some wine.

NIJO: Haven't you ever felt like that? You've all felt / like that. Nothing will ever happen again. I am dead already.

ISABELLA: You thought your life was over but it wasn't.

JOAN: You wish it was over.

GRET: Sad.

MARLENE: Yes, when I first came to London I sometimes . . . and when I got back from America I did. But only for a few hours. Not twenty years.

ISABELLA: When I was forty I thought my life was over. / Oh I was pitiful. I was sent

NIJO: I didn't say I felt it for twenty years. Not every minute.

ISABELLA: on a cruise for my health and I felt even worse. Pains in my bones, pins and needles in my hands, swelling behind the ears, and— oh, stupidity. I shook all over, indefinable terror. And Australia seemed to me a hideous country, the acacias stank like drains. / I

NIJO: You were homesick. (*Gret steals a bottle of wine.*)

ISABELLA: had a photograph taken for Hennie but I told her I wouldn't send it, my hair had fallen out and my clothes were crooked, I looked completely insane and suicidal.

NIJO: So did I, exactly, dressed as a nun. / I was wearing walking shoes for the first time.

ISABELLA: I longed to go home, / but home to what? Houses are so perfectly dismal.*

NIJO: I longed to go back ten years.

MARLENE: *I thought traveling cheered you both up.

ISABELLA: Oh it did / of course. It was on

NIJO: I'm not a cheerful person, Marlene. I just laugh a lot.

ISABELLA: the trip from Australia to the Sandwich Isles, I fell in love with the sea. There were rats in the cabin and ants in the food but suddenly it was like a new world. I woke up every morning happy, knowing there would be nothing to annoy me. No nervousness. No dressing.

NIJO: Don't you like getting dressed? I adored my clothes. / When I was chosen

MARLENE: You had prettier colors than Isabella.

NIJO: to give sake to His Majesty's brother, the Emperor Kameyana, on his formal visit, I wore raw silk pleated trousers and a seven-layered gown in shades of red, and two outer garments, / yellow lined with green

MARLENE: Yes, all that silk must have been very—(*The Waitress enters, clears the first course and exits.*)

JOAN: I dressed as a boy when I left home.*

NIJO: and a light green jacket. Lady Betto had a five-layered gown in shades of green and purple.

ISABELLA: *You dressed as a boy?

MARLENE: Of course, / for safety.

JOAN: It was easy, I was only twelve. / Also women weren't allowed in the library. We wanted to study in Athens.

MARLENE: You ran away alone?

JOAN: No, not alone, I went with my friend. / He was

NIJO: Ah, an elopement.

JOAN: sixteen but I thought I knew more science than he did and almost as much philosophy.

ISABELLA: Well I always traveled as a lady and I repudiated strongly any suggestion in the press that I was other than feminine.

MARLENE: I don't wear trousers in the office. / I could but I don't.

ISABELLA: There was no great danger to a woman of my age and appearance.

MARLENE: And you got away with it, Joan?

JOAN: I did then. (*The Waitress brings in the main course.*)

MARLENE: And nobody noticed anything?

JOAN: They noticed I was a very clever boy. / And

MARLENE: I couldn't have kept pretending for so long.

JOAN: when I shared a bed with my friend, that was ordinary—two poor students in a lodging house. I think I forgot I was pretending.

ISABELLA: Rocky Mountain Jim, Mr. Nugent, showed me no disrespect. He found it interesting, I think, that I could make scones and also lasso cattle. Indeed he declared his love for me, which was most distressing.

NIJO: What did he say? / We always sent poems first.

MARLENE: What did you say?

ISABELLA: I urged him to give up whiskey, / but he said it was too late.

MARLENE: Oh Isabella.

ISABELLA: He had lived alone in the mountains for many years.

MARLENE: But did you—? (*The Waitress goes.*)

ISABELLA: Mr. Nugent was a man that any woman might love but none could marry. I came back to England.

NIJO: Did you write him a poem when you left? / Snow on the mountains. My sleeves

MARLENE: Did you never see him again?

ISABELLA: No, never.

NIJO: are wet with tears. In England no tears, no snow.

ISABELLA: Well, I say never. One morning very early in Switzerland, it was a year later, I had a vision of him as I last saw him / in his trapper's clothes with his

NIJO: A ghost!

ISABELLA: hair round his face, and that was the day, / I learned later, he died with a

NIJO: Ah!

ISABELLA: bullet in his brain. / He just bowed to me and vanished.

MARLENE: Oh Isabella.

NIJO: When your lover dies—One of my lovers died. / The priest Ariake.

JOAN: My friend died. Have we all got dead lovers?

MARLENE: Not me, sorry.

NIJO (to Isabella): I wasn't a nun, I was still at court, but he was a priest, and when he came to me he dedicated his whole life to hell. / He knew that when he died he would fall into one of the three lower realms. And he died, he did die.

JOAN (to Marlene): I'd quarrelled with him over the teachings of John the Scot,° who held that our ignorance of God is the same as his ignorance of himself. He only knows what he creates because he creates everything he knows but he himself is above being—do you follow?

MARLENE: No, but go on.

NIJO: I couldn't bear to think / in what shape would he be reborn.*

JOAN: St. Augustine maintained that the Neo-Platonic Ideas are indivisible

ISABELLA: *Buddhism is really most uncomfortable.

JOAN: from God, but I agreed with John that the created world is essences derived from Ideas which derived from God. As Denys the Areopagite° said —the pseudo-Denys—first we give God a name, then deny it, / then reconcile the contradiction

NIJO: In what shape would he return?

JOAN: by looking beyond / those terms—

MARLENE: Sorry, what? Denys said what?

JOAN: Well we disagreed about it, we quarreled. And next day he was ill, / I was so annoyed with him

NIJO: Misery in this life and worse in the next, all because of me.

JOAN: all the time I was nursing him I kept going over the arguments in my mind. Matter is not a means of knowing the essence. The source of the species is the Idea. But then I realized he'd never understand my arguments again, and that night he died. John the Scot held that the individual disintegrates / and there is no personal immortality.

ISABELLA: I wouldn't have you think I was in love with Jim Nugent. It was yearning to save him that I felt.

MARLENE (to Joan): So what did you do?

John the Scot: Controversial ninth-century Irish religious philosopher.
Denys the Areopagite: First-century Greek religious philosopher.

JOAN: First I decided to stay a man. I was used to it. And I wanted to devote my life to learning. Do you know why I went to Rome? Italian men didn't have beards.

ISABELLA: The loves of my life were Hennie, my own pet, and my dear husband the doctor, who nursed Hennie in her last illness. I knew it would be terrible when Hennie died but I didn't know how terrible. I felt half of myself had gone. How could I go on my travels without that sweet soul waiting at home for my letters? It was Doctor Bishop's devotion to her in her last illness that made me decide to marry him. He and Hennie had the same sweet character. I had not.

NIJO: I thought His Majesty had sweet character because when he found out about Ariake he was so kind. But really it was because he no longer cared for me. One night he even sent me out to a man who had been pursuing me. / He lay awake on the other side of the screens and listened.

ISABELLA: I did wish marriage had seemed more of a step. I tried very hard to cope with the ordinary drudgery of life. I was ill again with carbuncles on the spine and nervous prostration. I ordered a tricycle, that was my idea of adventure then. And John himself fell ill, with erysipelas and anemia. I began to love him with my whole heart but it was too late. He was a skeleton with transparent white hands. I wheeled him on various seafronts in a bathchair. And he faded and left me. There was nothing in my life. The doctors said I had gout / and my heart was much affected.

NIJO: There was nothing in my life, nothing, without the Emperor's favor. The Empress had always been my enemy, Marlene, she said I had no right to wear three-layered gowns. / But I was the adopted daughter of my grandfather the Prime Minister. I had been publicly granted permission to wear thin silk.

JOAN: There was nothing in my life except my studies. I was obsessed with pursuit of the truth. I taught at the Greek School in Rome, which St. Augustine had made famous. I was poor, I worked hard, I spoke apparently brilliantly, I was still very young, I was a stranger, suddenly I was quite famous, I was everyone's favorite. Huge crowds came to hear me. The day after they made me cardinal I fell ill and lay two weeks without speaking, full of terror and regret. / But then I got up determined to

MARLENE: Yes, success is very . . .

JOAN: go on. I was seized again / with a desperate longing for the absolute.

ISABELLA: Yes, yes, to go on. I sat in Tobermory among Hennie's flowers and sewed a complete outfit in Jaeger flannel. / I was fifty-six years old.

NIJO: Out of favor but I didn't die. I left on foot, nobody saw me go. For the next twenty years I walked through Japan.

GRET: Walking is good. (*Meanwhile, the Waitress enters, pours lots of wine, then shows Marlene the empty bottle.*)

JOAN: Pope Leo died and I was chosen. All right then. I would be Pope. I would know God. I would know everything.

ISABELLA: I determined to leave my grief behind and set off for Tibet.

MARLENE: Magnificent all of you. We need some more wine, please, two bottles I think, Griselda isn't even here yet, and I want to drink a toast to you all. (*The Waitress exits.*)

ISABELLA: To yourself surely, / we're here to celebrate your success.

NIJO: Yes, Marlene.

JOAN: Yes, what is it exactly, Marlene?

MARLENE: Well it's not Pope but it is managing director.*

JOAN: And you find work for people.

MARLENE: Yes, an employment agency.

NIJO: *Over all the women you work with. And the men.

ISABELLA: And very well deserved too. I'm sure it's just the beginning of something extraordinary.

MARLENE: Well it's worth a party.

ISABELLA: To Marlene.*

MARLENE: And all of us.

JOAN: *Marlene.

NIJO: Marlene.

GRET: Marlene.

MARLENE: We've all come a long way. To our courage and the way we changed our lives and our extraordinary achievements. (*They laugh and drink a toast.*)

ISABELLA: Such adventures. We were crossing a mountain pass at seven thousand feet, the cook was all to pieces, the muleteers suffered fever and snow blindness. But even though my spine was agony I managed very well.*

MARLENE: Wonderful.

NIJO: *Once I was ill for four months lying alone at an inn. Nobody to offer a horse to Buddha. I had to live for myself, and I did live.

ISABELLA: Of course you did. It was far worse returning to Tobermory. I always felt dull when I was stationary. / That's why I could never stay anywhere.

NIJO: Yes, that's it exactly. New sights. The shrine by the beach, the moon shining on the sea. The goddess had vowed to save all living things. / She would even save the fishes. I was full of hope.

JOAN: I had thought the Pope would know everything. I thought God would speak to me directly. But of course he knew I was a woman.

MARLENE: But nobody else even suspected? (*The Waitress brings more wine and then exits.*)

JOAN: In the end I did take a lover again.*

ISABELLA: In the Vatican?

GRET: *Keep you warm.

NIJO: *Ah, lover.

MARLENE: *Good for you.

JOAN: He was one of my chamberlains. There are such a lot of servants when you're Pope. The food's very good. And I realized I did know the truth. Because whatever the Pope says, that's true.

NIJO: What was he like, the chamberlain?*

GRET: Big cock.

ISABELLA: Oh, Gret.

MARLENE: *Did he fancy you when he thought you were a fella?

NIJO: What was he like?

JOAN: He could keep a secret.

MARLENE: So you did know everything.

JOAN: Yes, I enjoyed being Pope. I consecrated bishops and let people kiss my feet. I received the King of England when he came to submit to the church. Unfortunately there were earthquakes, and some village reported it had rained blood, and in France there was a plague of giant grasshoppers, but I don't think that can have been my fault, do you?* (*Laughter.*) The grasshoppers fell on the English Channel / and were washed up on shore

NIJO: I once went to sea. It was very lonely. I realized it made very little difference where I went.

JOAN: and their bodies rotted and poisoned the air and everyone in those parts died. (*Laughter.*)

ISABELLA: *Such superstition! I was nearly murdered in China by a howling mob. They thought the barbarians ate babies and put them under railway sleepers to make the tracks steady, and ground up their eyes to make the lenses of cameras. / So they were shouting,

MARLENE: And you had a camera!

ISABELLA: "Child-eater, child-eater." Some people tried to sell girl babies to Europeans for cameras or stew! (*Laughter.*)

MARLENE: So apart from the grasshoppers it was a great success.

JOAN: Yes, if it hadn't been for the baby I expect I'd have lived to an old age like Theodora of Alexandria, who lived as a monk. She was accused by a girl / who fell in love with her of being the father of her child and—

NIJO: But tell us what happened to your baby. I had some babies.

MARLENE: Didn't you think of getting rid of it?

JOAN: Wouldn't that be a worse sin than having it? / But a Pope with a child was about as bad as possible.

MARLENE: I don't know, you're the Pope.

JOAN: But I wouldn't have known how to get rid of it.

MARLENE: Other Popes had children, surely.

JOAN: They didn't give birth to them.

NIJO: Well you were a woman.

JOAN: Exactly and I shouldn't have been a woman. Woman, children, and lunatics can't be Pope.

MARLENE: So the only thing to do / was to get rid of it somehow.

NIJO: You had to have it adopted secretly.

JOAN: But I didn't know what was happening. I thought I was getting fatter, but then I was eating more and sitting about, the life of a Pope is quite luxurious. I don't think I'd spoken to a woman since I was twelve. The chamberlain was the one who realized.

MARLENE: And by then it was too late.

JOAN: Oh I didn't want to pay attention. It was easier to do nothing.

NIJO: But you had to plan for having it. You had to say you were ill and go away.

JOAN: That's what I should have done I suppose.

MARLENE: Did you want them to find out?

NIJO: I too was often in embarrassing situations, there's no need for a scandal. My first child was His Majesty's, which unfortunately died, but my second was Akebono's. I was seventeen. He was in love with me when I was thirteen, he was very upset when I had to go the Emperor, it was very romantic, a lot of poems. Now His Majesty hadn't been near me for two months so he thought I was four months pregnant when I was really six, so when I reached the ninth month / I announced I was seriously ill,

JOAN: I never knew what month it was.

NIJO: and Akebono announced he had gone on a religious retreat. He held me round the waist and lifted me up as the baby was born. He cut the cord with a short sword, wrapped the baby in white and took it away. It was only a girl but I was sorry to lose it. Then I told the Emperor that the baby had miscarried because of my illness, and there you are. The danger was past.

JOAN: But, Nijo, I wasn't used to having a woman's body.

ISABELLA: So what happened?

JOAN: I didn't know of course that it was near the time. It was Rogation Day, there was always a procession. I was on the horse dressed in my robes and a cross was carried in front of me, and all the cardinals were following, and all the clergy of Rome, and a huge crowd of people. / We set off from St. Peter's to go

MARLENE: Total Pope. (*Gret pours the wine and steals the bottle.*)

JOAN: to St. John's. I had felt a slight pain earlier, I thought it was something I'd eaten, and then it came back, and came back more often. I thought when this is over I'll go to bed. There were still long gaps when I felt perfectly all right and I didn't want to attract attention to myself and spoil the ceremony. Then I suddenly realized what it must be. I had to last out till I could get home and hide. Then something changed, my breath started to catch, I couldn't plan things properly anymore. We were in a little street that goes between St. Clement's and the Colosseum, and I just had to get off the horse and sit down for a minute. Great waves of pressure were going through my body, I heard sounds like a cow lowing, they came out of my mouth. Far away I heard people screaming, "The Pope is ill, the Pope is dying." And the baby just slid out onto the road.*

MARLENE: The cardinals / won't have known where to put themselves.

NIJO: Oh dear, Joan, what a thing to do! In the street!

ISABELLA: *How embarrassing.

GRET: In a field, yah. (*They are laughing.*)

JOAN: One of the cardinals said, "The Antichrist!" and fell over in a faint. (*They all laugh.*)

MARLENE: So what did they do? They weren't best pleased.

JOAN: They took me by the feet and dragged me out of town and stoned me to death. (*They stop laughing.*)

MARLENE: Joan, how horrible.

JOAN: I don't really remember.

NIJO: And the child died too?

JOAN: Oh yes, I think so, yes. (*The Waitress enters to clear the plates. Pause. They start talking very quietly.*)

ISABELLA (*to Joan*): I never had any children. I was very fond of horses.

NIJO (*to Marlene*): I saw my daughter once. She was three years old. She wore a plum-red / small sleeved gown. Akebono's wife

ISABELLA: Birdie was my favorite. A little Indian bay mare I rode in the Rocky Mountains.

NIJO: had taken the child because her own died. Everyone thought I was just a visitor. She was being brought up carefully so she could be sent to the palace like I was. (*Gret steals her empty plate.*)

ISABELLA: Legs of iron and always cheerful, and such a pretty face. If a stranger led her she reared up like a bronco.

NIJO: I never saw my third child after he was born, the son of Ariake the priest. Ariake held him on his lap the day he was born and talked to him as if he could understand, and cried. My fourth child was Ariake's too. Ariake died before he was born. I didn't want to see anyone, I stayed alone in the hills. It was a boy again, my third son. But oddly enough I felt nothing for him.

MARLENE: How many children did you have, Gret?

GRET: Ten.

ISABELLA: Whenever I came back to England I felt I had so much to atone for. Hennie and John were so good. I did no good in my life. I spent years in self-gratification. So I hurled myself into committees, I nursed the people of Tobermory in the epidemic of influenza, I lectured the Young Women's Christian Association on Thrift. I talked and talked explaining how the East was corrupt and vicious. My travels must do good to someone besides myself. I wore myself out with good causes.

MARLENE (*pause*): Oh God, why are we all so miserable?

JOAN (*pause*): The procession never went down that street again.

MARLENE: They rerouted it specially?

JOAN: Yes they had to go all round to avoid it. And they introduced a pierced chair.

MARLENE: A pierced chair?

JOAN: Yes, a chair made out of solid marble with a hole in the seat / and it was

MARLENE: You're not serious.

JOAN: in the Chapel of the Savior, and after he was elected the Pope had to sit in it.

MARLENE: And someone looked up his skirts? / Not really!

ISABELLA: What an extraordinary thing.

JOAN: Two of the clergy / made sure he was a man.

NIJO: On their hands and knees!

MARLENE: A pierced chair!

GRET: Balls!

(*Griselda arrives unnoticed.*)

NIJO: Why couldn't he just pull up his robe?

JOAN: He had to sit there and look dignified.

MARLENE: You could have made all your chamberlains sit in it.*

GRET: Big one. Small one.

NIJO: Very useful chair at court.

ISABELLA: *Or the Laird of Tobermory in his kilt.

(*They are quite drunk. They get the giggles. Marlene notices Griselda and gets up to welcome her. The others go on talking and laughing. Gret crosses to Joan and Isabella and pours them wine from her stolen bottles. The Waitress gives out the menus.*)

MARLENE: Griselda! / There you are. Do you want to eat?

GRISELDA: I'm sorry I'm so late. No, no, don't bother.

MARLENE: Of course it's no bother. / Have you eaten?

GRISELDA: No really, I'm not hungry.

MARLENE: Well have some pudding.

GRISELDA: I never eat pudding.

MARLENE: Griselda, I hope you're not anorexic. We're having pudding, I am, and getting nice and fat.

GRISELDA: Oh if everyone is. I don't mind.

MARLENE: Now who do you know? This is Joan who was Pope in the ninth century, and Isabella Bird, the Victorian traveler, and Lady Nijo from Japan, Emperor's concubine and Buddhist nun, thirteenth century, nearer your own time, and Gret who was painted by Brueghel. Griselda's in Boccaccio and Petrarch and Chaucer because of her extraordinary marriage. I'd like profiteroles because they're disgusting.

JOAN: Zabaglione, please.

ISABELLA: Apple pie / and cream.

NIJO: What's this?

MARLENE: Zabaglione, it's Italian, it's what Joan's having, / it's delicious.

NIJO: A Roman Catholic / dessert? Yes please.

MARLENE: Gret?

GRET: Cake.

GRISELDA: Just cheese and biscuits, thank you. (*The Waitress exits.*)

MARLENE: Yes, Griselda's life is like a fairy story, except it starts with marrying the prince.

GRISELDA: He's only a marquis, Marlene.

MARLENE: Well everyone for miles around is his liege and he'd absolute lord of life and death and you were the poor but beautiful peasant girl and he whisked you off. / Near enough a prince.

NIJO: How old were you?

GRISELDA: Fifteen.

NIJO: I was brought up in court circles and it was still a shock. Had you ever seen him before?

GRISELDA: I'd seen him riding by, we all had. And he'd seen me in the fields with the sheep.*

ISABELLA: I would have been well suited to minding sheep.

NIJO: And Mr. Nugent riding by.

ISABELLA: Of course not, Nijo, I mean a healthy life in the open air.

JOAN: *He just rode up while you were minding the sheep and asked you to marry him?

GRISELDA: No, no, it was on the wedding day. I was waiting outside the door to see the procession. Everyone wanted him to get married so there'd be an heir to look after us when he died, / and at last he

MARLENE: I don't think Walter wanted to get married. It is Walter? Yes.

GRISELDA: announced a day for the wedding but nobody knew who the bride was, we thought it must be a foreign princess, we were longing to see her. Then the carriage stopped outside our cottage and we couldn't see the bride anywhere. And he came and spoke to my father.

NIJO: And your father told you to serve the Prince.

GRISELDA: My father could hardly speak. The Marquis said it wasn't an order, I could say no, but if I said yes I must always obey him in everything.

MARLENE: That's when you should have suspected.

GRISELDA: But of course a wife must obey her husband. / And of course I must obey the Marquis.*

ISABELLA: I swore to obey dear John, of course, but it didn't seem to arise. Naturally I wouldn't have wanted to go abroad while I was married.

MARLENE: *Then why bother to mention it at all? He'd got a thing about it, that's why.

GRISELDA: I'd rather obey the Marquis than a boy from the village.

MARLENE: Yes, that's a point.

JOAN: I never obeyed anyone. They all obeyed me.

NIJO: And what did you wear? He didn't make you get married in your own clothes? That would be perverse.*

MARLENE: Oh, you wait.

GRISELDA: *He had ladies with him who undressed me and they had a white silk dress and jewels for my hair.

MARLENE: And at first he seemed perfectly normal?

GRISELDA: Marlene, you're always so critical of him. / Of course he was normal, he was very kind.

MARLENE: But, Griselda, come on, he took your baby.

GRISELDA: Walter found it hard to believe I loved him. He couldn't believe I would always obey him. He had to prove it.

MARLENE: I don't think Walter likes women.

GRISELDA: I'm sure he loved me, Marlene, all the time.

MARLENE: He just had a funny way / of showing it.

GRISELDA: It was hard for him too.

JOAN: How do you mean he took away your baby?

NIJO: Was it a boy?

GRISELDA: No, the first one was a girl.

NIJO: Even so it's hard when they take it away. Did you see it at all?

GRISELDA: Oh yes, she was six weeks old.

NIJO: Much better to do it straight away.

ISABELLA: But why did your husband take the child?

GRISELDA: He said all the people hated me because I was just one of them. And now I had a child they were restless. So he had to get rid of the child to keep them quiet. But he said he wouldn't snatch her, I had to agree and obey and give her up. So when I was feeding her a man came in and took her away. I thought he was going to kill her even before he was out of the room.

MARLENE: But you let him take her? You didn't struggle?

GRISELDA: I asked him to give her back so I could kiss her. And I asked him to bury her where no animals could dig her up. / It was Walter's child to do what he

ISABELLA: Oh, my dear.

GRISELDA: liked with.*

MARLENE: Walter was bonkers.

GRET: Bastard.

ISABELLA: *But surely, murder.

GRISELDA: I had promised.

MARLENE: I can't stand this. I'm going for a pee.

(*Marlene goes out. The Waitress brings the dessert, serves it during the follow-ing, then exits*)

NIJO: No, I understand. Of course you had to, he was your life. And were you in favor after that?

GRISELDA: Oh yes, we were very happy together. We never spoke about what had happened.

ISABELLA: I can see you were doing what you thought was your duty. But didn't it make you ill?

GRISELDA: No, I was very well, thank you.

NIJO: And you had another child?

GRISELDA: Not for four years, but then I did, yes, a boy.

NIJO: Ah a boy. / So it all ended happily.

GRISELDA: Yes he was pleased. I kept my son till he was two years old. A peasant's grandson. It made the people angry. Walter explained.

ISABELLA: But surely he wouldn't kill his children / just because —

GRISELDA: Oh it wasn't true. Walter would never give in to the people. He wanted to see if I loved him enough.

JOAN: He killed his children / to see if you loved him enough?

NIJO: Was it easier the second time or harder?

GRISELDA: It was always easy because I always knew I would do what he said. (*Pause. They start to eat.*)

ISABELLA: I hope you didn't have any more children.

GRISELDA: Oh no, no more. It was twelve years till he tested me again.

ISABELLA: So whatever did he do this time? / My poor John, I never loved him enough, and he would never have dreamt . . .

GRISELDA: He sent me away. He said the people wanted him to marry someone else who'd give him an heir and he'd got special permis-sion from the Pope. So I said I'd go home to my father. I came with nothing / so I went with nothing. I took

NIJO: Better to leave if your master doesn't want you.

GRISELDA: off my clothes. He let me keep a slip so he wouldn't be shamed. And I walked home barefoot. My father came out in tears. Everyone was crying except me.

NIJO: At least your father wasn't dead. / I had nobody.

ISABELLA: Well it can be a relief to come home. I loved to see Hennie's sweet face again.

GRISELDA: Oh yes, I was perfectly content. And quite soon he sent for me again.

JOAN: I don't think I would have gone.

GRISELDA: But he told me to come. I had to obey him. He wanted me to help prepare his wedding. He was getting married to a young girl from France / and nobody except me knew how to arrange things the way he liked them.

NIJO: It's always hard taking him another woman. (*Marlene comes back.*)

JOAN: I didn't live a woman's life. I don't understand it.

GRISELDA: The girl was sixteen and far more beautiful than me. I could see why he loved her. / She had her younger brother with her as a page. (*The Waitress enters.*)

MARLENE: Oh God, I can't bear it. I want some coffee. Six coffees. Six brandies. / Double brandies. Straightaway. (*The Waitress exits.*)

GRISELDA: They all went into the feast I'd prepared. And he stayed behind and put his arms round me and kissed me. / I felt half asleep with the shock.

NIJO: Oh, like a dream.

MARLENE: And he said, "This is your daughter and your son."

GRISELDA: Yes.

JOAN: What?

NIJO: Oh. Oh I see. You got them back.

ISABELLA: I did think it was remarkably barbaric to kill them but you learn not to say anything. / So he had them brought up secretly I suppose.

MARLENE: Walter's a monster. Weren't you angry? What did you do?

GRISELDA: Well I fainted. Then I cried and kissed the children. / Everyone was making a fuss of me.

NIJO: But did you feel anything for them?

GRISELDA: What?

NIJO: Did you feel anything for the children?

GRISELDA: Of course, I loved them.

JOAN: So you forgave him and lived with him?

GRISELDA: He suffered so much all those years.

ISABELLA: Hennie had the same sweet nature.

NIJO: So they dressed you again?

GRISELDA: Cloth of gold.

JOAN: I can't forgive anything.

MARLENE: You really are exceptional, Griselda.

NIJO: Nobody gave me back my children. (*She cries.*)

(*The Waitress brings the brandies and then exits. During the following, Joan goes to Nijo.*)

ISABELLA: I can never be like Hennie. I was always so busy in England, a kind of business I detested. The very presence of people exhausted my emotional reserves. I could not be like Hennie however I tried. I tried and was as ill as could be. The doctor suggested a steel net to support my head, the weight of my own head was too much for my diseased spine. It is dangerous to put oneself in depressing circumstances. Why should I do it?

JOAN (*to Nijo*): Don't cry.

NIJO: My father and the Emperor both died in the autumn. So much pain.

JOAN: Yes, but don't cry.

NIJO: They wouldn't let me into the palace when he was dying. I hid in the room with his coffin, then I couldn't find where I'd left my shoes, I ran after the funeral procession in bare feet, I couldn't keep up. When I got there it was over, a few wisps of smoke in the sky, that's all that was left of him. What I want to know is, if I'd still been at court, would I have been allowed to wear full mourning?

MARLENE: I'm sure you would.

NIJO: Why do you say that? You don't know anything about it. Would I have been allowed to wear full mourning?

ISABELLA: How can people live in this dim pale island and wear our hideous clothes? I cannot and will not live the life of a lady.

NIJO: I'll tell you something that made me angry. I was eighteen, at the Full Moon Ceremony. They make a special rice gruel and stir it with their sticks, and then they beat their women across the loins so they'll have sons and not daughters. So the Emperor beat us all / very hard as

MARLENE: What a sod. (*The Waitress enters with the coffees.*)

NIJO: usual—that's not it, Marlene, that's normal, what made us angry he told his attendants they could beat us too. Well they had a wonderful time. / So Lady Genki and I made a plan, and the ladies

MARLENE: I'd like another brandy, please. Better make it six. (*The Waitress exits.*)

NIJO: all hid in his rooms, and Lady Mashimizu stood guard with a stick at the door, and when His Majesty came in Genki seized him and I beat him till he cried out and promised he would never order anyone to hit us again. Afterward there was a terrible fuss. The nobles were horrified. "We wouldn't even dream of stepping on Your Majesty's shadow." And I had hit him with a stick. Yes, I hit him with a stick.

(The Waitress brings the brandy bottle and tops up the glasses. Joan crosses in front of the table and back to her place while drunkenly reciting:)

JOAN: Suave, mari magno turantibus aequora ventis,
e terra magnum alterius spectare laborem;
non quia vexari quemquamst iucunda voluptas,
sed quibus ipse malis careas quia cernere suave est.
Suave etiam belli certamina magna tueri
per campos instructa tua sine parse pericli.
Sed nil dulcius est, bene quam munita tenere
edita doctrine sapientum temple serena, /
despicere uncle queas alios passimque videre
errare atque viam palantis quaerere vitae,°

GRISELDA: I do think—I do wonder—it would have been nicer if Walter hadn't had to.

ISABELLA: Why should I? Why should I?

MARLENE: Of course not.

NIJO: I hit him with a stick.

JOAN: certare ingenio, contendere nobilitate,
noctes atque dies niti praestante labore
ad summas emergere opes rerumque potiri.
O miseras hominum mentis, / o pectora caeca!*

ISABELLA: O miseras!

NIJO: *Pectora caeca!

JOAN: qualibus in tenebris vitae quantisque periclis
degitur hoc aevi quodcumquest! / none videre
nil aliud sibi naturam latrare, nisi utqui
corpore seiunctus dolor absit, mente fruatur . . . *(She subsides.)*

GRET: We come to hell through a big mouth. Hell's black and red. / It's

MARLENE *(to Joan)*: Shut up, pet.

GRISELDA: Hush, please.

ISABELLA: Listen, she's been to hell.

GRET: like the village where I come from. There's a river and a bridge and houses. There's places on fire like when the soldiers come. There's a big devil sat on a roof with a big hole in his arse and he's scooping

---

Suave, mari . . . quaerere vitae: Here and in her next several speeches, Joan quotes from the philosophical poem *De Rerum Natura (On the Nature of Things)* by first-century B.C. Roman philosopher Lucretius. The passage considers differences between the active and the contemplative life. As she becomes drunk, Joan's recitation grows more fragmentary and error-ridden.

stuff out of it with a big ladle and it's falling down on us, and it's money, so a lot of the women stop and get some. But most of us is fighting the devils. There's lots of little devils, our size, and we get them down all right and give them a beating. There's lots of funny creatures round your feet, you don't like to look, like rats and lizards, and nasty things, a bum with a face, and fish with legs, and faces on things that don't have faces on. But they don't hurt, you just keep going. Well we'd had worse, you see, we'd had the Spanish. We'd all had family killed. My big son die on a wheel. Birds eat him. My baby, a soldier run her through with a sword. I'd had enough, I was mad, I hate the bastards. I come out of my front door that morning and shout till my neighbors come out and I said, "Come on, we're going where the evil come from and pay the bastards out." And they all come out just as they was / from baking or

NIJO: All the ladies come.

GRET: washing in their aprons, and we push down the street and the ground opens up and we go through a big mouth into a street just like ours but in hell. I've got a sword in my hand from somewhere and I fill a basket with gold cups they drink out of down there. You just keep running on and fighting, / you didn't stop for nothing. Oh we give them devils such a beating.*

NIJO: Take that, take that.

JOAN: *Something something something mortisque timores
tum vacuum pectus—damn.
Quod si ridicula—
something something on and on and on
and something splendorem purpureai.

ISABELLA: I thought I would have a last jaunt up the west river in China. Why not? But the doctors were so very grave I just went to Morocco. The sea was so wild I had to be landed by ship's crane in a coal bucket. / My horse was a terror to me, a powerful black charger.

GRET: Coal bucket good.

JOAN: nos in luce timemus
something
terrorem

(Nijo is laughing and crying. Joan gets up and is sick. Griselda looks after her.)

GRISELDA: Can I have some water, please? *(The Waitress exits.)*

ISABELLA: So off I went to visit the Berber sheikhs in full blue trousers and great brass spurs. I was the only European woman ever to have seen the Emperor of Morocco. I was *(the Waitress brings the water)* seventy years old. What lengths to go to for a last chance of joy. I knew my return of vigor was only temporary, but how marvelous while it lasted.

Scene II

(*"Top Girls" Employment Agency. Monday morning. The lights come up on Marlene and Jeanine.*)

MARLENE: Right, Jeanine, you are Jeanine aren't you? Let's have a look. O's and A's.° / No A's, all those

JEANINE: Six O's.

MARLENE: O's you probably could have got an A. / Speeds, not brilliant, not too bad.

JEANINE: I wanted to go to work.

MARLENE: Well, Jeanine, what's your present job like?

JEANINE: I'm a secretary.

MARLENE: Secretary or typist?

JEANINE: I did start as a typist but the last six months I've been a secretary.

MARLENE: To?

JEANINE: To three of them, really, they share me. There's Mr. Ashford, he's the office manager, and Mr. Philly / is sales, and—

MARLENE: Quite a small place?

JEANINE: A bit small.

MARLENE: Friendly?

JEANINE: Oh it's friendly enough.

MARLENE: Prospects?

JEANINE: I don't think so, that's the trouble. Miss Lewis is secretary to the managing director and she's been there forever, and Mrs. Bradford / is—

MARLENE: So you want a job with better prospects?

JEANINE: I want a change.

MARLENE: So you'll take anything comparable?

JEANINE: No, I do want prospects. I want more money.

MARLENE: You're getting—?

JEANINE: Hundred.

MARLENE: It's not bad you know. You're what? Twenty?

JEANINE: I'm saving to get married.

MARLENE: Does that mean you don't want a long-term job, Jeanine?

JEANINE: I might do.

O's and A's: O-levels and A-levels (for Ordinary and Advanced), academic achievement exams usually taken by British students at ages sixteen and eighteen.

MARLENE: Because where do the prospects come in? No kids for a bit?

JEANINE: Oh no, not kids, not yet.

MARLENE: So you won't tell them you're getting married?

JEANINE: Had I better not?

MARLENE: It would probably help.

JEANINE: I'm not wearing a ring. We thought we wouldn't spend on a ring.

MARLENE: Saves taking it off.

JEANINE: I wouldn't take it off.

MARLENE: There's no need to mention it when you go for an interview. / Now, Jeanine, do you have a feel

JEANINE: But what if they ask?

MARLENE: for any particular kind of company?

JEANINE: I thought advertising.

MARLENE: People often do think advertising. I have got a few vacancies but I think they're looking for something glossier.

JEANINE: You mean how I dress? / I can

MARLENE: I mean experience.

JEANINE: dress different. I dress like this on purpose for where I am now.

MARLENE: I have a marketing department here of a knitwear manufacturer. / Marketing is near enough

JEANINE: Knitwear?

MARLENE: advertising. Secretary to the marketing manager, he's thirty-five, married, I've sent him a girl before and she was happy, left to have a baby, you won't want to mention marriage there. He's very fair I think, good at his job, you won't have to nurse him along. Hundred and ten, so that's better than you're doing now.

JEANINE: I don't know.

MARLENE: I've a fairly small concern here, father and two sons, you'd have more say potentially, secretarial and reception duties, only a hundred but the job's going to grow with the concern and then you'll be in at the top with new girls coming in underneath you.

JEANINE: What is it they do?

MARLENE: Lampshades. / This would be my first choice for you.

JEANINE: Just lampshades?

MARLENE: There's plenty of different kinds of lampshade. So we'll send you there, shall we, and the knitwear second choice. Are you free to go for an interview any day they call you?

JEANINE: I'd like to travel.

MARLENE: We don't have any foreign clients. You'd have to go elsewhere.

JEANINE: Yes I know. I don't really . . . I just mean . . .

MARLENE: Does your fiancé want to travel?

JEANINE: I'd like a job where I was here in London and with him and everything but now and then — I expect it's silly. Are there jobs like that?

MARLENE: There's personal assistant to a top executive in a multi-national. If that's the idea you need to be planning ahead. Is that where you want to be in ten years?

JEANINE: I might not be alive in ten years.

MARLENE: Yes but you will be. You'll have children.

JEANINE: I can't think about ten years.

MARLENE: You haven't got the speeds anyway. So I'll send you to these two shall I? You haven't been to any other agency? Just so we don't get crossed wires. Now, Jeanine, I want you to get one of these jobs, all right? If I send you that means I'm putting myself on the line for you. Your presentation's OK, you look fine, just be confident and go in there convinced that this is the best job for you and you're the best person for the job. If you don't believe it they won't believe it.

JEANINE: Do you believe it?

MARLENE: I think you could make me believe it if you put your mind to it.

JEANINE: Yes, all right.

Scene III

(*Joyce's back yard. Sunday afternoon. The house with a back door is upstage. Downstage is a shelter made of junk, made by children. The lights come up on two girls, Angie and Kit, who are squashed together in the shelter. Angie is sixteen, Kit is twelve. They cannot be seen from the house.*)

JOYCE (*off, calling from the house*): Angie. Angie, are you out there?

(*Silence. They keep still and wait. When nothing else happens they relax.*)

ANGIE: Wish she was dead.

KIT: Wanna watch *The Exterminator*?

ANGIE: You're sitting on my leg.

KIT: There's nothing on telly. We can have an ice cream. Angie?

ANGIE: Shall I tell you something?

KIT: Do you wanna watch *The Exterminator*?

ANGIE: It's X, innit?

KIT: I can get into Xs.

ANGIE: Shall I tell you something?

KIT: We'll go to something else. We'll go to Ipswich. What's on the Odeon?

ANGIE: She won't let me, will she.

KIT: Don't tell her.

ANGIE: I've no money.

KIT: I'll pay.

ANGIE: She'll moan though, won't she.

KIT: I'll ask her for you if you like.

ANGIE: I've no money, I don't want you to pay.

KIT: I'll ask her.

ANGIE: She don't like you.

KIT: I still got three pounds birthday money. Did she say she don't like me? I'll go by myself then.

ANGIE: Your mum don't let you. I got to take you.

KIT: She won't know.

ANGIE: You'd be scared who'd sit next to you.

KIT: No I wouldn't. She does like me anyway. Tell me then.

ANGIE: Tell you what?

KIT: It's you she doesn't like.

ANGIE: Well I don't like her so tough shit.

JOYCE (off): Angie. Angie. Angie. I know you're out there. I'm not coming out after you. You come in here. (Silence. Nothing happens.)

ANGIE: Last night when I was in bed. I been thinking yesterday could I make things move. You know, make things move by thinking about them without touching them. Last night I was in bed and suddenly a picture fell down off the wall.

KIT: What picture?

ANGIE: My gran, that picture. Not the poster. The photograph in the frame.

KIT: Had you done something to make it fall down?

ANGIE: I must have done.

KIT: But were you thinking about it?

ANGIE: Not about it, but about something.

KIT: I don't think that's very good.

ANGIE: You know the kitten?

KIT: Which one?

ANGIE: There only is one. The dead one.

KIT: What about it?

ANGIE: I heard it last night.

KIT: Where?

ANGIE: Out here. In the dark. What if I left you here in the dark all night?

KIT: You couldn't. I'd go home.

ANGIE: You couldn't.

KIT: I'd / go home.

ANGIE: No you couldn't, not if I said.

KIT: I could.

ANGIE: Then you wouldn't see anything. You'd just be ignorant.

KIT: I can see in the daytime.

ANGIE: No you can't. You can't hear it in the daytime.

KIT: I don't want to hear it.

ANGIE: You're scared that's all.

KIT: I'm not scared of anything.

ANGIE: You're scared of blood.

KIT: It's not the same kitten anyway. You just heard an old cat, / you just heard some old cat.

ANGIE: You don't know what I heard. Or what I saw. You don't know nothing because you're a baby.

KIT: You're sitting on me.

ANGIE: Mind my hair / you silly cunt.

KIT: Stupid fucking cow, I hate you.

ANGIE: I don't care if you do.

KIT: You're horrible.

ANGIE: I'm going to kill my mother and you're going to watch.

KIT: I'm not playing.

ANGIE: You're scared of blood. (*Kit puts her hand under dress, brings it out with blood on her finger.*)

KIT: There, see, I got my own blood, so. (*Angie takes Kit's hand and licks her finger.*)

ANGIE: Now I'm a cannibal. I might turn into a vampire now.

KIT: That picture wasn't nailed up right.

ANGIE: You'll have to do that when I get mine.

KIT: I don't have to.

ANGIE: You're scared.

KIT: I'll do it, I might do it. I don't have to just because you say. I'll be sick on you.

ANGIE: I don't care if you are sick on me, I don't mind sick. I don't mind blood. If I don't get away from here I'm going to die.

KIT: I'm going home.

ANGIE: You can't go through the house. She'll see you.

KIT: I won't tell her.

ANGIE: Oh great, fine.

KIT: I'll say I was by myself. I'll tell her you're at my house and I'm going there to get you.

ANGIE: She knows I'm here, stupid.

KIT: Then why can't I go through the house?

ANGIE: Because I said not.

KIT: My mum don't like you anyway.

ANGIE: I don't want her to like me. She's a slag.

KIT: She is not.

ANGIE: She does it with everyone.

KIT: She does not.

ANGIE: You don't even know what it is.

KIT: Yes I do.

ANGIE: Tell me then.

KIT: We get it all at school, cleverclogs. It's on television. You haven't done it.

ANGIE: How do you know?

KIT: Because I know you haven't.

ANGIE: You know wrong then because I have.

KIT: Who with?

ANGIE: I'm not telling you / who with.

KIT: You haven't anyway.

ANGIE: How do you know?

KIT: Who with?

ANGIE: I'm not telling you.

KIT: You said you told me everything.

ANGIE: I was lying wasn't I.

KIT: Who with? You can't tell me who with because / you never—

ANGIE: Sh.

(*Joyce has come out of the house. She stops halfway across the yard and listens. They listen.*)

JOYCE: You there Angie? Kit? You there Kitty? Want a cup of tea? I've got some chocolate biscuits. Come on now I'll put the kettle on. Want a choccy biccy, Angie? (*They all listen and wait.*) Fucking rotten little cunt. You can stay there and die. I'll lock the door.

(*They all wait. Joyce goes back to the house. Angie and Kit sit in silence for a while.*)

KIT: When there's a war, where's the safest place?

ANGIE: Nowhere.

KIT: New Zealand is, my mum said. Your skin's burned right off. Shall we go to New Zealand?

ANGIE: I'm not staying here.

KIT: Shall we go to New Zealand?

ANGIE: You're not old enough.

KIT: You're not old enough.

ANGIE: I'm old enough to get married.

KIT: You don't want to get married.

ANGIE: No but I'm old enough.

KIT: I'd find out where they were going to drop it and stand right in the place.

ANGIE: You couldn't find out.

KIT: Better than walking round with your skin dragging on the ground. Eugh. / Would you like walking round with your skin dragging on the ground?

ANGIE: You couldn't find out, stupid, it's a secret.

KIT: Where are you going?

ANGIE: I'm not telling you.

KIT: Why?

ANGIE: It's a secret.

KIT: But you tell me all your secrets.

ANGIE: Not the true secrets.

KIT: Yes you do.

ANGIE: No I don't.

KIT: I want to go somewhere away from the war.

ANGIE: Just forget the war.

KIT: I can't.

ANGIE: You have to. It's so boring.

KIT: I'll remember it at night.

ANGIE: I'm going to do something else anyway.

KIT: What? Angie, come on. Angie.

ANGIE: It's a true secret.

KIT: It can't be worse than the kitten. And killing your mother. And the war.

ANGIE: Well I'm not telling you so you can die for all I care.

KIT: My mother says there's something wrong with you playing with someone my age. She says why haven't you got friends your own age. People your own age know there's something funny about you. She says you're a bad influence. She says she's going to speak to your mother. (*Angie twists Kit's arm till she cries out.*)

ANGIE: Say you're a liar.

KIT: She said it not me.

ANGIE: Say you eat shit.

KIT: You can't make me. (*Angie lets go.*)

ANGIE: I don't care anyway. I'm leaving.

KIT: Go on then.

ANGIE: You'll all wake up one morning and find I've gone.

KIT: Go on then.

ANGIE: You'll wake up one morning and find I've gone.

KIT: Good.

ANGIE: I'm not telling you when.

KIT: Go on then.

ANGIE: I'm sorry I hurt you.

KIT: I'm tired.

ANGIE: Do you like me?

KIT: I don't know.

ANGIE: You do like me.

KIT: I'm going home. (*She gets up.*)

ANGIE: No you're not.

KIT: I'm tired.

ANGIE: She'll see you.

KIT: She'll give me a chocolate biscuit.

ANGIE: Kitty.

KIT: Tell me where you're going.

ANGIE: Sit down.

KIT (*sitting down again*): Go on then.

ANGIE: Swear?

KIT: Swear.

ANGIE: I'm going to London. To see my aunt.

KIT: And what?

ANGIE: That's it.

KIT: I see my aunt all the time.

ANGIE: I don't see my aunt.

KIT: What's so special?

ANGIE: It is special. She's special.

KIT: Why?

ANGIE: She is.

KIT: Why?

ANGIE: She is.

KIT: Why?

ANGIE: My mother hates her.

KIT: Why?

ANGIE: Because she does.

KIT: Perhaps she's not very nice.

ANGIE: She is nice.

KIT: How do you know?

ANGIE: Because I know her.

KIT: You said you never see her.

ANGIE: I saw her last year. You saw her.

KIT: Did I?

ANGIE: Never mind.

KIT: I remember her. That aunt. What's so special?

ANGIE: She gets people jobs.

KIT: What's so special?

ANGIE: I think I'm my aunt's child. I think my mother's really my aunt.

KIT: Why?

ANGIE: Because she goes to America, now shut up.

KIT: I've been to London.

ANGIE: Now give us a cuddle and shut up because I'm sick.
KIT: You're sitting on my arm.

(*They curl up in each other's arms. Silence. Joyce comes out of the house and comes up to them quietly.*)

JOYCE: Come on.
KIT: Oh hello.
JOYCE: Time you went home.
KIT: We want to go to the Odeon.
JOYCE: What time?
KIT: Don't know.
JOYCE: What's on?
KIT: Don't know.
JOYCE: Don't know much do you?
KIT: That all right then?
JOYCE: Angie's got to clean her room first.
ANGIE: No I don't.
JOYCE: Yes you do, it's a pigsty.
ANGIE: Well I'm not.
JOYCE: Then you're not going. I don't care.
ANGIE: Well I am going.
JOYCE: You've no money, have you?
ANGIE: Kit's paying anyway.
JOYCE: No she's not.
KIT: I'll help you with your room.
JOYCE: That's nice.
ANGIE: No you won't. You wait here.
KIT: Hurry then.
ANGIE: I'm not hurrying. You just wait. (*Angie goes slowly into the house. Silence.*)
JOYCE: I don't know. (*Silence.*) How's school then?
KIT: All right.
JOYCE: What are you now? Third year?
KIT: Second year.
JOYCE: Your mum says you're good at English. (*Silence.*) Maybe Angie should've stayed on.
KIT: She didn't like it.
JOYCE: I didn't like it. And look at me. If your face fits at school it's going to fit other places too. It wouldn't make no difference to Angie. She's not going to get a job when jobs are hard to get. I'd be sorry for anyone in charge of her. She'd better get married. I don't know who'd have her, mind. She's one of those girls might never leave home. What do you want to be when you grow up, Kit?

KIT: Physicist.

JOYCE: What?

KIT: Nuclear physicist.

JOYCE: Whatever for?

KIT: I could, I'm clever.

JOYCE: I know you're clever, pet. (*Silence.*) I'll make a cup of tea. (*Silence.*) Looks like it's going to rain. (*Silence.*) Don't you have friends your own age?

KIT: Yes.

JOYCE: Well then.

KIT: I'm old for my age.

JOYCE: And Angie's simple is she? She's not simple.

KIT: I love Angie.

JOYCE: She's clever in her own way.

KIT: You can't stop me.

JOYCE: I don't want to.

KIT: You can't, so.

JOYCE: Don't be cheeky, Kitty. She's always kind to little children.

KIT: She's coming so you better leave me alone.

(*Angie comes out. She has changed into an old best dress, slightly small for her.*)

JOYCE: What you put that on for? Have you done your room? You can't clean your room in that.

ANGIE: I looked in the cupboard and it was there.

JOYCE: Of course it was there, it's meant to be there. Is that why it was a surprise, finding something in the right place? I should think she's surprised, wouldn't you, Kit, to find something in her room in the right place.

ANGIE: I decided to wear it.

JOYCE: Not today, why? To clean your room? You're not going to the pictures till you've done your room. You can put your dress on after if you like. (*Angie picks up a brick.*) Have you done your room? You're not getting out of it, you know.

KIT: Angie, let's go.

JOYCE: She's not going till she's done her room.

KIT: It's starting to rain.

JOYCE: Come on, come on then. Hurry and do your room, Angie, and then you can go to the cinema with Kit. Oh it's wet, come on. We'll look up the time in the paper. Does your mother know, Kit, it's going to be a late night for you, isn't it? Hurry up, Angie. You'll spoil your dress. You make me sick. (*Joyce and Kit run into the house. Angie stays where she is. There is the sound of rain. Kit comes out of the house.*)

KIT (*shouting*): Angie. Angie, come on, you'll get wet. (*She comes back to Angie.*)

ANGIE: I put on this dress to kill my mother.

KIT: I suppose you thought you'd do it with a brick.

ANGIE: You can kill people with a brick. (*She puts the brick down.*)

KIT: Well you didn't, so.

ACT II   *Scene I*

(*"Top Girls" Employment Agency. Monday morning. There are three desks in the main office and a separate small interviewing area. The lights come up in the main office on Win and Nell who have just arrived for work.*)

NELL: Coffee coffee coffee coffee / coffee.

WIN: The roses were smashing. / Mermaid.

NELL: Ohhh.

WIN: Iceberg. He taught me all their names. (*Nell has some coffee now.*)

NELL: Ah. Now then.

WIN: He has one of the finest rose gardens in West Sussex. He exhibits.

NELL: He what?

WIN: His wife was visiting her mother. It was like living together.

NELL: Crafty, you never said.

WIN: He rang on Saturday morning.

NELL: Lucky you were free.

WIN: That's what I told him.

NELL: Did you hell.

WIN: Have you ever seen a really beautiful rose garden?

NELL: I don't like flowers. / I like swimming pools.

WIN: Marilyn. Esther's Baby. They're all called after birds.°

NELL: Our friend's late. Celebrating all weekend I bet you.

WIN: I'd call a rose Elvis. Or John Conteh.°

NELL: Is Howard in yet?

WIN: If he is he'll be bleeping us with a problem.

NELL: Howard can just hang on to himself.

WIN: Howard's really cut up.

NELL: Howard thinks because he's a fella the job was his as of right. Our Marlene's got far more balls than Howard and that's that.

WIN: Poor little bugger.

NELL: He'll live.

birds: Women (slang).
John Conteh: British boxing champion turned actor.

WIN: He'll move on.

NELL: I wouldn't mind a change of air myself.

WIN: Serious?

NELL: I've never been a staying-put lady. Pastures new.

WIN: So who's the pirate?

NELL: There's nothing definite.

WIN: Inquiries?

NELL: There's always inquiries. I'd think I'd got bad breath if there stopped being inquiries. Most of them can't afford me. Or you.

WIN: I'm all right for the time being. Unless I go to Australia.

NELL: There's not a lot of room upward.

WIN: Marlene's filled it up.

NELL: Good luck to her. Unless there's some prospects moneywise.

WIN: You can but ask.

NELL: Can always but ask.

WIN: So what have we got? I've got a Mr. Holden I saw last week.

NELL: Any use?

WIN: Pushy. Bit of a cowboy.

NELL: Goodlooker?

WIN: Good dresser.

NELL: High flyer?

WIN: That's his general idea certainly but I'm not sure he's got it up there.

NELL: Prestel wants six flyers and I've only seen two and a half.

WIN: He's making a bomb on the road but he thinks it's time for an office. I sent him to IBM but he didn't get it.

NELL: Prestel's on the road.

WIN: He's not overbright.

NELL: Can he handle an office?

WIN: Provided his secretary can punctuate he should go far.

NELL: Bear Prestel in mind then, I might put my head round the door. I've got that poor little nerd I should never had said I could help. Tender heart me.

WIN: Tender like old boots. How old?

NELL: Yes well forty-five.

WIN: Say no more.

NELL: He knows his place, he's not after calling himself a manager, he's just a poor little bod wants a better commission and a bit of sunshine.

WIN: Don't we all.

NELL: He's just got to relocate. He's got a bungalow in Dymchurch.

WIN: And his wife says.

NELL: The lady wife wouldn't care to relocate. She's going through the change.

WIN: It's his funeral, don't waste your time.

NELL: I don't waste a lot.

WIN: Good weekend you?

NELL: You could say.

WIN: Which one?

NELL: One Friday, one Saturday.

WIN: Aye—aye.

NELL: Sunday night I watched telly.

WIN: Which of them do you like best really?

NELL: Sunday was best, I like the Ovaltine.

WIN: Holden, Barker, Gardner, Duke.

NELL: I've a lady here thinks she can sell.

WIN: Taking her on?

NELL: She's had some jobs.

WIN: Services?

NELL: No, quite heavy stuff, electric.

WIN: Tough bird like us.

NELL: We could do with a few more here.

WIN: There's nothing going here.

NELL: No but I always want the tough ones when I see them. Hang on to them.

WIN: I think we're plenty.

NELL: Derek asked me to marry him again.

WIN: He doesn't know when he's beaten.

NELL: I told him I'm not going to play house, not even in Ascot.

WIN: Mind you, you could play house.

NELL: If I chose to play house I would play house ace.

WIN: You could marry him and go on working.

NELL: I could go on working and not marry him.

(*Marlene arrives.*)

MARLENE: Morning ladies. (*Win and Nell cheer and whistle.*) Mind my head.

NELL: Coffee coffee coffee.

WIN: We're tactfully not mentioning you're late.

MARLENE: Fucking tube.°

WIN: We've heard that one.

NELL: We've used that one.

WIN: It's the top executive doesn't come in as early as the poor working girl.

MARLENE: Pass the sugar and shut your face, pet.

WIN: Well I'm delighted.

tube: London underground train system.

NELL: Howard's looking sick.

WIN: Howard is sick. He's got ulcers and heart. He told me.

NELL: He'll have to stop then, won't he?

WIN: Stop what?

NELL: Smoking, drinking, shouting. Working.

WIN: Well, working.

NELL: We're just looking through the day.

MARLENE: I'm doing some of Pam's ladies. They've been piling up while she's away.

NELL: Half a dozen little girls and an arts graduate who can't type.

WIN: I spent the whole weekend at his place in Sussex.

NELL: She fancies his rose garden.

WIN: I had to lie down in the back of the car so the neighbors wouldn't see me go in.

NELL: You're kidding.

WIN· It was funny.

NELL: Fuck that for a joke.

WIN: It was funny.

MARLENE: Anyway they'd see you in the garden.

WIN: The garden has extremely high walls.

NELL: I think I'll tell the wife.

WIN: Like hell.

NELL: She might leave him and you could have the rose garden.

WIN: The minute it's not a secret I'm out on my ear.

NELL: Don't know why you bother.

WIN: Bit of fun.

NELL: I think it's time you went to Australia.

WIN: I think it's pushy Mr. Holden time.

NELL: If you've any really pretty bastards, Marlene, I want some for Prestel.

MARLENE: I might have one this afternoon. This morning it's all Pam's secretarial.

NELL: Not long now and you'll be upstairs watching over us all.

MARLENE: Do you feel bad about it?

NELL: I don't like coming second.

MARLENE: Who does?

WIN: We'd rather it was you than Howard. We're glad for you, aren't we, Nell?

NELL: Oh yes. Aces.

(*Louise enters the interviewing area. The lights crossfade to Win and Louise in the interviewing area. Nell exits.*)

WIN: Now, Louise, hello, I have your details here. You've been very loyal
  to the one job I see.

LOUISE: Yes I have.

WIN: Twenty-one years is a long time in one place.

LOUISE: I feel it is. I feel it's time to move on.

WIN: And you are what age now?

LOUISE: I'm in my early forties.

WIN: Exactly?

LOUISE: Forty-six.

WIN: It's not necessarily a handicap, well it is of course we have to face
  that, but it's not necessarily a disabling handicap, experience does
  count for something.

LOUISE: I hope so.

WIN: Now between ourselves is there any trouble, any reason why
  you're leaving that wouldn't appear on the form?

LOUISE: Nothing like that.

WIN: Like what?

LOUISE: Nothing at all.

WIN: No long-term understandings come to a sudden end, making for
  an insupportable atmosphere?

LOUISE: I've always completely avoided anything like that at all.

WIN: No personality clashes with your immediate superiors or inferiors?

LOUISE: I've always taken care to get on very well with everyone.

WIN: I only ask because it can affect the reference and it also affects
  your motivation, I want to be quite clear why you're moving on. So I
  take it the job itself no longer satisfies you. Is it the money?

LOUISE: It's partly the money. It's not so much the money.

WIN: Nine thousand is very respectable. Have you dependents?

LOUISE: No, no dependents. My mother died.

WIN: So why are you making a change?

LOUISE: Other people make changes.

WIN: But why are you, now, after spending most of your life in the one
  place?

LOUISE: There you are, I've lived for that company, I've given my life
  really you could say because I haven't had a great deal of social life,
  I've worked in the evenings. I haven't had office entanglements for the
  very reason you just mentioned and if you are committed to your work
  you don't move in many other circles. I had management status from
  the age of twenty-seven and you'll appreciate what that means. I've
  built up a department. And there it is, it works extremely well, and
  I feel I'm stuck there. I've spent twenty years in middle management. I've seen young men who I trained go on, in my own company

or elsewhere, to higher things. Nobody notices me, I don't expect it, I don't attract attention by making mistakes, everybody takes it for granted that my work is perfect. They will notice me when I go, they will be sorry I think to lose me, they will offer me more money of course, I will refuse. They will see when I've gone what I was doing for them.

WIN: If they offer you more money you won't stay?

LOUISE: No I won't.

WIN: Are you the only woman?

LOUISE: Apart from the girls of course, yes. There was one, she was my assistant, it was the only time I took on a young woman assistant, I always had my doubts. I don't care greatly for working with women, I think I pass as a man at work. But I did take on this young woman, her qualifications were excellent, and she did well, she got a department of her own, and left the company for a competitor where she's now on the board and good luck to her. She has a different style, she's a new kind of attractive well dressed — I don't mean I don't dress properly. But there is a kind of woman who is thirty now who grew up in a different climate. They are not so careful. They take themselves for granted. I have had to justify my existence every minute, and I have done so, I have proved — well.

WIN: Let's face it, vacancies are ones where you'll be in competition with younger men. And there are companies that will value your experience enough that you'll be in with a chance. There are also fields that are easier for a woman, there is a cosmetic company here where your experience might be relevant. It's eight and a half, I don't know if that appeals.

LOUISE: I've proved I can earn money. It's more important to get away. I feel it's now or never. I sometimes / think —

WIN: You shouldn't talk too much at an interview.

LOUISE: I don't. I don't normally talk about myself. I know very well how to handle myself in an office situation. I only talk to you because it seems to me this is different, it's your job to understand me, surely. You asked the questions.

WIN: I think I understand you sufficiently.

LOUISE: Well good, that's good.

WIN: Do you drink?

LOUISE: Certainly not. I'm not a teetotaler, I think that's very suspect, it's seen as being an alcoholic if you're teetotal. What do you mean? I don't drink. Why?

WIN: I drink.

LOUISE: I don't.

WIN: Good for you.

(*The lights crossfade to the main office with Marlene sitting at her desk. Win and Louise exit. Angie arrives in the main office.*)

ANGIE: Hello.

MARLENE: Have you an appointment?

ANGIE: It's me. I've come.

MARLENE: What? It's not Angie?

ANGIE: It was hard to find this place. I got lost.

MARLENE: How did you get past the receptionist? The girl on the desk, didn't she try to stop you?

ANGIE: What desk?

MARLENE: Never mind.

ANGIE: I just walked in. I was looking for you.

MARLENE: Well you found me.

ANGIE: Yes.

MARLENE: So where's your mum? Are you up in town for the day?

ANGIE: Not really.

MARLENE: Sit down. Do you feel all right?

ANGIE: Yes thank you.

MARLENE: So where's Joyce?

ANGIE: She's at home.

MARLENE: Did you come up on a school trip then?

ANGIE: I've left school.

MARLENE: Did you come up with a friend?

ANGIE: No. There's just me.

MARLENE: You came up by yourself, that's fun. What have you been doing? Shopping? Tower of London?

ANGIE: No, I just come here. I come to you.

MARLENE: That's very nice of you to think of paying your aunty a visit. There's not many nieces make that the first port of call. Would you like a cup of coffee?

ANGIE: No thank you.

MARLENE: Tea, orange?

ANGIE: No thank you.

MARLENE: Do you feel all right?

ANGIE: Yes thank you.

MARLENE: Are you tired from the journey?

ANGIE: Yes, I'm tired from the journey.

MARLENE: You sit there for a bit then. How's Joyce?

ANGIE: She's all right.

MARLENE: Same as ever.

ANGIE: Oh yes.

MARLENE: Unfortunately you've picked a day when I'm rather busy, if there's ever a day when I'm not, or I'd take you out to lunch and we'd go to Madame Tussaud's.° We could go shopping. What time do you have to be back? Have you got a day return?

ANGIE: No.

MARLENE: So what train are you going back on?

ANGIE: I came on the bus.

MARLENE: So what bus are you going back on? Are you staying the night?

ANGIE: Yes.

MARLENE: Who are you staying with? Do you want me to put you up for the night, is that it?

ANGIE: Yes please.

MARLENE: I haven't got a spare bed.

ANGIE: I can sleep on the floor.

MARLENE: You can sleep on the sofa.

ANGIE: Yes please.

MARLENE: I do think Joyce might have phoned me. It's like her.

ANGIE: This is where you work is it?

MARLENE: It's where I have been working the last two years but I'm going to move into another office.

ANGIE: It's lovely.

MARLENE: My new office is nicer than this. There's just the one big desk in it for me.

ANGIE: Can I see it?

MARLENE: Not now, no, there's someone else in it now. But he's leaving at the end of next week and I'm going to do his job.

ANGIE: Is that good?

MARLENE: Yes, it's very good.

ANGIE: Are you going to be in charge?

MARLENE: Yes I am.

ANGIE: I knew you would be.

MARLENE: How did you know?

ANGIE: I knew you'd be in charge of everything.

MARLENE: Not quite everything.

ANGIE: You will be.

MARLENE: Well we'll see.

ANGIE: Can I see it next week then?

MARLENE: Will you still be here next week?

ANGIE: Yes.

Madame Tussaud's: Wax museum; a popular London tourist attraction.

MARLENE: Don't you have to go home?
ANGIE: No.
MARLENE: Why not?
ANGIE: It's all right.
MARLENE: Is it all right?
ANGIE: Yes, don't worry about it.
MARLENE: Does Joyce know where you are?
ANGIE: Yes of course she does.
MARLENE: Well does she?
ANGIE: Don't worry about it.
MARLENE: How long are you planning to stay with me then?
ANGIE: You know when you came to see us last year?
MARLENE: Yes, that was nice wasn't it.
ANGIE: That was the best day of my whole life.
MARLENE: So how long are you planning to stay?
ANGIE: Don't you want me?
MARLENE: Yes yes, I just wondered.
ANGIE: I won't stay if you don't want me.
MARLENE: No, of course you can stay.
ANGIE: I'll sleep on the floor. I won't be any bother.
MARLENE: Don't get upset.
ANGIE: I'm not, I'm not. Don't worry about it.

(*Mrs. Kidd comes in.*)

MRS. KIDD: Excuse me.
MARLENE: Yes.
MRS. KIDD: Excuse me.
MARLENE: Can I help you?
MRS. KIDD: Excuse me bursting in on you like this but I have to talk to you.
MARLENE: I am engaged at the moment. / If you could go to reception —
MRS. KIDD: I'm Rosemary Kidd, Howard's wife, you don't recognize me
    but we did meet, I remember you of course / but you wouldn't —
MARLENE: Yes of course, Mrs. Kidd, I'm sorry, we did meet. Howard's
    about somewhere I expect, have you looked in his office?
MRS. KIDD: Howard's not about, no. I'm afraid it's you I've come to see if
    I could have a minute or two.
MARLENE: I do have an appointment in five minutes.
MRS. KIDD: This won't take five minutes. I'm very sorry. It is a matter of
    some urgency.
MARLENE: Well of course. What can I do for you?
MRS. KIDD: I just wanted a chat, an informal chat. It's not something I
    can simply — I'm sorry if I'm interrupting your work. I know office
    work isn't like housework / which is all interruptions.

MARLENE: No no, this is my niece. Angie. Mrs. Kidd.

MRS. KIDD: Very pleased to meet you.

ANGIE: Very well thank you.

MRS. KIDD: Howard's not in today.

MARLENE: Isn't he?

MRS. KIDD: He's feeling poorly.

MARLENE: I didn't know. I'm sorry to hear that.

MRS. KIDD: The fact is he's in a state of shock. About what's happened.

MARLENE: What has happened?

MRS. KIDD: You should know if anyone. I'm referring to you being appointed managing director instead of Howard. He hasn't been at all well all weekend. He hasn't slept for three nights. I haven't slept.

MARLENE: I'm sorry to hear that, Mrs. Kidd. Has he thought of taking sleeping pills?

MRS. KIDD: It's very hard when someone has worked all these years.

MARLENE: Business life is full of little setbacks. I'm sure Howard knows that. He'll bounce back in a day or two. We all bounce back.

MRS. KIDD: If you could see him you'd know what I'm talking about. What's it going to do to him working for a woman? I think if it was a man he'd get over it as something normal.

MARLENE: I think he's going to have to get over it.

MRS. KIDD: It's me that bears the brunt. I'm not the one that's been promoted. I put him first every inch of the way. And now what do I get? You women this, you women that. It's not my fault. You're going to have to be very careful how you handle him. He's very hurt.

MARLENE: Naturally I'll be tactful and pleasant to him, you don't start pushing someone around. I'll consult him over any decisions affecting his department. But that's no different, Mrs. Kidd, from any of my other colleagues.

MRS. KIDD: I think it is different, because he's a man.

MARLENE: I'm not quite sure why you came to see me.

MRS. KIDD: I had to do something.

MARLENE: Well you've done it, you've seen me. I think that's probably all we've time for. I'm sorry he's been taking it out on you. He really is a shit, Howard.

MRS. KIDD: But he's got a family to support. He's got three children. It's only fair.

MARLENE: Are you suggesting I give up the job to him then?

MRS. KIDD: It had crossed my mind if you were unavailable after all for some reason, he would be the natural second choice I think, don't you? I'm not asking.

MARLENE: Good.

MRS. KIDD: You mustn't tell him I came. He's very proud.

MARLENE: If he doesn't like what's happening here he can go and work somewhere else.

MRS. KIDD: Is that a threat?

MARLENE: I'm sorry but I do have some work to do.

MRS. KIDD: It's not that easy, a man of Howard's age. You don't care. I thought he was going too far but he's right. You're one of these ball-breakers, / that's what you

MARLENE: I'm sorry but I do have some work to do.

MRS. KIDD: are. You'll end up miserable and lonely. You're not natural.

MARLENE: Could you please piss off?

MRS. KIDD: I thought if I saw you at least I'd be doing something. (*Mrs. Kidd goes.*)

MARLENE: I've got to go and do some work now. Will you come back later?

ANGIE: I think you were wonderful.

MARLENE: I've got to go and do some work now.

ANGIE: You told her to piss off.

MARLENE: Will you come back later?

ANGIE: Can't I stay here?

MARLENE: Don't you want to go sightseeing?

ANGIE: I'd rather stay here.

MARLENE: You can stay here I suppose, if it's not boring.

ANGIE: It's where I most want to be in the world.

MARLENE: I'll see you later then.

(*Marlene goes. Shona and Nell enter the interviewing area. Angie sits at Win's desk. The lights crossfade to Nell and Shona in the interviewing area.*)

NELL: Is this right? You are Shona?

SHONA: Yeh.

NELL: It says here you're twenty-nine.

SHONA: Yeh.

NELL: Too many late nights, me. So you've been where you are for four years, Shona, you're earning six basic and three commission. So what's the problem?

SHONA: No problem.

NELL: Why do you want a change?

SHONA: Just a change.

NELL: Change of product, change of area?

SHONA: Both.

NELL: But you're happy on the road?

SHONA: I like driving.

NELL: You're not after management status?

SHONA: I would like management status.

NELL: You'd be interested in titular management status but not come off the road?

SHONA: I want to be on the road, yeh.

NELL: So how many calls have you been making a day?

SHONA: Six.

NELL: And what proportion of those are successful?

SHONA: Six.

NELL: That's hard to believe.

SHONA: Four.

NELL: You find it easy to get the initial interest do you?

SHONA: Oh yeh, I get plenty of initial interest.

NELL: And what about closing?

SHONA: I close, don't I?

NELL: Because that's what an employer is going to have doubts about with a lady as I needn't tell you, whether she's got the guts to push through to a closing situation. They think we're too nice. They think we listen to the buyer's doubts. They think we consider his needs and his feelings.

SHONA: I never consider people's feelings.

NELL: I was selling for six years, I can sell anything, I've sold in three continents, and I'm jolly as they come but I'm not very nice.

SHONA: I'm not very nice.

NELL: What sort of time do you have on the road with the other reps? Get on all right? Handle the chat?

SHONA: I get on. Keep myself to myself.

NELL: Fairly much of a loner are you?

SHONA: Sometimes.

NELL: So what field are you interested in?

SHONA: Computers.

NELL: That's a top field as you know and you'll be up against some very slick fellas there, there's some very pretty boys in computers, it's an American-style field.

SHONA: That's why I want to do it.

NELL: Video systems appeal? That's a high-flying situation.

SHONA: Video systems appeal OK.

NELL: Because Prestel have half a dozen vacancies I'm looking to fill at the moment. We're talking in the area of ten to fifteen thousand here and upwards.

SHONA: Sounds OK.

NELL: I've half a mind to go for it myself. But it's good money here if you've got the top clients. Could you fancy it do you think?

SHONA: Work here?

NELL: I'm not in a position to offer, there's nothing officially going just now, but we're always on the lookout. There's not that many of us. We could keep in touch.

SHONA: I like driving.

NELL: So the Prestel appeals.

SHONA: Yeh.

NELL: What about ties?

SHONA: No ties.

NELL: So relocation wouldn't be a problem.

SHONA: No problem.

NELL: So just fill me in a bit more could you about what you've been doing.

SHONA: What I've been doing. It's all down there.

NELL: The bare facts are down here but I've got to present you to an employer.

SHONA: I'm twenty-nine years old.

NELL: So it says here.

SHONA: We look young. Youngness runs in the family in our family.

NELL: So just describe your present job for me.

SHONA: My present job at present. I have a car. I have a Porsche. I go up the M1° a lot. Burn up the M1 a lot. Straight up the M1 in the fast lane to where the clients are, Staffordshire, Yorkshire, I do a lot in Yorkshire. I'm selling electric things. Like dishwashers, washing machines, stainless steel tubs are a feature and the reliability of the program. After sales service, we offer a very good after sales service, spare parts, plenty of spare parts. And fridges, I sell a lot of fridges specially in the summer. People want to buy fridges in the summer because of the heat melting the butter and you get fed up standing the milk in a basin of cold water with a cloth over, stands to reason people don't want to do that in this day and age. So I sell a lot of them. Big ones with big freezers. Big freezers. And I stay in hotels at night when I'm away from home. On my expense account. I stay in various hotels. They know me, the ones I go to. I check in, have a bath, have a shower. Then I go down to the bar, have a gin and tonic, have a chat. Then I go into the dining room and have dinner. I usually have fillet steak and mushrooms, I like mushrooms. I like smoked salmon very much. I like having a salad on the side. Green salad. I don't like tomatoes.

NELL: Christ what a waste of time.

SHONA: Beg your pardon?

NELL: Not a word of this is true, is it?

SHONA: How do you mean?

M1: The main north-south expressway connecting London to Yorkshire.

NELL: You just filled in the form with a pack of lies.
SHONA: Not exactly.
NELL: How old are you?
SHONA: Twenty-nine.
NELL: Nineteen?
SHONA: Twenty-one.
NELL: And what jobs have you done? Have you done any?
SHONA: I could though, I bet you.

(*The lights crossfade to the main office with Angie sitting as before. Win comes in to the main office. Shona and Nell exit.*)

WIN: Who's sitting in my chair?
ANGIE: What? Sorry.
WIN: Who's been eating my porridge?
ANGIE: What?
WIN: It's all right, I saw Marlene. Angie, isn't it? I'm Win. And I'm not going out for lunch because I'm knackered. I'm going to set me down here and have a yogurt. Do you like yogurt?
ANGIE: No.
WIN: That's good because I've only got one. Are you hungry?
ANGIE: No.
WIN: There's a café on the corner.
ANGIE: No thank you. Do you work here?
WIN: How did you guess?
ANGIE: Because you look as if you might work here and you're sitting at the desk. Have you always worked here?
WIN: No I was headhunted. That means I was working for another outfit like this and this lot came and offered me more money. I broke my contract, there was a hell of a stink. There's not many top ladies about. Your aunty's a smashing bird.
ANGIE: Yes I know.
MARLENE: Fan are you? Fan of your aunty's?
ANGIE: Do you think I could work here?
WIN: Not at the moment.
ANGIE: How do I start?
WIN: What can you do?
ANGIE: I don't know. Nothing.
WIN: Type?
ANGIE: Not very well. The letters jump up when I do capitals. I was going to do a CSE° in commerce but I didn't.

CSE: Certificate of Secondary Education; a less prestigious exam than O-levels, generally taken in vocational rather than academic subjects.

WIN: What have you got?

ANGIE: What?

WIN: CSE's, O's.

ANGIE: Nothing, none of that. Did you do all that?

WIN: Oh yes, all that, and a science degree funnily enough. I started out doing medical research but there's no money in it. I thought I'd go abroad. Did you know they sell Coca-Cola in Russia and Pepsi-Cola in China? You don't have to be qualified as much as you might think. Men are awful bullshitters, they like to make out jobs are harder than they are. Any job I ever did I started doing it better than the rest of the crowd and they didn't like it. So I'd get unpopular and I'd have a drink to cheer myself up. I lived with a fella and supported him for four years, he couldn't get work. After that I went to California. I like the sunshine. Americans know how to live. This country's too slow. Then I went to Mexico, still in sales, but it's no country for a single lady. I came home, went bonkers for a bit, thought I was five different people, got over that all right, the psychiatrist said I was perfectly sane and highly intelligent. Got married in a moment of weakness and he's inside now, he's been inside four years, and I've not been to see him too much this last year. I like this better than sales, I'm not really that aggressive. I started thinking sales was a good job if you want to meet people, but you're meeting people that don't want to meet you. It's no good if you like being liked. Here your clients want to meet you because you're the one doing them some good. They hope. (*Angie has fallen asleep. Nell comes in.*)

NELL: You're talking to yourself, sunshine.

WIN: So what's new?

NELL: Who is this?

WIN: Marlene's little niece.

NELL: What's she got, brother, sister? She never talks about her family.

WIN: I was telling her my life story.

NELL: Violins?

WIN: No, success story.

NELL: You've heard Howard's had a heart attack?

WIN: No, when?

NELL: I heard just now. He hadn't come in, he was at home, he's gone to hospital. He's not dead. His wife was here, she rushed off in a cab.

WIN: Too much butter, too much smoke. We must send him some flowers. (*Marlene comes in.*) You've heard about Howard?

MARLENE: Poor sod.

NELL: Lucky he didn't get the job if that's what his health's like.

MARLENE: Is she asleep?

WIN: She wants to work here.

MARLENE: Packer in Tesco° more like.
WIN: She's a nice kid. Isn't she?
MARLENE: She's a bit thick. She's a bit funny.
WIN: She thinks you're wonderful.
MARLENE: She's not going to make it.

Scene II

(*Joyce's kitchen. Sunday evening, a year earlier. The lights come up on Joyce, Angie, and Marlene. Marlene is taking presents out of a bright carrier bag. Angie has already opened a box of chocolates.*)

MARLENE: Just a few little things. / I've
JOYCE: There's no need.
MARLENE: no memory for birthdays have I, and Christmas seems to slip
    by. So I think I owe Angie a few presents.
JOYCE: What do you say?
ANGIE: Thank you very much. Thank you very much, Aunty Marlene.
    (*She opens a present. It is the dress from Act I, new.*) Oh look, Mum, isn't it
    lovely?
MARLENE: I don't know if it's the right size. She's grown up since I saw
    her. / I knew she was always
ANGIE: Isn't it lovely?
MARLENE: tall for her age.
JOYCE: She's a big lump.
MARLENE: Hold it up, Angie, let's see.
ANGIE: I'll put it on, shall I?
MARLENE: Yes, try it on.
JOYCE: Go on to your room then, we don't want / a strip show thank you.
ANGIE: Of course I'm going to my room, what do you think. Look, Mum,
    here's something for you. Open it, go on. What is it? Can I open it for
    you?
JOYCE: Yes, you open it, pet.
ANGIE: Don't you want to open it yourself? / Go on.
JOYCE: I don't mind, you can do it.
ANGIE: It's something hard. It's—what is it? A bottle. Drink is it? No, it's
    what? Perfume, look. What a lot. Open it, look, let's smell it. Oh it's
    strong. It's lovely. Put it on me. How do you do it? Put it on me.
JOYCE: You're too young.
ANGIE: I can play wearing it like dressing up.
JOYCE: And you're too old for that. Here, give it here, I'll do it, you'll tip
    the whole bottle over yourself / and we'll have you smelling all summer.

Tesco: A supermarket chain.

ANGIE: Put it on you. Do I smell? Put it on Aunty too. Put it on Aunty too. Let's all smell.

MARLENE: I didn't know what you'd like.

JOYCE: There's no danger I'd have it already, / that's one thing.

ANGIE: Now we all smell the same.

MARLENE: It's a bit of nonsense.

JOYCE: It's very kind of you Marlene, you shouldn't.

ANGIE: Now I'll put on the dress and then we'll see. (*Angie goes.*)

JOYCE: You've caught me on the hop with the place in the mess. / If you'd let me

MARLENE: That doesn't matter.

JOYCE: know you was coming I'd have got something in to eat. We had our dinner dinnertime. We're just going to have a cup of tea. You could have an egg.

MARLENE: No, I'm not hungry. Tea's fine.

JOYCE: I don't expect you take sugar.

MARLENE: Why not?

JOYCE: You take care of yourself.

MARLENE: How do you mean you didn't know I was coming?

JOYCE: You could have written. I know we're not on the phone but we're not completely in the dark ages, / we do have a postman.

MARLENE: But you asked me to come.

JOYCE: How did I ask you to come?

MARLENE: Angie said when she phoned up.

JOYCE: Angie phoned up, did she.

MARLENE: Was it just Angie's idea?

JOYCE: What did she say?

MARLENE: She said you wanted me to come and see you. / It was a couple of

JOYCE: Ha.

MARLENE: weeks ago. How was I to know that's a ridiculous idea? My diary's always full a couple of weeks ahead so we fixed it for this weekend. I was meant to get here earlier but I was held up. She gave me messages from you.

JOYCE: Didn't you wonder why I didn't phone you myself?

MARLENE: She said you didn't like using the phone. You're shy on the phone and can't use it. I don't know what you're like, do I?

JOYCE: Are there people who can't use the phone?

MARLENE: I expect so.

JOYCE: I haven't met any.

MARLENE: Why should I think she was lying?

JOYCE: Because she's like what she's like.

MARLENE: How do I know / what she's like?

JOYCE: It's not my fault you don't know what she's like. You never come and see her.

MARLENE: Well I have now / and you don't seem over the moon.*

JOYCE: Good. *Well I'd have got a cake if she'd told me. (*Pause.*)

MARLENE: I did wonder why you wanted to see me.

JOYCE: I didn't want to see you.

MARLENE: Yes, I know. Shall I go?

JOYCE: I don't mind seeing you.

MARLENE: Great, I feel really welcome.

JOYCE: You can come and see Angie any time you like, I'm not stopping you. / You

MARLENE: Ta ever so.

JOYCE: know where we are. You're the one went away, not me. I'm right here where I was. And will be a few years yet I shouldn't wonder.

MARLENE: All right. All right. (*Joyce gives Marlene a cup of tea.*)

JOYCE: Tea.

MARLENE: Sugar? (*Joyce passes Marlene the sugar.*) It's very quiet down here.

JOYCE: I expect you'd notice it.

MARLENE: The air smells different too.

JOYCE: That's the scent.

MARLENE: No, I mean walking down the lane.

JOYCE: What sort of air you get in London then?

(*Angie comes in, wearing the dress. It fits.*)

MARLENE: Oh, very pretty. / You do look pretty, Angie.

JOYCE: That fits all right.

MARLENE: Do you like the color?

ANGIE: Beautiful. Beautiful.

JOYCE: You better take it off, / you'll get it dirty.

ANGIE: I want to wear it. I want to wear it.

MARLENE: It is for wearing after all. You can't just hang it up and look at it.

ANGIE: I love it.

JOYCE: Well if you must you must.

ANGIE: If someone asks me what's my favorite color I'll tell them it's this. Thank you very much Aunty Marlene.

MARLENE: You didn't tell your mum you asked me down.

ANGIE: I wanted it to be a surprise.

JOYCE: I'll give you a surprise / one of these days.

ANGIE: I thought you'd like to see her. She hasn't been here since I was nine. People do see their aunts.

MARLENE: Is it that long? Doesn't time fly.

ANGIE: I wanted to.

JOYCE: I'm not cross.

ANGIE: Are you glad?

JOYCE: I smell nicer anyhow, don't I?

(*Kit comes in without saying anything, as if she lived there.*)

MARLENE: I think it was a good idea, Angie, about time. We are sisters
after all. It's a pity to let that go.

JOYCE: This is Kitty, / who lives up the road. This is Angie's Aunty Marlene.

KIT: What's that?

ANGIE: It's a present. Do you like it?

KIT: It's all right. / Are you coming out?*

MARLENE: Hello, Kitty.

ANGIE: *No.

KIT: What's that smell?

ANGIE: It's a present.

KIT: It's horrible. Come on.*

MARLENE: Have a chocolate.

ANGIE: *No, I'm busy.

KIT: Coming out later?

ANGIE: No.

KIT (*to Marlene*): Hello. (*Kit goes without a chocolate.*)

JOYCE: She's a little girl Angie sometimes plays with because she's the
only child lives really close. She's like a little sister to her really. Angie's
good with little children.

MARLENE: Do you want to work with children, Angie? / Be a teacher or a
nursery nurse?

JOYCE: I don't think she's ever thought of it.

MARLENE: What do you want to do?

JOYCE: She hasn't an idea in her head what she wants to do. / Lucky to
get anything.

MARLENE: Angie?

JOYCE: She's not clever like you. (*Pause.*)

MARLENE: I'm not clever, just pushy.

JOYCE: True enough. (*Marlene takes a bottle of whiskey out of the bag.*)
I don't drink spirits.

ANGIE: You do at Christmas.

JOYCE: It's not Christmas, is it?

ANGIE: It's better than Christmas.

MARLENE: Glasses?

JOYCE: Just a small one then.

MARLENE: Do you want some, Angie?

ANGIE: I can't, can I?

JOYCE: Taste it if you want. You won't like it. (*Angie tastes it.*)

ANGIE: Mmm.

MARLENE: We got drunk together the night your grandfather died.

JOYCE: We did not get drunk.

MARLENE: I got drunk. You were just overcome with grief.

JOYCE: I still keep up the grave with flowers.

MARLENE: Do you really?

JOYCE: Why wouldn't I?

MARLENE: Have you seen Mother?

JOYCE: Of course I've seen Mother.

MARLENE: I mean lately.

JOYCE: Of course I've seen her lately, I go every Thursday.

MARLENE (*to Angie*): Do you remember your grandfather?

ANGIE: He got me out of the bath one night in a towel.

MARLENE: Did he? I don't think he ever gave me a bath. Did he give you a bath, Joyce? He probably got soft in his old age. Did you like him?

ANGIE: Yes of course.

MARLENE: Why?

ANGIE: What?

MARLENE: So what's the news? How's Mrs. Paisley? Still going crazily? / And Dorothy. What happened to Dorothy?*

ANGIE: Who's Mrs. Paisley?

JOYCE: *She went to Canada.

MARLENE: Did she? What to do?

JOYCE: I don't know. She just went to Canada.

MARLENE: Well / good for her.

ANGIE: Mr. Connolly killed his wife.

MARLENE: What, Connolly at Whitegates?

ANGIE: They found her body in the garden. / Under the cabbages.

MARLENE: He was always so proper.

JOYCE: Stuck up git,° Connolly. Best lawyer money could buy but he couldn't get out of it. She was carrying on with Matthew.

MARLENE: How old's Matthew then?

JOYCE: Twenty-one. / He's got a motorbike.

MARLENE: I think he's about six.

ANGIE: How can he be six? He's six years older than me. / If he was six I'd be nothing, I'd be just born this minute.

JOYCE: Your aunty knows that, she's just being silly. She means it's so long since she's been here she's forgotten about Matthew.

ANGIE: You were here for my birthday when I was nine. I had a pink cake. Kit was only five then, she was four, she hadn't started school

---

git: Fool.

yet. She could read already when she went to school. You remember my birthday? / You remember me?

MARLENE: Yes, I remember the cake.

ANGIE: You remember me?

MARLENE: Yes, I remember you.

ANGIE: And Mum and Dad was there, and Kit was.

MARLENE: Yes, how is your dad? Where is he tonight? Up the pub?

JOYCE: No, he's not here.

MARLENE: I can see he's not here.

JOYCE: He moved out.

MARLENE: What? When did he? / Just recently?*

ANGIE: Didn't you know that? You don't know much.

JOYCE: *No, it must be three years ago. Don't be rude, Angie.

ANGIE: I'm not, am I, Aunty? What else don't you know?

JOYCE: You was in America or somewhere. You sent a postcard.

ANGIE: I've got that in my room. It's the Grand Canyon. Do you want to see it? Shall I get it? I can get it for you.

MARLENE: Yes, all right. (*Angie goes.*)

JOYCE: You could be married with twins for all I know. You must have affairs and break up and I don't need to know about any of that so I don't see what the fuss is about.

MARLENE: What fuss? (*Angie comes back with the postcard.*)

ANGIE: "Driving across the states for a new job in L.A. It's a long way but the car goes very fast. It's very hot. Wish you were here. Love from Aunty Marlene."

JOYCE: Did you make a lot of money?

MARLENE: I spent a lot.

ANGIE: I want to go to America. Will you take me?

JOYCE: She's not going to America, she's been to America, stupid.

ANGIE: She might go again, stupid. It's not something you do once. People who go keep going all the time, back and forth on jets. They go on Concorde and Laker and get jet lag. Will you take me?

MARLENE: I'm not planning a trip.

ANGIE: Will you let me know?

JOYCE: Angie, / you're getting silly.

ANGIE: I want to be American.

JOYCE: It's time you were in bed.

ANGIE: No it's not. / I don't have to go to bed at all tonight.

JOYCE: School in the morning.

ANGIE: I'll wake up.

JOYCE: Come on now, you know how you get.

ANGIE: How do I get? / I don't get anyhow.*

JOYCE: Angie. *Are you staying the night?

MARLENE: Yes, if that's all right. / I'll see you in the morning.

ANGIE: You can have my bed. I'll sleep on the sofa.

JOYCE: You will not, you'll sleep in your bed. / Think

ANGIE: Mum.

JOYCE: I can't see through that? I can just see you going to sleep / with us talking.

ANGIE: I would, I would go to sleep, I'd love that.

JOYCE: I'm going to get cross, Angie.

ANGIE: I want to show her something.

JOYCE: Then bed.

ANGIE: It's a secret.

JOYCE: Then I expect it's in your room so off you go. Give us a shout when you're ready for bed and your aunty'll be up and see you.

ANGIE: Will you?

MARLENE: Yes of course. (*Angie goes. Silence.*) It's cold tonight.

JOYCE: Will you be all right on the sofa? You can / have my bed.

MARLENE: The sofa's fine.

JOYCE: Yes the forecast said rain tonight but it's held off.

MARLENE: I was going to walk down to the estuary but I've left it a bit late. Is it just the same?

JOYCE: They cut down the hedges a few years back. Is that since you were here?

MARLENE: But it's not changed down the end, all the mud? And the reeds? We used to pick them up when they were bigger than us. Are there still lapwings?

JOYCE: You get strangers walking there on a Sunday. I expect they're looking at the mud and the lapwings, yes.

MARLENE: You could have left.

JOYCE: Who says I wanted to leave?

MARLENE: Stop getting at me then, you're really boring.

JOYCE: How could I have left?

MARLENE: Did you want to?

JOYCE: I said how, / how could I?

MARLENE: If you'd wanted to you'd have done it.

JOYCE: Christ.

MARLENE: Are we getting drunk?

JOYCE: Do you want something to eat?

MARLENE: No, I'm getting drunk.

JOYCE: Funny time to visit, Sunday evening.

MARLENE: I came this morning. I spent the day —

ANGIE (*off*): Aunty! Aunty Marlene!

MARLENE: I'd better go.

JOYCE: Go on then.

MARLENE: All right.

ANGIE (*off*): Aunty! Can you hear me? I'm ready.

(*Marlene goes. Joyce goes on sitting, clears up, sits again. Marlene comes back.*)

JOYCE: So what's the secret?

MARLENE: It's a secret.

JOYCE: I know what it is anyway.

MARLENE: I bet you don't. You always said that.

JOYCE: It's her exercise book.

MARLENE: Yes, but you don't know what's in it.

JOYCE: It's some game, some secret society she has with Kit.

MARLENE: You don't know the password. You don't know the code.

JOYCE: You're really in it, aren't you. Can you do the handshake?

MARLENE: She didn't mention a handshake.

JOYCE: I thought they'd have a special handshake. She spends hours writing that but she's useless at school. She copies things out of books about black magic, and politicians out of the paper. It's a bit childish.

MARLENE: I think it's a plot to take over the world.

JOYCE: She's been in the remedial class the last two years.

MARLENE: I came up this morning and spent the day in Ipswich. I went to see Mother.

JOYCE: Did she recognize you?

MARLENE: Are you trying to be funny?

JOYCE: No, she does wander.

MARLENE: She wasn't wandering at all, she was very lucid thank you.

JOYCE: You were very lucky then.

MARLENE: Fucking awful life she's had.

JOYCE: Don't tell me.

MARLENE: Fucking waste.

JOYCE: Don't talk to me.

MARLENE: Why shouldn't I talk? Why shouldn't I talk to you? / Isn't she my mother too?

JOYCE: Look, you've left, you've gone away, / we can do without you.

MARLENE: I left home, so what, I left home. People do leave home / it is normal.

JOYCE: We understand that, we can do without you.

MARLENE: We weren't happy. Were you happy?

JOYCE: Don't come back.

MARLENE: So it's just your mother is it, your child, you never wanted me round, / you were jealous

JOYCE: Here we go.

MARLENE: of me because I was the little one and I was clever.

JOYCE: I'm not clever enough for all this psychology / if that's what it is.

MARLENE: Why can't I visit my own family / without

JOYCE: Aah.

MARLENE: all this?

JOYCE: Just don't go on about Mum's life when you haven't been to see her for how many years. / I go

MARLENE: It's up to me.

JOYCE: and see her every week.

MARLENE: Then don't go and see her every week.

JOYCE: Somebody has to.

MARLENE: No they don't. / Why do they?

JOYCE: How would I feel if I didn't go?

MARLENE: A lot better.

JOYCE: I hope you feel better.

MARLENE: It's up to me.

JOYCE: You couldn't get out of here fast enough. (*Pause.*)

MARLENE: Of course I couldn't get out of here fast enough. What was I going to do? Marry a dairyman who'd come home pissed? / Don't you fucking this

JOYCE: Christ.

MARLENE: fucking that fucking bitch fucking tell me what to fucking do fucking.

JOYCE: I don't know how you could leave your own child.

MARLENE: You were quick enough to take her.

JOYCE: What does that mean?

MARLENE: You were quick enough to take her.

JOYCE: Or what? Have her put in a home? Have some stranger / take her would you rather?

MARLENE: You couldn't have one so you took mine.

JOYCE: I didn't know that then.

MARLENE: Like hell, / married three years.

JOYCE: I didn't know that. Plenty of people / take that long.

MARLENE: Well it turned out lucky for you, didn't it?

JOYCE: Turned out all right for you by the look of you. You'd be getting a few less thousand a year.

MARLENE: Not necessarily.

JOYCE: You'd be stuck here / like you said.

MARLENE: I could have taken her with me.

JOYCE: You didn't want to take her with you. It's no good coming back now, Marlene, / and saying—

MARLENE: I know a managing director who's got two children, she breast-feeds in the board room, she pays a hundred pounds a week on domestic help alone and she can afford that because she's an extremely high-powered lady earning a great deal of money.

JOYCE: So what's that got to do with you at the age of seventeen?

MARLENE: Just because you were married and had somewhere to live—

JOYCE: You could have lived at home. / Or live

MARLENE: Don't be stupid.

JOYCE: with me and Frank. / You

MARLENE: You never suggested.

JOYCE: said you weren't keeping it. You shouldn't have had it / if you wasn't

MARLENE: Here we go.

JOYCE: going to keep it. You was the most stupid, / for someone so clever you was the most stupid, get yourself pregnant, not go to the doctor, not tell.

MARLENE: You wanted it, you said you were glad, I remember the day, you said I'm glad you never got rid of it, I'll look after it, you said that down by the river. So what are you saying, sunshine, you don't want her?

JOYCE: Course I'm not saying that.

MARLENE: Because I'll take her, / wake her up and pack now.

JOYCE: You wouldn't know how to begin to look after her.

MARLENE: Don't you want her?

JOYCE: Course I do, she's my child.

MARLENE: Then what are you going on about / why did I have her?

JOYCE: You said I got her off you / when you didn't—

MARLENE: I said you were lucky / the way it—

JOYCE: Have a child now if you want one. You're not old.

MARLENE: I might do.

JOYCE: Good. (*Pause.*)

MARLENE: I've been on the pill so long / I'm probably sterile.

JOYCE: Listen when Angie was six months I did get pregnant and I lost it because I was so tired looking after your fucking baby / because she cried so

MARLENE: You never told me.

JOYCE: much—yes I did tell you— / and the doctor

MARLENE: Well I forgot.

JOYCE: said if I'd sat down all day with my feet up I'd've kept it / and that's the only chance I ever had because after that—

MARLENE: I've had two abortions, are you interested? Shall I tell you about them? Well I won't, it's boring, it wasn't a problem. I don't like messy talk about blood / and what a bad time we all had. I

JOYCE: If I hadn't had your baby. The doctor said.

MARLENE: don't want a baby. I don't want to talk about gynecology.

JOYCE: Then stop trying to get Angie off of me.

MARLENE: I come down here after six years. All night you've been saying I don't come often enough. If I don't come for another six years she'll be twenty-one, will that be OK?

JOYCE: That'll be fine, yes, six years would suit me fine. (*Pause.*)

MARLENE: I was afraid of this. I only came because I thought you wanted . . . I just want . . . (*She cries.*)

JOYCE: Don't grizzle,° Marlene, for God's sake. Marly? Come on, pet. Love you really. Fucking stop it, will you? (*She goes to Marlene.*)

MARLENE: No, let me cry. I like it. (*They laugh, Marlene begins to stop crying.*) I knew I'd cry if I wasn't careful.

JOYCE: Everyone's always crying in this house. Nobody takes any notice.

MARLENE: You've been wonderful looking after Angie.

JOYCE: Don't get carried away.

MARLENE: I can't write letters but I do think of you.

JOYCE: You're getting drunk. I'm going to make some tea.

MARLENE: Love you. (*Joyce goes to make tea.*)

JOYCE: I can see why you'd want to leave. It's a dump here.

MARLENE: So what's this about you and Frank?

JOYCE: He was always carrying on, wasn't he. And if I wanted to go out in the evening he'd go mad, even if it was nothing, a class, I was going to go to an evening class. So he had this girlfriend, only twenty-two poor cow, and I said go on, off you go, hoppit. I don't think he even likes her.

MARLENE: So what about money?

JOYCE: I've always said I don't want your money.

MARLENE: No, does he send you money?

JOYCE: I've got four different cleaning jobs. Adds up. There's not a lot round here.

MARLENE: Does Angie miss him?

JOYCE: She doesn't say.

MARLENE: Does she see him?

JOYCE: He was never that fond of her to be honest.

MARLENE: He tried to kiss me once. When you were engaged.

JOYCE: Did you fancy him?

MARLENE: No, he looked like a fish.

JOYCE: He was lovely then.

MARLENE: Ugh.

JOYCE: Well I fancied him. For about three years.

MARLENE: Have you got someone else?

JOYCE: There's not a lot round here. Mind you, the minute you're on your own, you'd be amazed how your friends' husbands drop by. I'd sooner do without.

MARLENE: I don't see why you couldn't take my money.

JOYCE: I do, so don't bother about it.

grizzle: Whimper.

MARLENE: Only got to ask.

JOYCE: So what about you? Good job?

MARLENE: Good for a laugh. / Got back

JOYCE: Good for more than a laugh I should think.

MARLENE: from the US of A a bit wiped out and slotted into this speedy employment agency and still there.

JOYCE: You can always find yourself work then?

MARLENE: That's right.

JOYCE: And men?

MARLENE: Oh there's always men.

JOYCE: No one special?

MARLENE: There's fellas who like to be seen with a high-flying lady. Shows they've got something really good in their pants. But they can't take the day to day. They're waiting for me to turn into the little woman. Or maybe I'm just horrible of course.

JOYCE: Who needs them.

MARLENE: Who needs them. Well I do. But I need adventures more. So on on into the sunset. I think the eighties are going to be stupendous.

JOYCE: Who for?

MARLENE: For me. / I think I'm going up up up.

JOYCE: Oh for you. Yes, I'm sure they will.

MARLENE: And for the country, come to that. Get the economy back on its feet and whoosh. She's a tough lady, Maggie.° I'd give her a job. / She just needs to hang

JOYCE: You voted for them, did you?

MARLENE: in there. This country needs to stop whining. / Monetarism is not

JOYCE: Drink your tea and shut up, pet.

MARLENE: stupid. It takes time, determination. No more slop. / And

JOYCE: Well I think they're filthy bastards.

MARLENE: who's got to drive it on? First woman prime minister. Terrifico. Aces. Right on. / You must admit. Certainly gets my vote.

JOYCE: What good's first woman if it's her? I suppose you'd have liked Hitler if he was a woman. Ms. Hitler. Got a lot done, Hitlerina. / Great adventures.

MARLENE: Bosses still walking on the worker's faces? Still dadda's little parrot? Haven't you learned to think for yourself? I believe in the individual. Look at me.

JOYCE: I am looking at you.

MARLENE: Come on, Joyce, we're not going to quarrel over politics.

Maggie: Margaret Thatcher, conservative British prime minister from 1979 to 1991.

JOYCE: We are though.

MARLENE: Forget I mentioned it. Not a word about the slimy unions will cross my lips. (*Pause.*)

JOYCE: You say Mother had a wasted life.

MARLENE: Yes I do. Married to that bastard.

JOYCE: What sort of life did he have? /

MARLENE: Violent life?

JOYCE: Working in the fields like an animal. / Why

MARLENE: Come off it.

JOYCE: wouldn't he want a drink? You want a drink. He couldn't afford whiskey.

MARLENE: I don't want to talk about him.

JOYCE: You started, I was talking about her. She had a rotten life because she had nothing. She went hungry.

MARLENE: She was hungry because he drank the money. / He used to hit her.

JOYCE: It's not all down to him / Their

MARLENE: She didn't hit him.

JOYCE: lives were rubbish. They were treated like rubbish. He's dead and she'll die soon and what sort of life / did they have?

MARLENE: I saw him one night. I came down.

JOYCE: Do you think I didn't? / They

MARLENE: I still have dreams.

JOYCE: didn't get to America and drive across it in a fast car. / Bad nights, they had bad days.

MARLENE: America, America, you're jealous. / I had to get out, I knew when I

JOYCE: Jealous?

MARLENE: was thirteen, out of their house, out of them, never let that happen to me, / never let him, make my own way, out.

JOYCE: Jealous of what you've done, you'd be ashamed of me if I came to your office, your smart friends, wouldn't you, I'm ashamed of you, think of nothing but yourself, you've got on, nothing's changed for most people, / has it?

MARLENE: I hate the working class / which is what

JOYCE: Yes you do.

MARLENE: you're going to go on about now, it doesn't exist any more, it means lazy and stupid. / I don't

JOYCE: Come on, now we're getting it.

MARLENE: like the way they talk. I don't like beer guts and football vomit and saucy tits / and brothers and sisters—

JOYCE: I spit when I see a Rolls Royce, scratch it with my ring / Mercedes it was.

MARLENE: Oh very mature—

JOYCE: I hate the cows I work for / and their dirty dishes with blanquette of fucking veau.

MARLENE: and I will not be pulled down to their level by a flying picket and I won't be sent to Siberia / or a loony bin just because I'm original. And I support

JOYCE: No, you'll be on a yacht, you'll be head of Coca-Cola and you wait, the eighties is going to be stupendous all right because we'll get you lot off our backs—

MARLENE: Reagan even if he is a lousy movie star because the reds are swarming up his map and I want to be free in a free world—

JOYCE: What? / What?

MARLENE: I know what I mean / by that—not shut up here.

JOYCE: So don't be round here when it happens because if someone's kicking you I'll just laugh. (*Silence.*)

MARLENE: I don't mean anything personal. I don't believe in class. Anyone can do anything if they've got what it takes.

JOYCE: And if they haven't?

MARLENE: If they're stupid or lazy or frightened, I'm not going to help them get a job, why should I?

JOYCE: What about Angie?

MARLENE: What about Angie?

JOYCE: She's stupid, lazy, and frightened, so what about her?

MARLENE: You run her down too much. She'll be all right.

JOYCE: I don't expect so, no. I expect her children will say what a wasted life she had. If she has children. Because nothing's changed and it won't with them in.

MARLENE: Them, them. / Us and them?

JOYCE: And you're one of them.

MARLENE: And you're us, wonderful us, and Angie's us / and Mum and Dad's us.

JOYCE: Yes, that's right, and you're them.

MARLENE: Come on, Joyce, what a night. You've got what it takes.

JOYCE: I know I have.

MARLENE: I didn't really mean all that.

JOYCE: I did.

MARLENE: But we're friends anyway.

JOYCE: I don't think so, no.

MARLENE: Well it's lovely to be out in the country. I really must make the effort to come more often. I want to go to sleep. I want to go to sleep. (*Joyce gets blankets for the sofa.*)

JOYCE: Goodnight then. I hope you'll be warm enough.

MARLENE: Goodnight. Joyce—

JOYCE: No, pet. Sorry. (*Joyce goes. Marlene sits wrapped in a blanket and has another drink. Angie comes in.*)

ANGIE: Mum?

MARLENE: Angie? What's the matter?

ANGIE: Mum?

MARLENE: No, she's gone to bed. It's Aunty Marlene.

ANGIE: Frightening.

MARLENE: Did you have a bad dream? What happened in it? Well you're awake now, aren't you, pet?

ANGIE: Frightening.

1982

"MASTER HAROLD"
. . . and the boys

ATHOL FUGARD [b. 1932]

Characters
WILLIE
SAM
HALLY

(*The St. George's Park Tea Room on a wet and windy Port Elizabeth afternoon.*)

(*Tables and chairs have been cleared and are stacked on one side except for one which stands apart with a single chair. On this table a knife, fork, spoon and side plate in anticipation of a simple meal, together with a pile of comic books.*)

(*Other elements: a serving counter with a few stale cakes under glass and a not very impressive display of sweets, cigarettes and cool drinks, etc.; a few cardboard advertising handouts—Cadbury's Chocolate, Coca-Cola—and a blackboard on which an untrained hand has chalked up the prices of Tea, Coffee, Scones, Milkshakes—all flavors—and Cool Drinks; a few sad ferns in pots; a telephone; an old-style jukebox.*)

(*There is an entrance on one side and an exit into a kitchen on the other.*)

(*Leaning on the solitary table, his head cupped in one hand as he pages through one of the comic books, is Sam. A black man in his mid-forties. He wears the white coat of a waiter. Behind him on his knees, mopping down the floor with a bucket of water and a rag, is Willie. Also black and about the same age as Sam. He has his sleeves and trousers rolled up.*)

(*The year: 1950.*)

WILLIE (*singing as he works*): "She was scandalizin' my name,
She took my money
She called me honey
But she was scandalizin' my name.
Called it love but was playin' a game. . . ."

(*He gets up and moves the bucket. Stands thinking for a moment, then, raising his arms to hold an imaginary partner, he launches into an intricate ballroom dance step. Although a mildly comic figure, he reveals a reasonable degree of accomplishment.*)

Hey, Sam.

(*Sam, absorbed in the comic book, does not respond.*)

Hey, Boet° Sam!

(*Sam looks up.*)

I'm getting it. The quickstep. Look now and tell me. (*He repeats the step.*) Well?

SAM (*encouragingly*): Show me again.

WILLIE: Okay, count for me.

SAM: Ready?

WILLIE: Ready.

SAM: Five, six, seven, eight. . . . (*Willie starts to dance.*) A-n-d one two three four . . . and one two three four. . . . (*Ad libbing as Willie dances.*) Your shoulders, Willie . . . your shoulders! Don't look down! Look happy, Willie! Relax, Willie!

WILLIE (*desperate but still dancing*): I am relax.

SAM: No, you're not.

WILLIE (*he falters*): Ag, no man, Sam! Mustn't talk. You make me make mistakes.

SAM: But you're stiff.

WILLIE: Yesterday I'm not straight . . . today I'm too stiff!

SAM: Well, you are. You asked me and I'm telling you.

WILLIE: Where?

SAM: Everywhere. Try to glide through it.

WILLIE: Glide?

SAM: Ja, make it smooth. And give it more style. It must look like you're enjoying yourself.

WILLIE (*emphatically*): I wasn't.

SAM: Exactly.

WILLIE: How can I enjoy myself? Not straight, too stiff and now it's also glide, give it more style, make it smooth. . . . Haai! Is hard to remember all those things, Boet Sam.

SAM: That's your trouble. You're trying too hard.

WILLIE: I try hard because it *is* hard.

SAM: But don't let me see it. The secret is to make it look easy. Ballroom must look happy, Willie, not like hard work. It must. . . . Ja! . . . it must look like romance.

WILLIE: Now another one! What's romance?

SAM: Love story with happy ending. A handsome man in tails, and in his arms, smiling at him, a beautiful lady in evening dress!

Boet: Brother.

WILLIE: Fred Astaire, Ginger Rogers.

SAM: You got it. Tapdance or ballroom, it's the same. Romance. In two weeks' time when the judges look at you and Hilda, they must see a man and a woman who are dancing their way to a happy ending. What I saw was you holding her like you were frightened she was going to run away.

WILLIE: Ja! Because that is what she wants to do! I got no romance left for Hilda anymore, Boet Sam.

SAM: Then pretend. When you put your arms around Hilda, imagine she is Ginger Rogers.

WILLIE: With no teeth? You try.

SAM: Well, just remember, there's only two weeks left.

WILLIE: I know, I know! (*To the jukebox.*) I do it better with music. You got sixpence for Sarah Vaughan?

SAM: That's a slow foxtrot. You're practicing the quickstep.

WILLIE: I'll practice slow foxtrot.

SAM (*shaking his head*): It's your turn to put money in the jukebox.

WILLIE: I only got bus fare to go home. (*He returns disconsolately to his work.*) Love story and happy ending! She's doing it all right, Boet Sam, but is not me she's giving happy endings. Fuckin' whore! Three nights now she doesn't come practice. I wind up gramophone, I get record ready and I sit and wait. What happens? Nothing. Ten o'clock I start dancing with my pillow. You try and practice romance by yourself, Boet Sam. Struesgod, she doesn't come tonight I take back my dress and ballroom shoes and I find me new partner. Size twenty-six. Shoes size seven. And now she's also making trouble for me with the baby again. Reports me to Child Wellfed, that I'm not giving her money. She lies! Every week I am giving her money for milk. And how do I know is my baby? Only his hair looks like me. She's fucking around all the time I turn my back. Hilda Samuels is a bitch! (*Pause.*) Hey, Sam!

SAM: Ja.

WILLIE: You listening?

SAM: Ja.

WILLIE: So what you say?

SAM: About Hilda?

WILLIE: Ja.

SAM: When did you last give her a hiding?

WILLIE (*reluctantly*): Sunday night.

SAM: And today is Thursday.

WILLIE (*he knows what's coming*): Okay.

SAM: Hiding on Sunday night, then Monday, Tuesday, and Wednesday she doesn't come to practice . . . and you are asking me why?

WILLIE: I said okay, Boet Sam!

SAM: You hit her too much. One day she's going to leave you for good.

WILLIE: So? She makes me the hell-in too much.

SAM (*emphasizing his point*): *Too* much and *too* hard. You had the same trouble with Eunice.

WILLIE: Because she also make the hell-in, Boet Sam. She never got the steps right. Even the waltz.

SAM: Beating her up every time she makes a mistake in the waltz? (*Shaking his head.*) No, Willie! That takes the pleasure out of ballroom dancing.

WILLIE: Hilda is not too bad with the waltz, Boet Sam. Is the quickstep where the trouble starts.

SAM (*teasing him gently*): How's your pillow with the quickstep?

WILLIE (*ignoring the tease*): Good! And why? Because it got no legs. That's her trouble. She can't move them quick enough, Boet Sam. I start the record and before halfway Count Basie is already winning. Only time we catch up with him is when gramophone runs down. (*Sam laughs.*) Haaikona, Boet Sam, is not funny.

SAM (*snapping his fingers*): I got it! Give her a handicap.

WILLIE: What's that?

SAM: Give her a ten-second start and then let Count Basie go. Then I put my money on her. Hot favorite in the Ballroom Stakes: Hilda Samuels ridden by Willie Malopo.

WILLIE (*turning away*): I'm not talking to you no more.

SAM (*relenting*): Sorry, Willie. . . .

WILLIE: It's finish between us.

SAM: Okay, okay . . . I'll stop.

WILLIE: You can also fuck off.

SAM: Willie, listen! I want to help you!

WILLIE: No more jokes?

SAM: I promise.

WILLIE: Okay. Help me.

SAM (*his turn to hold an imaginary partner*): Look and learn. Feet together. Back straight. Body relaxed. Right hand placed gently in the small of her back and wait for the music. Don't start worrying about making mistakes or the judges or the other competitors. It's just you, Hilda and the music, and you're going to have a good time. What Count Basie do you play?

WILLIE: "You the cream in my coffee, you the salt in my stew."

SAM: Right. Give it to me in strict tempo.

WILLIE: Ready?

SAM: Ready.

WILLIE: A-n-d . . . (*Singing.*)
"You the cream in my coffee.
You the salt in my stew.

You will always be my necessity.
I'd be lost without you. . . ." (*etc.*)

(*Sam launches into the quickstep. He is obviously a much more accomplished dancer than Willie. Hally enters. A seventeen-year-old white boy. Wet raincoat and school case. He stops and watches Sam. The demonstration comes to an end with a flourish. Applause from Hally and Willie.*)

HALLY: Bravo! No question about it. First place goes to Mr. Sam Semela.
WILLIE (*in total agreement*): You was gliding with style, Boet Sam.
HALLY (*cheerfully*): How's it, chaps?
SAM: Okay, Hally.
WILLIE (*springing to attention like a soldier and saluting*): At your service, Master Harold!
HALLY: Not long to the big event, hey!
SAM: Two weeks.
HALLY: You nervous?
SAM: No.
HALLY: Think you stand a chance?
SAM: Let's just say I'm ready to go out there and dance.
HALLY: It looked like it. What about you, Willie?

(*Willie groans.*)

What's the matter?
SAM: He's got leg trouble.
HALLY (*innocently*): Oh, sorry to hear that, Willie.
WILLIE: Boet Sam! You promised. (*Willie returns to his work.*)

(*Hally deposits his school case and takes off his raincoat. His clothes are a little neglected and untidy: black blazer with school badge, gray flannel trousers in need of an ironing, khaki shirt and tie, black shoes. Sam has fetched a towel for Hally to dry his hair.*)

HALLY: God, what a lousy bloody day. It's coming down cats and dogs out there. Bad for business, chaps. . . . (*Conspiratorial whisper.*) . . . but it also means we're in for a nice quiet afternoon.
SAM: You can speak loud. Your Mom's not here.
HALLY: Out shopping?
SAM: No. The hospital.
HALLY: But it's Thursday. There's no visiting on Thursday afternoons. Is my Dad okay?
SAM: Sounds like it. In fact, I think he's going home.
HALLY (*stopped short by Sam's remark*): What do you mean?
SAM: The hospital phoned.
HALLY: To say what?
SAM: I don't know. I just heard your Mom talking.

HALLY: So what makes you say he's going home?
SAM: It sounded as if they were telling her to come and fetch him.

(*Hally thinks about what Sam has said for a few seconds.*)

HALLY: When did she leave?
SAM: About an hour ago. She said she would phone you. Want to eat?

(*Hally doesn't respond.*)

Hally, want your lunch?
HALLY: I suppose so. (*His mood has changed.*) What's on the menu? . . . as if I don't know.
SAM: Soup, followed by meat pie and gravy.
HALLY: Today's?
SAM: No.
HALLY: And the soup?
SAM: Nourishing pea soup.
HALLY: Just the soup. (*The pile of comic books on the table.*) And these?
SAM: For your Dad. Mr. Kempston brought them.
HALLY: You haven't been reading them, have you?
SAM: Just looking.
HALLY (*examining the comics*): *Jungle Jim* . . . *Batman and Robin* . . . *Tarzan* . . . God, what rubbish! Mental pollution. Take them away.

(*Sam exits waltzing into the kitchen. Hally turns to Willie.*)

HALLY: Did you hear my Mom talking on the telephone, Willie?
WILLIE: No, Master Hally. I was at the back.
HALLY: And she didn't say anything to you before she left?
WILLIE: She said I must clean the floors.
HALLY: I mean about my Dad.
WILLIE: She didn't say nothing to me about him, Master Hally.
HALLY (*with conviction*): No! It can't be. They said he needed at least another three weeks of treatment. Sam's definitely made a mistake. (*Rummages through his school case, finds a book and settles down at the table to read.*) So, Willie!
WILLIE: Yes, Master Hally! Schooling okay today?
HALLY: Yes, okay. . . . (*He thinks about it.*) . . . No, not really. Ag, what's the difference? I don't care. And Sam says you've got problems.
WILLIE: Big problems.
HALLY: Which leg is sore?

(*Willie groans.*)

Both legs.
WILLIE: There is nothing wrong with my legs. Sam is just making jokes.

HALLY: So then you *will* be in the competition.

WILLIE: Only if I can find a partner.

HALLY: But what about Hilda?

SAM (*returning with a bowl of soup*): She's the one who's got trouble with her legs.

HALLY: What sort of trouble, Willie?

SAM: From the way he describes it, I think the lady gone a bit lame.

HALLY: Good God! Have you taken her to see a doctor?

SAM: I think a vet would be better.

HALLY: What do you mean?

SAM: What do you call it again when a racehorse goes very fast?

HALLY: Gallop?

SAM: That's it!

WILLIE: Boet Sam!

HALLY: "A gallop down the homestretch to the winning post." But what's that got to do with Hilda?

SAM: Count Basie always gets there first.

(*Willie lets fly with his slop rag. It misses Sam and hits Hally.*)

HALLY (*furious*): For Christ's sake, Willie! What the hell do you think you're doing?

WILLIE: Sorry, Master Hally, but it's him. . . .

HALLY: Act your bloody age! (*Hurls the rag back at Willie.*) Cut out the nonsense now and get on with your work. And you too, Sam. Stop fooling around.

(*Sam moves away.*)

No. Hang on. I haven't finished! Tell me exactly what my Mom said.

SAM: I have. "When Hally comes, tell him I've gone to the hospital and I'll phone him."

HALLY: She didn't say anything about taking my Dad home?

SAM: No. It's just that when she was talking on the phone. . . .

HALLY (*interrupting him*): No, Sam. They can't be discharging him. She would have said so if they were. In any case, we saw him last night and he wasn't in good shape at all. Staff nurse even said there was talk about taking more X-rays. And now suddenly today he's better? If anything, it sounds more like a bad turn to me . . . which I sincerely hope it isn't. Hang on . . . how long ago did you say she left?

SAM: Just before two . . . (*His wrist watch.*) . . . hour and a half.

HALLY: I know how to settle it. (*Behind the counter to the telephone. Talking as he dials.*) Let's give her ten minutes to get to the hospital, ten minutes to load him up, another ten, at the most, to get home, and another ten to get him inside. Forty minutes. They should have been home for at least half an hour already. (*Pause—he waits with the receiver to his ear.*) No reply, chaps. And you know why? Because she's at his bedside in hospital helping him pull through a bad turn. You definitely heard wrong.

SAM: Okay.

(*As far as Hally is concerned, the matter is settled. He returns to his table, sits down, and divides his attention between the book and his soup. Sam is at his school case and picks up a textbook.*)

Modern Graded Mathematics for Standards Nine and Ten. (*Opens it at random and laughs at something he sees.*) Who is this supposed to be?

HALLY: Old fart-face Prentice.

SAM: Teacher?

HALLY: Thinks he is. And believe me, that is not a bad likeness.

SAM: Has he seen it?

HALLY: Yes.

SAM: What did he say?

HALLY: Tried to be clever, as usual. Said I was no Leonardo da Vinci and that bad art had to be punished. So, six of the best, and his are bloody good.

SAM: On your bum?

HALLY: Where else? The days when I got them on my hands are gone forever, Sam.

SAM: With your trousers down!

HALLY: No. He's not quite that barbaric.

SAM: That's the way they do it in jail.

HALLY (*flicker of morbid interest*): Really?

SAM: Ja. When the magistrate sentences you to "strokes with a light cane."

HALLY: Go on.

SAM: They make you lie down on a bench. One policeman pulls down your trousers and holds your ankles, another one pulls your shirt over your head and holds your arms. . . .

HALLY: Thank you! That's enough.

SAM: . . . and the one that gives you the strokes talks to you gently and for a long time between each one. (*He laughs.*)

HALLY: I've heard enough, Sam! Jesus! It's a bloody awful world when you come to think of it. People can be real bastards.

SAM: That's the way it is, Hally.

HALLY: It doesn't *have* to be that way. There is something called progress, you know. We don't exactly burn people at the stake anymore.

SAM: Like Joan of Arc.

HALLY: Correct. If she was captured today, she'd be given a fair trial.

SAM: And then the death sentence.

HALLY (*a world-weary sigh*): I know, I know! I oscillate between hope and despair for this world as well, Sam. But things will change, you wait and see. One day somebody is going to get up and give history a kick up the backside and get it going again.

SAM: Like who?

HALLY (*after thought*): They're called social reformers. Every age, Sam, has got its social reformer. My history book is full of them.

SAM: So where's ours?

HALLY: Good question. And I hate to say it, but the answer is: I don't know. Maybe he hasn't even been born yet. Or is still only a babe in arms at his mother's breast. God, what a thought.

SAM: So we just go on waiting.

HALLY: Ja, looks like it. (*Back to his soup and the book.*)

SAM (*reading from the textbook*): "Introduction: In some mathematical problems only the magnitude. . . ." (*He mispronounces the word "magnitude."*)

HALLY (*correcting him without looking up*): Magnitude.

SAM: What's it mean?

HALLY: How big it is. The size of the thing.

SAM (*reading*): ". . . magnitude of the quantities is of importance. In other problems we need to know whether these quantities are negative or positive. For example, whether there is a debit or credit bank balance . . ."

HALLY: Whether you're broke or not.

SAM: ". . . whether the temperature is above or below Zero. . . ."

HALLY: Naught degrees. Cheerful state of affairs! No cash and you're freezing to death. Mathematics won't get you out of that one.

SAM: "All these quantities are called . . ." (*spelling the word*) . . . s-c-a-l. . . .

HALLY: Scalars.

SAM: Scalars! (*Shaking his head with a laugh.*) You understand all that?

HALLY (*turning a page*): No. And I don't intend to try.

SAM: So what happens when the exams come?

HALLY: Failing a maths exam isn't the end of the world, Sam. How many times have I told you that examination results don't measure intelligence?

SAM: I would say about as many times as you've failed one of them.

HALLY (*mirthlessly*): Ha, ha, ha.

SAM (*simultaneously*): Ha, ha, ha.

HALLY: Just remember Winston Churchill didn't do particularly well at school.

SAM: You've also told me that one many times.

HALLY: Well, it just so happens to be the truth.

SAM (*enjoying the word*): Magnitude! Magnitude! Show me how to use it.

HALLY (*after thought*): An intrepid social reformer will not be daunted by the magnitude of the task he has undertaken.

SAM (*impressed*): Couple of jaw-breakers in there!

HALLY: I gave you three for the price of one. Intrepid, daunted, and magnitude. I did that once in an exam. Put five of the words I had to explain in one sentence. It was half a page long.

SAM: Well, I'll put my money on you in the English exam.

HALLY: Piece of cake. Eighty percent without even trying.

SAM (*another textbook from Hally's case*): And history?

HALLY: So-so. I'll scrape through. In the fifties if I'm lucky.

SAM: You didn't do too badly last year.

HALLY: Because we had World War One. That at least has some action. You try to find that in the South African Parliamentary system.

SAM (*reading from the history textbook*): "Napoleon and the principle of equality." Hey! This sounds interesting. "After concluding peace with Britain in 1802, Napoleon used a brief period of calm to in-sti-tute . . ."

HALLY: Introduce.

SAM: ". . . many reforms. Napoleon regarded all people as equal before the law and wanted them to have equal opportunities for advancement. All ves-ti-ges of the feu-dal sys-tem with its oppression of the poor were abol-ished." Vestiges, feudal system, and abolished. I'm all right on oppression.

HALLY: I'm thinking. He swept away . . . abol-ished . . . the last remains . . . vestiges . . . of the bad old days . . . feudal system.

SAM: Ha! There's the social reformer we're waiting for. He sounds like a man of some magnitude.

HALLY: I'm not so sure about that. It's a damn good title for a book, though. A man of magnitude!

SAM: He sounds pretty big to me, Hally.

HALLY: Don't confuse historical significance with greatness. But maybe I'm being a bit prejudiced. Have a look in there and you'll see he's two chapters long. And hell! . . . has he only got dates, Sam, all of which you've got to remember! This campaign and that campaign, and then, because of all the fighting, the next thing is we get Peace Treaties all over the place. And what's the end of the story? Battle of Waterloo, which he loses. Wasn't worth it. No, I don't know about him as a man of magnitude.

SAM: Then who would you say was?

HALLY: To answer that, we need a definition of greatness, and I suppose that would be somebody who . . . somebody who benefited all mankind.

SAM: Right. But like who?

HALLY (*he speaks with total conviction*): Charles Darwin. Remember him? That big book from the library. *The Origin of the Species.*

SAM: Him?

HALLY: Yes. For his Theory of Evolution.

SAM: You didn't finish it.

HALLY: I ran out of time. I didn't finish it because my two weeks was up. But I'm going to take it out again after I've digested what I read. It's safe. I've hidden it away in the Theology section. Nobody ever goes in there. And anyway who are you to talk? You hardly even looked at it.

SAM: I tried. I looked at the chapters in the beginning and I saw one called "The Struggle for an Existence." Ah ha, I thought. At last! But what did I get? Something called the mistiltoe which needs the apple tree and there's too many seeds and all are going to die except one . . . ! No, Hally.

HALLY (*intellectually outraged*): What do you mean, No! The poor man had to start somewhere. For God's sake, Sam, he revolutionized science. Now we know.

SAM: What?

HALLY: Where we come from and what it all means.

SAM: And that's a benefit to mankind? Anyway, I still don't believe it.

HALLY: God, you're impossible. I showed it to you in black and white.

SAM: Doesn't mean I got to believe it.

HALLY: It's the likes of you that kept the Inquisition in business. It's called bigotry. Anyway, that's my man of magnitude. Charles Darwin! Who's yours?

SAM (*without hesitation*): Abraham Lincoln.

HALLY: I might have guessed as much. Don't get sentimental, Sam. You've never been a slave, you know. And anyway we freed your ancestors here in South Africa long before the Americans. But if you want to thank somebody on their behalf, do it to Mr. William Wilberforce.° Come on. Try again. I want a real genius.

(*Now enjoying himself, and so is Sam. Hally goes behind the counter and helps himself to a chocolate.*)

SAM: William Shakespeare.

HALLY (*no enthusiasm*): Oh. So you're also one of them, are you? You're basing that opinion on only one play, you know. You've only read my *Julius Caesar* and even I don't understand half of what they're talking

---

Mr. William Wilberforce: (1759–1833), British politician and humanitarian who campaigned for the abolition of the slave trade.

about. They should do what they did with the old Bible: bring the language up to date.

SAM: That's all you've got. It's also the only one *you've* read.

HALLY: I know. I admit it. That's why I suggest we reserve our judgment until we've checked up on a few others. I've got a feeling, though, that by the end of this year one is going to be enough for me, and I can give you the names of twenty-nine other chaps in the Standard Nine class of the Port Elizabeth Technical College who feel the same. But if you want him, you can have him. My turn now. (*Pacing.*) This is a damned good exercise, you know! It started off looking like a simple question and here it's got us really probing into the intellectual heritage of our civilization.

SAM: So who is it going to be?

HALLY: My next man . . . and he gets the title on two scores: social reform and literary genius . . . is Leo Nikolaevich Tolstoy.

SAM: That Russian.

HALLY: Correct. Remember the picture of him I showed you?

SAM: With the long beard.

HALLY (*trying to look like Tolstoy*): And those burning, visionary eyes. My God, the face of a social prophet if ever I saw one! And remember my words when I showed it to you? Here's a *man*, Sam!

SAM: Those were words, Hally.

HALLY: Not many intellectuals are prepared to shovel manure with the peasants and then go home and write a "little book" called *War and Peace*. Incidentally, Sam, he was somebody else who, to quote, ". . . did not distinguish himself scholastically."

SAM: Meaning?

HALLY: He was also no good at school.

SAM: Like you and Winston Churchill.

HALLY (*mirthlessly*): Ha, ha, ha.

SAM (*simultaneously*): Ha, ha, ha.

HALLY: Don't get clever, Sam. That man freed his serfs of his own free will.

SAM: No argument. He was a somebody, all right. I accept him.

HALLY: I'm sure Count Tolstoy will be very pleased to hear that. Your turn. Shoot. (*Another chocolate from behind the counter.*) I'm waiting, Sam.

SAM: I've got him.

HALLY: Good. Submit your candidate for examination.

SAM: Jesus.

HALLY (*stopped dead in his tracks*): Who?

SAM: Jesus Christ.

HALLY: Oh, come on, Sam!

SAM: The Messiah.

HALLY: Ja, but still . . . No, Sam. Don't let's get started on religion. We'll just spend the whole afternoon arguing again. Suppose I turn around and say Mohammed?

SAM: All right.

HALLY: You can't have them both on the same list!

SAM: Why not? You like Mohammed, I like Jesus.

HALLY: I *don't* like Mohammed. I never have. I was merely being hypothetical. As far as I'm concerned, the Koran is as bad as the Bible. No. Religion is out! I'm not going to waste my time again arguing with you about the existence of God. You know perfectly well I'm an atheist . . . and I've got homework to do.

SAM: Okay, I take him back.

HALLY: You've got time for one more name.

SAM (*after thought*): I've got one I know we'll agree on. A simple straightforward great Man of Magnitude . . . and no arguments. And *he* really *did* benefit all mankind.

HALLY: I wonder. After your last contribution I'm beginning to doubt whether anything in the way of an intellectual agreement is possible between the two of us. Who is he?

SAM: Guess.

HALLY: Socrates? Alexandre Dumas? Karl Marx? Dostoevsky? Nietzsche?

(*Sam shakes his head after each name.*)

Give me a clue.

SAM: The letter *P* is important. . . .

HALLY: Plato!

SAM: . . . and his name begins with an *F.*

HALLY: I've got it. Freud and Psychology.

SAM: No. I didn't understand him.

HALLY: That makes two of us.

SAM: Think of moldy apricot jam.

HALLY (*after a delighted laugh*): Penicillin and Sir Alexander Fleming! And the title of the book: *The Microbe Hunters.* (*Delighted.*) Splendid, Sam! Splendid. For once we are in total agreement. The major breakthrough in medical science in the Twentieth Century. If it wasn't for him, we might have lost the Second World War. It's deeply gratifying, Sam, to know that I haven't been wasting my time in talking to you. (*Strutting around proudly.*) Tolstoy may have educated his peasants, but I've educated you.

SAM: Standard Four to Standard Nine.

HALLY: Have we been at it as long as that?

SAM: Yep. And my first lesson was geography.

HALLY (*intrigued*): Really? I don't remember.

SAM: My room there at the back of the old Jubilee Boarding House. I had just started working for your Mom. Little boy in short trousers walks in one afternoon and asks me seriously: "Sam, do you want to see South Africa?" Hey man! Sure I wanted to see South Africa!

HALLY: Was that me?

SAM: . . . So the next thing I'm looking at a map you had just done for homework. It was your first one and you were very proud of yourself.

HALLY: Go on.

SAM: Then came my first lesson. "Repeat after me, Sam: Gold in the Transvaal, mealies in the Free State, sugar in Natal, and grapes in the Cape." I still know it!

HALLY: Well, I'll be buggered. So that's how it all started.

SAM: And your next map was one with all the rivers and the mountains they came from. The Orange, the Vaal, the Limpopo, the Zambezi. . . .

HALLY: You've got a phenomenal memory!

SAM: You should be grateful. That is why you started passing your exams. You tried to be better than me.

(*They laugh together. Willie is attracted by the laughter and joins them.*)

HALLY: The old Jubilee Boarding House. Sixteen rooms with board and lodging, rent in advance and one week's notice. I haven't thought about it for donkey's years . . . and I don't think that's an accident. God, was I glad when we sold it and moved out. Those years are not remembered as the happiest ones of an unhappy childhood.

WILLIE (*knocking on the table and trying to imitate a woman's voice*): "Hally, are you there?"

HALLY: Who's that supposed to be?

WILLIE: "What you doing in there, Hally? Come out at once!"

HALLY (*to Sam*): What's he talking about?

SAM: Don't you remember?

WILLIE: "Sam, Willie . . . is he in there with you boys?"

SAM: Hiding away in our room when your mother was looking for you.

HALLY (*another good laugh*): Of course! I used to crawl and hide under your bed! But finish the story, Willie. Then what used to happen? You chaps would give the game away by telling her I was in there with you. So much for friendship.

SAM: We couldn't lie to her. She knew.

HALLY: Which meant I got another rowing for hanging around the "servants' quarters." I think I spent more time in there with you chaps than anywhere else in that dump. And do you blame me? Nothing but bloody misery wherever you went. Somebody was always complaining about the food, or my mother was having a fight with Micky Nash because she'd caught her with a petty officer in her room. Maud Meiring was another one. Remember those two? They were prostitutes, you know. Soldiers and sailors from the troopships. Bottom fell out of the business when the war ended. God, the flotsam and jetsam that life washed up on our shores! No joking, if it wasn't for your room, I would have been the first certified ten-year-old in medical history. Ja, the memories are coming back now. Walking home from school and thinking: "What can I do this afternoon?" Try out a few ideas, but sooner or later I'd end up in there with you fellows. I bet you I could still find my way to your room with my eyes closed. (*He does exactly that.*) Down the corridor . . . telephone on the right, which my Mom keeps locked because somebody is using it on the sly and not paying . . . past the kitchen and unappetizing cooking smells . . . around the corner into the backyard, hold my breath again because there are more smells coming when I pass your lavatory, then into that little passageway, first door on the right and into your room. How's that?

SAM: Good. But, as usual, you forgot to knock.

HALLY: Like that time I barged in and caught you and Cynthia . . . at it. Remember? God, was I embarrassed! I didn't know what was going on at first.

SAM: Ja, that taught you a lesson.

HALLY: And about a lot more than knocking on doors, I'll have you know, and I don't mean geography either. Hell, Sam, couldn't you have waited until it was dark?

SAM: No.

HALLY: Was it that urgent?

SAM: Yes, and if you don't believe me, wait until your time comes.

HALLY: No, thank you. I am not interested in girls. (*Back to his memories. . . . Using a few chairs he re-creates the room as he lists the items.*) A gray little room with a cold cement floor. Your bed against that wall . . . and I now know why the mattress sags so much! . . . Willie's bed . . . it's propped up on bricks because one leg is broken . . . that wobbly little table with the washbasin and jug of water . . . Yes! . . . stuck to the wall above it are some pin-up pictures from magazines. Joe Louis. . . .

WILLIE: Brown Bomber. World Title. (*Boxing pose.*) Three rounds and knockout.

HALLY: Against who?

SAM: Max Schmeling.

HALLY: Correct. I can also remember Fred Astaire and Ginger Rogers, and Rita Hayworth in a bathing costume which always made me hot and bothered when I looked at it. Under Willie's bed is an old suitcase with all his clothes in a mess, which is why I never hide there. Your things are neat and tidy in a trunk next to your bed, and on it there is a picture of you and Cynthia in your ballroom clothes, your first silver cup for third place in a competition and an old radio which doesn't work anymore. Have I left out anything?

SAM: No.

HALLY: Right, so much for the stage directions. Now the characters. (*Sam and Willie move to their appropriate positions in the bedroom.*) Willie is in bed, under his blankets with his clothes on, complaining nonstop about something, but we can't make out a word of what he's saying because he's got his head under the blankets as well. You're on your bed trimming your toenails with a knife—not a very edifying sight— and as for me. . . . What am I doing?

SAM: You're sitting on the floor giving Willie a lecture about being a good loser while you get the checkerboard and pieces ready for a game. Then you go to Willie's bed, pull off the blankets and make him play with you first because you know you're going to win, and that gives you the second game with me.

HALLY: And you certainly were a bad loser, Willie!

WILLIE: Haai!

HALLY: Wasn't he, Sam? And so slow! A game with you almost took the whole afternoon. Thank God I gave up trying to teach you how to play chess.

WILLIE: You and Sam cheated.

HALLY: I never saw Sam cheat, and mine were mostly the mistakes of youth.

WILLIE: Then how is it you two was always winning?

HALLY: Have you ever considered the possibility, Willie, that it was because we were better than you?

WILLIE: Every time better?

HALLY: Not every time. There were occasions when we deliberately let you win a game so that you would stop sulking and go on playing with us. Sam used to wink at me when you weren't looking to show me it was time to let you win.

WILLIE: So then you two didn't play fair.

HALLY: It was for your benefit, Mr. Malopo, which is more than being fair. It was an act of self-sacrifice. (*To Sam.*) But you know what my best memory is, don't you?

SAM: No.

HALLY: Come on, guess. If your memory is so good, you must remember it as well.

SAM: We got up to a lot of tricks in there, Hally.

HALLY: This one was special, Sam.

SAM: I'm listening.

HALLY: It started off looking like another of those useless nothing-to-do afternoons. I'd already been down to Main Street looking for adventure, but nothing had happened. I didn't feel like climbing trees in the Donkin Park or pretending I was a private eye and following a stranger . . . so as usual: See what's cooking in Sam's room. This time it was you on the floor. You had two thin pieces of wood and you were smoothing them down with a knife. It didn't look particularly interesting, but when I asked you what you were doing, you just said, "Wait and see, Hally. Wait . . . and see". . . in that secret sort of way of yours, so I knew there was a surprise coming. You teased me, you bugger, by being deliberately slow and not answering my questions!

(Sam laughs.)

And whistling while you worked away! God, it was infuriating! I could have brained you! It was only when you tied them together in a cross and put that down on the brown paper that I realized what you were doing. "Sam is making a kite?" And when I asked you and you said, "Yes". . . ! *(Shaking his head with disbelief.)* The sheer audacity of it took my breath away. I mean, seriously, what the hell does a black man know about flying a kite? I'll be honest with you, Sam, I had no hopes for it. If you think I was excited and happy, you got another guess coming. In fact, I was shit-scared that we were going to make fools of ourselves. When we left the boarding house to go up onto the hill, I was praying quietly that there wouldn't be any other kids around to laugh at us.

SAM *(enjoying the memory as much as Hally)*: Ja, I could see that.

HALLY: I made it obvious, did I?

SAM: Ja. You refused to carry it.

HALLY: Do you blame me? Can you remember what the poor thing looked like? Tomato-box wood and brown paper! Flour and water for glue! Two of my mother's old stockings for a tail, and then all those bits and pieces of string you made me tie together so that we could fly it! Hell, no, that was now only asking for a miracle to happen.

SAM: Then the big argument when I told you to hold the string and run with it when I let go.

HALLY: I was prepared to run, all right, but straight back to the boarding house.

SAM *(knowing what's coming)*: So what happened?

HALLY: Come on, Sam, you remember as well as I do.

SAM: I want to hear it from you.

(Hally pauses. He wants to be as accurate as possible.)

HALLY: You went a little distance from me down the hill, you held it up ready to let it go. . . . "This is it," I thought. "Like everything else in my life, here comes another fiasco." Then you shouted, "Go, Hally!" and I started to run. (*Another pause.*) I don't know how to describe it, Sam. Ja! The miracle happened! I was running, waiting for it to crash to the ground, but instead suddenly there was something alive behind me at the end of the string, tugging at it as if it wanted to be free. I looked back . . . (*Shakes his head.*) . . . I still can't believe my eyes. It was flying! Looping around and trying to climb even higher into the sky. You shouted to me to let it have more string. I did, until there was none left and I was just holding that piece of wood we had tied it to. You came up and joined me. You were laughing.

SAM: So were you. And shouting, "It works, Sam! We've done it!"

HALLY: And we had! I was so proud of us! It was the most splendid thing I had ever seen. I wished there were hundreds of kids around to watch us. The part that scared me, though, was when you showed me how to make it dive down to the ground and then just when it was on the point of crashing, swoop up again!

SAM: You didn't want to try yourself.

HALLY: Of course not! I would have been suicidal if anything had happened to it. Watching you do it made me nervous enough. I was quite happy just to see it up there with its tail fluttering behind it. You left me after that, didn't you? You explained how to get it down, we tied it to the bench so that I could sit and watch it, and you went away. I wanted you to stay, you know. I was a little scared of having to look after it by myself.

SAM (*quietly*): I had work to do, Hally.

HALLY: It was sort of sad bringing it down, Sam. And it looked sad again when it was lying there on the ground. Like something that had lost its soul. Just tomato-box wood, brown paper and two of my mother's old stockings! But, hell, I'll never forget that first moment when I saw it up there. I had a stiff neck the next day from looking up so much.

(*Sam laughs. Hally turns to him with a question he never thought of asking before.*)

Why did you make that kite, Sam?

SAM (*evenly*): I can't remember.

HALLY: Truly?

SAM: Too long ago, Hally.

HALLY: Ja, I suppose it was. It's time for another one, you know.

SAM: Why do you say that?

HALLY: Because it feels like that. Wouldn't be a good day to fly it, though.

SAM: No. You can't fly kites on rainy days.

HALLY (*He studies Sam. Their memories have made him conscious of the man's presence in his life.*): How old are you, Sam?

SAM: Two score and five.

HALLY: Strange, isn't it?

SAM: What?

HALLY: Me and you.

SAM: What's strange about it?

HALLY: Little white boy in short trousers and a black man old enough to be his father flying a kite. It's not every day you see that.

SAM: But why strange? Because the one is white and the other black?

HALLY: I don't know. Would have been just as strange, I suppose, if it had been me and my Dad . . . cripple man and a little boy! Nope! There's no chance of me flying a kite without it being strange. (*Simple statement of fact—no self-pity.*) There's a nice little short story there. "The Kite-Flyers." But we'd have to find a twist in the ending.

SAM: Twist?

HALLY: Yes. Something unexpected. The way it ended with us was too straightforward . . . me on the bench and you going back to work. There's no drama in that.

WILLIE: And me?

HALLY: You?

WILLIE: Yes me.

HALLY: You want to get into the story as well, do you? I got it! Change the title: "Afternoons in Sam's Room". . . expand it and tell all the stories. It's on its way to being a novel. Our days in the old Jubilee. Sad in a way that they're over. I almost wish we were still in that little room.

SAM: We're still together.

HALLY: That's true. It's just that life felt the right size in there . . . not too big and not too small. Wasn't so hard to work up a bit of courage. It's got so bloody complicated since then.

(*The telephone rings. Sam answers it.*)

SAM: St. George's Park Tea Room . . . Hello, Madam . . . Yes, Madam, he's here. . . . Hally, it's your mother.

HALLY: Where is she phoning from?

SAM: Sounds like the hospital. It's a public telephone.

HALLY (*relieved*): You see! I told you. (*The telephone.*) Hello, Mom . . . Yes . . . Yes no fine. Everything's under control here. How's things with poor old Dad? . . . Has he had a bad turn? . . . What? . . . Oh, God! . . . Yes, Sam told me, but I was sure he'd made a mistake. But what's this all about, Mom? He didn't look at all good last night. How can he get better so quickly? . . . Then very obviously you must say no. Be firm with him. You're the boss. . . . You know what it's going to be like if he comes home. . . . Well then, don't blame me when I fail my exams at the end of the year. . . . Yes! How am I expected to be fresh for school when I spend half the night massaging his gammy leg? . . . So am

I! . . . So tell him a white lie. Say Dr. Colley wants more X-rays of his stump. Or bribe him. We'll sneak in double tots of brandy in future. . . . What? . . . Order him to get back into bed at once! If he's going to behave like a child, treat him like one. . . . All right, Mom! I was just trying to . . . I'm sorry. . . . I said I'm sorry. . . . Quick, give me your number. I'll phone you back. (*He hangs up and waits a few seconds.*) Here we go again! (*He dials.*) I'm sorry, Mom. . . . Okay. . . . But now listen to me carefully. All it needs is for you to put your foot down. Don't take no for an answer. . . . Did you hear me? And whatever you do, don't discuss it with him. . . . Because I'm frightened you'll give in to him. . . . Yes, Sam gave me lunch. . . . I ate all of it! . . . No, Mom not a soul. It's still raining here. . . . Right, I'll tell them. I'll just do some homework and then lock up. . . . But remember now, Mom. Don't listen to anything he says. And phone me back and let me know what happens. . . . Okay. Bye, Mom. (*He hangs up. The men are staring at him.*) My Mom says that when you're finished with the floors you must do the windows. (*Pause.*) Don't misunderstand me, chaps. All I want is for him to get better. And if he was, I'd be the first person to say: "Bring him home." But he's not, and we can't give him the medical care and attention he needs at home. That's what hospitals are there for. (*Brusquely.*) So don't just stand there! Get on with it!

(*Sam clears Hally's table.*)

You heard right. My Dad wants to go home.

SAM: Is he better?

HALLY (*sharply*): No! How the hell can he be better when last night he was groaning with pain? This is not an age of miracles!

SAM: Then he should stay in hospital.

HALLY (*seething with irritation and frustration*): Tell me something I don't know, Sam. What the hell do you think I was saying to my Mom? All I can say is fuck-it-all.

SAM: I'm sure he'll listen to your Mom.

HALLY: You don't know what she's up against. He's already packed his shaving kit and pajamas and is sitting on his bed with his crutches, dressed and ready to go. I know him when he gets in that mood. If she tries to reason with him, we've had it. She's no match for him when it comes to a battle of words. He'll tie her up in knots. (*Trying to hide his true feelings.*)

SAM: I suppose it gets lonely for him in there.

HALLY: With all the patients and nurses around? Regular visits from the Salvation Army? Balls! It's ten times worse for him at home. I'm at school and my mother is here in the business all day.

SAM: He's at least got you at night.

HALLY (*before he can stop himself*): And we've got him! Please! I don't want to talk about it anymore. (*Unpacks his school case, slamming down books on the table.*) Life is just a plain bloody mess, that's all. And people are fools.

SAM: Come on, Hally.

HALLY: Yes, they are! They bloody well deserve what they get.

SAM: Then don't complain.

HALLY: Don't try to be clever, Sam. It doesn't suit you. Anybody who thinks there's nothing wrong with this world needs to have his head examined. Just when things are going along all right, without fail someone or something will come along and spoil everything. Somebody should write that down as a fundamental law of the Universe. The principle of perpetual disappointment. If there is a God who created this world, he should scrap it and try again.

SAM: All right, Hally, all right. What you got for homework?

HALLY: Bullshit, as usual. (*Opens an exercise book and reads.*) "Write five hundred words describing an annual event of cultural or historical significance."

SAM: That should be easy enough for you.

HALLY: And also plain bloody boring. You know what he wants, don't you? One of their useless old ceremonies. The commemoration of the landing of the 1820 Settlers, or if it's going to be culture, Carols by Candlelight every Christmas.

SAM: It's an impressive sight. Make a good description, Hally. All those candles glowing in the dark and the people singing hymns.

HALLY: And it's called religious hysteria. (*Intense irritation.*) Please, Sam! Just leave me alone and let me get on with it. I'm not in the mood for games this afternoon. And remember my Mom's orders . . . you're to help Willie with the windows. Come on now, I don't want any more nonsense in here.

SAM: Okay, Hally, okay.

(*Hally settles down to his homework; determined preparations . . . pen, ruler, exercise book, dictionary, another cake . . . all of which will lead to nothing.*)

(*Sam waltzes over to Willie and starts to replace tables and chairs. He practices a ballroom step while doing so. Willie watches. When Sam is finished, Willie tries.*)

Good! But just a little bit quicker on the turn and only move in to her after she's crossed over. What about this one?

(*Another step. When Sam is finished, Willie again has a go.*)

Much better. See what happens when you just relax and enjoy yourself? Remember that in two weeks' time and you'll be all right.

WILLIE: But I haven't got partner, Boet Sam.

SAM: Maybe Hilda will turn up tonight.

WILLIE: No, Boet Sam. (*Reluctantly.*) I gave her a good hiding.

SAM: You mean a bad one.

WILLIE: Good bad one.

SAM: Then you mustn't complain either. Now you pay the price for losing your temper.

WILLIE: I also pay two pounds ten shilling entrance fee.

SAM: They'll refund you if you withdraw now.

WILLIE (*appalled*): You mean, don't dance?

SAM: Yes.

WILLIE: No! I wait too long and I practice too hard. If I find me new partner, you think I can be ready in two weeks? I ask Madam for my leave now and we practice every day.

SAM: Quickstep nonstop for two weeks. World record, Willie, but you'll be mad at the end.

WILLIE: No jokes, Boet Sam.

SAM: I'm not joking.

WILLIE: So then what?

SAM: Find Hilda. Say you're sorry and promise you won't beat her again.

WILLIE: No.

SAM: Then withdraw. Try again next year.

WILLIE: No.

SAM: Then I give up.

WILLIE: Haaikona, Boet Sam, you can't.

SAM: What do you mean, I can't? I'm telling you: I give up.

WILLIE (*adamant*): No! (*Accusingly.*) It was you who start me ballroom dancing.

SAM: So?

WILLIE: Before that I use to be happy. And is you and Miriam who bring me to Hilda and say here's partner for you.

SAM: What are you saying, Willie?

WILLIE: You!

SAM: But me what? To blame?

WILLIE: Yes.

SAM: Willie . . . ? (*Bursts into laughter.*)

WILLIE: And now all you do is make jokes at me. You wait. When Miriam leaves you is my turn to laugh. Ha! Ha! Ha!

SAM (*he can't take Willie seriously any longer*): She can leave me tonight! I know what to do. (*Bowing before an imaginary partner.*) May I have the pleasure? (*He dances and sings.*)
"Just a fellow with his pillow . . .
Dancin' like a willow . . .
In an autumn breeze. . . ."

WILLIE: There you go again!

(*Sam goes on dancing and singing.*)

Boet Sam!

SAM: There's the answer to your problem! Judges' announcement in two weeks' time: "Ladies and gentlemen, the winner in the open section . . . Mr. Willie Malopo and his pillow!"

(*This is too much for a now really angry Willie. He goes for Sam, but the latter is too quick for him and puts Hally's table between the two of them.*)

HALLY (*exploding*): For Christ's sake, you two!

WILLIE (*still trying to get at Sam*): I donner you, Sam! Struesgod!

SAM (*still laughing*): Sorry, Willie . . . Sorry. . . .

HALLY: Sam! Willie! (*Grabs his ruler and gives Willie a vicious whack on the bum.*) How the hell am I supposed to concentrate with the two of you behaving like bloody children!

WILLIE: Hit him too!

HALLY: Shut up, Willie.

WILLIE: He started jokes again.

HALLY: Get back to your work. You too, Sam. (*His ruler.*) Do you want another one, Willie?

(*Sam and Willie return to their work. Hally uses the opportunity to escape from his unsuccessful attempt at homework. He struts around like a little despot, ruler in hand, giving vent to his anger and frustration.*)

Suppose a customer had walked in then? Or the Park Superintendent. And seen the two of you behaving like a pair of hooligans. That would have been the end of my mother's license, you know. And your jobs? Well, this is the end of it. From now on there will be no more of your ballroom nonsense in here. This is a business establishment, not a bloody New Brighton dancing school. I've been far too lenient with the two of you. (*Behind the counter for a green cool drink and a dollop of ice cream. He keeps up his tirade as he prepares it.*) But what really makes me bitter is that I allow you chaps a little freedom in here when business is bad and what do you do with it? The foxtrot! Specially you, Sam. There's more to life than trotting around a dance floor and I thought at least you knew it.

SAM: It's a harmless pleasure, Hally. It doesn't hurt anybody.

HALLY: It's also a rather simple one, you know.

SAM: You reckon so? Have you ever tried?

HALLY: Of course not.

SAM: Why don't you? Now.

HALLY: What do you mean? Me dance?

SAM: Yes. I'll show you a simple step—the waltz—then you try it.

HALLY: What will that prove?

SAM: That it might not be as easy as you think.

HALLY: I didn't say it was easy. I said it was simple—like in simple-minded, meaning mentally retarded. You can't exactly say it challenges the intellect.

SAM: It does other things.

HALLY: Such as?

SAM: Make people happy.

HALLY (*the glass in his hand*): So do American cream sodas with ice cream. For God's sake, Sam, you're not asking me to take ballroom dancing serious, are you?

SAM: Yes.

HALLY (*sigh of defeat*): Oh, well, so much for trying to give you a decent education. I've obviously achieved nothing.

SAM: You still haven't told me what's wrong with admiring something that's beautiful and then trying to do it yourself.

HALLY: Nothing. But we happen to be talking about a foxtrot, not a thing of beauty.

SAM: But that is just what I'm saying. If you were to see two champions doing, two masters of the art . . . !

HALLY: Oh God, I give up. So now it's also art!

SAM: Ja.

HALLY: There's a limit, Sam. Don't confuse art and entertainment.

SAM: So then what is art?

HALLY: You want a definition?

SAM: Ja.

HALLY (*He realizes he has got to be careful. He gives the matter a lot of thought before answering.*): Philosophers have been trying to do that for centuries. What is Art? What is Life? But basically I suppose it's . . . the giving of meaning to matter.

SAM: Nothing to do with beautiful?

HALLY: It goes beyond that. It's the giving of form to the formless.

SAM: Ja, well, maybe it's not art, then. But I still say it's beautiful.

HALLY: I'm sure the word you mean to use is entertaining.

SAM (*adamant*): No. Beautiful. And if you want proof come along to the Centenary Hall in New Brighton in two weeks' time.

(*The mention of the Centenary Hall draws Willie over to them.*)

HALLY: What for? I've seen the two of you prancing around in here often enough.

SAM (*he laughs*): This isn't the real thing, Hally. We're just playing around in here.

HALLY: So? I can use my imagination.

SAM: And what do you get?

HALLY: A lot of people dancing around and having a so-called good time.

SAM: That all?

HALLY: Well, basically it is that, surely.

SAM: No, it isn't. Your imagination hasn't helped you at all. There's a lot more to it than that. We're getting ready for the championships, Hally, not just another dance. There's going to be a lot of people, all right, and they're going to have a good time, but they'll only be spectators, sitting around and watching. It's just the competitors out there on the dance floor. Party decorations and fancy lights all around the walls! The ladies in beautiful evening dresses!

HALLY: My mother's got one of those, Sam, and, quite frankly, it's an embarrassment every time she wears it.

SAM (*undeterred*): Your imagination left out the excitement.

(*Hally scoffs.*)

Oh, yes. The finalists are not going to be out there just to have a good time. One of those couples will be the 1950 Eastern Province Champions. And your imagination left out the music.

WILLIE: Mr. Elijah Gladman Guzana and his Orchestral Jazzonions.

SAM: The sound of the big band, Hally. Trombone, trumpet, tenor and alto sax. And then, finally, your imagination also left out the climax of the evening when the dancing is finished, the judges have stopped whispering among themselves and the Master of Ceremonies collects their scorecards and goes up onto the stage to announce the winners.

HALLY: All right. So you make it sound like a bit of a do. It's an occasion. Satisfied?

SAM (*victory*): So you admit that!

HALLY: Emotionally yes, intellectually no.

SAM: Well, I don't know what you mean by that, all I'm telling you is that it is going to be *the* event of the year in New Brighton. It's been sold out for two weeks already. There's only standing room left. We've got competitors coming from Kingwilliamstown, East London, Port Alfred.

(*Hally starts pacing thoughtfully.*)

HALLY: Tell me a bit more.

SAM: I thought you weren't interested . . . intellectually.

HALLY (*mysteriously*): I've got my reasons.

SAM: What do you want to know?

HALLY: It takes place every year?

SAM: Yes. But only every third year in New Brighton. It's East London's turn to have the championships next year.

HALLY: Which, I suppose, makes it an even more significant event.

SAM: Ah ha! We're getting somewhere. Our "occasion" is now a "significant event."

HALLY: I wonder.

SAM: What?

HALLY: I wonder if I would get away with it.

SAM: But what?

HALLY (*to the table and his exercise book*): "Write five hundred words describing an annual event of cultural or historical significance." Would I be stretching poetic license a little too far if I called your ballroom championships a cultural event?

SAM: You mean . . . ?

HALLY: You think we could get five hundred words out of it, Sam?

SAM: Victor Sylvester has written a whole book on ballroom dancing.

WILLIE: You going to write about it, Master Hally?

HALLY: Yes, gentlemen, that is precisely what I am considering doing. Old Doc Bromely—he's my English teacher—is going to argue with me, of course. He doesn't like natives. But I'll point out to him that in strict anthropological terms the culture of a primitive black society includes its dancing and singing. To put my thesis in a nutshell: The war-dance has been replaced by the waltz. But it still amounts to the same thing: the release of primitive emotions through movement. Shall we give it a go?

SAM: I'm ready.

WILLIE: Me also.

HALLY: Ha! This will teach the old bugger a lesson. (*Decision taken.*) Right. Let's get ourselves organized. (*This means another cake on the table. He sits.*) I think you've given me enough general atmosphere, Sam, but to build the tension and suspense I need facts. (*Pencil poised.*)

WILLIE: Give him facts, Boet Sam.

HALLY: What you called the climax . . . how many finalists?

SAM: Six couples.

HALLY (*making notes*): Go on. Give me the picture.

SAM: Spectators seated right around the hall. (*Willie becomes a spectator.*)

HALLY: . . . and it's a full house.

SAM: At one end, on the stage, Gladman and his Orchestral Jazzonions. At the other end is a long table with the three judges. The six finalists go onto the dance floor and take up their positions. When they are ready and the spectators have settled down, the Master of Ceremonies goes to the microphone. To start with, he makes some jokes to get people laughing. . . .

HALLY: Good touch. (*As he writes.*) ". . . creating a relaxed atmosphere which will change to one of tension and drama as the climax is approached."

SAM (*onto a chair to act out the M.C.*): "Ladies and gentlemen, we come now to the great moment you have all been waiting for this evening. . . . The finals of the 1950 Eastern Province Open Ballroom Dancing Championships. But first let me introduce the finalists! Mr. and Mrs. Welcome Tchabalala from Kingwilliamstown . . ."

WILLIE (*he applauds after every name*): Is when the people clap their hands and whistle and make a lot of noise, Master Hally.

SAM: "Mr. Mulligan Njikelane and Miss Nomhle Nkonyeni of Grahams-town; Mr. and Mrs. Norman Nchinga from Port Alfred; Mr. Fats Bokolane and Miss Dina Plaatjies from East London; Mr. Sipho Dugu and Mrs. Mable Magada from Peddie; and from New Brighton our very own Mr. Willie Malopo and Miss Hilda Samuels."

(*Willie can't believe his ears. He abandons his role as spectator and scrambles into position as a finalist.*)

WILLIE: Relaxed and ready to romance!

SAM: The applause dies down. When everybody is silent, Gladman lifts up his sax, nods at the Orchestral Jazzonions. . . .

WILLIE: Play the jukebox please, Boet Sam!

SAM: I also only got bus fare, Willie.

HALLY: Hold it, everybody. (*Heads for the cash register behind the counter.*) How much is in the till, Sam?

SAM: Three shillings. Hally . . . Your Mom counted it before she left.

(*Hally hesitates.*)

HALLY: Sorry, Willie. You know how she carried on the last time I did it. We'll just have to pool our combined imaginations and hope for the best. (*Returns to the table.*) Back to work. How are the points scored, Sam?

SAM: Maximum of ten points each for individual style, deportment, rhythm, and general appearance.

WILLIE: Must I start?

HALLY: Hold it for a second, Willie. And penalties?

SAM: For what?

HALLY: For doing something wrong. Say you stumble or bump into somebody . . . do they take off any points?

SAM (*aghast*): Hally . . . !

HALLY: When you're dancing. If you and your partner collide into another couple.

(*Hally can get no further. Sam has collapsed with laughter. He explains to Willie.*)

SAM: If me and Miriam bump into you and Hilda. . . .

(*Willie joins him in another good laugh.*)

Hally, Hally . . . !

HALLY (*perplexed*): Why? What did I say?

SAM: There's no collisions out there, Hally. Nobody trips or stumbles or bumps into anybody else. That's what that moment is all about. To be one of those finalists on that dance floor is like . . . like being in a dream about a world in which accidents don't happen.

HALLY (*genuinely moved by Sam's image*): Jesus, Sam! That's beautiful!

WILLIE (*can endure waiting no longer*): I'm starting!

(*Willie dances while Sam talks.*)

SAM: Of course it is. That's what I've been trying to say to you all afternoon. And it's beautiful because that is what we want life to be like. But instead, like you said, Hally, we're bumping into each other all the time. Look at the three of us this afternoon: I've bumped into Willie, the two of us have bumped into you, you've bumped into your mother, she bumping into your Dad. . . . None of us knows the steps and there's no music playing. And it doesn't stop with us. The whole world is doing it all the time. Open a newspaper and what do you read? America has bumped into Russia, England is bumping into India, rich man bumps into poor man. Those are big collisions, Hally. They make for a lot of bruises. People get hurt in all that bumping, and we're sick and tired of it now. It's been going on for too long. Are we never going to get it right? . . . Learn to dance life like champions instead of always being just a bunch of beginners at it?

HALLY (*deep and sincere admiration of the man*): You've got a vision, Sam!

SAM: Not just me. What I'm saying to you is that everybody's got it. That's why there's only standing room left for the Centenary Hall in two weeks' time. For as long as the music lasts, we are going to see six couples get it right, the way we want life to be.

HALLY: But is that the best we can do, Sam . . . watch six finalists dreaming about the way it should be?

SAM: I don't know. But it starts with that. Without the dream we won't know what we're going for. And anyway I reckon there are a few people who have got past just dreaming about it and are trying for something real. Remember that thing we read once in the paper about the Mahatma Gandhi? Going without food to stop those riots in India?

HALLY: You're right. He certainly was trying to teach people to get the steps right.

SAM: And the Pope.

HALLY: Yes, he's another one. Our old General Smuts° as well, you know. He's also out there dancing. You know, Sam, when you come to think

---

General Smuts: (1870–1950), South African statesman who helped create the Union of South Africa and the United Nations. Smuts was also a soldier in the Boer War against the British.

of it, that's what the United Nations boils down to . . . a dancing school for politicians!

SAM: And let's hope they learn.

HALLY (*a little surge of hope*): You're right. We mustn't despair. Maybe there's some hope for mankind after all. Keep it up, Willie. (*Back to his table with determination.*) This is a lot bigger than I thought. So what have we got? Yes, our title: "A World Without Collisions."

SAM: That sounds good! "A World Without Collisions."

HALLY: Subtitle: "Global Politics on the Dance Floor." No. A bit too heavy, hey? What about "Ballroom Dancing as a Political Vision"?

(*The telephone rings. Sam answers it.*)

SAM: St. George's Park Tea Room . . . Yes, Madam . . . Hally, it's your Mom.

HALLY (*back to reality*): Oh, God, yes! I'd forgotten all about that. Shit! Remember my words, Sam? Just when you're enjoying yourself, someone or something will come along and wreck everything.

SAM: You haven't heard what she's got to say yet.

HALLY: Public telephone?

SAM: No.

HALLY: Does she sound happy or unhappy?

SAM: I couldn't tell. (*Pause.*) She's waiting, Hally.

HALLY (*to the telephone*): Hello, Mom . . . No, everything is okay here. Just doing my homework. . . . What's your news? . . . You've what? . . . (*Pause. He takes the receiver away from his ear for a few seconds. In the course of Hally's telephone conversation, Sam and Willie discreetly position the stacked tables and chairs. Hally places the receiver back to his ear.*) Yes, I'm still here. Oh, well, I give up now. Why did you do it, Mom? . . . Well, I just hope you know what you've let us in for. . . . (*Loudly.*) I said I hope you know what you've let us in for! It's the end of the peace and quiet we've been having. (*Softly.*) Where is he? (*Normal voice.*) He can't hear us from in there. But for God's sake, Mom, what happened? I told you to be firm with him. . . . Then you and the nurses should have held him down, taken his crutches away. . . . I know only too well he's my father! . . . I'm not being disrespectful, but I'm sick and tired of emptying stinking chamber pots full of phlegm and piss. . . . Yes, I do! When you're not there, he asks *me* to do it. . . . If you really want to know the truth, that's why I've got no appetite for my food. . . . Yes! There's a lot of things you don't know about. For your information, I still haven't got that science textbook I need. And you know why? He borrowed the money you gave me for it. . . . Because I didn't want to start another fight between you two. . . . He says that every time. . . . All right, Mom! (*Viciously.*) Then just remember to start hiding your bag away again, because he'll be at your purse before long for money for booze. And when he's well enough to come down here, you better keep an eye on the till as well, because that is also going to develop a leak. . . . Then don't complain to me when he starts his old tricks. . . . Yes, you do. I get it from you on one side and from him on the other, and it makes life hell for me. I'm not going to be the peacemaker anymore. I'm warning you now: when the two of you start fighting again, I'm leaving home. . . . Mom, if you start crying, I'm going to put down the receiver. . . . Okay. . . . (*Lowering his voice to a vicious whisper.*) Okay, Mom. I heard you. (*Desperate.*) No. . . . Because I don't want to. I'll see him when I get home! Mom! . . . (*Pause. When he speaks again, his tone changes completely. It is not simply pretense. We sense a genuine emotional conflict.*) Welcome home, chum! . . . What's that? . . . Don't be silly, Dad. You being home is just about the best news in the world. . . . I bet you are. Bloody depressing there with everybody going on about their ailments, hey! . . . How you feeling? . . . Good. . . . Here as well, pal. Coming down cats and dogs. . . . That's right. Just the day for a kip and a toss in your old Uncle Ned. . . . Everything's just hunky-dory on my side, Dad. . . . Well, to start with, there's a nice pile of comics for you on the counter. . . . Yes, old Kemple brought them in. *Batman and Robin, Submariner* . . . just your cup of tea. . . . I will. . . . Yes, we'll spin a few yarns tonight. . . . Okay, chum, see you in a little while. . . . No, I promise. I'll come straight home. . . . (*Pause—his mother comes back on the phone.*) Mom? Okay. I'll lock up now. . . . What? . . . Oh, the brandy . . . Yes, I'll remember! . . . I'll put it in my suitcase now, for God's sake. I know well enough what will happen if he doesn't get it. . . . (*Places a bottle of brandy on the counter.*) I *was* kind to him, Mom. I didn't say anything nasty! . . . All right. Bye. (*End of telephone conversation. A desolate Hally doesn't move. A strained silence.*)

SAM (*quietly*): That sounded like a bad bump, Hally.

HALLY (*Having a hard time controlling his emotions. He speaks carefully.*): Mind your own business, Sam.

SAM: Sorry. I wasn't trying to interfere. Shall we carry on? Hally? (*He indicates the exercise book. No response from Hally.*)

WILLIE (*also trying*): Tell him about when they give out the cups, Boet Sam.

SAM: Ja! That's another big moment. The presentation of the cups after the winners have been announced. You've got to put that in.

(*Still no response from Hally.*)

WILLIE: A big silver one, Master Hally, called floating trophy for the champions.

SAM: We always invite some big-shot personality to hand them over. Guest of honor this year is going to be His Holiness Bishop Jabulani of the All African Free Zionist Church.

(*Hally gets up abruptly, goes to his table, and tears up the page he was writing on.*)

HALLY: So much for a bloody world without collisions.

SAM: Too bad. It was on its way to being a good composition.

HALLY: Let's stop bullshitting ourselves, Sam.

SAM: Have we been doing that?

HALLY: Yes! That's what all our talk about a decent world has been . . . just so much bullshit.

SAM: We did say it was still only a dream.

HALLY: And a bloody useless one at that. Life's a fuckup and it's never going to change.

SAM: Ja, maybe that's true.

HALLY: There's no maybe about it. It's a blunt and brutal fact. All we've done this afternoon is waste our time.

SAM: Not if we'd got your homework done.

HALLY: I don't give a shit about my homework, so, for Christ's sake, just shut up about it. (*Slamming books viciously into his school case.*) Hurry up now and finish your work. I want to lock up and get out of here. (*Pause.*) And then go where? Home-sweet-fucking-home. Jesus, I hate that word.

(*Hally goes to the counter to put the brandy bottle and comics in his school case. After a moment's hesitation, he smashes the bottle of brandy. He abandons all further attempts to hide his feelings. Sam and Willie work away as unobtrusively as possible.*)

Do you want to know what is really wrong with your lovely little dream, Sam? It's not just that we are all bad dancers. That does happen to be perfectly true, but there's more to it than just that. You left out the cripples.

SAM: Hally!

HALLY (*now totally reckless*): Ja! Can't leave them out, Sam. That's why we always end up on our backsides on the dance floor. They're also out there dancing . . . like a bunch of broken spiders trying to do the quickstep! (*An ugly attempt at laughter.*) When you come to think of it, it's a bloody comical sight. I mean, it's bad enough on two legs . . . but one and a pair of crutches! Hell, no, Sam. That's guaranteed to turn that dance floor into a shambles. Why you shaking your head? Picture it, man. For once this afternoon let's use our imaginations sensibly.

SAM: Be careful, Hally.

HALLY: Of what? The truth? I seem to be the only one around here who is prepared to face it. We've had the pretty dream, it's time now to wake up and have a good long look at the way things really are. Nobody knows the steps, there's no music, the cripples are also out there tripping up everybody and trying to get into the act, and it's all called the All-Comers-How-to-Make-a-Fuckup-of-Life Championships. (*Another ugly laugh.*) Hang on, Sam! The best bit is still coming. Do you know what the winner's trophy is? A beautiful big chamber pot with roses on the side, and it's full to the brim with piss. And guess who I think is going to be this year's winner.

SAM (*almost shouting*): Stop now!

HALLY (*suddenly appalled by how far he has gone*): Why?

SAM: Hally? It's your father you're talking about.

HALLY: So?

SAM: Do you know what you've been saying?

(*Hally can't answer. He is rigid with shame. Sam speaks to him sternly.*)

No, Hally, you mustn't do it. Take back those words and ask for forgiveness! It's a terrible sin for a son to mock his father with jokes like that. You'll be punished if you carry on. Your father is your father, even if he is a . . . cripple man.

WILLIE: Yes, Master Hally. Is true what Sam say.

SAM: I understand how you are feeling, Hally, but even so. . . .

HALLY: No, you don't!

SAM: I think I do.

HALLY: And I'm telling you you don't. Nobody does. (*Speaking carefully as his shame turns to rage at Sam.*) It's your turn to be careful, Sam. Very careful! You're treading on dangerous ground. Leave me and my father alone.

SAM: I'm not the one who's been saying things about him.

HALLY: What goes on between me and my Dad is none of your business!

SAM: Then don't tell me about it. If that's all you've got to say about him, I don't want to hear.

(*For a moment Hally is at loss for a response.*)

HALLY: Just get on with your bloody work and shut up.

SAM: Swearing at me won't help you.

HALLY: Yes, it does! Mind your own fucking business and shut up!

SAM: Okay. If that's the way you want it, I'll stop trying.

(*He turns away. This infuriates Hally even more.*)

HALLY: Good. Because what you've been trying to do is meddle in something you know nothing about. All that concerns you in here, Sam, is to try and do what you get paid for—keep the place clean and serve the customers. In plain words, just get on with your job. My mother is right. She's always warning me about allowing you to get too familiar. Well, this time you've gone too far. It's going to stop right now.

(*No response from Sam.*)

You're only a servant in here, and don't forget it.

(*Still no response. Hally is trying hard to get one.*)

And as far as my father is concerned, all you need to remember is that he is your boss.

SAM (*needled at last*): No, he isn't. I get paid by your mother.

HALLY: Don't argue with me, Sam!

SAM: Then don't say he's my boss.

HALLY: He's a white man and that's good enough for you.

SAM: I'll try to forget you said that.

HALLY: Don't! Because you won't be doing me a favor if you do. I'm telling you to remember it.

(*A pause. Sam pulls himself together and makes one last effort.*)

SAM: Hally, Hally . . . ! Come on now. Let's stop before it's too late. You're right. We *are* on dangerous ground. If we're not careful, somebody is going to get hurt.

HALLY: It won't be me.

SAM: Don't be so sure.

HALLY: I don't know what you're talking about, Sam.

SAM: Yes, you do.

HALLY (*furious*): Jesus, I wish you would stop trying to tell me what I do and what I don't know.

(*Sam gives up. He turns to Willie.*)

SAM: Let's finish up.

HALLY: Don't turn your back on me! I haven't finished talking.

(*He grabs Sam by the arm and tries to make him turn around. Sam reacts with a flash of anger.*)

SAM: Don't do that, Hally! (*Facing the boy.*) All right, I'm listening. Well? What do you want to say to me?

HALLY (*pause as Hally looks for something to say*): To begin with, why don't you also start calling me Master Harold, like Willie.

SAM: Do you mean that?

HALLY: Why the hell do you think I said it?

SAM: And if I don't?

HALLY: You might just lose your job.

SAM (*quietly and very carefully*): If you make me say it once, I'll never call you anything else again.

HALLY: So? (*The boy confronts the man.*) Is that meant to be a threat?

SAM: Just telling you what will happen if you make me do that. You must decide what it means to you.

HALLY: Well, I have. It's good news. Because that is exactly what Master Harold wants from now on. Think of it as a little lesson in respect, Sam, that's long overdue, and I hope you remember it as well as you do your geography. I can tell you now that somebody who will be glad to hear I've finally given it to you will be my Dad. Yes! He agrees with my Mom. He's always going on about it as well. "You must teach the boys to show you more respect, my son."

SAM: So now you can stop complaining about going home. Everybody is going to be happy tonight.

HALLY: That's perfectly correct. You see, you mustn't get the wrong idea about me and my Dad, Sam. We also have our good times together. Some bloody good laughs. He's got a marvelous sense of humor. Want to know what our favorite joke is? He gives out a big groan, you see, and says: "It's not fair, is it, Hally?" Then I have to ask: "What, chum?" And then he says: "A nigger's arse". . . and we both have a good laugh.

(*The men stare at him with disbelief.*)

What's the matter, Willie? Don't you catch the joke? You always were a bit slow on the uptake. It's what is called a pun. You see, fair means both light in color and to be just and decent. (*He turns to Sam.*) I thought *you* would catch it, Sam.

SAM: Oh ja, I catch it all right.

HALLY: But it doesn't appeal to your sense of humor.

SAM: Do you really laugh?

HALLY: Of course.

SAM: To please him? Make him feel good?

HALLY: No, for heavens sake! I laugh because I think it's a bloody good joke.

SAM: You're really trying hard to be ugly, aren't you? And why drag poor old Willie into it? He's done nothing to you except show you the respect you want so badly. That's also not being fair, you know . . . and *I* mean just or decent.

WILLIE: It's all right, Sam. Leave it now.

SAM: It's me you're after. You should just have said "Sam's arse". . . because that's the one you're trying to kick. Anyway, how do you know it's not fair? You've never seen it. Do you want to? (*He drops his trousers and underpants and presents his backside for Hally's inspection.*) Have a good look. A real Basuto arse . . . which is about as nigger as they can come. Satisfied? (*Trousers up.*) Now you can make your Dad even happier when you go home tonight. Tell him I showed you my arse and he is quite right. It's not fair. And if it will give him an even better laugh next time, I'll also let *him* have a look. Come, Willie, let's finish up and go.

(*Sam and Willie start to tidy up the tea room. Hally doesn't move. He waits for a moment when Sam passes him.*)

HALLY (*quietly*): Sam . . .

(*Sam stops and looks expectantly at the boy. Hally spits in his face. A long and heartfelt groan from Willie. For a few seconds Sam doesn't move.*)

SAM (*taking out a handkerchief and wiping his face*): It's all right, Willie.

(*To Hally.*)

Ja, well, you've done it . . . Master Harold. Yes, I'll start calling you that from now on. It won't be difficult anymore. You've hurt yourself, Master Harold. I saw it coming. I warned you, but you wouldn't listen. You've just hurt yourself *bad.* And you're a coward, Master Harold. The face you should be spitting in is your father's . . . but you used mine, because you think you're safe inside your fair skin . . . and this time I don't mean just or decent. (*Pause, then moving violently toward Hally.*) Should I hit him, Willie?

WILLIE (*stopping Sam*): No, Boet Sam.

SAM (*violently*): Why not?

WILLIE: It won't help, Boet Sam.

SAM: I don't want to help! I want to hurt him.

WILLIE: You also hurt yourself.

SAM: And if he had done it to you, Willie?

WILLIE: Me? Spit at me like I was a dog? (*A thought that had not occurred to him before. He looks at Hally.*) Ja. Then I want to hit him. I want to hit him hard!

(*A dangerous few seconds as the men stand staring at the boy. Willie turns away, shaking his head.*)

But maybe all I do is go cry at the back. He's little boy, Boet Sam. Little *white* boy. Long trousers now, but he's still little boy.

SAM (*his violence ebbing away into defeat as quickly as it flooded*): You're right. So go on, then: groan again, Willie. You do it better than me. (*To Hally.*) You don't know all of what you've just done . . . Master Harold. It's not just that you've made me feel dirtier than I've ever been in my life . . . I mean, how do I wash off yours and your father's filth? . . . I've also failed. A long time ago I promised myself I was going to try and do something, but you've just shown me . . . Master Harold . . . that I've failed. (*Pause.*) I've also got a memory of a little white boy when he was still wearing short trousers and a black man, but they're not flying a kite. It was the old Jubilee days, after dinner one night. I was in my room. You came in and just stood against the wall, looking down at the ground, and only after I'd asked you what you wanted, what was wrong, I don't know how many times, did you speak and even then so softly I almost didn't hear you. "Sam, please help me to go and fetch my Dad." Remember? He was dead drunk on the floor of the Central Hotel Bar. They'd phoned for your Mom, but you were the only one at home. And do you remember how we did it? You went in first by yourself to ask permission for me to go into the bar. Then I loaded him onto my back like a baby and carried him back to the boarding house with you following behind carrying his crutches. (*Shaking his head as he remembers.*) A crowded Main Street with all the people watching a little white boy following his drunk father on a nigger's back! I felt for that little boy . . . Master Harold. I felt for him. After that we still had to clean him up, remember? He'd messed in his trousers, so we had to clean him up and get him into bed.

HALLY (*great pain*): I love him, Sam.

SAM: I know you do. That's why I tried to stop you from saying these things about him. It would have been so simple if you could have just despised him for being a weak man. But he's your father. You love him and you're ashamed of him. You're ashamed of so much! . . . And now that's going to include yourself. That was the promise I made to myself: to try and stop that happening. (*Pause.*) After we got him to bed you came back with me to my room and sat in a corner and carried on just looking down at the ground. And for days after that! You hadn't done anything wrong, but you went around as if you owed the world an apology for being alive. I didn't like seeing that! That's not the way a boy grows up to be a man! . . . But the one person who should have been teaching you what that means was the cause of your shame. If you really want to know, that's why I made you that kite. I wanted you to look up, be proud of something, of yourself . . . (*bitter smile at the memory*) . . . and you certainly were that when I left you with it up there on the hill. Oh, ja . . . something else! . . . If you ever do write it as a short story, there *was* a twist in our ending. I couldn't sit down there and stay with you. It was a "Whites Only" bench. You were too young, too excited to notice then. But not anymore. If you're not careful . . . Master Harold . . . you're going to be sitting up there by yourself for a long time to come, and there won't be a kite in the sky. (*Sam has got nothing more to say. He exits into the kitchen, taking off his waiter's jacket.*)

WILLIE: Is bad. Is all bad in here now.

HALLY (*books into his school case, raincoat on*): Willie . . . (*It is difficult to speak.*) Will you lock up for me and look after the keys?

WILLIE: Okay.

(*Sam returns. Hally goes behind the counter and collects the few coins in the cash register. As he starts to leave. . . .*)

SAM: Don't forget the comic books.

(*Hally returns to the counter and puts them in his case. He starts to leave again.*)

SAM (*to the retreating back of the boy*): Stop . . . Hally. . . .

(*Hally stops, but doesn't turn to face him.*)

Hally . . . I've got no right to tell you what being a man means if I don't behave like one myself, and I'm not doing so well at that this afternoon. Should we try again, Hally?

HALLY: Try what?

SAM: Fly another kite, I suppose. It worked once, and this time I need it as much as you do.

HALLY: It's still raining, Sam. You can't fly kites on rainy days, remember.

SAM: So what do we do? Hope for better weather tomorrow?

HALLY (*helpless gesture*): I don't know. I don't know anything anymore.

SAM: You sure of that, Hally? Because it would be pretty hopeless if that was true. It would mean nothing has been learnt in here this afternoon, and there was a hell of a lot of teaching going on . . . one way or the other. But anyway, I don't believe you. I reckon there's one thing you know. You don't *have* to sit up there by yourself. You know what that bench means now, and you can leave it any time you choose. All you've got to do is stand up and walk away from it.

(*Hally leaves. Willie goes up quietly to Sam.*)

WILLIE: Is okay, Boet Sam. You see. Is . . . (*he can't find any better words*) . . . is going to be okay tomorrow. (*Changing his tone.*) Hey, Boet Sam! (*He is trying hard.*) You right. I think about it and you right. Tonight I find Hilda and say sorry. And make promise I won't beat her no more. You hear me, Boet Sam?

SAM: I hear you, Willie.

WILLIE: And when we practice I relax and romance with her from beginning to end. Nonstop! You watch! Two weeks' time: "First prize for promising newcomers: Mr. Willie Malopo and Miss Hilda Samuels." (*Sudden impulse.*) To hell with it! I walk home. (*He goes to the jukebox, puts in a coin and selects a record. The machine comes to life in the gray*

twilight, blushing its way through a spectrum of soft, romantic colors.) How
did you say it, Boet Sam? Let's dream. (*Willie sways with the music and
gestures for Sam to dance.*)

(*Sarah Vaughan sings.*)

"Little man you're crying,
I know why you're blue,
Someone took your kiddy car away;
Better go to sleep now,
Little man you've had a busy day." (*etc., etc.*)
You lead. I follow.

(*The men dance together.*)

"Johnny won your marbles,
Tell you what we'll do;
Dad will get you new ones right away;
Better go to sleep now,
Little man you've had a busy day."

1982

The Piano Lesson

AUGUST WILSON [b. 1945]

Gin my cotton
Sell my seed
Buy my baby
Everything she need —SKIP JAMES

Characters

DOAKER
BOY WILLIE
LYMON
BERNIECE
MARETHA
AVERY
WINING BOY
GRACE

The Setting: *The action of the play takes place in the kitchen and parlor of the house where Doaker Charles lives with his niece, Berniece, and her eleven-year-old daughter, Maretha. The house is sparsely furnished, and although there is evidence of a woman's touch, there is a lack of warmth and vigor. Berniece and Maretha occupy the upstairs rooms. Doaker's room is prominent and opens onto the kitchen. Dominating the parlor is an old upright piano. On the legs of the piano, carved in the manner of African sculpture, are mask-like figures resembling totems. The carvings are rendered with a grace and power of invention that lifts them out of the realm of craftsmanship and into the realm of art. At left is a staircase leading to the upstairs.*

ACT 1   *Scene 1*

(The lights come up on the Charles household. It is five o'clock in the morning. The dawn is beginning to announce itself, but there is something in the air that belongs to the night. A stillness that is a portent, a gathering, a coming together of something akin to a storm. There is a loud knock at the door.)

BOY WILLIE (*offstage, calling*): Hey, Doaker . . . Doaker!

(*He knocks again and calls.*)

   Hey, Doaker! Hey, Berniece! Berniece!

(*Doaker enters from his room. He is a tall, thin man of forty-seven, with severe features, who has for all intents and purposes retired from the world though he works full-time as a railroad cook.*)

DOAKER: Who is it?

BOY WILLIE: Open the door, nigger! It's me . . . Boy Willie!

DOAKER: Who?

BOY WILLIE: Boy Willie! Open the door!

(*Doaker opens the door and Boy Willie and Lymon enter. Boy Willie is thirty years old. He has an infectious grin and a boyishness that is apt for his name. He is brash and impulsive, talkative and somewhat crude in speech and manner. Lymon is twenty-nine. Boy Willie's partner, he talks little, and then with a straightforwardness that is often disarming.*)

DOAKER: What you doing up here?

BOY WILLIE: I told you, Lymon. Lymon talking about you might be sleep. This is Lymon. You remember Lymon Jackson from down home? This my Uncle Doaker.

DOAKER: What you doing up here? I couldn't figure out who that was. I thought you was still down in Mississippi.

BOY WILLIE: Me and Lymon selling watermelons. We got a truck out there. Got a whole truckload of watermelons. We brought them up here to sell. Where's Berniece?

(*Calls.*)

   Hey, Berniece!

DOAKER: Berniece up there sleep.

BOY WILLIE: Well, let her get up.

(*Calls.*)

   Hey, Berniece!

DOAKER: She got to go to work in the morning.

BOY WILLIE: Well she can get up and say hi. It's been three years since I seen her.

(*Calls.*)

   Hey, Berniece! It's me . . . Boy Willie.

DOAKER: Berniece don't like all that hollering now. She got to work in the morning.

BOY WILLIE: She can go on back to bed. Me and Lymon been riding two days in that truck . . . the least she can do is get up and say hi.

DOAKER (*looking out the window*): Where you all get that truck from?

BOY WILLIE: It's Lymon's. I told him let's get a load of watermelons and bring them up here.

LYMON: Boy Willie say he going back, but I'm gonna stay. See what it's like up here.

BOY WILLIE: You gonna carry me down there first.

LYMON: I told you I ain't going back down there and take a chance on that truck breaking down again. You can take the train. Hey, tell him Doaker, he can take the train back. After we sell them watermelons he have enough money he can buy him a whole railroad car.

DOAKER: You got all them watermelons stacked up there no wonder the truck broke down. I'm surprised you made it this far with a load like that. Where you break down at?

BOY WILLIE: We broke down three times! It took us two and a half days to get here. It's a good thing we picked them watermelons fresh.

LYMON: We broke down twice in West Virginia. The first time was just as soon as we got out of Sunflower. About forty miles out she broke down. We got it going and got all the way to West Virginia before she broke down again.

BOY WILLIE: We had to walk about five miles for some water.

LYMON: It got a hole in the radiator but it runs pretty good. You have to pump the brakes sometime before they catch. Boy Willie have his door open and be ready to jump when that happens.

BOY WILLIE: Lymon think that's funny. I told the nigger I give him ten dollars to get the brakes fixed. But he thinks that funny.

LYMON: They don't need fixing. All you got to do is pump them till they catch.

(*Berniece enters on the stairs. Thirty-five years old, with an eleven-year-old daughter, she is still in mourning for her husband after three years.*)

BERNIECE: What you doing all that hollering for?

BOY WILLIE: Hey, Berniece. Doaker said you was sleep. I said at least you could get up and say hi.

BERNIECE: It's five o'clock in the morning and you come in here with all this noise. You can't come like normal folks. You got to bring all that noise with you.

BOY WILLIE: Hell, I ain't done nothing but come in and say hi. I ain't got in the house good.

BERNIECE: That's what I'm talking about. You start all that hollering and carry on as soon as you hit the door.

BOY WILLIE: Aw hell, woman, I was glad to see Doaker. You ain't had to come down if you didn't want to. I come eighteen hundred miles to see my sister I figure she might want to get up and say hi. Other than that you can go back upstairs. What you got, Doaker? Where your bottle? Me and Lymon want a drink.

(*To Berniece.*)

This is Lymon. You remember Lymon Jackson from down home.

LYMON: How you doing, Berniece. You look just like I thought you looked.

BERNIECE: Why you all got to come in hollering and carrying on? Waking the neighbors with all that noise.

BOY WILLIE: They can come over and join the party. We fixing to have a party. Doaker, where your bottle? Me and Lymon celebrating. The Ghosts of the Yellow Dog got Sutter.

BERNIECE: Say what?

BOY WILLIE: Ask Lymon, they found him the next morning. Say he drowned in his well.

DOAKER: When this happen, Boy Willie?

BOY WILLIE: About three weeks ago. Me and Lymon was over in Stoner County when we heard about it. We laughed. We thought it was funny. A great big old three-hundred-and-forty-pound man gonna fall down his well.

LYMON: It remind me of Humpty Dumpty.

BOY WILLIE: Everybody say the Ghosts of the Yellow Dog pushed him.

BERNIECE: I don't want to hear that nonsense. Somebody down there pushing them people in their wells.

DOAKER: What was you and Lymon doing over in Stoner County?

BOY WILLIE: We was down there working. Lymon got some people down there.

LYMON: My cousin got some land down there. We was helping him.

BOY WILLIE: Got near about a hundred acres. He got it set up real nice. Me and Lymon was down there chopping down trees. We was using Lymon's truck to haul the wood. Me and Lymon used to haul wood all around them parts.

(*To Berniece.*)

Me and Lymon got a truckload of watermelons out there.

(*Berniece crosses to the window to the parlor.*)

Doaker, where your bottle? I know you got a bottle stuck up in your room. Come on, me and Lymon want a drink.

(*Doaker exits into his room.*)

BERNIECE: Where you all get that truck from?

BOY WILLIE: I told you it's Lymon's.

BERNIECE: Where you get the truck from, Lymon?

LYMON: I bought it.

BERNIECE: Where he get that truck from, Boy Willie?

BOY WILLIE: He told you he bought it. Bought it for a hundred and
    twenty dollars. I can't say where he got that hundred and twenty dol-
    lars from . . . but he bought that old piece of truck from Henry Porter.
    (*To Lymon.*) Where you get that hundred and twenty dollars from,
    nigger?

LYMON: I got it like you get yours. I know how to take care of money.

(*Doaker brings a bottle and sets it on the table.*)

BOY WILLIE: Aw hell, Doaker got some of that good whiskey. Don't give
    Lymon none of that. He ain't used to good whiskey. He liable to get
    sick.

LYMON: I done had good whiskey before.

BOY WILLIE: Lymon bought that truck so he have him a place to sleep.
    He down there wasn't doing no work or nothing. Sheriff looking for
    him. He bought that truck to keep away from the sheriff. Got Stovall
    looking for him too. He down there sleeping in that truck ducking and
    dodging both of them. I told him come on let's go up and see my sister.

BERNIECE: What the sheriff looking for you for, Lymon?

BOY WILLIE: The man don't want you to know all his business. He's my
    company. He ain't asking you no questions.

LYMON: It wasn't nothing. It was just a misunderstanding.

BERNIECE: He in my house. You say the sheriff looking for him, I wanna
    know what he looking for him for. Otherwise you all can go back out
    there and be where nobody don't have to ask you nothing.

LYMON: It was just a misunderstanding. Sometimes me and the sheriff
    we don't think alike. So we just got crossed on each other.

BERNIECE: Might be looking for him about that truck. He might have
    stole that truck.

BOY WILLIE: We ain't stole no truck, woman. I told you Lymon bought it.

DOAKER: Boy Willie and Lymon got more sense than to ride all the way
    up here in a stolen truck with a load of watermelons. Now they might
    have stole them watermelons, but I don't believe they stole that truck.

BOY WILLIE: You don't even know the man good and you calling him a
    thief. And we ain't stole them watermelons either. Them old man
    Pitterford's watermelons. He give me and Lymon all we could load for
    ten dollars.

DOAKER: No wonder you got them stacked up out there. You must have
    five hundred watermelons stacked up out there.

BERNIECE: Boy Willie, when you and Lymon planning on going back?

BOY WILLIE: Lymon say he staying. As soon as we sell them watermelons I'm going on back.

BERNIECE (*starts to exit up the stairs*): That's what you need to do. And you need to do it quick. Come in here disrupting the house. I don't want all that loud carrying on around here. I'm surprised you ain't woke Maretha up.

BOY WILLIE: I was fixing to get her now.

(*Calls.*)

Hey, Maretha!

DOAKER: Berniece don't like all that hollering now.

BERNIECE: Don't you wake that child up!

BOY WILLIE: You going up there . . . wake her up and tell her her uncle's here. I ain't seen her in three years. Wake her up and send her down here. She can go back to bed.

BERNIECE: I ain't waking that child up . . . and don't you be making all that noise. You and Lymon need to sell them watermelons and go on back.

(*Berniece exits up the stairs.*)

BOY WILLIE: I see Berniece still try to be stuck up.

DOAKER: Berniece alright. She don't want you making all that noise. Maretha up there sleep. Let her sleep until she get up. She can see you then.

BOY WILLIE: I ain't thinking about Berniece. You hear from Wining Boy? You know Cleotha died?

DOAKER: Yeah, I heard that. He come by here about a year ago. Had a whole sack of money. He stayed here about two weeks. Ain't offered nothing. Berniece asked him for three dollars to buy some food and he got mad and left.

LYMON: Who's Wining Boy?

BOY WILLIE: That's my uncle. That's Doaker's brother. You heard me talk about Wining Boy. He play piano. He done made some records and everything. He still doing that, Doaker?

DOAKER: He made one or two records a long time ago. That's the only ones I ever known him to make. If you let him tell it he a big recording star.

BOY WILLIE: He stopped down home about two years ago. That's what I hear. I don't know. Me and Lymon was up on Parchman Farm doing them three years.

DOAKER: He don't never stay in one place. Now, he been here about eight months ago. Back in the winter. Now, you subject not to see him for another two years. It's liable to be that long before he stop by.

BOY WILLIE: If he had a whole sack of money you liable never to see him. You ain't gonna see him until he get broke. Just as soon as that sack of money is gone you look up and he be on your doorstep.

LYMON (*noticing the piano*): Is that the piano?

BOY WILLIE: Yeah . . . look here, Lymon. See how it's carved up real nice and polished and everything? You never find you another piano like that.

LYMON: Yeah, that look real nice.

BOY WILLIE: I told you. See how it's polished? My mama used to polish it every day. See all them pictures carved on it? That's what I was talking about. You can get a nice price for that piano.

LYMON: That's all Boy Willie talked about the whole trip up here. I got tired of hearing him talk about the piano.

BOY WILLIE: All you want to talk about is women. You ought to hear this nigger, Doaker. Talking about all the women he gonna get when he get up here. He ain't had none down there but he gonna get a hundred when he get up here.

DOAKER: How your people doing down there, Lymon?

LYMON: They alright. They still there. I come up here to see what it's like up here. Boy Willie trying to get me to go back and farm with him.

BOY WILLIE: Sutter's brother selling the land. He say he gonna sell it to me. That's why I come up here. I got one part of it. Sell them watermelons and get me another part. Get Berniece to sell that piano and I'll have the third part.

DOAKER: Berniece ain't gonna sell that piano.

BOY WILLIE: I'm gonna talk to her. When she see I got a chance to get Sutter's land she'll come around.

DOAKER: You can put that thought out your mind. Berniece ain't gonna sell that piano.

BOY WILLIE: I'm gonna talk to her. She been playing on it?

DOAKER: You know she won't touch that piano. I ain't never known her to touch it since Mama Ola died. That's over seven years now. She say it got blood on it. She got Maretha playing on it though. Say Maretha can go on and do everything she can't do. Got her in an extra school down at the Irene Kaufman Settlement House. She want Maretha to grow up and be a schoolteacher. Say she good enough she can teach on the piano.

BOY WILLIE: Maretha don't need to be playing on no piano. She can play on the guitar.

DOAKER: How much land Sutter got left?

BOY WILLIE: Got a hundred acres. Good land. He done sold it piece by piece, he kept the good part for himself. Now he got to give that up. His brother come down from Chicago for the funeral . . . he up there in Chicago got some kind of business with soda fountain equipment. He anxious to sell the land, Doaker. He don't want to be bothered with it. He called me to him and said cause of how long our families done known each other and how we been good friends and all, say he wanted to sell the land to me. Say he'd rather see me with it than Jim Stovall. Told me he'd let me have it for two thousand dollars cash money. He don't know I found out the most Stovall would give him for it was fifteen hundred dollars. He trying to get that extra five hundred out of me telling me he doing me a favor. I thanked him just as nice. Told him what a good man Sutter was and how he had my sympathy and all. Told him to give me two weeks. He said he'd wait on me. That's why I come up here. Sell them watermelons. Get Berniece to sell that piano. Put them two parts with the part I done saved. Walk in there. Tip my hat. Lay my money down on the table. Get my deed and walk on out. This time I get to keep all the cotton. Hire me some men to work it for me. Gin my cotton. Get my seed. And I'll see you again next year. Might even plant some tobacco or some oats.

DOAKER: You gonna have a hard time trying to get Berniece to sell that piano. You know Avery Brown from down there don't you? He up here now. He followed Berniece up here trying to get her to marry him after Crawley got killed. He been up here about two years. He call himself a preacher now.

BOY WILLIE: I know Avery. I know him from when he used to work on the Willshaw place. Lymon know him too.

DOAKER: He after Berniece to marry him. She keep telling him no but he won't give up. He keep pressing her on it.

BOY WILLIE: Avery think all white men is bigshots. He don't know there some white men ain't got as much as he got.

DOAKER: He supposed to come past here this morning. Berniece going down to the bank with him to see if he can get a loan to start his church. That's why I know Berniece ain't gonna sell that piano. He tried to get her to sell it to help him start his church. Sent the man around and everything.

BOY WILLIE: What man?

DOAKER: Some white fellow was going around to all the colored people's houses looking to buy up musical instruments. He'd buy anything. Drums. Guitars. Harmonicas. Pianos. Avery sent him past here. He looked at the piano and got excited. Offered her a nice price. She turned him down and got on Avery for sending him past. The man kept on her about two weeks. He seen where she wasn't gonna sell it, he gave her his number and told her if she ever wanted to sell it to call him first. Say he'd go one better than what anybody else would give her for it.

BOY WILLIE: How much he offer her for it?

DOAKER: Now you know me. She didn't say and I didn't ask. I just know it was a nice price.

LYMON: All you got to do is find out who he is and tell him somebody else wanna buy it from you. Tell him you can't make up your mind who to sell it to, and if he like Doaker say, he'll give you anything you want for it.

BOY WILLIE: That's what I'm gonna do. I'm gonna find out who he is from Avery.

DOAKER: It ain't gonna do you no good. Berniece ain't gonna sell that piano.

BOY WILLIE: She ain't got to sell it. I'm gonna sell it. I own just as much of it as she does.

BERNIECE (*offstage, hollers*): Doaker! Go on get away. Doaker!

DOAKER (*calling*): Berniece?

(*Doaker and Boy Willie rush to the stairs, Boy Willie runs up the stairs, passing Berniece as she enters, running.*)

DOAKER: Berniece, what's the matter? You alright? What's the matter?

(*Berniece tries to catch her breath. She is unable to speak.*)

DOAKER: That's alright. Take your time. You alright. What's the matter?

(*He calls.*)

Hey, Boy Willie?

BOY WILLIE (*offstage*): Ain't nobody up here.

BERNIECE: Sutter . . . Sutter's standing at the top of the steps.

DOAKER (*calls*): Boy Willie!

(*Lymon crosses to the stairs and looks up. Boy Willie enters from the stairs.*)

BOY WILLIE: Hey Doaker, what's wrong with her? Berniece, what's wrong? Who was you talking to?

DOAKER: She say she seen Sutter's ghost standing at the top of the stairs.

BOY WILLIE: Seen what? Sutter? She ain't seen no Sutter.

BERNIECE: He was standing right up there.

BOY WILLIE (*entering on the stairs*): That's all in Berniece's head. Ain't nobody up there. Go on up there, Doaker.

DOAKER: I'll take your word for it. Berniece talking about what she seen. She say Sutter's ghost standing at the top of the steps. She ain't just make all that up.

BOY WILLIE: She up there dreaming. She ain't seen no ghost.

LYMON: You want a glass of water, Berniece? Get her a glass of water, Boy Willie.

BOY WILLIE: She don't need no water. She ain't seen nothing. Go on up there and look. Ain't nobody up there but Maretha.

DOAKER: Let Berniece tell it.

BOY WILLIE: I ain't stopping her from telling it.

DOAKER: What happened, Berniece?

BERNIECE: I come out my room to come back down here and Sutter was standing there in the hall.

BOY WILLIE: What he look like?

BERNIECE: He look like Sutter. He look like he always look.

BOY WILLIE: Sutter couldn't find his way from Big Sandy to Little Sandy. How he gonna find his way all the way up here to Pittsburgh? Sutter ain't never even heard of Pittsburgh.

DOAKER: Go on, Berniece.

BERNIECE: Just standing there with the blue suit on.

BOY WILLIE: The man ain't never left Marlin County when he was living . . . and he's gonna come all the way up here now that he's dead?

DOAKER: Let her finish. I want to hear what she got to say.

BOY WILLIE: I'll tell you this. If Berniece had seen him like she think she seen him she'd still be running.

DOAKER: Go on, Berniece. Don't pay Boy Willie no mind.

BERNIECE: He was standing there . . . had his hand on top of his head. Look like he might have thought if he took his hand down his head might have fallen off.

LYMON: Did he have on a hat?

BERNIECE: Just had on that blue suit . . . I told him to go away and he just stood there looking at me . . . calling Boy Willie's name.

BOY WILLIE: What he calling my name for?

BERNIECE: I believe you pushed him in the well.

BOY WILLIE: Now what kind of sense that make? You telling me I'm gonna go out there and hide in the weeds with all them dogs and things he got around there . . . I'm gonna hide and wait till I catch him looking down his well just right . . . then I'm gonna run over and push him in. A great big old three-hundred-and-forty-pound man.

BERNIECE: Well, what he calling your name for?

BOY WILLIE: He bending over looking down his well, woman . . . how he know who pushed him? It could have been anybody. Where was you when Sutter fell in his well? Where was Doaker? Me and Lymon was over in Stoner County. Tell her, Lymon. The Ghosts of the Yellow Dog got Sutter. That's what happened to him.

BERNIECE: You can talk all that Ghosts of the Yellow Dog stuff if you want. I know better.

LYMON: The Ghosts of the Yellow Dog pushed him. That's what the people say. They found him in his well and all the people say it must be the Ghosts of the Yellow Dog. Just like all them other men.

BOY WILLIE: Come talking about he looking for me. What he come all the way up here for? If he looking for me all he got to do is wait. He could have saved himself a trip if he looking for me. That ain't nothing but in Berniece's head. Ain't no telling what she liable to come up with next.

BERNIECE: Boy Willie, I want you and Lymon to go ahead and leave my house. Just go on somewhere. You don't do nothing but bring trouble with you everywhere you go. If it wasn't for you Crawley would still be alive.

BOY WILLIE: Crawley what? I ain't had nothing to do with Crawley getting killed. Crawley three time seven. He had his own mind.

BERNIECE: Just go on and leave. Let Sutter go somewhere else looking for you.

BOY WILLIE: I'm leaving. Soon as we sell them watermelons. Other than that I ain't going nowhere. Hell, I just got here. Talking about Sutter looking for me. Sutter was looking for that piano. That's what he was looking for. He had to die to find out where that piano was at . . . If I was you I'd get rid of it. That's the way to get rid of Sutter's ghost. Get rid of that piano.

BERNIECE: I want you and Lymon to go on and take all this confusion out of my house!

BOY WILLIE: Hey, tell her, Doaker. What kind of sense that make? I told you, Lymon, as soon as Berniece see me she was gonna start something. Didn't I tell you that? Now she done made up that story about Sutter just so she could tell me to leave her house. Well, hell, I ain't going nowhere till I sell them watermelons.

BERNIECE: Well why don't you go out there and sell them! Sell them and go on back!

BOY WILLIE: We waiting till the people get up.

LYMON: Boy Willie say if you get out there too early and wake the people up they get mad at you and won't buy nothing from you.

DOAKER: You won't be waiting long. You done let the sun catch up with you. This the time everybody be getting up around here.

BERNIECE: Come on, Doaker, walk up here with me. Let me get Maretha up and get her started. I got to get ready myself. Boy Willie, just go on out there and sell them watermelons and you and Lymon leave my house.

(*Berniece and Doaker exit up the stairs.*)

BOY WILLIE (*calling after them*): If you see Sutter up there . . . tell him I'm down here waiting on him.

LYMON: What if she see him again?

BOY WILLIE: That's all in her head. There ain't no ghost up there.

(*Calls.*)

Hey, Doaker . . . I told you ain't nothing up there.

LYMON: I'm glad he didn't say he was looking for me.

BOY WILLIE: I wish I would see Sutter's ghost. Give me a chance to put a whupping on him.

LYMON: You ought to stay up here with me. You be down there working his land . . . he might come looking for you all the time.

BOY WILLIE: I ain't thinking about Sutter. And I ain't thinking about staying up here. You stay up here. I'm going back and get Sutter's land. You think you ain't got to work up here. You think this the land of milk and honey. But I ain't scared of work. I'm going back and farm every acre of that land.

(*Doaker enters from the stairs.*)

I told you there ain't nothing up there, Doaker. Berniece dreaming all that.

DOAKER: I believe Berniece seen something. Berniece levelheaded. She ain't just made all that up. She say Sutter had on a suit. I don't believe she ever seen Sutter in a suit. I believe that's what he was buried in, and that's what Berniece saw.

BOY WILLIE: Well, let her keep on seeing him then. As long as he don't mess with me.

(*Doaker starts to cook his breakfast.*)

I heard about you, Doaker. They say you got all the women looking out for you down home. They be looking to see you coming. Say you got a different one every two weeks. Say they be fighting one another for you to stay with them.

(*To Lymon.*)

Look at him, Lymon. He know it's true.

DOAKER: I ain't thinking about no women. They never get me tied up with them. After Coreen I ain't got no use for them. I stay up on Jack Slattery's place when I be down there. All them women want is somebody with a steady payday.

BOY WILLIE: That ain't what I hear. I hear every two weeks the women all put on their dresses and line up at the railroad station.

DOAKER: I don't get down there but once a month. I used to go down there every two weeks but they keep switching me around. They keep switching all the fellows around.

BOY WILLIE: Doaker can't turn that railroad loose. He was working the railroad when I was walking around crying for sugartit. My mama used to brag on him.

DOAKER: I'm cooking now, but I used to line track. I pieced together the Yellow Dog stitch by stitch. Rail by rail. Line track all up around there. I lined track all up around Sunflower and Clarksdale. Wining Boy

worked with me. He helped put in some of that track. He'd work it for
six months and quit. Go back to playing piano and gambling.

BOY WILLIE: How long you been with the railroad now?

DOAKER: Twenty-seven years. Now, I'll tell you something about the railroad. What I done learned after twenty-seven years. See, you got
North. You got West. You look over here you got South. Over there you
got East. Now, you can start from anywhere. Don't care where you at.
You got to go one of them four ways. And whichever way you decide to
go they got a railroad that will take you there. Now, that's something
simple. You think anybody would be able to understand that. But
you'd be surprised how many people trying to go North get on a train
going West. They think the train's supposed to go where they going
rather than where it's going.

Now, why people going? Their sister's sick. They leaving before they
kill somebody . . . and they sitting across from somebody who's leaving to keep from getting killed. They leaving cause they can't get satisfied. They going to meet someone. I wish I had a dollar for every time
that someone wasn't at the station to meet them. I done seen that a lot.
In between the time they sent the telegram and the time the person get
there . . . they done forgot all about them.

They got so many trains out there they have a hard time keeping
them from running into each other. Got trains going every whichaway.
Got people on all of them. Somebody going where somebody just left.
If everybody stay in one place I believe this would be a better world.
Now what I done learned after twenty-seven years of railroading is
this . . . if the train stays on the track . . . it's going to get where it's
going. It might not be where you going. If it ain't, then all you got to do
is sit and wait cause the train's coming back to get you. The train don't
never stop. It'll come back every time. Now I'll tell you another
thing . . .

BOY WILLIE: What you cooking over there, Doaker? Me and Lymon's
hungry.

DOAKER: Go on down there to Wylie and Kirkpatrick to Eddie's restaurant. Coffee cost a nickel and you can get two eggs, sausage, and grits
for fifteen cents. He even give you a biscuit with it.

BOY WILLIE: That look good what you got. Give me a little piece of that
grilled bread.

DOAKER: Here . . . go on take the whole piece.

BOY WILLIE: Here you go, Lymon . . . you want a piece?

(*He gives Lymon a piece of toast. Maretha enters from the stairs.*)

BOY WILLIE: Hey, sugar. Come here and give me a hug. Come on give
Uncle Boy Willie a hug. Don't be shy. Look at her, Doaker. She done got
bigger. Ain't she got big?

DOAKER: Yeah, she getting up there.

BOY WILLIE: How you doing, sugar?

MARETHA: Fine.

BOY WILLIE: You was just a little old thing last time I seen you. You remember me, don't you? This your Uncle Boy Willie from down South. That there's Lymon. He my friend. We come up here to sell watermelons. You like watermelons?

(*Maretha nods.*)

We got a whole truckload out front. You can have as many as you want. What you been doing?

MARETHA: Nothing.

BOY WILLIE: Don't be shy now. Look at you getting all big. How old is you?

MARETHA: Eleven. I'm gonna be twelve soon.

BOY WILLIE: You like it up here? You like the North?

MARETHA: It's alright.

BOY WILLIE: That there's Lymon. Did you say hi to Lymon?

MARETHA: Hi.

LYMON: How you doing? You look just like your mama. I remember you when you was wearing diapers.

BOY WILLIE: You gonna come down South and see me? Uncle Boy Willie gonna get him a farm. Gonna get a great big old farm. Come down there and I'll teach you how to ride a mule. Teach you how to kill a chicken, too.

MARETHA: I seen my mama do that.

BOY WILLIE: Ain't nothing to it. You just grab him by his neck and twist it. Get you a real good grip and then you just wring his neck and throw him in the pot. Cook him up. Then you got some good eating. What you like to eat? What kind of food you like?

MARETHA: I like everything . . . except I don't like no black-eyed peas.

BOY WILLIE: Uncle Doaker tell me your mama got you playing that piano. Come on play something for me.

(*Boy Willie crosses over to the piano followed by Maretha.*)

Show me what you can do. Come on now. Here . . . Uncle Boy Willie give you a dime . . . show me what you can do. Don't be bashful now. That dime say you can't be bashful.

(*Maretha plays. It is something any beginner first learns.*)

Here, let me show you something.

(*Boy Willie sits and plays a simple boogie-woogie.*)

See that? See what I'm doing? That's what you call the boogie-woogie. See now . . . you can get up and dance to that. That's how good it sound. It sound like you wanna dance. You can dance to that. It'll hold you up. Whatever kind of dance you wanna do you can dance to that right there. See that? See how it go? Ain't nothing to it. Go on you do it.

MARETHA: I got to read it on the paper.

BOY WILLIE: You don't need no paper. Go on. Do just like that there.

BERNIECE: Maretha! You get up here and get ready to go so you be on time. Ain't no need you trying to take advantage of company.

MARETHA: I got to go.

BOY WILLIE: Uncle Boy Willie gonna get you a guitar. Let Uncle Doaker teach you how to play that. You don't need to read no paper to play the guitar. Your mama told you about that piano? You know how them pictures got on there?

MARETHA: She say it just always been like that since she got it.

BOY WILLIE: You hear that, Doaker? And you sitting up here in the house with Berniece.

DOAKER: I ain't got nothing to do with that. I don't get in the way of Berniece's raising her.

BOY WILLIE: You tell your mama to tell you about that piano. You ask her how them pictures got on there. If she don't tell you I'll tell you.

BERNIECE: Maretha!

MARETHA: I got to get ready to go.

BOY WILLIE: She getting big, Doaker. You remember her, Lymon?

LYMON: She used to be real little.

(There is a knock on the door. Doaker goes to answer it. Avery enters. Thirty-eight years old, honest and ambitious, he has taken to the city like a fish to water, finding in it opportunities for growth and advancement that did not exist for him in the rural South. He is dressed in a suit and tie with a gold cross around his neck. He carries a small Bible.)

DOAKER: Hey, Avery, come on in. Berniece upstairs.

BOY WILLIE: Look at him . . . look at him . . . he don't know what to say. He wasn't expecting to see me.

AVERY: Hey, Boy Willie. What you doing up here?

BOY WILLIE: Look at him, Lymon.

AVERY: Is that Lymon? Lymon Jackson?

BOY WILLIE: Yeah, you know Lymon.

DOAKER: Berniece be ready in a minute, Avery.

BOY WILLIE: Doaker say you a preacher now. What . . . we supposed to call you Reverend? You used to be plain old Avery. When you get to be a preacher, nigger?

LYMON: Avery say he gonna be a preacher so he don't have to work.

BOY WILLIE: I remember when you was down there on the Willshaw place planting cotton. You wasn't thinking about no Reverend then.

AVERY: That must be your truck out there. I saw that truck with them watermelons, I was trying to figure out what it was doing in front of the house.

BOY WILLIE: Yeah, me and Lymon selling watermelons. That's Lymon's truck.

DOAKER: Berniece say you all going down to the bank.

AVERY: Yeah, they give me a half day off work. I got an appointment to talk to the bank about getting a loan to start my church.

BOY WILLIE: Lymon say preachers don't have to work. Where you working at, nigger?

DOAKER: Avery got him one of them good jobs. He working at one of them skyscrapers downtown.

AVERY: I'm working down there at the Gulf Building running an elevator. Got a pension and everything. They even give you a turkey on Thanksgiving.

LYMON: How you know the rope ain't gonna break? Ain't you scared the rope's gonna break?

AVERY: That's steel. They got steel cables hold it up. It take a whole lot of breaking to break that steel. Naw, I ain't worried about nothing like that. It ain't nothing but a little old elevator. Now, I wouldn't get in none of them airplanes. You couldn't pay me to do nothing like that.

LYMON: That be fun. I'd rather do that than ride in one of them elevators.

BOY WILLIE: How many of them watermelons you wanna buy?

AVERY: I thought you was gonna give me one seeing as how you got a whole truck full.

BOY WILLIE: You can get one, get two. I'll give you two for a dollar.

AVERY: I can't eat but one. How much are they?

BOY WILLIE: Aw, nigger, you know I'll give you a watermelon. Go on, take as many as you want. Just leave some for me and Lymon to sell.

AVERY: I don't want but one.

BOY WILLIE: How you get to be a preacher, Avery? I might want to be a preacher one day. Have everybody call me Reverend Boy Willie.

AVERY: It come to me in a dream. God called me and told me he wanted me to be a shepherd for his flock. That's what I'm gonna call my church . . . The Good Shepherd Church of God in Christ.

DOAKER: Tell him what you told me. Tell him about the three hobos.

AVERY: Boy Willie don't want to hear all that.

LYMON: I do. Lots a people say your dreams can come true.

AVERY: Naw. You don't want to hear all that.

DOAKER: Go on. I told him you was a preacher. He didn't want to believe me. Tell him about the three hobos.

AVERY: Well, it come to me in a dream. See . . . I was sitting out in this railroad yard watching the trains go by. The train stopped and these three hobos got off. They told me they had come from Nazareth and was on their way to Jerusalem. They had three candles. They gave me one and told me to light it . . . but to be careful that it didn't go out. Next thing I knew I was standing in front of this house. Something told me to go knock on the door. This old woman opened the door and said they had been waiting on me. Then she led me into this room. It was a big room and it was full of all kinds of different people. They looked like anybody else except they all had sheep heads and was making noise like sheep make. I heard somebody call my name. I looked around and there was these same three hobos. They told me to take off my clothes and they give me a blue robe with gold thread. They washed my feet and combed my hair. Then they showed me these three doors and told me to pick one.

I went through one of them doors and that flame leapt off that candle and it seemed like my whole head caught fire. I looked around and there was four or five other men standing there with these same blue robes on. Then we heard a voice tell us to look out across this valley. We looked out and saw the valley was full of wolves. The voice told us that these sheep people that I had seen in the other room had to go over to the other side of this valley and somebody had to take them. Then I heard another voice say, "Who shall I send?" Next thing I knew I said, "Here I am. Send me." That's when I met Jesus. He say, "If you go, I'll go with you." Something told me to say, "Come on. Let's go." That's when I woke up. My head still felt like it was on fire . . . but I had a peace about myself that was hard to explain. I knew right then that I had been filled with the Holy Ghost and called to be a servant of the Lord. It took me a while before I could accept that. But then a lot of little ways God showed me that it was true. So I became a preacher.

LYMON: I see why you gonna call it the Good Shepherd Church. You dreaming about them sheep people. I can see that easy.

BOY WILLIE: Doaker say you sent some white man past the house to look at that piano. Say he was going around to all the colored people's houses looking to buy up musical instruments.

AVERY: Yeah, but Berniece didn't want to sell that piano. After she told me about it . . . I could see why she didn't want to sell it.

BOY WILLIE: What's this man's name?

AVERY: Oh, that's a while back now. I done forgot his name. He give Berniece a card with his name and telephone number on it, but I believe she throwed it away.

(*Berniece and Maretha enter from the stairs.*)

BERNIECE: Maretha, run back upstairs and get my pocketbook. And wipe that hair grease off your forehead. Go ahead, hurry up.

(*Maretha exits up the stairs.*)

How you doing, Avery? You done got all dressed up. You look nice. Boy
Willie, I thought you and Lymon was going to sell them watermelons.

BOY WILLIE: Lymon done got sleepy. We liable to get some sleep first.

LYMON: I ain't sleepy.

DOAKER: As many watermelons as you got stacked up on that truck out
there, you ought to have been gone.

BOY WILLIE: We gonna go in a minute. We going.

BERNIECE: Doaker. I'm gonna stop down there on Logan Street. You
want anything?

DOAKER: You can pick up some ham hocks if you going down there. See
if you can get the smoked ones. If they ain't got that get the fresh ones.
Don't get the ones that got all that fat under the skin. Look for the long
ones. They nice and lean.

(*He gives her a dollar.*)

Don't get the short ones lessen they smoked. If you got to get the fresh
ones make sure that they the long ones. If they ain't got them smoked
then go ahead and get the short ones.

(*Pause.*)

You may as well get some turnip greens while you down there. I got
some buttermilk . . . if you pick up some cornmeal I'll make me some
cornbread and cook up them turnip greens.

(*Maretha enters from the stairs.*)

MARETHA: We gonna take the streetcar?

BERNIECE: Me and Avery gonna drop you off at the settlement house.
You mind them people down there. Don't be going down there show-
ing your color. Boy Willie, I done told you what to do. I'll see you later,
Doaker.

AVERY: I'll be seeing you again, Boy Willie.

BOY WILLIE: Hey, Berniece . . . what's the name of that man Avery sent
past say he want to buy the piano?

BERNIECE: I knew it. I knew it when I first seen you. I knew you was up
to something.

BOY WILLIE: Sutter's brother say he selling the land to me. He waiting on
me now. Told me he'd give me two weeks. I got one part. Sell them
watermelons get me another part. Then we can sell that piano and I'll
have the third part.

BERNIECE: I ain't selling that piano, Boy Willie. If that's why you come
up here you can just forget about it.

(*To Doaker.*)

Doaker, I'll see you later. Boy Willie ain't nothing but a whole lot of mouth. I ain't paying him no mind. If he come up here thinking he gonna sell that piano then he done come up here for nothing.

(*Berniece, Avery, and Maretha exit the front door.*)

BOY WILLIE: Hey, Lymon! You ready to go sell these watermelons.

(*Boy Willie and Lymon start to exit. At the door Boy Willie turns to Doaker.*)

Hey, Doaker . . . if Berniece don't want to sell that piano . . . I'm gonna cut it in half and go on and sell my half.

(*Boy Willie and Lymon exit.*)

(*The lights go down on the scene.*)

Scene 2

(*The lights come up on the kitchen. It is three days later. Wining Boy sits at the kitchen table. There is a half-empty pint bottle on the table. Doaker busies himself washing pots. Wining Boy is fifty-six years old. Doaker's older brother, he tries to present the image of a successful musician and gambler, but his music, his clothes, and even his manner of presentation are old. He is a man who looking back over his life continues to live it with an odd mixture of zest and sorrow.*)

WINING BOY: So the Ghosts of the Yellow Dog got Sutter. That just go to show you I believe I always lived right. They say every dog gonna have his day and time it go around it sure come back to you. I done seen that a thousand times. I know the truth of that. But I'll tell you outright . . . if I see Sutter's ghost I'll be on the first thing I find that got wheels on it.

(*Doaker enters from his room.*)

DOAKER: Wining Boy!

WINING BOY: And I'll tell you another thing . . . Berniece ain't gonna sell that piano.

DOAKER: That's what she told him. He say he gonna cut it in half and go on and sell his half. They been around here three days trying to sell them watermelons. They trying to get out to where the white folks live but the truck keep breaking down. They go a block or two and it break down again. They trying to get out to Squirrel Hill and can't get around the corner. He say soon as he can get that truck empty to where he can set the piano up in there he gonna take it out of here and go sell it.

WINING BOY: What about them boys Sutter got? How come they ain't farming that land?

DOAKER: One of them going to school. He left down there and come North to school. The other one ain't got as much sense as that frying pan over yonder. That is the dumbest white man I ever seen. He'd stand in the river and watch it rise till it drown him.

WINING BOY: Other than seeing Sutter's ghost how's Berniece doing?

DOAKER: She doing alright. She still got Crawley on her mind. He been dead three years but she still holding on to him. She need to go out here and let one of these fellows grab a whole handful of whatever she got. She act like it done got precious.

WINING BOY: They always told me any fish will bite if you got good bait.

DOAKER: She stuck up on it. She think it's better than she is. I believe she messing around with Avery. They got something going. He a preacher now. If you let him tell it the Holy Ghost sat on his head and heaven opened up with thunder and lightning and God was calling his name. Told him to go out and preach and tend to his flock. That's what he gonna call his church. The Good Shepherd Church.

WINING BOY: They had that joker down in Spear walking around talking about he Jesus Christ. He gonna live the life of Christ. Went through the Last Supper and everything. Rented him a mule on Palm Sunday and rode through the town. Did everything . . . talking about he Christ. He did everything until they got up to that crucifixion part. Got up to that part and told everybody to go home and quit pretending. He got up to the crucifixion part and changed his mind. Had a whole bunch of folks come down there to see him get nailed to the cross. I don't know who's the worse fool. Him or them. Had all them folks come down there . . . even carried the cross up this little hill. People standing around waiting to see him get nailed to the cross and he stop everything and preach a little sermon and told everybody to go home. Had enough nerve to tell them to come to church on Easter Sunday to celebrate his resurrection.

DOAKER: I'm surprised Avery ain't thought about that. He trying every little thing to get him a congregation together. They meeting over at his house till he get him a church.

WINING BOY: Ain't nothing wrong with being a preacher. You got the preacher on one hand and the gambler on the other. Sometimes there ain't too much difference in them.

DOAKER: How long you been in Kansas City?

WINING BOY: Since I left here. I got tied up with some old gal down there.

(Pause.)

You know Cleotha died.

DOAKER: Yeah, I heard that last time I was down there. I was sorry to hear that.

WINING BOY: One of her friends wrote and told me. I got the letter right here.

(*He takes the letter out of his pocket.*)

I was down in Kansas City and she wrote and told me Cleotha had died. Name of Willa Bryant. She say she know cousin Rupert.

(*He opens the letter and reads.*)

Dear Wining Boy: I am writing this letter to let you know Miss Cleotha Holman passed on Saturday the first of May she departed this world in the loving arms of her sister Miss Alberta Samuels. I know you would want to know this and am writing as a friend of Cleotha. There have been many hardships since last you seen her but she survived them all and to the end was a good woman whom I hope have God's grace and is in His Paradise. Your cousin Rupert Bates is my friend also and he give me your address and I pray this reaches you about Cleotha. Miss Willa Bryant. A friend.

(*He folds the letter and returns it to his pocket.*)

They was nailing her coffin shut by the time I heard about it. I never knew she was sick. I believe it was that yellow jaundice. That's what killed her mama.

DOAKER: Cleotha wasn't but forty-some.

WINING BOY: She was forty-six. I got ten years on her. I met her when she was sixteen. You remember I used to run around there. Couldn't nothing keep me still. Much as I loved Cleotha I loved to ramble. Couldn't nothing keep me still. We got married and we used to fight about it all the time. Then one day she asked me to leave. Told me she loved me before I left. Told me, Wining Boy, you got a home as long as I got mine. And I believe in my heart I always felt that and that kept me safe.

DOAKER: Cleotha always did have a nice way about her.

WINING BOY: Man that woman was something. I used to thank the Lord. Many a night I sat up and looked out over my life. Said, well, I had Cleotha. When it didn't look like there was nothing else for me, I said, thank God, at least I had that. If ever I go anywhere in this life I done known a good woman. And that used to hold me till the next morning.

(*Pause.*)

What you got? Give me a little nip. I know you got something stuck up in your room.

DOAKER: I ain't seen you walk in here and put nothing on the table. You done sat there and drank up your whiskey. Now you talking about what you got.

WINING BOY: I got plenty money. Give me a little nip.

(*Doaker carries a glass into his room and returns with it half-filled. He sets it on the table in front of Wining Boy.*)

WINING BOY: You hear from Coreen?

DOAKER: She up in New York. I let her go from my mind.

WINING BOY: She was something back then. She wasn't too pretty but she had a way of looking at you made you know there was a whole lot of woman there. You got married and snatched her out from under us and we all got mad at you.

DOAKER: She up in New York City. That's what I hear.

(*The door opens and Boy Willie and Lymon enter.*)

BOY WILLIE: Aw hell . . . look here! We was just talking about you. Doaker say you left out of here with a whole sack of money. I told him we wasn't going see you till you got broke.

WINING BOY: What you mean broke? I got a whole pocketful of money.

DOAKER: Did you all get that truck fixed?

BOY WILLIE: We got it running and got halfway out there on Centre and it broke down again. Lymon went out there and messed it up some more. Fellow told us we got to wait till tomorrow to get it fixed. Say he have it running like new. Lymon going back down there and sleep in the truck so the people don't take the watermelons.

LYMON: Lymon nothing. You go down there and sleep in it.

BOY WILLIE: You was sleeping in it down home, nigger! I don't know nothing about sleeping in no truck.

LYMON: I ain't sleeping in no truck.

BOY WILLIE: They can take all the watermelons. I don't care. Wining Boy, where you coming from? Where you been?

WINING BOY: I been down in Kansas City.

BOY WILLIE: You remember Lymon? Lymon Jackson.

WINING BOY: Yeah, I used to know his daddy.

BOY WILLIE: Doaker say you don't never leave no address with nobody. Say he got to depend on your whim. See when it strike you to pay a visit.

WINING BOY: I got four or five addresses.

BOY WILLIE: Doaker say Berniece asked you for three dollars and you got mad and left.

WINING BOY: Berniece try and rule over you too much for me. That's why I left. It wasn't about no three dollars.

BOY WILLIE: Where you getting all these sacks of money from? I need to be with you. Doaker say you had a whole sack of money . . . turn some of it loose.

WINING BOY: I was just fixing to ask you for five dollars.

BOY WILLIE: I ain't got no money. I'm trying to get some. Doaker tell you about Sutter? The Ghosts of the Yellow Dog got him about three weeks ago. Berniece done seen his ghost and everything. He right upstairs.

(*Calls.*)

Hey Sutter! Wining Boy's here. Come on, get a drink!

WINING BOY: How many that make the Ghosts of the Yellow Dog done got?

BOY WILLIE: Must be about nine or ten, eleven or twelve. I don't know.

DOAKER: You got Ed Saunders. Howard Peterson. Charlie Webb.

WINING BOY: Robert Smith. That fellow that shot Becky's boy . . . say he was stealing peaches . . .

DOAKER: You talking about Bob Mallory.

BOY WILLIE: Berniece say she don't believe all that about the Ghosts of the Yellow Dog.

WINING BOY: She ain't got to believe. You go ask them white folks in Sunflower County if they believe. You go ask Sutter if he believe. I don't care if Berniece believe or not. I done been to where the Southern cross the Yellow Dog and called out their names. They talk back to you, too.

LYMON: What they sound like? The wind or something?

BOY WILLIE: You done been there for real, Wining Boy?

WINING BOY: Nineteen thirty. July of nineteen thirty I stood right there on that spot. It didn't look like nothing was going right in my life. I said everything can't go wrong all the time . . . let me go down there and call on the Ghosts of the Yellow Dog, see if they can help me. I went down there and right there where them two railroads cross each other . . . I stood right there on that spot and called out their names. They talk back to you, too.

LYMON: People say you can ask them questions. They talk to you like that?

WINING BOY: A lot of things you got to find out on your own. I can't say how they talked to nobody else. But to me it just filled me up in a strange sort of way to be standing there on that spot. I didn't want to leave. It felt like the longer I stood there the bigger I got. I seen the train coming and it seem like I was bigger than the train. I started not to move. But something told me to go ahead and get on out the way. The train passed and I started to go back up there and stand some more. But something told me not to do it. I walked away from there feeling like a king. Went on and had a stroke of luck that run on for three years. So I don't care if Berniece believe or not. Berniece ain't got to believe. I know cause I been there. Now Doaker'll tell you about the Ghosts of the Yellow Dog.

DOAKER: I don't try and talk that stuff with Berniece. Avery got her all tied up in that church. She just think it's a whole lot of nonsense.

BOY WILLIE: Berniece don't believe in nothing. She just think she believe. She believe in anything if it's convenient for her to believe. But when that convenience run out then she ain't got nothing to stand on.

WINING BOY: Let's not get on Berniece now. Doaker tell me you talking about selling that piano.

BOY WILLIE: Yeah . . . hey, Doaker, I got the name of that man Avery was talking about. The man what's fixing the truck gave me his name. Everybody know him. Say he buy up anything you can make music with. I got his name and his telephone number. Hey, Wining Boy, Sutter's brother say he selling the land to me. I got one part. Sell them watermelons get me the second part. Then . . . soon as I get them watermelons out that truck I'm gonna take and sell that piano and get the third part.

DOAKER: That land ain't worth nothing no more. The smart white man's up here in these cities. He cut the land loose and step back and watch you and the dumb white man argue over it.

WINING BOY: How you know Sutter's brother ain't sold it already? You talking about selling the piano and the man's liable to sold the land two or three times.

BOY WILLIE: He say he waiting on me. He say he give me two weeks. That's two weeks from Friday. Say if I ain't back by then he might gonna sell it to somebody else. He say he wanna see me with it.

WINING BOY: You know as well as I know the man gonna sell the land to the first one walk up and hand him the money.

BOY WILLIE: That's just who I'm gonna be. Look, you ain't gotta know he waiting on me. I know. Okay. I know what the man told me. Stovall already done tried to buy the land from him and he told him no. The man say he waiting on me . . . he waiting on me. Hey, Doaker . . . give me a drink. I see Wining Boy got his glass.

(*Doaker exits into his room.*)

Wining Boy, what you doing in Kansas City? What they got down there?

LYMON: I hear they got some nice-looking women in Kansas City. I sure like to go down there and find out.

WINING BOY: Man, the women down there is something else.

(*Doaker enters with a bottle of whiskey. He sets it on the table with some glasses.*)

DOAKER: You wanna sit up here and drink up my whiskey, leave a dollar on the table when you get up.

BOY WILLIE: You ain't doing nothing but showing your hospitality. I know we ain't got to pay for your hospitality.

WINING BOY: Doaker say they had you and Lymon down on the Parchman Farm. Had you on my old stomping grounds.

BOY WILLIE: Me and Lymon was down there hauling wood for Jim Miller and keeping us a little bit to sell. Some white fellows tried to run us off of it. That's when Crawley got killed. They put me and Lymon in the penitentiary.

LYMON: They ambushed us right there where that road dip down and around that bend in the creek. Crawley tried to fight them. Me and Boy Willie got away but the sheriff got us. Say we was stealing wood. They shot me in my stomach.

BOY WILLIE: They looking for Lymon down there now. They rounded him up and put him in jail for not working.

LYMON: Fined me a hundred dollars. Mr. Stovall come and paid my hundred dollars and the judge say I got to work for him to pay him back his hundred dollars. I told them I'd rather take my thirty days but they wouldn't let me do that.

BOY WILLIE: As soon as Stovall turned his back, Lymon was gone. He down there living in that truck dodging the sheriff and Stovall. He got both of them looking for him. So I brought him up here.

LYMON: I told Boy Willie I'm gonna stay up here. I ain't going back with him.

BOY WILLIE: Ain't nobody twisting your arm to make you go back. You can do what you want to do.

WINING BOY: I'll go back with you. I'm on my way down there. You gonna take the train? I'm gonna take the train.

LYMON: They treat you better up here.

BOY WILLIE: I ain't worried about nobody mistreating me. They treat you like you let them treat you. They mistreat me I mistreat them right back. Ain't no difference in me and the white man.

WINING BOY: Ain't no difference as far as how somebody supposed to treat you. I agree with that. But I'll tell you the difference between the colored man and the white man. Alright. Now you take and eat some berries. They taste real good to you. So you say I'm gonna go out and get me a whole pot of these berries and cook them up to make a pie or whatever. But you ain't looked to see them berries is sitting in the white fellow's yard. Ain't got no fence around them. You figure anybody want something they'd fence it in. Alright. Now the white man come along and say that's my land. Therefore everything that grow on it belong to me. He tell the sheriff, "I want you to put this nigger in jail as a warning to all the other niggers. Otherwise first thing you know these niggers have everything that belong to us."

BOY WILLIE: I'd come back at night and haul off his whole patch while he was sleep.

WINING BOY: Alright. Now Mr. So and So, he sell the land to you. And he come to you and say, "John, you own the land. It's all yours now. But them is my berries. And come time to pick them I'm gonna send my boys over. You got the land . . . but them berries, I'm gonna keep them. They mine." And he go and fix it with the law that them is his berries. Now that's the difference between the colored man and the white man. The colored man can't fix nothing with the law.

BOY WILLIE: I don't go by what the law say. The law's liable to say anything. I go by if it's right or not. It don't matter to me what the law say. I take and look at it for myself.

LYMON: That's why you gonna end up back down there on the Parchman Farm.

BOY WILLIE: I ain't thinking about no Parchman Farm. You liable to go back before me.

LYMON: They work you too hard down there. All that weeding and hoeing and chopping down trees. I didn't like all that.

WINING BOY: You ain't got to like your job on Parchman. Hey, tell him, Doaker, the only one got to like his job is the waterboy.

DOAKER: If he don't like his job he need to set that bucket down.

BOY WILLIE: That's what they told Lymon. They had Lymon on water and everybody got mad at him cause he was lazy.

LYMON: That water was heavy.

BOY WILLIE: They had Lymon down there singing:

(*Sings.*)

O Lord Berta Berta O Lord gal oh-ah
O Lord Berta Berta O Lord gal well

(*Lymon and Wining Boy join in.*)

Go 'head marry don't you wait on me oh-ah
Go 'head marry don't you wait on me well
Might not want you when I go free oh-ah
Might not want you when I go free well

BOY WILLIE: Come on, Doaker. Doaker know this one.

(*As Doaker joins in the men stamp and clap to keep time. They sing in harmony with great fervor and style.*)

O Lord Berta Berta O Lord gal oh-ah
O Lord Berta Berta O Lord gal well

Raise them up higher, let them drop on down oh-ah
Raise them up higher, let them drop on down well
Don't know the difference when the sun go down oh-ah
Don't know the difference when the sun go down well

Berta in Meridan and she living at ease oh-ah
Berta in Meridan and she living at ease well
I'm on old Parchman, got to work or leave oh-ah
I'm on old Parchman, got to work or leave well

O Alberta, Berta, O Lord gal oh-ah
O Alberta, Berta, O Lord gal well

When you marry, don't marry no farming man oh-ah
When you marry, don't marry no farming man well
Everyday Monday, hoe handle in your hand oh-ah
Everyday Monday, hoe handle in your hand well

When you marry, marry a railroad man, oh-ah
When you marry, marry a railroad man, well
Everyday Sunday, dollar in your hand oh-ah
Everyday Sunday, dollar in your hand well

O Alberta, Berta, O Lord gal oh-ah
O Alberta, Berta, O Lord gal well

BOY WILLIE: Doaker like that part. He like that railroad part.

LYMON: Doaker sound like Tangleye. He can't sing a lick.

BOY WILLIE: Hey, Doaker, they still talk about you down on Parchman. They ask me, "You Doaker Boy's nephew?" I say, "Yeah, me and him is family." They treated me alright soon as I told them that. Say, "Yeah, he my uncle."

DOAKER: I don't never want to see none of them niggers no more.

BOY WILLIE: I don't want to see them either. Hey, Wining Boy, come on play some piano. You a piano player, play some piano. Lymon wanna hear you.

WINING BOY: I give that piano up. That was the best thing that ever happened to me, getting rid of that piano. That piano got so big and I'm carrying it around on my back. I don't wish that on nobody. See, you think it's all fun being a recording star. Got to carrying that piano around and man did I get slow. Got just like molasses. The world just slipping by me and I'm walking around with that piano. Alright. Now, there ain't but so many places you can go. Only so many road wide enough for you and that piano. And that piano get heavier and heavier. Go to a place and they find out you play piano, the first thing they want to do is give you a drink, find you a piano, and sit you right down. And that's where you gonna be for the next eight hours. They ain't gonna let you get up! Now, the first three or four years of that is fun. You can't get enough whiskey and you can't get enough women and you don't never get tired of playing that piano. But that only last so long. You look up one day and you hate the whiskey, and you hate the women, and you hate the piano. But that's all you got. You can't do nothing else. All you know how to do is play that piano. Now, who am I? Am I me? Or am I the piano player? Sometime it seem like the only thing to do is shoot the piano player cause he the cause of all the trouble I'm having.

DOAKER: What you gonna do when your troubles get like mine?

LYMON: If I knew how to play it, I'd play it. That's a nice piano.

BOY WILLIE: Whoever playing better play quick. Sutter's brother say he waiting on me. I sell them watermelons. Get Berniece to sell that piano. Put them two parts with the part I done saved . . .

WINING BOY: Berniece ain't gonna sell that piano. I don't see why you don't know that.

BOY WILLIE: What she gonna do with it? She ain't doing nothing but letting it sit up there and rot. That piano ain't doing nobody no good.

LYMON: That's a nice piano. If I had it I'd sell it. Unless I knew how to play like Wining Boy. You can get a nice price for that piano.

DOAKER: Now I'm gonna tell you something, Lymon don't know this . . . but I'm gonna tell you why me and Wining Boy say Berniece ain't gonna sell that piano.

BOY WILLIE: She ain't got to sell it! I'm gonna sell it! Berniece ain't got no more rights to that piano than I do.

DOAKER: I'm talking to the man . . . let me talk to the man. See, now . . . to understand why we say that . . . to understand about that piano . . . you got to go back to slavery time. See, our family was owned by a fellow named Robert Sutter. That was Sutter's grandfather. Alright. The piano was owned by a fellow named Joel Nolander. He was one of the Nolander brothers from down in Georgia. It was coming up on Sutter's wedding anniversary and he was looking to buy his wife . . . Miss Ophelia was her name . . . he was looking to buy her an anniversary present. Only thing with him . . . he ain't had no money. But he had some niggers. So he asked Mr. Nolander to see if maybe he could trade off some of his niggers for that piano. Told him he would give him one and a half niggers for it. That's the way he told him. Say he could have one full grown and one half grown. Mr. Nolander agreed only he say he had to pick them. He didn't want Sutter to give him just any old nigger. He say he wanted to have the pick of the litter. So Sutter lined up his niggers and Mr. Nolander looked them over and out of the whole bunch he picked my grandmother . . . her name was

Berniece . . . same like Berniece . . . and he picked my daddy when he wasn't nothing but a little boy nine years old. They made the trade-off and Miss Ophelia was so happy with that piano that it got to be just about all she would do was play on that piano.

WINING BOY: Just get up in the morning, get all dressed up and sit down and play on that piano.

DOAKER: Alright. Time go along. Time go along. Miss Ophelia got to missing my grandmother . . . the way she would cook and clean the house and talk to her and what not. And she missed having my daddy around the house to fetch things for her. So she asked to see if maybe she could trade back that piano and get her niggers back. Mr. Nolander said no. Said a deal was a deal. Him and Sutter had a big falling out about it and Miss Ophelia took sick to the bed. Wouldn't get out of the bed in the morning. She just lay there. The doctor said she was wasting away.

WINING BOY: That's when Sutter called our granddaddy up to the house.

DOAKER: Now, our granddaddy's name was Boy Willie. That's who Boy Willie's named after . . . only they called him Willie Boy. Now, he was a worker of wood. He could make you anything you wanted out of wood. He'd make you a desk. A table. A lamp. Anything you wanted. Them white fellows around there used to come up to Mr. Sutter and get him to make all kinds of things for them. Then they'd pay Mr. Sutter a nice price. See, everything my granddaddy made Mr. Sutter owned cause he owned him. That's why when Mr. Nolander offered to buy him to keep the family together Mr. Sutter wouldn't sell him. Told Mr. Nolander he didn't have enough money to buy him. Now . . . am I telling it right, Wining Boy?

WINING BOY: You telling it.

DOAKER: Sutter called him up to the house and told him to carve my grandmother and my daddy's picture on the piano for Miss Ophelia. And he took and carved this . . .

(*Doaker crosses over to the piano.*)

See that right there? That's my grandmother, Berniece. She looked just like that. And he put a picture of my daddy when he wasn't nothing but a little boy the way he remembered him. He made them up out of his memory. Only thing . . . he didn't stop there. He carved all this. He got a picture of his mama . . . Mama Esther . . . and his daddy, Boy Charles.

WINING BOY: That was the first Boy Charles.

DOAKER: Then he put on the side here all kinds of things. See that? That's when him and Mama Berniece got married. They called it jumping the broom. That's how you got married in them days. Then he got here when my daddy was born . . . and here he got Mama Esther's funeral . . . and down here he got Mr. Nolander taking Mama Berniece and my daddy away down to his place in Georgia. He got all kinds of things what happened with our family. When Mr. Sutter seen the piano with all them carvings on it he got mad. He didn't ask for all that. But see . . . there wasn't nothing he could do about it. When Miss Ophelia seen it . . . she got excited. Now she had her piano and her niggers too. She took back to playing it and played on it right up till the day she died. Alright . . . now see, our brother Boy Charles . . . that's Berniece and Boy Willie's daddy . . . he was the oldest of us three boys. He's dead now. But he would have been fifty-seven if he had lived. He died in 1911 when he was thirty-one years old. Boy Charles used to talk about that piano all the time. He never could get it off his mind. Two or three months go by and he be talking about it again. He be talking about taking it out of Sutter's house. Say it was the story of our whole family and as long as Sutter had it . . . he had us. Say we was still in slavery. Me and Wining Boy tried to talk him out of it but it wouldn't do any good. Soon as he quiet down about it he'd start up again. We seen where he wasn't gonna get it off his mind . . . so, on the Fourth of July, 1911 . . . when Sutter was at the picnic what the county give every year . . . me and Wining Boy went on down there with him and took that piano out of Sutter's house. We put it on a wagon and me and Wining Boy carried it over into the next county with Mama Ola's people. Boy Charles decided to stay around there and wait until Sutter got home to make it look like business as usual.

Now, I don't know what happened when Sutter came home and found that piano gone. But somebody went up to Boy Charles's house and set it on fire. But he wasn't in there. He must have seen them coming cause he went down and caught the 3:57 Yellow Dog. He didn't know they was gonna come down and stop the train. Stopped the train and found Boy Charles in the boxcar with four of them hobos. Must have got mad when they couldn't find the piano cause they set the boxcar afire and killed everybody. Now, nobody know who done that. Some people say it was Sutter cause it was his piano. Some people say it was Sheriff Carter. Some people say it was Robert Smith and Ed Saunders. But don't nobody know for sure. It was about two months after that that Ed Saunders fell down his well. Just upped and fell down his well for no reason. People say it was the ghost of them men who burned up in the boxcar that pushed him in his well. They started calling them the Ghosts of the Yellow Dog. Now, that's how all that got started and that why we say Berniece ain't gonna sell that piano. Cause her daddy died over it.

BOY WILLIE: All that's in the past. If my daddy had seen where he could have traded that piano in for some land of his own, it wouldn't be sitting up here now. He spent his whole life farming on somebody else's land. I ain't gonna do that. See, he couldn't do no better. When he come along he ain't had nothing he could build on. His daddy ain't had nothing to give him. The only thing my daddy had to give me was that piano. And he died over giving me that. I ain't gonna let it sit up there and rot without trying to do something with it. If Berniece can't see that, then I'm gonna go ahead and sell my half. And you and Wining Boy know I'm right.

DOAKER: Ain't nobody said nothing about who's right and who's wrong. I was just telling the man about the piano. I was telling him why we say Berniece ain't gonna sell it.

LYMON: Yeah, I can see why you say that now. I told Boy Willie he ought to stay up here with me.

BOY WILLIE: You stay! I'm going back! That's what I'm gonna do with my life! Why I got to come up here and learn to do something I don't know how to do when I already know how to farm? You stay up here and make your own way if that's what you want to do. I'm going back and live my life the way I want to live it.

(*Wining Boy gets up and crosses to the piano.*)

WINING BOY: Let's see what we got here. I ain't played on this thing for a while.

DOAKER: You can stop telling that. You was playing on it the last time you was through here. We couldn't get you off of it. Go on and play something.

(*Wining Boy sits down at the piano and plays and sings. The song is one which has put many dimes and quarters in his pocket, long ago, in dimly remembered towns and way stations. He plays badly, without hesitation, and sings in a forceful voice.*)

WINING BOY: (*Singing.*)
I am a rambling gambling man
I gambled in many towns
I rambled this wide world over
I rambled this world around
I had my ups and downs in life
And bitter times I saw
But I never knew what misery was
Till I lit on old Arkansas.

I started out one morning
to meet that early train

He said, "You better work for me
I have some land to drain.
I'll give you fifty cents a day,
Your washing, board and all
And you shall be a different man
In the state of Arkansas."

I worked six months for the rascal
Joe Herrin was his name
He fed me old corn dodgers
They was hard as any rock
My tooth is all got loosened
And my knees begin to knock
That was the kind of hash I got
In the state of Arkansas.

Traveling man
I've traveled all around this world
Traveling man
I've traveled from land to land
Traveling man
I've traveled all around this world
Well it ain't no use
writing no news
I'm a traveling man.

(*The door opens and Berniece enters with Maretha.*)

BERNIECE: Is that . . . Lord, I know that ain't Wining Boy sitting there.
WINING BOY: Hey, Berniece.
BERNIECE: You all had this planned. You and Boy Willie had this planned.
WINING BOY: I didn't know he was gonna be here. I'm on my way down home. I stopped by to see you and Doaker first.
DOAKER: I told the nigger he left out of here with that sack of money, we thought we might never see him again. Boy Willie say he wasn't gonna see him till he got broke. I looked up and seen him sitting on the doorstep asking for two dollars. Look at him laughing. He know it's the truth.
BERNIECE: Boy Willie, I didn't see that truck out there. I thought you was out selling watermelons.
BOY WILLIE: We done sold them all. Sold the truck too.
BERNIECE: I don't want to go through none of your stuff. I done told you to go back where you belong.
BOY WILLIE: I was just teasing you, woman. You can't take no teasing?
BERNIECE: Wining Boy, when you get here?
WINING BOY: A little while ago. I took the train from Kansas City.

BERNIECE: Let me go upstairs and change and then I'll cook you something to eat.

BOY WILLIE: You ain't cooked me nothing when I come.

BERNIECE: Boy Willie, go on and leave me alone. Come on, Maretha, get up here and change your clothes before you get them dirty.

(*Berniece exits up the stairs, followed by Maretha.*)

WINING BOY: Maretha sure getting big, ain't she, Doaker. And just as pretty as she want to be. I didn't know Crawley had it in him.

(*Boy Willie crosses to the piano.*)

BOY WILLIE: Hey, Lymon . . . get up on the other side of this piano and let me see something.

WINING BOY: Boy Willie, what is you doing?

BOY WILLIE: I'm seeing how heavy this piano is. Get up over there, Lymon.

WINING BOY: Go on and leave that piano alone. You ain't taking that piano out of here and selling it.

BOY WILLIE: Just as soon as I get them watermelons out that truck.

WINING BOY: Well, I got something to say about that.

BOY WILLIE: This my daddy's piano.

WINING BOY: He ain't took it by himself. Me and Doaker helped him.

BOY WILLIE: He died by himself. Where was you and Doaker at then? Don't come telling me nothing about this piano. This is me and Berniece's piano. Am I right, Doaker?

DOAKER: Yeah, you right.

BOY WILLIE: Let's see if we can lift it up, Lymon. Get a good grip on it and pick it up on your end. Ready? Lift!

(*As they start to move the piano, the sound of Sutter's Ghost is heard. Doaker is the only one to hear it. With difficulty they move the piano a little bit so it is out of place.*)

BOY WILLIE: What you think?

LYMON: It's heavy . . . but you can move it. Only it ain't gonna be easy.

BOY WILLIE: It wasn't that heavy to me. Okay, let's put it back.

(*The sound of Sutter's Ghost is heard again. They all hear it as Berniece enters on the stairs.*)

BERNIECE: Boy Willie . . . you gonna play around with me one too many times. And then God's gonna bless you and West is gonna dress you. Now set that piano back over there. I done told you a hundred times I ain't selling that piano.

BOY WILLIE: I'm trying to get me some land, woman. I need that piano to get me some money so I can buy Sutter's land.

BERNIECE: Money can't buy what that piano cost. You can't sell your soul for money. It won't go with the buyer. It'll shrivel and shrink to know that you ain't taken on to it. But it won't go with the buyer.

BOY WILLIE: I ain't talking about all that, woman. I ain't talking about selling my soul. I'm talking about trading that piece of wood for some land. Get something under your feet. Land the only thing God ain't making no more of. You can always get you another piano. I'm talking about some land. What you get something out the ground from. That's what I'm talking about. You can't do nothing with that piano but sit up there and look at it.

BERNIECE: That's just what I'm gonna do. Wining Boy, you want me to fry you some pork chops?

BOY WILLIE: Now, I'm gonna tell you the way I see it. The only thing that make that piano worth something is them carvings Papa Willie Boy put on there. That's what make it worth something. That was my great-grandaddy. Papa Boy Charles brought that piano into the house. Now, I'm supposed to build on what they left me. You can't do nothing with that piano sitting up here in the house. That's just like if I let them watermelons sit out there and rot. I'd be a fool. Alright now, if you say to me, Boy Willie, I'm using that piano. I give out lessons on it and that help me make my rent or whatever. Then that be something else. I'd have to go on and say, well, Berniece using that piano. She building on it. Let her go on and use it. I got to find another way to get Sutter's land. But Doaker say you ain't touched that piano the whole time it's been up here. So why you wanna stand in my way? See, you just looking at the sentimental value. See, that's good. That's alright. I take my hat off whenever somebody say my daddy's name. But I ain't gonna be no fool about no sentimental value. You can sit up here and look at the piano for the next hundred years and it's just gonna be a piano. You can't make more than that. Now I want to get Sutter's land with that piano. I get Sutter's land and I can go down and cash in the crop and get my seed. As long as I got the land and the seed then I'm alright. I can always get me a little something else. Cause that land give back to you. I can make me another crop and cash that in. I still got the land and the seed. But that piano don't put out nothing else. You ain't got nothing working for you. Now, the kind of man my daddy was he would have understood that. I'm sorry you can't see it that way. But that's why I'm gonna take that piano out of here and sell it.

BERNIECE: You ain't taking that piano out of my house.

(*She crosses to the piano.*)

Look at this piano. Look at it. Mama Ola polished this piano with her tears for seventeen years. For seventeen years she rubbed on it till her hands bled. Then she rubbed the blood in . . . mixed it up with the rest of the blood on it. Every day that God breathed life into her body she rubbed and cleaned and polished and prayed over it. "Play something for me, Berniece. Play something for me, Berniece." Every day. "I cleaned it up for you, play something for me, Berniece." You always talking about your daddy but you ain't never stopped to look at what his foolishness cost your mama. Seventeen years' worth of cold nights and an empty bed. For what? For a piano? For a piece of wood? To get even with somebody? I look at you and you're all the same. You, Papa Boy Charles, Wining Boy, Doaker, Crawley . . . you're all alike. All this thieving and killing and thieving and killing. And what it ever lead to? More killing and more thieving. I ain't never seen it come to nothing. People getting burned up. People getting shot. People falling down their wells. It don't never stop.

DOAKER: Come on now, Berniece, ain't no need in getting upset.

BOY WILLIE: I done a little bit of stealing here and there, but I ain't never killed nobody. I can't be speaking for nobody else. You all got to speak for yourself, but I ain't never killed nobody.

BERNIECE: You killed Crawley just as sure as if you pulled the trigger.

BOY WILLIE: See, that's ignorant. That's downright foolish for you to say something like that. You ain't doing nothing but showing your ignorance. If the nigger was here I'd whup his ass for getting me and Lymon shot at.

BERNIECE: Crawley ain't knew about the wood.

BOY WILLIE: We told the man about the wood. Ask Lymon. He knew all about the wood. He seen we was sneaking it. Why else we gonna be out there at night? Don't come telling me Crawley ain't knew about the wood. Them fellows come up on us and Crawley tried to bully them. Me and Lymon seen the sheriff with them and give in. Wasn't no sense in getting killed over fifty dollars' worth of wood.

BERNIECE: Crawley ain't knew you stole that wood.

BOY WILLIE: We ain't stole no wood. Me and Lymon was hauling wood for Jim Miller and keeping us a little bit on the side. We dumped our little bit down there by the creek till we had enough to make a load. Some fellows seen us and we figured we better get it before they did. We come up there and got Crawley to help us load it. Figured we'd cut him in. Crawley trying to keep the wolf from his door . . . we was trying to help him.

LYMON: Me and Boy Willie told him about the wood. We told him some fellows might be trying to beat us to it. He say let me go back and get my thirty-eight. That's what caused all the trouble.

BOY WILLIE: If Crawley ain't had the gun he'd be alive today.

LYMON: We had it about half loaded when they come up on us. We seen the sheriff with them and we tried to get away. We ducked around near the bend in the creek . . . but they was down there too. Boy Willie say let's give in. But Crawley pulled out his gun and started shooting. That's when they started shooting back.

BERNIECE: All I know is Crawley would be alive if you hadn't come up there and got him.

BOY WILLIE: I ain't had nothing to do with Crawley getting killed. That was his own fault.

BERNIECE: Crawley's dead and in the ground and you still walking around here eating. That's all I know. He went off to load some wood with you and ain't never come back.

BOY WILLIE: I told you, woman . . . I ain't had nothing to do with . . .

BERNIECE: He ain't here, is he? He ain't here!

(Berniece hits Boy Willie.)

I said he ain't here. Is he?

(Berniece continues to hit Boy Willie, who doesn't move to defend himself, other than back up and turning his head so that most of the blows fall on his chest and arms.)

DOAKER *(grabbing Berniece)*: Come on, Berniece . . . let it go, it ain't his fault.

BERNIECE: He ain't here, is he? Is he?

BOY WILLIE: I told you I ain't responsible for Crawley.

BERNIECE: He ain't here.

BOY WILLIE: Come on now, Berniece . . . don't do this now. Doaker get her. I ain't had nothing to do with Crawley . . .

BERNIECE: You come up there and got him!

BOY WILLIE: I done told you now. Doaker, get her. I ain't playing.

DOAKER: Come on. Berniece.

(Maretha is heard screaming upstairs. It is a scream of stark terror.)

MARETHA: Mama! . . . Mama!

(The lights go down to black. End of Act One.)

ACT 2   *Scene 1*

(The lights come up on the kitchen. It is the following morning. Doaker is ironing the pants to his uniform. He has a pot cooking on the stove at the same time. He is singing a song. The song provides him with the rhythm for his work and he moves about the kitchen with the ease born of many years as a railroad cook.)

DOAKER:
  Gonna leave Jackson Mississippi
  and go to Memphis

and double back to Jackson
Come on down to Hattiesburg
Change cars on the Y. D.
coming through the territory to
Meridian
and Meridian to Greenville
and Greenville to Memphis
I'm on my way and I know where

Change cars on the Katy
Leaving Jackson
and going through Clarksdale
Hello Winona!
Courtland!
Bateville!
Como!
Senitobia!
Lewisberg!
Sunflower!
Glendora!
Sharkey!
And double back to Jackson
Hello Greenwood
I'm on my way Memphis
Clarksdale
Moorhead
Indianola
Can a highball pass through?
Highball on through sir
Grand Carson!
Thirty First Street Depot
Fourth Street Depot
Memphis!

(*Wining Boy enters carrying a suit of clothes.*)

DOAKER: I thought you took that suit to the pawnshop?
WINING BOY: I went down there and the man tell me the suit is too old.
  Look at this suit. This is one hundred percent silk! How a silk suit
  gonna get too old? I know what it was he just didn't want to give me
  five dollars for it. Best he wanna give me is three dollars. I figure a silk
  suit is worth five dollars all over the world. I wasn't gonna part with it
  for no three dollars so I brought it back.
DOAKER: They got another pawnshop up on Wylie.

WINING BOY: I carried it up there. He say he don't take no clothes. Only thing he take is guns and radios. Maybe a guitar or two. Where's Berniece?

DOAKER: Berniece still at work. Boy Willie went down there to meet Lymon this morning. I guess they got that truck fixed, they been out there all day and ain't come back yet. Maretha scared to sleep up there now. Berniece don't know, but I seen Sutter before she did.

WINING BOY: Say what?

DOAKER: About three weeks ago. I had just come back from down there. Sutter couldn't have been dead more than three days. He was sitting over there at the piano. I come out to go to work . . . and he was sitting right there. Had his hand on top of his head just like Berniece said. I believe he broke his neck when he fell in the well. I kept quiet about it. I didn't see no reason to upset Berniece.

WINING BOY: Did he say anything? Did he say he was looking for Boy Willie?

DOAKER: He was just sitting there. He ain't said nothing. I went on out the door and left him sitting there. I figure as long as he was on the other side of the room everything be alright. I don't know what I would have done if he had started walking toward me.

WINING BOY: Berniece say he was calling Boy Willie's name.

DOAKER: I ain't heard him say nothing. He was just sitting there when I seen him. But I don't believe Boy Willie pushed him in the well. Sutter here cause of that piano. I heard him playing on it one time. I thought it was Berniece but then she don't play that kind of music. I come out here and ain't seen nobody, but them piano keys was moving a mile a minute. Berniece need to go on and get rid of it. It ain't done nothing but cause trouble.

WINING BOY: I agree with Berniece. Boy Charles ain't took it to give it back. He took it cause he figure he had more right to it than Sutter did. If Sutter can't understand that . . . then that's just the way that go. Sutter dead and in the ground . . . don't care where his ghost is. He can hover around and play on the piano all he want. I want to see him carry it out the house. That's what I want to see. What time Berniece get home? I don't see how I let her get away from me this morning.

DOAKER: You up there sleep. Berniece leave out of here early in the morning. She out there in Squirrel Hill cleaning house for some bigshot down there at the steel mill. They don't like you to come late. You come late they won't give you your carfare. What kind of business you got with Berniece?

WINING BOY: My business. I ain't asked you what kind of business you got.

DOAKER: Berniece ain't got no money. If that's why you was trying to catch her. She having a hard enough time trying to get by as it is. If she go ahead and marry Avery . . . he working every day . . . she go ahead and marry him they could do alright for themselves. But as it stands she ain't got no money.

WINING BOY: Well, let me have five dollars.

DOAKER: I just give you a dollar before you left out of here. You ain't gonna take my five dollars out there and gamble and drink it up.

WINING BOY: Aw, nigger, give me five dollars. I'll give it back to you.

DOAKER: You wasn't looking to give me five dollars when you had that sack of money. You wasn't looking to throw nothing my way. Now you wanna come in here and borrow five dollars. If you going back with Boy Willie you need to be trying to figure out how you gonna get train fare.

WINING BOY: That's why I need the five dollars. If I had five dollars I could get me some money.

(*Doaker goes into his pocket.*)

Make it seven.

DOAKER: You take this five dollars . . . and you bring my money back here too.

(*Boy Willie and Lymon enter. They are happy and excited. They have money in all of their pockets and are anxious to count it.*)

DOAKER: How'd you do out there?

BOY WILLIE: They was lining up for them.

LYMON: Me and Boy Willie couldn't sell them fast enough. Time we got one sold we'd sell another.

BOY WILLIE: I seen what was happening and told Lymon to up the price on them.

LYMON: Boy Willie say charge them a quarter more. They didn't care. A couple of people give me a dollar and told me to keep the change.

BOY WILLIE: One fellow bought five. I say now what he gonna do with five watermelons? He can't eat them all. I sold him the five and asked him did he want to buy five more.

LYMON: I ain't never seen nobody snatch a dollar fast as Boy Willie.

BOY WILLIE: One lady asked me say, "Is they sweet?" I told her say, "Lady, where we grow these watermelons we put sugar in the ground." You know, she believed me. Talking about she had never heard of that before. Lymon was laughing his head off. I told her, "Oh, yeah, we put the sugar right in the ground with the seed." She say, "Well, give me another one." Them white folks is something else . . . ain't they, Lymon?

LYMON: Soon as you holler watermelons they come right out their door. Then they go and get their neighbors. Look like they having a contest to see who can buy the most.

WINING BOY: I got something for Lymon.

(*Wining Boy goes to get his suit. Boy Willie and Lymon continue to count their money.*)

BOY WILLIE: I know you got more than that. You ain't sold all them watermelons for that little bit of money.

LYMON: I'm still looking. That ain't all you got either. Where's all them quarters?

BOY WILLIE: You let me worry about the quarters. Just put the money on the table.

WINING BOY (*entering with his suit*): Look here, Lymon . . . see this? Look at his eyes getting big. He ain't never seen a suit like this. This is one hundred percent silk. Go ahead . . . put it on. See if it fit you.

(*Lymon tries the suit coat on.*)

Look at that. Feel it. That's one hundred percent genuine silk. I got that in Chicago. You can't get clothes like that nowhere but New York and Chicago. You can't get clothes like that in Pittsburgh. These folks in Pittsburgh ain't never seen clothes like that.

LYMON: This is nice, feel real nice and smooth.

WINING BOY: That's a fifty-five-dollar suit. That's the kind of suit the bigshots wear. You need a pistol and a pocketful of money to wear that suit. I'll let you have it for three dollars. The women will fall out their windows they see you in a suit like that. Give me three dollars and go on and wear it down the street and get you a woman.

BOY WILLIE: That looks nice, Lymon. Put the pants on. Let me see it with the pants.

(*Lymon begins to try on the pants.*)

WINING BOY: Look at that . . . see how it fits you? Give me three dollars and go on and take it. Look at that, Doaker . . . don't he look nice?

DOAKER: Yeah . . . that's a nice suit.

WINING BOY: Got a shirt to go with it. Cost you an extra dollar. Four dollars you got the whole deal.

LYMON: How this look, Boy Willie?

BOY WILLIE: That look nice . . . if you like that kind of thing. I don't like them dress-up kind of clothes. If you like it, look real nice.

WINING BOY: That's the kind of suit you need for up here in the North.

LYMON: Four dollars for everything? The suit and the shirt?

WINING BOY: That's cheap. I should be charging you twenty dollars. I give you a break cause you a homeboy. That's the only way I let you have it for four dollars.

LYMON (*going into his pocket*): Okay . . . here go the four dollars.

WINING BOY: You got some shoes? What size you wear?

LYMON: Size nine.

WINING BOY: That's what size I got! Size nine. I let you have them for three dollars.

LYMON: Where they at? Let me see them.

WINING BOY: They real nice shoes, too. Got a nice tip to them. Got pointy toe just like you want.

(*Wining Boy goes to get his shoes.*)

LYMON: Come on, Boy Willie, let's go out tonight. I wanna see what it looks like up here. Maybe we go to a picture show. Hey, Doaker, they got picture shows up here?

DOAKER: The Rhumba Theater. Right down there on Fullerton Street. Can't miss it. Got the speakers outside on the sidewalk. You can hear it a block away. Boy Willie know where it's at.

(*Doaker exits into his room.*)

LYMON: Let's go to the picture show, Boy Willie. Let's go find some women.

BOY WILLIE: Hey, Lymon, how many of them watermelons would you say we got left? We got just under a half a load . . . right?

LYMON: About that much. Maybe a little more.

BOY WILLIE: You think that piano will fit up in there?

LYMON: If we stack them watermelons you can sit it up in the front there.

BOY WILLIE: I'm gonna call that man tomorrow.

WINING BOY (*returns with his shoes*): Here you go . . . size nine. Put them on. Cost you three dollars. That's a Florsheim shoe. That's the kind Staggerlee wore.

LYMON (*trying on the shoes*): You sure these size nine?

WINING BOY: You can look at my feet and see we wear the same size. Man, you put on that suit and them shoes and you got something there. You ready for whatever's out there. But is they ready for you? With them shoes on you be the King of the Walk. Have everybody stop to look at your shoes. Wishing they had a pair. I'll give you a break. Go on and take them for two dollars.

(*Lymon pays Wining Boy two dollars.*)

LYMON: Come on, Boy Willie . . . let's go find some women. I'm gonna go upstairs and get ready. I'll be ready to go in a minute. Ain't you gonna get dressed?

BOY WILLIE: I'm gonna wear what I got on. I ain't dressing up for these city niggers.

(*Lymon exits up the stairs.*)

That's all Lymon think about is women.

WINING BOY: His daddy was the same way. I used to run around with him. I know his mama too. Two strokes back and I would have been his daddy! His daddy's dead now . . . but I got the nigger out of jail one time. They was fixing to name him Daniel and walk him through the Lion's Den. He got in a tussle with one of them white fellows and the sheriff lit on him like white on rice. That's how the whole thing come about between me and Lymon's mama. She knew me and his daddy used to run together and he got in jail and she went down there and took the sheriff a hundred dollars. Don't get me to lying about where she got it from. I don't know. The sheriff looked at that hundred dollars and turned his nose up. Told her, say, "That ain't gonna do him no good. You got to put another hundred on top of that." She come up there and got me where I was playing at this saloon . . . said she had all but fifty dollars and asked me if I could help. Now the way I figured it . . . without that fifty dollars the sheriff was gonna turn him over to Parchman. The sheriff turn him over to Parchman it be three years before anybody see him again. Now I'm gonna say it right . . . I will give anybody fifty dollars to keep them out of jail for three years. I give her the fifty dollars and she told me to come over to the house. I ain't asked her. I figure if she was nice enough to invite me I ought to go. I ain't had to say a word. She invited me over just as nice. Say, "Why don't you come over to the house?" She ain't had to say nothing else. Them words rolled off her tongue just as nice. I went on down there and sat about three hours. Started to leave and changed my mind. She grabbed hold to me and say, "Baby, it's all night long." That was one of the shortest nights I have ever spent on this earth! I could have used another eight hours. Lymon's daddy didn't even say nothing to me when he got out. He just looked at me funny. He had a good notion something had happened between me an' her. L. D. Jackson. That was one bad-luck nigger. Got killed at some dance. Fellow walked in and shot him thinking he was somebody else.

(*Doaker enters from his room.*)

Hey, Doaker, you remember L. D. Jackson?

DOAKER: That's Lymon's daddy. That was one bad-luck nigger.

BOY WILLIE: Look like you ready to railroad some.

DOAKER: Yeah, I got to make that run.

(*Lymon enters from the stairs. He is dressed in his new suit and shoes, to which he has added a cheap straw hat.*)

LYMON: How I look?

WINING BOY: You look like a million dollars. Don't he look good, Doaker? Come on, let's play some cards. You wanna play some cards?

BOY WILLIE: We ain't gonna play no cards with you. Me and Lymon gonna find some women. Hey, Lymon, don't play no cards with Wining Boy. He'll take all your money.

WINING BOY (*to Lymon*): You got a magic suit there. You can get you a woman easy with that suit . . . but you got to know the magic words. You know the magic words to get you a woman?

LYMON: I just talk to them to see if I like them and they like me.

WINING BOY: You just walk right up to them and say, "If you got the harbor I got the ship." If that don't work ask them if you can put them in your pocket. The first thing they gonna say is, "It's too small." That's when you look them dead in the eye and say, "Baby, ain't nothing small about me." If that don't work then you move on to another one. Am I telling him right, Doaker?

DOAKER: That man don't need you to tell him nothing about no women. These women these days ain't gonna fall for that kind of stuff. You got to buy them a present. That's what they looking for these days.

BOY WILLIE: Come on, I'm ready. You ready, Lymon? Come on, let's go find some women.

WINING BOY: Here, let me walk out with you. I wanna see the women fall out their window when they see Lymon.

(*They all exit and the lights go down on the scene.*)

Scene 2

(*The lights come up on the kitchen. It is late evening of the same day. Berniece has set a tub for her bath in the kitchen. She is heating up water on the stove. There is a knock at the door.*)

BERNIECE: Who is it?

AVERY: It's me, Avery.

(*Berniece opens the door and lets him in.*)

BERNIECE: Avery, come on in. I was just fixing to take my bath.

AVERY: Where Boy Willie? I see that truck out there almost empty. They done sold almost all them watermelons.

BERNIECE: They was gone when I come home. I don't know where they went off to. Boy Willie around here about to drive me crazy.

AVERY: They sell them watermelons . . . he'll be gone soon.

BERNIECE: What Mr. Cohen say about letting you have the place?

AVERY: He say he'll let me have it for thirty dollars a month. I talked him out of thirty-five and he say he'll let me have it for thirty.

BERNIECE: That's a nice spot next to Benny Diamond's store.

AVERY: Berniece . . . I be at home and I get to thinking you up here an' I'm down there. I get to thinking how that look to have a preacher that ain't married. It makes for a better congregation if the preacher was settled down and married.

BERNIECE: Avery . . . not now. I was fixing to take my bath.

AVERY: You know how I feel about you, Berniece. Now . . . I done got the place from Mr. Cohen. I get the money from the bank and I can fix it up real nice. They give me a ten cents a hour raise down there on the job . . . now Berniece, I ain't got much in the way of comforts. I got a hole in my pockets near about as far as money is concerned. I ain't never found no way through life to a woman I care about like I care about you. I need that. I need somebody on my bond side. I need a woman that fits in my hand.

BERNIECE: Avery, I ain't ready to get married now.

AVERY: You too young a woman to close up, Berniece.

BERNIECE: I ain't said nothing about closing up. I got a lot of woman left in me.

AVERY: Where's it at? When's the last time you looked at it?

BERNIECE (*stunned by his remark*): That's a nasty thing to say. And you call yourself a preacher.

AVERY: Anytime I get anywhere near you . . . you push me away.

BERNIECE: I got enough on my hands with Maretha. I got enough people to love and take care of.

AVERY: Who you got to love you? Can't nobody get close enough to you. Doaker can't half say nothing to you. You jump all over Boy Willie. Who you got to love you, Berniece?

BERNIECE: You trying to tell me a woman can't be nothing without a man. But you alright, huh? You can just walk out of here without me—without a woman—and still be a man. That's alright. Ain't nobody gonna ask you, "Avery, who you got to love you?" That's alright for you. But everybody gonna be worried about Berniece. "How Berniece gonna take care of herself? How she gonna raise that child without a man? Wonder what she do with herself. How she gonna live like that?" Everybody got all kinds of questions for Berniece. Everybody telling me I can't be a woman unless I got a man. Well, you tell me, Avery—you know—how much woman am I?

AVERY: It wasn't me, Berniece. You can't blame me for nobody else. I'll own up to my own shortcomings. But you can't blame me for Crawley or nobody else.

BERNIECE: I ain't blaming nobody for nothing. I'm just stating the facts.

AVERY: How long you gonna carry Crawley with you, Berniece? It's been over three years. At some point you got to let go and go on. Life's got all kinds of twists and turns. That don't mean you stop living. That don't mean you cut yourself off from life. You can't go through life carrying Crawley's ghost with you. Crawley's been dead three years. Three years, Berniece.

BERNIECE: I know how long Crawley's been dead. You ain't got to tell me that. I just ain't ready to get married right now.

AVERY: What is you ready for, Berniece? You just gonna drift along from day to day. Life is more than making it from one day to another. You gonna look up one day and it's all gonna be past you. Life's gonna be gone out of your hands—there won't be enough to make nothing with. I'm standing here now, Berniece—but I don't know how much longer I'm gonna be standing here waiting on you.

BERNIECE: Avery, I told you . . . when you get your church we'll sit down and talk about this. I got too many other things to deal with right now. Boy Willie and the piano . . . and Sutter's ghost. I thought I might have been seeing things, but Maretha done seen Sutter's ghost, too.

AVERY: When this happen, Berniece?

BERNIECE: Right after I came home yesterday. Me and Boy Willie was arguing about the piano and Sutter's ghost was standing at the top of the stairs. Maretha scared to sleep up there now. Maybe if you bless the house he'll go away.

AVERY: I don't know, Berniece. I don't know if I should fool around with something like that.

BERNIECE: I can't have Maretha scared to go to sleep up there. Seem like if you bless the house he would go away.

AVERY: You might have to be a special kind of preacher to do something like that.

BERNIECE: I keep telling myself when Boy Willie leave he'll go on and leave with him. I believe Boy Willie pushed him in the well.

AVERY: That's been going on down there a long time. The Ghosts of the Yellow Dog been pushing people in their wells long before Boy Willie got grown.

BERNIECE: Somebody down there pushing them people in their wells. They ain't just upped and fell. Ain't no wind pushed nobody in their well.

AVERY: Oh, I don't know. God works in mysterious ways.

BERNIECE: He ain't pushed nobody in their wells.

AVERY: He caused it to happen. God is the Great Causer. He can do anything. He parted the Red Sea. He say I will smite my enemies. Reverend Thompson used to preach on the Ghosts of the Yellow Dog as the hand of God.

BERNIECE: I don't care who preached what. Somebody down there pushing them people in their wells. Somebody like Boy Willie. I can see him doing something like that. You ain't gonna tell me that Sutter just upped and fell in his well. I believe Boy Willie pushed him so he could get his land.

AVERY: What Doaker say about Boy Willie selling the piano?

BERNIECE: Doaker don't want no part of that piano. He ain't never wanted no part of it. He blames himself for not staying behind with Papa Boy Charles. He washed his hands of that piano a long time ago. He didn't want me to bring it up here—but I wasn't gonna leave it down there.

AVERY: Well, it seems to me somebody ought to be able to talk to Boy Willie.

BERNIECE: You can't talk to Boy Willie. He been that way all his life. Mama Ola had her hands full trying to talk to him. He don't listen to nobody. He just like my daddy. He get his mind fixed on something and can't nobody turn him from it.

AVERY: You ought to start a choir at the church. Maybe if he seen you was doing something with it—if you told him you was gonna put it in my church—maybe he'd see it different. You ought to put it down in the church and start a choir. The Bible say "Make a joyful noise unto the Lord." Maybe if Boy Willie see you was doing something with it he'd see it different.

BERNIECE: I done told you I don't play on that piano. Ain't no need in you to keep talking this choir stuff. When my mama died I shut the top on that piano and I ain't never opened it since. I was only playing it for her. When my daddy died seem like all her life went into that piano. She used to have me playing on it . . . had Miss Eula come in and teach me . . . say when I played it she could hear my daddy talking to her. I used to think them pictures came alive and walked through the house. Sometime late at night I could hear my mama talking to them. I said that wasn't gonna happen to me. I don't play that piano cause I don't want to wake them spirits. They never be walking around in this house.

AVERY: You got to put all that behind you, Berniece.

BERNIECE: I got Maretha playing on it. She don't know nothing about it. Let her go on and be a schoolteacher or something. She don't have to carry all of that with her. She got a chance I didn't have. I ain't gonna burden her with that piano.

AVERY: You got to put all of that behind you, Berniece. That's the same thing like Crawley. Everybody got stones in their passway. You got to step over them or walk around them. You picking them up and carry-ing them with you. All you got to do is set them down by the side of the road. You ain't got to carry them with you. You can walk over there right now and play that piano. You can walk over there right now and

God will walk over there with you. Right now you can set that sack of stones down by the side of the road and walk away from it. You don't have to carry it with you. You can do it right now.

(*Avery crosses over to the piano and raises the lid.*)

Come on, Berniece . . . set it down and walk away from it. Come on, play "Old Ship of Zion." Walk over here and claim it as an instrument of the Lord. You can walk over here right now and make it into a celebration.

(*Berniece moves toward the piano.*)

BERNIECE: Avery . . . I done told you I don't want to play that piano. Now or no other time.

AVERY: The Bible say, "The Lord is my refuge . . . and my strength!" With the strength of God you can put the past behind you, Berniece. With the strength of God you can do anything! God got a bright tomorrow. God don't ask what you done . . . God ask what you gonna do. The strength of God can move mountains! God's got a bright tomorrow for you . . . all you got to do is walk over here and claim it.

BERNIECE: Avery, just go on and let me finish my bath. I'll see you tomorrow.

AVERY: Okay, Berniece. I'm gonna go home. I'm gonna go home and read up on my Bible. And tomorrow . . . if the good Lord give me strength tomorrow . . . I'm gonna come by and bless the house . . . and show you the power of the Lord.

(*Avery crosses to the door.*)

It's gonna be alright, Berniece. God say he will soothe the troubled waters. I'll come by tomorrow and bless the house.

(*The lights go down to black.*)

Scene 3

(*Several hours later. The house is dark. Berniece has retired for the night. Boy Willie enters the darkened house with Grace.*)

BOY WILLIE: Come on in. This my sister's house. My sister live here. Come on, I ain't gonna bite you.

GRACE: Put some light on. I can't see.

BOY WILLIE: You don't need to see nothing, baby. This here is all you need to see. All you need to do is see me. If you can't see me you can feel me in the dark. How's that, sugar?

(*He attempts to kiss her.*)

GRACE: Go on now . . . wait!

BOY WILLIE: Just give me one little old kiss.

GRACE (*pushing him away*): Come on, now. Where I'm gonna sleep at?

BOY WILLIE: We got to sleep out here on the couch. Come on, my sister
   don't mind. Lymon come back he just got to sleep on the floor. He run
   off with Dolly somewhere he better stay there. Come on, sugar.

GRACE: Wait now . . . you ain't told me nothing about no couch. I
   thought you had a bed. Both of us can't sleep on that little old couch.

BOY WILLIE: It don't make no difference. We can sleep on the floor. Let
   Lymon sleep on the couch.

GRACE: You ain't told me nothing about no couch.

BOY WILLIE: What difference it make? You just wanna be with me.

GRACE: I don't want to be with you on no couch. Ain't you got no bed?

BOY WILLIE: You don't need no bed, woman. My granddaddy used to
   take women on the backs of horses. What you need a bed for? You just
   want to be with me.

GRACE: You sure is country. I didn't know you was this country.

BOY WILLIE: There's a lot of things you don't know about me. Come on,
   let me show you what this country boy can do.

GRACE: Let's go to my place. I got a room with a bed if Leroy don't come
   back there.

BOY WILLIE: Who's Leroy? You ain't said nothing about no Leroy.

GRACE: He used to be my man. He ain't coming back. He gone off with
   some other gal.

BOY WILLIE: You let him have your key?

GRACE: He ain't coming back.

BOY WILLIE: Did you let him have your key?

GRACE: He got a key but he ain't coming back. He took off with some
   other gal.

BOY WILLIE: I don't wanna go nowhere he might come. Let's stay here.
   Come on, sugar.

(*He pulls her over to the couch.*)

Let me heist your hood and check your oil. See if your battery needs
charged.

(*He pulls her to him. They kiss and tug at each other's clothing. In their anxiety
they knock over a lamp.*)

BERNIECE: Who's that . . . Wining Boy?

BOY WILLIE: It's me . . . Boy Willie. Go on back to sleep. Everything's
   alright.

(*To Grace.*)

That's my sister. Everything's alright, Berniece. Go on back to sleep.

BERNIECE: What you doing down there? What you done knocked over?

BOY WILLIE: It wasn't nothing. Everything's alright. Go on back to sleep.

(*To Grace.*)

That's my sister. We alright. She gone back to sleep.

(*They begin to kiss. Berniece enters from the stairs dressed in a nightgown. She cuts on the light.*)

BERNIECE: Boy Willie, what you doing down here?

BOY WILLIE: It was just that there lamp. It ain't broke. It's okay. Everything's alright. Go on back to bed.

BERNIECE: Boy Willie, I don't allow that in my house. You gonna have to take your company someplace else.

BOY WILLIE: It's alright. We ain't doing nothing. We just sitting here talking. This here is Grace. That's my sister Berniece.

BERNIECE: You know I don't allow that kind of stuff in my house.

BOY WILLIE: Allow what? We just sitting here talking.

BERNIECE: Well, your company gonna have to leave. Come back and talk in the morning.

BOY WILLIE: Go on back upstairs now.

BERNIECE: I got an eleven-year-old girl upstairs. I can't allow that around here.

BOY WILLIE: Ain't nobody said nothing about that. I told you we just talking.

GRACE: Come on . . . let's go to my place. Ain't nobody got to tell me to leave but once.

BOY WILLIE: You ain't got to be like that, Berniece.

BERNIECE: I'm sorry, Miss. But he know I don't allow that in here.

GRACE: You ain't got to tell me but once. I don't stay nowhere I ain't wanted.

BOY WILLIE: I don't know why you want to embarrass me in front of my company.

GRACE: Come on, take me home.

BERNIECE: Go on, Boy Willie. Just go on with your company.

(*Boy Willie and Grace exit. Berniece puts the light on in the kitchen and puts on the teakettle. Presently there is a knock at the door. Berniece goes to answer it. Berniece opens the door. Lymon enters.*)

LYMON: How you doing, Berniece? I thought you'd be asleep. Boy Willie been back here?

BERNIECE: He just left out of here a minute ago.

LYMON: I went out to see a picture show and never got there. We always end up doing something else. I was with this woman she just wanted

to drink up all my money. So I left her there and came back looking for
Boy Willie.

BERNIECE: You just missed him. He just left out of here.

LYMON: They got some nice-looking women in this city. I'm gonna like it
up here real good. I like seeing them with their dresses on. Got them
high heels. I like that. Make them look like they real precious. Boy
Willie met a real nice one today. I wish I had met her before he did.

BERNIECE: He come by here with some woman a little while ago. I told
him to go on and take all that out of my house.

LYMON: What she look like, the woman he was with? Was she a brown-
skinned woman about this high? Nice and healthy? Got nice hips on her?

BERNIECE: She had on a red dress.

LYMON: That's her! That's Grace. She real nice. Laugh a lot. Lot of fun to
be with. She don't be trying to put on. Some of these woman act like
they the Queen of Sheba. I don't like them kind. Grace ain't like that.
She real nice with herself.

BERNIECE: I don't know what she was like. He come in here all drunk
knocking over the lamp, and making all kind of noise. I told them to
take that somewhere else. I can't really say what she was like.

LYMON: She real nice. I seen her before he did. I was trying not to act like
I seen her. I wanted to look at her a while before I said something. She
seen me when I come into the saloon. I tried to act like I didn't see her.
Time I looked around Boy Willie was talking to her. She was talking to
him kept looking at me. That's when her friend Dolly came. I asked her
if she wanted to go to the picture show. She told me to buy her a drink
while she thought about it. Next thing I knew she done had three
drinks talking about she too tired to go. I bought her another drink,
then I left. Boy Willie was gone and I thought he might have come
back here. Doaker gone, huh? He say he had to make a trip.

BERNIECE: Yeah, he gone on his trip. This is when I can usually get me
some peace and quiet, Maretha asleep.

LYMON: She look just like you. Got them big eyes. I remember her when
she was in diapers.

BERNIECE: Time just keep on. It go on with or without you. She going on
twelve.

LYMON: She sure is pretty. I like kids.

BERNIECE: Boy Willie say you staying . . . what you gonna do up here in
this big city? You thought about that?

LYMON: They never get me back down there. The sheriff looking for me.
All because they gonna try and make me work for somebody when I
don't want to. They gonna try and make me work for Stovall when
he don't pay nothing. It ain't like that up here. Up here you more or
less do what you want to. I figure I find me a job and try to get set up

and then see what the year brings. I tried to do that two or three times down there . . . but it never would work out. I was always in the wrong place.

BERNIECE: This ain't a bad city once you get to know your way around.

LYMON: Up here is different. I'm gonna get me a job unloading boxcars or something. One fellow told me say he know a place. I'm gonna go over there with him next week. Me and Boy Willie finish selling them watermelons I'll have enough money to hold me for a while. But I'm gonna go over there and see what kind of jobs they have.

BERNIECE: You shouldn't have too much trouble finding a job. It's all in how you present yourself. See now, Boy Willie couldn't get no job up here. Somebody hire him they got a pack of trouble on their hands. Soon as they find that out they fire him. He don't want to do nothing unless he do it his way.

LYMON: I know. I told him let's go to the picture show first and see if there was any women down there. They might get tired of sitting at home and walk down to the picture show. He say he wanna look around first. We never did get down there. We tried a couple of places and then we went to this saloon where he met Grace. I tried to meet her before he did but he beat me to her. We left Wining Boy sitting down there running his mouth. He told me if I wear this suit I'd find me a woman. He was almost right.

BERNIECE: You don't need to be out there in them saloons. Ain't no telling what you liable to run into out there. This one liable to cut you as quick as that one shoot you. You don't need to be out there. You start out that fast life you can't keep it up. It makes you old quick. I don't know what them women out there be thinking about.

LYMON: Mostly they be lonely and looking for somebody to spend the night with them. Sometimes it matters who it is and sometimes it don't. I used to be the same way. Now it got to matter. That's why I'm here now. Dolly liable not to even recognize me if she sees me again. I don't like women like that. I like my women to be with me in a nice and easy way. That way we can both enjoy ourselves. The way I see it we the only two people like us in the world. We got to see how we fit together. A woman that don't want to take the time to do that I don't bother with. Used to. Used to bother with all of them. Then I woke up one time with this woman and I didn't know who she was. She was the prettiest woman I had ever seen in my life. I spent the whole night with her and didn't even know it. I had never taken the time to look at her. I guess she kinda knew I ain't never really looked at her. She must have known that cause she ain't wanted to see me no more. If she had wanted to see me I believe we might have got married. How come you ain't married? It seem like to me you would be married. I remember

Avery from down home. I used to call him plain old Avery. Now he
Reverend Avery. That's kinda funny about him becoming a preacher. I
like when he told about how that come to him in a dream about them
sheep people and them hobos. Nothing ever come to me in a dream
like that. I just dream about women. Can't never seem to find the right
one.

BERNIECE: She out there somewhere. You just got to get yourself ready
to meet her. That's what I'm trying to do. Avery's alright. I ain't really
got nobody in mind.

LYMON: I get me a job and a little place and get set up to where I can
make a woman comfortable I might get married. Avery's nice. You
ought to go ahead and get married. You be a preacher's wife you won't
have to work. I hate living by myself. I didn't want to be no strain on
my mama so I left home when I was about sixteen. Everything I tried
seem like it just didn't work out. Now I'm trying this.

BERNIECE: You keep trying it'll work out for you.

LYMON: You ever go down there to the picture show?

BERNIECE: I don't go in for all that.

LYMON: Ain't nothing wrong with it. It ain't like gambling and sinning. I
went to one down in Jackson once. It was fun.

BERNIECE: I just stay home most of the time. Take care of Maretha.

LYMON: It's getting kind of late. I don't know where Boy Willie went off
to. He's liable not to come back. I'm gonna take off these shoes. My
feet hurt. Was you in bed? I don't mean to be keeping you up.

BERNIECE: You ain't keeping me up. I couldn't sleep after that Boy Willie
woke me up.

LYMON: You got on that nightgown. I likes women when they wear them
fancy nightclothes and all. It makes their skin look real pretty.

BERNIECE: I got this at the five-and-ten-cents store. It ain't so fancy.

LYMON: I don't too often get to see a woman dressed like that.

(*There is a long pause. Lymon takes off his suit coat.*)

Well, I'm gonna sleep here on the couch. I'm supposed to sleep on the
floor but I don't reckon Boy Willie's coming back tonight. Wining Boy
sold me this suit. Told me it was a magic suit. I'm gonna put it on
again tomorrow. Maybe it bring me a woman like he say.

(*He goes into his coat pocket and takes out a small bottle of perfume.*)

I almost forgot I had this. Some man sold me this for a dollar. Say it
come from Paris. This is the same kind of perfume the Queen of
France wear. That's what he told me. I don't know if it's true or not. I
smelled it. It smelled good to me. Here . . . smell it see if you like it.
I was gonna give it to Dolly. But I didn't like her too much.

BERNIECE (*takes the bottle*): It smells nice.

LYMON: I was gonna give it to Dolly if she had went to the picture with me. Go on, you take it.

BERNIECE: I can't take it. Here . . . go on you keep it. You'll find somebody to give it to.

LYMON: I wanna give it to you. Make you smell nice.

(*He takes the bottle and puts perfume behind Berniece's ear.*)

They tell me you supposed to put it right here behind your ear. Say if you put it there you smell nice all day.

(*Berniece stiffens at his touch. Lymon bends down to smell her.*)

There . . . you smell real good now.

(*He kisses her neck.*)

You smell real good for Lymon.

(*He kisses her again. Berniece returns the kiss, then breaks the embrace and crosses to the stairs. She turns and they look silently at each other. Lymon hands her the bottle of perfume. Berniece exits up the stairs. Lymon picks up his suit coat and strokes it lovingly with the full knowledge that it is indeed a magic suit. The lights go down on the scene.*)

Scene 4

(*It is late the next morning. The lights come up on the parlor. Lymon is asleep on the sofa. Boy Willie enters the front door.*)

BOY WILLIE: Hey, Lymon! Lymon, come on get up.

LYMON: Leave me alone.

BOY WILLIE: Come on, get up, nigger! Wake up, Lymon.

LYMON: What you want?

BOY WILLIE: Come on, let's go. I done called the man about the piano.

LYMON: What piano?

BOY WILLIE (*dumps Lymon on the floor*): Come on, get up!

LYMON: Why you leave, I looked around and you was gone.

BOY WILLIE: I come back here with Grace, then I went looking for you. I figured you'd be with Dolly.

LYMON: She just want to drink and spend up your money. I come on back here looking for you to see if you wanted to go to the picture show.

BOY WILLIE: I been up at Grace's house. Some nigger named Leroy come by but I had a chair up against the door. He got mad when he couldn't get in. He went off somewhere and I got out of there before he could come back. Berniece got mad when we came here.

LYMON: She say you was knocking over the lamp busting up the place.

BOY WILLIE: That was Grace doing all that.

LYMON: Wining Boy seen Sutter's ghost last night.

BOY WILLIE: Wining Boy's liable to see anything. I'm surprised he found the right house. Come on, I done called the man about the piano.

LYMON: What he say?

BOY WILLIE: He say to bring it on out. I told him I was calling for my sister, Miss Berniece Charles. I told him some man wanted to buy it for eleven hundred dollars and asked him if he would go any better. He said yeah, he would give me eleven hundred and fifty dollars for it if it was the same piano. I described it to him again and he told me to bring it out.

LYMON: Why didn't you tell him to come and pick it up?

BOY WILLIE: I didn't want to have no problem with Berniece. This way we just take it on out there and it be out the way. He want to charge twenty-five dollars to pick it up.

LYMON: You should have told him the man was gonna give you twelve hundred for it.

BOY WILLIE: I figure I was taking a chance with that eleven hundred. If I had told him twelve hundred he might have run off. Now I wish I had told him twelve-fifty. It's hard to figure out white folks sometimes.

LYMON: You might have been able to tell him anything. White folks got a lot of money.

BOY WILLIE: Come on, let's get it loaded before Berniece come back. Get that end over there. All you got to do is pick it up on that side. Don't worry about this side. You wanna stretch you' back for a minute?

LYMON: I'm ready.

BOY WILLIE: Get a real good grip on it now.

(*The sound of Sutter's Ghost is heard. They do not hear it.*)

LYMON: I got this end. You get that end.

BOY WILLIE: Wait till I say ready now. Alright. You got it good? You got a grip on it?

LYMON: Yeah, I got it. You lift up on that end.

BOY WILLIE: Ready? Lift!

(*The piano will not budge.*)

LYMON: Man, this piano is heavy! It's gonna take more than me and you to move this piano.

BOY WILLIE: We can do it. Come on—we did it before.

LYMON: Nigger—you crazy! That piano weighs five hundred pounds!

BOY WILLIE: I got three hundred pounds of it! I know you can carry two hundred pounds! You be lifting them cotton sacks! Come on lift this piano!

(*They try to move the piano again without success.*)

LYMON: It's stuck. Something holding it.

BOY WILLIE: How the piano gonna be stuck? We just moved it. Slide you' end out.

LYMON: Naw—we gonna need two or three more people. How this big old piano get in the house?

BOY WILLIE: I don't know how it got in the house. I know how it's going out though! You get on this end. I'll carry three hundred and fifty pounds of it. All you got to do is slide your end out. Ready?

(*They switch sides and try again without success. Doaker enters from his room as they try to push and shove it.*)

LYMON: Hey, Doaker . . . how this piano get in the house?

DOAKER: Boy Willie, what you doing?

BOY WILLIE: I'm carrying this piano out the house. What it look like I'm doing? Come on, Lymon, let's try again.

DOAKER: Go on let the piano sit there till Berniece come home.

BOY WILLIE: You ain't got nothing to do with this, Doaker. This my business.

DOAKER: This is my house, nigger! I ain't gonna let you or nobody else carry nothing out of it. You ain't gonna carry nothing out of here without my permission!

BOY WILLIE: This is my piano. I don't need your permission to carry my belongings out of your house. This is mine. This ain't got nothing to do with you.

DOAKER: I say leave it over there till Berniece come home. She got part of it too. Leave it set there till you see what she say.

BOY WILLIE: I don't care what Berniece say. Come on, Lymon. I got this side.

DOAKER: Go on and cut it half in two if you want to. Just leave Berniece's half sitting over there. I can't tell you what to do with your piano. But I can't let you take her half out of here.

BOY WILLIE: Go on, Doaker. You ain't got nothing to do with this. I don't want you starting nothing now. Just go on and leave me alone. Come on, Lymon. I got this end.

(*Doaker goes into his room. Boy Willie and Lymon prepare to move the piano.*)

LYMON: How we gonna get it in the truck?

BOY WILLIE: Don't worry about how we gonna get it on the truck. You got to get it out the house first.

LYMON: It's gonna take more than me and you to move this piano.

BOY WILLIE: Just lift up on that end, nigger!

(*Doaker comes to the doorway of his room and stands.*)

DOAKER (*quietly with authority*): Leave that piano set over there till Berniece come back. I don't care what you do with it then. But you gonna leave it sit over there right now.

BOY WILLIE: Alright . . . I'm gonna tell you this, Doaker. I'm going out of here . . . I'm gonna get me some rope . . . find me a plank and some wheels . . . and I'm coming back. Then I'm gonna carry that piano out of here . . . sell it and give Berniece half the money. See . . . now that's what I'm gonna do. And you . . . or nobody else is gonna stop me. Come on, Lymon . . . let's go get some rope and stuff. I'll be back, Doaker.

(*Boy Willie and Lymon exit. The lights go down on the scene.*)

Scene 5

(*The lights come up. Boy Willie sits on the sofa, screwing casters on a wooden plank. Maretha is sitting on the piano stool. Doaker sits at the table playing solitaire.*)

BOY WILLIE (*to Maretha*): Then after that them white folks down around there started falling down their wells. You ever seen a well? A well got a wall around it. It's hard to fall down a well. You got to be leaning way over. Couldn't nobody figure out too much what was making these fellows fall down their well . . . so everybody says the Ghosts of the Yellow Dog must have pushed them. That's what everybody called them four men what got burned up in the boxcar.

MARETHA: Why they call them that?

BOY WILLIE: Cause the Yazoo Delta railroad got yellow boxcars. Sometime the way the whistle blow sound like an old dog howling so the people call it the Yellow Dog.

MARETHA: Anybody ever see the Ghosts?

BOY WILLIE: I told you they like the wind. Can you see the wind?

MARETHA: No.

BOY WILLIE: They like the wind you can't see them. But sometimes you be in trouble they might be around to help you. They say if you go where the Southern cross the Yellow Dog . . . you go to where them two railroads cross each other . . . and call out their names . . . they say they talk back to you. I don't know, I ain't never done that. But Uncle Wining Boy he say he been down there and talked to them. You have to ask him about that part.

(*Berniece has entered from the front door.*)

BERNIECE: Maretha, you go on and get ready for me to do your hair.

(*Maretha crosses to the steps.*)

Boy Willie, I done told you to leave my house.

(*To Maretha.*)

Go on, Maretha.

(*Maretha is hesitant about going up the stairs.*)

BOY WILLIE: Don't be scared. Here, I'll go up there with you. If we see Sutter's ghost I'll put a whupping on him. Come on, Uncle Boy Willie going with you.

(*Boy Willie and Maretha exit up the stairs.*)

BERNIECE: Doaker—what is going on here?

DOAKER: I come home and him and Lymon was moving the piano. I told them to leave it over there till you got home. He went out and got that board and them wheels. He say he gonna take that piano out of here and ain't nobody gonna stop him.

BERNIECE: I ain't playing with Boy Willie. I got Crawley's gun upstairs. He don't know but I'm through with it. Where Lymon go?

DOAKER: Boy Willie sent him for some rope just before you come in.

BERNIECE: I ain't studying Boy Willie or Lymon—or the rope. Boy Willie ain't taking that piano out this house. That's all there is to it.

(*Boy Willie and Maretha enter on the stairs. Maretha carries a hot comb and a can of hair grease. Boy Willie crosses over and continues to screw the wheels on the board.*)

MARETHA: Mama, all the hair grease is gone. There ain't but this little bit left.

BERNIECE (*gives her a dollar*): Here . . . run across the street and get another can. You come straight back, too. Don't you be playing around out there. And watch the cars. Be careful when you cross the street.

(*Maretha exits out the front door.*)

Boy Willie, I done told you to leave my house.

BOY WILLIE: I ain't in you' house. I'm in Doaker's house. If he ask me to leave then I'll go on and leave. But consider me done left your part.

BERNIECE: Doaker, tell him to leave. Tell him to go on.

DOAKER: Boy Willie ain't done nothing for me to put him out of the house. I told you if you can't get along just go on and don't have nothing to do with each other.

BOY WILLIE: I ain't thinking about Berniece.

(*He gets up and draws a line across the floor with his foot.*)

There! Now I'm out of your part of the house. Consider me done left your part. Soon as Lymon come back with that rope. I'm gonna take that piano out of here and sell it.

BERNIECE: You ain't gonna touch that piano.

BOY WILLIE: Carry it out of here just as big and bold. Do like my daddy would have done come time to get Sutter's land.

BERNIECE: I got something to make you leave it over there.

BOY WILLIE: It's got to come better than this thirty-two-twenty.

DOAKER: Why don't you stop all that! Boy Willie, go on and leave her alone. You know how Berniece get. Why you wanna sit there and pick with her?

BOY WILLIE: I ain't picking with her. I told her the truth. She the one talking about what she got. I just told her what she better have.

BERNIECE: That's alright, Doaker. Leave him alone.

BOY WILLIE: She trying to scare me. Hell, I ain't scared of dying. I look around and see people dying every day. You got to die to make room for somebody else. I had a dog that died. Wasn't nothing but a puppy. I picked it up and put it in a bag and carried it up there to Reverend C. L. Thompson's church. I carried it up there and prayed and asked Jesus to make it live like he did the man in the Bible. I prayed real hard. Knelt down and everything. Say ask in Jesus' name. Well, I must have called Jesus' name two hundred times. I called his name till my mouth got sore. I got up and looked in the bag and the dog still dead. It ain't moved a muscle! I say, "Well, ain't nothing precious." And then I went out and killed me a cat. That's when I discovered the power of death. See, a nigger that ain't afraid to die is the worse kind of nigger for the white man. He can't hold that power over you. That's what I learned when I killed that cat. I got the power of death too. I can command him. I can call him up. The white man don't like to see that. He don't like for you to stand up and look him square in the eye and say, "I got it too." Then he got to deal with you square up.

BERNIECE: That's why I don't talk to him, Doaker. You try and talk to him and that's the only kind of stuff that comes out his mouth.

DOAKER: You say Avery went home to get his Bible?

BOY WILLIE: What Avery gonna do? Avery can't do nothing with me. I wish Avery would say something to me about this piano.

DOAKER: Berniece ain't said about that. Avery went home to get his Bible. He coming by to bless the house see if he can get rid of Sutter's ghost.

BOY WILLIE: Ain't nothing but a house full of ghosts down there at the church. What Avery look like chasing away somebody's ghost?

(*Maretha enters the front door.*)

BERNIECE: Light that stove and set that comb over there to get hot. Get something to put around your shoulders.

BOY WILLIE: The Bible say an eye for an eye, a tooth for a tooth, and a life for a life. Tit for tat. But you and Avery don't want to believe that.

You gonna pass up that part and pretend it ain't in there. Everything else you gonna agree with. But if you gonna agree with part of it you got to agree with all of it. You can't do nothing halfway. You gonna go at the Bible halfway. You gonna act like that part ain't in there. But you pull out the Bible and open it and see what it say. Ask Avery. He a preacher. He'll tell you it's in there. He the Good Shepherd. Unless he gonna shepherd you to heaven with half the Bible.

BERNIECE: Maretha, bring me that comb. Make sure it's hot.

(Maretha brings the comb. Berniece begins to do her hair.)

BOY WILLIE: I will say this for Avery. He done figured out a path to go through life. I don't agree with it. But he done fixed it so he can go right through it real smooth. Hell, he liable to end up with a million dollars that he done got from selling bread and wine.

MARETHA: OWWWWWW!

BERNIECE: Be still, Maretha. If you was a boy I wouldn't be going through this.

BOY WILLIE: Don't you tell that girl that. Why you wanna tell her that?

BERNIECE: You ain't got nothing to do with this child.

BOY WILLIE: Telling her you wished she was a boy. How's that gonna make her feel?

BERNIECE: Boy Willie, go on and leave me alone.

DOAKER: Why don't you leave her alone? What you got to pick with her for? Why don't you go on out and see what's out there in the streets? Have something to tell the fellows down home.

BOY WILLIE: I'm waiting on Lymon to get back with that truck. Why don't you go on out and see what's out there in the streets? You ain't got to work tomorrow. Talking about me . . . why don't you go out there? It's Friday night.

DOAKER: I got to stay around here and keep you all from killing one another.

BOY WILLIE: You ain't got to worry about me. I'm gonna be here just as long as it takes Lymon to get back here with that truck. You ought to be talking to Berniece. Sitting up there telling Maretha she wished she was a boy. What kind of thing is that to tell a child? If you want to tell her something tell her about that piano. You ain't even told her about that piano. Like that's something to be ashamed of. Like she supposed to go off and hide somewhere about that piano. You ought to mark down on the calendar the day that Papa Boy Charles brought that piano into the house. You ought to mark that day down and draw a circle around it . . . and every year when it come up throw a party. Have a celebration. If you did that she wouldn't have no problem in life. She could walk around here with her head held high. I'm talking about a big party!

Invite everybody! Mark that day down with a special meaning. That way she know where she at in the world. You got her going out here thinking she wrong in the world. Like there ain't no part of it belong to her.

BERNIECE: Let me take care of my child. When you get one of your own then you can teach it what you want to teach it.

(*Doaker exits into his room.*)

BOY WILLIE: What I want to bring a child into this world for? Why I wanna bring somebody else into all this for? I'll tell you this . . . If I was Rockefeller I'd have forty or fifty. I'd make one every day. Cause they gonna start out in life with all the advantages. I ain't got no advantages to offer nobody. Many is the time I looked at my daddy and seen him staring off at his hands. I got a little older I know what he was thinking. He sitting there saying, "I got these big old hands but what I'm gonna do with them? Best I can do is make a fifty-acre crop for Mr. Stovall. Got these big old hands capable of doing anything. I can take and build something with these hands. But where's the tools? All I got is these hands. Unless I go out here and kill me somebody and take what they got . . . it's a long row to hoe for me to get something of my own. So what I'm gonna do with these big old hands? What would you do?"

See now . . . if he had his own land he wouldn't have felt that way. If he had something under his feet that belonged to him he could stand up taller. That's what I'm talking about. Hell, the land is there for everybody. All you got to do is figure out how to get you a piece. Ain't no mystery to life. You just got to go out and meet it square on. If you got a piece of land you'll find everything else fall right into place. You can stand right up next to the white man and talk about the price of cotton . . . the weather, and anything else you want to talk about. If you teach that girl that she living at the bottom of life, she's gonna grow up and hate you.

BERNIECE: I'm gonna teach her the truth. That's just where she living. Only she ain't got to stay there.

(*To Maretha.*)

Turn you' head over to the other side.

BOY WILLIE: This might be your bottom but it ain't mine. I'm living at the top of life. I ain't gonna just take my life and throw it away at the bottom. I'm in the world like everybody else. The way I see it everybody else got to come up a little taste to be where I am.

BERNIECE: You right at the bottom with the rest of us.

BOY WILLIE: I'll tell you this . . . and ain't a living soul can put a come back on it. If you believe that's where you at then you gonna act that way. If you act that way then that's where you gonna be. It's as simple as that. Ain't no mystery to life. I don't know how you come to believe that stuff. Crawley didn't think like that. He wasn't living at the bottom of life. Papa Boy Charles and Mama Ola wasn't living at the bottom of life. You ain't never heard them say nothing like that. They would have taken a strap to you if they heard you say something like that.

(*Doaker enters from his room.*)

Hey, Doaker . . . Berniece say the colored folks is living at the bottom of life. I tried to tell her if she think that . . . that's where she gonna be. You think you living at the bottom of life? Is that how you see yourself?

DOAKER: I'm just living the best way I know how. I ain't thinking about no top or no bottom.

BOY WILLIE: That's what I tried to tell Berniece. I don't know where she got that from. That sound like something Avery would say. Avery think cause the white man give him a turkey for Thanksgiving that makes him better than everybody else. That's gonna raise him out of the bottom of life. I don't need nobody to give me a turkey. I can get my own turkey. All you have to do is get out my way. I'll get me two or three turkeys.

BERNIECE: You can't even get a chicken let alone two or three turkeys. Talking about get out your way. Ain't nobody in your way.

(*To Maretha.*)

Straighten your head, Maretha! Don't be bending down like that. Hold your head up!

(*To Boy Willie.*)

All you got going for you is talk. You' whole life that's all you ever had going for you.

BOY WILLIE: See now . . . I'll tell you something about me. I done strung along and strung along. Going this way and that. Whatever way would lead me to a moment of peace. That's all I want. To be as easy with everything. But I wasn't born to that. I was born to a time of fire.

The world ain't wanted no part of me. I could see that since I was about seven. The world say it's better off without me. See, Berniece accept that. She trying to come up to where she can prove something to the world. Hell, the world a better place cause of me. I don't see it like Berniece. I got a heart that beats here and it beats just as loud as the next fellow's. Don't care if he black or white. Sometime it beats louder. When it beats louder, then everybody can hear it. Some people get scared of that. Like Berniece. Some people get scared to hear a nigger's heart beating. They think you ought to lay low with that heart. Make it beat quiet and go along with everything the way it is. But my mama ain't birthed me for nothing. So what I got to do? I got to mark my passing on the road. Just like you write on a tree, "Boy Willie was here."

That's all I'm trying to do with that piano. Trying to put my mark on the road. Like my daddy done. My heart say for me to sell that piano and get me some land so I can make a life for myself to live in my own way. Other than that I ain't thinking about nothing Berniece got to say.

(*There is a knock at the door. Boy Willie crosses to it and yanks it open thinking it is Lymon. Avery enters. He carries a Bible.*)

BOY WILLIE: Where you been, nigger? Aw . . . I thought you was Lymon. Hey, Berniece, look who's here.

BERNIECE: Come on in, Avery. Don't you pay Boy Willie no mind.

BOY WILLIE: Hey . . . Hey, Avery . . . tell me this . . . can you get to heaven with half the Bible?

BERNIECE: Boy Willie . . . I done told you to leave me alone.

BOY WILLIE: I just ask the man a question. He can answer. He don't need you to speak for him. Avery . . . if you only believe on half the Bible and don't want to accept the other half . . . you think God let you in heaven? Or do you got to have the whole Bible? Tell Berniece . . . if you only believe in part of it . . . when you see God he gonna ask you why you ain't believed in the other part . . . then he gonna send you straight to Hell.

AVERY: You got to be born again. Jesus say unless a man be born again he cannot come unto the Father and who so ever heareth my words and believeth them not shall be cast into a fiery pit.

BOY WILLIE: That's what I was trying to tell Berniece. You got to believe in it all. You can't go at nothing halfway. She think she going to heaven with half the Bible.

(*To Berniece.*)

You hear that . . . Jesus say you got to believe in it all.

BERNIECE: You keep messing with me.

BOY WILLIE: I ain't thinking about you.

DOAKER: Come on in, Avery, and have a seat. Don't pay neither one of them no mind. They been arguing all day.

BERNIECE: Come on in, Avery.

AVERY: How's everybody in here?

BERNIECE: Here, set this comb back over there on that stove.

(*To Avery.*)

Don't pay Boy Willie no mind. He been around here bothering me since I come home from work.

BOY WILLIE: Boy Willie ain't bothering you. Boy Willie ain't bothering nobody. I'm just waiting on Lymon to get back. I ain't thinking about you. You heard the man say I was right and you still don't want to believe it. You just wanna go and make up anythin'. Well there's Avery . . . there's the preacher . . . go on and ask him.

AVERY: Berniece believe in the Bible. She been baptized.

BOY WILLIE: What about that part that say an eye for an eye a tooth for a tooth and a life for a life? Ain't that in there?

DOAKER: What they say down there at the bank, Avery?

AVERY: Oh, they talked to me real nice. I told Berniece . . . they say maybe they let me borrow the money. They done talked to my boss down at work and everything.

DOAKER: That's what I told Berniece. You working every day you ought to be able to borrow some money.

AVERY: I'm getting more people in my congregation every day. Berniece says she gonna be the Deaconess. I get me my church I can get married and settled down. That's what I told Berniece.

DOAKER: That be nice. You all ought to go ahead and get married. Berniece don't need to be by herself. I tell her that all the time.

BERNIECE: I ain't said nothing about getting married. I said I was thinking about it.

DOAKER: Avery get him his church you all can make it nice.

(*To Avery.*)

Berniece said you was coming by to bless the house.

AVERY: Yeah, I done read up on my Bible. She asked me to come by and see if I can get rid of Sutter's ghost.

BOY WILLIE: Ain't no ghost in this house. That's all in Berniece's head. Go on up there and see if you see him. I'll give you a hundred dollars if you see him. That's all in her imagination.

DOAKER: Well, let her find that out then. If Avery blessing the house is gonna make her feel better . . . what you got to do with it?

AVERY: Berniece say Maretha seen him too. I don't know, but I found a part in the Bible to bless the house. If he is here then that ought to make him go.

BOY WILLIE: You worse than Berniece believing all that stuff. Talking about . . . if he here. Go on up there and find out. I been up there I ain't seen him. If you reading from that Bible gonna make him leave out of Berniece imagination, well, you might be right. But if you talking about . . .

DOAKER: Boy Willie, why don't you just be quiet? Getting all up in the man's business. This ain't got nothing to do with you. Let him go ahead and do what he gonna do.

BOY WILLIE: I ain't stopping him. Avery ain't got no power to do nothing.

AVERY: Oh, I ain't got no power. God got the power! God got power over everything in His creation. God can do anything. God say, "As I commandeth so it shall be." God said, "Let there be light," and there was light. He made the world in six days and rested on the seventh. God's got a wonderful power. He got power over life and death. Jesus raised Lazareth from the dead. They was getting ready to bury him and Jesus told him say, "Rise up and walk." He got up and walked and the people made great rejoicing at the power of God. I ain't worried about him chasing away a little old ghost!

(*There is a knock at the door. Boy Willie goes to answer it. Lymon enters carrying a coil of rope.*)

BOY WILLIE: Where you been? I been waiting on you and you run off somewhere.

LYMON: I ran into Grace. I stopped and bought her drink. She say she gonna go to the picture show with me.

BOY WILLIE: I ain't thinking about no Grace nothing.

LYMON: Hi, Berniece.

BOY WILLIE: Give me that rope and get up on this side of the piano.

DOAKER: Boy Willie, don't start nothing now. Leave the piano alone.

BOY WILLIE: Get that board there, Lymon. Stay out of this, Doaker.

(*Berniece exits up the stairs.*)

DOAKER: You just can't take the piano. How you gonna take the piano? Berniece ain't said nothing about selling that piano.

BOY WILLIE: She ain't got to say nothing. Come on, Lymon. We got to lift one end at a time up on the board. You got to watch so that the board don't slide up under there.

LYMON: What we gonna do with the rope?

BOY WILLIE: Let me worry about the rope. You just get up on this side over here with me.

(*Berniece enters from the stairs. She has her hand in her pocket where she has Crawley's gun.*)

AVERY: Boy Willie . . . Berniece . . . why don't you all sit down and talk this out now?

BERNIECE: Ain't nothing to talk out.

BOY WILLIE: I'm through talking to Berniece. You can talk to Berniece till you get blue in the face, and it don't make no difference. Get up on that side, Lymon. Throw that rope around there and tie it to the leg.

LYMON: Wait a minute . . . wait a minute, Boy Willie. Berniece got to say. Hey, Berniece . . . did you tell Boy Willie he could take this piano?

BERNIECE: Boy Willie ain't taking nothing out of my house but himself. Now you let him go ahead and try.

BOY WILLIE: Come on, Lymon, get up on this side with me.

(*Lymon stands undecided.*)

Come on, nigger! What you standing there for?

LYMON: Maybe Berniece is right, Boy Willie. Maybe you shouldn't sell it.

AVERY: You all ought to sit down and talk it out. See if you can come to an agreement.

DOAKER: That's what I been trying to tell them. Seem like one of them ought to respect the other one's wishes.

BERNIECE: I wish Boy Willie would go on and leave my house. That's what I wish. Now, he can respect that. Cause he's leaving here one way or another.

BOY WILLIE: What you mean one way or another? What's that supposed to mean? I ain't scared of no gun.

DOAKER: Come on, Berniece, leave him alone with that.

BOY WILLIE: I don't care what Berniece say. I'm selling my half. I can't help it if her half got to go along with it. It ain't like I'm trying to cheat her out of her half. Come on, Lymon.

LYMON: Berniece . . . I got to do this . . . Boy Willie say he gonna give you half of the money . . . say he want to get Sutter's land.

BERNIECE: Go on, Lymon. Just go on . . . I done told Boy Willie what to do.

BOY WILLIE: Here, Lymon . . . put that rope up over there.

LYMON: Boy Willie, you sure you want to do this? The way I figure it . . . I might be wrong . . . but I figure she gonna shoot you first.

BOY WILLIE: She just gonna have to shoot me.

BERNIECE: Maretha, get on out the way. Get her out the way, Doaker.

DOAKER: Go on, do what your mama told you.

BERNIECE: Put her in your room.

(*Maretha exits to Doaker's room. Boy Willie and Lymon try to lift the piano. The door opens and Wining Boy enters. He has been drinking.*)

WINING BOY: Man, these niggers around here! I stopped down there at Seefus. . . . These folks standing around talking about Patchneck Red's coming. They jumping back and getting off the sidewalk talking about Patchneck Red this and Patchneck Red that. Come to find out . . . you know who they was talking about? Old John D. from up around Tyler! Used to run around with Otis Smith. He got everybody scared of him. Calling him Patchneck Red. They don't know I whupped the nigger's head in one time.

BOY WILLIE: Just make sure that board don't slide, Lymon.

LYMON: I got this side. You watch that side.

WINING BOY: Hey, Boy Willie, what you got? I know you got a pint stuck up in your coat.

BOY WILLIE: Wining Boy, get out the way!

WINING BOY: Hey, Doaker. What you got? Gimme a drink. I want a drink.

DOAKER: It look like you had enough of whatever it was. Come talking about "What you got?" You ought to be trying to find somewhere to lay down.

WINING BOY: I ain't worried about no place to lay down. I can always find me a place to lay down in Berniece's house. Ain't that right, Berniece?

BERNIECE: Wining Boy, sit down somewhere. You been out there drinking all day. Come in here smelling like an old polecat. Sit on down there, you don't need nothing to drink.

DOAKER: You know Berniece don't like all that drinking.

WINING BOY: I ain't disrespecting Berniece. Berniece, am I disrespecting you? I'm just trying to be nice. I been with strangers all day and they treated me like family. I come in here to family and you treat me like a stranger. I don't need your whiskey. I can buy my own. I wanted your company, not your whiskey.

DOAKER: Nigger, why don't you go upstairs and lay down? You don't need nothing to drink.

WINING BOY: I ain't thinking about no laying down. Me and Boy Willie fixing to party. Ain't that right, Boy Willie? Tell him. I'm fixing to play me some piano. Watch this.

(*Wining Boy sits down at the piano.*)

BOY WILLIE: Come on, Wining Boy! Me and Lymon fixing to move the piano.

WINING BOY: Wait a minute . . . wait a minute. This a song I wrote for Cleotha. I wrote this song in memory of Cleotha.

(*He begins to play and sing.*)

Hey little woman what's the matter with you now
Had a storm last night and blowed the line all down

Tell me how long
Is I got to wait
Can I get it now
Or must I hesitate

It takes a hesitating stocking in her hesitating shoe
It takes a hesitating woman wanna sing the blues

Tell me how long
Is I got to wait
Can I kiss you now
Or must I hesitate.

BOY WILLIE: Come on, Wining Boy, get up! Get up, Wining Boy! Me and Lymon's fixing to move the piano.

WINING BOY: Naw . . . Naw . . . you ain't gonna move this piano!

BOY WILLIE: Get out the way, Wining Boy.

(*Wining Boy, his back to the piano, spreads his arms out over the piano.*)

WINING BOY: You ain't taking this piano out the house. You got to take me with it!

BOY WILLIE: Get on out the way, Wining Boy! Doaker get him!

(*There is a knock on the door.*)

BERNIECE: I got him, Doaker. Come on, Wining Boy. I done told Boy Willie he ain't taking the piano.

(*Berniece tries to take Wining Boy away from the piano.*)

WINING BOY: He got to take me with it!

(*Doaker goes to answer the door. Grace enters.*)

GRACE: Is Lymon here?

DOAKER: Lymon.

WINING BOY: He ain't taking that piano.

BERNIECE: I ain't gonna let him take it.

GRACE: I thought you was coming back. I ain't gonna sit in that truck all day.

LYMON: I told you I was coming back.

GRACE: (*Sees Boy Willie.*) Oh, hi, Boy Willie. Lymon told me you was gone back down South.

LYMON: I said he was going back. I didn't say he had left already.

GRACE: That's what you told me.

BERNIECE: Lymon, you got to take your company someplace else.

LYMON: Berniece, this is Grace. That there is Berniece. That's Boy Willie's sister.

GRACE: Nice to meet you.

(*To Lymon.*)

I ain't gonna sit out in that truck all day. You told me you was gonna take me to the movie.

LYMON: I told you I had something to do first. You supposed to wait on me.

BERNIECE: Lymon, just go on and leave. Take Grace or whoever with you. Just go on get out my house.

BOY WILLIE: You gonna help me move this piano first, nigger!

LYMON: (*To Grace.*) I got to help Boy Willie move the piano first.

(*Everybody but Grace suddenly senses Sutter's presence.*)

GRACE: I ain't waiting on you. Told me you was coming right back. Now you got to move a piano. You just like all the other men.

(*Grace now senses something.*)

Something ain't right here. I knew I shouldn't have come back up in this house.

(*Grace exits.*)

LYMON: Hey, Grace! I'll be right back, Boy Willie.

BOY WILLIE: Where you going, nigger?

LYMON: I'll be back. I got to take Grace home.

BOY WILLIE: Come on, let's move the piano first!

LYMON: I got to take Grace home. I told you I'll be back.

(*Lymon exits. Boy Willie exits and calls after him.*)

BOY WILLIE: Come on, Lymon! Hey . . . Lymon! Lymon . . . come on!

(*Again, the presence of Sutter is felt.*)

WINING BOY: Hey, Doaker, did you feel that? Hey, Berniece . . . did you get cold? Hey, Doaker . . .

DOAKER: What you calling me for?

WINING BOY: I believe that's Sutter.

DOAKER: Well, let him stay up there. As long as he don't mess with me.

BERNIECE: Avery, go on and bless the house.

DOAKER: You need to bless that piano. That's what you need to bless. It ain't done nothing but cause trouble. If you gonna bless anything go on and bless that.

WINING BOY: Hey, Doaker, if he gonna bless something let him bless everything. The kitchen . . . the upstairs. Go on and bless it all.

BOY WILLIE: Ain't no ghost in this house. He need to bless Berniece's head. That's what he need to bless.

AVERY: Seem like that piano's causing all the trouble. I can bless that. Berniece, put me some water in that bottle.

(*Avery takes a small bottle from his pocket and hands it to Berniece, who goes into the kitchen to get water. Avery takes a candle from his pocket and lights it. He gives it to Berniece as she gives him the water.*)

Hold this candle. Whatever you do make sure it don't go out.

O Holy Father we gather here this evening in the Holy Name to cast out the spirit of one James Sutter. May this vial of water be empowered with thy spirit. May each drop of it be a weapon and a shield against the presence of all evil and may it be a cleansing and blessing of this humble abode.

Just as Our Father taught us how to pray so He say, "I will prepare a table for you in the midst of mine enemies," and in His hands we place ourselves to come unto his presence. Where there is Good so shall it cause Evil to scatter to the Four Winds.

(*He throws water at the piano at each commandment.*)

AVERY: Get thee behind me, Satan! Get thee behind the face of Righteousness as we Glorify His Holy Name! Get thee behind the Hammer of Truth that breaketh down the Wall of Falsehood! Father. Father. Praise. Praise. We ask in Jesus' name and call forth the power of the Holy Spirit as it is written . . .

(*He opens the Bible and reads from it.*)

I will sprinkle clean water upon thee and ye shall be clean.

BOY WILLIE: All this old preaching stuff. Hell, just tell him to leave.

(*Avery continues reading throughout Boy Willie's outburst.*)

AVERY: I will sprinkle clean water upon you and you shall be clean: from all your uncleanliness, and from all your idols, will I cleanse you. A new heart also will I give you, and a new spirit will I put within you: and I will take out of your flesh the heart of stone, and I will give you a heart of flesh. And I will put my spirit within you, and cause you to walk in my statutes, and ye shall keep my judgments, and do them.

(*Boy Willie grabs a pot of water from the stove and begins to fling it around the room.*)

BOY WILLIE: Hey Sutter! Sutter! Get your ass out this house! Sutter! Come on and get some of this water! You done drowned in the well, come on and get some more of this water!

(*Boy Willie is working himself into a frenzy as he runs around the room throwing water and calling Sutter's name. Avery continues reading.*)

BOY WILLIE: Come on, Sutter!

(*He starts up the stairs.*)

Come on, get some water! Come on, Sutter!

(*The sound of Sutter's Ghost is heard. As Boy Willie approaches the steps he is suddenly thrown back by the unseen force, which is choking him. As he struggles he frees himself, then dashes up the stairs.*)

BOY WILLIE: Come on, Sutter!

AVERY (*continuing*): A new heart also will I give you and a new spirit will I put within you: and I will take out of your flesh the heart of stone, and I will give you a heart of flesh. And I will put my spirit within you, and cause you to walk in my statutes, and ye shall keep my judgments, and do them.

(*There are loud sounds heard from upstairs as Boy Willie begins to wrestle with Sutter's Ghost. It is a life-and-death struggle fraught with perils and faultless terror. Boy Willie is thrown down the stairs. Avery is stunned into silence. Boy Willie picks himself up and dashes back upstairs.*)

AVERY: Berniece, I can't do it.

(*There are more sounds heard from upstairs. Doaker and Wining Boy stare at one another in stunned disbelief. It is in this moment, from somewhere old, that Berniece realizes what she must do. She crosses to the piano. She begins to play. The song is found piece by piece. It is an old urge to song that is both a commandment and a plea. With each repetition it gains in strength. It is intended as an exorcism and a dressing for battle. A rustle of wind blowing across two continents.*)

BERNIECE (*singing*):
    I want you to help me
    I want you to help me
    I want you to help me
    I want you to help me
    I want you to help me
    I want you to help me
    Mama Berniece
    I want you to help me
    Mama Esther
    I want you to help me
    Papa Boy Charles
    I want you to help me
    Mama Ola
    I want you to help me

    I want you to help me
    I want you to help me
    I want you to help me
    I want you to help me
    I want you to help me
    I want you to help me
    I want you to help me
    I want you to help me

(*The sound of a train approaching is heard. The noise upstairs subsides.*)

BOY WILLIE: Come on, Sutter! Come back, Sutter!

(*Berniece begins to chant:*)

BERNIECE:
  Thank you.
  Thank you.
  Thank you.

(*A calm comes over the house. Maretha enters from Doaker's room. Boy Willie enters on the stairs. He pauses a moment to watch Berniece at the piano.*)

BERNIECE:
  Thank you.
  Thank you.

BOY WILLIE: Wining Boy, you ready to go back down home? Hey, Doaker, what time the train leave?

DOAKER: You still got time to make it.

(*Maretha crosses and embraces Boy Willie.*)

BOY WILLIE: Hey Berniece . . . if you and Maretha don't keep playing on that piano . . . ain't no telling . . . me and Sutter both liable to be back.

(*He exits.*)

BERNIECE: Thank you.

(*The lights go down to black.*)

1987

A Brief History of Western Theater

Words and phrases highlighted in **boldface** are defined in the Glossary of Dramatic and Critical Terms (pp. 729–737).

In earlier centuries, when only a small part of the populace was literate, theater was one of the primary venues for passing down the great stories and traditions of culture to new generations. At different times and in different parts of the world, drama and theater have served a variety of functions — from teaching history and legend, to promoting religious and spiritual values, to simply offering a break from daily toil and worry. At its best, theater performs many of these functions simultaneously. What is sometimes called "the tradition" of Western theater is really any number of traditions that compete with one another, contribute to one another, and jostle one another in and out of vogue. Any attempt to cover 2,500 years of cultural history in a few pages will, of course, be incomplete. This overview, however, identifies and provides a context for some general trends and important moments in Western drama.

While the history presented here was unfolding in Europe and America, theater and drama in other parts of the world were likewise developing and changing to respond to evolving social and cultural circumstances. Indeed, some have contended that theater, in some form, is a practice that is universal to all human culture. Until fairly recently, however (perhaps the last hundred or so years), there was fairly little cross-pollination between the different regional and world traditions. For the sake of brevity and simplicity, therefore, this history concerns itself with the theater that finds its roots in ancient Greece and continues to thrive in Europe and North America.

Little is really known about the origins of Western theater, and much that has been written on the subject is essentially educated guesswork. The most commonly repeated theory, which owes its authority to the Greek philosopher Aristotle (384–322 B.C.), is that drama arose as part of religious rituals in honor of Dionysus, the ancient Greek god of wine. This theory holds that at some point in the history of these rituals, a member of the chorus, singing or chanting hymns in honor of the god, stepped forward to interact with the chorus as an actor in the role of the god. The addition of a second actor and eventually a third allowed for increased conflict and complexity in these interactions and more varied types of story that could be dramatized.

It is certain that at the height of Greek drama, in the fifth century B.C., plays were performed in Athens as a part of the annual spring festival known as the City Dionysia, when playwrights competed for prizes in **tragedy**. The huge outdoor amphitheater in which the plays were presented seated as many as 15,000 spectators. The all-male casts consisted of few actors (often playing multiple roles) and a **chorus** of twelve to fifteen. Actors wore large masks with exaggerated features, and the chorus danced and sang its way through highly stylized **odes**. Such **conventions**, though they seem rather artificial to today's audiences, would have made it possible for audience members seated far from the action to enjoy the **spectacle** of performance. The plays of three great tragic authors from this period—Aeschylus (525–456 B.C.), Sophocles (496–406 B.C.), and Euripides (480–406 B.C.)—are still regularly performed around the world. Greek **comedy** is now divided into **old comedy**, with Aristophanes (c. 448–c. 385 B.C.) providing its leading examples, and **new comedy**, as practiced by Menander (342–292 B.C.).

Like much in Greek culture, Greek drama was admired by the Romans, who adopted the basic Greek dramatic **genres** and adapted them to suit Roman culture and character. The great exemplar of Roman tragedy was Seneca (4 B.C.–A.D. 65), whose plays combined bloody **plots**, often centered on revenge, with sophisticated rhetoric and a sense of the stoicism for which his culture was famous. His works were probably intended more for reading than for performance. The comic playwrights Plautus (c. 254–184 B.C.) and Terence (c. 190–159 B.C.) wrote fast-paced, witty comedies that made heavy use of **stock characters**. Though Roman drama is not much performed today, it was greatly admired during the European Renaissance and influenced many authors of that period, including Shakespeare.

After the fall of Rome (A.D. 476), the tragedies and comedies of antiquity went largely unread and unperformed for hundreds of years. Drama, however, still played a part in medieval cultural life, beginning with brief performances within Roman Catholic church services as early as the tenth century. In England, particularly, two main forms of drama helped to teach religious values and stories to a largely illiterate populace. Mystery plays (so named because they were produced by craft guilds, whose mysteries were known only to members, and because they dramatized religious mysteries) told incidents from the Bible and were performed on religious feast days beginning in the fourteenth century. While these mystery plays and the related genre of miracle plays taught particular stories of biblical characters and saints, morality plays—**allegories** of good and evil with names like *Everyman, Wisdom,* and *The Castle of Perseverance*—

imparted general precepts of behavior and belief. A more secular tradition of folk performances existed at this time as well, but written records and scripts for these do not survive as they do for the forms of drama supported by the church. Performances of medieval drama, though often highly skilled and elaborate, were by and large amateur affairs and took place in church courtyards, market squares, and other open public spaces.

The European Renaissance (which occurred from roughly the fourteenth through the seventeenth centuries) brought significant changes to all aspects of culture, including the theater. The rediscovery of the great classical comedies and tragedies provided models for ambitious secular dramas; professional theater companies began to flourish, first on the continent and then in England; and buildings once again began to be constructed specifically for the purpose of housing dramatic performances. By the late 1500s, the great flowering of Elizabethan drama was well underway in England. William Shakespeare (1564–1616) is regarded as the brightest star of this period, but he had plenty of company among prolific and skilled dramatists. Some well-known names among authors of tragedy are Thomas Kyd (1558–1594), Christopher Marlowe (1564–1593), John Webster (1580–1634), and John Ford (1586–1640). Ben Jonson (1572–1637), Francis Beaumont (1584–1616), and John Fletcher (1579–1625) wrote some of the era's best comedies, the latter two often collaborating.

The mid- to late seventeenth century is considered one of the great ages of comedy in Europe, particularly in France and England. In France, the plays of such authors as Molière (1622–1673) shone a satirical light on the manners and mores of members of the upper-class society who made up audiences. (Unfortunately, the reputation of the theater as entertainment primarily for the wealthy and influential has never entirely been shaken, which has kept too many people away from playhouses.) The year 1660 was particularly important for English drama, for it was when the theaters reopened after eighteen years of closure during the English civil war and a period of Puritan rule. With their reopening, English theaters for the first time showcased the talents of women, both on stage as actresses and off stage in the person of Aphra Behn (c. 1640–1689), the most popular playwright of the day. Behn's work, like that of her contemporaries, tended to be comedies dramatizing witty battles between the sexes and a gentle **satire** of contemporary behavior.

By the nineteenth century, theater in Europe had branched into many competing popular strands, with **melodrama** and **realism** among the most significant. Though its roots were in musical productions of the late seventeenth century, melodrama flourished (and indeed continues to do so, particularly in certain movie and television genres) with a predominantly middle-class audience who enjoyed suspenseful plots and clear heroes and villains. A more intellectual strain of drama was exemplified by such authors as Henrik Ibsen (1828–1906) in Norway, August Strindberg (1849–1912) in Sweden, and Anton Chekhov (1860–1904) in Russia—authors whose best-remembered works tend to dramatize the lives and problems of ordinary men and women dealing with the real problems of contemporary life. Important dramatic voices in England as the nineteenth century drew to a close included Oscar Wilde (1854–1900), whose light-seeming plays contain a wealth of social satire, and George Bernard Shaw (1856–1950), who remained an active writer and committed political reformer throughout his long life.

The early to mid–twentieth century was a particularly difficult time for Europe. Long-held religious and cultural certainties could no longer be counted on, World War I wrought devastation on the continent on a scale never before seen, and as that conflict ground to an end, a worldwide influenza epidemic eventually killed even more people than the war had. The theater, along with the rest of the art world, responded to the fragmentation and fear in ways that are collectively referred to as *modernism*. In France, Antonin Artaud (1896–1948) proposed his **theater of cruelty**, while Eugene Ionesco (1912–1994) began to produce plays that are still recognized as classics of the **theater of the absurd**. In the unsettled aftermath of various social and political tragedies, the stage was set for the horrors of World War II, from concentration camps to nuclear weapons. Perhaps the theatrical voice that spoke out most loudly against the growing Nazi menace was the German communist Bertolt Brecht (1898–1956), who hoped his **epic theater** would raise the political consciousness of the common people.

During these same years, American playwrights chose to work in ways that made less obvious and dramatic breaks with their predecessors. Musicals, sentimental comedies, and **well-made plays** based on domestic relations dominated the popular stage, while various versions of realism were in ascendancy among those serious American playwrights who had the most lasting influence on the stage. Playwrights including Susan Glaspell (1882–1948), Eugene O'Neill (1888–1953), Tennessee Williams (1911–1983), Arthur Miller (b. 1915), and Lorraine Hansberry (1930–1965) brought to life the struggles, and often the tragedies, of ordinary Americans. Though each of these authors worked in part within the conventions of realistic drama, each also sought to stretch the bounds of that drama, as when Glaspell chose to focus on the problems of women, or when Miller incorporated **expressionist** elements of dream and fantasy into his otherwise realistic *Death of a Salesman*. Some of the most interesting and controversial productions in the American theater of this period were created under the Depression era back-to-work program known as the Federal Theater Project.

Since the middle of the twentieth century, experimentation has continued to thrive on world stages, but many seemingly new theatrical expressions have their roots in the works of previous generations. Theater of the absurd has moved closer to the mainstream through the efforts of such successful writers as Samuel Beckett (1906–1989) and Harold Pinter (b. 1930). The flashback scenes in the popular *M. Butterfly* by David Henry Hwang (b. 1957) are often reminiscent of the more dreamlike and expressionistic works of Miller or Williams. The powerful influence of Brecht can be seen in works ranging from the plays of Caryl Churchill (b. 1939) to the anti–Vietnam War pageants of America's experimental Bread and Puppet Theater Company. Some critics claim that all theater is political by its nature as a collaborative art form, and certainly even domestic dramas often work with highly politicized themes, as with the treatment of race issues in plays by Athol Fugard (b. 1932) or August Wilson (b. 1945).

By the end of the twentieth century, popular new types of theater, particularly in America, included extended monologues such as Spaulding Gray's *Swimming to Cambodia,* Anna Deveare Smith's *Fires in the Mirror,* and Eve Ensler's *The Vagina Monologues.* At the other extreme, mixed-media **performance art** often downplays plot and the verbal elements of theater, focusing instead on music and wild visual spectacle. Popular American performance artists include Laurie Anderson and the Blue Man Group. Though theater has increasingly had to compete with movies and television for the hearts, minds, and money of patrons, live theater has its own special contribution to make. The theater tradition bequeathed to us by the ancient Greeks continues to thrive, and it will surely do so well into the future.

Biographical and Textual Notes

ARISTOPHANES [c. 448–c. 385 B.C.]

The best-known writer of Greek comedies, Aristophanes was a master of the irreverent satirical form now known as old comedy. Little is known with certainty about his life, but his writing clearly reflects the troubled times through which he lived, during the decline of the Athenian city-state and the long and deeply destructive Peloponnesian war (431–404 B.C.). Only eleven of his more than forty plays survive. His writings were a source of laughter but also dealt with many serious intellectual issues — for instance, courts and juries in *The Wasps* (422), the excesses of philosophers in *The Clouds* (423), and literature itself (particularly playwriting) in *The Frogs* (405). Many of his works satirized prominent contemporary Athenians, which occasionally caused trouble for Aristophanes. His dominant theme, though, is war, the overriding concern for most Greeks of his day, and *Lysistrata* (411) is the best known of his antiwar plays. His work makes clear that rowdy entertainment is not incompatible with serious social and political messages, while at the same time it reminds us of the importance of laughter.

Lysistrata is probably the most frequently performed Greek comedy today, and it remains controversial as well as funny. The women of Athens, Sparta, and other Greek city-states, under the leadership of Lysistrata, band together in an attempt to end the long wars that are robbing them of their husbands, lovers, and sons. Despite women's inferior position in the social hierarchy, they take over the city treasury and, more devastating, decide to withhold sex until the men agree to make peace. Some of the funniest scenes in *Lysistrata* occur as men and women suffer the torment of separation, and both the humor and the gender politics were no doubt heightened in the original productions by the fact that women's roles were played by male actors on the classical Greek stage. Frank discussions of the desires of both sexes, as well as the men's enormous and plainly visible erections, demonstrate the bawdry typical of much Greek comedy. More than a classic battle between the sexes, though, the play uses comedy to take on the most serious of topics — the devastating consequences of war. Consider particularly Lysistrata's speech on how war affects women (p. 66). There are inconsistencies within the play — not the least of which is that the women begin their sex strike because their men are away, and yet when the strike occurs, the men are suddenly present

711

to be tormented by it. But in spite of these problems, *Lysistrata* remains a classic in part for its perennially important themes and in part for its sheer entertainment value.

SAMUEL BECKETT [1906–1989]

It is hard to overestimate the influence that Samuel Beckett exerted over mid-twentieth-century theater in Europe, inspiring as he did subsequent generations of bold, spare playmaking. Born near Dublin, Beckett moved to France in the late 1920s, fought against the Nazis with the French resistance, and remained in France after the war, writing in both French and English. Though the author himself was most proud of his prose works—long and difficult novels including the trilogy *Molloy, Malone Dies,* and *The Unname-able* (1951–1953)—his reputation as a great writer rests principally on his plays. He is perhaps the greatest exponent of what came to be known as theater of the absurd. His first success came with *Waiting for Godot* (1952), a play that thoroughly upset established notions of plot and genre and that suggested the future direction of Beckett's work. As his playwriting career progressed, his works grew shorter, more enigmatic, and more self-consciously experimental. Many of Beckett's works present a bleak world—the postapocalyptic landscape of *Endgame* (1957), the nearly empty room in which the protagonist of *Krapp's Last Tape* (1958) "converses" with audio-tapes of his earlier self, the barren plain of *Happy Days* (1961) on which the unflappably upbeat Winnie spends her days literally buried up to her waist and later up to her neck in sand. In addition to writing, Beckett directed early productions of several of his plays and tried to preserve his original vision by maintaining strict control over subsequent productions.

Endgame is in many ways characteristic of Beckett's work. A bleak setting, disaffected and physically restricted characters, a static plot, repetitions, pauses, and elliptical language are all hallmarks of the playwright's style. Though Beckett is, as always, very specific about the setting of *Endgame,* directors have created various interpretations, including staging the play on sets made to resemble the inside of a skull (making the whole story the fantasy or nightmare of the paralyzed Hamm) and the platform of an abandoned subway station. Despite his specificity, though, the playwright explains very little. What has happened to the land to leave it so barren? How could this unnamed catastrophe affect even the quality of the light? How did Hamm and Clov survive? What, exactly, is their relationship? How accurate are their memories of the past? Why are Hamm's parents enclosed in trash bins? How do the characters expect to survive with their supplies rapidly running out? Time moves irrevocably on, but we are still in the dark as the play draws to an end. At the closing tableau, our questions are unanswered. Did Clov really see a boy approaching in the barren landscape, or have his eyes deceived him again? Has Clov really left? If so, what will become of Hamm? The word *endgame* refers to the closing moves of a chess match, but what sort of game has been played here, and who, if anyone, has won? Typically, Beckett's audience leaves the theater shaken and thoughtful but not really enlightened.

ANTON CHEKHOV [1860–1904]

Though he trained as a doctor and continued to practice medicine throughout most of his short adult life, Anton Chekhov devoted much of his energy to writing, and most of his success came from his literary pursuits. In his twenties, he began to publish short stories, many of which remain classics to this day, and comic sketches for the stage. During the last years of his life, while battling the tuberculosis that would eventually kill him, Chekhov penned his great full-length plays — *The Seagull* (1896), *Uncle Vanya* (1879), *The Three Sisters* (1901), and *The Cherry Orchard* (1903). Chekhov's plays were not immediately accessible to audiences of his day, accustomed as they were to the clearly drawn heroes and villains of melodrama. But his work was championed by the great actor and director Konstantin Stanislavsky of the Moscow Art Theater, and in time the playwright became one of the most respected in Russian theater. Existing in a space between comedy and tragedy, Chekhov's plays present characters drawn from the author's close observation of real people, with all their intermingled goodness, covetousness, vanity, and generosity. Though often his characters' motives are mixed, and rarely might they be considered fully admirable people, they stay with us because they seem so real.

The Cherry Orchard, Chekhov's last play, was written in 1903 and first performed in 1904. In act 2, the middle-aged and vaguely foolish Gaev says simply, "I am a man of the eighties," and therein lies much of the sorrowful mood of the play. A number of characters — Gaev, his sister Madame Ranevskaya, the old servant Firs — live in the past. Others — including the driven merchant Lopakhin, the visionary perpetual student Trofimov, and the impressionable young girl Anya — seem able to think only of the future. Nobody seems comfortable in the play's present moment, a time when the old political and social certainties of generations past are rapidly disintegrating, but the new order has yet to truly emerge. Chekhov insisted that *The Cherry Orchard* was a comedy, but it is hardly a laugh riot, and it doesn't have the happy ending typical of the genre. From the pure white of the blossoming orchard to the enigmatic sound of a breaking string, which twice occurs, the strange symbolism of the play creates an uneasy, often melancholy mood. But that mood never rises to the lofty heights associated with real tragedy. Moments of seriousness are often undercut with trivial, even comic, actions: a character munches a cucumber, falls down a flight of stairs, crushes a hat box with a suitcase. In the end, there is neither a comic reintegration nor a tragic fall to alter the characters' destinies. While circumstances change, the characters remain fundamentally the same, to the end unable to settle comfortably into the world they must inhabit.

CARYL CHURCHILL [b. 1938]

Caryl Churchill was born in England and moved with her family to Canada during World War II. She returned to England to attend Oxford University, and there she began writing plays for student production. After college, she pursued her writing in only a low-key fashion, penning short works, mostly for radio, while she stayed home to raise children. By the mid-1970s, she was beginning to produce full-length works on the London stage, chiefly at the Royal Court Theatre, a venue well known for its support of promising new writers. As she became established among Britain's leading playwrights, the strength and audacity of her voice continued to grow, and by the mid-1980s, she had begun to experiment with form, music, and choreography in many of her works. Churchill's range as an author can be seen in some of her best-known plays: *Cloud Nine* (1979) explores sexuality and sexual politics, *Top Girls* (1982) critiques a newly emerging definition of success for women, *Fen* (1983) examines the lives of the rural poor, *Serious Money* (1987) offers a biting critique of free-market capitalist ideology, and *The Skriker* (1994) combines a modern fable with elements of ancient British folklore.

Though now known for her commitment to the causes of both socialism and feminism, Churchill says she came late and slowly to politics. One of these more political plays, *Top Girls*, was first performed in 1982, a time when women in England, as in America, were increasingly internalizing the traditionally "male" values of the business world—self-reliance, hard work, and money making. Marlene embraces these values, while her sister Joyce remains bound to the ideals traditionally associated with both her gender and her working-class roots. Young Angie, who is poised to inherit her elders' place, ends the play repeating the single word "frightening," and Churchill certainly leaves us with a profound understanding of why both Marlene's and Joyce's worlds might frighten the young girl. For some readers and audiences, the fantasy dinner party that begins the play has proved problematic, laced as it is with Churchill's signature overlapping dialogue and seemingly connected only tangentially with the rest of the play. This initial scene, though, is integral to the play's design and deals just as much as the rest of the play does with the choices that women make in life. The joyous mood with which the party begins quickly dissolves, and what appeared to be a celebration of women's achievements becomes a critique of the varied cultural values held by the vastly different women, including Marlene herself.

ATHOL FUGARD [b. 1932]

Athol Fugard was born to an Afrikaans mother and an English father in Cape Province, South Africa, and grew up as a part of the privileged white minority under the system of racial segregation known as apartheid. In the late 1950s, Fugard began to work as both an actor and a playwright in an integrated theater group. Racial mixing was not permitted on stage at the time, though, so the company encountered legal difficulties. Collaboration with black performers and writers, however, helped to develop Fugard's talents and secure his place in the theatrical world. *The Blood Knot* (1961), which he performed with Zakes Moake, is a controversial play about two brothers, one of whom is light enough to pass as white. Fugard also collaborated in improvisational workshops with black actors and writers John Kani and Winston Ntshona to create plays including *Sizwe Bansi Is Dead* (1972) and *The Island* (1974). His solo writing efforts have been no less significant, including some of his best-known works — *A Lesson from Aloes* (1978), *"MASTER HAROLD" . . . and the boys* (1982), and *Valley Song* (1996, his first major postapartheid play). The backdrop of Fugard's plays typically displays his interest in social and political issues, including the racial and social class injustices that have defined so much of South African life. But more significantly, his works are about the struggles in the minds and hearts of real people, and that focus, even more than his political awareness, has made him a major voice in world theater.

"MASTER HAROLD" . . . and the boys is the most autobiographical of Fugard's works, with much of Hally's character, as well as his powerful and troubled relationship with Sam, reminiscent of Fugard's life. The playwright, however, did not merely transfer his memories to the script. Rather, he transformed them into an enduring fiction with resonance beyond the apartheid South Africa that serves as the play's backdrop. The play is about race and class issues, to be sure, but it is even more about people, family, and personal relationships. Fugard's artistry includes skillful manipulation of symbols, as in the scene when Sam and Hally compare their vivid memories of flying a kite together years earlier. Likewise Sam's passion for ballroom dancing suggests more than a cultural difference separating him from Hally. As he describes the dancers working together to create something beautiful, he clearly laments that such grace and unity do not exist in everyday life, and finally even strong-minded and generally optimistic Sam is forced to admit that his envisioned "world without collisions" is still only "a dream." Though

things have improved for South Africa's black majority since the end of apartheid, Sam's dream will probably never be fully realized, and *"MASTER HAROLD"... and the boys* remains a powerful examination of forces that both unite and divide people.

SUSAN GLASPELL [1882–1948]

Born, raised, and educated in Iowa, Susan Glaspell came to be associated with Massachusetts, where she and her husband, George Cram Cook, founded the Provincetown Players on Cape Cod. This small theater company was influential in giving a start to several serious playwrights, most notably Eugene O'Neill, and promoting realist dramas at a time when sentimental comedy and melodrama still dominated the stage. She began her writing career publishing short stories and novels, including the critically acclaimed *Fidelity* (1915). Glaspell's first several plays, including *Trifles* (1916), were one acts, and with them she began her lifelong interest in writing about the lives and special circumstances of women. She went on to write and produce a number of full-length plays as well, among the best known being *The Inheritors* (1921) and *Alison's House* (1930), which was based loosely on the life of Emily Dickinson and won a Pulitzer Prize. Though some of her work was more lighthearted, much of it dealt with serious issues of the day. Respected in her own time, Glaspell's writing fell out of fashion until it was "rediscovered" by feminist scholars and critics in the 1960s.

Trifles was first produced by the Provincetown Players in 1916, and a year later Glaspell transformed it into a short story entitled "A Jury of Her Peers," an ironic title given that when the story was written, women were not allowed to serve on juries in most states. This irony—the extreme separation of men's and women's worlds—lies at the center of *Trifles*, a play whose brevity belies its depth and its power to move an audience. Though at its heart the play is a murder mystery, it moves far beyond the fairly narrow conventions of that genre to present social commentary, both on contemporary relations between the sexes and on issues of loyalty and morality. Today, the blustering, arrogant men seem almost cartoonish in their ignorance, but we must remember that nothing in their upbringing or training has prepared them to think of "women's things"—preserves, birdcages, quilts—as anything but trifles. Likewise, the women are more complex than they may first appear and not only because their experiences allow them to see the "clues" that are invisible to the men. At the climax of the play, these women face a moral dilemma: should they share what they have discovered with their husbands, or should their loyalty lie with the accused woman? While Glaspell allows us to see the reasons for their choice, only we can decide if we believe their actions to be right.

HENRIK IBSEN [1828–1906]

Henrik Ibsen was born and raised in Skien, Norway, and he is still principally associated with that country, though he also lived for an extended
period in Italy, where he did much of his writing. His earliest literary successes were the poetic plays *Brand* (1865) and *Peer Gynt* (1867), which were
intended as closet dramas, though both eventually were performed on stage.
His real breakthrough, though, came in the late 1870s, when he began to
write realistic dramas that are sometimes called *problem plays* because they
explore contemporary social issues and problems. Some of the problems
Ibsen chose to depict, however, were too controversial for the theater of his
day—the subjugation of women in marriage in *A Doll House* (1879), vene-
real disease and incest in *Ghosts* (1881), the will of an individual against
social and political pressure in *An Enemy of the People* (1882). This subject
matter led some critics in Norway and abroad to protest against public performances of these works. Despite their controversial nature, though, or perhaps because of it, these were the plays that secured Ibsen's reputation as
one of the most influential playwrights of the late nineteenth century.
Important later works by Ibsen include *The Wild Duck* (1884), *Hedda Gabler*
(1890, probably his most performed play today), and *The Master Builder*
(1892). Many of his works resemble the type of tightly structured, plot-driven
theatrical device known as the *well-made play*, but his work contains subtleties of characterization and theme that help it rise above commonplace
theatrical experience.

Now that separation and divorce have become everyday occurrences, it is
hard to imagine the sensation caused by *A Doll House* when it was first performed in 1879. When Ibsen gave his audiences a peek into a troubled home,
they clearly did not like what they saw—a young family torn apart by deceit
and inequality and a stern condemnation of entrenched nineteenth-century
notions concerning the absolute sanctity of marriage. Yet despite the outcry
against his play, clearly something about it touched a chord with the public,
and *A Doll House* has gone on to become one of the great standards of the
theater. The curtain opens on a scene of seeming comfort—the home of a
middle-class family on its way up in the social world and the approach of a
joyous Christmas celebration. Almost immediately, however, we realize that
all is not well behind the façade of stability and happiness. Though Nora's
character growth is the centerpiece of the play, Ibsen was not merely advo-
cating women's rights. For him, Nora was a person first and a woman, wife,
and mother only secondarily, and as such she was entitled to develop to the
full extent of her abilities. It is not Nora's growth that finally tears her marriage apart; rather, it is the fact that her father and her husband, however
unwittingly, have stunted her natural development for so long that she

remains an emotional child well into her adult years. We may sympathize with Helmer's vulnerability and despair at the close of the play, but it is difficult for us to share his moment of optimism. Though domestic in scale, *A Doll House* strikes readers and theatrical audiences alike as a true modern tragedy.

ARTHUR MILLER [b. 1915]

Born and raised in New York and educated at the University of Michigan, Arthur Miller is recognized as one of the most important American dramatists. This reputation rests largely on plays written relatively early in his career, including *All My Sons* (1947, winner of the New York Drama Critics' Circle Award), *Death of a Salesman* (1949, winner of both the Drama Critics' Circle Award and the Pulitzer Prize), *The Crucible* (1953), and *A View from the Bridge* (1955). Though he continued to write after the mid-1950s, his output slowed somewhat, and his later works proved less popular with both critics and the public. Miller's writing shows clearly his social and political commitments. *The Crucible*, for instance, uses a story about the Salem witch-craft trials to comment on the persecution of suspected communists by Senator Joseph McCarthy and the House Un-American Activities Committee. His best work never fails, though, to combine this sort of social commentary with the believable characters and compelling stories that make for powerful theater, so a play like *The Crucible* outlives its original context and remains a drama classic. In addition to his plays, Miller's essays on the theater, particularly on the nature of modern tragedy, provide a rich source for students and devotees of drama.

Miller gave his best-known play, *Death of a Salesman*, the subtitle *Certain Private Conversations in Two Acts and a Requiem*, and perhaps it is this sense of overheard private conversations that gives the play its feeling of intimacy. The playwright skillfully weaves together techniques of realism and expressionism so that we see not only the interior workings of the Lomans' household but also the working of Willy Loman's troubled mind. The play's title leaves no room for suspense as to the fate awaiting Willy, but we are compelled nonetheless by his disintegration and are sympathetic to the troubles of his wife and sons. Though his decline and ultimate death are brought on by his own actions—particularly by his tenacious adherence to a code of bourgeois American values that does not suit his talents but also by his short temper, his infidelity, and his unequal treatment of his sons—Willy remains, nevertheless, a tragic figure for most audiences. Indeed, in a famous essay written shortly after the play's premier, Miller argued that, regardless of historical definitions of tragedy, a common man, no less than a king, could be a tragic hero. As his family gathers around his grave for the brief requiem scene, they still cannot agree on what sort of a man Willy was, but we feel keenly their different sorts of pain and loss.

WILLIAM SHAKESPEARE [1564–1616]

Widely regarded as the most influential writer not only of English drama but of English literature as a whole, William Shakespeare was a significant voice in the great flowering of theater during the English Renaissance. Born to a comfortable middle-class family in Stratford-upon-Avon, his early life remains largely a mystery, though this has not prevented much speculation throughout the years. It is likely that he attended the local grammar school, where his training would have included a good foundation in grammar, rhetoric, logic, and classical, chiefly Latin, literature. Such an education would be of great benefit to him as he developed his writing talents. By 1590, he had begun his career in the theater as an actor, a writer, and eventually a part owner of a theater company. His collected works include thirty-seven plays — comedies, tragedies, histories, and romances — as well as many poems, most notably the famous cycle of 154 sonnets. By the time Shakespeare died at the age of fifty-two, he was acknowledged as a leading light of the Elizabethan stage and had become successful enough to have purchased a coat of arms for his family home.

It has been said that a performance of *Hamlet* takes place somewhere on earth every day of every year, but this is, if anything, an understatement of the play's popularity and importance. Probably no other play in history has been subjected to such an array of productions and adaptations — both stage and film — and the depth of critical scrutiny as *Hamlet*. Tragedies of revenge were common enough in Shakespeare's England, but *Hamlet* clearly goes beyond its bloody antecedents to present complex psychological studies of its characters. Hamlet must face the death of his beloved father, a ghostly visitation, his mother's betrayal (as Hamlet sees it) of her marriage vows, the disintegration of his relationship with Ophelia, and the treachery of his old friends Rosencrantz and Guildenstern. Certainly these would be difficult problems for any man to face, but Hamlet is not just a man like any other. He is also the rightful heir to the throne of Denmark, and his uncle's act of fratricide has robbed him not only of his father but also of his crown.

The complexities of the text leave open many opportunities for interpretation within individual productions, as a single example can demonstrate. Following the influence of Freudian psychology, many twentieth-century productions played on the popular notion that Hamlet suffers from an Oedipus complex — a desire to eliminate his father because of his partially repressed sexual interest in his mother. The film versions directed by Laurence Olivier (1948, also starring Olivier in the title role) and Franco

Zeffirelli (1990, starring Mel Gibson) both make much of this Freudian interpretation, vividly depicting sexual tension in the scenes between Gertrude
and Hamlet, particularly the confrontation in Gertrude's bedroom (act 3,
scene 4). Other productions, however, including Kenneth Branagh's uncut
film version (1996), downplay this possibility, making Ophelia the clear center of Hamlet's sexual interest. In other examples of interpretive flexibility,
directors and actors must clarify the dubious nature of Hamlet's madness
and the degree to which Gertrude was complicit in the murder of her first
husband. Offering as it does such fertile ground for thought and analysis, it
is easy to see what has made *Hamlet* such an enduring classic.

SOPHOCLES [c. 496–c. 406 B.C.]

Sophocles was not the first important voice to emerge in drama, but as a representative of classical Greek tragedy, it is hard to imagine a more important
figure. Indeed, his works were considered such models of the craft that
Aristotle based much of his *Poetics* on an analysis of *Oedipus Rex*. Sophocles
was born to a wealthy Athenian family and became active in many aspects of
civic life as a soldier, a priest, and a statesman. Today, however, he is remembered principally for his achievements as a playwright. During a long and
distinguished career, he won first prize in the Greek drama competitions
more often than any other writer. Though there is evidence that he wrote
over 120 plays, only seven have survived in their entirety, along with frag-
ments of many others. In his plays, Sophocles wrestled with some of the
most important issues of his time and indeed of all time—the conflict
between fate and free will; between public and private morality; and between
duty to the family, the state, and the gods—giving his work enduring appeal.

Oedipus Rex (*Oedipus the King*, first performed in 430 B.C.), is one of
Sophocles' three Theban plays, the others being *Antigone* (441 B.C.) and
Oedipus at Colonus (401 B.C., first performed posthumously). The famous
story of Oedipus and his tragically fated family was already well known to
Sophocles' contemporaries, so the audience derived its pleasure not from suspense but from foreknowledge. Indeed, the central mechanism of *Oedipus
Rex* relies on complex layers of irony, including the audience's awareness of
what awaits the characters. Oedipus uses his own will, as Laius and Jocasta
did before him, in an attempt to avoid the fate (Greek *moira*) that has been
prophesied for him, and yet this apparent use of free will actually brings
about that fate. In addition, the characters actively seek the knowledge they
expect will save them, but this knowledge ultimately destroys them. Clearly,
though, Sophocles did not simply mean to argue that free will is an illusion or
that ignorance is preferable to knowledge. Rather, he plays on the audience's
desire to resolve seeming contradictions and asks us to untangle for ourselves

the complexities of Oedipus's dilemma. Contrasting images of sight and blindness highlight the ironies of the play: the blind prophet Tiresias sees truth more clearly than any of the sighted characters, while Oedipus is at first figuratively blind to his true identity and ultimately blinds himself physically because he cannot bear sight of the truth he has sought so long.

TENNESSEE WILLIAMS [1911–1983]

Born Thomas Lanier Williams in Columbia, Mississippi, as a child Williams moved with his family to St. Louis. His childhood was not easy: his parents were ill matched, the family had little money, and both he and his beloved sister, Rose, suffered from depression and medical problems. It took Williams three attempts at college before he finished, finally earning a degree in playwriting from the University of Iowa at the age of twenty-four. His earliest efforts at writing were unsuccessful, but in 1944 *The Glass Menagerie* opened in Chicago and later began a very successful run in New York, winning the prestigious Drama Critics' Circle Award. Other successes followed, including *A Streetcar Named Desire* (1947, which won a Pulitzer Prize and also helped launch the career of its young star, Marlon Brando), *Cat on a Hot Tin Roof* (1955), and *Suddenly Last Summer* (1958). The American stage in the 1940s and 1950s was not yet ready to accept overt homosexuality, so Williams transformed his own tortured searching for sexual and emotional fulfillment into plays with remarkably frank heterosexual themes. This frankness and a dreamy, poetic sense of language are key elements of his style. In his later years, Williams suffered from drug and alcohol problems and was occasionally institutionalized for these and the crippling depressions that continued to plague him. Though his later work never achieved the popular success of his early plays, Williams's reputation in the American theater is secure.

Many critics have claimed that Williams used his writing as a sort of therapy, a way to come to grips with the difficulties of his life. Certainly *The Glass Menagerie* is strongly autobiographical and examines many of the issues that haunted him and his family. Mildly crippled and painfully shy Laura Wingfield is very much based on Rose Williams, down to the fact that Williams's sister would lose herself in a fantasy world among her collection of glass animals. Laura's brother, Tom, who serves as a sort of narrator and through whose memory the play is filtered, is likewise a projection of the playwright himself. Both children are a disappointment to their mother, Amanda Wingfield, who is herself the sort of complex character an audience can neither wholly admire nor easily dismiss or dislike. No member of the family is happy in his or her circumstances, and as a result each retreats into a different sort of dream life. *The Glass Menagerie* provides ample evidence of the lyricism for which Williams is known, in which language creates a powerful mood while revealing character. The play also offers special rewards for those who read it, as opposed to seeing it on stage. The unusually specific descriptions and stage directions create vivid pictures in the minds of readers, allowing us to experience the play fully in our imaginations.

AUGUST WILSON [b. 1945]

Born and raised in the Hill District, an African American section of Pittsburgh that provides the backdrop to many of his plays, August Wilson has come to be seen as one of the most important, and certainly one of the most award-winning, voices on the contemporary American stage. He was the son of a mixed-race marriage, but his white father was not in the household when Wilson was growing up. He dropped out of high school but continued to read widely and began his serious writing with poetry, the rhythms of which can still be heard in his plays. In the 1960s, he became involved in the black power movement and also began to turn his writing talents to the stage. His best-known work is his cycle of historical plays examining important elements of African American experience, with one play set in each decade of the twentieth century. Among these are *Ma Rainy's Black Bottom* (1985), *Fences* (1987), *Joe Turner's Come and Gone* (1988), *The Piano Lesson* (1990), and *Seven Guitars* (1996). Each of these plays won the New York Drama Critics' Circle Award, and two of them—*Fences* and *The Piano Lesson*—also earned Wilson Pulitzer Prizes for drama.

As in much of Wilson's work, there is a metaphor at the center of *The Piano Lesson*—in this case the intricately carved antique piano, which clearly stands for far more than the fine musical instrument it actually is, representing both the family's history of enslavement and its strength to move beyond this history. Boy Willie's desire to sell the piano may at first appear self-serving or crassly materialistic, but we can hardly fault his desire to ensure his family's future security or the pride he would feel in owning a piece of the land on which his ancestors worked as slaves. Berniece's position is also valid, though: it is important for all families to honor their heritage, but it is particularly so for African Americans, who have had so much of their history violently erased. How, then, should the family choose between the two mutually exclusive positions, each of which is ultimately right? When the supernatural enters the story in the form of the ghost story subplot, it provides more than just the thrill of the unknown. Taking us to the spiritual plane, Wilson reminds us that more than a piece of family lore, a piece of land, or even a piece of history is at stake here: along with the literal ghost, the family must figure out how to exorcise the figurative ghosts of the past, or they must learn to live with their haunting.

List of Selected Video Resources

ARISTOPHANES

Lysistrata. 97 minutes, color, 1987. VHS, Beta. A contemporary adaptation, shot on location at the Acropolis. In Greek with English subtitles. With Jenny Karezi and Costas Kazakos. Directed by Georgos Zervoulakos. Distributed by Insight Media.

SAMUEL BECKETT

Endgame. 96 minutes, color, 1992. VHS. *Endgame* is presented by the University of Maryland in collaboration with PBS. Presented by the San Quentin Drama Workshop. Part of Visual Press's Beckett Directs Beckett series, based on an original stage production. With Bud Thorpe, Rick Cluchey, and Teresita Garcia Suro. Directed for film by Robert Bilheimer. Distributed by Smithsonian Institution Press.

Beckett Film Project: Endgame. 84 minutes, color, 2001. DVD. This series contains productions of all nineteen of Samuel Beckett's stage plays. With Michael Gambon, David Thewlis, Charles Simon, and Jean Anderson. Directed by Conor McPherson. Produced and distributed by Blue Angel Films for RTÉ in association with Channel 4 and the Irish Film Board.

ANTON CHEKHOV

The Cherry Orchard, Part I: Chekhov, Innovator of Modern Drama. 21 minutes, color and black-and-white, 1968. VHS, Beta, 16 mm film. Select scenes with discussion led by Norris Houghton. Distributed by Encyclopaedia Britannica Educational Corp.

The Cherry Orchard, Part II: Comedy or Tragedy? 21 minutes, color and black-and-white, 1967. VHS, Beta, 16 mm film. Norris Houghton discusses Chekhov's technique of dramatization of interior actions. Distributed by Encyclopaedia Britannica Educational Corp.

The Cherry Orchard. 135 minutes, color, 1999. This adaptation of Chekhov's drama began playing in American theaters in February 2002. However, as this book goes to press, the film has not yet been released on video. With Charlotte Rampling, Alan Bates, Katrin Cartlidge, and Owen

Teale. Written and directed by Michael Cacoyannis. Distributed by Kino International.

CARYL CHURCHILL

Top Girls.   175 minutes, color, 1996. VHS. A 1991 BBC performance, followed by interviews with the playwright and the actors and director involved in the production. With Deborah Findlay, Beth Goddard, Cecily Hobbs, and Sarah Lam. Directed by Max Stafford-Clark. Distributed by Open University.

ATHOL FUGARD

"MASTER HAROLD" . . . and the boys.   90 minutes, color, 1984. VHS, Beta. A made-for-cable production. With Zakes Mokae and Matthew Broderick. Directed by Michael Lindsay-Hogg. Distributed by Warner Home Video.

SUSAN GLASPELL

A Jury of Her Peers.   30 minutes, color, 1980. VHS. Based on the short-story version of *Trifles.* Directed by Sally Heckel. Distributed by Home Vision.

HENRIK IBSEN

A Doll's House.   89 minutes, black-and-white, 1959. VHS, Beta. An original television production. With Julie Harris, Christopher Plummer, Jason Robards, Hume Cronyn, Eileen Heckart, and Richard Thomas. Directed by James Costigan. Distributed by MGM/UA Entertainment.

A Doll's House.   98 minutes, color, 1973. VHS, 16 mm film. Controversial for explicit scenes only referred to in Ibsen's text. With Jane Fonda, Edward Fox, and Trevor Howard. Directed by Joseph Losey. Distributed by Prism Entertainment.

A Doll's House.   93 minutes, color, 1973. VHS. A more faithful translation, this version was held out of general release when it was first made because of the competition from the Jane Fonda version. With Claire Bloom, Anthony Hopkins, and Ralph Richardson. Directed by Patrick Garland. Adapted by Christopher Hampton. Distributed by AIMS Multimedia.

ARTHUR MILLER

Death of a Salesman.   120 minutes, color, 1966. VHS. Acclaimed television production in which Cobb and Duncock re-create their original Broadway roles as Willy and Linda Loman. With Lee J. Cobb, Mildred Duncock, George

Segal, and James Farentino. Directed by Alex Segal. Distributed by Insight Media.

Death of a Salesman.   135 minutes, color, 1985. VHS, Beta. Award-winning made-for-television adaptation of the play. With Dustin Hoffman, John Malkovich, Charles Durning, and Stephen Lang. Directed by Volker Schlondorff. Distributed by Facets Multimedia and Warner Home Video.

WILLIAM SHAKESPEARE

Hamlet.   153 minutes, black-and-white, 1948. VHS, Beta, laser disc, DVD. Olivier's classic interpretation, which set the standard for twentieth-century productions of *Hamlet.* Filmed in Elsinore, Denmark. With Laurence Olivier, Basil Sydney, Felix Aylmer, Jean Simmons, Stanley Holloway, Peter Cushing, and Christopher Lee. Voice of John Gielgud. Directed by Laurence Olivier. Distributed by Paramount Home Video.

Hamlet.   135 minutes, color, 1990. VHS. A fast-paced, witty, and accessible *Hamlet,* though some purists find the cuts too radical. With Mel Gibson, Glenn Close, Alan Bates, Paul Scofield, Ian Holm, and Helena Bonham-Carter. Directed by Franco Zeffirelli. Distributed by Warner Home Video.

Hamlet.   165 minutes, color, 1990. VHS, DVD. A PBS Great Performances presentation of Joseph Papp's New York Shakespeare Festival production. With Kevin Kline, Francis James, Brian Murray, and Diana Venora. Directed by Kevin Kline. Distributed by Broadway Theatre Archive.

Hamlet.   242 minutes, color, 1996. VHS, Laser disc. A star-studded cast in a landmark production, the first filmed version of *Hamlet* to use an uncut version of Shakespeare's play. With Kenneth Branagh, Kate Winslet, Julie Christie, and Derek Jacobi. Directed by Kenneth Branagh. Distributed by Columbia Tristar Home Video.

Hamlet.   112 minutes, color, 2000. VHS, DVD. The action of *Hamlet* updated and transposed to modern-day New York City. With Ethan Hawke, Kyle MacLachlan, Sam Shepherd, Bill Murray, and Julia Stiles. Directed by Michael Almereyda. Distributed by Buena Vista Home Entertainment.

SOPHOCLES

Oedipus Rex.   87 minutes, color, 1957. VHS, 16 mm film. Elaborate masks, sets, and choral movement used to re-create the feel of an ancient Greek production. With Douglas Campbell, Douglas Rain, Eric House, and Eleanor Stuart. Directed by Tyrone Guthrie. Based on William Yeats's translation. Distributed by Water Bearer Films.

Oedipus the King.   45 minutes, color, 1975. VHS, Beta, 16 mm film. Set in the fifth century B.C. Theatre of Amphiaraion by the Athens Classical Theatre Company. Includes an English soundtrack. With Anthony Quayle, James Mason, Claire Bloom, and Ian Richardson. Directed by Harold Mantell. Distributed by Films for the Humanities and Sciences.

TENNESSEE WILLIAMS

The Glass Menagerie.   134 minutes, color, 1987. VHS, Beta, DVD. Well-acted and well-received adaptation based on the Broadway revival. With Joanne Woodward, Karen Allen, John Malkovich, and James Naughton. Directed by Paul Newman. Distributed by Universal Studios Home Video.

AUGUST WILSON

The Piano Lesson.   99 minutes, color, 1994. VHS. A made-for-television Hallmark Hall of Fame production. With Alfre Woodard, Charles Dutton, and Courtney Vance. Directed by Lloyd Richards. Distributed by Republic Pictures Home Video.

Directory of Distributors

AIMS Multimedia, 9710 DeSoto Avenue, Chatsworth, CA 91311-4409, (818) 773-4300, (800) 367-2467

Blue Angel Films, see local retailer.

Broadway Theatre Archive, see local retailer.

Buena Vista Home Entertainment, 500 South Buena Vista Street, Burbank, CA 91521, (800) 723-4763

Columbia Tristar Home Video, see local retailer.

Encyclopaedia Britannica Educational Corporation, 310 South Michigan Avenue, Chicago, IL 60604, (312) 347-7900, (800) 621-3900

Facets Multimedia, Inc., 1517 West Fullerton Avenue, Chicago, IL 60614, (773) 281-9075, (800) 331-6197

Films for the Humanities and Sciences, P.O. Box 2053, Princeton, NJ 08543-2053, (609) 275-1400, (800) 257-5126

Home Vision, 5547 North Ravenswood Avenue, Chicago, IL 60640-1199, (312) 878-2600, (800) 826-3456

Insight Media, 2162 Broadway, New York, NY 10024, (212) 721-6316

Kino International, 333 West 39th Street, Suite 503, New York, NY 10018, (212) 629-6880, (800) 562-3330

MGM/UA, see local retailer.

Open University, Berrill Building, Walton Hall, Milton Keynes, MK7 6AA UK, (44 0) 1908 858793

Paramount Home Video, see local retailer.

Prism Entertainment, 1888 Century Park East, Suite 350, Los Angeles, CA 90067, (310) 277-3270

Republic Pictures Home Video, see local retailer.

Smithsonian Institution Press, 470 L'Enfante Plaza, Suite 7100, Washington, DC 20650, (202) 287-3738

Universal Studios Home Video, see local retailer.

Warner Home Video, see local retailer.

Water Bearer Films, 48 West 21st Street, Suite 301, New York, NY 10010, (212) 242-8686, (800) 551-8304

Glossary of Dramatic
and Critical Terms

Words and phrases highlighted in **boldface** are also defined here.

Absurd, theater of the Theatrical style, prominent in the mid–twentieth century, that seeks to dramatize the absurdity of modern life. **Conventions** of the style include disjointed or elliptical plotlines, disaffected characters, non**naturalistic** dialogue, and often **black comedy.** Proponents include Eugene Ionesco and Samuel Beckett.

Act One of the principle divisions of a full-length play. Plays of the Renaissance are commonly divided into five acts. Although four acts enjoyed a brief period of popularity in the nineteenth century, two or three acts are more typical of modern and contemporary drama.

Agon The central conflict in a play. In Greek drama, the agon is a formal structural component, often a debate between two characters or parts of the **chorus.**

Allegory An extended metaphor; a play, often religious, in which characters stand not only for themselves but for abstract concepts, such as death or knowledge. Allegorical plays were popular in medieval times.

Alternative theater Any theater—most often political or experimental—that sets itself up in opposition to the **conventions** of the mainstream theater of its time.

Anagnorisis A significant recognition or discovery by a character, usually the **protagonist,** that moves the **plot** forward by changing the circumstances of a play.

Antagonist The character (or, less often, the force) that opposes the **protagonist.**

Anticlimax A disappointingly trivial occurrence where a **climax** would usually happen. An anticlimax can achieve comic effect or disrupt audience expectations of dramatic structure.

Antihero   A character playing a hero's part but lacking the grandeur typically associated with a **hero**. Such a character may be comic or may exist to force the audience to reconsider its notions of heroism.

Antistrophe   The second part of a choral **ode** in Greek drama. The antistrophe was traditionally sung as the **chorus** moved **stage left** to **stage right**.

Aside   A brief bit of dialogue spoken by a character to the audience or to him- or herself and assumed to be unheard by other characters on stage.

Black comedy   A type of comedy in which the traditional material of tragedy (that is, suffering or even death) is staged to provoke laughter.

Blank verse   Unrhymed iambic pentameter (ten-syllable lines of verse with five strong beats per line). Blank verse was commonly employed by English playwrights of the Renaissance, including Shakespeare, and remained a popular verse form for those writing poetic dramas, including T. S. Eliot in the twentieth century.

Blocking   The process of determining the stage positions, movement, and groupings for the actors. Blocking generally is proposed in rehearsal by the director and may be negotiated and reworked by the actors themselves.

Canon   The group of literary works that form the backbone of a cultural tradition. *12 Plays: A Portable Anthology* presents a brief canon of Western drama.

Catastrophe   The final movement of a **tragedy**, which brings about the fall or death of the **protagonist**. In plays other than classical tragedy, the place of the catastrophe is filled by the **denouement**.

Catharsis   A purging of the spectators' emotions through the actions of pity and fear. Aristotle argued in his *Poetics* that catharsis is the natural, and beneficial, outcome of viewing a **tragedy**.

Characterization   The process by which writer and actor make a character distinct and believable to an audience. One of the six **elements of drama** identified by Aristotle.

Chorus   In classical Greek theater, the group of actors who perform in the **orchestra** and whose functions might include providing **exposition**, confronting or questioning the **protagonist**, and commenting on the action of the play. Much of the **spectacle** of Greek drama lay in the singing and dancing of the chorus. In theater of other times and places, particularly the Renaissance, the functions of the Greek chorus are sometimes given to a single character identified by the name "Chorus."

Climax   The turning point at which a play switches from **rising action** to **falling action**.

Closet drama   A play intended to be read rather than performed.

Comedy   Originally, any play that ends with the characters in a better condition than they began, though the term is now used more frequently to describe a play intended to be funny. Traditional comedy is generally distinguished by low or ordinary characters (as opposed to the great men and women of tragedy), humble style, a series of events or role reversals that create chaos and upheaval, and a conclusion or **denouement** that marks a return to normal and often a reintegration of society (such as a wedding or other formal celebration).

Comic relief   A funny scene or character in an otherwise serious play, intended to provide the audience with a momentary break from the heavier themes of tragedy.

Commedia dell'arte   Semi-improvised comedy, relying heavily on **stock characters** and **stage business**, performed originally by traveling Italian players in the sixteenth and seventeenth centuries.

Complication   One of the traditional elements of **plot**. Complication occurs when someone or something opposes the **protagonist**.

Confidant   A character, major or minor, to whom another character confides secrets so that the audience can "overhear" the transaction and be apprised of unseen events.

Convention   An unstated rule or code. Tacit acceptance of theatrical conventions prevents the audience from being distracted by unrealistic features that are necessarily part of any theater experience. Greek audiences, for instance, accepted the convention of the **chorus**, while Renaissance audiences accepted the use of **blank verse**. Today's audiences readily accept the convention of the **fourth wall** in realistic drama and of songs in musical comedy.

Cruelty, theater of   Term coined by Antonin Artaud in the early twentieth century to describe a type of theater using light, sound, **spectacle,** and other primarily nonverbal forms of communication, intended to shock audiences out of complacency through images of cruelty and destruction.

Denouement   Literally, "unknotting." The end of a play or other literary work, in which all elements of the **plot** are brought to their necessary conclusion.

Deus ex machina   Literally, "god out of the machine," referring to the mechanized system used to lower an actor playing a god onto the stage in classical Greek drama. Today it is generally used disparagingly to indicate careless plotting and an unbelievable **resolution** for a play.

Diction   The specific words chosen by an author for a character. One of the six **elements of drama** identified by Aristotle.

Downstage   The part of the stage closest to the audience.

Dramatic irony   The particular variety of **irony** in which the audience has more knowledge of the truth than do the characters.

Elements of drama   The six features identified by Aristotle in his *Poetics* as descriptive of and necessary to drama. They are, in order of the importance assigned to them by Aristotle, **plot**, **characterization**, **theme**, **diction**, **melody**, and **spectacle**.

Empathy   The ability of the audience to relate to, or even experience, the emotions of the characters on stage.

Epic theater   The name given by Bertold Brecht to a theatrical style emphasizing the relationship between form and ideology. It is characterized by brief scenes, narrative breaks, political and historical themes, an analytical (rather than emotional) tone, and characters with whom it is difficult to feel **empathy**. Though considered **alternative theater** when it was new, many of its **conventions** have since been adopted by mainstream dramatists.

Epilogue   A final speech or scene after the main action of the play has ended. An epilogue generally sums up or comments on the meaning of the play.

Episode   In Greek drama, the scenes of dialogue that occur between the choral **odes**. Now, any small unit of drama that has its own completeness and internal unity.

Exposition   The means of filling in the audience on events that occur off stage or before the play's beginning. Clumsily handled exposition, in which characters talk at length about things they normally would not, is the cause of much bad drama.

Expressionism Nonrealistic playmaking style using exaggerated or otherwise unreal gestures, light, and sound. Expressionistic techniques are often used to convey a sense of memory, dream, or fantasy.

Falling action The action after the **climax** in a traditionally structured play, as the tension lessens and the play moves toward the **catastrophe** or **denouement**.

Farce A type of **comedy** relying on exaggerated characters, extreme situations, fast and accelerating pacing, and often sexual innuendo.

Feminist theater Any play or theater whose primary object is to shine light on the issues of women's rights and sexism.

Foil A character who exists chiefly to set off or display, usually by opposition, the important character traits of the **protagonist** or another important person.

Fourth wall The theatrical **convention**, dating from the nineteenth century, whereby the audience seems to be looking and listening through an invisible fourth wall, usually into a room in a private residence. The fourth wall is primarily associated with **realism** and domestic dramas.

Genre A basic type of a play or other work of literature. While the most basic genres are **comedy** and **tragedy**, many others are recognized, including **tragicomedy**, **romance**, **melodrama**, and so on.

Hamartia Sometimes translated as "tragic flaw," more properly an error or general character trait that leads to the downfall of a character in **tragedy**.

Hero, heroine Sometimes used to refer to any **protagonist**, the term more properly applies only to a great figure from legend or history or to a character who performs in a remarkably honorable and selfless manner.

Hubris An arrogance or inflated sense of self that can lead to a character's downfall. The **protagonists** of **tragedy** often suffer from hubris.

Imitation Since Aristotle, drama has been differentiated from fiction because it relies on an imitation (Greek *mimesis*) of human actions rather than a narration of them.

Interlude A brief, usually comic, performance inserted between the **acts** of a play or between courses at a formal banquet. Interludes were most popular during the Renaissance.

Irony   The effect achieved when the true meaning of an utterance or action is different from, often opposed to, the surface meaning. In drama, irony can create tension between characters or between a character and the audience. See also **dramatic irony**.

Melodrama   A type of play employing broadly drawn heroes and villains, suspenseful plots, music, and a triumph of good over evil. Melodrama thrived throughout the nineteenth century and continued its popularity into the twentieth.

Melody   One of the six **elements of drama** identified by Aristotle. Since the Greek **chorus** communicated through song and dance, melody was an important part of even the most serious play, though it is now largely confined to musical comedy.

Motivation   What drives a character to act in a particular way. To be convincing to an audience, an actor must understand and make clear the character's motivation.

Naturalism, naturalistic   A style of writing or acting meant to mimic closely the patterns of ordinary life.

New comedy   An ancient form of **comedy** based on forbidden (but ultimately successful) love and employing **stock characters**. New comedy is particularly associated with the Greek playwright Menander (342–292 B.C.)

Ode   A multipart song sung by the **chorus** of Greek drama. A classical ode consists of a **strophe** followed by an **antistrophe** and sometimes by a final section called the *epode*.

Old comedy   Comedy, such as that of Aristophanes, employing raucous (sometimes coarse) humor, elements of **satire** and **farce**, and often a critique of contemporary persons or political and social norms.

One act   A short play that is complete in one **act**.

Orchestra   In Greek theater, the playing area in front of the stage proper, where the chorus performed their songs and dances. Later, a pit for musicians in front of the stage.

Performance art   Loose term for a variety of performance types that defy traditional categories of play, monologue, musical act, and so on. The term arose in the late twentieth century as a catch-all to name the growing number of nontraditional performances, many of which addressed controversial subjects and themes.

Peripeteia   A reversal or change of fortune for a character, for better or worse.

Plot   The action that takes place within the play. Of the six **elements of drama** identified by Aristotle, he considered plot to be the most important. Typical elements of the plot include a **prologue** or **exposition**, **rising action**, **complication**, **climax**, **falling action**, and **catastrophe** or **denouement**.

Prologue   A speech or scene before the beginning of the **plot** proper.

Properties, props   Any movable objects, beyond scenery and costumes, needed for the performance of a play. Early drama was performed with few props, but as theater moved toward **realism**, props took on greater importance.

Proscenium arch   An arch across the front of a stage, sometimes with a curtain. The proscenium frames the action and provides a degree of separation between actors and audience.

Protagonist   The lead character of a play, though not necessarily a **hero** in the classic sense.

Realism   Any drama (or other art) that seeks to closely mimic real life. Realism more specifically refers to a sort of drama that rose in opposition to **melodrama** in the late nineteenth and early twentieth century and that attempted to avoid some of the more artificial **conventions** of theater and present the problems of ordinary people living their everyday lives.

Recognition   See **Anagnorsis**.

Resolution   A satisfying outcome that effectively ends the conflict of a play.

Rising action   The increasingly tense and complicated action leading up to the **climax** in a traditionally structured play.

Romance   A play neither wholly comic nor wholly tragic, often containing elements of the supernatural. The best-known examples are Shakespeare's late plays, such as *The Winter's Tale* and *The Tempest*, which have a generally comic structure but are more ruminative in theme and spirit than traditional **comedy**.

Satire   The type of drama or other literature employing **comedy** and **irony** to mock a particular human characteristic or social institution. Generally, a satirist wants the audience not only to laugh but also to change its opinions or actions.

Scene   One of the secondary divisions, within an **act**, of a play.

Set   The stage dressing for a play, consisting of backdrops, furniture, and similar large items.

Soliloquy   A speech delivered by a character who is alone on stage or otherwise out of hearing of the other characters. Since the character is effectively speaking to him- or herself, a soliloquy often serves as a window into the character's mind and heart.

Spectacle   The purely visual elements of a play, including the **sets**, costumes, **props**, lighting, and special effects. Of the six **elements of drama** identified by Aristotle, he considered spectacle to be the least important.

Stage business   Minor physical activity performed by actors on stage, often involving **props**, intended to strengthen **characterization** or modulate tension in a play.

Stage directions   Written instructions in the script telling actors how to move on the stage or how to deliver a particular line. To facilitate reading of scripts and distinguish them from dialogue, stage directions are typically placed in parentheses and written in italics.

Stage left, stage right   Area of the stage as seen from the point of view of an actor facing the audience. Stage left, therefore, is on the audience's right-hand side, and vice versa.

Stichomythia   Short lines of dialogue quickly alternating between two characters.

Stock character   Any of a number of traditional characters easily identified by a single, stereotypical characteristic. Stock characters include innocent young women, rakish young men, clever servants, and so forth.

Strophe   The first part of a choral **ode** in Greek drama. The strophe was traditionally sung as the **chorus** moved **stage right** to **stage left**.

Subplot   A secondary **plot** that exists beside the main plot and involves the minor characters. In **tragedy**, particularly, there might be a subplot to provide **comic relief**.

Subtext   The unspoken meaning, sense, or **motivation** for a scene or character.

Symbolism   A device whereby an object or event suggests meaning beyond its immediate, physical presence. Symbolism exists in all genres of literature, but in drama it might include visual or sound elements as well as language.

Theater in the round   A theatrical design wherein a circular stage is completely surrounded by seating for the audience.

Theater of the absurd, of cruelty   See **Absurd, theater of the; Cruelty, theater of.**

Theme   The central idea(s) explored by a play or literary work. One of the six **elements of drama** identified by Aristotle.

Tragedy   A play in which the **plot** moves from relative stability to death or other serious sorrow for the **protagonist**. A traditional tragedy is written in a grand style and shows a **hero** of high social stature brought down by **peripeteia** or events beyond his or her control.

Tragicomedy   A play in which **tragedy** and **comedy** are mingled in roughly equal proportion.

Unities   The elements of a play that help an audience to understand the play as a unified whole. Aristotle commented on the unities of time (the action of a play usually takes place within approximately one day) and action (the play should have a single principle plot line). Renaissance critics added a third unity—unity of place (the play has only one main setting). Though Aristotle intended these as merely observations about the most successful dramas he had seen, some later playwrights took them as inflexible laws of drama and were highly constrained by this interpretation.

Upstage   As an adjective, adverb, or noun, the part of the stage farthest from the audience, at the back of the playing area. As a verb, to draw the audience's attention away from another actor on stage.

Well-made play   A type of play that rose to prominence in the nineteenth century and that relied for its effect on clever, causal plotting and a series of startling discoveries or revelations rather than on subtleties of character or language.

Tennessee Williams. *The Glass Menagerie* (play and production notes). Copyright 1945 by Tennessee Williams and Edwina D. Williams. Copyright renewed 1973 by Tennessee Williams. Used by permission of Random House, Inc.

August Wilson. *The Piano Lesson.* Copyright © 1988, 1990 by August Wilson. Used by permission of Dutton Signet, a division of Penguin Putnam Inc.